HERBERT A. SIMON

HERBERT A. SIMON

Critical Evaluations in Business and Management

Edited by
John C. Wood and
Michael C. Wood

Volume III

Routledge
Taylor & Francis Group

LONDON AND NEW YORK

First published 2007
by Routledge
2 Park Square, Milton Park, Abingdon, OX14 4RN UK

Simultaneously published in the USA and Canada
by Routledge
270 Madison Avenue, New York, NY 10016

Routledge is an imprint of the Taylor & Francis Group, an informa business

Editorial material and selection © 2007 John C. Wood and Michael C. Wood;
individual owners retain copyright in their own material

Typeset in 10/12pt Times by Graphicraft Limited, Hong Kong
Printed and bound in Great Britain by
TJI Digital, Padstow, Cornwall

British Library Cataloguing in Publication Data
A catalogue record for this book is available from the British Library

Library of Congress Cataloging in Publication Data
A catalog record for this book has been requested

ISBN10: 0-415-32587-0 (Set)
ISBN10: 0-415-40631-5 (Volume III)

ISBN13: 978-0-415-32587-5 (Set)
ISBN13: 978-0-415-40631-4 (Volume III)

Publisher's Note
References within each chapter are as they appear in the original complete work

CONTENTS

v

CONTENTS

ACKNOWLEDGEMENTS

The publishers would like to thank the following for permission to reprint their material:

M. F. Shakun, 'Unbounded rationality', *Group Decision and Negotiation*, 10 (2001), 97–118. Reprinted with kind permission from Springer Science and Business Media. © 2001 Kluwer Academic Publishers.

Reprinted from *Journal of Economic Psychology*, 23, Y. Hanoch, 'Neither an angel nor an ant: emotion as an aid to bounded rationality', pp. 1–25, Copyright 2002, with permission from Elsevier.

Reprinted from *Journal of Economic Psychology*, 24, N. J. Foss, 'Bounded rationality in the economics of organization: "much cited and little used"', pp. 245–264, Copyright 2003, with permission from Elsevier.

Reprinted from *Journal of Economic Psychology*, 26, R. Muramatsu and Y. Hanoch, 'Emotions as a mechanism for boundedly rational agents: the fast and frugal way', pp. 201–221, Copyright 2005, with permission from Elsevier.

Reprinted from 'Unprogrammed decision making' by P. Soelberg, *Industrial Management Review* (MIT Sloan Management Review), 8: 2 (1967), 19–29, by permission of publisher. Copyright © 1967 by Massachusetts Institute of Technology. All rights reserved.

T. Tammi, 'Simon's and Siegel's responses to the 'mixed strategy anomaly': a missed case in the sensitivity of economics to empirical evidence', *Cambridge Journal of Economics*, 27: 1 (2003), 85–96, reprinted by permission of the Cambridge Political Economy Society.

M. A. Goodrich, W. C. Stirling and E. R. Boer, 'Satisficing revisited', *Minds and Machines*, 10: 1 (2000), 79–110. Reprinted with kind permission from Springer Science and Business Media. © 2000 Kluwer Academic Publishers.

Reprinted from *Journal of Economic Psychology*, 24, R. Franz, 'Herbert Simon: artificial intelligence as a framework for understanding intuition', pp. 265–277, Copyright 2003, with permission from Elsevier.

Reprinted from *Journal of Economic Psychology*, 24, R. N. Langlois, 'Cognitive comparative advantage and the organization of work: lessons from Herbert Simon's vision of the future', pp. 167–187, Copyright 2003, with permission from Elsevier.

L. F. Dennard, 'Neo-Darwinism and Simon's bureaucratic antihero', *Administration & Society*, 26: 4 (1995), 464–487. Copyright 1995 by Sage Publications, Inc. Reprinted by permission of Sage Publications, Inc.

T. W. Zawidzki, 'Competing models of stability in complex, evolving systems: Kauffman vs. Simon', *Biology and Philosophy*, 13 (1998), 541–554. Reprinted with kind permission from Springer Science and Business Media. © 1998 Kluwer Academic Publishers.

Reprinted from *Journal of Economic Psychology*, 24, T. Knudsen, 'Simon's selection theory: why docility evolves to breed successful altruism', pp. 229–244. Copyright 2003, with permission from Elsevier.

Lawrence Erlbaum Associates, Inc., for permission to reprint R. Shaw, 'The agent-environment interface: Simon's indirect or Gibson's direct coupling?' *Ecological Psychology*, 15: 1 (2003), 37–106.

The University of Chicago for permission to reprint S. Downes, 'Herbert Simon's computational models of scientific discovery', *in PSA: Proceedings of the Biennial Meeting of the Philosophy of Science Association*, (vol. one: Contributed Papers), 1990, pp. 97–108. Copyright © 1990 by the Philosophy of Science Association.

Reprinted from *Evaluation and Program Planning*, 12, J. Z. Shapiro, 'Contextual limits on validity attainment: an artificial science perspective on program evaluation', pp. 367–374, Copyright 1989, with permission from Elsevier.

Reprinted from *Journal of Economic Psychology*, 22, P. E. Earl, 'Simon's travel theorem and the demand for live music', pp. 335–358, Copyright 2001, with permission from Elsevier.

T. J. Lowi, 'The state in political science: how we become what we study', *American Political Science Review*, 86: 1 (1992), 1–7. © American Political Science Association, reproduced with permission.

Herbert A. Simon, 'The state of American political science: Professor Lowi's view of our discipline', *PS: Political Science and Politics*, 26: 1 (1993), 49–51. © American Political Science Association, reproduced with permission.

T. J. Lowi, 'A review of Herbert Simon's review of my view of the discipline', *PS: Political Science and Politics*, 26: 1 (1993), 51–52. © American Political Science Association, reproduced with permission.

ACKNOWLEDGEMENTS

Disclaimer

The publishers have made every effort to contact authors/copyright holders of works reprinted in *Herbert A. Simon: Critical Evaluations in Business and Management*. This has not been possible in every case, however, and we would welcome correspondence from those individuals/companies whom we have been unable to trace.

49

UNBOUNDED RATIONALITY

Melvin F. Shakun

Source: *Group Decision and Negotiation*, 10 (2001), 97–118.

Abstract

The paper discusses bounded and unbounded rationality in purposeful complex adaptive systems (PCAS) modeled by the Evolutionary Systems Design (ESD) framework. Due to Herbert Simon, bounded rationality is the rationality of cognition. Unbounded rationality is the generalized rationality of connectedness represented mathematically, of spirituality, and of right decision/negotiation. Operational procedures for defining/solving and validating a problem in group decision and negotiation under unbounded rationality are discussed. With human PCAS as a focus, the paper more generally considers rationality in multiagent systems with natural and/or artificial agents.

1. Purposeful complex adaptive systems

Adaptive systems use change (changing action) to cope with change in the environment or internally to attain purpose. Such systems have been termed "artificial" (Simon 1996). They include human-made artifacts – thus a science of the artificial is a science of design – and humans themselves, in terms of behavior. When adaptation includes change through cybernetic positive feedback/feedforward and self-organization as well as cybernetic negative feedback/feedforward, we say the system is complex. Adaptive systems that can choose their own purposes are purposeful.

Both cybernetic and self-organizing, purposeful complex adaptive systems (PCAS) solve problems defined by choosing and delivering purposes to participants (Shakun 1996). PCAS involve multiplayer, multicriteria, ill-structured, evolving dynamic problems in which agents (players) both cooperate and conflict. Individuals, groups, organizations and economies are PCAS. Here we focus on individuals and groups. Processes[1] exhibited by PCAS constitute policy making, negotiation, individual and group decision,

1

and multiagent problem solving with human and/or artificial agents all viewed as design of PCAS.

2. Evolutionary systems design

Following Shakun (1999a), Evolutionary Systems Design (ESD) is a universal (culture independent) general problem solving, formal modeling/design framework[2] (a methodology) for PCAS. The ESD general framework (problem representation or structure) can be applied in defining and solving specific problems and can be computer implemented (Bui and Shakun 1996, Lewis and Shakun 1996) as a group/negotiation support system.[3] Formally, the ESD problem representation (model) for PCAS is a system involving relations between the following sets of elements: (1) **players, agents**, negotiators or decision makers in a group (coalition); (2) **values** or broadly stated desires; (3) operational **goals**, or specific expressions of these values; (4) decisions, actions, or **controls** taken to achieve these goals; (5) **criteria** based on goals for evaluating the effectiveness of decisions; (6) **individual preferences** defined on criteria; and (7) **group or coalition preference** defined on individual preferences. Sometimes goals and controls are the same. Not all agents in a PCAS are necessarily active in choosing purposes. For example, for a multiagent system with all artificial agents, an associated PCAS may be considered consisting of human designer and artificial agents with purposes chosen by the designer and/or some or all of the artificial agents.

In the ESD framework, the relations between the sets of elements can be represented by two evolving hierarchies of relations.[4] These hierarchies may be in the form of trees or other graphs. The hierarchy 1 relation (see Figure 1) is a framework for evolving, that is, for defining the general problem in the sense of defining values to be delivered to group members in the form of operational goal variables by exercising control variables. Hierarchy 1 is concerned with what Fisher, Ury, and Patton (1991) call *interests*. The hierarchy 2 relation (see Figure 2) is a framework for finding a solution – finding the levels or particular values of the control and goal variables – to the evolved general problem at any stage. Hierarchy 2 is concerned with what Fisher, Ury and Patton call *positions*. Together, hierarchies 1 and 2 represent a general framework for defining and solving an evolved problem. These relations or structures are beliefs held by a negotiator (decision maker). Beliefs, that is, relations can evolve; hence, the concept of an evolving problem representation. Players design the problem representation. *Problem solving* is *system design* (and vice versa) of PCAS, formally with ESD by designing the problem representation. A solution has been found when in control, goal, criteria, individual preference and group preference spaces the intersection of the group (coalition) target (what it wants) and the group feasible technology (what it can get) is a single set or point.

2

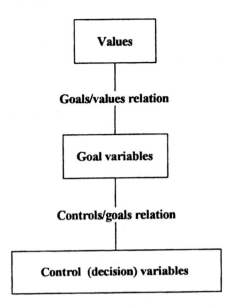

Figure 1 Hierarchy 1 relation between control variables, goal variables, and values.

The formal representation (hierarchies 1 and 2) can be individual or group. The formal group (joint) problem representation is based on the union of individual-player problem representations. If the latter are not fully shared (made public) by individuals in the group, the public group problem representation will be incomplete (Shakun 1990). In this case, each player privately can subjectively estimate missing information; in other words, establish his private group problem representation. Thus, with ESD negotiation support can be provided for an individual and/or for the group. The group searches for a solution to an evolved problem.[5]

ESD involves evolution of the group problem representation, i.e., evolution of the sets of elements and their relations through **cybernetics/ self-organization**: (a) problem adaptation through learning associated with cybernetic negative feedback/feedforward, as through information-sharing and concession-making; and (b) problem restructuring or reframing (evolution) associated with cybernetic positive feedback/feedforward and self-organization. Cybernetics/self-organization can be described by mathematical relations. In ESD, PCAS are modeled as a dynamical system (problem representation) expressing the two evolving hierarchies of relations as an evolving difference game with a moving present.[6] Players and self-organization design the problem representation. Cybernetics/self-organization defines complexity in PCAS.

3

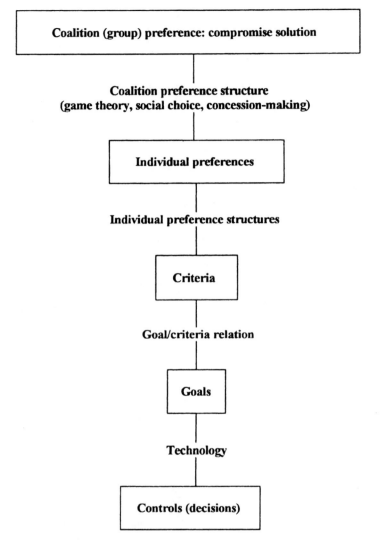

Figure 2 Hierarchy 2 relation between controls, goals, criteria, individual preferences, and coalition preference.

When satisfactory solutions (agreements) are not forthcoming, problem restructuring (reframing) is a key approach. Problem restructuring involves redefining the structure (sets of elements and their relations) in hierarchies 1 and 2. Regarding restructuring, the group problem representation can have bifurcation points at which there is a choice of branch (problem structure).

Table 1 Cybernetics/self-organization in group problem restructuring.

Problem representation driven to bifurcation by:	Selection of problem structure at bifurcation by:	
	Cybernetic control	Self-organization
Cybernetic control	cybernetics (description 1)	cybernetic self-organization (description 2)
Self-organization	self-organization cybernetics (description 4)	self-organization (description 3)

Shakun (1996) describes four possibilities for restructuring with cybernetics/self-organization shown in Table 1.

Restructuring may be supported using a heuristic controls/goals/values referral process (for descriptions 1, 2, and 4) and other domain-independent methodological knowledge (Shakun 1991). Examples are given in Shakun (1988, 1991, 1995, 1996). Other artificial intelligence restructuring methods, such as those of Sycara (1991) using case-based reasoning and related procedures, and of Kersten *et al.* (1991) using rule-based techniques are complementary approaches.

The ESD heuristic controls/goals/values referral process constituting domain-independent methodological knowledge is based on the idea that a value, goal variable, or control variable can serve as a reference or focal point for relating or referring other values, goal variables, and control variables in restructuring the controls/goals/values relation in hierarchy 1.

In hierarchy 1, consider the goals/values relation as a matrix which shows which values (rows) are delivered by which goal variables (columns) for individual players in a group. For a given player, an entry of 1 as an element of the matrix indicates that the player is "for" the row value being delivered by the column goal variable, i.e., he/she favors both the value and the goal variable as an operational expression of the value. An entry of 0 indicates the player is against the value being delivered by the goal variable. An entry of * indicates the player is neutral or does not perceive the value as being delivered by the goal variable. The entries for a given player can change, and the sets of values and goal variables can evolve using the goals/values referral process.

In other words, we are relating two sets (lists), values (rows) and goal variables (columns). ESD makes use of heuristics (rules of thumb) for changing the two sets and their relation in problem restructuring.

Some heuristics for the referral process stated for values and goal variables (control variables can also be used) are as follows (Shakun 1988, Ch. 13):

1. Given a particular value (row) and looking at the goal variables (columns), is there any other new goal variable that also delivers the value, or should an existing goal variable be dropped?

2. Given a particular goal variable (column) and looking at the values (rows), is there any other new value that is also delivered by the goal or shall an existing value be dropped?
3. Given a particular value (row), is there any other new value (more general or less general) that also expresses this value?
4. Is there any other additional value that is important in this problem or should an existing value be dropped?
5. Given a particular goal variable (column), is there any other goal variable that is suggested by this goal?
6. Is there any other additional goal variable that is important in this problem or should an existing one be dropped?
7. Is there any other additional player who should now be included in the group (coalition) goals/values relation or should one be dropped?

Overall, ESD supports consensus-seeking, i.e., moving towards the same preferred (desired) solution for all players in the group. Of course, in practice if consensus is not achieved, compromise provides a solution.

Finding compromise solutions when conflict is present is a basic support activity for ESD. Various game theory, social choice and concession-making approaches are available (Shakun 1988, 1990). For the use of case-based reasoning to find compromises, see Sycara (1990) and for rule-based techniques, see Kersten et al. (1988).

Social-emotional aspects of ESD are discussed by Faure, Le Dong, and Shakun (1990). It is possible to include social-emotional aspects as well as task aspects in the problem representation.

3. Intelligence, information processing, embodied cognitive science and ESD

Intelligence defined as adaptive behavior (changing behavior to cope with change in the environment or internally to attain purpose) has been studied using the sense-think-act cognitivistic paradigm constituting the information processing theory of mind. Cognitivism views cognition as computation operating on a symbolic representation of a real world situation. This approach constituting classical cognitive science (classical view of intelligence) is being challenged by the sense-motor (act) paradigm of embodied cognitive science (see Pfeifer and Scheier 1999 for extensive discussion). Here cognition and intelligence emerge from the interaction of an embodied agent (as human, animal, artificial – having a physical body) with an environment. Embodied cognitive science has been motivated by difficulties in applying classical cognitive science to design of autonomous artificial agents. Ideally, such agents are complete, i.e., autonomous, self-sufficient, embodied and situated, characteristics observed in natural biological agents as animals and humans. Proponents of embodied cognitive science argue for its use as a paradigm for artificial agent design and intelligence in general. The information processing paradigm is powerful in understanding many aspects of human intelligence. It is less powerful as a paradigm for intelligence in animals and robots. Humans, at the top of the evolutionary intelligence chain, surpass animals in intelligence while retaining animalistic behavior characteristics.[7] Humans have bodies that interact with their environment. The embodied cognitive science paradigm can be useful in explaining aspects of human intelligence, e.g., infant development. Considering intelligence in general, from the embodied cognitive science viewpoint thinking and intuition emerge in the interaction of an embodied agent and its environment through agent sensory-motor coordination. Nunez (1999) argues, via a conceptual mapping "Time Events are Things in Space", for a full embodiment approach to all human cognition, not only to low-level cognitive tasks as visual scanning and locomotion, but also to high-level cognition such as concepts, logic and theories. The embodiment paradigm provides an alternative to the information processing view of intelligence. We view the two paradigms as complementary with their use depending on the problem. ESD accommodates both.

As discussed in sections 1, 2, and 3, ESD is proposed as a modeling/design framework for PCAS with natural and/or artificial agents. Natural agents may be human, animal, plant or matter (e.g., rock, water). Artificial agents (robots, softbots (software agents), computers and artifacts in general) are designed by human or by other natural or artificial agents. Agents have various degrees of autonomy (freedom from external control). They have various levels of consciousness discussed below. Sections 4 through 9 in discussing connectedness, consciousness, right (spiritual) decision/negotiation, and bounded and unbounded rationality in relation to ESD are focused on human agents. Section 10 gives concluding remarks on human unbounded rationality; then considers an ESD consciousness theory of intelligence and rationality for natural and artificial agents.

4. Right problem solving and connectedness

Defining and solving a "right" or correct problem rather than a "wrong" problem in purposeful complex adaptive systems is central to overall procedural rationality – how decisions should be or are made using reasonable procedures – in individual and group decision/negotiation processes. A right decision/negotiation outcome is a solution to a right problem that can be explicit or implicit.

Right problems, right decisions/negotiations and, speaking generally, rightness are associated with connectedness. Connectedness is generally required for right problem solving and is delivered by right problem solving, as discussed below. Connectedness is a dynamic subjective experience of an individual agent. Mathematically, we represent connectedness of an individual agent i with an individual agent j (in Two – see below) as a relation expressed by a matrix $Z = [z (i, j, t)]$. At time t, if an individual agent i experiences connectedness with an individual agent j, then $z (i, j, t) = 1$; otherwise $z (i, j, t) = 0$ signifying non-connectedness. There is also the experience of connectedness or non-connectedness of agent i holistically with all there is, a one-element set we shall call One (below). Mathematically, for n individual agents, we represent this connectedness as a relation expressed by a $(n \times 1)$ matrix $Z^* = [z^* (i, t)]$. At time t, if individual agent i experiences connectedness with the one-element set One, then $z^* (i, t) = 1$; otherwise $z^* (i, t) = 0$ signifying non-connectedness. Connectedness of an individual agent i with individual agents j as represented in Z promotes connectedness of agent i with One as represented in Z^* and vice versa. Further, connectedness of agents in Z and Z^* reinforces continued connectedness in Z and Z^*, respectively.

The concept of connectedness represented mathematically is fundamental to our approach to right problem solving and unbounded rationality. Some readers emphasizing traditional science while allowing subjectivity in decision/negotiation may prefer to follow our approach using the connectedness concept without employing the related terms spirituality and consciousness below that for many readers will enhance understanding. Our work in decision/negotiation is operational. While embracing modern science, we go beyond traditional scientific considerations and consider the full context of human experience (consciousness).[8]

Following Shakun (1999a), right problem solving is associated with spirituality. Spirituality is consciousness experiencing connectedness with One. Human consciousness is self-organizing[9] response capacity with awareness embodying inner, subjective, qualitative experience[10] (qualia), and manifesting purpose, cognition, affection (emotion, feeling), conation (action) and spirituality. From the viewpoint of materialism, it is an emergent property of the neuronal system; there are other views.[11]

One represents all there is, the absolute, the implicate order, the quantum vacuum, emptiness, God. Two represents the process of all there is, the relative, the explicate order, excitations of the quantum vacuum. Two comes from One manifesting itself as energy, matter and consciousness. These concepts of One and Two accommodate science, various religions, spiritual practices and philosophies. Consciousness experiences connectedness with One, i.e., spirituality, as unity with One, as emergence of One from Two, and as manifestation of Two from One.[12] When consciousness is experiencing connectedness with One, then cognition, affection and conation (as manifestations of consciousness) experience connectedness as oneness, love and perfect action, respectively, integrally bound as oneness/love/perfect action.[13] One and Two remain a mystery. However, through consciousness we know something about them and want to make right decisions, i.e., consonant with them, with our nature. Purpose is inherent in consciousness.

Purpose is expressed through cognition, affection and conation. Through implemented right decisions in Two, we find One, at the same time acting as co-designing agents of One. This defines ultimate purpose in Two (ultimate value in hierarchy 1) – spirituality, consciousness experiencing connectedness with One manifesting oneness/love/perfect action, i.e., to live Two as One. Humans as PCAS try to live Two as One through right decision/negotiation, i.e., problem solving under oneness/love/perfect action, thus providing meaning as relation (structure, system) among problem elements. Right problem solving creates what Zukav (2000) calls authentic power.

What we normally term decision making (conscious decision making) is a manifestation of consciousness. As such, the decision process operates through cognition, affection and conation and is an emergent property. Interaction of unconsciousness neuronal processors exerts upward control on the decision process while the latter exerts downward control on the former. Downward causation involves conscious processing of the decision problem through cognition, affection and conation that influences unconscious neuronal processing. Upward causation, i.e., emergence of an evolving decision problem comes from interacting neuronal processors. Thus, decision is an output of a complex adaptive system of neurons, yet purposeful in that consciousness is aware of One and Two and can choose values, goals and design hierarchies 1 and 2.

The work of MacLean (1990) on the triune brain (see endnote 7) indicates that the reality of a mathematical cognitive problem representation (a product of the neocortex) – its believability for a human – depends on a co-functioning limbic system, the seat of affection. For something to exist for a human requires an affective feeling. Thus, the evolving ESD problem representation characterizing the design/decision process that expresses consciousness is cognitive and affective, and also conative through implementation of the current or present decision (Shakun 1992). Purpose, action, emotion, cognition and spirituality are inherent in human consciousness. The volume edited by Nunez and Freeman (1999) argues for the primacy of intention (purpose), action (via embodiment) and emotion in reclaiming (understanding) cognition, contending that the cognitivistic paradigm – cognition as computation – is insufficient. We note that the MacLean model involves the evolutionary formation sequence: first, reptilian complex (action); then, limbic system (emotion); then, neocortex (cognition).

One view: A self-organizing homogeneity break in One, manifest in the big bang, results in Two. Two signifies at least two elements. In Two, human consciousness emerges, and further creates elements of Two and their relations, thus creating (designing) systems and problems. Broadly, ecology is concerned with relations in Two. The relative, Two increases complexity (response capacity or consciousness) evolving toward the absolute, One through cybernetics/self-organization (section 2), a problem defining/solving process of cooperative control (design) subject to self-organization. Thus,

Two comes from One, and One comes from Two. Right problem defining/solving is the design of Two towards One.

A problem is defined by relations between elements in Two. With ESD these relations in Two are formally represented by evolving hierarchies 1 and 2 which are redesigned at the present moment. Relations are beliefs held by a decision maker. Rightness in problems and decisions imply rightness in problem relations (beliefs). Rightness comes from spirituality, consciousness experiencing connectedness with One. In turn, making right decisions delivers connectedness with One experienced as the emergence of One from Two. The absence of experiencing connectedness with One (experiencing non-connectedness) is experienced by cognition, affection and conation as separateness, fear and non-connected action, respectively, integrally bound as separateness/fear/non-connected action. Conflicts in information (uncertainty), values, goals, and controls are potential sources of separateness/fear/non-connected action and associated threat cycles and deadlocks. Strong existing separateness/fear/non-connected action circuit patterns in the neuronal system are also sources.

Strong circuit patterns are often established in childhood. When a parent (or other person) experiences oneness/love extending it naturally to the child, the child experiences oneness/love reinforcing internally what is naturally there. Many associates of oneness/love such as self-trust and self-esteem go with this reinforcing process. This reinforcing process works for separateness/fear as well. Later however, separateness/fear can be attenuated. Oneness/love circuit patterns naturally always there can be reinforced. Awareness and learning are key in later change.

Thoughts (cognition), feelings (affection) and decisions (conation) constitute an experientially synchronous flow, the now of consciousness. If consciousness is tuned into the process of all there is, we can experience what is termed "psychological flow" (Csikszentmihalyi 1990), being in the moment. Psychological flow and stillness are the same, time stops, we are in the moment and experience connectedness to One. One is always in the moment, without time. Two, the relative is in time. Problems are in Two, not in One.

Thus, right decisions/negotiations come from oneness (oneness/love/perfect action)[14] and deliver oneness. *Integrated Problem Solving and Oneness (IPSO)* means problem solving through oneness and oneness through problem solving. ESD is IPSO. Problem solving is systems design (and vice versa).

As noted, Two implies two elements, at least. In fact, human consciousness perceives many sets of elements in Two. If we consider the set of human agents, then human consciousness identifies subsets of agents (national, ethnic or other groups) within which agents share common elements in other sets (e.g., values, goals, actions) and their relations (expressed cognitively in hierarchies 1 and 2), thus characterizing such subsets of agents as cultures.[15] This defines culture and diversity in culture. Fundamentally diversity arises with two agents (as Adam and Eve) – every two people are different, diverse. With diversity comes the need for tolerance and conflict resolution. Conflict resolution as right group decision comes from spirituality, oneness. If agents in Two experience their diversity as oneness, e.g., as different excitations of One allowing each agent to experience a different potential, then ideally conflict between agents can fall away. There can be consensus, the same preferred (desired) solution for all agents. In practice, if consensus is not achieved, compromise provides a solution (hierarchy 2). Shakun (1999b) discusses intercultural group decision/negotiation with ESD and computer support.

4.1. Modes of consciousness; oneness/love, separateness/fear

Since right decisions/negotiations come from and deliver oneness/love (oneness/love/perfect action – see footnote 14), some discussion of the latter and its absence, separateness/fear is in order. We relate our work to some concepts discussed by Pransky (1995). When our consciousness is tuned into our memory, we are in what Pransky calls *computer* mode of consciousness. Here we can use knowledge and reasoning for problem defining/solving. Our consciousness experiences oneness/love or separateness/fear. If, when in computer mode, we clear (free up) our mind by letting present thoughts and feelings go, i.e., let go of the passing-moment contents (past, present or future) – exit from our memory – we naturally go into *receiver* mode. Here we are in our spirituality, experiencing the present moment as present, being in the moment, consciousness experiencing oneness/love. We are in touch with our ultimate purpose in Two, to live Two as One.[16]

While in receiver mode, we may experience passing transient thoughts and feelings of separateness/fear that come and go by. We may think of such a transient as a brief departure from receiver mode into computer mode and back again. Pransky suggests receiver mode as a way of life. However, when in receiver mode. consciousness knows when to switch into computer mode to access knowledge in memory.[17] If accessible knowledge in memory is insufficient for problem defining/solving, then going into receiver mode opens the way for problem self-organization inherent in the process of all there is. A discontinuous increase in consciousness associated with problem restructuring may occur. At each moving present (now) consciousness chooses receiver mode or computer mode. When previously in receiver mode, the choice now of mode made by consciousness is self-organizing; when in computer mode, the choice is cybernetic or self-organizing. The interplay of computer and receiver modes and cybernetics/self-organization are mutually reflective and drive problem evolution, represented formally in ESD by evolving hierarchies 1 and 2, to and at the edge of chaos where restructuring (evolution) takes place.[18]

In addition to letting present thoughts and feelings go, we can also "escape" from computer mode and enter receiver mode by focusing on external or internal stimuli perceived by the senses (as sight, hearing, smell, taste, touch, and combinations). In psychology, this is the orienting reflex. Some object, a scene in nature, etc. can provide such a stimulus. The breath can provide entry to receiver mode as in meditation; so can physical exercise, as jogging. Stepping back and becoming an observer of oneself and others is another technique.

With ESD, cybernetic control or self-organization may facilitate escape from computer mode to receiver mode. For example, in problem restructuring with description 2 (table 1, section 2), the heuristic referral process can facilitate cybernetic transition from computer to receiver mode for selection of problem structure. Self-organization drives this transition in descriptions 3 and 4. By definition, with description 4 we go back into computer mode after receiver mode. With description 1, we stay in computer mode.

Separateness/fear in computer mode is being out of the moment, out of experiencing oneness/love. If we clear our mind, let go of fear, we naturally go into receiver mode. Clearing our mind can be aided by loving-kindness (compassion) toward ourselves and others, and faith (belief) in One from which love will rise again. In receiver mode we are again in touch with our purpose to live Two as One. In other words, we are again in our spirituality, in the moment, experiencing oneness/love. There is no room for separateness/fear in the moment – there it does not exist. The title of Jampolsky's (1979) book, *Love is Letting Go of Fear*, puts it simply. Letting go, not following fear brings oneness/love.

Birch (1993) suggests three ways to transit from fear (in our personality) to love (in our spirituality): Stop (take a break, relax, meditate, etc); laugh ("If it's this bad, it's got to be funny", select funny books, movies, etc.); loving intelligence (combining kindness toward ourselves and others with intelligence – cognitive, affective, conative – to pursue purpose as a challenge). Fear and its associates – threat, anxiety, anger, separateness, etc. – are no fun, we suffer. However, fear alerts us and wants to protect us. It is adaptive. Nevertheless, we are best protected and beyond that fulfilled and happy with inner peace by living in our love-based spirituality which knows best what to do, in the moment following our purpose as a challenge, and experiencing oneness/love. If fear signals potential danger, we can thank it but immediately let it go to transit to oneness/love in receiver mode for our best protection. If we are aware that we dwelling in fear (have a fear problem), we can detach from it, observe it, thank it for trying to protect us and let it go as we again follow our purpose in oneness/love.

Right problem solving requires oneness/love, not separateness/fear. However, paradoxically, as Chodron (1997) points out "fear"[19] is a natural reaction to moving closer to the "truth" – to sustaining oneness. Chodron, proceeding from a Buddhist perspective, recommends moving toward and through fear rather than running from it; getting to know fear and its inevitable partner, hope; replacing hope and fear with hopelessness and confidence. Hopelessness is the ground, i.e., we are groundless. Loving-kindness toward ourselves (*maitri*) helps us move through fear to our spirituality. Chodron suggests coming back to bare bones: Relaxing with the present moment, with hopelessness, with death and accepting impermanence. Moving through and from fear (from ego, personality) means transiting to our spirituality, to oneness/love/perfect action. Our connectedness with One, is always there. It is choiceless in that it is the default state. For spirituality, consciousness experiencing connectedness with One, we merely have to choose to "awake", be open[20] to connectedness in receiver mode or in oneness/love/perfect action computer mode. For Chodron, "the path is the goal – the moment-by-moment evolution of our experience".

When we solve problems, rightness requires us to be in our spirituality – consciousness experiencing oneness, connectedness with One. If we are in separateness/fear we try to transit to oneness/love for right problem solving. Oneness/love promotes problem solving and negotiation – expressed formally in the ESD problem representation – that is at the same time right.

5. Problems

When relationships in Two challenge the continuity of our ultimate purpose, living Two as One, we have a problem and a specific purpose to define and solve it. A problem always has a representation (cognitive, visual, verbal, emotional, etc.), aspects of which can be expressed in a formal problem representation as in ESD.

6. Bounded rationality

The contributions of Herbert Simon to bounded rationality are well known, as noted by Munier, Selten *et al.* (1999). Simon (1955, 1956) points out that commonly in real-world decision situations cognitive limitations with respect to computational capability and knowledge of the environment necessarily mean that human rationality is bounded. Instead of optimizing – making optimal choices as by maximizing a utility function – decision makers satisfices, i.e., achieve a threshold level of satisfaction that is good enough. Simon (1978, 1986) distinguishes between substantive rationality – the term in economics for making optimal choices – and procedural rationality, the reasonableness under bounded rationality of procedures used in decision making associated with satisficing. He identifies procedural rationality with psychology. Simon (1995, 1996) discussing the information processing theory of mind argues that these procedures involve (1) *recognition* based on a large body of knowledge, a large memory accessed by an index (a discrimination net) that recognizes different stimuli, and (2) *heuristic search* based on various search techniques through spaces of possibilities. According to Simon, recognition and heuristic search can explain problem solving, intuition, insight and cognitive aspects of creativity. These mechanisms, recognition and heuristic search, are developed through learning.

7. Cognitive, generalized and right (spiritual) rationalities

In common, dictionary usage, rationality of actions (behavior, decisions) means that actions are reasonable (are based on reason) with regard to producing ends (goals), i.e., the actions/goals relation is reasonable. The rationality terms introduced in section 6, as substantive and procedural rationality, are consistent with this common, dictionary meaning. The emphasis is on reasoning – on cognition, so we use the term *cognitive* (C) rationality. It is bounded. We use the term *generalized* (G) rationality to extend rationality to reasonableness validated not only by cognition, but also by affection and conation. Generalized rationality is bounded rationality. *Right* (R) or *spiritual* rationality is generalized rationality under oneness/love/perfect action manifest with consciousness experiencing connectedness with One. Spiritual rationality is unbounded rationality (section 8). These rationality definitions apply to individuals.

Actions and goals are examples of purpose. If a purpose 1 produces a purpose 2 as validated by cognition, the purpose 1/purpose 2 relation[21] is cognitive rational; if validated by cognition, affection and conation, it is generalized rational; if validated by cognition, affection and conation under oneness/love, it is right (spiritual).

Cognitive, generalized, right and non-CGR can be used to characterize (1) *procedures* for defining/solving a problem, and (2) the resulting *problem/solution* itself.

Cognitive procedural rationality or what is commonly termed simply as procedural rationality means that procedures for defining/solving a problem are cognitively reasonable. Generalized procedural rationality means that procedures are generalized reasonable (satisfy generalized rationality as validated by cognition, affection and conation). Right (spiritual) procedural rationality means that procedures are right (satisfy generalized procedural rationality under oneness/love). Otherwise, procedures are non-CGR.

Cognitive, generalized, right and non-CGR procedures so executed tend to produce cognitive, generalized, right and non-CGR problems, respectively. In any case, the resulting generated problem (representation) is tested (validated) and characterized as cognitive, generalized, right rational or non-CGR.[22] Thus, overall procedural rationality (what Simon simply terms procedural rationality) involves testing and characterizing the rationality of both defining/solving procedures and the problem/solution itself. Operational procedures for testing and characterizing procedural rationality and problem rationality as cognitive, generalized, right and non-CGR are discussed in section 9.

In ESD, the problem representation is a system involving relations between sets of elements (hierarchies 1 and 2). The sets – values, goals, controls, criteria, individual preferences and group preference – are purposes of agents. The above definitions for cognitive, generalized and right (spiritual) rationalities and non-CGR apply to the ESD problem representation, as well as to the procedures for defining that representation.

In ESD, all procedures are viewed as *search procedures* – search for (design of) the problem and for a solution to the problem as defined (found) at any present moment. Occurring in both hierarchies 1 and 2, search proceeds through cybernetics/self-organization – at any time may be (1) cybernetic or (2) self-organizing. Cybernetic search is search with control and is based on knowledge. Cybernetic search can involve (a) recognition or (b) heuristic search. With cybernetic search, the search principle being used is known. When the search principle is not known, then search is self-organizing. ESD adds self-organizing search to the recognition and heuristic search procedures discussed by Simon (1995, 1996) and noted in section 6.

In ESD, cybernetic heuristic search procedures are among the evolutionary generating procedures (Shakun 1992, 1999a) for generating, examining, changing (evolving), and retaining a relation in hierarchies 1 and 2. They simultaneously provide cognitive validation for the procedure defining the relation and for the resulting relation itself. In addition to cognitive validation, generalized and right rationalities require affective validation – does this procedure or relation feel reasonable and reasonable/right, respectively, and conative validation – as commitment to implementation of the procedure or relation as reasonable and reasonable/right, respectively.

With cybernetic recognition, an incoming problem stimulus (chunk) is processed by an index (recognition capability) that recognizes it (its features having been previously stored in long term memory) and accesses knowledge associated with it. Knowledge stored by topics (nodes) is linked associatively with other knowledge (Simon 1995, 1996). Search through recognition can find knowledge that is problem evolving.

Cybernetic heuristic search, cybernetic recognition and self-organizing search often work together. For example, in problem restructuring in hierarchy 1, the ESD goals/values referral process (an evolutionary generating procedure) may be used to restructure the goals/values relation. Heuristics in the form of domain-independent methodological knowledge control the system (problem representation) to a bifurcation point (descriptions 1 and 2 in Table 1). With description (1), cybernetics, problem restructuring at the bifurcation point can follow from recognition and retrieval of knowledge from memory. With description (2), cybernetic self-organization, problem restructuring at the bifurcation point is self-organizing rather than based on knowledge retrieved from memory. With description (3), self-organization,

15

self-organizing fluctuations drive the problem representation to a bifurcation point and also generate the new structure the problem representation now follows. With description (4), self-organizing cybernetics, self-organization drives the problem representation to a bifurcation point where selection (cybernetic control) of the new problem structure can follow from recognition and retrieval of knowledge from memory.

A different example of the use of heuristic knowledge is where it is used for cybernetic control of search in defined spaces of possibilities. For example, in a defined hierarchy 2, heuristic search might be used to find satisfactory solutions to nonlinear programming problems. Optimization using algorithms may be viewed as a special case of heuristics.

8. Unbounded rationality

Here we summarize and apply our discussion of rationality to an individual in individual or group decision making, and define unbounded rationality. For that individual, right procedural rationality means that *procedures* are right, i.e., satisfy general rationality (reasonableness as validated by cognition, affection and conation) under oneness/love. Thus, operationally, initiation of problem definition and solution with right procedural rationality means an individual is in or transits to oneness/love – connectedness with One, using techniques as suggested in section 4.1. Later, if an individual has been experiencing connectedness with One but loses it, he tries to reconnect before continuing problem definition and solution. Sometimes an individual must initiate or continue decision making while in separateness/fear (if possible he tries to avoid this). In this case, the individual preferably uses generalized procedural rationality, i.e., generalized reasonable procedures but not right, and failing this uses cognitive or non-CGR procedures, interspersing these procedures with attempts to transit to oneness/love. Sometimes the problem solving process itself (cybernetics/self-organization search in ESD) can facilitate transit to oneness/love[23] permitting right procedural rationality. Whatever the process (problem definition procedure) the individual tests the problem definition and solution (representation) that evolves for rightness. If the evolved problem is right, it delivers oneness/love.

Thus, rightness is applicable to procedures for (1) defining a problem, and for (2) validating (testing) the resulting problem/solution itself. Since right procedural rationality tends to produce right problems, right problem definition and solution generally requires and delivers connectedness with One, spirituality, the ultimate purpose in Two (ultimate value in hierarchy 1) to live Two as One. In other words, problem definition and solution with connectedness with One is open, expansive and less constrained than with non-connectedness, generating more and superior solutions for delivering connectedness with One.

Human unbounded rationality is defined as right or spiritual rationality, the generalized rationality of connectedness with consciousness experiencing connectedness with One manifesting oneness/love/perfect action. Individual unbounded rationality is achieved when an individual or group problem definition and solution is right for that individual.

9. Operationalizing unbounded rationality in group decision and negotiation

For group decision and negotiation, current computer technology allows same-place/same-time work and telework. With telework, group members are distributed physically in space and/or time, i.e., function at different places and/or times. In any case, prior to group problem solving a facilitator briefs the group on the concept of right decision/negotiation, explaining that in principle the group tries to make a right decision, one that is right for all individuals in the group, if possible. Each individual in the group tries to be in oneness/love, connectedness with One. For this, the facilitator may suggest techniques as suggested in section 4.1. If an individual is experiencing connectedness with One, he bases his suggested procedures to the group on right procedural rationality for defining and solving a right group problem. Otherwise, an individual preferably bases his suggested procedures on generalized procedural rationality, i.e., generalized reasonable procedures, but not right, for defining and solving the group problem. If an individual is using generalized procedural rationality, he tries to transit to oneness/love (perhaps with facilitator support) to attain right procedural rationality. If an individual does not base his suggested procedures on generalized or right procedural rationalities (e.g., he bases them on cognitive rationality or affective rationality), he tries to change to generalized or, preferably, to right procedural rationality.

With regard to (1) his own procedural rationality, (2) that of other individuals considering their procedural suggestions, and (3) that of the group considering the procedures actually adopted by the group, each individual can judge whether for him the procedural rationality is right, generalized, cognitive, non-CGR or a mix of these over time. We describe the test (validation) for right procedural rationality. The tests for generalized, cognitive and non-CGR rationalities are similar, less comprehensive versions omitting those elements of right procedural rationality that do not apply.

The test (validation) for right procedural rationality starts with an individual asking himself whether he is experiencing connectedness to One, and replying affirmatively. Then the procedure under test is validated jointly through cognition, affection and conation by the individual questioning himself as follows: Is this procedure (1) cognitively reasonable – is it reasonable in defining/solving the problem under oneness, (2) affectively reasonable

17

– does it feel reasonable under love, and (3) conatively reasonable – am I committed to implementing it under perfection action?

Whatever the (procedure) process, an individual can test a group problem representation that evolves for rightness (or other rationalities). Shakun (1992, 1999a) suggests that validation by an individual of problem represen-tation rightness requires his validation of the rightness of the relations (beliefs) constituting it (with ESD, hierarchies 1 and 2). If all relations are right, the problem representation is right. Operational procedures for an individual testing rightness of a relation involve testing through (1) cognition – is this relation cognitively reasonable and does it deliver oneness, as validated by specified cybernetic/self-organization procedures (evolutionary heuristics or generating procedures) for examining, changing (evolving) and retaining the relations, (2) affection – is this relation affectively reasonable and does it deliver love, feel right, and (3) conation – is this relation conatively reason-able and does it deliver perfect action as commitment to implementation? Shakun (1992, 1999a) discusses some evolutionary generating procedures (e.g., the heuristic controls/goals/values referral process). He considers cases of fully and not-fully-shared information among individuals in the group.[24] Sometimes the evolved group problem is right (i.e., right as judged by all individuals in the group), sometimes it is right for some individuals but not for others, and sometimes it is right for no one. If the evolved problem is right as judged by a particular individual, it delivers oneness/love to him. If it is right for all individuals, it delivers oneness/love to the group. If it is not right for some or all individuals in the group, cybernetics/self-organization search can continue until a right problem is defined and solved leading to implementation of a right solution. Solutions that are not right (wrong) for at least some individuals, as judged respectively by them, are not infrequently implemented in practice. Still transit to oneness/love is possible for ensuing problem solving.

As to practice, Shakun (1999b) discusses how a group may apply the ESD general framework in defining and solving a specific problem. With the help of a facilitator, the group may create and execute a process (procedure) meeting script for the problem that applies ESD implemented by a com-puter group support system (GSS). The meeting script can involve both electronic and non-electronic activities. The meeting script is the detailed agenda or procedural sequence (hopefully, judged by all individuals as fol-lowing right procedural rationality, but not necessarily) that the group chooses in developing the ESD group problem representation (formally, hierarchies 1 and 2).[25] Script management is dynamic including adjustment of meeting scripts "on the fly" during meetings (Keleman, Lewis, and Garcia 1993). Lewis (1995) discusses a general purpose GSS, MeetingWorks for Windows, that has a set of software tools (generate, organize, cross-impact, etc.) for group meeting support. Originally for same-place/same-time work, Meetingworks has been extended to group telework that can be performed on the Internet. Lewis and Shakun (1996) create and execute an illustrative group meeting script with MeetingWorks.[26]

Shakun (1999b) discusses how ESD and MeetingWorks constitute a formal basis for a group ESD computer culture for intercultural problem solving and negotiation. The procedure (process) to be used is outlined by the meeting script. The content consists of the inputed sets of elements and their relations. Content depends of process (procedure) and vice versa, and both are dependent on spirituality[27] and culture[28] as parameters. The evolved ESD group problem representation is thus spirituality and culture dependent on both procedure (process) and content. It is tested for rightness, etc. as noted above in this section.

Finally, we note that spirituality is the source for ethics. ESD, as a formal modeling/design framework for right means (actions) and ends (goals, values), provides a useful methodology for ethics and ethics provides values, goals, and actions for ESD.

10. Concluding remarks

10.1. Human unbounded rationality

Spirituality is consciousness experiencing connectedness with One manifesting oneness/love/perfect action. Two is impermanent. As humans, our connectedness with One is always there. It is choiceless in that it is the default state. For spirituality, experiencing connectedness with One, we merely have to choose to "awake", be open to connectedness in receiver mode or in oneness/love/perfect action computer mode (Chodron 1997, Shakun 1999a). Right problem solving generally requires and delivers spiritual rationality, the generalized rationality of connectedness with One.

Human unbounded rationality is spiritual rationality. Spiritual rationality is the rationality that ultimately matters, that requires and delivers spirituality, our ultimate purpose (ultimate value) in Two to live Two as One. Human unbounded rationality is achievable even with cognitive limitations, i.e., even under Simon's bounded rationality.

10.2. An ESD consciousness theory of intelligence and rationality for natural and artificial agents

From a classical perspective, mind and computer are mutual metaphors wherein intelligence (defined as adaptive behavior) is modeled by cognition viewed as computation operating on symbols (information processing). Thus, the classical approach is a cognitive computational (information processing) theory of intelligence. When to this classical perspective we add our discussions of embodied cognitive science, consciousness and rationality, we are led to consider an ESD consciousness theory of intelligence and rationality applicable to all agents. This includes natural agents (human, animal, plant and matter) and artificial agents (robots, softbots, computers and artifacts in general).

Natural agents have consciousness defined as self-organizing response capacity with awareness embodying inner, subjective, qualitative experience (qualia). Agents have energy/matter and consciousness, i.e., have energy/matter/qualia at different levels. Energy/matter/qualia evolve cumulatively manifesting purpose, conation (response/action via body), affection (emotion, feeling), cognition and human spirituality.[29] The evolution of consciousness may be described as nested evolution with each succeeding consciousness level including or nesting the preceding ones. Humans have all the above consciousness levels. Late mammals have all levels but human spirituality, i.e., evolve cumulatively up to and including cognition. Early mammals evolve to affection (emotion). Reptiles, other lower animals, insects, plants and matter evolve to conation (response/action via body). They all have purpose – to live Two as One. Natural rationality, MacLean's brain model (footnote 7), and the Great Chain (Nest) of Being (footnote 8) all represent consciousness as nested evolution.

Explicitly, *natural rationality* following consciousness evolves cumulatively as purposeful rationality, conative rationality, affective rationality, cognitive rationality, and human spiritual (right) rationality. Humans are capable of all of these rationalities. Late mammals have evolved cumulative capabilities up to and including cognitive rationality, i.e., have generalized rationality capability. Early mammals have capabilities up to and including affective rationality. Reptiles, other lower animals, insects, plants and matter have evolved capability up to conative rationality. They all have purposeful rationality – to live Two as One.

While natural agents are cumulatively capable of their respective rationalities, they do not necessarily employ all of them. For example, some humans employ only or primarily affective rationality in developing procedures for defining a problem and validating the resulting problem/solution. Some humans use only or primarily cognitive rationality. For the ultimate purpose in Two to live Two as One, what we have recommended in sections 7 through 9 is that humans try to employ their rationality capability to the fullest extent possible, ideally using spiritual (right) rationality, an ideal that is realizable.

The classical information processing theory of intelligence uses only the cognitive computational manifestation of consciousness as a theory of intelligence for both human and artificial agents. This cognitive computational theory of intelligence while very useful is incomplete. The ESD consciousness theory of intelligence and rationality described above is based on natural consciousness and rationality, and in particular, that of humans whose evolution of consciousness and rationality is at present the most advanced and comprehensive. Thus, it can serve as an intelligence/

rationality framework for artificial agents, as well as other natural agents.

PCAS whether individual or multiagent, whether natural or artificial (or both in multiagent systems) can be modeled/designed using the ESD consciousness theory of intelligence and rationality that accommodates the various levels of consciousness and rationality discussed above and with which unbounded rationality is possible. With the ESD approach to PCAS, modeling and designing means not only defining and solving a problem given human (more generally, natural) and/or artificial agents having various rationality capabilities in a given multiagent system, but also modeling/designing the agents and multiagent system as well.

In closing, we note that with regard to modeling/designing artificial agents, human and artificial designers have relied primarily on cognition – on the classical cognitive computational (information processing) theory of intelligence. Newer approaches include introducing conation (action via embodiment) as in embodied cognitive science. Here cognition emerges from interaction of an embodied agent and an environment through sensory-motor coordination (section 4). Picard (1997) discusses affection (emotion, feeling) in artificial agents. For a discussion of spirituality in artificial agents, see Kurzwell (1999). Research continues.

Notes

1 A system is a set of elements and their relations. A process is a time description of a system, i.e., a dynamical system.

2 With ESD sensemaking as discussed by Weick and Meader (1993) is integral to formal modelling.

3 The terms group support system (GSS) and negotiation support system (NSS) are sometimes used to emphasize support of different aspects of task-oriented group processes. Group members may be distributed physically in space and/or time, i.e., function at a distance at different places and/or times in telework problem solving and negotiation. In this case, the terms distributed GSS or NSS are applicable.

4 Mathematically, a relation is a subset of a Cartesian product of sets.

5 Formal problem relations (always explicit) are expressed by the formal group problem representation. There are always also informal relations, those not expressed in the formal group problem representation, that may be explicit or implicit. The popular expression "no problem" means that the problem is solved.

6 The mathematical model problem representation (dynamical system) is given by relations (5), (6), (7), (8), (9) and a goals/criteria relation in Shakun (1988), chapter 1. A coalition (group) C plays a game in time over a planning horizon against the set $\bar{C}$ of all other players not in C who themselves can form one or more coalitions. The game has a moving present and is an evolving difference game. (Dynamical (described in time) systems in discrete (continuous) time with two or more players are called difference (differential) games). Relation (5) is represented in hierarchy 1 which shows the controls/goals/values relation. Relation (6) is represented in hierarchy 2 as the individual and group (coalition C) preference structures. Relations (7), (8), (9) are represented in hierarchy 2 by the

technology relation between controls and goals. The goals/criteria relation is also represented in hierarchy 2. The relations (5), (6), (7), (8), (9) and the goals/criteria relation model cybernetics/self organization.

7   The triune brain model of MacLean (1990) involves three evolutionary forma-tions – R-complex (reptilian complex), limbic system, and neocortex associated with reptilian-behavior (reptiles), emotion (early mammals), and cognitive func-tions (late mammals), respectively. Reptilian behaviors observed in humans are described by MacLean. They include special forms of behavior as establishment of territory, challenge displays, submissive displays, courtship behavior, and so on, and general interoperative forms of behavior that come into play in several different contexts and may involve several special forms of behavior.

8   For example, the full context of human experience (consciousness) suggests being open to Wilbur (1998) who discussed the need for integration of science (and the other differentiations of modernity, i.e., art and morals) with the Great Chain (Nest) of Being of the "perennial philosophy" or "ageless wisdom". The Great Chain (Nest) reaches from matter to body to mind to soul to spirit with each succeeding level enveloping or nesting the preceding ones. Soul, if accepted, may be viewed as the relation between One (Father – spirit) and Two (Mother – matter, body, mind) manifesting yang (masculinity) and yin (femininity). Consciousness, One and Two are discussed below; see also McLaughlin and Davidson (1994).

9   For some, God is the organizer of consciousness.

10 Chalmers (1995) defines consciousness as subjective experience reserving the term "awareness" for the simultaneously occurring objective, physical (neural) correlates. He speculates that subjective experience and physical neural process-ing are simultaneous aspects of a single information state.

11 An emergent property or output is a new property transcending, or going bey-ond, the properties of the inputs (components) used in modeling it. Zohar and Marshall (1994) consider consciousness as an emergent property of quantum processing in the brain. De Quincey (1997), in reviewing Hameroff, Kaszniak and Scott (1996), raises two challenges for the study of consciousness. The first involves the fundamental nature of reality (ontology). De Quincey discusses four approaches: materialism (matter/energy is primary and consciousness emerges); dualism (both matter and consciousness exist independently and separately); idealism (consciousness is primary and matter emerges); and panpsychism, panexperientialism, radical naturalism or double-aspectism (reality is intrinsic-ally both matter and consciousness which are not separate). The second chal-lenge concerns how we obtain knowledge about consciousness (epistemology). De Quincey notes three approaches: the third-person (objective) approach, the first-person (subjective, what consciousness feels like within), and the second-person (intersubjective, I-thou relation). See also De Quincey (2000a, b).

12 Connectedness with One is inclusive of knowing (Shakun 1992). Knowing is consciousness experiencing connectedness with One as manifestation of Two from One.

13 In classical Chinese philosophy (Lau 1961, Merton 1969), wu wei (meaning liter-ally "without action", wu meaning "nothing") is the name for perfect action/non-action. Wu wei means perfect action for any action (conation) in Two in perfect harmony with, i.e., connected with, One (Tao), and non-action for any action in Two not connected with One.

14 We use the terms "oneness" or "oneness/love" as short for oneness/love/perfect action, and "separateness" or "separateness/fear" as short for separateness/fear/non-connected action.

15 Values, goals and actions are cognitive sets. Agents of a culture also share emotional (Faure, Le Dong and Shakun (1990), reptilian (Shakun 1992), and spiritual (Shakun 1999a) elements that, if desired, can be expressed cognitively as values, goals and actions in the ESD problem representation (hierarchies 1 and 2).

16 Through memory and spiritual knowing, the computer and receiver modes of consciousness encompass modes associated with the left (analytic, rational, logical, sequential) and right (intuitive, holistic, simultaneous, gestalt) hemispheres of the brain.

17 The knowledge in memory may reside in an agent's personal memory or in extended computer memory.

18 The edge of chaos is the phase transition between the order (stability) and disorder (instability, chaos) zones of operation of a complex adaptive system. The edge of chaos is the space of creativity (novelty). See Stacy (1996).

19 Chodron considers that fear is rooted in fear of death.

20 In Buddhism, openness or emptiness in Two means not fixating or holding on to anything.

21 The purpose 1/purpose 2 relation constitutes meaning Shakun (1988). Motivation refers to meaning and purpose. Attention connects motivation and emotion with cognition (Simon 1994).

22 An example of non-CGR rationality is affective rationality applying to procedures or problems validated only by affection.

23 In ESD, for example, the heuristic controls/goals/values referral process can facilitate transit from separateness/fear in computer mode to oneness/love in that mode or receiver mode.

24 In the general case of not-fully-shared (nonshared) information among individuals in a group, each individual can judge the rightness for him of his own private group problem representation, as well as the rightness for him of the incomplete public one. If for all individuals the respective private group problem representations are right for each of them and a group compromise solution has been found by the group, then a right group problem has been defined and solves, although it is publicly represented incompletely.

   Regarding the public representation, if each individual judges that the incomplete public group problem representation is right for him, it follows that the incomplete public individual problem representations as judged by the respective individuals are right for them, and that the incomplete public group representation is right as far as it goes but is incomplete.

   In the special case of full information sharing, the public group problem representation is complete. All individuals have the same private group problem representation, that is, the public one. In this case, if each individual judges that the public group problem representation is right for him, then the public group problem representation is right and complete. If a compromise solution has been found, the group publicly knows the complete group problem it has defined and solved, and it is a right one.

25 Rubenstein (1998) models formally some procedural aspects of cognitive bounded rationality that can be incorporated into the procedure meeting script. Creation of a procedure script is applicable to individual decision making, as well as to group decision making.

26 Of course, other general-purpose GSS, e.g., GroupSystems, can be used with ESD. More specialized negotiation capability as NEGOTIATOR can be added (Bui and Shakun 1996).

27 Spirituality dependent means that procedure and content are dependent on whether individuals are in or out of spirituality, i.e., they are dependent on consciousness mode – oneness/love (in spirituality) or separateness/fear (out of spirituality).
28 Culture can mean any one culture or that of a multicultural group. See Shakun (1996b).
29 Agents, in general, experience connectedness with One and thus, by definition, spirituality, but at the human spirituality level non-connectedness and spirituality become a significant variable for consciousness.

References

Birch, J. (1993). *Loving Change*. Putney, Vermont: StressPress.
Bui, T., and Shakun, M. F. (1996). "Negotiation Processes, Evolutionary Systems Design and NEGOTIATOR," *Group Decision and Negotiation* 5(4–6).
Chalmers, D. J. (1995). "The Puzzle of Conscious Experience," *Scientific American* 273(6), December.
Chodron, P. (1997). *When Things Fall Apart*. Boston, MA: Shambhala Publications.
Csikszentmihalyi, M. (1990). *Flow: The Psychology of Experience*. New York: Harper Perennial.
De Quincey, C. (1997). "Consciousness: The Final Frontier," *IONS Noetic Sciences Review* 42, Summer.
De Quincey, C. (2000a). "Consciousness: Truth or Wisdom," *IONS Noetic Sciences Review* 51, March–June.
De Quincey, C. (2000b). "Conceiving the Inconceivable: Fishing for Consciousness with a Net of Miracles," *Journal of Consciousness Studies* 7(4).
Faure, G. O., Le Dong, V., and Shakun, M. F. (1990). "Social-Emotional Aspects of Negotiation," *European Journal of Operational Research* 46(2), 177–180.
Fisher, R., Ury, W., and Patton, B. (1991). *Getting to Yes*. New York: Penguin Books.
Hameroff, S. R., Kaszniak, A. W., and Scott, A. C. (eds.) (1996). *Toward a Science of Consciousness: The First Tucson Discussions and Debates*. Cambridge, MA: The MIT Press.
Jampolsky, G. G. (1979). *Love is Letting Go of Fear*. Millbrae, CA: Celestial Arts.
Keleman, K. S., Lewis, L. F., and Garcia, J. E. (1993). "Script Management: A link Between Group Support Systems and Organizational Learning," *Small Group Research* 24(4), 566–582.
Kersten, G. E. *et al.* (1988). "Representing the Negotiation Problem with a Rule-Based Formalism," *Theory and Decision* 25(3), 225–257.
Kersten, G. E. *et al.* (1991). "Restructurable Representations of Negotiation," *Management Science* 37(October), 1269–1290.
Kurzwell, R. (1999). *The Age of Spiritual Machines*. New York: Viking Penguin.
Lau, D. C. (trans.) (1961). *Lao Tzu, Tao Te Ching*. Hammondsworth, England: Penguin Books.
Lewis, L. F. (1995). *Group Support Systems: A Brief Introduction*. Bellingham, Washington: MeetingWorks Associates.
Lewis, L. F., and Shakun, M. F. (1996). "Using MeetingWorks for Windows Group Support System to Implement Evolutionary Systems Design," *Group Decision and Negotiation* 5(4–6).

MacLean, P. D. (1990). *The Triune Brain in Evolution.* New York: Plenum Press.

McLaughlin, C., and Davidson, G. (1994). *Spiritual Politics.* New York: Ballantine Books.

Merton, T. (1969). *The Way of Chuang Tzu.* New York: New Directions.

Munier, B., Selten, R. *et al.* (1999). "Bounded Rationality Modeling," Note de Recherche GRID 99–01, Departement d'Economie et Gestion, Ecole Normale Supieure, Cachan, France.

Nunez, R. (1999). "Could the Future Taste Purple? Reclaiming Mind, Body and Cognition," *in* R. Nunez and Freeman (eds.).

Nunez, R., and Freeman W. J. (eds.). (1999). *Reclaiming Cognition: The Primacy of Action, Intention and Emotion. Journal of Consciousness Studies* 6(11–12), November/December.

Pfeifer, R., and Scheier, C. (1999). *Understanding Intelligence.* Cambridge, MA: The MIT Press.

Picard, R. W. (1997). *Affective Computing.* Cambridge, MA: The MIT Press.

Pransky, G. S. (1995). *Living in Mental Well Being*, Parts One and Two, *Audiotapes.* LaConner, Washington: Pransky and Associates.

Rubenstein, A. (1998). *Modeling Bounded Rationality.* Cambridge, MA: The MIT Press.

Shakun, M. F. (1988). *Evolutionary Systems Design: Policy Making Under Complexity and Group Decision Support Systems.* Oakland, CA: Holden-Day.

Shakun, M. F. (1990). "Group Decision and Negotiation Support in Evolving, Nonshared Information Contexts," *Theory and Decision* 28(3), 275–288.

Shakun, M. F. (1991). "Airline Buyout: Evolutionary Systems Design and Problem Restructuring in Group Decision and Negotiation," *Management Science* 37(10), 1291–1303.

Shakun, M. F. (1992). "Defining a Right Problem in Group Decision and Negotiation: Feeling and Evolutionary Generating Procedures," *Group Decision and Negotiation* 1(1), 27–40.

Shakun, M. F. (1995). "Restructuring a Negotiation with Evolutionary Systems Design," *Negotiation Journal* 11(2), 145–150.

Shakun, M. F. (1996a). "Modeling and Supporting Task-Oriented Group Processes: Purposeful Complex Adaptive Systems and Evolutionary Systems Design," *Group Decision and Negotiation* 5(4–6), 305–317.

Shakun, M. F. (1996b). "Intercultural Group Decision and Negotiation with ESD and Computer Support," *Proceedings of the 1996 IEEE International Conference on Systems, Man and Cybernetics.* Beijing, October 14–17, 1996.

Shakun, M. F. (1999a). "Consciousness, Spirituality and Right Decision/Negotiation in Purposeful Complex Adaptive Systems," *Group Decision and Negotiation* 8(1), 1–15.

Shakun, M. F. (1999b). "An ESD Computer Culture for Intercultural Problem Solving and Negotiation," *Group Decision and Negotiation* 8(3), 237–249.

Simon, H. A. (1955). "A Behavioral Model of Rational Choice," *Quarterly Journal of Economics* 66, 99–118.

Simon, H. A. (1956). "Rational Choice and the Structure of the Environment," *Psychological Review* 63, 129–138.

Simon, H. A. (1978). "Rationality as Process and Product of Thought," *American Economic Review* 68(2), 1–16.

Simon, H. A. (1986). "Rationality in Psychology and Economics", *in* R. M. Hogarth, and M. W. Reder (eds.), *Rational Choice: The Contrast between Economics and Psychology*. Chicago, IL: The University of Chicago Press, pp. 25–40.

Simon, H. A. (1994). "The Bottleneck of Attention: Connecting Thought with Motivation", *in* W. D. Spaulding (ed.), *Integrative Views on Motivation, Cognition and Emotion*. Lincoln, NE: University of Nebraska Press, pp. 1–21.

Simon, H. A. (1995). "The Information Processing Theory of Mind," *American Psychologist* 50, 507–508.

Simon, H. A. (1996). *The Sciences of the Artificial*, 3rd ed. Cambridge, MA: The MIT Press.

Stacey, R. D. (1996). *Complexity and Creativity in Organizations*. San Francisco, CA: Berrett-Koehler Publishers.

Sycara, K. P. (1990). "Negotiation Planning: An AI Approach," *European Journal of Operational Research* 46(2), 216–234.

Sycara, K. P. (1991). "Problem Restructuring in Negotiation," *Management Science* 37(October), 1248–1268.

Weik, K. E., and Meader, D. K. (1993). "Sensemaking and Group Support Systems", *in* L. M. Jessup, and J. S. Valacich (eds.), *Group Support Systems: New Perspectives*. New York: Macmillan Publishing Company.

Wilbur, K. (1998). *The Marriage of Sense and Soul*. New York: Random House.

Yu, P. L. (1995). *Habitual Domains*. Shawnee Missions, Kansas: Highwater Editions.

Zohar, D., and Marshall, I. (1994). *The Quantum Society*, New York: William Morrow.

Zukav, G. (2000). *Soul Stories*. New York: Simon & Schuster.

50

NEITHER AN ANGEL
NOR AN ANT

Emotion as an aid to bounded rationality

Yaniv Hanoch

Source: *Journal of Economic Psychology*, 23, (2002): 1–25.

Abstract

The role of emotion as a source of bounded rationality has been largely ignored. Following Herbert Simon, economists as well as psychologists have mainly focused on cognitive constraints while neglecting to integrate the growing body of research on emotion which indicates that reason and emotion are interconnected. Accordingly, the present paper aims to bridge the existing gap. By establishing a link between the two domains of research, emotion and bounded rationality, it will be suggested that emotions work together with rational thinking in two distinct ways, and thereby function as an additional source of bounded rationality. The aim, therefore, is not to offer an alternative to bounded rationality; rather, the purpose is to elaborate and supplement themes emerging out of bounded rationality.

1. Introduction

A survey by Lewin (1996) provides an historical analysis regarding economists' departure from Bentham's original formulation of the utility construct, where emotions played a significant role, and reliant instead on cognitive factors. Rabin's (1998) survey "Psychology and Economics" has, on the other hand, little to say about emotions. This is a neglect characteristic of economists. Although cognitive psychology and economics have influenced one another as in the work of Tversky and Kahneman (1973, 1974), no similar exchange of ideas has taken place nor has any prominent figure arisen to establish a bond between emotion and economic theories (Elster, 1998). As this lacuna has only lately been acknowledged (Earl, 1986a, 1990;

Elster, 1999; Etzioni, 1988; Frank, 1988; Loewenstein, 2000), few attempts have been made to bridge the existing gap. Bounded Rationality has been one area where little exchange of ideas between emotion and economic theorists has taken place.

Simon's (1947, 1955, 1982a), and others' (Conlisk, 1996; March, 1978), concept of Bounded Rationality (hereafter BR) has received much attention ever since it was first introduced – Simon, for example, won the Nobel Prize in economics in 1978. In fact, BR has become a prominent theory influencing many domains of research including economics, political science, psychology, and artificial intelligence. One of Simon's main concerns in developing the concept of BR, was to explain human reasoned thinking and behavior. In a way, he disagreed with prevailing models of human rationality and irrationality, arguing that they fell short in their ability to depict a realistic representation of human behavior. He wrote, for example, that:

> We may deem behavior irrational because, although it serves some particular impulse, it is inconsistent with other goals that we may deem more important. We may deem it irrational because the actor is proceeding on incorrect facts or ignoring whole areas of relevant facts. We may deem it irrational because the actor has not drawn the correct conclusions from the facts. We may deem it irrational because the actor has failed to consider important alternative courses of action. If the action involves the future, as most action does, we may deem it irrational because we don't think the actor uses the best methods for forming expectations or for adapting to uncertainty. All of these forms of irrationality play important roles in the lives of every one of us, but I think it is misleading to call them irrationality. They are better viewed as forms of bounded rationality.
> (Simon, 1985, p. 297)

Simon's argument can be divided into two domains (March, 1978), both aimed, among other things, at bringing psychology and economics closer together. The first, articulated in his paper of 1955, argues that rationality is constrained, hence bounded, since we possess limited computational ability and selective memory and perception. The second line of argument, developed in his paper of 1956, concerns economists' neglecting to integrate environmental factors into their consideration of rationality. He asserts that "we might hope to discover, by careful examination of some of the fundamental structural characteristics of the environment, some further clues as to the nature of the approximating mechanisms used in decision making" (cf. Simon, 1956, p. 130).

Simon's focus on cognitive capabilities as the sole source of BR is in accord with the research mode in psychology and economics. On the one hand he maintains that "people have reasons for what they do; they have motivations and use reason (well or badly) to respond to these motivations and reach their goal" (cf. Simon, 1987, pp. 25–26), and on the other hand he argues that "reason is wholly instrumental. It cannot tell us where to go; at best it can tell us how to get there. It is a gun for hire that can be employed in the service of whatever goals we have, good or bad" (1983, pp. 7–8). Indeed, people use reason to respond to these motivations, but they also use emotions. What sets the stage is our emotional mechanism, while one function of reason is to explore the possible paths to get there. That is, while ends cannot be determined logically by reason (Hare, 1963; Popper, 1962), once ends are determined, it is the role of reason to take us there. "In circumstances sufficiently known", Shackle (1972, p. 135) argues, "reason may tell what action will lead to what end. But reason will not tell what end ought to be chosen".

Working mainly within the cognitive framework and concentrating on ends rather than process, it is not surprising that economists have neglected to examine the role emotions might play in BR. Aside from scattered research (Kaufman, 1999; Pieters & van Raaij, 1988; Simon, 1967, 1982b) little has been done to incorporate the growing body of research on emotion into the domain of BR, nor have emotion theorist tried to integrate BR into their discourse. Reading the literature on BR, one might suspect that emotions do not exist, or that their contribution is, at best, minimal. Indeed, Davis (1996) and Dennard (1995) have criticized Simon's work for portraying humans' behavior in a cold manner, thus creating a unidimensional view. Davis writes that Simon's depiction of the supremacy of rationality ignores aspects of "democracy, justice, equality and so forth" (1996, p. 44). Dennard, likewise, asserts that "neo-Darwinists, like Simon, enamored of skills, techniques, tasks, and programs, have made light of the very human need for idealism and aspiration – emotional dispositions that could lead to a more humane world than which rational economics can conceptually master" (1995, p. 464). Adopting Simon's work, these authors argue, presents individuals as an inferior image of Mr. Spock – unemotional but without Spock's information processing capacities (Earl, 2001).

Emotions, we hope to show, can be seen to function as a vital mechanism. We suggest that emotions operate with rational thinking in two distinct modes: (i) they restrict the range of options contemplated and evaluated; (ii) they focus the agent's attention on specific parameters or aspects of the information. The aim is to illustrate the junctions at which emotions and bounded rationality conjoin, without committing to the stronger claim that emotions have a beneficial and/or deleterious effect. They might have both.

Integrating emotions into the BR equation might provide an additional source of explanation pertaining to how humans, despite their limited cognitive ability, function as well as they do. The questions of how a person decides when to start and/or stop evaluating relevant information, of which information he or she decides to incorporate into the equation, and which bites of information receive priorities still need an adequate answer (but see below Simon's notion of satisficing). At least partially, however, the answer is through emotions.

2. Subjective expected utility

BR has emerged, in part, as a reaction to the Subjective Expected Utility (SEU) model (von Neumann & Morgenstern, 1947). Researchers working in the field of decision-making (Zey, 1992) and rationality (Brown, 1978; Elster, 1984) have come to realize that SEU offers only limited explanation power. Although the theory has been beneficial in many ways, it does not provide an accurate description of the human mind.

There are several assumptions underlying SEU. Firstly, a person is assumed to possess a well-defined utility function. Hence, it is presumed that people can assign values as an indicator of their preference towards different stimuli or events in a given scenario (present and future). Secondly, it presupposes that individuals are faced with a well-defined cluster of options from which to choose. SEU does not require the entire scenario to be a one-time occasion, but as Simon indicates, "may entail sequences of choices or strategies in which each subchoice will be made only at a specified time using the information available at that time" (1983, p. 12). Thirdly, it maintains that individuals can provide uniform mutual probabilities distribution to all events (Macleod, 1996). Finally, it predicts that the decision-maker will pick the option, or the strategy that delivers the highest expected value, in terms of his utility function, of a set of events consequent upon the strategy. Although the theory has many problems that make it close to impossible to use in a straightforward way, it has certainly made a major contribution to economic theory.

There are four basic objections to SEU. The theory assumes that the individual comprehensively examines the entire range of possibilities; that he grasps the whole spectrum of options open to him at present as well as far into the future; that he comprehends the results of each of the alternatives possible, at least up to the point of being able to assign a joint probability distribution to future states of the world; and, in Simon's words, "that he has reconciled or balanced all his conflicting partial values and synthesized them into a single coherent utility function that orders, by his reference for them, all these future states of the world" (1983, p. 13).

Researchers (Arrow, 1992; Hollins & Nell, 1975; March, 1994) have presented numerous challenges to the above assumptions. The shortcomings of the theory come from several fronts. Firstly, all possible alternatives are not known (Levi, 1997). Even among the known alternatives, the outcomes attached to each are not known. Secondly, some issues never reach the agent making the decision. Thirdly, Some problems that do reach the agents but are evaluated or defined as insignificant and irrelevant. Finally, agents' information may be lacking, unrelated, too complicated, and too vast.

March (1978) has raised several additional problems with SEU. He maintains that the properties of taste (which might bear a closer relationship to emotional evaluation rather than to rational deliberation), as depicted in standard theories of choice, seem inconsistent with the observation of both individuals' and organizations' choice behavior (see also Etzioni, 1992, pp. 14–17). Tastes, according to normative description, are absolute, stable, consistent, precise, exogenous, and relevant (March, 1978, pp. 595–596). Yet, individuals are not always consistent in their tastes; tastes tend to change throughout life; choices are made without respect to taste, and at times are contrary to our tastes (such as when our tastes contradict societal norms or laws); tastes are not precise, and tastes are partially determined endogenously (March, 1978). By juxtaposing neoclassical economics and bounded rationality, March not only points out the shortcoming of SEU, but also argues that theory of choice must have a better understanding of the intricacy of preference processing. This is due to the fact that "goals and preferences are at the same time premises for and outcomes of human and organizational choice" (Augier & Kreiner, 2000, p. 675). It is not surprising, then, that Simon claims that "SEU theory has never been applied, nor will it, by any human" (1983, p. 14).

3. Bounded rationality

The problems inherent in SEU have driven the search for an alternative model. One model to emerge in the late 1940s is Simon's Bounded Rationality (cf. Simon, 1947). One aim of BR is to overcome the obstacles presented in SEU and to introduce a model that can more accurately describe the manner in which we make decisions. A basic notion that will be exceedingly important in the rest of the paper is that we are living in an unpredictable world, with limited knowledge of that world, and with limited processing capabilities. One of Simon's intentions in developing BR was to illustrate the restricted ability we have as rational agents. He argues that "human beings have neither the facts nor the consistent structure of values nor the reasoning power at their disposal that would be required, even in these relatively simple situations, to apply SEU models" (1983, p. 17).

One important factor operating in the process of decision making is our effort investment. If one is looking into investing a large sum of money, for example, one is expected to examine the matter seriously by exploring the various options, risks, interest, etc. One must devote resources in the form of time and effort to investigating the various aspects of that investment. After one has gathered the relevant information (if one can gather all relevant information), one still needs to conduct an evaluation, and perhaps re-check one's ideas. What we are stating here is that when we are faced with a decision we have to devote many resources – time, money, energy, etc. – to it.

BR does not assume that one has to make choices that reach far into the future, that encompasses the whole spectrum of human values, and in which each problem is interconnected with all the other problems in the world. On the contrary, the environment in which we live is one characterized by the unique nature of each problem. At different times we make decisions concerning our biological needs (e.g., hunger), physiological needs (e.g., sleep) and psychological needs (e.g., love). Luckily, we seldom need to resolve all these problems at once. Maslow's ideas regarding hierarchy of needs capitalize precisely on this point. We can, of course, be hungry and tired at the same time, but the most urgent need must be satisfied first (Robbins, 1984, pp. 114–115). You will, if you are starving, probably eat before you will go to bed. While we have many needs that at times co-occur we act as if one is more pressing than the other (Jáiuregui, 1995).

In most of the day-to-day scenarios we encounter, we can comprehend or assimilate only a fraction of the variables or stimuli present: that is, we are limited in our information-processing capacities. We can assimilate, pay attention, focus, and perform one, or at most a few, functions simultaneously. As Heiner (1983) pointed out, the nature of uncertainty is imbedded in the fact that individuals cannot unravel all the complexity of the decision problem they face – which is one reason they cannot choose the best option.

The above description of the world might present, however, difficulties. We can speculate that the mechanism for reasoning "is adaptive" and was sufficient at one point to function within the boundaries just described. The caveman's environment was not saturated with information to the degree that ours is today. Simon claims that in fact very little was happening most of the time, although action had to be periodically taken to deal with our basic needs such as finding food, securing protection, and raising children. Rational mechanisms could focus on dealing with one or with a few problems at a time, with the expectation that when other problems arose there would be time to deal with those too. Furthermore, the argument advanced by Heiner builds on the notion that our simple ways of dealing with the environment make it easier for others to predict our behavior. That is, "the factors that standard theory places in the error term are in fact what is producing regularity, while optimizing will tend to produce sophisticated deviation from these patterns" (Heiner, 1983, p. 585).

One question we can ask is what mechanisms an organism needs in order to employ a reasonable kind of bounded rationality? The first obvious answer might be: a mechanism which discriminates between the various types of incoming information and which allows one to focus one's attention on a selective set of information. Further, we need a mechanism endowed with the ability to generate alternatives: a large part of our problem-solving consists of searching for alternatives or improvements on the alternatives we

32

already have. The third mechanism we might need is one with a capacity for gathering facts about the environment in which we live and an ability to draw inferences from these observations. The last mechanism an organism might need is a start and stop rule.

Simon has provided one possibility pertaining to the above questions: instead of optimizing, as suggested by SEU, people search for a "good enough" solution (see Radner, 1975). One should note, however, that "bounded rationality is not the study of optimization in relation to task environment" (Simon, 1991, p. 35). Instead, satisficing, as Gigerenzer and Todd argue, "is a method for making a choice from a set of alternatives encountered sequentially when one does not know much about the possibilities ahead of time" (1999, p. 13). The idea is that although optimal solutions might exist (as in a game of chess), human limited cognitive capacities render it close to impossible, if not impossible, to find them. Instead of searching all possible alternatives, computing utility function for each strategy, and memorizing all the facts, one decides according to simpler mechanism: satisficing. Satisficing creates mental "shortcuts" that allows the decision maker to end the search once he or she encounters an alternative that meets or exceeds a specific aspiration level (Earl, 1983, pp. 78–81). Satisficing, according to March, "is less of a decision rule than a search rule. It specifies the conditions under which search is triggered or stops, and it directs search to areas of failure" (1994, p. 27).

4. Emotions as an aid to bounded rationality

Research on emotions, both in theory and in empirical finding, has proliferated greatly in the last three decades (Ekman & Davidson, 1994; Izard, 1977; Frijda, 1986; Lazarus, 1991; Oatley, 1992). While emotions have traditionally been predominately judged to be disorganized and irrational, more up-to-date theories have struggled to argue the opposite (De Sousa, 1987; Leeper, 1948). Indeed, emotions have, in recent years, been portrayed as rational (Lyons, 1980; Turski, 1994), as functional (Ben-Ze'ev, 2000; LeDoux, 1996), and as a necessary tool in decision-making (Charland, 1998; Damasio, 1994; Picard, 1997). In light of these changes, the purpose of this study is to show that the emotions constitute a phenomenon that supplements themes arising out of bounded rationality, and hence satisfies Elster's first issue concerning rationality and the emotions (see Elster, 1999, pp. 283–284). What we mean by this is that emotions function as an information processing mechanism with their own internal logic, working in conjunction with rational calculation. By restricting the range of options considered (reducing the load on short and long term memory), by focusing on certain variables (certain stimuli receive higher ranking order), and by initiating and terminating the evaluation process (working as a satisficing mechanism), emotions supplement the insufficiencies of reason. In other words, while humans' rationality is limited in its information processing capacity (Simon, 1982a, 1967), emotions serve as one of the tools, designed by evolution, by which we manage to function as well as we do (Panksepp, 1996; Plutchik, 1980; Tooby & Cosmides, 1990).

5. Emotions as a prioritizing mechanism

5.1. Attention as a scarce resource

One of the problems raised by Simon is which goal an agent must attend to first, given the multiple goals we have (i.e., why goal X has higher order ranking than goal Y). One needs a system that will create a hierarchical order of prioritization and postponement. What is the mechanism of that system?[1] While we acknowledge that more than one mechanism might underline this procedure, currently we aim to deal with only one: our emotions. Following Oatley and Johnson-Laird (1987), we propose that emotions are part of the arsenal available to us to find our way in a world with multiple goals – given its constraints of time, energy, and other resources. This last point, constraints on resources, has generally been overlooked by economists. Berger (1989), following Simon (1978) and March (1982), argues that we should treat attention as a scarce resource, and as such, should accredit attention a more prominent place in economics. Attention playing a crucial role in coordinating behavior, in knowledge, and in communication – is therefore important in all economic phenomena. Since attentional deployment "cannot be explained by recourse to calculation with respect to underlying objects constituting the economic environment" (Berger, 1989, p. 220), we need to investigate other mechanisms that shed light on the phenomenon. Furthermore, because reason "can't select our final goals, nor can it mediate for us in pure conflicts over what final goal to pursue – we have to settle these issues in some other way" (Simon, 1983, p. 106). One other way, we maintain, is via our emotions.

People tend to have, simultaneously, several goals. At times these goals contradict one another; at times they have no relationship with each other; sometimes they have some bearing on one another, and at other times are the first step to achieving a higher ranking goal (e.g., to save money [subgoal 1], in order to retire comfortably [goal 1]). One way in which emotions function is to divert a particular course of action being taken in order to pursue a more urgent objective. That is, while one might be in the course of pursuing goal X, emotional arousal can subvert attention in order to pursue goal Y. Thus, emotions can function as a mechanism for establishing a hierarchy of goals by pressing us to pursue goals that have high survival value while setting aside less urgent ones. In the words of Simon, "emotion can . . . distract you from your current focus of thought, and call your attention to something else that presumably needs attention right now" (1983,

p. 21). Focusing and directing our attention is one of the fundamental roles played by our emotions. Like thirst or hunger, all emotion informs us that something in the environment needs our immediate attention and resources.

To see how the mechanism works, the research done by LeDoux (1994) and others (Berkowitz, 1993; Panksepp, 1982) can be of assistance. They maintain that information processing can occur in two different channels. The first, the emotional channel, is shorter though less precise ("quick but dirty" as LeDoux terms it); the second, the rational, is slower, though more precise. Evolution has, in a sense, given us two options: (i) act fast, with the risk of making mistakes, or (ii) act slowly, though with more precision. There are advantages, of course, to each option. (For a discussion on the tradeoff between accuracy and information gathering, see Heiner, 1986.)[2] But in cases of danger, as Zajonc points out, "the decision to run must be made on the basis of minimal cognitive engagement" (1980, p. 156). The "decision" on which path to take is executed automatically with no conscious awareness. Information 'is moving through each neural network simultaneously, and depending on the meaning attached to the information, we can react either in a preprogrammed way (Ekman, 1992; Panksepp, 1982), or we can further evaluate the information. That is, if the information carries with it a particular signal such as danger, then an emotional schema is activated, which produces a reaction; but if the information does not fit a preprogrammed criterion, a more elaborate deliberation can occur. We are not, of course, in control of the process. We cannot decide whether to activate the emotional program or to rely on our rational thinking. In a sense, the emotional system is designed to react to stimuli (i.e., predators) in a schematic fashion with "the most-likely-to-succeed behavior" (LeDoux, 1996, p. 175).

An example might help to illustrate the above point. Imagine you are walking in the forest, enjoying the sites, smells, and tranquility of the surroundings. Your goal might be, say, to pick berries, or to reach the top of a mountain. While hiking, you suddenly see an object resembling a snake. Before you have time to think things over you jump backwards. The process of jumping back emanated not from rational thinking about the nature of the object, nor from rationally thinking about the options available to you. Rather, as LeDoux maintains (see also Darwin, 1965), the entire process is regulated and orchestrated by our emotional mechanism. These reactions have been shaped by evolution and occur automatically (Griffiths, 1997). When danger looms, it is highly advantageous to respond quickly. The time saved by activating the emotional centers, rather than waiting for rational decision, "may be the difference between life and death" (LeDoux, 1996, p. 166). Since rational thinking takes a longer time, deploying the emotional mechanism to govern the procedure has the potential to save our life. Thus, while goal X (picking berries) was governing our actions, emotional arousal has shifted the course of the plan, and created a new plan or a goal: staying alive.

This description, in turn, can be viewed as a satisficing mechanism, providing one potential response to "the infinite regress" problem. The infinite regress problem deals with the problem that "if we can economize on economizing, than we economize on economizing on economizing, and so on" (Conlisk, 1996, p. 687).

Let us consider the infinite regress problem from the following example. In cases of danger (perhaps a predator or a suspicious figure in a dark street), the decision to stop evaluating information (or choosing the best strategy) and to act is activated automatically, with no, or little, cognitive evaluation. The decision-maker does not need to consider additional information; she does not have to decide how to decide how to decide . . . as Lipman (1991) has suggested. There is simply no time to thoroughly evaluate the situation, if one wants to make it home. There is no time to contemplate the precise nature of the object (whether the man in the dark street is your friend or a potential killer). There is no time to gather additional information (should I wait and look closely at his face?) – given the imprecise nature of the person's perception of the situation, which determines the choice procedure. There is no time to calculate probabilities in order to estimate the chances of the stranger being a foe, or to investigate the various potential escape routes. Instead, all the decision-maker needs is a good enough approximation or even a single cue to activate the emotional mechanism, which in turn produces reaction. One does not search for an optimal solution, for an attached cost to this search might be the agent's life (Zajonc, 1980).

In a way, one can argue that the decision to run (or freeze) is in fact the optimal strategy. Thus it is the rational one from a normative perspective, where "normative" here denotes the appropriate response in the given situations. The only difference is that the agent did not have to intellectually calculate or to find the best alternative, for there is an additional mechanism that has done the "job" for him: namely evolution. As Tooby and Cosmides (2000, p. 1172) argue "natural selection retained neural structures on their ability to create adaptively organized relationships between information and behavior (e.g., the sight of a predator activates inference procedures that cause the organism to hide or flee) or between information and physiology (e.g., the sight of a predator increases the organism's heart rate, in preparation for flight)". What Tooby and Cosmides argue, we believe, is that evolution has already done the calculation for us. It has "found," through the process of natural selection, the best procedure for dealing with danger. In the words of Ekman (1999) "each emotion thus prompts us in a direction which, in the course of evolution, has done better than other solutions in recurring circumstances that are relevant to goals" (p. 46).

Elster (1999) asks why the emotional mechanism has a priority in situations of danger. It is not, he maintains, that reason cannot respond as quickly or as well, but that "in reality, of course, that's not how we cope with novelty or bitter-tasting food – not because the program is unfeasible but because natural selection has wired us differently" (Elster, 1999, p. 291). The emotions carry out the operation not because they have a better adaptive mechanism, nor a better solution than reason can fathom. The reason emotional mechanism reacts first is because we have evolved that way.

5.2. Emotion, bounded rationality, and consumer research

Thus far it might seem that emotions could set priorities only in extreme cases of danger or fear. This is not the case. Elster (1999) has provided an example from everyday life in which he sees the integration of emotion into decision making. Coming back from a vacation and sorting through his mail, Elster must decide which piece of mail to deal with first. He must have a mechanism by which he decides whether paying his bills (as he does) should come before answering his friends. Instead of contemplating a large set of possibilities, scenarios, and their consequences, he rather follows a few rules of thumb. In deciding the order in which he will deal with the mail – old letters must be answered first, bills must be paid, etc. – "emotional tags and pulls certainly play a role" Elster concludes (1999, p. 296).

A similar case, regarding consumers' decision making can be found in the work done by Shiv and Fedorikhin (1999). In their research, subjects had to choose between a chocolate cake and a fruit salad. The authors argue that chocolate cake is "associated with more intense positive affect but less favorable cognitions", while the fruit salad is "associated with less favorable affect but more favorable cognitions" (p. 278). When subjects had little information they were more prone to choose the chocolate cake, hence indicating that affective evaluation provokes a greater impact on choice. The results of this study, according to the authors, suggest that "under conditions where the consumer does not allocate processing resources to the decision-making task, she/he is more likely to choose based on affect rather than on cognition" (1999, p. 288).

The notion that emotions play a more significant role in decision making gain further support from research on high-risk sporting activities, where knowledge is often restricted or limited. Participants in risky sport activities such as skydiving and water rafting do not have the time or know-how to work out how to deal with the information they encounter. Decisions to make the first sky jump, for example, are often guided by emotional factors rather than on rational calculations of cost and benefit. Research by Celsi, Rose, and Leigh (1993) on skydiving (though the same logic, the authors maintain, can be applied to other risky sports such as mountain climbing) indicates that explaining risky behavior requires a multidimensional perspective. Yet, what is evident from their research is that the underlining motivation to engage in such risky sports stems from emotional factors rather than rational calculation. The costs are relatively easy to indicate prior to the jump: money, time, potential injury and death. The benefits, however, are not only harder to quantify but are difficult to envision, let alone evaluate. The thrill of the free fall, the relief upon the opening of the canopy, the sense of community (including the rites of passage), are a few of the variables that the first-timer maybe oblivious too. Comments such as "no one understands us and why we do it, only other people that skydive truly understand" (Celsi et al., 1993, p. 14), are not atypical to hear. That is to say, novice skydivers rarely have all the facts required to make a rational decision – at least one that conforms to SEU theory.

Arnold and Price (1993) report similar results from research on river rafting. Although the experience is costly, both in money and time, "people do not appear to think about it carefully" (p. 24). Individuals are motivated to engage in river rafting activities in order to have fun, get away from it all, and, like first time jumpers, they are often just carried along with family members or friends. An illustrative case comes from a wealthy client and his family who were disappointed to find that the water in the Green River was not green but muddy, and that the scenery was not a lush forest but a desert. So disappointed was the client that he requested a helicopter to take him and his family out of there. But, at the end of the trip "the family was 'ecstatic' . . . and later wrote that the trip had brought them together" (1993, p. 40). In fact, inexperienced customers are ill-informed on most, if not all, aspects regarding such trips. Yet, the river rafting industry is growing. As in the case of skydiving, the decision to participate in river rafting is elicited by emotional expectations, rather than on rational deliberation of pros and cons.

5.3. Emotion and "cold" calculated machines

Elster's example, discussed above, is but one of many that we can think of. Imagine, for example, a doctor driving to her work at a local hospital. She has at least one goal in mind: to get to work on time. While driving, however, she observes a car accident in which she suspects there might be injuries. Stopping her car and checking whether she is needed will probably become a higher order goal; hence, coming to work on time will lose its primacy. Let us imagine further that one of the individuals involved in the accident is a handsome man, one our doctor finds very attractive. After making sure he is not hurt, and treating the other individuals, our doctor might change her priorities and converse with the man, although her tardiness will only increase. In this case, coming to work on time drops even lower down the ladder of importance. Her goals have changed due to different emotions: care for others, and sexual attractiveness.

38

One might argue that our doctor is exhibiting a perfect example of SEU. Looking at a beautiful woman/man might generate a certain type of intellectual thought process, yet, without emotional arousal (sexual attraction, love, desire, etc.) one has no reason to advance towards the woman/man. We are attracted to a particular person since we feel (physically or otherwise), something towards that person. We are motivated to form a relationship with that person on grounds of emotional desire (Ben-Ze'ev, 2000). Of course, rational calculation can manifest itself in one form or another (as in rationalizing our decision), yet the underlining motivation stems from emotions.

Let us imagine, next, that our doctor and the man get married. A few years down the road, the doctor has an accident in which she suffers a severe brain injury leaving her comatose. In fact, the doctors treating her see no chance of recovery. If the doctor's husband were to follow SEU theory, the rational thing to do might be to leave his wife and search for a new partner. Yet in real life husbands and wives, frequently not only stay with their ill spouse – defying SEU expectations – but also visit them often providing for them for many years. Leaving emotions such as love out of the equation would portray humans as cold calculating machines, as argued by Davis and Dennard.

In one of his papers, Simon (1967, pp. 31–32) provides a theoretical computer program simulating the commands needed in order to reach a destination, designated in the model as block 1400. One potential problem with Simon's computer-generated illustration is that it does not take into account an individual's emotional makeup, and, hence, all the subroutines possible (see Dennett, 1987). If we were to insert our doctor into Simon's computer simulation, she would have driven straight to work, not feeling the need to stop. What that person lacks, as Charland (1998) has shown in the case of Mr. Spock, is emotion to guide her through the labyrinth of life. There is no doubting that the computer is better than humans at certain calculations, but many of the decisions that humans make so effortlessly would render the biggest and strongest computers immobile. One reason is the "use of feelings and intuition to *guide* reasoning and decision making" (Picard, 1997, p. 218; italic is mine).

One should note that the argument above does not consider the question of whether computers can (or could at some point in the future) feel and exhibit emotions. Rather, the argument is that in order for computers to accurately simulate human behavior in general, and decision making in particular, they must incorporate emotional abilities (Levine & Leven, 1992, p. viii).

Picard's idea might coincide with Keynes (1936) notion of "animal spirit" in *The General Theory of Employment, Interest and Money*. He argues that not all decisions are based on "a weighted average of quantitative benefits multiplied by quantitative probabilities" (p. 161), but rather on a "spontaneous urge to action rather than inaction" (ibid.). Decisions made while facing uncertainties, such as venturing to the Moon or constructing a factory, cannot be grounded solely on the precise calculation of future benefits, for support for such calculation does not exist. "It is our innate urge to activity which makes the wheels go round, our rational selves choosing between the alternatives as best we are able, calculating where we can, but often falling back for our motive on whim or sentiment or chance" (p. 163). Keynes' argument was later rephrased by Simon ("a gun for hire"), and echoes Hume's dictum that "Reason is, and ought only be the slave of passions, and can never pretend to any other office than to serve and obey them (Hume, 1978/1740, book II, part III, section III, p. 415; but see Matthews, 1991).[3] The point we argue here (see also, Marchionatti, 1999, and references therein) is that while reason can be employed to search for the best alternatives, if our "animal spirits are dimmed and the spontaneous optimism falters . . . enterprise will fade and die" (Keynes, 1936, p. 162).

5.4. Emotion and imagination

Shackle (1961) has advanced another line of argument against SEU, which he terms potential surprise theory. Briefly stated, potential surprise theory argues that "decisions are based upon a comparison of imagination. Expectation is *thought* taking place in the present but having a content labelled with future dates" (1969, p. 14, italics in the original). That is, instead of *calculating* what will happen, Shackle argues that individuals *imagine* what can happen. "Only potential surprise called up in the mind, and assessed, in the moment when decision is made, is relevant for the decision, and alone can have any bearing or influence on it" (1969, p. 69). Yet, he is fully aware of the role emotion plays within this new decision theory (Augier & Kreiner, 2000). Probability, he writes, "cannot discriminate or express degrees of possibility. Potential surprise is, precisely, the expression, *in terms of feeling*, of degree of surprise (1969, p. 76, italics are mine).

Two aspects of Shackle's theory are of importance: surprise and imagination. First, surprise, as Ortony *et al.* (1988, pp. 32, 125–127) argue, is not an emotion but a cognitive state (see also, Ben-Ze'ev, 2000, p. 56). For example, an agent might be surprised to find that there are no penguins in England, yet remain indifferent to such information. On the other hand, imagination is relevant both for generating emotion and for making decisions. Ben-Ze'ev (2000, Chapter 7), for example, argues that imagination is a key factor in generating a specific emotion and in the intensity of that emotion. Fear and hope, he argues, "entail imagining a future alternative to the present one" (p. 191; see also Elster, 1999, on counterwishful thinking in children's play). The work done by Peter Earl on the relationship between imagination, creativity and decision-making by individuals (Earl, 1983) and in the corporate environment (Earl, 1984) illustrates how imagination can assist decision making processes, and how rigidity (or lack of imagination) can hinder performance.

The point is that the emotional values attached to the imagined future situation can affect the decision taken in the present moment. Schwarz and Clore (1983, 1988) have constructed a "How do I feel about it?" heuristic, in which they argue that people inspect their feelings in order to evaluate targets. That is, individuals do not question the emotional state they are in (good or bad) at that moment, but rather the emotional responses to a future target of decision (e.g., how do I feel about Chinese food?). Imagined scenarios involving a strong negative emotional reaction such as anxiety might be excluded from further consideration, while positive ones will be more likely to be entertained (Isen & Geva, 1987; Isen & Patrick, 1983). For example, in trying to decide how to invest money (or move to a new job), one imagines the various risks and benefits attached to each option. If, for instance, the agent feels intense fear due to the risks involved in one option, he or she might exclude this option, while choosing a safer line of investment (for a similar perspective see Earl, 1983, pp. 165–167; 175–180; Lopes, 1987).

Pham (1998) has found that peoples' decisions to go to the movies were heavily based on their emotional attitude towards the target, i.e., the movie. As Pham writes "looking at affect as a source of information helps us understand how consumers can use their feeling to guide their decisions" (1998, p. 156). Consumers, according to this view, hold representations of targets in their mind and use the feelings that these representations generate as an additional source of information in the decision making process. Further evidence can be derived from research on phobic behavior, where the phobia (reluctance to fly, for example) stems from imagining the negative outcomes associated with flying. As Shackle has argued "what is action but the response to feelings? What action would there be if there were no desires, no consciousness of dissatisfaction, no longing for 'good state of mind'? What is motive, except emotion?" (1972, p. 135). He concludes by saying: "We chose, and take, action is pursuit of an end. What is an end if not something upon which our desire concentrates our thought and effort? . . . Reason, logic, are in themselves purely formal, without force" (ibid.).

Antonio Damasio (1994) in his book, *Descartes' Error*, presents compelling data indicating that emotions are vital to decision making (but see Elster, 1999). His evidence stems from work with patients who have suffered damage to their frontal lobes. Due to this damage, these patients have become "emotionally flat", while retaining all of their cognitive abilities. They do, however, exhibit one particular flaw: they lose their decision-making abilities. In a series of experiments, they (Bachara, Damasio, Damasio, & Anderson, 1994; Bachara, Damasio, Tranel, & Damasio, 1997) show that individuals suffering from a lesion to their frontal lobe are incapable of making decisions, and that those they do make are generally faulty. The explanation provided by Damasio is that these patients are insensitive to future consequences. They are concerned with the here and now, not reflecting on the possible outcomes of their actions. Not being able to assign emotional value to future outcomes renders these outcomes meaningless. Accordingly, outcomes that carry no emotional value, apparently cannot be part of the equation.

In a particular incident, one patient ruminated for half an hour over when to set his next appointment. During the deliberation process, he evaluated every imaginable parameter: from alternative appointments times to variants in weather conditions. Damasio belief that his patient would have continued deliberating the pros and cons of each option *ad infinitum*, if he, Damasio, had not intervened. This patient, like the others treated by Damasio, illustrates the limits of pure reason. Without emotions, one could ruminate over trivial matters until one had exhausted all possibilities. One would not be able to form a prioritizing mechanism.

Langer (1989, pp. 199–200), describing choosing a restaurant, poses the same difficulties as Damasio. Should she eat in a Chinese restaurant, and if so, in which one? There are advantages to each of the restaurants she thinks of: food is better in one, atmosphere in the other, one is closer, the other less expensive. The SEU model, she argues, assumes that it can provide the right answer, for the decision can be grounded on rational deliberation. But generating more options does not help, for there is no rational stopping rule, and, therefore, she advocates a more intuitive processing. "We can then work on making the decision right rather than obsess about making the right decision" (p. 200).

6. Emotions as a focusing mechanism

6.1. Emotion and information

In making a decision, as Simon (1983) has argued, we rarely possess all the relevant information, nor do we hold an exhaustive, detailed, picture of all possibilities and their probabilities. Rather, we hold a general portrait of our life, of where we would like to be, and of the resources available to us.

For instance, when we are about to purchase a house we have a clear idea about our financial resources, the area we would like to live in, preferred residential type, etc. (see, for example, Earl, 1986a, pp. 176–178; 202–203). We might have several other criteria in mind (e.g., the view from the living room, schools in the vicinity, or the proximity of the nearest hospital), though we are unlikely to contemplate a broad spectrum of possibilities that might affect our decision. When thinking about the house we would like to purchase, we focus our attention on issues pertaining to houses, not concerning ourselves with furniture. In other words, one focuses ones attention, or mental resources, on a limited set of variables and among those entertained some will have a higher value than others.

When the author of this paper suggested to a friend that she should re-examine her decision to purchase a house, after a leading Israeli newspaper claimed it was less advantageous than investing in the bank, she insisted that it was of no interest to her. In fact, she wasn't willing to consider (or hear) other options such as renting and investing her money in a more profitable enterprise. Her main concern was with feelings of security, that is, knowing that she owns the place, and that no one can take it away from her, or ask her to leave on short notice.

The above example – though it should be taken with caution – has two possible ramifications. First, it can illustrate the point advanced by Earl (1983, 1986b, 1992) on how cognitive dissonance (Festinger, 1957) and personal construct theory (Kelly, 1967) can be applied to the economic domain (see also Etzioni, 1988). And second, as Shiv and Fedorikhin (1999) have argued, "if affective and cognitive reactions have opposite valences, then they are likely to act in opposite directions (one promoting choice, the other promoting rejection)" (1999, p. 281). In the example given above, the reluctance to even consider other alternatives (such as renting) was blocked due to emotional considerations, namely feeling of insecurity, which can reduce the risk of cognitive dissonance.

6.2. Emotion, uncertainty and creativity

The world we live in presents endless possibilities, options and variables that, in theory, can affect any decision we make, but generally do not. In a sense, we are living in what Simon (1983) has called an "empty world". In this "empty" world, we discriminate between variables; we choose to focus on some while neglecting others. Langer (1989) has termed this phenomenon "mindlessness." She presents ample evidence suggesting that people see what they want to see, clouding their judgments in the process. She maintains that rational "fixation" can lead to mental rigidity, preventing individuals from exploring possible alternatives, reaching favorable decisions, and being creative. March (1971) advanced a similar line of argument, criticizing rational choice theories for their inflexible assumptions regarding preferences and goals, for they confine our ability to generate new aims and change our preference ordering. Play, according to March, "relaxes that insistence to allow us to act 'unintelligently' or 'irrationally', or 'foolishly' to explore alternative ideas of possible purposes and alternative concepts of behavioral consistency . . . while maintaining our basic commitment to the necessity of intelligence" (March, 1971, p. 568). These authors argue, therefore, that we should allow foolishness, playfulness, and intuition to gain a more prominent role in decisions making, problem-solving, and creativity (Langer, 1989, Chapter 7; March, 1971). Schumpeter, likewise, writes that under conditions of uncertainty "the success of everything depends on intuition, the capacity of seeing things in a way which afterwards proves to be true, even though it cannot be established at the moment" (Schumpeter, 1934, p. 85). Intuition, therefore, can function as a heuristic mechanism, allowing the agent to reach a decision based on minimal amounts of information. For example, Simon (1983, 25–27) describes how chess masters can respond with a strong move (often the best one) after looking at the board for only 5–10 seconds.

Let us examine one of Langer's examples where the commitment to rational decision making, as advocated by SEU, is brought to the fore. One day Langer arrived late to a meeting of a committee formed to award a prize for teaching. The committee faced a dilemma: there were five nominees but only three to five letters of recommendation for each. The problem was how to make a sensible decision in light of the limited information before them. Langer, realizing the problematic nature of information gathering, formulated a series of hypothetical questions designed to show that no amount of information would, in fact, be satisfactory, nor that they could agree on what information should be collected. Should they examine current students, or maybe those who finished the course two years ago? Should they ask poor students or excellent students? Langer's point was that decision making could hardly ever be "based on enough information" (p. 147). Instead of searching for all relevant information, she suggested that a rule of thumb would be used.

Given that in most cases such as the one described by Langer there are no absolutely right or absolutely wrong criteria to choose from, one might ask how we attach values to each criterion? One mechanism that determines the saliency of variables is, we propose, our emotions.

Damasio suggest a similar line of reasoning in which he argues the following:

> Imagine that before you apply any kind of cost/benefit analysis to the premises, and before you reason toward the solution of the problem, something quite important happens: When the bad outcome connected with a given response option comes into mind, however fleetingly, you experience an unpleasant feeling. Because the feeling is about the body, I gave the phenomenon the technical term *somatic* state ("soma" is Greek for body); and because it "marks" an image, I called it a *marker*... What does the *somatic marker* achieve? It forces attention on the negative outcome to which a given action may lead, and functions as an automated alarm signal which says: Beware of danger ahead of you if you choose the option which leads to this outcome. The signal may lead you to reject, *immediately*, the negative course of action and thus make you choose among other alternatives.
>
> (1994, p. 174; italics in the original)

Later on, Damasio argues that:

> [S]omatic markers do not deliberate for us. They assist the deliberation process by highlighting some options (either dangerous or favorable), and eliminating them rapidly from subsequent consideration. You may think of it as a system for automated qualification of predictions, which acts, whether you want it or not, to evaluate the extremely diverse scenarios of the anticipated future before you. Think of it as a basic biasing device.
>
> (ibid.)

Consider the following example. In deliberating whether to agree to Joe's proposal of marriage, Jane has many questions to consider (see also Gigerenzer & Todd, 1999, pp. 7–8). Is Joe the right one? Will he be a good father? Will he satisfy her psychological and sexual needs? One can easily come up with numerous additional questions, which will hamper any system trying to figure out answers to these questions. Jane, obviously, cannot provide a definitive answer to many of the potential questions. She must make a choice by deliberating on a few, maybe a minimal set, of questions. She must decide which parameters are of importance to her, and which can be ignored. But how does the system manage to reduce the number of questions asked? (e.g., is providing psychological and sexual needs more important than being a good father?) In other words, what is the mechanism by which the system reduces its load, so that it can both function and provide meaningful answers?

Since there are no right or wrong answers to the question of which parameters are more important – one might want money, the other babies – one way in which we generate a value system is via our emotions.[4] Etzioni, for example, offers a Normative/Affective theory of decision making in which emotions play precisely that role. He says that:

> the majority of choices people make, including economic ones, are completely or largely based on normative-affective considerations not merely with regard to selection of goals but also of means, and that the limited zones in which other, logical empirical (L/E), considerations are paramount, are themselves defined by N/A factors that legitimate and otherwise motivate such decision-making.
>
> (1988, p. 126)

Without emotions to generate both values and preferences, reason – as shown by Damasio's patients – is an arbitrary mechanism lost in a sea of theoretical possibilities and consequences. Intellectual reasoning without emotions, then, seems to be next to impossible (Charland, 1998). That is why De Sousa (1996, p. 331) argues that "without the ability to care about the [future or hypothetical] situations evoked by the reasoning, the values involved never get to move the agent in accord with his 'knowledge'".

Similar ideas are expressed in the research conducted by Isen and her colleagues (Isen & Levin, 1972; Isen, Shalker, Clark, & Karp, 1978; Isen, Means, Patrick, & Nowicki, 1982). She argues, for example, that good mood facilitates problem-solving in several ways. It "reduces the load on working memory: to reduce the complexity of decision situations and the difficulty of tasks, by adopting the simplest strategy possible, considering the fewest number of alternatives possible, and doing little or no checking of information, hypotheses, and tentative conclusions" (Isen *et al.*, 1982, p. 258).

Emotions, by attaching values to each variable, restrict the range of options entertained. Parameters receiving low emotional values are ignored, for they have no (or less) significance for the evaluator, while parameters receiving high emotional values are brought to the front of our attention. Those, and only those, variables which reach the final round are inserted into the equation.

Etzioni (1988) considers the question of how we decide what to eat for dinner. The typical American teenager will chose hamburger over snails[5] every day, since she *loves* hamburgers, while snails are *disgusting*. We would expect a French teenager to make a different selection. Similar logic, Etzioni argues, can explain why Americans choose to work in the US, and not, for example, in Canada. Wages and tax rates are not the only parameters entering into the equation; patriotism may also be a factor. Our choice, in these cases, is restricted by emotional evaluation: high emotional ranking means a possibility, while low emotional ranking is not considered. Our American teenager does not have to "think" about all the possible foods available to her. She only has to think about the food she loves. It does not matter how many rational arguments one offers American children regarding the merits of spinach and broccoli. They are unlikely to replace hamburgers from the top of their list.

Ritzer (1993), following Max Weber's work on formal rationality, adds a sociological perspective. In his book, *The McDonaldization of Society*, he analyses a diverse spectrum of American institutions: universities, fast-food chains, the automobile industry, hospitals, banks, amusement parks, etc. He shows that their commitment to rationality in the form of efficiency, predictability, and quantifiable measures has had dire consequences.

Firstly, it dehumanizes workers and customers alike. The assembly line presents a clear notion of the conditions in which fast food and car manufacture employees work; and produces, therefore, the sense of alienation that exists in such work environments. The feeling of alienation leads, among other things, to high employee turnover (the typical worker in a fast food restaurant lasts only four months), workers' retaliation, and low productivity levels. Feelings of alienation are not restricted to those who work on the assembly line. Carr (1994) reports similar findings, where management pressure to increase productivity and efficiency (in the name of rationality) in the education sector in Australia, has led to "emotional fallout". This "emotional fallout" included an array of symptoms such as high levels of anxiety, stress, and depression.

The second point argued by Ritzer is that commitment to rationality can lead to irrational behavior. Rationality, in the form advocated and exercised by the McDonaldization process, often leads to "inefficiency, unpredictability, incalculability, and loss of control" (1993, p. 121). Ritzer illustrates that the "promise" of speed, efficiency, cheapness, and controllability is often an illusion rather than a reality, and that cold, calculated rationality can lead to disastrous consequences. In one well-known case, the auto manufacture's Ford rushed the production of the Pinto because of competition from small foreign car manufactures, "despite the fact that production tests had indicated that its fuel system would rupture easily in a rear-end collision" (p. 144). Since the assembly-line machinery was already in place, they decided to go ahead and produce the car without the safety alterations. Ford's decision was based on a quantitative comparison between fixing the defective fuel system and the lives that would be lost. "They estimated that the defects would lead to 180 deaths and about the same number of injuries. Placing a value, or rather a cost, to them of $200,000 per person, Ford decided that the total cost from these deaths and injuries would be less than the $11 per car it would cost to repair the defect" (ibid.).

Macleod (1996) offers a similar idea to the one suggested by Etzioni's. Macleod maintains that in the morning, when deciding what to wear, we seldom if ever evaluate the entire spectrum of dress options. We eliminate rather quickly many of the alternatives available to us and pick the ones that "look right." Otherwise, dressing in the morning would be a close to impossible task, taking us days to decide what to wear. What Macleod suggests, we assume, is that the "look right" criterion can be viewed as a satisficing mechanism. It is one kind of a stopping rule, indicating to the decision maker that article A is satisfactory, hence there is no need to further evaluate other dress options.

Rook's (1985) work on ritual behavior provides additional support. In his study, where hair care activities figure prominently (on hairstyle choice, see also Parsons, 2000, p. 143), subjects' grooming behavior was examined. His findings indicates, that while respondents were most satisfied with their hair (compared to other body parts), fixing one's hair was the most frustrating activity (p. 259). The discrepancy between his subjects' responses is indicative of the emotional importance attached to one's hair. For young adults, grooming is more than just a cleaning procedure. It reflects on their identity as determined by peer pressure and the need to look just right. In fact, when subjects were asked to write creative stories about two pictures, most of the stories were loaded with emotional (good and bad) connotations, yet reflected little rational deliberation. Drawing from Erikson's work – which interprets ritual behavior as stemming from, among other things, feeling of shame, guilt, inferiority, confusion and isolation – Rook concludes that grooming behavior "contrasts sharply with the various static and naive behavioral models that depict consumers as rational and constructive attribute maximizers" (1985, p. 262).

One should note that the suggestions by Etzioni and Macleod adopted here are not intended to reflect probabilities but matters of taste and emotional preference. The possibilities contemplated are not to be understood as having higher probabilities. If the menu contains both hamburger and broccoli or one's wardrobe contains both yellow and black shirts, both options are as probable. We do not mean that the decision making has to compute the probabilities of their occurrence, rather that ranking should be understood as reflecting the agent's subjective emotional evaluation. In other words, emotions do not compute probabilities, reason does.

That is not to say that parameters with low emotional values are of no importance. The importance attached to each stimulus is, by it's nature, a subjective not an objective one – which is one reason why emotions have been viewed as irrational. Emotions create a personal and subjective set of values that differ from one person to another. Furthermore, at certain times, negative emotional reactions can be overcome and choices made contrary to emotional evaluation.

7. Conclusion

"In order to have a complete theory of human rationality, we have to understand the role emotion plays in it" (Simon, 1983, p. 29). Not many economists have paid enough attention to the above assertion. In fact, it seems as if many have completely ignored it. The general tendency to focus on cognitive abilities and functions and to ignore the played role by emotion has given us a one-sided picture. In this paper I have tried to make the first steps towards integrating emotion into the field of bounded rationality. By arguing that our emotional mechanism processes information along with rational thinking, I suggest that it aids mental deliberation in two ways. This is not to argue that emotions are necessarily involved in all of the cognitive functioning. It is possible to remember, imagine, and make calculations without any emotional involvement. The condition under which there is positive and/or negative "co-operation" between mental deliberation and emotions remain to be empirically investigated. What seems to be the case thus far is that emotions play a vital role in supplementing our limited computational abilities. Further evidence might suggest that the role emotions play in decision making, for example, is much more significant than has previously been acknowledged.

Finally, if Thaler's prediction is correct, "that economists will devote more attention to the study of emotions" (cf. Thaler, 2000, p. 139), than economists must familiarize themselves with psychological, neurological and philosophical research on emotion. This is one area where, by utilizing existing research and findings, economists can economize.

Acknowledgements

I wish to thank Aaron Ben-Ze'ev, Peter Earl, Joe Nugent, Ofer Raban, and two anonymous reviewers for critical comments and helpful suggestions.

Notes

1 If we had only one goal, this issue would not arise. Yet seldom, if ever, do humans have a single goal in mind (Ortony, *et al.*, 1988; Simon, 1983).
2 One should be aware that acting slowly does not guarantee more accurate decisions for two reasons. First, information might become outdated as the environment changes; and second, accumulation of information can result in system overload, since the agent might not be able to analyze the immense accumulated data.
3 According to Matthews (1991), Keynes admired Hume who has also used the term animal spirit, though the idea of animal spirit is probably taken from Descartes (p. 106).
4 Gigerenzer and Todd (1999) advance a slightly different explanation. They propose that love serves "as a powerful stopping rule that ends the current search for a partner" (p. 31). In other words, falling in love serves as a sufficient condition to committing oneself. One needs not evaluate the entire spectrum of options or conduct a cost–benefit analysis. One only needs a single cue: to fall in love.
5 That is, unless the individual is a vegetarian. People decision to adopt a vegetarian diet poses another difficulty for SEU theory. Research by Beardsworth and Keil's (1992) show how prior to shifting into a vegetarian diet, individuals lack a definite knowledge in several domains. Individuals are not sure how family, friends, and co-workers will react (some are hostile while others welcome the dietary change), how to deal with criticism (e.g., how come you are wearing leather shows?), and what to have for dinner. Their findings indicate that this lack of knowledge is responsible, at least partially, for the gradual conversion patterns. Furthermore, conversion into vegetarianism varies from moral beliefs (cruelty to animals), nutritional beliefs (meat is bad for you), too social factors (their spouse made the change). In either case, rational deliberation was not a major influencing force. In their concluding remark, the authors argue that "the adoption of vegetarianism, in whatever form is appropriate to each individual's unique concern and predicament, would seem to be at root an exercise in the management of anxiety" (Beardsworth & Keil, 1992, p. 290; see also, Kalof, Dietz, Stern, & Guagnano, 1999).

References

Arnold, E. J., & Price, L. L. (1993). River magic: Extraordinary experience and extended service encounter. *Journal of Consumer Research, 20*, 24–45.
Arrow, K. J. (1992). Rationality of self and others in an economic system. In M. Zey (Ed.), *Decision making: Alternatives to rational choice models* (pp. 63–77). Newbury Park: Sage.

Augier, M., & Kreiner, K. (2000). Rationality, imagination and intelligence: Some boundaries in human decision-making. *Industrial and Corporate Change, 9*, 659–681.

Bachara, A., Damasio, A. R., Damasio, H., & Anderson, S. (1994). Insensitivity to future consequences following damage to human prefrontal cortex. *Cognition, 50*, 7–12.

Bachara, A., Damasio, A., Tranel, D., & Damasio, A. R. (1997). Deciding advantageously before knowing the advantageous strategy. *Science, 275*, 1293–1295.

Beardsworth, A., & Keil, T. (1992). The vegetarian option: Varieties, conversions, motives and careers. *The Sociological Review, 40*, 253–293.

Ben-Ze'ev, A. (2000). *The subtlety of the emotion.* Cambridge, MA: MIT Press.

Berger, L. A. (1989). Economics and hermeneutics. *Economics and Philosophy, 5*, 209–233.

Berkowitz, L. (1993). Towards a general theory of anger and emotional aggression: Implications of the cognitive neoassociationistic perspective for the analysis of anger and other emotions. In R. S. Wyer, & T. K. Srull (Eds.), *Advances in social cognition* (pp. 1–46). Hillsdale: Erlbaum.

Brown, H. I. (1978). On being rational. *American Philosophical Quarterly, 14*, 241–248.

Carr, A. N. (1994). The "emotional fallout" of the new efficiency movement in public administration in Australia: A case study. *Administration and Society, 26*, 344–358.

Celsi, R. L., Rose, R. L., & Leigh, T. W. (1993). An exploration of high-risk leisure consumption through skydiving. *Journal of Consumer Research, 20*, 1–23.

Charland, L. C. (1998). Is Mr. Spock mentally competent? Competence to consent and emotion. *Philosophy, Psychiatry and Psychology, 5*, 67–81.

Conlisk, J. (1996). Why bounded rationality? *Journal of Economic Literature, 34*, 669–700.

Damasio, A. (1994). *Descartes' error: Emotion, reason, and the human brain.* New York: Putnam.

Darwin, C. (1965). *The expression of the emotion in man and animals (1872).* Chicago: University of Chicago Press.

Davis, C. R. (1996). The administrative rational model and public organizational theory. *Administration and Society, 28*, 39–60.

Dennard, L. F. (1995). Neo-Darwinism and Simon's bureaucratic antihero. *Administration and Society, 26*, 464–487.

Dennett, D. C. (1987). Cognitive wheels: The frame problem in AI. In Z. Pylyshyn (Ed.), *The Robot's dilemma: The frame problem and other problems of holism in artificial intelligence.* Norwood, NJ: Ablex.

De Sousa, R. (1987). *The rationality of emotions.* Cambridge, MA: MIT Press.

De Sousa, R. (1996). A review of Descartes' Error: Emotion, reason and the human brain. *Cognition and Emotion, 10*, 329–333.

Earl, P. (1983). *The economic imagination: Towards a behavioral theory of choice.* Brighton: Wheatsheaf.

Earl, P. (1984). *The corporate imagination: How big companies make mistakes.* Brighton: Wheatsheaf.

Earl, P. (1986a). *Lifestyle economics: Consumer behavior in a turbulent world.* Brighton: Wheatsheaf.

Earl, P. (1986b). A behavioral analysis of demand elasticities. *Journal of Economic Studies, 13*, 20–37.

Earl, P. (1990). Economics and psychology: A survey. *The Economic Journal, 100*, 718–755.

Earl, P. (1992). On the complementarity of economic applications of cognitive dissonance theory and personal construct psychology. In S. E. G. Lea, P. Webley, & B. M. Young (Eds.), *New directions in economic psychology: Theory, experiment and application* (pp. 49–65). Hants: Edward Elgar.

Earl, P. (2001). *The legacy of Herbert A. Simon in economic analysis'* (Vol. 2). Cheltenhma: Edward Elgar.

Ekman, P. (1992). An argument for basic emotions. *Cognition and Emotion, 6*, 169–200.

Ekman, P. (1999). Basic Emotions. In T. Dalgleish, & M. J. Power (Eds.), *Handbook of cognition and emotion* (pp. 45–60). Chichester: Wiley.

Ekman, P., & Davidson, R. (1994). *The nature of emotions*. Oxford: Oxford University Press.

Elster, J. (1984). *Ulysses and the sirens*. Cambridge: Cambridge University Press.

Elster, J. (1998). Emotions and economic theory. *Journal of Economic Literature, 36*, 47–74.

Elster, J. (1999). *Alchemies of the mind: Rationality and the emotions*. Cambridge: Cambridge University Press.

Etzioni, A. (1988). Normative–affective factors: Toward a new decision-making modal. *Journal of Economic Psychology, 9*, 125–150.

Etzioni, A. (1992). Socio-economics: Select policy implications. In S. E. G. Lea, P. Webley, & B. M. Young (Eds.), *New directions in economic psychology: Theory experiment and application* (pp. 13–27). Hants: Edward Elgar.

Festinger, L. (1957). *A theory of cognitive dissonance*. Stanford: Stanford University Press.

Frank, R. (1988). *Passions within reason*. New York: Norton.

Frijda, N. H. (1986). *The emotions*. Cambridge: Cambridge University Press.

Gigerenzer, G., The ABC Research Group & Todd, M. P. (1999). *Simple heuristics that make us smart*. New York: Oxford University Press.

Griffiths, P. E. (1997). *What emotions really are*. Chicago: University of Chicago Press.

Hare, R. M. (1963). *Freedom and reason*. Oxford: Oxford University Press.

Heiner, R. A. (1983). The origin of predictable behavior. *American Economic Review, 73*, 560–595.

Heiner, R. A. (1986). The economics of information when decision are imperfect. In A. J. MacFadyen, & H. W. MacFadyen (Eds.), *Economic psychology: Intersections in theory and application* (pp. 293–350). Amsterdam: Elsevier.

Hollins, M., & Nell, E. J. (1975). *Rational economic man: A philosophical critique of neo-classical economics*. Cambridge: Cambridge University Press.

Hume, D. (1978). *A treatise on human nature (1740)*. Oxford: Clarendon Press.

Isen, M. A., & Patrick, R. (1983). The effect of positive feelings on risk taking: When the chips are down. *Organizational Behavior and Human Decision Process, 31*, 194–202.

Isen, M. A., & Geva, N. (1987). The influence of positive effect on acceptable level of risk: The person with a large canoe has a large worry. *Organizational Behavior and Human Decision Process, 39*, 145–154.

Isen, M. A., & Levin, P. F. (1972). The effects of feeling good on helping: Cookies and kindness. *Journal of Personality and Social Psychology, 21,* 384–388.

Isen, M. A., Means, B., Patrick, R., & Nowicki, G. (1982). Some factors influencing decision-making strategy and risk taking. In M. S. Clark, & S. Fiske (Eds.), *Affect and cognition* (pp. 243–261). Hillsdale, NJ: Lawrence Erlbaum.

Isen, M. A., Shalker, T. E., Clark, M., & Karp, L. (1978). Affect, accessibility of material in memory, and behavior: A cognitive loop? *Journal of Personality and Social Psychology, 36,* 1–12.

Izard, C. A. (1977). *Human emotions.* New York: Plenum Press.

Jáuregui, J. A. (1995). *The emotional computer.* Oxford: Blackwell.

Kalof, L., Dietz, T., Stern, P. C., & Guagnano, G. A. (1999). Social psychological and structural influences on vegetarian beliefs. *Rural Sociology, 64,* 500–511.

Kaufman, B. E. (1999). Emotional arousal as a source of bounded rationality. *Journal of Economic Behavior and Organization, 38,* 135–144.

Kelly, H. H. (1967). Attribution theory in social psychology. In D. Levine (Ed.), *Nebraska symposium on motivation* (pp. 192–241). Lincoln, NE: University of Nebraska Press.

Keynes, J. M. (1936). *The general theory of employment, interest and money.* London: Macmillan Press (References are to Vol. VII of the Collected Writings of John Maynard Keynes).

Langer, E. J. (1989). *Mindfulness.* Reading, MA: Merloyd Lawrence.

Lazarus, R. S. (1991). *Emotion and adaptation.* New York: Oxford University Press.

LeDoux, J. (1994). Emotion, memory and the brain. *Scientific American, 270,* 32–39.

LeDoux, J. (1996). *The emotional brain.* New York: Simon and Schuster.

Leeper, R. W. (1948). A motivational theory of emotion to replace "emotion as disorganize response". *Psychological Review, 44,* 2–21.

Levi, I. (1997). *The covenant of reason.* Cambridge: Cambridge University Press.

Levine, D. S., & Leven, S. J. (1992). Preface. In D. S. Levine, & S. J. Leven (Eds.), *Motivation, emotion, and goal direction in neural network* (pp. vii–xvi). Hillsdale, NJ: Lawrence Erlbaum.

Lewin, S. B. (1996). Economics and psychology: lessons for our own day from the early twentieth century. *Journal of Economic Literature, 34,* 1293–1323.

Lipman, B. L. (1991). How to decide how to decide how to . . . : Modeling limited rationality. *Econometrica, 59,* 1105–1125.

Loewenstein, G. (2000). Emotions in economic theory and economic behavior. *The American Economic Review, 90,* 426–432.

Lopes, L. L. (1987). Between hope and fear: The psychology of risk. *Advances in Experimental Psychology, 24,* 255–295.

Lyons, W. (1980). *Emotion.* Cambridge: Cambridge University Press.

Macleod, B. W. (1996). Decision, contract, and emotion: Some economics for a complex and confusing world. *Canadian Journal of Economics, 4,* 788–810.

March, J. M. (1971). The technology of foolishness. In J. G. March (Ed.), *The pursuit of organizational intelligence (1988).* Basil Blackwell: Oxford.

March, J. M. (1978). Bounded rationality, ambiguity, and the engineering of choice. *The Bell Journal of Economics, 9,* 587–608.

March, J. M. (1982). Theories of choice and making decisions. *Society, 20,* 29–39.

March, J. M. (1994). *A primer on decision making.* New York: The Free Press.

Marchionatti, R. (1999). On Keynes' animal spirits. *Kyklos, 52,* 415–439.

Matthews, R. (1991). Animal Spirits. In T. G. J. Meeks (Ed.), *Thoughtful economic man: Essays on rationality, moral rules and benevolence* (pp. 103–125). Cambridge: Cambridge University Press.

Oatley, K. (1992). *Best laid schemes: The psychology of emotions.* Cambridge: Cambridge University Press.

Oatley, K., & Johnson-Laird, P. N. (1987). Towards a cognitive theory of emotions. *Cognition and Emotion, 1,* 29–50.

Ortony, A., Clore, G. L., & Collins, A. (1988). *The cognitive structure of emotions.* Cambridge: Cambridge University Press.

Panksepp, J. (1982). Towards a general psychological theory of emotion. *Behavioral and Blain Science, 5,* 407–467.

Panksepp, J. (1996). Affective neuroscience: a paradigm to study the animate circuits of human emotion. In R. Kavanaugh, B. Zimmerberg, & S. Fein (Eds.), *Emotion: Interdisciplinary perspective* (pp. 29–60). Hillsdale, NJ: Lawrence Erlbaum.

Parsons, S. D. (2000). Shackle and the project of the Enlightenment: Reason, time and imagination. In P. E. Earl, & S. F. Frowen (Eds.), *Economics as an art of thought: Essays in memory of GLS shackle* (pp. 124–148). London: Routledge.

Pham, M. T. (1998). Representativeness, relevance, and the use of feelings in decision making. *Journal of Consumer Research, 25,* 144–159.

Picard, S. (1997). *Affective computing.* Cambridge, MA: MIT Press.

Pieters, R. G. M., & van Raaij, W. F. (1988). The role of affect in economic behavior. In R. G. M. Pieters, & W. F. van Raaij (Eds.), *Handbook of economic psychology* (pp. 109–142). Netherlands: Kluwer Academic Publishers.

Plutchik, R. (1980). *A psychoevolutionary synthesis.* New York: Harper & Row.

Popper, K. (1962). *Conjectures and refutations.* London: Routledge & Kegan Paul.

Rabin, M. (1998). Psychology and economics. *Journal of Economic Literature, 36,* 11–46.

Radner, R. (1975). Satisficing. *Journal of Mathematical Economics, 2,* 153–162.

Ritzer, G. (1993). *The McDonaldization of society.* California: Pine Forge Press.

Robbins, L. (1984). *An essay on the nature and significance of economic science.* London: Macmillan. Reprinted in D. M. Hausman (Ed.), *The philosophy of economics* (pp. 113–140). Cambridge: Cambridge University Press.

Rook, D. W. (1985). The ritual dimension of consumer behavior. *Journal of Consumer Research, 12,* 251–264.

Schwarz, N., & Clore, G. L. (1983). Mood, misattribution, and judgment of well-being: Informative and directive functions of affective states. *Journal of Personality and Social Psychology, 45,* 513–523.

Schwarz, N., & Clore, G. L. (1988). How do I feel about it? The informative function of affective states. In K. Fiedler, & J. Forgas (Eds.), *Affect, cognition, and social behavior* (pp. 44–62). Toronto: Hogrefe.

Schumpeter, J. A. (1934). *Theory of economic development.* London: George Allen & Unwin.

Shackle, G. L. S. (1961). *Decision, order and time in human affairs.* Cambridge: Cambridge University Press.

Shackle, G. L. S. (1972). *Epistemics and economics: A critique of economic doctrines.* Cambridge: Cambridge University Press.

Shiv, B., & Fedorikhin, A. (1999). Heart and mind in conflict: The interplay of affect and cognition in consumer decision making. *Journal of Consumer Research, 26,* 278–292.

Simon, H. A. (1947). *Administrative behavior.* New York: Macmillan.

Simon, H. A. (1955). A behavioral model of rational choice. *Quarterly Journal of Economics, 69,* 99–118.

Simon, H. A. (1956). Rational choice, and the structure of the environment. *Psychological Review, 63,* 129–138.

Simon, H. A. (1967). Motivational and emotional controls of cognition. *Psychological Review, 74,* 29–39.

Simon, H. A. (1978). Rationality as process and as product of thought. *American Economic Review, 68,* 1–16.

Simon, H. A. (1982a). *Models of bounded rationality.* Cambridge, MA: MIT Press.

Simon, H. A. (1982b). Comments. In M. S. Clark, & S. Fiske (Eds.), *Affect and cognition.* Hillsdale, NJ: Lawrence Erlbaum.

Simon, H. A. (1983). *Reason in human affairs.* Stanford, CA: Stanford University Press.

Simon, H. A. (1985). Human nature in politics: The dialogue of psychology with political science. *American Political Science Review, 79,* 293–304.

Simon, H. A. (1987). Rationality in psychology and economics. In R. M. Hogarth, & M. W. Reder (Eds.), *Rational choice: The contrast between economics and psychology* (pp. 25–40). Chicago: University of Chicago Press.

Simon, H. A. (1991). Cognitive architectures and rational analysis: Comment. In K. VanLehn (Ed.), *Architectures for intelligence* (pp. 25–39). Hillsdale, NJ: Erlbaum.

Thaler, R. H. (2000). From homo economicus to homo sapiens. *Journal of Economic Perspectives, 14,* 133–141.

Tooby, J., & Cosmides, L. (1990). The past explains the present: Emotional adaptations and the structure of ancestral environment. *Ethology and Sociobiology, 11,* 375–424.

Tooby, J., & Cosmides, L. (2000). Toward mapping the evolved functional organization of mind and brain. In M. S. Gazzaniga (Ed.), *The new cognitive neurosciences* (pp. 1167–1270). Cambridge, MA: MIT Press.

Turski, W. G. (1994). *Toward a rationality of emotions.* Athens, OH: Ohio University Press.

Tversky, A., & Kahneman, D. (1973). Availability: A heuristic for judging frequency and probability. *Cognitive Psychology, 4,* 207–232.

Tversky, A., & Kahneman, D. (1974). Judgment under uncertainty: Heuristic and biases. *Science, 185,* 1124–1131.

von Neumann, J., & Morgenstern, O. (1947). *Theory of games and economic behavior.* Princeton, NJ: Princeton University Press.

Zajonc, R. B. (1980). Feeling and thinking: Preferences need no Inferences. *American Psychologist, 2,* 151–175.

Zey, M. (1992). Criticism of rational choice theory. In M. Zey (Ed.), *Decision making: Alternatives to rational choice model* (pp. 9–31). Newbury Park: Sage.

51

BOUNDED RATIONALITY IN THE ECONOMICS OF ORGANIZATION

'Much cited and little used'

Nicolai J. Foss

Source: *Journal of Economic Psychology*, 24 (2003), 245–264.

Abstract

Herbert Simon was the apostle of bounded rationality. He very often illustrated bounded rationality in the context of the theory of the firm, and was, of course, a major contributor to organizational theory. However, in spite of Simon's efforts, I argue that bounded rationality has been only incompletely absorbed in the economics of organization, is little used for substantive purposes, and mostly serves a rhetorical function. In order to substantiate these claims, I discuss and compare alternative approaches to integrating bounded rationality with the theory of economic organization. I argue that in general bounded rationality is treated "thinly," and is actually not necessary for producing the main insights of these theories. The paper ends with a brief discussion of how to proceed with integrating richer notions of bounded rationality with the theory of economic organization.

1. Introduction

There is one, and arguably only one, field of economics where Herbert Simon's Grand Theme of bounded rationality (henceforth, "BR") seem continuously to have been an important factor; in fact, to have been important ever since the inception of that field. The field in question is the economics of organization. Thus, BR played a role in such seminal early contributions as Williamson (1971), a founding paper in transaction cost economics, and in Nelson and Winter (1973), a founding paper in formal evolutionary economics as well as an important precursor of the "organizational capabilities approach" (Langlois & Foss, 1999). Marschak and Radner (1972), the founding contribution to team theory, also made use of BR (although there was little direct inspiration from Simon in this case). Given this, it is not surprising that BR continues to be frequently invoked in contemporary contributions to these streams of research. Indeed, many contributors to the economics of organization view BR as crucially important. "But for bounded rationality," Williamson (1996a, p. 36) argues, "all issues of organization collapse in favor of comprehensive contracting of either Arrow-Debreu or mechanism design kinds"; hence, to him BR is a *necessary* ingredient of a theory of organization.[1]

However, in spite of all of this, the main themes of this paper are that Simon's Grand Theme of bounded rationality, first, has been rather incompletely absorbed in the economics of organization; second, does not constitute a necessary part of theorizing on economic organization and mostly serves a rhetorical function; and, third, that part of the reason for this is that Simon and those who have followed his lead did not develop a distinct, affirmative program for incorporating bounded rationality in the economics of organization that would be satisfactory to most economists. Not only are these themes related, they are also provocative, and may give rise to all sorts of objections – for example, does not transaction cost economics (Williamson, 1996b) make use of BR; for example, is not the crucial notion of incomplete contracts founded on this? Is not it the case that the evolutionary approach to the firm (Nelson & Winter, 1982) as well as related approaches (e.g., Conner & Prahalad, 1996) are directly founded on BR? Did not Simon write paper after paper, involving the theory of the firm and urging economists to substitute BR for substantive rationality (Simon, 1976, 1978, 1979)? And did not he note that "[n]othing is more fundamental in setting our research agenda and informing our research methods than our view of the nature of the human beings whose behavior we are studying" (Simon, 1985, p. 303), a view that has also been very strongly stressed by Williamson, arguably the flag-bearer of the whole field of the economics of organization, as a reason to take BR seriously (e.g., Williamson, 1985)?

Against such objections I shall argue that in the modern economics of organization there are few serious attempts to precisely define BR, and examine its implications for economic organization. This is not surprising, since – as it is being used in the contemporary economics of organization – bounded rationality is not necessary for producing the central results of these theories. Rather, the status of bounded rationality is the rhetorical one of lending credence to other, more central analytical concepts, notably organizational capabilities and incomplete contracts. I develop this theme in the context of both the organizational capabilities/evolutionary economics approach (Section 2, *Bounded rationality in the organizational capabilities approach*), and the transaction cost and contract theory approaches (Section 3, *Bounded rationality in transaction cost economics and contract theory*).

Attention is then turned to the reasons why Simon's Grand Theme of bounded rationality has been so incompletely absorbed and used, some of which arguably has to do with Simon never putting forward a specific program for incorporating bounded rationality in the economics of organization, at least not in a way that economists have been willing to accept (Section 4, *Why is bounded rationality much cited and little used?*).

This paper should by no means be read as an attack on BR per se; rather, it is a critique of the current way in which BR is used. Actually, we need more of bounded rationality in the economics of organization, not less. However, this will require beginning from better founded conceptualizations of BR, and of how BR may be put to use in the economics of organization. There are many potentially enlightening ways in which BR models may be built and used in the economics of organization, and I briefly discuss these at the end of the paper (Section 5, *Whither bounded rationality in the economics of organization?*).

2. Bounded rationality in the organizational capabilities approach[2]

2.1. Briefly on the organizational capabilities approach

It is appropriate to begin a discussion of the role of BR in the modern economics of organization with the organizational capabilities approach, because this is the approach that is conventionally most directly associated with BR (Nelson & Winter, 1982; Fransman, 1994; Hodgson, 1998; Conner & Prahalad, 1996; Brousseau, 2000). The "organizational capabilities approach" is shorthand for a set of approaches to the behavior and organization of firms that lie somewhat in-between economics and strategic management and organization, including "dynamic capabilities," "competence-based," and "resource-based" approaches, and, of course, the "evolutionary theory of the firm."[3] These approaches share a number of characteristics, notably an emphasis on experiential, localized, and socially held knowledge and learning processes as a key aspect of the firm. It is such knowledge that explains firm heterogeneity, and various aspects of competitive advantage, particularly differential innovation performance. As Langlois and Foss (1999) point out, the above approaches are also united in their attempt to increasingly go beyond their traditional *explananda* (i.e., the sources of competitive advantage, localized innovative activity, and general rigidity of firm behavior) to also include issues, notably the boundaries of the firm, that have traditionally been considered the turf of the more mainstream economics of organization. At the heart of these stories are the characteristics, notably tacitness, of the knowledge that is embedded in organizational capabilities (Kogut & Zander, 1992; Langlois, 1992). As Kogut and Zander (1992) argue, firms know more than their contracts can tell, as it were, which

renders contracting infeasible for certain kinds of knowledge-intensive transactions (see also Langlois, 1992). Such transactions are instead internalized
within the firm.

BR is at the root of these stories, it is sometimes argued (Loasby, 1991;
Fransman, 1994), because BR implies that learning processes will go on differently in different firms, resulting in differences across accumulated bodies
of knowledge; however, it is seldom made clear in exactly what sense BR is
foundational. The organizational capabilities approach builds on numerous
sources, most obviously the works of Philip Selznick, Alfred Chandler, Edith
Penrose, G. B. Richardson, and Nelson and Winter (1982) (see Foss, 1997,
for a sampling). However, of these sources, Nelson and Winter are actually the only writers to explicitly address and stress BR. Understanding the
role of BR in the organizational capabilities should therefore begin by
considering its role in Nelson and Winter.

2.2. *Bounded rationality in Nelson and Winter*

Quite early in Nelson and Winter (1982), namely when discussing "the need
for an evolutionary theory," the authors observe that their "... basic
critique of orthodoxy is connected with the BR problem" (p. 36). Given
this, it is not surprising that they establish direct links, and are strongly
indebted, to the behavioralist notion that short and medium run firm behavior
is determined by relatively simple decision rules (Cyert & March, 1963).
They also make use of behavioralist models of satisficing search. However,
they go significantly beyond behavioralism by examining populations of
firms with differing decision rules, by addressing the interplay between changing external environments and changing decision rules, and by trying to
bring BR together with tacit knowledge.

Nelson and Winter's main problem with "orthodox" theory, and particularly the neoclassical theory of the firm is that – if it enters at all –
heterogeneity is at best exogenously determined. To paraphrase their argument, in the setting of the (basic) neoclassical theory of the firm, it has to be
in this way, because the production set is assumed to be not only given (or
at best changing through given technological progress functions or similar
constructs), but also to be fully transparent. To bring out the differences
between mainstream and evolutionary conceptions of productive activities,
Nelson and Winter devote a whole chapter (4) to an analysis of skills, that
is, the "... capability for a smooth sequence of coordinated behavior that is
ordinarily effective relative to its objectives, given the context in which it
normally occurs" (Nelson & Winter, 1982, p. 73). The attractions of the
notion of skill are apparent. It provides a direct link to the behavioralist
notion that behavior is strongly guided by relatively rigid decision rules. It
also allows them to bring considerations of tacit knowledge into the picture
and to develop a strong critique of the "blueprint" view of neoclassical

production function theory. Finally, it helps them to establish a link between individual action and organizational behavior. That link is initiated in a rather straightforward way by the observation that "... directly relevant to our development here is the value of individual behavior as a *metaphor* for organizational behavior" (Nelson & Winter, 1982, p. 72; emphasis in original).[4] In turn, "organizational behavior" is addressed in terms of "routines" that serve as direct (metaphorical) equivalents to individual skills. Like skills, routines represent stable sequences of actions (i.e., they coordinate actions) that are triggered by certain stimuli in certain contexts and which, in a sense, serve as memories for the organizations that embody them.

At first glance, BR appears to be quite crucial to Nelson and Winter's argument (Fransman, 1994). Thus, firm members can only learn routines through practicing them; routines are simply repeated until they become too dysfunctional; learning is myopic; search is satisficing; etc. All of these rather strong ideas would seem to install a prominent place for a rationality that is very bounded indeed. However, after reading Nelson and Winter one is left with the feeling that what ultimately interests them is not really BR per se in the sense of a commitment to investigating specific models of boundedly rational individual behaviors and tracing the effects of these on organizational outcomes. What interest them is rather tacit knowledge and its embodiment in their firm-level analogy to individual skills, namely routines, and how employing these notions assists the understanding of sluggish organizational adaptation. To be sure, Nelson and Winter do mention and discuss BR to the extent that this helps them introducing the behavioralist notion of decision rules. Clearly such decision rules may be analyzed as manifestations of BR. However, agent level decision rules say nothing about organizational behavior per se. What permits the link to be established is the use of the skill metaphor. The aggregation problem, which is quite problematic in the presence of the variety of behaviors implied by the notion of BR, is, if not entirely suppressed, then largely sidestepped, by means of the analogy from skills to organizational routine. Thus, the whole construct works from an initial assumption about BR, goes from there to behavioralist decision rules, combines this with ideas on tacit knowledge as embodied in skilled behavior, and then transfers individually BR and skills to the level of routines and organizational capabilities.

There are a number of problematic consequences of this exercise. First, tacit knowledge and BR become indiscriminately lumped together. It is important to stress that tacit knowledge and BR represent different kinds of assumptions and do not necessarily imply each other. Thus, there can be tacit rules for maximization, as Machlup (1946) argued. Or, agents can cope with BR by means of fully explicit operating procedures. While one can certainly construct an argument that boundedly rational agents make use of experientially produced – and "skilled" – decision rules that are likely to embody a good deal of tacit knowledge, there is no necessary connection between BR and tacit knowledge. Second, and perhaps more seriously, BR on the level of the individual agent becomes suppressed so that the aggregate notions of routines and capabilities (i.e., collections of routines) are without any clear foundations in individual behavior. For example, it is not clear in principle whether organization-level routinization is produced by interaction effects among the members of a team or whether it is ultimately founded in aspects of individual cognition (Egidi, 2000, p. 2; for further discussion, see Foss, 2003).

In the end, BR is more a sort of background argument that – in combination with other assumptions about tacit knowledge and skilled human behavior – serves to make plausible the notion of organizational routine (including search routines), and therefore the sluggish organizational adaptation that is crucial in Nelson and Winter's evolutionary story. In fact, it is the concept of routine as the carrier of socialle held tacit knowledge, rather than individual BR that is centerstage in their discussion. There is nothing wrong with this per se. For the purposes of Nelson and Winter (1982) it is perfectly rational. However, as I argue next, transferring the notions of routines and organizational capabilities to other purposes may be highly problematic.

2.3. The organizational capabilities approach and economic organization

The argument here is that certain characteristics of Nelson and Winter (1982) were carried over into the organizational capabilities approach, characteristics that are quite appropriate for the purpose of building a theory of rigidity in firm behavior as a part of a broader evolutionary story, but which are much less appropriate for the purpose of building a theory of economic organization.[5] These characteristics have been discussed above. They are the strong emphasis on aggregate entities, notably routines and organizational capabilities, an emphasis that comes at the expense of attention to individual behaviors. This emphasis derives from Nelson and Winter's attempt to establish a *metaphorical* solution to the aggregation problem of moving from the level of the agent to the level of the organization. Because they fully recognize the metaphorical character of this maneuver, they do not commit the mistake of conflating an ontological claim with a useful research heuristic. Later contributors to the organizational capabilities approach may not have been as careful here as Nelson and Winter.

The problems seem to emerge as soon as ideas on organizational routines and capabilities are transferred from their original place in the analysis of a population of firms to an analysis of the behavior and, particularly, organization of individual firms. While these notions have indeed been of value for the understanding of, for example, the sources of competitive advantage, their application to economic organization is more problematic. For example, Kogut and Zander (1992) argue directly from tacit knowledge embodied in organizational capabilities to the boundaries of the firm. The argument is that "firms know more than their contracts can tell." Apparently, the boundaries of the firm are determined by economizing with the costs of trying to communicate tacit knowledge.[6] However, there is no attempt to address this is in terms of comparative contracting. What exactly is it that cannot be written in contracts? Even if the costs of writing contract are prohibitive, why cannot relational contracting, involving highly incomplete contracts, between independent parties handle the transfer of knowledge? Why is it only vertical integration that economizes with what are presumably writing and communication costs? No compelling answers are given to such questions.

There is a related difficulty in most of the organizational capabilities literature, particularly as it applies to economic organization, namely that knowledge inside firms is *assumed* be homogeneous (or communicable at very low cost), while knowledge between firms ("differential capabilities") is taken to be (very) heterogeneous (and therefore very costly to communicate) (e.g., Winter, 1986, p. 175). It is hard to accept this assumption as a generally true one. There are many examples of firms where the bandwidth of the communication channels between some business unit of the firm and external firm (e.g., buyer or seller) is much higher than the bandwidth between the unit and, say, corporate headquarters. Moreover, the implicit assumption that knowledge in hierarchies can be taken, at least as a first approximation, to be communicable at zero cost makes it hard to understand hierarchical organization, since with zero cost communication the managerial task has no economic rationale (Demsetz, 1991; Casson, 1994).

However, it is easy to see that such an assumption easily slips into the analysis when the units of analysis are routines or organizational capabilities. It is then easy to postulate that "firms know more than their contracts can tell" and that all organizational aspects are "intertwined in a functioning routine." If instead the analysis had started from individual choice behavior, the argument that communication costs within, for example, certain business units may be lower than the communication costs between employees in the unit and employees in a supplier firm, might have been derived as an outcome of a properly specified model instead of being postulated. This is an indication that the emphasis on aggregate entities characteristic of the organizational capabilities approach makes a micro-analytic understanding of economic organization difficult.

Ironically, it turns out that much of the organizational capabilities approach is vulnerable to much the same critique that Winter (1991) forcefully launched against the neoclassical theory of the firm. Specifically, and

borrowing directly from Winter, it is in potential "conflict with methodological individualism" (p. 181) (because of the emphasis on routines and
organizational capabilities), ". . . provides no basis for explaining economic
organization" (p. 183) (because transaction costs and comparative contracting are not considered), lacks "realism" (because of its "unrealistic" treatment
of decision-making as entirely guided by routines), and provides a "simp-
listic treatment of its focal concern" (e.g., because it is simply assumed that
it is easier to gather, combine, source, etc. knowledge inside firms than
between firms). The main underlying problem, it has been argued here, is
that too little attention is devoted to boundedly rational *individual* decision-
making. As I argue next, in transaction cost economics and contract theory,
BR is also not really modeled in any serious way. This gives rise to somewhat similar problems. Here, too, it is in actuality a background argument
that in combination with other assumptions helps to rationalize other, supposedly more central, phenomena. And as recent theoretical debate has
suggested (e.g., Tirole, 1999), it is not clear whether those stories that claim
to rely on BR in order to be able to explain key aspects of economic organization can actually accomplish this.

3. Bounded rationality in transaction cost economics
and contract theory

3.1. Bounded rationality: Spanners in the works
of complete contracting

Although the more mainstream economics of organization, particularly transaction cost economics (Williamson, 1996b), may have been one of the first
areas where the notion of BR was systematically applied in theorizing, later
developments do not seem to have gone significantly beyond Simon (1951),
Marschak and Radner (1972) and Williamson (1975). If anything, the
use, or at least invocation, of the notion of BR may actually have declined.[7]
To some extent this is because the mainstream economics of organization
has developed into a highly formal and axiomatic enterprise, and BR has a
bad reputation of only being given to formalization if that formalization is
fundamentally ad hoc and the axiomatic basis is unclear or non-existent.
That reputation may not be justified (Rubinstein, 1998), but most economists of organization (particularly contract theorists) act as if it is. Hart
(1990, 700–701) sums up the sentiments of many formal economists when
he argues that

> . . . I do not think that bounded rationality is necessary for a theory
> of organizations. This is fortunate because developing a theory of
> bounded rationality in a bilateral or multilateral setting seems even
> more complicated than developing such a theory at the individual

level; and the latter task has already proved more than enough for economists to handle.

In fact, some parts of the economics of organization, particularly contract theory, bear little substantial imprint of BR. Its only real job, if it is used at all, is to explain in a loose way why some contingencies may be left out of a contract.

It is commonly held that transaction cost economics provides more room for BR than simply this (e.g., Brousseau & Fares, 2000). There is something to this claim; for example, Williamson (1975) does invoke BR in connection with, for example, explaining the M-form. Still, however, Williamson refrains from being explicit about how to model BR. He is quite explicit here, noting that "[e]conomizing on bounded rationality takes two forms. One concerns decision processes and the other involves governance structures. The use of heuristic problem-solving . . . is a decision process response" (Williamson, 1985, p. 46). The latter "form" is not central, however, in transaction cost economics, which ". . . is principally concerned . . . with the economizing consequences of assigning transactions to governance structures in a discriminating way."[8] Thus, Williamson is interested in making use of bounded rationality for the purpose of explaining the existence and boundaries of firms rather than for the purposes of explaining administrative *behavior*, as in Simon (1947).[9] He is not interested in BR as a "decision process response." What Williamson says he is interested in is, of course, how BR help to explain the choice between governance structures[10] which has to do with the role of BR in explaining incomplete contracts and therefore the hold-up problem around which his thinking revolves. For the purpose of explaining why contracts are incomplete, Williamson thinks that it is not necessary to model BR itself. It may be asserted as a "background assumption" that while vital – indeed, necessary – does not need to be explicated itself. Milgrom and Roberts (1992, p. 128), as well as most other mainstream economists of organization who invoke BR, adopt the same procedure.

Thus, BR enters organizational economics reasoning in a loose background sort of way, in which it lends credence to exogeneously imposing constraints on the feasible contracting space, but is not being modeled itself. It supplies the rhetorical function of lending intuitive support to the notion of incomplete contracts. A Simonian information processing argument is sometimes invoked here (Hart, 1990, p. 698; Schwartz, 1992, p. 80). Thus, if agents do not have the mental capacity to think through the whole decision tree – for example, in complicated bilateral trading relations – it seems reasonable to assume that some of the branches of the tree (such as those relating to some future uses of assets) cannot be represented in a contract; the contract is left incomplete. However, agents are supposed to deal with this manifestation of BR in a substantively rational manner, as many critics have pointed out since Dow (1987).

Because BR tends to be simply used as convenient spanners in the works of incomplete contracting, we are seldom or never given deep explanations in the economics of organization of what it actually is; it is merely a label for a convenient deviation from the "fully rational" contracting outcome. As Dow (1987) observed, this approach provokes a lurking suspicion of a basic inconsistency, for whereas BR is loosely invoked as a background assumption (yet still a necessary one), there is no hesitation to appeal to substantive rationality when the choice between governance structures must be rationalized.[11] I discuss this next.

3.2. Bounded rationality, transaction costs and economic organization: The incomplete contract controversy

A recent theoretical debate on the coherence and foundations of incomplete contract theory – the "incomplete contract controversy" (Tirole, 1999) – is quite pertinent to the issues under consideration here. The debate concerns whether satisfactory foundations for incomplete contracts are offered in the works of Hart and associates (e.g., Grossman & Hart, 1986; Hart & Moore, 1990; Hart, 1995). At the core of this debate is the explanatory tension between invoking transaction costs – which may be understood as a consequence of BR – on the one hand and postulating farsighted and substantively rational contracting on the other hand. However, whereas Dow (1987) and other critics interpreted this as an inconsistency in transaction cost economics, Maskin and Tirole show something else: There is no formal inconsistency; however, the use of transaction costs (i.e., BR) does not provide additional explanatory insight relative to models that make no use of these.

Organizational issues have motivated the upsurge in incomplete contract modeling during the last decade. In fact, the founding incomplete contract paper, namely Grossman and Hart (1986), was explicitly motivated by an attempt to model the emphasis in transaction cost economics on asset specificity as a key determinant of the scope of the firm. The key problem in these models are that the parties' *ex ante* incentives may be misaligned when contracts are not complete in situations where the parties to a relation have to undertake specific and complementary investments in that relation. Of course, this is closely related to the hold-up problem of transaction cost economics (Williamson, 1996b). And as in the case of transaction cost economics, there is an appeal to transaction costs, whether arising from the inability to perfectly anticipate or describe all relevant contingencies or enforce contract terms (all of which may derive from BR[12]). The point of contention in the incomplete contracts controversy is whether transaction costs constrain the set of feasible contracting outcomes relative to the complete contracting benchmark. If this is *not* the case, transaction costs (i.e., BR) do not suffice to establish the possibility of inefficient investment patterns. Therefore, they do not suffice to establish a role for ownership, and in turn for a theory of the boundaries of the firm.

The argument builds on the assumption in the incomplete contract approach that although valuations may not be verifiable by a court of law, they may still be observable by the parties. This implies that trade can be conditioned on message games between the parties. These games are designed *ex ante* in such a way that they can effectively describe *ex post* (where bargaining is efficient) all the trades that were not described *ex ante*. A further crucial step in the argument is accepting the typical contract theory assumption that parties allocate property rights and choose investments so that their expected utilities are maximized, knowing (at least probabilistically) how payoffs relate to allocations of property rights and levels of investment (i.e., they can perform "dynamic programming"). Given this, Maskin and Tirole (1999) provide sufficient conditions under which the undescribability of c ontingencies does *not* restrict the payoffs that can be achieved. This is their "irrelevance of transaction costs" theorem.

There are further rounds to the debate (e.g., Hart & Moore, 1999). However, it is not necessary to go into these to see that the debate has potentially far-reaching implications for the use of BR in the economics of organization. Thus, Maskin and Tirole (1999) show that there is no *logical* inconsistency involved in assuming that payoffs are fully foreseeable, yet parties are ignorant about the sources of that utility. If you like, Savage and Simon are compatible (see, however, Kreps (1996) for some acerbic comments on this). However, they *also* show that, within the relevant modeling frameworks, very little, and perhaps no, economic content is added by introducing considerations of BR. Note that the Maskin and Tirole critique is also *potentially* damning for transaction cost economics to the extent that it relies on a substantively rational story of the design of efficient governance structures and to the extent that misaligned investment incentives are crucial here, too.[13]

It is not warranted to generalize from a single episode in an ongoing theoretical discussion that has not yet reached a definitive conclusion. However, in the light of the debate, it is tempting to conjecture that the reason why the mainstream economics of organization has not yet succeeded in providing a convincing explanation of the key issues of economic organization – particularly the boundaries of the firm – is that it fundamentally stays close to the basic complete contracting model and allows for very little room for BR, and, at any rate, does not engage in any modeling of BR on the level of the individual agent. Thus, while the treatment of BR in the mainstream economics of organization is completely different from the organizational capabilities approach, there is the same lack of consideration with BR on the level of the individual agent, and the same kind of problems with respect to the *explananda* of the theories emerge.

4. Why is bounded rationality much cited and little used?

4.1. The puzzle of organizational economists' limited use of bounded rationality

BR, it has been argued, is very much a background assumption that is introduced m order to help explaining, in an "intuitive" way, other, more central, insights and concepts. At first glance, this rather limited use of BR in the economics of organization is surprising, considering the importance of Simon for the whole field (and also for the neighbouring field of organization theory), and the energy and effort that he invested here. Thus, in a series of methodologically oriented papers, delivered at very prestiguous occasions (i.e., Ely and Nobel lectures), Simon (1976, 1978, 1979, 1997) worked hard to convince economists to take seriously his Grand Theme of BR. His examples of BR and its implications quite often involved the business firm. Indeed, he sometimes took the notion of "administrative man" to be *synonymous* with a boundedly rational agent. Of course, Simon himself published prolifically on firms and other organizations (e.g., Simon, 1947, 1951, 1991, 1997; March & Simon, 1958). Given all this, how can it be that organizational economists have been reluctant to be serious about BR? There seem to be three dominant reasons for this, one having to do with the way BR tends to be defined, namely negatively rather than positively; one historical, having to do with Simon's influence on economists' thinking on BR; and one having to do with the difficulty of aligning BR with the basic machinery of neoclassical microeconomics and game theory.

4.2. Negative and positive definitions of rationality

A fundamental problem in many discussions of BR is that the concept tends to be defined negatively rather than positively.[14] Taking account of Simon's total *oeuvre*, he can hardly be accused of doing this; for example, his work with Newell (Newell & Simon, 1972) very concretely goes into bounded rationality. However, Simon's more methodological papers that he wrote for an economics audience (Simon, 1976, 1978, 1979), and which are the only Simon papers on BR that most economists are likely to know, come close to defining BR in a negative manner. He is acutely aware of the problem (Simon, 1979, p. 502), referring to earlier work in which BR was in fact defined as a "residual category":

> In *Administrative Behavior*, bounded rationality is largely characterized as a residual category – rationality is bounded when it falls short of omniscience. . . . There was needed a more positive and formal characterization of the mechanisms of choice under conditions of bounded rationality.

The theory of satisficing search is, of course, one such characterization, and it, as well as other instances of behavioral decision theory, is discussed in Simon (1978, 1979). It has often been argued that a basic problem with satisficing search is that there is virtually nothing in the theory itself about the merits of alternative search procedures. Simon explicitly argues that in order to understand the relative advantages of different procedures, it is necessary to step outside of economics, and consider, for example, work on integer programming. However, his comments on the subject are extremely vague, and he chooses to "... leave the topics of computational complexity and heuristic search with these sketchy remarks. What implications these developments in the theory of procedural rationality will have for economics . . . remain to be seen" (Simon, 1978, p. 12).

Thus, in those writings for economists that were published simultaneously with the take-off of organizational economics, Simon did, in fact, not provide a positive definition of bounded rationality that could have supplied a building block for modeling exercises in organizational economics. His writings from the 1950s that were published in economics journals and were quite specific about the nature of BR were not known, or at least not used.

4.3. Simon's influence

There can be little doubt that Simon has had a quite overwhelming influence on those economists who have taken an interest in firms and organization. Because Simon is a towering figure not only with respect to developing the notion of BR, but also with respect to applying this notion in organizational analysis (Simon, 1947; March & Simon, 1958), his work is easily seen as exemplary by an economist taken up with firm organization. However, although Simon in his more methodologically oriented papers directed at economists (Simon, 1976, 1978, 1979) typically illustrate BR by means of examples drawn from firms, these examples are typically very broad (e.g., centralization vs. decentralization, maximizing decisions vs. rules of thumb) and largely taken from the works of other contributors, such as Cyert and March (1963). Notably, when Simon talks to economists about BR (in Simon, 1976, 1978, 1979), it is typically much less specific and elaborated than when he tells scholars in psychology or artificial intelligence about the same subject (e.g., Simon, 1982; Newell and Simon, 1982). One of his latest papers on organizational issues (Simon, 1991) surprisingly does not go into BR *at all*, but mostly takes issue with various themes in organizational economics, notably the assumption of opportunism. The fact is that there is not much in Simon's methodological papers that may instruct economists wanting to build a BR research program in the economics of organization about the exact nature of the hard core assumption itself. Neither is there much in Simon's methodological writings for economists resembling a positive heuristic, describing how theories of economic organization, building on this already vague notion, should be constructed. It is a very plausible inference that this has contributed to the absence of a distinct BR research program in the economics of organization.

4.4. Aligning bounded rationality with mainstream economics

The most obvious reason why economists of organization have at best worked with strongly watered-down versions of BR is because of the well-known difficulties of aligning BR with the basic machinery of neoclassical microeconomics and game theory (Conlisk, 1996; Rabin, 1998; Camerer, 1998). Of course, it was the belief that BR simply could not be aligned with mainstream economics, and that BR implied a very strong critique of this body of theory that made Simon so critical of it. And, indeed, fundamental notions and modeling principles of mainstream, such as subjective expected utility, common priors, rational expectations/dynamic programming, backward induction, etc., are not too easily aligned, to say the least, with fundamental findings of cognitive psychology (such as gain–loss asymmetries, role-biased expectations, etc.). Moreover, from the mainstream economist point of view, there is a price to be paid in terms of analytical tractability and clarity to the extent that one wishes to factor findings from cognitive psychology into economic models. Hence, the use of watered-down versions of BR in the economics of organization, in which BR occupies at best a small corner of the model, as it were, and the rest is taken up by common priors, dynamic programming, etc. Now, a possible problem with this explanation turns on the above observation that other economists have been less reluctant to work with much more explicit models of BR, notably scholars in behavioral finance and behavioral law and economics, and with considerable success (as well as controversy). It is arguable that their comparative success is caused by their willingness to use more explicit and detailed views of BR, drawn from cognitive psychology. Is this also an attractive route for organizational economists? This is briefly discussed in the following section.

5. Whither bounded rationality in the economics of organization?

5.1. Towards "thicker" notions of bounded rationality in the economics of organization

In general, the BR research effort may be understood as an attempt to elaborate and examine the insights that (1) the human capacity to process information is quite limited, (2) humans try to economize on cognitive effort by relying on short-cuts, and (3) because of (1) and (2), as well as other factors, such as the influence of emotions on cognition, human cognition and judgment is subject to a wide range of biases and errors. Note in passing that Simon's Grand theme concerned (1) and (2); he never took much of an interest in, for example, the biases literature of Tversky, Kahneman, Thaler, etc. (e.g., Tversky & Kahneman, 1987; Kahneman, Knetsch, & Thaler, 1990), although he was aware of it.[15] In short, he was never out to do the kind of "behavioral economics" associated today with, for example, Thaler and Rabin. Going from level (1) to level (3) means adding increasing content to the description of boundedly rational man. Thus, the limited capacity information processor (or the adaptive problem-solvers discussed in Newell & Simon, 1972) is a more anonymous entity than the agent who comes equipped with reference level biases, adaptive preferences and the like. Economists of organization have taken an interest in (1), have been less occupied with (2), and have almost entirely neglected (3). An attempt to bring BR more explicitly into the economics of should consider (2) and perhaps (3), since, according to the argument of this paper, the very "thin" versions (essentially (1) above) that organizational economists have worked with so far have resuited in essentially no explanatory value-added, and it seems to be a reasonable expectation that being explicit about BR may yield more such value added.

5.2. *Speculations on modeling approaches*

One way of classifying approaches to modeling BR in the context of economic organization relates to the three levels of research in BR mentioned above. Thus, corresponding to level (1) are the approaches that have been critically discussed in previous sections. Corresponding to level (2), there are a number of papers around that try to further insight in economic organization by building on Simonian ideas on problem-solving and heuristic search, most of which are written by evolutionary economists (i.e., fall within the organizational capabilities approach) and involve the use of NK-modeling, classifier systems and the like (Marengo, Dosi, Legrenzi, & Pasquali (2000) is fairly representative). While this, usually highly abstract, literature has developed interesting results on organizational structure (idem.), it has so far said very little about other issues of economic organization. Whether it can be extended to questions that relate to, for example, the boundaries of the firm remains to be seen.

There is a third possible approach that corresponds to level (3) above, but which is closer to transaction cost economics and contract theory than to the organizational capabilities approach.[16] It, too, is loosely reflected in a few recent papers (such as Carmichael & MacLeod, 1999; Mookerji, 1998; Williamson, 1998). The research strategy of this approach may be described as (a) consider the massive body of largely psychology-based research science on biases to human cognition and judgment (summarized for economists by Conlisk, 1996; Camerer, 1998; Rabin, 1998); (b) identify the regularities in how human decision-making systematically differs from the Savage model; (c) treat these deviations as sources of transaction costs; and (d) examine the implications for comparative contracting and the choice of governance structures.

A similar argument has recently been sketched by Williamson (1998), who argues that taking more account of the relevant psychological literature will improve the understanding of organization "... as an instrument for utilizing varying cognitive and behavioral propensities to best advantage" (Williamson, 1998, p. 12). However, he seems mostly intent on demonstrating that the many findings on biased cognition and judgment are entirely consistent with "[t]he transaction cost economics triple for describing human actors – BR, farsighted contracting, and opportunism." He therefore refrains from inquiring into how *specifically* these findings may add to and complement the transaction cost economics approach. However, looking at this in a more detailed manner will improve our knowledge of the ways in which organizations may be instruments for utilizing varying cognitive and behavioral propensities to "best advantage." Much of that can be accomplished simply through specialization and assignment, which are the most obvious ways in which organization economize with BR. However, this observation is not a license to be complacent about the above-mentioned psychological findings. Thus, organizations also economize on BR by curbing the less fortunate manifestations and consequences of biases and errors in decision making, time-variant preferences, over-confidence biases, and the like, all of which may persist even with an extensive level of specialization.

Thus, a broad implication is that paying more attention to such behavioral aspects allows for a richer understanding of the managerial task. In addition to performance assessment, the tasks of the tasks of the manager may also include correcting biases in judgment, curbing problems of procrastination and impulsiveness, influencing organizational expectations, and manipulating preferences. Another implication is that more room is created for *ex post* governance than is usual in the economics of organization: If indeed agents cannot perfectly foresee all contingencies and calculate the payoffs of their relations or if their estimates of these payoffs are biased, unintended consequences are likely to follow. In turn, this may give rise to haggling, as the parties try to adjust. The costs of haggling may be reduced by means of *ex post* mechanisms, such as the authority relation. While entirely consistent with transaction cost economics, such an approach would provide a better explanation of why exactly *ex post* haggling costs arise. A third implication is that the design of incentive schemes may have to respect that risk-preferences are often context-dependent, which means that the efficiency of incentive contracts, which partly relies on shifting risks between parties, is context dependent, and that some kinds of incentive contracts may in some contexts have perverse consequences.

Considerations of space do not allow going into this at any length.[17] However, the reasoning hopefully serve to indicate the main thrust of the argument: it is possible to tell stories about economic organization that pay much more attention to BR, but still does not fundamentally break with explanatory fundamentals of organizational economics, that is, keeps intact an economizing orientation, methodological individualism, a focus on the costs of transacting, and comparative contracting. However, taking account of "thicker" notions of BR than is standard fare in organizational economics and the organizational capabilities approach means that there are certain research heuristics in the economics of organization that becomes problematic, notably the use of rational expectations/dynamic programming. On the other hand new heuristics may be added, such as the idea that biases to cognition and judgment, etc. may be analyzed as determinants of transaction costs on a par with the usual determinants identified in the economics of organization. With respect to the outcomes of theorizing, the conjecture here is that the introduction of biases to cognition and judgment means that the set of feasible outcomes is different from what is described in the economics of organization, for example, because reference level biases constrain this set (for more on this, see Foss, 2001).

Of course, the set of approaches to modeling BR is a huge one, including, for example, the "fast and frugal heuristics" approach developed in Gigerenzer and Todd (2001), or the axiomatic approach in Rubinstein (1998). Thus, the examples that have been discussed here merely constitute a small subset. The purpose has merely been to suggest that there *are* positive approaches to BR, some of which may potentially be usefully in organizational economics research.

6. Conclusions

I have argued that although many contributors to the economics of organization have agreed on the importance of BR to their subject area, upon closer inspection it turns out that there is little agreement on (1) what is the nature of BR, (2) how it should be modeled, and (3) its implications for the behavior and organization of firms. Because of the absence of a distinct, positive program for incorporating BR in the economics of organization – the lack of which may be partly attributed to Simon's own vagueness on the matter – economists have worked with BR in a non-substantive manner, merely invoking BR to provide intuition for, more central, higher-level concepts. In both the mainstream economics of organization and in the organizational capabilities approach, boundedly rational individual behavior is in actuality not modeled, which results in explanatory problems for these approaches.

However, it has also been noted that the situation is far from hopeless. In actuality, there is plenty of research in BR, and some of the foremost symbol manipulators of the economics profession have lately taken an active interest (e.g., Rubinstein, 1998). However, those economists who wish to make more room for BR in the economics of organization does not necessarily have to wait for the latest models with finite automata and the like. There are plenty of conceptualizations of BR – "stylized facts," if you like – out there, many of which are amply supported by extensive empirical research in psychology, and which may be fed into economic models in the form of context dependent preferences, framing effects, etc. (e.g., Carmichael & MacLeod, 1999; Mookerji, 1998). However, so far efforts within such a program have been few and scattered. This is perhaps not so surprising. Often central concepts can live a life for a long time without being defined with much precision and their exact role in theorizing not being clearly identified. The most obvious example is that of transaction costs. Another one is BR, at least as it has been used in organizational economics. Transaction cost economics had what is in effect a four or five decades long gestation period after Coase (1937) before it could finally take off in the hands of, primarily, Oliver Williamson. Perhaps BR, introduced in economics at a much later time, needs a similar gestation period. And it may also need its Oliver Williamson, so that, being duly "operationalized," BR can finally be not only cited, but also used in a more substantive manner.

Acknowledgements

I am grateful to Mie Augier, Peter Earl, John Finch, James March, Luigi Marengo, and Uskali Mäki and two anonymous reviewers of this journal for comments on earlier versions of the paper, and to Oliver Williamson and Henrik Lando for discussion of a central point. All errors, obscurities, etc. are solely my responsibility.

Notes

1 BR is also frequently invoked and discussed in important contemporary contributions to contract theory (Milgrom & Roberts, 1992; Hart, 1990), including important recent work on the foundations of incomplete contract theory (Hart & Moore, 1999; Maskin & Tirole, 1999; Tirole, 1999).
2 This section draws on Foss (2003).
3 Some representative authors are Richardson (1972), Conner (1991), Langlois (1992), Foss (1993), Fransman (1994), and Conner and Prahalad (1996).
4 As an anonymous reviewer pointed out, this solution may be more than merely metaphorical. Winter (the likely main author of the chapters in Nelson & Winter, 1982, on firm behavior and organization) was employed at RAND (to work on the science policy debates that were raging in US in 1950s and 1960s). At RAND it was commonly held that the computer was a "scale-free" model of organization, whether this be at the level of the mind or at the level of firms. With such a background, it may have been natural to jump directly from "routines" (i.e., "programmed" sequences of actions) at the level of the individual to routines at the level of the firm.

5 Foss (1996) discusses other problems with organizational capabilities theories as theories of economic organization.

6 This is the story told by Demsetz (1991) and Langlois (1992). Thus, Langlois invokes the concept of "dynamic transaction costs," which are communication costs that arise because of "dis-similar" (Richardson, 1972) capabilities in a vertical structure of firms. Efficient economic organization minimizes such costs (as well as other more "traditional" transaction costs, allowance being made for possible tradeoffs between these).

7 For example, in Williamson's work, bounded rationality arguably loomed larger in Williamson (1975) than it does in Williamson (1996b).

8 Here, Simon seems justified in his critique that ". . . the new institutional economics has not drawn heavily from the empirical work in organizations and decision-making for its auxiliary assumptions" (Simon, 1991, p. 27).

9 For a fascinating, personal statement on the Carnegie influence on the development of transaction cost economics, see Williamson (1996b).

10 However, if that is the case, one wonders why it is necessary to exclude a concern with decision process responses, since one might expect different governance structures to exhibit different decision process properties.

11 This asymmetry is discussed in greater detail in Foss and Foss (2000).

12 In the last case (non-verifiability), it is the enforcing party, such as a judge, that is boundedly rational.

13 However, much depends on the specific analytical structure being adopted. The Maskin and Tirole "irrelevance" result holds for a certain class of very specific modeling approaches. The result can only be held to be critical for transaction cost economics to the extent that these approaches may be taken to fairly accurately portray the analytical structure of transaction cost economics. Oliver Williamson denies that this is the case (personal communication).

14 Of course, the problem is inherent in the name of the concept itself, and Simon may have committed a fundamental labeling blunder here. This may explain why he, from about the mid-1970s often used the notion of "procedural rationality" rather than BR.

15 Communication with Mie Augier. Also, Simon was apparently not interested in the role of emotions in cognition, either.

16 Much of team theory may be described as unfolding the consequences of level 2 BR for organizations; see, for example, Sah and Stiglitz (1988) and Radner (1996).

17 See Foss (2001) for a slightly more detailed discussion pertaining to inertia in organizations, leadership behavior and team organization.

References

Brousseau, E. (2000). New Institutional economics and evolutionary economics: What convergences. In Paper for the LINK/MPI Workshop on Cognition and Rationality in the Theory of the Firm, Jena, 25–27 September, 2000.

Brousseau, E., & Fares, M. (2000). Incomplete contract theory and new institutional economics approaches to contracts: Substitutes or complements. In Claude Ménard (Ed.), *Institutions, contracts, and organizations: Perspectives from new institutional economics*. Aldershot: Edward Elgar.

Camerer, C. (1998). Bounded rationality in individual decision making. *Experimental Economics, 1*, 163–183.

Carmichael, L., & MacLeod, W. B. (1999). Caring about sunk costs: A behavioral solution to hold-up problems with small stakes. University of Southern California Law School, Olin Working Paper 99-19.

Casson, M. (1994). Why are firms hierarchical? *International Journal of the Economics of Business*, *1*, 43–81.

Coase, R. H. (1937). The nature of the firm. *Economica (N.S.)*, *4*, 386–405.

Conlisk, J. (1996). Why bounded rationality? *Journal of Economic Literature*, *34*, 669–700.

Conner, K. R. (1991). A historical comparison of resource-based theory and five schools of thought within industrial organization economics: Do we have a new theory of the firm? *Journal of Management*, *17*, 121–154.

Conner, K. R., & Prahalad, C. K. (1996). A resource-based theory of the firm: Knowledge vs. opportunism. *Organization Science*, *7*, 477–501.

Cyert, R. M., & March, J. G. (1963). *A behavioral theory of the firm*, Englewood Cliffs: Prentice-Hall.

Demsetz, H. (1991). The nature of the film revisited. In Oliver E. Williamson & Sidney G. Winter (Eds.), *The nature of the firm: Origins, evolution, and development*. Oxford: Basil Blackwell.

Dow, G. K. (1987). The function of authority in transaction cost economics. *Journal of Economic Behavior and Organization*, *8*, 13–38.

Egidi, M. (2000). Biases in organizational behavior. Unpublished paper.

Foss, N. J. (1993). Theories of the firm: Contractual and competence perspectives. *Journal of Evolutionary Economics*, *3*, 127–144.

Foss, N. J. (1996). Knowledge-based approaches to the theory of the firm: Some critical comments. *Organization Science*, *7*, 470–476.

Foss, N. J. (1997). *Resources, firms, and strategies*. Oxford: Oxford University Press.

Foss, N. J. (2001). Bounded rationality in the economics of organization: Present use and (some) future possibilities. *Journal of Management and Governance*.

Foss, N. J. (2003). Bounded rationality and tacit knowledge in the organizational capabilities approach: An evaluation and a stocktaking. *Industrial and Corporate Change*. (forthcoming).

Foss, K., & Foss, N. (2000). Theoretical isolation in contract theory: Suppressing margins and entrepreneurship. *Journal of Economic Methodology*, *7*, 313–339.

Fransman, M. (1994). Information, knowledge, vision and theories of the firm. In G. Dosi, D. J. Teece, & J. Chytry (Eds.), *Technology, organization, and competitiveness*. Oxford: Oxford University Press.

Gigerenzer, G., & Todd, P. M. (Eds.). (2001). *Simple heuristics that make us smart*. Oxford: Oxford University Press.

Grossman, S., & Hart, O. (1986). The costs and benefits of ownership: A theory of vertical integration. *Journal of Political Economy*, *94*, 691–719.

Hart, O. (1990). Is 'Bounded Rationality' an important element of a theory of institutions? *Journal of Institutional and Theoretical Economics*, *146*, 696–702.

Hart, O. (1995). *Firms, contracts, and financial structure*. Oxford: Clarendon Press.

Hart, O., & Moore, J. (1990). Property rights and the nature of the firm. *Journal of Political Economy*, *98*, 1119–1158.

Hart, O., & Moore, J. (1999). Foundations of incomplete contracts. *Review of Economic Studies*, *66*, 115–138.

Hodgson, G. (1998). Competence and contract in the theory of the firm. *Journal of Economic Behavior and Organization, 35*, 179–202.

Kahneman, D., Knetsch, J. L., & Thaler, R. H. (1990). Experimental tests of the endowment effect and the Coase theorem. *Journal of Political Economy, 98*, 1325–1348.

Kogut, B., & Zander, U. (1992). Knowledge of the firm, combinative capabilities, and the replication of technology. *Organization Science, 3*, 383–397.

Kreps, D. M. (1996). Markets and hierarchies and (mathematical) economic theory. *Industrial and Corporate Change, 5*, 561–595.

Langlois, R. N. (1992). Transaction cost economics in real time. *Industrial and Corporate Change, 1*, 99–127.

Langlois, R. N., & Foss, N. J. (1999). Capabilities and governance: The rebirth of production in the theory of economic organization. *Kyklos, 52*, 201–218.

Loasby, B. J. (1991). *Equilibrium and evolution.* Manchester: Manchester University Press.

Machlup, F. (1946). Marginal analysis and empirical research. *American Economic Review, 36*, 519–554.

March, J. G., & Simon, H. A. (1958). *Organizations.* New York: Wiley.

Marengo, L., Dosi, G., Legrenzi, P., & Pasquali, C. (2000). The structure of problem-solving knowledge and the structure of organizations. *Industrial and Corporate Change, 9*, 757–788.

Marschak, J., & Radner, R. (1972). *The theory of teams.* New Haven, CT: Yale University Press.

Maskin, E., & Tirole, J. (1999). Unforeseen contingencies and incomplete contracts. *Review of Economic Studies, 66*, 83–114.

Milgrom, P., & Roberts, J. (1992). *Economics, organization, and management.* Englewood Cliffs, NJ: Prentice-Hall.

Mookerji, S. (1998). Ambiguity aversion and incompleteness of contractual form. *American Economic Review, 88*, 1207–1231.

Nelson, R. R., & Winter, S. G. (1973). Toward an evolutionary theory of economic capabilities. *American Economic Review, 63*, 440–449.

Nelson, R. R., & Winter, S. G. (1982). *An evolutionary theory of economic change.* Cambridge, MA: The Belknap Press.

Newell, A., & Simon, H. A. (1972). *Human problem solving.* Englewood Cliffs, NJ: Prentice-Hall.

Rabin, M. (1998). Psychology and economics. *Journal of Economic Literature, 36*, 11–46.

Radner, R. (1996). Bounded rationality, indeterminacy, and the theory of the firm. *Economic Journal, 106*, 1360–1373.

Richardson, G. B. (1972). The organisation of industry. *Economic Journal, 82*, 883–896.

Rubinstein, A. (1998). *Modeling bounded rationality.* Cambridge, MA: MIT Press.

Sah, R. K., & Stiglitz, J. E. (1988). The architecture of economic systems: Hierarchies and polyarchies. *American Economic Review, 76*, 716–727.

Schwartz, A. (1992). Legal contract theories and incomplete contracts. In L. Werin & H. Wijkander (Eds.), *Contract economics.* Blackwell: Oxford.

Simon, H. A. (1947). *Administrative behavior.* New York: Macmillan.

Simon, H. A. (1951). A formal theory of the employment contract. *Econometrica*, *19*, 293–305.

Simon, H. A. (1976). From 'bounded' to 'procedural' rationality. In Spiro Latsis (Ed.), *Method and appraisal in economics*. Cambridge: Cambridge University Press.

Simon, H. A. (1978). Rationality as process and a product of thought. *American Economic Review*, *68*, 1–14.

Simon, H. A. (1979). Rational decision making in business organizations. *American Economic Review*, *69*, 493–513.

Simon, H. A. (1982). *Models of bounded rationality*. Cambridge, MA: MIT Press.

Simon, H. A. (1985). Human nature in politics. *American Political Science Review*, *79*, 293–304.

Simon, H. A. (1991). Organizations and markets. *Journal of Economic Perspectives*, *5*, 25–44.

Simon, H. A. (1997). *An empirically based microeconomics*. Cambridge: Cambridge University Press.

Tirole, J. (1999). Incomplete contracts: Where do we stand? *Econometrica*, *67*, 741–781.

Tversky, A., & Kahneman, D. (1987). Rational choice and the framing of decisions. In R. M. Hogarth & M. Reder (Eds.), *Rational choice: The contrast between economics and psychology*. Chicago: University of Chicago Press.

Williamson, O. E. (1971). The vertical integration of production: Market failure considerations. *American Economic Review*, *61*, 112–123.

Williamson, O. E. (1975). *Markets and hierarchies*. New York: Free Press.

Williamson, O. E. (1985). *The economic institutions of capitalism*. New York: Free Press.

Williamson, O. E. (1996a). *The mechanisms of governance*. Oxford: Oxford University Press.

Williamson, O. E. (1996b). Transaction cost economics and the carnegie connection. *Journal of Economic Behavior and Organization*, *31*, 149–155.

Williamson, O. E. (1998). Human actors and economic organization. In Paper for the 1998 Paris ISNIE conference.

Winter, S. G. (1986). The research program of the behavioral theory of the firm: Orthodox critique and evolutionary perspective. In B. Gilad & S. Kaish (Eds.), *Handbook of behavioral microeconomics, vol. A*. Greenwich: JAI Press.

Winter, S. G. (1991). On coase, competence, and the corporation. In O. E. Williamson & S. G. Winter (Eds.), *The nature of the firm: Origins, evolution, and development*. Oxford: Basil Blackwell.

52

EMOTIONS AS A MECHANISM FOR BOUNDEDLY RATIONAL AGENTS

The fast and frugal way

Roberta Muramatsu and Yaniv Hanoch

Source: *Journal of Economic Psychology*, 26 (2005), 201–221.

Abstract

Herbert Simon has warned us that an explanatory account of human rationality must identify the significance of emotions for choice behavior. Customarily emphasizing the cognitive dimensions of decision making, relatively few researchers have paid close attention to specifying the complex ways in which emotion may shape human thinking and decisions. Accordingly, this paper is an attempt to follow Simon's suggestion and specify how emotions can enter into the theory of bounded rationality. To accomplish our task, we capitalize on Rom Harré's work on causal powers, from which we propose a strategy to study the significance of emotion in decision-making processes. In an attempt to elaborate on an explanation of behavior by mechanism, we discuss a version of bounded rationality recently put forward by Gigerenzer, Todd, and the ABC Research Group [Simple Heuristics that Make us Smart, Oxford University Press, New York, 1999] and Gigerenzer and Selten [Bounded Rationality: The Adaptive Toolbox, MIT Press, Cambridge, MA, 2001, pp. 1–12], the so-called adaptive toolbox of fast and frugal heuristics. Coupled with insights from evolutionary psychology and neuroscience, this version of bounded rationality gives us a better grasp of the functional role of emotions within the human decision machinery.

Hence, in order to have anything like a complete theory of human rationality, we have to understand what role emotion plays in it.

(Herbert Simon, *Reason in Human Affairs*, p. 29)

1. Introduction

In his book *Reason in Human Affairs*, Herbert Simon (1983) warns us that an explanatory account of human rationality must identify the significance of emotions for choice behavior. Customarily emphasizing the cognitive dimensions of decision making, relatively few researchers have paid close attention to specifying the complex ways in which emotions influence human thinking and decisions (including Simon himself; but see Simon, 1967, 1983). Accordingly, we aim to follow Simon's advice and propose to specify how emotions can be accommodated into the theory of bounded rationality (BR). Integrating emotions into the BR framework could illuminate the underlying mental processes that govern human decision making.

Emotions, we argue, play a central role in guiding and regulating choice behavior, by virtue of their capacity to modulate numerous cognitive and physiological activities. By coordinating specific instances of cognitive processing and physiological functioning, emotions are one of the tools that allow agents to make (often) adaptive inferences and choices (Levenson, 1999). Since we view emotions as constituting part of the adaptive toolbox of specialized heuristic processes, we entertain the notion that they can be studied as content and domain specific. With this in mind, an account of decision making – in terms of a mechanism composed of specialized cognitive processes that are governed by emotions – will be provided. It is worthwhile to stress that our paper calls into question the view that emotions are but sand in the decision machinery. Instead, we offer a framework that can assist in evaluating the cases in which emotions lead to fast and adaptive behavior responses.

The paper is structured as follows. In Section 2 we discuss the philosophical guidelines necessary for studying the causal relevance of emotions, maintaining that emotions can be studied as a network of interacting cognitive and physiological processes (with neural underpinnings) that produce stable and predictable behavior patterns. To do so, we spell out certain enabling and triggering conditions that emotions may satisfy in order to have the causal power of guiding individual judgments and decisions. In the third section, we clarify the confusion surrounding the notion of BR. Our interpretation of BR closely follows Gigerenzer, Todd, and the ABC Research Group's (1999) notion of the adaptive toolbox of heuristics. This vision of BR implies that emotions, seen as a constellation of domain-specific heuristics, are among the building blocks of the configuration of our mental architecture. Sections 4 and 5 will, respectively, discuss the theoretical and methodological implications emerging from our discussion with a focus on ongoing research in behavioral economics. Section 6 will wrap up the argument and concluding remarks will follow.

2. Philosophical guidelines: Emotions as causally powerful processes

A growing number of students of epistemology and economic methodology have labored hard to show that an explanatory account of behavior is meant to uncover the mechanisms or processes that produce the phenomenon under study (Elster, 1983; Machamer, Darden, & Craver, 2000; Muramatsu, 2004). According to this view, an "explanation by mechanism" is the most promising way to elucidate how the *explanandum* comes about and what it is that makes the phenomenon occur in the way that it does. Our argument is built upon the idea that an explanatory account of choice behavior requires us to uncover mental processes or mechanisms productive of judgment and decision making in the real world.

It is important to acknowledge that many philosophers disagree on a precise account of what a mechanism is. We suggest an interpretation of mechanism that is applicable to the explanatory purposes of behavioral scientists (including economists and psychologists). A mechanism for a behavior can be understood as a system made up of processes (with specific inner properties) that interact in a systematic fashion to generate a non-random behavioral output (Glennan, 2002; Machamer *et al.*, 2000). In our opinion, the merit of an explanation that captures a mechanism (also known as explanation by mechanism) lies in its ability to offer scientists firmer ground for distinguishing genuinely causal relations from spurious correlations; law-like generalizations from accidental ones; real effects from artifacts, and so forth.

To work out an explanation of decision making that describes a mechanism significant for rational behavior, and why (and how) specific emotional processes are causally productive of choice behavior, we will capitalize on Harré's (1970) work on causal powers. He argues that ascribing to a thing or a person a causal power requires that we specify whether such a thing or a person satisfies certain enabling and triggering conditions.

2.1. Enabling conditions and emotions

According to Harré, enabling conditions are those requirements that, when satisfied, allow one to hypothesize that a thing (or a person) has a causal power; it is in a state of readiness or has a certain inner disposition to act (Harré, 1970; Harré & Madden, 1975). To illustrate, take the case of dynamite. Dynamite has the power to explode[1] because of its inner chemical components that have certain properties, such as nitroglycerin. Quite analogously, it can be suggested that emotions equip individuals with the capacity

79

to make quick inferences and decisions by virtue of their properties that give rise to changes in cognitive and physiological functioning.

Ample research has shown that emotions affect various cognitive processes. For the purposes of this paper, it is sufficient to touch briefly on three of them: (i) attention, (ii) learning, and (iii) memory.

There is empirical evidence that emotions play an important role in focusing agents' attention on the most urgent and important pieces of information within a particular environmental structure, while overlooking more peripheral ones (Faucher & Tappolet, 2002). To paraphrase Simon, emotions play a central role in directing our attention – they distract us from our current thoughts and actions and call our attention to tasks that require our immediate attention (1983, p. 21; for a discussion on the need to treat attention as a scarce resource and the difficulties of explaining attention allocation by standard choice framework, see Berger, 1989).[2] For example, the elicitation of fear prompts agents to focus their attention on the importance of the incoming stimulus (while ignoring all other pieces of information), with the aim of properly allocating efforts to search for fast and effective solutions (Öhman & Mineka, 2001). Holland and Gallagher (1999, p. 68) tell us that via attention-directing processes emotions also deploy needed resources for learning.[3] Taken together, "these functions increase the likelihood that the most appropriate cues will control behavior" (Holland & Gallagher, 1999). Cognitive neuroscientists have also found that the amygdala – a key brain structure of emotional processing – is involved is assessing the significance of an incoming stimulus that subsequently influences attention and reaction.

A growing corpus of evidence shows how emotions exert a substantive influence on learning (LeDoux, 1996; Mineka & Cook, 1988). The conscious affective component of an emotion process and the bodily expression associated with it enable individuals to learn from their own experiences and from others' interactions within the environment. This quality of emotions facilitates individuals' inferences about the consequences associated with an alternative course of action. Consider these illustrations. Soldiers respond quickly and automatically to the sound of bullets because previous experiences taught them to appraise this as a cue for danger. Young children who see their parents and friends fearful of swimming in a particular lake might infer that this is a dangerous thing to do without having to examine it on their own. According to Damasio, "emotions of all shades eventually help connect homeostatic regulation and survival 'values' to numerous events and objects in our autobiographical experience" (Damasio, 1999, pp. 54–55). The influence of emotions in this version of cognitive processing highlights the plausibility of Damasio's (1994) somatic marker hypothesis, where the feeling component of emotions serves as a source of inference about the expected hedonic consequences of various options.

Memory processes are intimately related to learning and they are also influenced by emotion. This is partially due to their role in activating and regulating activities involved in encoding, storing, and retrieving information about important events. Research on emotion and memory shows that the activation of emotions affects the ways in which individuals reconstruct previously experienced situations. Experimental psychologists have stressed that individuals tend to remember more easily events that triggered strong emotions in comparison to incidents that were emotionally neutral (Bower, 1981). Based on a series of experiments, Bower (1981; Bower & Cohen, 1982) suggests that individuals in whom happy feelings are induced tend to remember pleasant events more easily and more precisely than unpleasant ones, whereas individuals experiencing unhappy feelings tend to recall sad incidents in a more accurate manner – a phenomenon known as mood recall congruency. In essence, the idea is that "people's feeling affects what records they can retrieve from memory. People can best retrieve events originally learned in a particular mood by somehow reinstating or returning to that same mood" (Bower & Cohen, 1982, p. 214). That is, emotional events are typically better recalled in comparison to non-emotional events (Christianson, 1992). One explanation of this phenomenon has been the idea that emotional information has privileged access to processing resources, which could possibly lead to better memory formation (Dolcos & Cabeza, 2002).

Another line of research found that during high emotional states animals and humans release high levels of β-adrenergic hormones – hormones that are a central ingredient in modulating memory storage and are largely connected to activation of the amygdala (Cahill, 2000). More recently, researchers have found that "the degree to which the activity of the human amygdala related to memory increased almost linearly with the degree of subjective arousal induced by the stimuli" (Packard & Cahill, 2001, p. 754). Canli *et al.* (1998, using functional magnetic resonance imaging) have drawn a similar conclusion, arguing that amygdala activation improves memory as a function of the level of emotional intensity – either positive or negative – of an experience. The above ideas fit nicely with recent neuroscientists' findings that the amygdala has strong and extensive connections with other brain regions involved with memory, such as the hippocampus and lateral prefrontal cortex (LeDoux, 1996; Panksepp, 1998). Though he lacked the necessary sophisticated machinery to test his thesis, William James foreshadowed these modern finding: "An impression may be so exciting emotionally as almost to leave a scar upon the cerebral tissues . . . The primitive impression has been accompanied by extraordinary degree of attention, either as being horrible or delightful" (James, 1890, quoted in Hamann, 2001, p. 394).

With this in mind, it can be suggested that emotional processing brings about changes in mental and bodily functioning that are necessary for effective and adaptive responses. But emotions can only exercise such capacity if they meet some extrinsic requirements called triggering conditions.

2.2. *Triggering conditions for emotional processing*

Harré (1970) emphasized that a thing or person has the power to generate a behavior pattern by virtue of its inner properties. Recall the above example of the dynamite – the capacity for explosion is understood in terms of its chemical properties. The existence of these internal attributes, however, does not guarantee the actual exercise of the capacity. Unless a dynamite stick is lighted, it will not perform its capacity for explosion. We extend this line of reasoning to our discussion of the causal powers of emotions.

To us, some triggering conditions, under which some emotion programs operate, resemble Sperber's (1996) initialization conditions. The latter amount to the mental representations that are outputs of sensory and conceptual processes. The functional role of these sensory and conceptual processes is to supply information for one's detection and categorization of an incoming stimulus. With regard to emotion systems, the initialization factors are content-specific mental representations that jointly detect and categorize recurrent adaptive problems a species has confronted throughout its evolutionary history. When such mental representations inform an agent about a recurrent danger or opportunity with survival value, a specialized and specific emotion program will be activated to prepare the agent to behave adaptively. That is, the emotional system produces physiological and cognitive activities that allow agents to behave adaptively. For example, the initialization of the disgust program prepares an agent to avoid the danger of being poisoned by food. This would reveal that there is some content specificity in the conditions that initialize the operation of a specialized emotion system.

The actual triggers of behavior are here assumed to be the mental algorithms activated by the experiences of an emotion. The underlying idea is that an emotion focuses an agent's attention on a selective search for alternatives. It also conditions one's aspiration level by altering perceived goal prioritization and as such determines a criterion by which an agent will make a satisfactory selection of action. Even though the above conditions might generate adaptive behavior, they might also generate maladaptive or biased responses. The latter may occur when the structure of one's chosen choice strategy fails to match the structure of the task environment. Fear, for example, will give rise to an adaptive behavioral response if an emotion-eliciting stimulus (a predator) prompts one to select a choice strategy (at the sight of an approaching lion, run away!) that matches with the structure of a certain environment (e.g. African savannah). When the structure of the decision heuristic is not in tune with the structure of the environment (in which the task is embedded), maladaptive responses will take place. Kelly's work (1955) could offer an additional angle on the role of emotions within the decision-making process. From Kelly's perspective, it is not only how the environmental cues trigger emotional programs, but how agents construct or view the environment that, in return, affects what emotional program is likely to be activated. This framework suggests that when external conditions (which might be similar to our notion of triggering conditions) are aligned with a person's core construct, decisions will tend to follow a more reflective procedure. In contrast, an emotion-driven behavior is expected to occur when a chasm exists between a person's core construct and the environmental challenges she or he faces (1955, p. 495; for an application of Kelly's work in an economic framework see Earl, 1983, 1986). Examined from this point of view, dysfunctional behavior could be explained as a function of a person's core constructs in relation to the task at hand.

As we can see, a perspective on causal powers highlights the significance of emotions for judgment and decision making in the real world. To some extent, the above conceptual apparatus offers a first step toward an explanation of choice behavior that spells out how emotions shape the various components and inner workings of the decision machinery.

2.3. From mechanism to discourse and back

Harré's (1970) account of causal powers was driven by his enthusiasm for the philosophical doctrine of scientific realism. The latter maintains that we can best explain a phenomenon by unveiling its generative (causal) processes or mechanism and therefore approximate to the truth about the explanandum phenomenon under study. This attitude toward theorizing and explanation promises to improve our understanding of the place of the explanandum in the causal structure of the world (Salmon, 1984).

In the 1980s, however, Harré began raising doubts about the adequacy of a psychological explanation of behavior that captures its underlying causal cognitive processes or mechanisms (Harré, 1983; Harré & Gillett, 1994). This line of explanation, Harré believed, is embedded in a vision of psychological theorizing that reified a non-social account of human action and led to an undersocialized view of humans as a bunch of hidden mechanisms. Inspired by Wittgenstein's (1953) and Vygotsky's (1962) writings, Harré argues for a turn in the study of psychology called the "Second Cognitive Revolution" (Harré, 2001). He characterizes this movement as the abandonment of the form of scientific realism, which motivated earlier cognitive scientists to account for behavior in terms of hidden cognitive mechanisms (with causal powers). Furthermore, he claims that conversation rather than information processing is the key player of human cognition. Thus, he argued that to avoid the danger of conflating causal relations with social rules and regularities that shape psychological phenomenon one needs to employ a different conceptual strategy: a shift from the information-processing approach to a conversational perspective on human thought and action. This led Harré to reject his earlier ideas about scientific psychological explanations and to regard himself as being a conversational realist. Harré came to argue that psychological phenomena are to be explained in terms of social exchange and negotiation processes of symbolic (linguistic) representations, which are in turn shaped by rules of conversation (rather than cognitive processes).

We are not convinced that the conversational alternative to realism can resolve the metaphysical problems associated with the issue of causality in behavioral theorizing and explanation. In addition, Harré seems to make a very partial characterization of the state-of-the-art in contemporary cognitive science. He argues that adherents of the second cognitive revolution have abandoned the information-processing approach to cognition in favor of a neural-processes approach. This is a bold claim that requires empirical substantiation. As far as we can see, current researchers do not reject the computer metaphor suggested by Simon, but rather have shifted their focus to the study of neural processes as a source of information about cognitive processes (mental algorithms) that might be causally productive of behavior. Even though some concentrate on describing behavioral phenomena at the neural level, most recognize the need for complementary levels of explanations of processes and mechanisms so as to avoid the implications of reductive materialism (cf. Marr, 1982).

The merit of recent developments in cognitive sciences is to enhance our understanding of the inextricable links between emotion and cognition. Based on an information-processing framework that is grounded in specialized neural structures, we can argue that the Lazarus–Zajonc debate in the 1980s concerning the primacy of cognition over emotion produced more heat than light. This is partly so because there is now evidence lending support to both sides. It seems that an individual cannot react emotionally unless an incoming stimulus is identified and promptly (automatically, unconsciously) appraised as carrying a specific value. If this is so, Lazarus (1984) is correct in his argument that some type of cognition (information processing) precedes elicitation of an emotional response. But we can also think of studies that substantiate Zajonc's (1980) thesis that some basic emotions prepare an individual to respond immediately (in a reflex-like fashion) before she or he has formed any awareness of the information. Finally, some have attributed the discrepancy between the two approaches to the way Lazarus and Zajonc define and employ the terms "cognition" and "emotion" (Nussbaum, 2001; Parkinson & Manstead, 1992). The "heuristic surplus value" of an information-processing approach grounded in neuroscience is that it informs us why and how emotion and cognition are inextricably linked conceptual categories.

The neuroscientist's research strategy, we believe, allows us to extend the information-processing metaphor and add to our understanding of why and how emotion and cognition work together to produce behavior. From this perspective, an emotion amounts to a content- and domain-specific processing system that is activated if and when certain sensory and conceptual inputs are met. Besides, an information-processing approach to the mental architecture of the brain presupposes a different conceptualization of cognition: It refers to all brain information-processing activities.[4] As a result, emotions can be viewed as information-processing systems just like memory and perception. However, they differ from each other by the peculiarities of their mode of processing (e.g. controlled, automatic, informationally encapsulated) and the functions they serve.

LeDoux (1996), for example, has specified two complementary neural pathways involved in detection (appraisal) of a dangerous stimulus: the short road (thalamus–amygdala) and the long road (thalamus–neocortex–amygdala). They seem to work parallel to one another. However, the emotional system will "take over" depending on the nature of the input received. He tries to explain what is at stake:

> In situations of danger, it is very useful to be able to respond quickly. The time saved by the amygdala in acting on the thalamic information, rather than waiting for the cortical input, can be the difference between life and death . . . From the point of view of survival, it is better to respond to potentially dangerous events as if they were in fact the real things than to fail to respond.
>
> (1996, p. 166)

Quite similarly, Damasio (1994) also studies the cognitive architecture of the brain in order to understand the interconnections between emotion and cognition. Based on systematic research with patients suffering from brain lesions, he found that the neural structures used for emotion processing – amygdala, orbital cortex, and anterior cingulate cortex – also play an important role in processing activities involved with higher forms of cognition like decision making.

The developments in emotion research reported above challenge Harré's claim regarding the possibility of providing a mechanistic explanation of psychological phenomena. Our proposed guidelines offer some grounds for the study of specific processes and mechanisms significant for choice behavior. Our conceptual framework is fine tuned with the causal picture of human thinking and acting that contemporary behavioral scientists endorse. More importantly, it provides a theorizing strategy that aims to offer understanding of why (and how) we should put together emotion, cognition, and motivation as powerful constituents of the trilogy of the mind.

3. A place for emotions in the BR framework

The concept of bounded rationality has been used in quite a broad fashion and it makes reference to very different things (even Simon (1992, p. 18) acknowledges the vagueness of the term). Rather than committing to one definition, Simon tackles the issue by contrasting BR with the neoclassical economic approach to rational behavior, while advocating a more realistic account of human decision-making behavior.

Simon's theory has gained popularity among economists and other decision researchers (Camerer, 1995; Conlisk, 1996). However, most economists tend to interpret BR as synonymous with optimization under constraints. This follows from the idea that agents make choices that involve time constraints and limited knowledge and cognitive capabilities. From this standpoint, individuals are assumed to calculate an optimal stopping rule (Stigler, 1961).[5] It seems to us that a careful reading of Simon's work reveals the problems with this vision of BR. Optimization under constraints requires even more demanding cognitive processing than the approach idealized by standard rational choice theory. In his writings on BR in the 1980s and 1990s, Simon rejected such interpretations (Simon, 1983, 1992) because of their reliance on an Olympian version of rationality.

Another popular interpretation of BR makes reference to human irrationality.[6] This phenomenon is often related to violations of Bayesian reasoning or deviations from expected utility theory (Kahneman, Slovic, & Tversky, 1982; Thaler, 1991). Although a broad notion of BR seems to accommodate empirical evidence about cognitive errors, there is no need to equate BR with the heuristics and biases program. As we understand it, this conceptualization would reduce the scope of BR theory (see Gigerenzer & Selten, 2001).

3.1. Rationality as an adaptive toolbox: A fast and frugal alternative

Another model of BR (see Gigerenzer et al., 1999) has been built on Simon's (1990, p. 7) understanding of behavior as a pair of scissors whose blades are an agent's computational facilities and the structure of the environment. More recently, Gigerenzer et al. (1999) have elaborated on this vision of BR. One interesting implication of Gigerenzer et al.'s alternative concerns the evaluation of two complementary routes to the study of human (bounded) rationality, on the one hand examining the mind's architecture with the hope of capturing the principles that govern decisions in the real world; and on the other hand, studying what lies outside the mind – the environmental structure – that exert influence on proximate mechanisms for behavior.

The above interpretation of BR is embedded in a theoretical perspective called the adaptive toolbox of fast and frugal heuristics (Gigerenzer & Selten, 2001; Gigerenzer et al., 1999). It assumes that individuals rely on decision strategies that economize on an agent's cognitive processing capabilities, since they exploit information within particular environmental structures. One may wonder in what sense heuristics are thought to be fast and frugal. They are fast because they rely on few cues, thus dispensing with much computational effort. They are frugal for they make selective search for cues and alternatives within the environment using a minimal number or at times a single cue. The core premises (P) of the adaptive toolbox framework can be summarized as follows:

- P_1. *Psychological plausibility*. The adaptive toolbox is built upon realistic assumptions about human behavior that specify the processes whereby real people make judgments and choices. The idea is to offer richer descriptions of decision behavior by making explicit reference to real humans' cognitive, behavioral, social, and emotional repertoires.
- P_2. *Domain specificity*. The adaptive toolbox of heuristics, as the name suggests, is assumed to be a collection of mental shortcuts – composed of cognitive and affective building blocks that deal with specific information-processing tasks.
- P_3. *Ecological rationality*. At the conceptual level, one implication of the view of rationality as a pair of scissors concerns the notion of ecological rationality. The latter is defined by its degree of fit with the real world. From this perspective, performance of a certain outcome is evaluated in terms of the match between a heuristic and the structure of the task environment. To put it another way, a heuristic will be ecologically rational to the degree that it is adapted to the structure of a specific environment.

The above theoretical perspective on bounded rationality attempts to unveil the (causal) processes underlying actual behavior. It assumes that actual decision makers rely on heuristic processes, which provide three functions: (i) a searching rule, (ii) a stopping rule, and (iii) a decision rule.

Search for information amounts to a twofold process of exploration: The decision maker first must discover the options available and then look for cues to evaluate and rank the possible alternatives.

Models of BR are built on the premise that information search is selective and necessarily ends at some point. Therefore, they try to specify what stopping rules look like. Some seem to dispense with the fiction of optimization, such as Simon's satisficing heuristic, which assumes that information search stops when the first alternative that meets or exceeds an agent's aspiration level is found. Gigerenzer and his colleagues have discovered heuristics simpler than satisficing, such as the Take-The-Best heuristic (TTB). It specifies that a search for alternatives ends as soon as one encounters a cue that discriminates between two options (Gigerenzer *et al.*, 1999).

Behavioral models inspired by Simon's ideas also assume that an individual selects a satisfactory course of action based on specific choice criteria, typically called selection decision heuristics. By virtue of the domain specificity and simplicity of such mental procedures, they often trigger quick and effective responses. Our next task is to show that emotions serve as the building blocks of certain fast and frugal heuristics.

Finally, Kaufman (1999; but see Hanoch, 2002a) presents an additional source of bounded rationality, one that stems from high emotional arousal rather than the traditional cognitive constraints. According to Kaufman, emotions, or rather high emotional arousal, can interfere with rational thinking, for it hinders one's success in various tests and in problem solving.

3.2. Emotions as built-in and learned computational devices

In what follows, we discuss two important functions of emotions – cognitive guidance and behavior preparation – from an evolutionary perspective. It is argued that emotions exert systematic influence on thinking and choice. Just like a toolbox of specialized cognitive shortcuts, emotions give direction to search, stopping, and decision rules that produce choice behavior. This perspective revives Simon's (1967, 1983) view that emotions play a role in information processing: They alter one's goal prioritization (Simon, 1967), determine the relative salience of aspects of a task (Hanoch, 2002b), shape cost–benefit assessments (Loewenstein, Weber, Hsee, & Welch, 2001), often tell us when to stop processing information (Ketelaar & Todd, 2000), and "rule out of court" or render unthinkable many options for the decision maker (Earl, 1986, pp. 96–100).

We can think of at least three reasons for studying the rationality of emotion on the basis of its functionality and fit with the task environment. First, it helps to clarify under what conditions an emotion leads to effective behavior and under what conditions it fails to do so. Second, it exposes the complex connections between emotions and cognition. Finally, by specifying the processes that people actually rely on in drawing inferences and making decisions, we can improve our understanding of how rationality works in the real world and the role emotions play within rationality.

To illuminate the functionality of emotions, we draw upon recent insights from evolutionary psychology. According to Tooby and Cosmides (1995, p. 1189), the mind resembles a "confederation of hundreds or thousands of functionally dedicated computers, designed to solve problems endemic to the Pleistocene, [more than it resembles] a single general purpose computer equipped with a small number of general purpose procedures." More recently Cosmides and Tooby (2000) have compared the human mind to a crowded zoo of specialized programs – emotions being some of them. Just like a specialized cognitive program that guides and coordinates behavioral processes, emotions are a vital component of our mental architecture.

To understand the "logic" of emotion, we use the example of one emotion: disgust (Rozin, Haidt, & McCauley, 1993). Detection of an incoming stimulus that is appraised as a potentially significant danger of ingesting harmful food will elicit a specialized computation program called disgust. This "program" has evolved to resolve (at least one) recurrent adaptive information-processing problem: how to distinguish healthy from noxious food and to avoid being poisoned by contaminated food (for a discussion on the role of disgust in the moral domain see Haidt, 2001). From an evolutionary cognitive perspective, we assume that individuals whose mental architecture accommodates the disgust program tend to achieve higher reproductive success than others unable to experience the emotion of disgust. As Rozin *et al.* (1993) rightly put the issue, the disposition to feel disgust can be taken as a comparative advantage. This is because this specialized computational program enables an individual to automatically detect and appraise the ecological significance of an important stimulus (harmful food); to be ready to concentrate physiological and cognitive efforts on search for alternative ways that have led to adaptive outcomes (throughout the course of the species' evolutionary history); and to make quick cue-based inferences and choices about the consequences associated with salient courses of action. It is in this sense that it can be said that a disgust program plays a functional role that it is to solve a recurrent information-processing problem with adaptive implications. As a result we are inclined to disagree with the view that there can only be a selective pressure operating on the evolution of emotion programs (e.g. disgust) when individuals are able to "cognize much" about the emotional reactions, states, and behaviors. Alternatively, we think that some emotional programs have been shaped by natural selection to help individuals resolve adaptive problems observed as far back as the Pleistocene era (rather than to represent some bits of information about an important event). Likewise, anger is an example of a specialized program that helps individuals resolve a recurrent adaptive problem of self-binding commitment. The emotional reactions to violations of an approved norm and the negative feeling of anger guarantee credible promises of social cooperation in environments that lack the necessary (modern) legal apparatus to guarantee binding contractual relations (Frank, 1988).

Quite similarly, Kelly (1955, pp. 502–508; see also Elster, 1999) suggests that guilt serves as an alarm signal that inform us when we are about to depart (or already have) from one of our core structures; and anxiety emerges when events appear to lie outside our core construct systems, motivating us to keep within the confines of familiar and controllable environments. Kelly's main concern, in contrast to the one focused on here, lay with individuals striving to preserve and maintain their self-concept, image, or identity, rather than preserving the physical self, thus it seems that his writing might reflect on issues that rest outside the framework developed here. However, recent research on impulsive purchasing by Dittmar and Drury (2000) fits very nicely with Kelly's ideas concerning personal construct, attempts to regulate anxiety, and desires to maintain self-identity. In their study, Dittmar and Drury argued that material goods are linked to a person's self-concept for they convey important information about one's personal and social identity. Impulse buying can be explained, accordingly, by consumers' desires to regulate emotions (Elliott, 1994), express a sense of uniqueness and self-identity (Dittmar, 1992), and increase ones self-image rather than by price or usefulness (Dittmar & Drury, 2000).

These examples illuminate situations in which emotional reactions can be ecologically rational. Emotion programs were selected for because they gave rise to action patterns that are good solutions to domain-specific adaptive problems, for they are well engineered to carry out evolved functions. As Tooby and Cosmides (2000) argue:

> Natural selection has retained neural structures on their ability to create adaptively organized relationships between information and behavior (e.g., the sight of a predator activates inference procedures that cause the organism to hide or flee) or between information and physiology (e.g., the sight of a predator increases the organism's heart beat rate, in preparation for flight).
>
> (p. 1172)

This evolutionary approach offers us an insightful strategy for grasping the role of emotions in human rationality. It is worthwhile to stress that an explanatory evolutionary account of behavior promises to uncover proximate and ultimate causes of behavior. Both sets of causes need to be spelled out for us to have a complete understanding of a phenomenon (Mayr, 1988, p. 28). Roughly, proximate causes (e.g. emotions and norms) refer to processes (cognitive and physiological) that trigger or initiate a particular behavior pattern. Ultimate causes, in turn, refer to those that reveal the adaptive value of a particular design trait.

Marr (1982) argues that there are three levels of analysis within an evolutionary explanation of the human mind. They correspond to the algorithmic, the hardware implementation, and the computational levels of analysis. He maintains that the first two levels capture proximate causes. The computational level, in turn, is expected to uncover ultimate mechanisms. Marr emphasizes that we need to devote careful attention to the third level to understand the nature of information processing (Marr, 1982, p. 27). Our discussion of the significance of emotions for bounded rationality is centered upon the algorithmic level. Remember that our assumption is that emotions function as cue-based heuristic processes that provide solutions to specific decision tasks.

More recently, cognitive neuroscientists have contributed to an account of emotions at the hardware level. By specifying the neural pathways (physical properties) through which emotions modulate real judgments and decisions, brain researchers identify neural structures that are involved in both emotion processing and decision making. The amygdala and the ventromedial prefrontal cortex are involved with automatic, fast, and involuntary information processing often associated with processing of emotionally arousing tasks and cues. But these same structures also play a central role in controlled, complex, voluntary systems of information processing, often associated with higher-order cognitive activities like planning and decision making (Adolphs & Damasio, 2001, p. 29). Adolphs and Damasio's research provides additional support for our view that emotions are the foundation of bounded rationality. As they frame the issue,

> Through circuits including components of amygdala, striatum, and basal forebrain, emotion may thus help to select particular aspects of the stimulus environment for disproportionate allocation of cognitive processing resources; namely, an organism should be designed to preferentially process information about those aspects of its environment that are most salient to its immediate survival and well-being.
>
> (Adolphs & Damasio, 2001, p. 33)

The above passage suggests that a description of the neural machinery reinforces our thesis that emotions are proximate mechanisms for boundedly rational behavior. Unfortunately, little can be said about ultimate processes or mechanisms. This is partly because this research agenda is still in its infancy, with many questions still to be tackled. A complete account of the nature of emotion processing and its significance for human behavior might require us to completely map emotion programs onto the complex adaptive tasks that their domain-specific heuristics were designed to solve – a task that far exceeds the scope of this paper.

4. Theoretical implications

Analyzing the significance of emotions for decision making carries several implications for the study of human BR. In this section, we briefly consider some ideas that arise from our suggested perspective on explanation by mechanism and BR.

The study of emotions as activators of domain-specific heuristic processes that lead to quick and adaptive decisions goes against a long-standing tradition that contrasts emotion with human rationality. Our approach calls for re-conceptualizing the links between emotion, thinking, and rationality, for emotions can lead to ecologically rational outcomes. However, our argument does not imply that emotions never distort thinking and choice patterns. To be fair, there is yet no full understanding of the conditions that cause emotions to enhance or undermine the rationality of human judgments and decisions. With that in mind, let us discuss some conditions under which emotions do lead to adaptive outcomes.

The very elicitation of a specialized emotion program is dependent on the way an organism's situation detector module explores information about an external (or internal) stimulus (which can be shaped by evolution as well as culture). The cluster of perceptual and conceptual processes that constitute the system evolved to extract information about environmental regularities and therefore to enable an individual to draw inferences about the available prospects and to decide on a satisfactory alternative.

To put it differently, the function of the situation detector is to promote quick evaluations about whether a particular stimulus represents a "friend or foe." When the detector system perceives an ecologically important threat or opportunity, a specialized emotion program will be activated. This process puts into motion changes in cognitive and physiological functioning so as to produce quick and adaptive behaviors. It can be said that emotions will lead to distorted outcomes (they are non-functional) when they give rise to mental procedures that fail to exploit relevant pieces of information in the environment (in which the task is embedded) and therefore select a behavioral strategy that is not a proper solution to the faced decision problem.

It is worthwhile to stress that our proposed criterion to evaluate performance is not based on internal consistency but on a sort of external correspondence.[7] In a sense, this deviates from the standard analysis of economic rationality as expected utility maximization. Gigerenzer et al. (1999) claim that studies of rationality in the real world should replace the coherence criterion with a correspondence one, where performance is assessed in terms of the match between a strategy and an environment.

Despite our sympathy toward the alternative notion of ecological rationality, it is doubtful that it can perfectly replace the view of rationality as inner consistency. The standard interpretation of rationality as coherence has important descriptive and normative dimensions that are not captured by ecological rationality. For that reason, we believe that coherence should be supplemented rather than replaced by correspondence. Both carry insights about the "rationality requirements on the nature of human reflection regarding what one should want, [believe], value or aim at" (Sen, 1994/ 1987, pp. 13–14, no. 9).

Another theoretical implication of our proposed approach to rationality concerns a different understanding of rational decision making. Unlike the paradigmatic notion of rationality as (expected) utility maximization, the "two-blade" conception of BR portrays decision making as a sequence of cognitive and emotional processes (with a neural counterpart) rather than the outcome of the optimization of a general-purpose algorithm (expected utility maximization).

5. Methodological implications

What are the methodological implications of conceiving emotions as one of the building blocks underlying the theory of bounded rationality? To address this issue, we need to explain what we mean by methodology.

Economists make at least two uses of the term "methodology." One has to do with the study of analytical tools for theoretical elaboration; and another concerns the analysis of models and theories at the "metatheoretical level." We are here interested in reflecting on the second "view" of methodology. We attempt to scrutinize philosophical issues related to pragmatic considerations that drive economic theorizing and the purposes of scientific explanations.

There seems to be agreement that formal tractability and parsimony are two pragmatic considerations that are valued highly during model or theory construction. Economists often appeal to tractability and parsimony as reasons against psychologizing decision theory and specifying psychological mechanisms that give rise to observed behavior. Camerer (1995, p. 676) has wisely drawn our attention to the fact that we cannot know how much tractability is lost in the generation of behavioral decision models without trying them out. One of the advantages of our proposed treatment of emotions, in terms of domain-specific heuristics, lies in its ability to offer a way of avoiding the tractability problem.

It is also likely that economists of conservative inclination would point out to us that a BR perspective cum evolutionary insight carries a deleterious implication – a heuristic approach is expected to conflict with the economist's goal of explaining behavior by means of parsimonious formulations. To call this line of reasoning into question, Rabin's (1998) work can be of help. He offers substantial evidence that economists respond to simple psychological hypotheses by constructing baroque alternative explanations of phenomena relying exclusively on traditional economic assumptions. Rabin's comment might resonate with Adam Smith's earlier work on the "origin, development, and replacement of the first astronomical system" (discussed in Skinner, 1979, p. 114) – work that could reflect on the development of theories in other domains. This early astronomical system was acceptable as long as no other heavenly bodies were discovered. More bodies, however, have been found "leading to gradual increase in the number of spheres needed to account for them until a situation reached where the theory itself attained a degree of complexity that rendered it unacceptable to the imagination: unacceptable because it violated the basic condition of simplicity" (Skinner, 1979, p. 114).

In our interpretation, one consequence of developing an alternative theoretical perspective (one that captures the underlying mechanism governing behavior) concerns the prospect of improving the predictive and explanatory powers of economic theories and models. Unlike mainstream economists, we share the behavioral economists' skepticism and their interest in explaining how individuals actually make choices within and outside the market reality.

Behavioral economists acknowledge that the economic theory of choice has broader scope but it has failed to predict important phenomena even at the microeconomic and macroeconomic levels (Loewenstein, O'Donoghue, & Rabin, 1999; Thaler, 1992). In an effort to accommodate rational choice anomalies, behavioral economists have come up with models of choice built upon refined psychological assumptions (e.g. hyperbolic discounting, preference reversal). Some of them have overcome problems with tractability and parsimony to hypothesize (and test) explicitly psychological processes productive of recurrent puzzles within the body of economic choice theory, such as the cooperation even in large groups with impersonal (anonymous) interactions. For example, in a recent paper, Fehr and Gachter (2002) try to explain their experimental findings of high rates of social cooperation by hypothesizing a behavioral process called altruistic punishment. They claim that an individual's behavioral predispositions to reciprocate cooperative attitudes and to punish defectors even at a personal cost are what ultimately sustain the emergence and perpetuation of prosociality.[11] They go on to stress that emotions – anger, guilt, and shame – constitute proximate causes (mechanisms) of altruistic punishment and therefore of cooperative behaviors. To us, such a research strategy is a promising way of exploring the roles of emotions and bounded rationality in the real economic world, characterized by complex causal interdependencies.

6. Conclusion

Until quite recently, the economic discourse has been largely mute on the role of emotions in decision making. It was almost taken for granted that if emotions play any part in reasoning, it would be to put sand into the rational choice machinery. How could emotional reactions lead to non-random rational outcomes?

Starting in the late 1950s, researchers on decision making began to question the Olympian model of rationality and argued that real agents have limited memory, time, and cognitive capabilities. At the same time, another group of choice theorists emphasized that there was no need to specify the processes or mechanisms whereby individuals come to make decisions – for they lead to outcomes consistent with the expected utility maximization algorithm (Friedman & Savage, 1948).

Inspired by Simon's (1967, 1983) theory of BR and recent developments within neuroscience and evolutionary psychology, we have advanced the thesis (instead of argued) that emotions need to be explicitly incorporated in formal models of boundedly rational choice. To substantiate our argument, we have showed that emotional processes perform activities that put into motion information-processing activities, which antecede actual decision making.

Via our discussion on the enabling and triggering conditions under which the emotional mechanism works, we highlighted the complex ways in which emotions might modulate behavior. This philosophical analysis was meant to pave the way to the claim that emotions constitute important building blocks of our mental architecture. Just like activators of domain-specific algorithms, emotions mobilize search, stopping, and choice heuristics. Emotions pick up and highlight certain cues within a given environment; they interrupt on-going activities; and they initiate cognitive and physiological changes to respond to these opportunities or hazards.

We have offered one framework that can be utilized to explore the circumstances under which emotions lead to effective and nonfunctional outcomes, while acknowledging the need for further attempts to integrate emotion into theories of choice behavior. This discussion attempted to reinforce our claim that economic explanations of human behavior could flourish by paying closer attention to the role of emotions. Elster (1999), Frank (1988), Loewenstein *et al.* (2001), and Thaler (2000) are among the researchers who have stressed that explanatory accounts of various instances of economic behavior – ranging from cooperation to intertemporal choice to decision making under risk – require us to dig deeper into the nature and structure of agents' preferences, beliefs (expectations), and rationality.

Even though more empirical research is necessary for us to understand exactly how emotions shape decision problems posed by economic reality, we hope that our analysis highlights the need to treat emotions as cognitive and motivational foundations of human judgment and decision making.

Acknowledgements

The authors contributed equally to the research and are listed in random order. The research was supported by CAPES Foundation to the first author, and a Minerva fellowship to the second author. We would like to thank Simon Kemp, Anita Todd, Jack Vromen, Andreas Wilke, and two anonymous reviewers for comments on earlier drafts. An earlier version of this paper was presented at the seminar of Fundación Urrutia and UNED in Madrid.

Notes

1 It is common to describe emotional reaction and expression as 'an explosion.' Being able to invoke such emotional reactions might provide an advantage, as they can allow agents to create the necessary conditions to cause others to 'explode'.

2 Koestler's (1967) example of driving under different conditions can be illustrative, especially when we consider the need to switch from unconscious to conscious operations. Experienced drivers do not need to pay much attention to driving; they perform the act effortlessly, as if it were second nature, and thus can devote their entire attention to the traffic around them. On the other hand, when faced with an emergency or difficult driving conditions, drivers suddenly have to pay close attention to their own actions, reducing in the process the level of attention that can be allocated to the traffic.

3 Among economists, it is worth noting Shackle's (1961) earlier attempt to incorporate attention into his theory of choice under uncertainty. Shackle's intuition, though he made no reference to emotions, was based on the idea that to catch our attention the various options or outcomes before us need to offer both plausible and substantial gains (or losses) from our present reference point. More recently, DellaVigna and Pollet (2003) have offered an interesting discussion regarding whether investors pay enough attention to long-term fundamentals.

4 According to Cosmides and Tooby (2000, p. 98), "the term cognition is often used to refer to a particular subset of information processing – roughly the effortful, conscious, voluntary, deliberate . . . However, from an evolutionary cognitive perspective, . . . cognition refers to a language describing all of the brain's operations, including emotion and reasoning . . . If the brain evolved as a system of information processing relations, then emotions are in an evolutionary sense, best understood as information processing relations (programs)."

5 Stated briefly, the idea is that one stops searching for information about prospects when the cost of further information is greater than or equal to the benefit of gaining additional information.

6 Anticipating the confusion that might arise, Simon wrote: "We may deem behavior irrational because, although it serves some particular impulse, it is inconsistent with other goals that we may deem more important. We may deem it irrational because the actor is proceeding on incorrect facts or ignoring whole areas of relevant facts. We may deem it irrational because the actor has not drawn the correct conclusions from the facts. We may deem it irrational because the actor has failed to consider important alternative courses of action. If the action involves the future, as most action does, we may deem it irrational because we do not think the actor uses the best methods for forming expectations or for adapting to uncertainty. All of these forms of irrationality play important roles in the lives of every one of us, but I think it is misleading to call them irrationality. They are better viewed as forms of bounded rationality" (1985, p. 297).

7 Sen (1994/1987) provides an interesting discussion about consistence-based and correspondence-based criteria of rationality.

8 Based on an evolutionary definition of altruism – any act that increases the average payoff of the group to the detriment of one's own payoff – Fehr and Gachter interpret individuals willing to punish defectors or free-riders even at a personal cost as displaying altruistic behavior.

References

Adolphs, R., & Damasio, A. (2001). The interaction of affect and cognition: A neurobiological perspective. In J. Forgas (Ed.), *Handbook of affect and social cognition* (pp. 27–49). Hillsdale, NJ: Erlbaum.

Berger, L. A. (1989). Economics and hermeneutics. *Economics and Philosophy, 5,* 209–233.

Bower, G. H. (1981). Mood and memory. *American Psychologist, 36,* 129–148.

Bower, G. H., & Cohen, P. R. (1982). Emotional influence in memory and thinking: Data and theory. In M. S. Clark & S. T. Fiske (Eds.), *Affect and cognition: The seventeenth annual Carnegie symposium on cognition* (pp. 291–331). Mahwah, NJ: Erlbaum.

Cahill, L. (2000). Modulation of long-term memory storage in humans by emotional arousal: Adrenergic activation and the amygdala. In J. P. Aggleton (Ed.), *The amygdala: Functional analysis* (pp. 425–445). Oxford: Oxford University Press.

Camerer, C. (1995). Individual decision-making. In J. H. Kagel & A. E. Roth (Eds.), *Handbook of experimental economics* (pp. 587–703). Princeton, NJ: Princeton University Press.

Canli, T., Zhao, Z., Desmond, J. E., Kang, E., Gross, J., & Gabrieli, J. D. (1998). Hemispheric asymmetry for emotional stimuli detected with fMRI. *Neuroreport, 9*, 3233–3239.

Christianson, S. A. (1992). Emotional stress and eyewitness memory: A critical review. *Psychological Bulletin, 112*, 284–309.

Conlisk, J. (1996). Why bounded rationality? *Journal of Economic Literature, 34*, 669–700.

Cosmides, L., & Tooby, J. (2000). Evolutionary psychology and the emotions. In J. M. Haviland-Jones (Ed.), *Handbook of emotions, Part I: Interdisciplinary foundations* (2nd ed., pp. 3–134). New York: Guilford Press.

Damasio, A. R. (1994). *Descartes' error: Emotion, reason, and the human brain.* New York: Putnam.

Damasio, A. R. (1999). *The feeling of what happens: Body and emotion in the making of consciousness.* Orlando, FL: Harcourt Brace.

DellaVigna, S., Pollet, J. (2003). *Attention, demographics, and the stock market,* December 1. Available: http://emlab.berkeley.edu/users/sdellavi/wp/attention.pdf.

Dittmar, H. (1992). The social psychology of material possessions: To have is to be. Hemel Hempstead: Harvester Wheatsheaf & New York: St. Martin Press.

Dittmar, H., & Drury, J. (2000). Self-image – is it in the bag. A qualitative comparison between "ordinary" and excessive" consumers. *Journal of Economic Psychology, 21*, 109–142.

Dolcos, F., & Cabeza, R. (2002). Event-related potentials of emotional memory: Encoding pleasant, unpleasant, and neutral pictures. *Cognitive, Affective & Behavioral Neurosciences, 2*, 252–263.

Earl, P. (1983). *The Economic Imagination: Towards a Behavioral Theory of Choice.* Brighton: Wheatsheaf.

Earl, P. (1986). *Lifestyle economics: Consumer behavior in a turbulent world.* Brighton: Wheatsheaf.

Elliott, R. (1994). Addictive consumption: Function and fragmentation in postmodernity. *Journal of Consumer Policy, 17*, 159–179.

Elster, J. (1983). *Explaining technical change.* Cambridge: Cambridge University Press.

Elster, J. (1999). *Alchemies of the mind: Rationality and the emotions.* Cambridge: Cambridge University Press.

Faucher, L., & Tappolet, C. (2002). Fear and the focus of attention. *Consciousness and Emotion, 3*, 105–144.

Fehr, E., & Gachter, S. (2002). Altruistic punishment in humans. *Nature, 415*, 137–140.

Frank, R. (1988). *Passions within reason.* New York: Norton.

Friedman, M., & Savage, L. (1948). The utility analysis of choice involving risk. *The Journal of Political Economy, LVI*, 279–304.

Gigerenzer, G., & Selten, R. (2001). Rethinking rationality. In G. Gigerenzer & R. Selten (Eds.), *Bounded rationality: The adaptive toolbox* (pp. 1–12). Cambridge, MA: MIT Press.

Gigerenzer, G., Todd, P. M., & the ABC Research Group (1999). *Simple heuristics that make us smart.* New York: Oxford University Press.

Glennan, S. (2002). Rethinking mechanistic explanation. *Philosophy of Science*, *69*, S342–S353.

Haidt, J. (2001). The emotional dog and its rational tail: A social intuitionist approach to moral judgment. *Psychological Review*, *108*, 814–834.

Hamann, S. T. (2001). Cognitive and neural mechanisms of emotional memory. *Trends in Cognitive Sciences*, *9*, 394–400.

Hanoch, Y. (2002a). The effects of emotions on bounded rationality: A comment on Kaufman. *Journal of Economic Behavior and Organization*, *49*(1), 131–135.

Hanoch, Y. (2002b). "Neither an angel nor an ant": Emotion as an aid to bounded rationality. *Journal of Economic Psychology*, *23*, 1–25.

Harré, R. (1970). Powers. *British Journal of Philosophy of Science*, *21*, 81–101.

Harré, R. (1983). *Personal being*. Oxford: Blackwell.

Harré, R. (2001). The rediscovery of the human mind. *Proceedings of the 50th anniversary conference of the Korean Psychological Association*, Seoul. Available: www.massey.ac.nz/~alock/virtual/korea.htm.

Harré, R., & Gillett, G. (1994). *The discursive mind*. London: Sage.

Harré, R., & Madden, E. (1975). *Causal powers: A theory of natural necessity*. Oxford: Basil Blackwell.

Holland, P. C., & Gallagher, M. (1999). Amygdala circuitry in attentional and representational processes. *Trends in Cognitive Science*, *3*, 65–73.

Kahneman, D., Slovic, P., & Tversky, A. (1982). *Judgment under uncertainty: Heuristics and biases*. Cambridge: Cambridge University Press.

Kaufman, B. E. (1999). Emotional arousal as a source of bounded rationality. *Journal of Economic Behavior and Organization*, *38*, 135–144.

Kelly, G. A. (1955). *The psychology of personal constructs*. New York: Norton.

Ketelaar, T., & Todd, P. M. (2000). Framing our thoughts: Ecological rationality evolutionary psychology's answer to the frame problem. In H. R. Holcomb (Ed.), *Conceptual challenges in evolutionary psychology: Innovative research strategies* (pp. 179–211). Norwell, MA: Kluwer.

Koestler, A. (1967). *The ghost in the machine*. London: Hutchinson.

Lazarus, R. S. (1984). On the primacy of cognition. *American Psychologist*, *39*, 124–129.

LeDoux, J. (1996). *The emotional brain*. New York: Simon and Schuster.

Levenson, R. W. (1999). The interpersonal functions of emotion. *Cognition and Emotion*, *13*, 481–504.

Loewenstein, G., O'Donoghue, T., & Rabin, M. (1999). *Projection bias in predicting future preferences*, September 20. Available: http://elsa.berkely.edu/users/rabin/papers.html.

Loewenstein, G., Weber, E., Hsee, C., & Welch, N. (2001). Risk as feelings. *Psychological Bulletin*, *127*, 267–286.

Machamer, P., Darden, L., & Craver, C. (2000). Thinking about mechanisms. *Philosophy of Science*, *67*, 1–25.

Marr, D. (1982). *Vision: A computational investigation into the human representation and processing of visual information*. New York: W.H. Freeman.

Mayr, E. (1988). Cause and effect in biology. In E. Mayr (Ed.), *Toward a new philosophy of biology* (pp. 24–37). Harvard: Harvard University Press.

Mineka, S., & Cook, M. (1988). Social learning and the acquisition of snake fear in monkeys. In T. Zentall & B. Galef (Eds.), *Social learning: Psychological and biological perspectives* (pp. 51–73). Hillsdale, NJ: Erlbaum.

Muramatsu, R. (2004). Emotions in action: An inquiry into the psychobiological foundations of decision-making. Unpublished doctoral dissertation. Erasmus University of Rotterdam, Rotterdam.

Nussbaum, M. (2001). *Upheavals of thought: The intelligence of emotions*. Cambridge: Cambridge University Press.

Öhman, A., & Mineka, S. (2001). Fears, phobias, and preparedness: Toward an evolved module of fear and fear learning. *Psychological Review, 108*, 483–522.

Packard, M. G., & Cahill, L. C. (2001). Affective modulation of multiple memory systems. *Current Opinion in Neurobiology, 11*, 752–755.

Panksepp, J. (1998). *Affective neuroscience: The foundations of human and animal emotions*. Oxford: Oxford University Press.

Parkinson, B., & Manstead, A. S. R. (1992). Appraisal as a cause of emotion. In M. C. Clark (Ed.), *Review of personality and social psychology* (Vol. 13, pp. 122–149). Newbury Park, CA: Sage.

Rabin, M. (1998). Psychology and economics. *Journal of Economic Literature, 36*, 11–46.

Rozin, P., Haidt, J., & McCauley, C. R. (1993). Disgust. In M. Lewis & J. Haviland (Eds.), *Handbook of emotions* (1st ed., pp. 575–594). New York: Guilford Press.

Salmon, W. (1984). *Scientific explanation and the causal structure of the world*. Princeton, NJ: Princeton University Press.

Sen, A. (1994). *On ethics and economics*. Oxford: Blackwell (Original work published 1987).

Shackle, G. L. S. (1961). *Decision, order and time in human affairs*. Cambridge: Cambridge University Press.

Simon, H. A. (1967). Motivational and emotional controls of cognition. *Psychological Review, 74*, 29–39.

Simon, H. A. (1983). *Reason in human affairs*. Stanford, CA: Stanford University Press.

Simon, H. A. (1990). Invariants of human behavior. *Annual Review of Psychology, 41*, 1–19.

Simon, H. A. (1992). Scientific discovery as problem solving. In M. Egidi & R. Marris (Eds.), *Economics, bounded rationality and the cognitive revolution*. Aldershot: Edward Elgar.

Skinner, A. S. (1979). Adam Smith: An aspect of modern economics. *Scottish Journal of Political Economy, 26*, 109–125.

Sperber, D. (1996). *Explaining culture: A naturalistic approach*. Oxford: Oxford University Press.

Stigler, G. J. (1961). The economics of information. *Journal of Political Economy, 69*, 213–225.

Thaler, R. H. (1991). *Quasi rational economics*. Russell Sage Foundation.

Thaler, R. H. (1992). *The winner's curse: Anomalies and paradoxes of economic life*. Princeton, NJ: Princeton University Press.

Thaler, R. H. (2000). From Homo economicus to Homo sapiens. *Journal of Economic Perspectives, 14*, 133–141.

Tooby, J., & Cosmides, L. (1995). Mapping the evolved functional organization of mind and brain. In M. S. Gazzaniga (Ed.), *The cognitive neurosciences* (pp. 1185–1997). Cambridge, MA: MIT Press.

Tooby, J., & Cosmides, L. (2000). Toward mapping the evolved functional organization of mind and brain. In M. S. Gazzaniga (Ed.), *The new cognitive neurosciences* (pp. 1167–1270). Cambridge, MA: MIT Press.

Vygotsky, L. S. (1962). *Thought and language*. Cambridge, MA: Harvard University Press.

Wittgenstein, L. (1953). *Philosophical investigations (G. E. M. Anscombe & G. H. von Wright, Trans.)*. Oxford: Blackwell.

Zajonc, R. B. (1980). Feeling and thinking: Preferences need no inferences. *American Psychologist, 2*, 151–175.

53

EVALUATING THE RELATIVE IMPORTANCE OF VARIABLES*

Hubert M. Blalock, Jr

Source: *American Sociological Review*, 26 (1961), 866–874.

Two distinct criteria are discussed for evaluating the relative importance of several independent variables in determining the variation in a dependent variable. The quantitative criterion is used primarily with numerical data, whereas the causal criterion often appears in theoretical arguments. Simon's method for making causal inferences from correlational data may offer potentialities for combining these criteria. The indiscriminate use of partial correlations and a single multiple regression equation can yield misleading conclusions in evaluating importance. Instead, an entire set of simultaneous equations is needed.

It has become almost a truism to say that the social scientist must deal with large numbers of variables. In the exploratory phases of any given discipline, one of the most difficult tasks is that of merely locating those variables which seem to be most important in accounting for the variation in some dependent variable. At later stages, however, it becomes increasingly necessary to attempt to evaluate the relative importance of such variables, if only for the practical reason that both theorists and empiricists must limit themselves to a reasonable number of explanatory variables.

The purpose of the present paper is to raise certain questions about the criteria used to determine the relative importance of a number of "independent" variables and to suggest that the indiscriminate use of multiple regression and partial correlational techniques to evaluate importance

* This research was conducted while the writer was supported by a Social Science Research Council Postdoctoral Research Training Fellowship.

can, on occasion, yield highly misleading conclusions.[1] It will be argued that a technique proposed by H. A. Simon for making causal inferences from correlational data offers certain potentialities for overcoming these difficulties.[2]

Two criteria for evaluating importance

There are at least two very different sorts of criteria used in evaluating importance. To oversimplify somewhat, the first criterion is usually applied when the social scientist is dealing with actual numerical data, whereas the second seems to be implied in certain types of theoretical discussions. Unfortunately, the two criteria do not necessarily lead to similar decisions; at least as often as not, they can be expected to yield exactly opposite conclusions.

The quantitative criterion

The first type of criterion seems to be purely empirical. Some sort of measure of association between an independent and dependent variable is computed. If there are several independent variables, their relative importance is assessed by comparing measures of association of each independent variable with the dependent variable, usually controlling for all of the remaining independent variables. The measure of association may be some sort of correlation coefficient, in which case the respective partials are compared. Or the measure may involve a prediction equation in which slopes are used to measure the change in the dependent variable produced by a given change in an independent variable. In the case of multiple regression analysis, one can compute beta weights which indicate the change in the dependent variable produced by standardized changes in each independent variable controlling for all the remaining variables. Usually, although not always, the conclusions reached using partial correlations will be essentially similar to those arrived at using beta weights.[3] For our purposes we shall therefore consider these various measures of association as involving a single type of criterion which, for convenience, we shall refer to as the *quantitative criterion* for evaluating the importance of variables.

One extremely significant point about this quantitative criterion deserves special emphasis. The importance of a given independent variable is always a function of the amount of variation in that variable. This is perhaps most obvious in the case of regression coefficients, where we are interested in the amount of change in the dependent variable produced by a given change in an independent variable. But the magnitude of a correlation coefficient also depends on the extent of variation in the independent variable, though this fact is sometimes not explicitly recognized.

The same argument would apply to purely theoretical attempts to assess importance. For example, in explaining minority discrimination it would seem to be meaningless to claim that economic variables are more important than religious ideologies, or even that a plantation economy is more important than Catholic ideology in explaining the position of Negroes in Brazil. Some basis for comparison must always be made. Thus one might argue that the *differences* between the economies of Brazil and the American South were more important than *differences* between Catholic and Protestant ideologies in accounting for differences in discrimination. Similarly, one would not ask whether temperature is more important than volume in determining the pressure of a gas in an enclosed space. But one could assess the change produced in pressure by a given change in either temperature or volume, and one might then answer the question as to which of these specific changes had the greatest effect on pressure.[4] The quantitative criterion of importance can be applied only to *specific* cases and not to abstract relationships among variables.

The causal criterion

Let us now turn to a second criterion of importance, one which does not appear explicitly in discussions in the literature but which nevertheless seems to be used in various theoretical arguments. This criterion involves the causal ordering among variables and will be labeled the *causal criterion*. Briefly put, if A causes B and B in turn causes C, it may be argued that A is more important than B in determining C since A is a more ultimate cause, whereas B is merely an immediate cause. Thus if the nature of the economy is seen to determine in part the details of the socialization process, which in turn affect specific beliefs concerning the nature of God, then economic variables are considered the more important of the two. Similarly, if the Northward migration of Negroes makes possible a more vigorous protest movement which, in turn, leads to lesser discrimination, then it is this migration rather than any social psychological leadership variables which is conceived to be most important. Or in Linton's discussion of social change among the Tanala-Betsileo the most important factor in determining a change in mental outlook and personality would be taken to be the change from dry to wet rice, since it was presumably this change which set in motion a chain reaction ultimately resulting in changes in personality.[5]

It can immediately be seen that this type of causal criterion is both sensible, in some sense, and yet capable of leading to endless debate. If pushed to the extreme, it would lead to absurd conclusions since if

$$A \rightarrow B \rightarrow C \rightarrow \ldots \rightarrow K \rightarrow L$$

then A is a more important factor than K in determining L regardless of the weaknesses in any part of the causal chain and regardless of the strength of the relationship between K and L. It can be shown for such a simple causal chain that intercorrelations among various pairs of variables become weaker and weaker the further removed the variables are from one another in the chain.[6] Thus

$$|r_{AL}| \leq |r_{BL}| \leq |r_{KL}|$$

and in this particular case the quantitative and causal criteria lead to opposite conclusions.

Perhaps the adherent of the quantitative criterion would argue that it is theoretically meaningless or at least unwise to become involved with the problem of evaluating the relative importances of variables which stand in some sort of causal relationship to each other. It might be claimed that we must recognize that some causes are more immediate than others and that one can legitimately compare only those variables which have the same degree of immediacy. The contrary argument, however, would obviously be that such an ideal is neither practically nor theoretically possible. Since, in reality, most variables with which the social scientist deals are linked in a rather complex causal network, the criterion one uses must reflect this fact and cannot ignore completely the problem of causation. To say that an immediate cause is the most important factor, merely because it is most highly associated with the dependent variable, is to take an absurdly extreme position.

Ideally, it might be desirable to develop a single criterion for evaluating importance which, somehow or another, would combine the desirable features of both the quantitative and causal criteria. It would also be advantageous if this single criterion could be stated with sufficient precision that it could be applied unambiguously to relatively complicated multivariate causal networks. For the present, we can only indicate the direction in which a fruitful search for a combined criterion might be made. A quantitative technique is needed which can take into consideration the various causal relationships among "independent" variables. Before discussing such a technique, however, we shall first consider the kinds of questions that can and cannot be answered by ordinary multiple regression methods.

Single multiple regression equations versus Simon's method

The contrast between laboratory experiments and real life situations is of course well known. In the laboratory, the scientist raises a series of hypothetical questions concerning the covariation among several variables with other relevant variables remaining constant or, at least, with the supposed effects of these other variables somehow being taken into consideration. The multiple regression equation has been designed with this ideal in mind. In multiple regression we can investigate the amount of change produced in a single dependent variable Y by a given change in any particular independent variable X: with the effects of the remaining variables controlled. If beta weights are used, we may compare the relative changes in the dependent variable for standardized changes in the various independent variables, each time with the effects of the other variables controlled. Likewise, one may use the square of the partial correlation coefficient to give the proportion of variation in the dependent variable associated with any given independent variable after adjusting for the effects of the remaining variables.[7]

The use of such beta weights or partial correlations enables one to answer the hypothetical question as to what would happen to the dependent variable *if* all but one of the independent variables were to remain fixed. If we cannot conceive of a laboratory situation in which all but one of the independent variables were literally held constant, we can at least imagine survey data for which there are some cases having identical values for all but one of these independent variables. Within each of these sets of cases, we could then investigate the relationship between the dependent variable and the remaining independent variable.[8] Actually, in using a regression equation we conceive of a distribution of Y's for *fixed* values of X_i. In other words, the various values of X_i are taken as givens and the Y's are predicted from these values.[9] For example, if we thought of a student as having certain abilities and certain motivational tendencies which would remain constant during his four years of college, we than might use scores on various tests designed to measure these traits in order to predict his performance. The predicted performance would be the mean performance level for all students having exactly his combination of abilities and motivation. Or we might ask questions of the following type: "If a student's abilities were to remain the same, how will his performance be affected by a given change in his motivation?"

But we can also ask a very different type of question, one which at first glance seems to be similar to the above question. We may ask, "What is the change, or expected change, produced in Y by a given change in a particular X_i, given the fact that certain of the other supposedly independent variables also may be affected by this change in X_i?" The single regression equation with Y as the dependent variable takes into consideration the *correlations* among the various X's, but it begs the question of the *direction of causality* among these variables. Presumably, they are merely thought not to be causally dependent on Y, although there is nothing in the mathematical formula for the regression equation to prevent one from interchanging Y with any of the X's. Such a single equation does not permit one to distinguish between situations in which X_1 causes X_2 and those where X_2 causes X_1.

In raising this second kind of question we seem to be coming closer to real-life situations in which there is a complex causal network where not only is Y causally dependent on the various X's, but some of these X's in turn are causally dependent on certain of the others. Thus if a particular

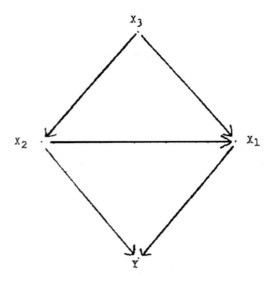

Figure 1

change in one X occurs, not only may there be a direct effect on Y, but there may be effects on some of the remaining X's and therefore an additional indirect effect on Y. In fact, there may be no direct effect on Y at all but only a series of indirect effects. For example, we may have a causal pattern as indicated in Figure 1.

To represent such a causal network we need not one but a number of separate equations which, when taken simultaneously, can be used to predict changes in Y. For example, assuming linearity, the network in Figure 1 can be represented by the following set of equations:

$$Y = a_1 + b_{11}X_1 + b_{12}X_2 + e_1$$
$$X_1 = a_2 + b_{22}X_2 + b_{23}X_3 + e_2$$
$$X_2 = a_3 + b_{33}X_3 + e_3$$

where the e's represent the effects of all variables not taken into consideration in the causal model.[10]

If X_3 were to change there would be direct effects on X_1 and X_2 but only an indirect effect on Y. If X_2 were to change there would be no effect on X_3 but both X_1 and Y would be changed, and furthermore the total effect on Y would stem not only from the direct effect of X_2 but from the change in X_1 as well. In any given case we could estimate the change in Y by making use of the complete set of equations. Thus if X_3 changes by one unit, X_2 will change b_{33} units. The change in X_1 will then be $b_{22}b_{33} + b_{23}$, the second term being due to X_3 directly and the first to the indirect effect through X_2. We can now predict a change in Y in a similar manner. This change will be

$$b_{11}(b_{22}b_{33} + b_{23}) + b_{12}b_{33}$$

Suppose, however, that we had asked about the change in Y for a change in X_3, presupposing that X_1 and X_2 remained constant. It can be shown that in such an instance we would have reached the conclusion that Y would not change.[11] This is both correct and misleading unless we clearly understand that we have raised an hypothetical question which may, in real life, be absurd. At least if we are to produce a change in X_3 without corresponding changes in X_1 and X_2, we must introduce certain *other* variables in the laboratory situation which exactly counteract the effects of X_3. The major point is that although the use of a single prediction equation may be useful in answering the type of hypothetical question which can be answered in laboratory experiments, we must not be tempted to use such a method in answering more complex questions in which we take into consideration the causal relationships among the variables which have been treated as independent. In this latter instance, which we recognize as being perhaps more realistic for most problems with which the social scientist deals, we need to work with an entire *set* of equations rather than with a single equation and a single dependent variable.

A method proposed by H. A. Simon for making causal inferences from correlational data makes use of such a set of simultaneous equations.[12] In the present paper it will be sufficient merely to outline the essentials of Simon's method since the procedure has been discussed at greater length elsewhere.[13] Simon restricts himself to linear models, but in principle his argument is quite general. Basically, the method involves writing an equation for each variable in the system taken as a possible dependent variable. Some of the regression coefficients can then be set equal to zero if there is no *direct* link between the two variables concerned. If certain assumptions can be made about outside variables which may possibly have disturbing effects, one can then make use of this set of equations rather than the single regression equation. A series of prediction equations can be derived which can be used to test the adequacy of any given causal model. Once a given model has been decided upon, the method can then be used to enable one to estimate not only the direct effects of a change in one variable but the indirect effects as well.

Direction of causality and the use of controls

If we wish to combine the quantitative and causal criteria of importance, we must decide upon the conditions under which we should or should not control for other "independent" variables. Such a decision will presumably depend upon the assumed causal ordering among these variables. Let us suppose that Simon's method, or perhaps some other technique of a similar nature, ahs been used to test the goodness of fit of a particular causal model to the empirical data. We are then in a position to commit ourselves on a particular causal model and can next raise questions as to the use of controls.

The question of when and when not to control for a given variable seems to be considerably more complex than is often recognized. Here, it will be sufficient to point out that the answer depends on whether one is primarily interested in determining the relative importance of certain variables or whether one's concern is with problems of interpretation or specification.[14] Where one is attempting to assess importance, and interest centers therefore on indirect as well as direct effects of some independent variable, it would seem to make little sense to control for intervening variables. But can any really general rules be established enabling one to decide when to control? Before such rules can be laid down, we would have to know considerably more about the behavior of both the correlation and regression coefficients under various assumptions about causal models and outside variables. In the present paper, the best we can do is to indicate the direction in which the answer would seem to lie.

Suppose we had only three variables related causally as in Figure 2. According to the causal criterion of importance, X_1 would automatically be more important than X_2. At first glance, it might seem as though the quantitative criterion would point to the same conclusion, but we must remember that the direct relationship between X_2 and Y might be much stronger than those between X_1 and X_2, on the one hand, and X_1 and Y on the other. How, then, would we compare the relative importance of X_1 and X_2? Would we compare $r_{y1.2}$ with $r_{y2.1}$?[15] Or would we use r_{y1} versus $r_{y2.1}$? Probably the latter if we reasoned that the relationship between X_2 and Y is partly

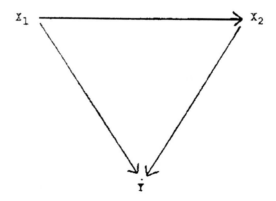

Figure 2

spurious and if we wished to take into consideration both the direct and indirect effects of X_1. We see, however, that when decisions must be made about controls, the quantitative criterion of importance is by no means unambiguous. Also, our decision as to controls may depend on whether our measure of importance involves correlation or regression co-efficients. For instance under the assumptions required for Simon's method, it can be shown that if the arrow between X_1 and Y were erased the magnitude of $r_{y2.1}$ would be less than that of r_{y2}. But the comparable betas would be identical, indicating no change in the slope of the relationship between X_2 and Y when X_1 is controlled.

In the case of the three variable chain $X_1 \rightarrow X_2 \rightarrow Y$, a control for the intervening variable X_2 will produce a zero value for both the partial correlation and beta between X_1 and Y if the assumptions for Simon's method are met. In this very simple case we have a rather obvious and dramatic instance in which the automatic use of multiple regression might lead to absurd conclusions. In more complex situations, however, it may be much more difficult to keep track of what is happening.

Suppose we had a situation involving five variables, with the causal model as indicated in Figure 3. In another paper, the author concluded, using Simon's method, that this particular causal model represented a better fit to certain empirical data than several other models.[16] To discuss the particular variables concerned would introduce considerations which are extraneous to the present argument. Instead, let us assume the causal model to be correct and focus attention on the numerical values of the various correlation coefficients which are also given in Figure 3. In this particular instance both causal and quantitative criteria for importance would seem to point to X_1 as the most important variable in determining Y. Not only is the zero-order coefficient between X_1 and Y larger than any other

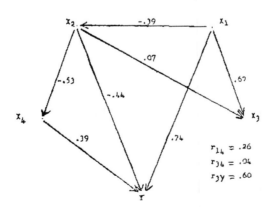

Figure 1

correlation, but X_1 is taken as either a direct or an indirect cause of all the other variables.

What if we had more or less indiscriminately related Y to each of these independent variables, with controls on each of the remaining variables? Of course with a best-fitting causal model in front of us, there would be little reason for carrying out such an operation. Among other things, we would perhaps argue that controlling for X_3 makes little sense in that the relationship between X_3 and Y is spurious.[17] This is, in fact, the major argument in favor of some such attempt to assess the causal interrelationships among variables. For if we were to relate X_1 to Y, controlling for X_2, X_3, and X_4, we would find that the correlation would be reduced from .74 to .33. Furthermore with controls on the other three variables, the correlation between X_3 and Y would be changed from .60 to .38, and we might be led to the conclusion that with "all relevant variables controlled," X_3 is slightly more important than X_1. Using the figure, however, and admitting the possibility of a direct causal link between X_3 and Y, it would undoubtedly seem more reasonable to compare $r_{y3.12}$ with r_{y1} rather than $r_{y1.234}$. Likewise, r_{y1} might also be compared with $r_{y2.1}$ and with $r_{y4.12}$ if one wished to combine the quantitative and causal criteria.

As indicated above, the development of a single criterion combining the desirable features of both the quantitative and causal criteria of importance would seem to depend on our being able to set forth a completely unambiguous set of rules specifying the conditions under which we should control in the general multivariate case. Tentatively, we may suggest that one should control only for those variables which are assumed to be causally prior to the independent variable in question.[18] Note, however, that in the case of Figure 3 there is a possible ambiguity as to whether to control for X_4 in relating X_3 to Y, though such a control would probably make little sense in this instance. Once the mathematical implications of Simon's method have been more thoroughly worked out it is hoped that such issues can be satisfactorily resolved. It may also be possible to see more clearly the relative advantages and disadvantages of using slopes as contrasted with correlation coefficients as measures of relative importance.

A note on reciprocal causation

We have completely ignored thus far the problem of reciprocal causation. Ideally, we must always allow for the possibility of two-way causation and also for the fact that a causal relationship may be stronger in one direction than in the other. If we raise the hypothetical question as to how much change we would expect in one variable given a change in the other, we may reach the theoretical conclusion that a change in either variable would affect the other. For example it might be argued that not only would certain types of changes in the economy lead to changes in the socialization process, but, likewise, if changes in the latter type of variable were to occur, the economy would also be affected. If, for some reason, all children in America were brought up in Gandhian fashion and taught to scorn material goods, there would undoubtedly be certain major changes in the American economy.

In raising such hypothetical questions we are not attempting to assess the *likelihood* of a given initial change in one or the other of these variables. We have simply asked what would happen to the economy *if* certain changes were made in the socialization process. When we pose the question of the likelihood of such a change, we immediately run into the problem of the relationship of each of these two variables to *other* factors. In real-life situations it may turn out that we practically always find changes in the economy followed by changes in socialization, rather than the other way around. This does not invalidate the assumption that there is reciprocal causation involved; it may merely indicate that initial changes in the one variable are easier to achieve or are more likely than changes in the other variable. In some other type of social system, perhaps one in which children are trained at a very early age by agents of the state, a consciously developed plan to modify socialization may have important effects on the economy. Again we need to distinguish the hypothetical question involving presumed changes from the kind of question we are apt to ask about an actual situation occurring outside the laboratory of the scientist. This does not mean that the answers to the scientist's hypothetical questions may not ultimately provide answers to more complex problems. For our purposes it is sufficient to emphasize that the two types of questions need to be clearly distinguished.

If two-way causation is assumed, the problems of evaluating relative importance and of deciding on the use of control variables become much more complex. Also, Simon's method yields results which have not as yet been systematically investigated by the writer. Considerably more attention needs to be given to the question of reciprocal causation before the various issues raised in the present paper cap be resolved.

Concluding remarks

Two criteria for evaluating the importance of variables, a quantitative and a causal criterion, have been discussed. Also, the distinction has been made between the kinds of questions that may be answered by ordinary regression analysis and those requiring the use of an entire set of simultaneous equations which allow for possible causal relationships among the supposedly independent variables. If one wants to make use of the purely quantitative criterion for evaluating importance, thereby begging the question of the causal interrelationships among independent variables, one may legitimately make use of beta weights or partial correlations. In so doing, one will obtain answers to the hypothetical question, "What is the relationship between the dependent variable and any given independent variable, assuming fixed values for the remaining independent variables?"

If one wishes to combine the two criteria for importance by somehow assessing the indirect as well as the direct effects of changes in any of the independent variables, one must first commit oneself to an appropriate causal model. Simon's method for making causal inferences from correlational data provides us with a procedure for evaluating the degree to which a given set of data actually fits such a causal model. The next step is to decide whether or not to control for a particular variable when relating some other factor to the dependent variable. Ultimately, it may prove possible to provide a completely unambiguous set of rules for making such a decision.

It may turn out that rather than searching for such a single combined criterion of importance, it will be more fruitful to think in terms of an orderly sequence of specific questions, each of which permits a relatively simple answer. A list of such questions might be as follows:

1. What is the *causal ordering* among all of the variables included in the system? (Simon's method provides a goodness-of-fit test for evaluating the adequacy of any given causal model.)
2. Given these assumptions about the causal network, what is the relative magnitude of each *direct* relationship? (Here, some rules for controlling for remaining variables would be required.)
3. Given these assumptions about the causal network and given the measures of each direct relationship, what is the *total effect*, direct and indirect, of a change in one variable on any other variable in the system? (Here, if we are using slopes to measure effects, we would need to make use of an entire set of simultaneous equations as was done illustratively above.)
4. Given the answers to the above three questions, which variables are *most likely* to change under given circumstances? (Answers to this question may involve variables not included in the causal system but may also help to resolve debates over reciprocal causation.)
5. Given answers to the first three questions, what is the *easiest* way to produce a given change in a dependent variable? (This is the practical question involved in social engineering.)

The kind of program of specific questions outlined above may seem to require a degree of knowledge which is completely unrealistic to expect of the social sciences in the near future. Perhaps, however, the explicit statement of an ideal will make it less tempting for an individual social scientist to assess the relative importance of variables by merely shrugging off the question of causal relationships among independent variables. Nor will he be as likely to go ahead more or less blindly controlling for all relevant variables without stopping to ask himself what kinds of questions he can hope to answer in such a manner or whether he is actually posing the kinds of questions he really wishes to have answered.

Notes

1 This general point is not new, of course. See especially Arnold M. Rose, "A Weakness of Partial Correlation in Sociological Studies," *American Sociological Review*, 14 (August, 1949), pp. 536–539.

2 Herbert A. Simon, "Spurious Correlation: A Causal Interpretation," *Journal of the American Statistical Association*, 49 (September, 1954), pp. 467–479.

3 For example, if a relationship is nonlinear or if the dispersion about the regression equation does not remain constant from one point of the curve to the next, certain peculiar results may be obtained. For an excellent discussion of the use of beta weights as an alternative to partial correlation see Donold J. Bogue and D. L. Harris, *Comparative Population and Urban Research via Multiple Regression and Covariance Analysis*, Oxford, Ohio: Scripps Foundation, 1954, pp. 3–18.

4 The scientist could also attempt to answer the practical question whether it would be *easier* to produce a given change in pressure by changing the volume or temperature. Several persons have pointed out to the writer that the ease with which a change can be made in a given variable may somehow affect one's evaluation of its importance. This suggests a possible third criterion of importance, but one which will not be discussed in the present paper.

5 See Ralph Linton, "The Tanala of Madagascar," in Abram Kardiner, *The Individual and His Society*, New York: Columbia University, 1939, pp. 251–290.

6 See Simon, *op. cit.*

7 Actually, controlling by means of partial correlations involves an adjusting operation which is somewhat different from literally holding the control variables constant. But the actual method of controlling is not of concern to us in the present discussion.

8 The criticism of the indiscriminate use of controls also applies to controls involving contingency tables as well as to partial correlations. Our discussion is in terms of correlation coefficients primarily for purposes of clarity of presentation.

9 The usual distinction is being made here between the regression equation and the least squares equation used for purposes of estimation.

10 For a discussion of the rationale for describing causal relationships in terms of a set of simultaneous equations see Herbert A. Simon, "Causal Ordering and Identifiability," Chap. 3 in *Studies in Econometric Methods* (Cowles Commission Monograph 14).

11 This can be shown by making use of Simon's method which is described in the following paragraph. This method requires the assumption that the various e's are uncorrelated, i.e., that possible outside disturbing influences have essentially random effects on the relationships among the variables included in the causal system. Some such assumptions about outside variables are of course always necessary if one is to make causal inferences.

12 See Herbert A. Simon, "Spurious Correlation: A Causal Interpretation," *loc. cit.*

13 *Ibid.* See also Hubert M. Blalock, Jr., *Social Statistics*, New York: McGraw-Hill, 1960, pp. 337–343, and Hubert M. Blalock, Jr., "Correlation and Causality: The Multivariate Case," *Social Forces*, 39 (March, 1961), pp. 246–251.

14 For an excellent discussion of these other types of controlling situations see Herbert Hyman, *Survey Design and Analysis*, Glencoe: The Free Press, 1955,

pp. 275–329. Where interpretation is the goal, a control for an intervening variable may legitimately be made in order to see whether or not the partial reduces to zero. If such a partial is zero in the three-variable case, and if certain assumptions can be made both about the causal ordering among the three variables and also about variables not included in the system, it may then be concluded that there is no *direct* link between the independent and dependent variables.

15 We are using this somewhat unconventional notation to emphasize that Y has been taken as the single dependent variable. The symbol $r_{y1.2}$ means the correlation between Y and X_1, controlling for X_2.

16 Blalock, "Correlation and Causality: the Multivariate Case," *loc. cit.*

17 Actually, the data indicate that it may be reasonable to draw an additional arrow from X_3 to Y, in which case this relationship—as measured by r_{y3}—is only partly spurious.

18 This proposal is certainly not original. See Rose, *op. cit.*

54

UNPROGRAMMED
DECISION MAKING*

Peer O. Soelberg

Source: *Industrial Management Review*, 8:2 (1967), 19–29.

Abstract

The paper presents a framework for describing human problem solving and decision making processes. The analysis departs from traditional utility and probability theory. It suggests that decision values are better described as partially ordered sets of constraining goal attributes, and that decision uncertainty may be adequately represented as ranges of "likely" values on each alternative's uncertain goal attributes. The resulting decision process model is fitted to the protocols of several points-in-time interviews of M.I.T. graduate students making job decisions. A set of key hypotheses in this fitted model are then tested on another sample of graduate students the following year. The model suggests how managers' unprogrammed decision making may be improved.

The research reported below has implications for management practice if one accepts the following three propositions: (1) information processing and decision making are central functions of modern organizations; (2) in order to improve management decision making it is useful to know how organizations presently make decisions;[1] (3) as long as people remain the chief instrument of corporate policy, a key feature of management decision making will be the choice processes of individual human beings.

* The paper summarizes findings and conclusions from the author's recent book, *A Study of Decision Making: Job Choice*, Massachusetts Institute of Technology, 1966, xix + 465 pp.

This paper is a report on how individuals make important, difficult and highly judgmental decisions. It has become customary to contrast so-called unprogrammed with more highly programmed types of decisions.[2] The latter are choices or actions that follow routinely from the decision maker's application of explicit decision rules to whatever stimulus or input data face him in his task environment.

The management of most companies' daily operations abounds with highly programmed decisions. Consider merely the routinized rules that normally guide the everyday management of inventories, production schedules, machine and manpower allocations, cost estimation, mark-up pricing, etc. A famous description of highly programmed decision making is G. P. E. Clarkson's portfolio selection study, in which he demonstrated that the investment decisions made by a bank trust officer were so well programmed that his decisions could be predicted by a computer six months after his investment rules had been elicited by an interviewer and described as a computer program.[3]

In contrast, this study focuses on highly unprogrammed decision making, a subject that usually gets relegated to the mystical realm of managerial "judgment."[4] Every day critical decisions are produced for which the decision maker can explicate no identifiable rules or pre-programmed decision procedure. This is not to say that a person may not be following some sort of generalized guidelines when rendering his so-called judgment. But if you asked him directly, he would insist that the unprogrammed problem confronting him had to be solved in its own unique context. Moreover, observing him solve the problem, you would find:

- The decision maker applied few special-purpose rules when arriving at his choice.
- The decision maker might not even be able to specify, *a priori*, the nature of an ideal solution to his problem.
- A number of the decision criteria that he wished to apply were not operational before he tackled the problem.
- Many of his choice alternatives were unknown when he started out.
- Information about the alternatives' consequences and relative worth was not immediately available from the task environment.

Yet it is precisely this type of unstructured or unprogrammed decision making that forms the basis for allocating billions of dollars worth of resources in our economy every year. Ironically, until we understand the nature of such human decision processes better, our sophisticated computer technology will be of slight aid in making these types of decision. In other words, the potential payoff to management of a scientific understanding of the economic, psychological, and socio-political "laws" of non-programmed human judgment is enormous.

Available theories

Traditional economists have long tried to get along with little more than the concepts of "utility" and "probability" for explaining unprogrammed choice among uncertain alternatives.[5] A utility function is an assumed linear preference ordering of all possible combinations of the goods and services that a person values, and as such is felt by economists to be an adequate basis for describing any decision maker's value structure. Likewise, objective (or personal) distributive probability measures are felt to capture the essence of how decision makers think about the "factual" connections which they are believed to perceive between each of the available solution alternatives and the possible, but uncertain, consequences of their choosing a specific alternative.[6] It does not take much observation of decision makers in action to convince oneself that the mathematical elegance of the probability-utility concepts may be a deceptive property that easily can mislead anyone interested in arriving at empirically testable descriptions of decision behavior.

The best known exception to traditional probability-utility theory appears in the work of Herbert Simon. The latter's notion of limited rationality, his "means-ends satisficing" model of information processing and his insistence on attaining a close correspondence between the intermediate outputs of his process simulation models of problem solving, and observable verbal behavior, have significantly reoriented and vitalized social science research on decision making.[7]

Simon characterizes unprogrammed decision making in terms of the following three-phase process model:[8]

Intelligence

Finding occasions for making a decision;

Design

Finding, inventing, developing, and analyzing alternative courses of action;

Choice

Selecting a particular course of action from those available.

In our research we used the following, slightly expanded phase structure as a framework for analyzing unprogrammed decision processes:[9]

Participation

The decision maker is somehow induced to work in a given task environment, in which he is then motivated to attain one or more non-trivial objectives.

117

Recognition and definition

The decision maker surveys his task environment, discovers, selects or is somehow provided with problems, and then defines operationally the particular problem he intends to solve.[10]

Understanding

The decision maker investigates his task environment, trying to develop an appropriate set of event classifications (i.e., concepts) in order to formulate and test hypotheses about the apparent cause-effect relationships in the environment. The latter in turn suggest design operators for, or help generate, viable solution alternatives.

Design and evaluation

The decision maker develops or searches for alternative courses of action. Rather than estimating probabilities to attach to a set of mutually exclusive consequences associated with each alternative, the decision maker searches "within" each alternative until he feels he has enough information about each important goal attribute of that alternative, or until he exhausts his search resources. If the alternative is not rejected, the decision maker assigns some value measure or range of possible values, to each goal attribute, but does not yet compare these values across goal attributes and alternatives.

Choice reduction

The decision maker reduces his set of investigated viable decision alternatives to a single one, i.e., he makes a choice.

Implementation

The decision maker introduces and manages his solution in the task environment.[11]

Feedback and control

The decision maker receives and evaluates information from the task environment regarding the effects of his implemented decision, and if required, either changes his problem definition, modifies his goals or strategies, or takes appropriate follow-up action. Thus non-linear dynamics is introduced into the decision making process.[12]

This framework was our point of departure for re-examining the literature of decision making and problem solving in search of testable hypotheses that would either make operational or be incompatible with our process outline.

Research strategy

In order to explore empirically the detail structure of the above generalized decision process, we should obviously have to investigate, at great length, the information processes of a large number of decision makers solving many different types of problems. The specific unprogrammed decision situation we chose to study sought to focus on decision makers who were:

1. Well-trained for problem solving, as well as able and motivated to talk at some length about their information processing while they were actually engaged in producing their decisions;
2. Highly involved with the problem confronting them, it being personally important for each to reach the "right" decision;
3. Quite unfamiliar with the type of problem with which they were faced; they had encountered few such problems before and did not expect to do so again in the near future;
4. Engaged in making the decision over a long period of time (several weeks) in order to minimize possible observer measurement effects, yet allow a number of observations to be made at different phases of the decision process;
5. Easily and inexpensively accessible to the investigator in reasonable number (in order to minimize our idiosyncratic interpretation of data from individuals, by enabling immediate cross-comparison of the thinkingaloud protocols of a fairly large sample of decision makers).

The above criteria for choice of subjects were designed to help us focus on as pure and "uncontaminated" a set of decision process observations as we thought could be found in industrial practice. M.I.T. Sloan School of Management Master's and doctoral candidates, making post-graduate job decisions, fitted this bill reasonably well. In addition to satisfying our research criteria, these subjects would allow us readily to test whatever rejectable hypotheses might be generated by our initial phase of investigation, on succeeding years' samples of graduating management aspirants.

Initially our goal was to design a longitudinal (i.e. periodic "over time") questionnaire that could chart efficiently and adequately the course of our subjects' job decision processes. For that purpose we put together an elaborate set of questions, which took three or four hours every week to complete. This was clearly too long, trying as it did to cover every possible theoretical contingency. For example, one part of the questionnaire was derived from probabilistic utility theory. In this part the decision maker was asked to identify, weight, and then rate whatever goal dimensions he felt entered into his decision. In turned out that the goal weights which the subjects provided during decision making could not be trusted; the reported weights varied quite unreliably both with respect to the specific alternatives that the decision maker referred to when answering the goal weight questions, and with the temporal phasing of the decision process.

We therefore had to give up the questionnaire as a poor job. It had become obvious that unless our questionnaire was made up largely of items that were closely compatible with the manner in which the decision maker actually stored and manipulated his decision information "internally," during his own thinking about the problem, the answers he provided to our questions would, for explanatory as well as predictive purposes, be spurious at best and entirely misleading at worst.

We therefore resolved to rely, almost exclusively at first, on periodic, open-ended, and highly detailed interviews with the decision makers. These interviews provided our first insight into some rather surprising aspects of unprogrammed decision making. Preliminary analysis of nearly 100 open-ended interviews, each ranging from one-half hour to two and one-half hours in length, with 20 different decision makers over three- to five-month choice periods, provided the basis for our first Generalizable Decision Processing model (for short, GDP-I).[13] The latter was first presented at Carnegie Institute of Technology in June, 1964.

Each interview protocol was thereafter reduced to comparable format by the following three-step method: First, each protocol was transcribed verbatim and its decision phase structure, according to GDP-I, was annotated in the margin. Thereafter the relevant protocol contents were summarized in a synoptic coding language derived directly from the variables and process hypotheses of GDP-I. This provided us with decision process data that were comparable across subjects. Finally the current state of each person's decision making and his active solution alternatives, at that point in time, were entered on a multidimensional, Gantt type process chart. The standardized data produced by the last two steps of the analysis served as our basis for quantifying each protocol. Fitting these data to the hypotheses of our generalizable decision process model provided (*post hoc*) support for a number of GDP-I hypotheses, relating principally to the phases in our above process outline, labelled Design and Evaluation, and Choice Reduction. The more interesting hypotheses that were supported by the data are summarized below:

- The decision maker defines his career problem by deriving an ideal solution to it, which in turn guides his planning of a set of operational criteria for evaluating specific job alternatives.
- The decision maker believes *a priori* that he will make his decision by weighting all relevant factors with respect to each alternative, and then "add up numbers" in order to identify the best one. In fact, he does not

generally do this; and if he does, it is done *after* he has made an "implicit" selection among alternatives.

- The decision maker will search in parallel for alternatives, by activating one or more "alternatives generators" – procedures which, once activated, allow him to search passively, by deciding whether or not to follow up investigating particular ones of a stream of alternatives presented by his generators.

- The decision maker will usually be evaluating more than one alternative at any one point in time, each evaluation consisting of a *series* of investigation and evaluation cycles.

- Evaluation during the search phase takes the form of screening each alternative along a number of non-compared goal dimensions; no evidence of factor weighting is apparent at this stage.

- Search will not necessarily halt as soon as the decision maker has identified an acceptable alternative (one that is not rejected by his various screening criteria); conversely, when he ends his search for new alternatives, he will usually have more than a single acceptable alternative in his "active roster."

- When the subject terminates his search for new alternatives before his search resources run out, he will already have identified a favorite alternative in his roster of acceptable alternatives; this alternative (his choice candidate) can be identified by considering his primary goal attributes (usually one or two) alone.

- At the point of search termination a person generally will *not* have compared his alternatives with one another, will not possess a transitive rank ordering of alternatives, and will refuse to admit that his implicit choice has been made.

- Before a decision maker will recognize his choice explicitly, he will engage in a sometimes quite lengthy (two or three months) confirmation processing of his roster of acceptable alternatives; alternatives *will* get compared to each other, factor by factor.

- During confirmation processing the roster of acceptable alternatives, if greater than two, quickly will be reduced to two alternatives – the choice candidate and a "confirmation candidate." If only one alternative, the choice candidate, is viable at this time, the decision maker will try to obtain another acceptable alternative (confirmation candidate) as soon as possible "in order to have something to compare it with."

- Confirmation processing aims to resolve the residual uncertainties and problems connected with the choice candidate, and to arrive at a decision rule which shows unequivocally that the choice candidate dominates the confirmation candidate – Pareto dominance being the ideal goal strived for.

- During confirmation processing a great deal of perceptual and interpretational distortion takes place in favor of the choice candidate, to the detriment of the confirmation candidate; goal attribute "weights" are arrived at, or changed, to fit the perceived data and the desired decision outcome.

- The decision is "made" when a satisfactorily Pareto dominant decision rule has been constructed, or when the decision maker runs up against an inescapable time deadline during confirmation processing.

Limited generality of the problem studied

Though our process hypotheses of job decision making have been stated in readily generalizable form, it should be obvious that the GDP-I model, as it stands, is by no means applicable to *any* unprogrammed problem situation. Some of the characteristics limiting the problem situations to which our hypotheses should apply are the following:

The alternatives are well-defined and separately identifiable. Instances of unprogrammed decision alternatives that are not well-defined are common in research and development work, for example. In such a case, the problem solver must laboriously seek out at least one feasible alternative before he can begin to choose among alternatives. His prime objective is not to select a "best" alternative among several acceptable ones, but merely to invent a single solution that works. For GDP-I to be applicable without modification, the task environment must be susceptible to the use of "search generators," procedures that present the decision maker with streams of reasonable alternatives, thus allowing him to search passively for alternatives by screening out undesirable possibilities.

Another limitation of our job choice study as a basis for generalizing about human decision processes may derive from the interactive relationship of the job seeker versus his alternatives. The latter are by no means passive pebbles to be picked at leisure. Whether or not a job possibility is to be a viable alternative for the decision maker depends on the employer's making an offer. Nevertheless, we *could* (to preserve generality) relegate the question of whether or not an alternative is "viable" to being just another goal attribute to be evaluated by the decision maker.

A third limiting characteristic of the class of decisions described above derives from the fact that the choices we studied were individual processes, largely controlled by single persons. The social or interpersonal aspects of organizational decision making are therefore not captured by the GDP-I model. Indeed, studying and providing for the effects of interpersonal group variables represents, in the author's opinion, the single most promising direction in which the GDP-I model should be developed.

A fourth obvious limit of generalizing from any model derived from observations of job decisions derives from the definiteness, or discreteness, with which solutions to the defined problem are arrived at. In contrast, we easily can think of decision problems to which solutions are found only gradually, or for which decisions have to be made repeatedly (in which case we might expect homeostatic decision rules to develop that would help the decision maker *adapt* to a preferred alternative).

A follow-up study

Our initial study provided insight into the information processes of unprogrammed human job decisions and laid the groundwork for the design of a predictively valid questionnaire instrument for testing some of the key hypotheses in the GDP-I model. In contrast to the protocol "curve fitting" exercise reported above, our follow-up investigation was thus truly a "prediction study." All hypotheses, with process-valid measures of their variables, were specified a priori. Moreover, disregarding our personal belief in the GDP-I model, most other decision models yielded small prior likelihoods that the hypotheses we set out to test were in fact true. To most orthodox theorists our predictions would appear to be "shots in the dark."

To keep the study manageable we focused on the Design, Evaluation, and Choice Reduction phases of the decision framework outlined above. We were particularly intrigued with the confirmation process that had been identified in the interview protocols. We wanted to test our ability to identify the onset of confirmation processing, which, if it took the form we were postulating, should enable us to predict the job decisions that people would make far in advance of their admission that they had made up their minds. The following six hypotheses, therefore, are merely consecutive building blocks of one long process hypothesis, derived to establish the existence of the confirmation process. A longitudinal job choice questionnaire was designed with quadruple redundancy checks for each item, to operationalize the variables in the hypotheses. The hypotheses, derived from GDP-I, took the following form:

1. Search for new alternatives ends a significant period of time before the decision maker (referred to as Dm) is willing to admit having made his decision.
2. In observation periods prior to the end of his search for new alternatives, Dm will, more often than not, already have available one or more acceptable choice alternatives.
3. When Dm ends his search for new alternatives, he will report significant uncertainty about which alternative he will select as his choice.
4. Should Dm not have obtained a firm job offer from more than one acceptable alternative at the time of search termination, he will have tried hard, and will usually have obtained, at least one other acceptable offer (according to GDP-I, in order to have something with which to compare his choice candidate) by the time he is ready to announce his decision.

5. When Dm ends his search for new alternatives, his favorite alternative can be identified by asking him a set of simple questions. When Dm's subsequent confirmation processing of alternatives ends, i.e. at the time of choice announcement, his decision will be to select that alternative.
6. Effective or perceptive dissonance reduction, in the form of a "spreading apart" of Dm's liking for his accepted versus rejected alternatives, will *not* generally be observed after choice has been announced.

Those familiar with aspiration-level, sequential search choice models may recall that according to this theory the first four hypotheses should not be reasonable. Similarly, according to cognitive dissonance reduction theory, the sixth proposition would be disturbing.

Results of the follow-up study

Below we can no more than summarize the findings pertaining to the above six hypotheses, based on data from 256 questionnaire response sets provided by 32 members of the 1965 graduating class of M.I.T. Sloan School of Management Master's and doctoral candidates. Each decision maker in the sample provided answers to eight biweekly questionnaires over the period in which he made his job decision. (For a small number of persons – a different subset with respect to each hypothesis – the path of their decision processes, as recorded by the questionnaires, provided inadequate data with which to test a given hypothesis. Thus each total reported below may add to less than 32.)

Hypothesis 1. Twenty-seven of 31 Dms (87 per cent) terminated the search for new alternatives 10 days or more before the date on which they reported having made their decision. Fifteen of 31 Dms terminated search three weeks or more before choice was made.

Hypothesis 2. Using a highly conservative measure of an alternative's acceptability, 17 of 24 Dms (74 per cent) reported having available one or more acceptable alternatives two weeks or more before they terminated search for new alternatives.

Hypothesis 3. The average personal probability distribution of 28 Dms reporting, at time of search termination, regarding the likelihood that they would choose either the alternatives that we independently had identified as being their "choice candidate," their second most preferred alternative, and "all other alternatives," was respectively: (.29, .24, .47). In other words, great uncertainty was expressed by Dms at the time of search termination regarding which alternative they were to choose.

Hypothesis 4. Thirteen of 16 Dms (81 per cent) who did not have, or had not been promised, an offer from more than one alternative at time of search termination, did report having at least one such other offer in hand before they made their decision.

Hypothesis 5. Twenty-five and one-half of 29 Dms (87 per cent) (one-half since one Dm could reasonably be classified either way) eventually selected as their final decision that alternative which at the time of search termination, one to 12 weeks earlier (median of three weeks), had independently been identified as their favorite alternative, i.e. choice candidate.

Hypothesis 6. *No* Dm reported a consistent dissonance reduction "spreading apart" of his liking for accepted versus rejected alternatives over the periods of observation immediately following decision commitment. However, two Dms exhibited what we might call latent dissonance reduction, i.e. one which took effect two or more weeks *after* Dm had committed himself to the decision. Nine of 26 Dms (35 per cent) showed an *initial* "spreading apart" effect of their relative liking for alternatives, a gap which, however, was reduced again in subsequent periods of observation. Ten of 26 Dms (38 per cent) exhibited no change whatever in their reported liking differentials in the observation periods following choice. The remaining five exhibited post-choice dissonance *expansion*, i.e. they narrowed down their liking differential between alternatives after they had made their decision.

In summary, the six decision process hypotheses described above were supported rather convincingly by the data in our longitudinal prediction study.

Chief implications for a theory

Below are some of our study's more central implications for decision theory, which may not be obvious from the above, severely summarized report of our findings.

First, scalar utility theory is a poor way of representing the structure of human values. Decision value attributes are usually multidimensional; they are not compared or substituted for each other during choice. No stable utility weighting function can be elicited from a decision maker prior to his selection of a preferred alternative, nor do such weights appear to enter into each person's decision processing. His non-comparison of goal attributes during the alternatives screening and selection phase also obviates the decision maker's need for, and the reasonableness of our postulating the existence of, a multidimensional utility indifference map.

Second, probability theory, either in its objective frequency or personal estimate Bayesian form, does not provide adequate representation of how our decision makers perceived and dealt with uncertainty during their unprogrammed decision making. The "probability" indices with which our highly trained decision makers provided us were neither additive nor cardinally scaled. It seems that a decision maker does not normally think of his choice alternatives in terms of multiple consequences, each of which is then seen to depend conditionally on a specific reaction to his decision by the task environment. Instead he thinks of each choice alternative in terms of a set of non-comparable goal attributes. Uncertainty in this context is more appropriately represented in terms of equally likely *ranges* of a specific alternative's rating along its various uncertain goal attributes. In other words decision uncertainty rarely takes the form of a "pure" or probability-risk *consequence* uncertainty. More commonly, uncertainty – a non-additive quantity – is associated with the decision maker's personal evaluation of an alternative's uncertain attributes.

The mathematics of how most decision makers compare such multiple-attribute uncertainty-ranged alternatives is quite simple, but unfortunately would take too much space to illustrate here.[14] By the same token of limited rationality, one might argue that it is the simplicity of Dm's information processing computations that effectively prevents him from operating with the *m* conditional probability distributions for each alternative which, according to distributive probability theory, the decision maker *should* be associating with each multiconsequence, multivalued alternative.

Third, search for alternatives is a parallel process, i.e. several potentially acceptable alternatives are considered by the decision maker at one time. This contrasts with the hypothesis of sequential search aspiration level models. In addition, a subject's evaluation of an alternative is a multistage affair; at each step new information is collected and evaluated about a subset of attributes of the given alternative. In other words, search *within* alternatives is as important a process for us to understand formally as the traditionally described search *across* alternatives.

During the search phase the decision maker does not view his evaluation of alternatives as final. Alternatives that fall short on important goal attributes are rejected immediately. But acceptable alternatives are merely put into the decision maker's "active roster," with little or no systematic comparison performed across the different acceptable alternatives, until the person is ready to make his final decision. In other words, the decision maker may well continue to search for new alternatives, even though he has already discovered a perfectly satisfactory one (one that was not rejected by any of his important goal attributes).

Fourth, making the final decision, what we have called decision confirmation, takes place *after* the decision maker has terminated search for new alternatives. This appears to be a highly involved and affectively a most painful process for a person to engage in. This is the period during which the decision maker has to reject alternatives that seem perfectly satisfactory to him, in some ways perhaps better than the one he finally ends up choosing. It is at this point that the decision maker is forced systematically to *compare* patently non-comparable alternatives.

It is a major thesis of this study that persons generally solve this problem in the simplest manner conceivable, by not entering into this difficult period of decision making until one of the alternatives can be identified as an implicit "favorite." In other words, decision making during its confirmation phase is an *exercise in prejudice*, of making sure that one's implicit favorite will indeed be the "right" choice. This proposition gives the key to a surprising degree of predictability in decision making, demonstrated with the data of Hypothesis 5 above, in which we predicted 87 per cent of the career jobs taken two to eight weeks before the decision makers would admit that they had reached a decision.

It is not feasible here to go into detail regarding the nature of confirmation processing,[15] yet the following are some of its more outstanding characteristics:

The criteria that the decision maker uses for identifying his favorite alternative are very few; not more than one or two of what we have called *prime* goal attributes account for most of the observed variance.

The decision maker's comparison among alternatives quickly reduces to a pro-con argument between two, and only two alternatives (see Hypothesis 4), the object of the decision maker being to bring his perception of the facts, and his evaluation of goal attributes, into line with his predisposition that the preferred choice candidate dominates his second-best alternative (which we call the confirmation candidate) on all important goal attributes, secondary and primary.

The decision maker finally makes his decision when he has constructed a satisfactory decision rule – a goal weighting function, if you please – that enables him to *explain* the Pareto dominance of his choice candidate (unless, of course, the decision maker is forced by some deadline to make his decision before that time. If so, he will still choose his choice candidate, but with much more expressed uncertainty about the "rightness" of his decision).

Fifth, dissonance reduction, in the sense that it has been described by Leon Festinger,[16] must be viewed as a conditional phenomenon. In a loose sense, confirmation processing might be viewed as part of the decision maker's "dissonance reduction" process. But according to Festinger, the onset of dissonance reduction awaits the decision maker's *commitment* to his choice, which in our data is synonymous with the point of the person's choice announcement. In this study dissonance reduction after that point in time was observed in only 35 per cent of the cases; in all of them the effect dissipated during subsequent periods of observations.

We propose as a testable explanation of our observations: Post-choice dissonance reduction will be observed only when the person, at the time of choice commitment, is not satisfied with his confirmation decision rule – i.e. with the intellectual rationale for why he chose the way he did. Thus

127

dissonance reduction constitutes an *affective* compensation on the part of the decision maker for his lack of a socially acceptable, cognitive justification for his behavior.

This hypothesis also explains the observed second-order dissonance reduction effect: With time we expect all men to be able to invent better and better rationales for why they behaved as they did. Correspondingly, we should observe that any initial affective (dissonance reduction) compensation, with which a person first may be protecting his decision, will be dissolved over time as his intellectual argument gets better.

Implications for management practice

Let us conclude by considering briefly some lessons of these findings for management. The reader can surely think of some other implications; nevertheless, here are a few obvious ones:

1. Our generalizable decision process model (GDP-I) should help a manager to recognize when others have reached an implicit decision, i.e. when they are merely confirming their favorite alternative. Such knowledge should enable managers not to waste time or resources or lose face by remaining party to a choice process that for most purposes has already been closed. This lesson should be particularly useful in situations where a manager or his company has been cast in the role of "confirmation candidate" by the decision maker.[17]
2. The existence of a confirmation process that goes into effect prior to public choice commitment emphasizes the desirability of getting one's alternatives into the decision process early. On bids for government research and development contracts, for example, Edward Roberts has uncovered evidence that a bidding company needs to get in there well before the official invitation to bid on a contract has left the government agency – that at this time one can predict with disturbing success which firm will get the contract, simply by looking at the order of names on the list of those invited to bid.[18]
3. The confirmation process also suggests a way of manipulating decision deadlines in a manager's favor. If he has evidence that his company happens to be his adversary's favorite alternative, the manager can safely clinch the deal by imposing a stringent deadline on decision making, trust to dissonance reduction to carry the day, and save himself time, needless anxiety, and the risk of that rare alternative arriving on the decision maker's horizon in time to upset the apple cart.
4. The existence of the confirmation process also explains the often observed asymmetry of administrative decision making. Once made, decisions are usually very hard to unmake, or to get remade. A most obvious explanation of this is that a manager balks at having to go

through all the pain of changing his tailor-made decision rule to fit a new pair of alternatives. (That *might* sound too much like "rationalizing," and thus go against the grain of men who like to think of themselves as orderly, rational decision makers.) Besides, the decision rule offers ready arguments, in *m* dimensions, why few alternatives can be expected to be as good as the chosen one. And these arguments get themselves strengthened and elaborated as time passes – partly through the self-fulfilling prophecy which will bias all future interactions between a manager and his rejected versus accepted alternatives.

The implication for action is that a manager must "watch" his own subsequent interactions with a rejected alternative, such as a subordinate he has not promoted, in order to avoid setting up self-fulfilling chains of interactions between himself and the rejectee. Similarly, the latter should take the manager's post-choice prejudices somewhat "philosophically," and not see the latter's behaviors as necessarily reflecting a personalized form of beastliness.

5. Our description of the nature of the confirmation process also offers a complementary explanation of the observed difficulty of changing people's cognitive attitudes. As soon as the manager is successful in winning a battle on one secondary point in the decision maker's rule, the latter will quickly mend his breach, either by pooh-poohing that particular goal attribute, or by countering with a compensating argument along some other goal dimension. Only if the manager can zero in on the decision maker's *primary* goal attributes (often carried around in a person's head quite inaccessibly, in the form of some uncommunicable existentialist "feel" for the problem situation), can the manager hope to change a person's decision behavior. Even then, the manager faces the difficult task of demonstrating convincingly to his opponent that this person's old favorite is indeed dominated by the manager's own favorite alternative. (This proposition might, incidentally, help explain why public debates are so ineffective as a means of changing anyone's political allegiance or voting behavior.)

Improvement of management decision

This study has implications for how management decision making might be improved. Three of these implications are given below:

1. A manager should work on integrating his formal models of rational decision making with his intuitive, judgmental, common sense manner of solving choice problems and seek to adapt the former to fit the latter, rather than submit to a bastardization of his intuition in the name of some modern mathematical technique. Mechanical aids to management decision, like computer-based management information systems, will

(and should) be resisted to the extent that their structure is incompatible either with the manner in which a manager codes relevant information for his own use, or the manner in which the manager intuitively feels that information should be reduced for arriving at a decision.

To be more specific, a formal goal attribute weighting scheme, an imposed set of operating decision rules, or an explicit framework for estimating and operating with personal probabilities, will be circumvented by reasonable managers, we hypothesize, to the extent that the area in which the technique is to be applied has not been carefully chosen to match the structure of the decision maker's intuitive (culturally learned) process of working through multivalued and uncertain decision alternatives. This is *not* to say, however, that a manager should not try to educate his personal decision-making judgment, although the question of which are the more effective techniques for accomplishing this remains a hotly debated issue in our schools of management. We would recommend that a major part of the manager's initial effort in this regard be directed toward a more explicit understanding of his personal processes of exercising managerial judgment in a variety of decision situations.

2. One way that a manager might start training himself to make better decisions would be to become more aware of his personal predispositions and prejudices (i.e. of his prime goals) when operating in different task contexts. Rapid feedback regarding his apparent decision behavior from people whom the manager trusts and respects should be of much aid in that regard. The attempt to avoid forming opinions early about complex sets of alternatives seems from anecdotal evidence to create an uncomfortable state of tension in most people. Perhaps the manager might try devising private "holding" heuristics to allow "sufficient" unbiased information about his available alternatives to be collected, and to prevent him from modifying his decision criteria until he has reached an explicit decision to start doing so. (A counter-argument, which we do not advocate, is that decision making and action taking under time pressure is so difficult to get accomplished under any circumstances, that a manager needs to use all the short-cuts and tension-reducing rules of thumb that he can devise, just to make a decision, even if in some cases such heuristics will lead him to very biased solutions.)

3. Our theory leads us to expect that different managers will exhibit different degrees of the tendency to commit themselves to alternatives early in the decision process. Perhaps such a predisposition could be effectively counteracted simply by pointing out to a manager that this is the way he tends to operate. But perhaps the characteristic is sufficiently difficult or expensive to change that we should consider developing standard laboratory testing problems to help screen out of

critical managerial positions those persons who too early, on too meager evidence, jump to conclusions about solutions to complex problems.

Notes

1 The second proposition parallels the now familiar argument regarding why engineers ought to know the science underlying their engineering rules of thumb. The less validated the engineering principles are, the more an engineer needs to understand the science on which his practice rests.
2 See [5], pp. 169–182.
3 See [2].
4 It is of interest to note that, prior to Clarkson's study, the trust officer also felt that his investment decisions were highly unprogrammed and "judgmental."
5 See [1].
6 See [7], pp. 200–278.
7 See [8], [9], [11], [12] and [13].
8 See [10].
9 The process framework is described in greater detail in [14].
10 Problem recognition for the decision maker may arise from: (1) the discovery of a barrier to progress toward an objective, (2) a request from others within the organization, (3) a performance indicator dropping below a target level, (4) perception of a previously "coded problem" pattern. Problem definition for the decision maker may take these forms: (1) a description of differences between status and goal along one or more attributes, (2) a description of strategy associated with a previously encountered problem with a similar stimulus configuration, (3) a prescription of an ideal solution to the encountered problem.
11 This phase of decision making, usually critical for practical purposes, is customarily left out of formal decision models (the consequences of which operations research consultants have had to discover the hard way).
12 See [4].
13 See [14], Chapter III.
14 See [14], Chapter VI.
15 See [14], Chapter III.
16 See [3].
17 As the IMR was going to press the author received the following letter from the chairman of the department of management of a large eastern university. "It may interest you to know that we used the results of your study in our faculty recruiting this year. If a prospective faculty member selects you as number one, there is little you have to do. If he selects you as number two, however, there is little you can do to change this. I found that people who had us as number one on their lists were quite willing to provide a number of clues to the effect that they would be willing to join us. On the other hand, those who saw fit not to join our faculty, were, in general, quite non-committal about their intentions. It is on this basis that I made my predictions as to whether we were number one or at some lower ranking in the applicant's mind. This model worked perfectly."
18 See [6].

References

1 Arrow, K. J. "Utility, Attitudes, Choices: A Review Note," *Econometrica*, 1958, pp. 1–23.

2 Clarkson, G. P. E. *Portfolio Selection: A Simulation of Trust Investment.* Englewood Cliffs, N.J.: Prentice-Hall, 1962.

3 Festinger, L. *Conflict, Choice and Dissonance Reduction.* Stanford University Press, 1964.

4 Forrester, J. A. *Industrial Dynamics.* New York: John Wiley & Sons, Inc., 1961.

5 March, J. G. and Simon, H. A. *Organizations.* New York: John Wiley & Sons, Inc., 1958.

6 Roberts, E. B. "Questioning the Cost/Effectiveness of the R & D Procurement Process," in M. Yovits *et al.* (eds.), *Research Program Effectiveness.* New York: Gordon and Breach, 1966.

7 Rothenberg, J. F. *The Measurement of Social Welfare.* Englewood Cliffs, N.J.: Prentice-Hall, 1961.

8 Simon, H. A. *Administrative Behavior.* New York: MacMillan, 1947.

9 ——. *Models of Man.* New York: John Wiley & Sons, Inc., 1957.

10 ——. *New Science of Management Decision.* New York: Harper, 1966.

11 ——. "Theories of Decision Making in Economics and Behavioral Science," *American Economic Review*, XLIX (1959), pp. 255–283.

12 ——. *The Shape of Automation.* New York: Harper, 1966.

13 ——. Newell, A. and Shaw, J. C. "Elements of a Theory of Human Problem Solving," *Psychological Review*, LXV (1958), pp. 151–166.

14 Soelberg, P. *A Study of Decision Making: Job Choice.* Cambridge, Mass: MIT, 1966.

55

SIMON'S AND SIEGEL'S RESPONSES TO THE 'MIXED STRATEGY ANOMALY'

A missed case in the sensitivity of economics to empirical evidence

Timo Tammi*

Source: *Cambridge Journal of Economics*, 27:1 (2003), 85–96.

In some of their papers published in the 1950s, Herbert Simon and Sidney Siegel responded to the so-called mixed strategy anomaly in ways which deserve more attention. They produced not only (i) immediate defences of the economic theory of their own time, but also (ii) ideas and solutions that have later turned out to be significant contributions to the development of the economic theory of choice and decision-making and the separation of experimental economics from experimental psychology. These observations suggest that economics can be more responsive to empirical anomalies than has been assumed. Furthermore, knowledge of the desirable responsiveness to anomalies can provide means of avoiding the non-desirable immunity to anomalies.

The official rhetoric of economics places considerable emphasis on the sensitivity of theories and theorising to relevant items of empirical evidence. One manifestation of such sensitivity is a responsiveness to empirical

* Two anonymous referees are thanked for their helpful comments on an earlier draft of this paper. The research has been supported financially by the Academy of Finland.

anomalies and to apparent empirical disconfirmations. Many reports show, however, that economists do not pay adequate attention to anomalies and disconfirming empirical data.[1] Although some scholars (see Backhouse 1997, pp. 205–15; Goldfarb 1995, 1997; Smithin, 1995) have gone beyond the official rhetoric and its failure to analyse how economics really maintains its sensitivity, there are gaps in our knowledge of the responsiveness of economics to anomalies, This kind of gap can easily bias our understanding of economics as a scientific discipline.

The empirical performance of economics is one of the questions addressed in Hausman and Mongin's (1997) study of the full-cost pricing controversy and of research into the phenomenon of preference reversal (see also Hausman, 1991, 1992, ch. 13; Mongin, 1992). Their study was motivated by the fact that responses to empirical anomalies are central in assessing the scientific status of economics and that the philosophy of science does not seem to provide adequate guidance to the ways in which economists ought to respond to such anomalies. On the basis of their case studies, Hausman and Mongin conclude that 'the fact that conventional economics tends to ignore past anomalies points, we think, to a failure of economics as a science rather than a failure of philosophy of science to advise economists' (1997, p. 270).

The present paper focuses on a case which deviates from Hausman and Mongin's conclusion. First, it describes an episode in the 1950s in which two *versatile social scientists*—Herbert Simon and Sidney Siegel—responded to a psychological anomaly in economic theory by producing solutions which were both (i) immediate defences of the economic theory of the day and (ii) sources of eventual progress in economics. Second, the present study accentuates the importance of carrying out detailed investigations into the impacts of anomalies on economics. It seems that the length of the interval between the appearance of the anomaly and the consequences of it is the key to a better understanding of the role of anomalies in economics.

The case in point is the debate over the results of numerous psychological Bernoulli-choice experiments throughout the 1940s and 1950s. The so-called 'mixed strategy anomaly' (known also as the 'probability matching puzzle') resulted from the fact that, in experiments, subjects adopted a mixed strategy (splitting one's predictions in some proportion), although the von Neumann–Morgenstern-type economic theory, which appeared in the 1940s, predicted that subjects would adopt a pure strategy (consistently predicting the more frequent alternative). The anomaly also emerged at the multidisciplinary Santa Monica seminar in 1952, and it stimulated further debate in the 1950s. The actual responses which later had some influence on economics were, however, provided by Simon and Siegel, whose connections with economics were somewhat unusual. Simon received his PhD in political science in 1943 but worked during the 1940s and 1950s on several projects to do with mathematical economics and econometrics, organisational decision-making and cognitive psychology. Siegel, on the other hand, received his PhD in psychology in 1953 and worked—again in collaboration with economists—during the 1950s on individual decision-making and non-parametric statistics for social sciences. Simon's and Siegel's various responses together form a set of solutions and ideas. First, both produced different solutions to accommodate the anomaly as part of the economic theory of that time. Second, Simon applied his earlier distinction between subjective and objective rationality to a game-theoretic environment. Third, Siegel developed this distinction in a direction which contributed to (i) the formulation of the methodological requirements of an economically meaningful experiment, and also to (ii) the formalisation of a decision-cost theory which could serve as an auxiliary theory within a utility theoretical framework.

1. The appearance of the anomaly

1.1 On the 'psychology question' and the 'stir' behind the Santa Monica conference

In economics, the first half of the twentieth century was a period of increasing formalisation. One of the important features in the formalisation was the increased interaction between mathematicians and economists. A case in point was von Neumann and Morgenstern's co-authored work *Theory of Games and Economic Behavior* (1944/1947). The work indicated a step backward to the cardinal utility approach, since it provided an axiomatic system and the conclusion that, whenever axioms hold true, people will behave in a way which facilitates the maximisation of the expected interval-scale utility. The work included an indication of how one can construct cardinal utilities on the basis of preferences among gambles. This was subsequently made operational by Friedman and Savage (1948).

Previous debate between economists and psychologists in the early decades of the twentieth century had resulted in the elimination of psychological hedonism from economic theory (see Coats, 1976; Lewin, 1996, p. 1310). This shift to an ordinalist interpretation of preferences (without reference to pleasures) was accompanied by even stronger efforts on the part of Samuelson (1948) and Houthakker (1950) to render economics totally independent of psychology and the theoretical notion of utility. There were, however, some important exceptions to this anti-psychological trend in economics in the middle decades of the century. First, as already stated, the rise of the expected utility approach involved a step back toward the cardinalist theory of preferences. Second, psychologists did not suspend their critical exploration of economic theory. As Lewin (1996, p. 1315) points out, numerous psychologists made attempts to derive utility functions experimentally during the 1930s and expected utility functions in the 1940s and 1950s. As a response to these activities—in particular, to the work by Thurstone (1931)—

Wallis and Friedman (1942) pointed to the absence of the kind of control and motivation that could be expected to be characteristic of an experiment in economics. Some experiments consisted of attempts to incorporate economic incentives in decision-making experiments (see Rousseas and Hart, 1951; Mosteller and Nogee, 1951). Third, in an invited paper published in the *American Economic Review* in 1959, Simon reviewed the psychologically inspired investigation into decision-making and business behaviour and also the new ideas of cognitive psychology and artificial intelligence having relevance for economics (Simon, 1959).

From the point of view of decision-making theory and the development of experimental economics, two important conferences were organised in 1952. One was the Santa Monica conference, which is described immediately below. The other was the Paris conference, where the participants were presented with the famous Allais paradox for the first time. Both conferences have turned out to have had a considerable influence on the development of utility theory and decision-making theories (for a discussion of the role played by the Paris conference, see Guala, 2000).

The Santa Monica conference was organised in order to increase the formalisation and mathematisation of the social sciences, and not only the conference organisers but also its participants were well established and influential in their field. The original proposal to stage the conference was made by the University of Michigan, and it was further supported by the Ford Foundation, the Office for Naval Research, the RAND Corporation and the Cowles Commission (Thrall *et al.*, 1954, p. v). Amongst the contributors were the economists Debreu, Hildreth, Koopmans, Marschak, Morgenstern and Radner, the psychologists Bush, Coombs and Estes, the mathematicians Karlin, Nash, Shapley and von Neumann, and the statisticians/decision theorists Mosteller and Raiffa (pp. 329, 331). Simon, who also attended the conference, describes the general atmosphere of the conference in the following way:

> I believe that the 1952 Santa Monica conference came out of the general stir about the whole range of things that was then sometimes put under the label of cybernetics. RAND was at the centre of that stir, and just about everyone involved had close connections with the RAND group and/or the Cowles Commission. This was a response not only to the von Neumann and Morgenstern [von Neumann and Morgenstern (1944)] (which was itself a response to these developments), but to the whole postwar interest in the applications of mathematics to human affairs—which encompassed computers, servomechanism theory, information theory, mathematical economics, mathematical learning theory, game theory, brain architecture, robots, and operations research (I am sure I have omitted some items). To the extent that some of the

people interested in these matters had backgrounds in various areas of empirical science, they brought empirical techniques, including experimentation, into the picture.

(Simon in Smith, 1992, pp. 254–5)

In other words, several 'intellectual programmes' in their early stages (game theory, expected utility, psychology vs economics, decision theory, experimental economics) had their own individual but related cognitive agendas. At the time, Simon himself was interested in decision-making and in the mathematising of the social sciences. He was particularly interested in game theory and rationality, but was not directly involved in experimentation in those areas. In the latter half of the 1940s, he also participated in the Cowles Commission seminars (along with economists) and began work as a consultant with the Rand Corporation (see ch. 9–11 in Simon, 1991). Sidney Siegel, on the other hand, was a key figure in the incorporation of experimentation into economics. As Smith's (1992) brief interview material (including his own remarks) shows, early contributors to experimental economics such as Shubik, Smith and (James) Friedman were influenced by the ideas which Siegel put forward in private conversations and also in the works which he co-authored with Fouraker on bargaining and group decision-making. In a sense, then, Simon and Siegel were acting in environments where they were encouraged to promote their own agendas and where there were audiences to whom they could address their results.[2]

1.2 The appearance of the anomaly at the Santa Monica conference

The mixed strategy anomaly (hereafter MSA) first appeared at the Santa Monica conference when William Estes, a psychologist, presented his own version of what was known as a psychological asymptotic learning theory. The theory was supported by evidence gathered from numerous Bernoulli-choice experiments. Estes's presentation was followed by the game theorists' critical—but only oral—reaction to the results of the experiments. Merrill Flood responded to the criticism by clarifying the nature of the disagreement. Estes's (1954) and Flood's (1954) papers were subsequently published in the Thrall et al. (1954) conference proceedings.

The Estes model of learning applies to a binary choice situation where an individual attempts to predict which of the alternative outcomes will occur when the actual sequence of occurrences is random. The model suggests that individuals' predictions converge towards the true probabilities of the outcomes. Accordingly, in a Bernoulli-choice experiment a subject chooses between A_1 and A_2 which are associated with events E_1 and E_2. If the subject chooses A_i and the event E_i occurs, he is rewarded with probability π_i.

137

The data collected in previous Bernoulli-choice experiments and in Estes's own experiments supported the predictions of the model. In particular, Estes underlined the difference between the predictions of learning theory and utility theory. For example, in a case where $\pi_1 = 0.25$ and $\pi_2 = 0.75$, the Estes model predicts that an individual will settle down at a relatively steady level where they predict E_1 in 25% and E_2 in 75% of the trials. This yields an expectation of $0.25(0.25) + 0.75(0.75) = 62.5\%$ correct predictions, whereas the 'pure strategy' in the expected utility sense (predicting the more frequent event in all trials) would yield an expectation of $0(0.25) + 1.0(0.75) = 75\%$ correct predictions. Thus, Estes (p. 136) concluded that 'in a simple decision process the human subjects tend to behave in accordance with the principles of associative learning and not, in general, in the most rational manner as "rational" is conventionally defined'.

It is reported by Flood (1954, pp. 287, 289), Davis (1954, pp. 10, 17), and Simon (1956A, p. 267) that Estes's presentation gave rise to a certain amount of discussion at the conference. First, the game theorists argued that the behaviour observed by Estes was irrational, since only a pure strategy (always predicting the more frequent alternative) would maximise the expected utility. Flood then presented two objections to the arguments put forward by the game theorists. First, a Bernoulli-choice type situation would not serve as the application of a game-theoretic analysis, since an individual would always use a mixed strategy. This is obvious, after all, since, when an individual aims at achieving a perfect score, say, in a (90;10) experiment, the only way actually to achieve that perfect score would be to choose E_1 90% of the time and E_2 10% of the time (Flood, 1954, p. 288). Secondly, Flood argued that a game-theoretic analysis would be inapplicable as long as the individual is not convinced that the experimental stimulus is generated by a stationary stochastic process. This will turn out to be the case since, when the individual believes that there is a predictable pattern, it is obvious that s/he has concluded that a pure strategy would provide no way of discovering the pattern (*ibid.*).

2. The second wave: Simon's and Siegel's responses to the anomaly

Three papers produced by Simon in the 1950s are more or less directly related to MSA. In Simon (1955), he presents definitions of 'approximate' rationality which are less demanding than 'the global rationality of Economic Man'. Following this, Simon (1956B) cites the Thrall *et al.* (1954) conference volume as an instance of the growing interest in decision-making. In particular, this paper makes the distinction between 'satisficing' and 'optimising', and it suggests that more attention should be paid to perception and cognition in constructing a theory of decision-making. Simon (1956A) is then a direct response to the discussions held at the Santa Monica conference:

In order to gain a better understanding of the concept of *rationality* underlying these two bodies of theory [game theory and learning theory], it would be interesting to construct a situation in which predictions made from these theories could be compared and then checked against experimental data on actual behavior. One situation of this kind received considerable attention at the Santa Monica Conference on Decision Processes [references omitted]. The experiment is one involving partial reinforcement [the Bernoulli-trial experiment] ... Estes reports several experiments that confirm predictions from his theory.

When this experimental situation was described to a number of game theorists at the Santa Monica conference, they pointed out that a *rational* individual would first estimate, by experimenting, which of the two alternatives had the greatest probability of reward, and would subsequently always select that alternative which would not be predicted by the Estes theory.

(pp. 267–8)

Simon then provides a game-theoretical derivation of Estes's results by including certain assumptions and by excluding others. As stated in the Estes model, π_1 is the probability that A_1 will be rewarded (note that this means a psychic reward for a successful trial) and π_2 is the probability that A_2 will be rewarded. The point is that Estes assumes that the reward probabilities are not known to the individual and not known to be variable; in fact, individuals are not informed that the sequences they face are random (Estes, 1954, p. 127). Simon replaces these assumptions with the following (Simon, 1956A, p. 269):

(i)   The subject takes as given and fixed the π corresponding to the alternative he has chosen on the last trial. That is, he assumes the probability of reward to be π_1 or π_2, if he persists in choosing again A_1 or A_2, as the case may be.

(ii) The subject expects that if he *shifts* from the alternative just chosen to the other one, the probability of reward is unknown and dependent on a strategy of nature.

(iii) The subject does not wish to persist in his present behavior if there is a good chance of increased reward from shifting. He measures his success on each trial not from the reward received, but from the difference between the reward actually received and the reward that *could* have been attained if he had outguessed nature. In the terminology of L. J. Savage, he wishes to minimise his *regret*.

On the basis of these assumptions Simon then constructs the interpretation that the behaviour predicted by the Estes model is identical with the behaviour of a rational individual aiming at 'minimaxing' her regret (p. 271). However, Simon points out that the actual lesson to be learnt from the analysis is the distinction to be made between subjective rationality and objective rationality: the former refers to behaviour that is rational in terms of the perceptual and evaluative premises of the individual, while the latter refers to behaviour that is rational 'as viewed by the experimenter' (p. 271). In particular:

> To the experimenter who knows that the rewards attached to the two behaviors A_1 and A_2 are random, with constant probabilities, it appears unreasonable that the subject should not learn to behave in such a way as to maximise this expected gain—always to choose A_1. To the subject who perceives the situation as one in which the probabilities may change, and who is more intent on outwitting the experimenter (or nature) than on maximising expected gain, rationality is something quite different.
>
> (*Ibid.*)

In responding to the mixed strategy anomaly, Siegel focused on the utilities which he saw as inherent in the tasks which subjects performed in the Bernoulli-choice experiments. He constructed a theoretical model on the basis of this insight and conducted a series of experiments to test the model and to stimulate its development. This research was reported in four papers (Siegel, 1959, 1961; Siegel and Goldstein, 1959; Siegel and Andrews, 1962). The following passage describes his approach:

> It is reasonable to suppose that when a person is in a situation in which the only payoff attached to the outcomes is the satisfaction of having his prediction confirmed by the event or the dissatisfaction of having his prediction disconfirmed by it, making a correct prediction of the rarer event has greater utility for the person than making a correct prediction of the more frequent event. The person derives satisfaction from playing a game with the machine, trying to outwit it. Moreover, there is the matter of monotony, both kinesthetic and cognitive: predicting the more frequent event on all trials would engender the monotony of pressing the same button . . . in trial after trial for hundreds of trials, in addition to the monotony of the same cognitive response (e.g., left light) in trial after trial. Under such circumstances, a subject may maximise the expected utility by matching his response ratio to the actual probabilities of the occurrence of the two events. For him, the cost of an incorrect prediction is very low, whereas the gain from this strategy in terms of other utilities, such as the utility of gambling and the utility of variability, may be relatively high. By choosing a mixed

strategy (i.e., splitting his predictions in some proportion), such a subject may maximize his own total satisfaction. If such an account is correct, then a decision-making model and the Estes model could yield the same predictions concerning the stable state (asymptotic) behavior of a person in a two-choice no payoff situation.

(Siegel, 1959, pp. 305–6)

This passage outlines the basic idea in Siegel's (pp. 306–13) derivation of the model as capable of accounting for different sources of utility. One version of the model involves the utility of predicting correctly and the utility of varying one's responses (or relieving monotony). In addition, the second version of the model involves the utility of gambling (which the first version assumes to be negligible in its effect, since for some people the utility of gambling is positive while for others it is negative). The third version differs from first two in that (i) the model involves the utility of 'reflecting' or 'reproducing,' in some manner, the information within the event system and (ii) the model ignores the utility of varying responses and of gambling.

The first model provides simple predictions and is assessed in the light of experimental data. Its main point is that, when the marginal utility of a correct prediction equals the marginal utility of varying one's responses, the first model produces the same prediction as the Estes model (pp. 307–8). In contrast, if monetary rewards or costs are added to the outcomes (which was not done in the previous experiments) and if, therefore, the utility of a correct prediction increases or the negative utility of an incorrect prediction increases, then the predictions diverge from the Estes model (p. 308). An experiment was set up under the following three conditions (p. 314): (1) *no payoff*: a psychic reward for being correct (or the costs of being wrong); (2) *reward*: a psychic reward/cost and a monetary reward consisting of receiving five cents for each correct prediction; (3) *risk*: a psychic reward/cost and a monetary reward (as above) or cost consisting of the loss of five cents for each incorrect prediction.

Siegel's hypothesis is that the probability of predicting the more frequent event tends towards unity when the rewards and costs of correct and incorrect predictions are increased. In other words: p^* (no payoff) < p^* (reward) < p^* (risk). In the experiment where $\pi = 0.70$ the mean observed values were the following: 0.70 (no payoff); 0.77 (reward); 0.93 (risk). The increase in the utilities/disutilities, as a consequence of the incorporation of monetary rewards and costs, influences the behaviour of the individual in the Bernoulli-choice experiment.

To sum up, Siegel holds that people do not maximise the expected number of correct predictions precisely because they maximise their total utility in a situation where the disutility of an incorrect prediction is very low and the utilities of gambling and variability may be very high. In this case, both the Siegel model and the Estes model would yield the same predictions. On the other hand, if monetary rewards or cost are attached to the outcomes, then the utility of predicting correctly or the disutility of predicting incorrectly may dominate over other utilities. This means that an individual may adopt the pure strategy predicted by game theory.

3. On the impacts of MSA upon economics

In responding to MSA and in commenting on its broader significance, Simon and Siegel produced a number of solutions and ideas, some of which can be regarded as *conventional solutions* to the anomaly (since they were defences of economic theory in the 1950s). Another group of the solutions and ideas was *non-conventional* in the sense that they were not adopted by the mainstream economics of the day. These non-conventional results have, however, later exerted an influence both on the interaction between economics and psychology and on the present-day nature of experimental economics. Moreover, these influences are related to some of the major questions of economics, such as the extension of a utility theoretical framework and the construction of an alternative to expected utility theory (EUT).

The non-conventional solutions and ideas are related to the deeper questions of the notion of rationality in economics. One way to put the distinction between subjective and objective rationality is to say that, as far as one can demand that EUT should describe actual decision-making behaviour, objective rationality of the kind recognised by economic theorists and experimentalists is incomplete and requires modification. Hence, perhaps, it would seem that an auxiliary theory could complete EUT and link subjective rationality to objective rationality. However, psychologists have not attempted to complement EUT but have pointed to the necessity of a new theory. In consequence, by focusing on the 'elaborate and detailed picture of the rational actor's cognitive processes' (Simon, 1959, p. 272), more evidence was produced against EUT. A well-known alternative to EUT which pays attention to the details of the cognitive processes is Kahneman and Tversky's (1979) prospect theory. This line of research conducted by psychologists—and also another, known as behavioural economics (see Yang and Lester, 1995, Loewenstein, 1999)—has built on Simon's rather than Siegel's ideas.[3]

Not surprisingly, it becomes apparent that Siegel's decision-cost approach came closer to mainstream economics than Simon's approach. Siegel's contribution can be interpreted as an effort to expand the utility theoretical framework by converting the restrictive assumption of negligible decision costs into a formal model of how the level of decision costs impact upon an individual's behaviour. Thus, in this way, and at the same time by relying on the established practice of developing 'logico-mathematical theories' (see Musgrave, 1981, p. 383), objective rationality has been supplemented with subjective rationality by staying within the expected utility framework.

A methodological reading of Siegel's works is also applicable. Through this kind of reading, Siegel's analysis serves as an example of how to introduce monetary incentives to make a decision-making experiment economically meaningful. The established current textbook characterisation for good practice in experimental economics quite clearly reflects Siegel's ideas: (i) subjects should perceive the relationship between available decisions and the payoff outcomes connected with them, and (ii) the rewards must be high enough to overcome the subjective costs of decision-making (see Davis and Holt, 1993, pp. 24–5). Although the requirement of salient monetary rewards is well established among experimental economists, the exact magnitudes of the rewards and the proper structure of the reward system have come in for intensive discussion (see Harrison, 1989, and the subsequent debate involving Merlo and Schotter, 1992; Friedman, 1992; and Harrison, 1992; see also Tammi, 1999). With no exaggeration, it can, however, be argued that Siegel's experiments were among the first to use monetary rewards to control the influence of the disturbing factors in an experiment.

The most prominent advocate of Siegel's ideas has been Vernon Smith. Smith (1976, p. 276) credits Siegel (1961) with demonstrating the methodological aspect of decision costs, while Smith (1978) states the need for an auxiliary theory of decision costs to supplement the utility theoretical framework. He also credits Siegel (1961) with showing the inadequacy of both traditional utility theory (without decision costs) and the psychologists' non-utilitarian theories, and for demonstrating the explanatory power of utility theory when it is extended to include decision costs (Smith, 1978, p. 76). Siegel's pioneering work is also mentioned in Smith's later contributions (Smith, 1982, 1991) and also in Friedman and Sunder's (1994) textbook account of the separation of experimental economics from experimental psychology. Finally, Smith and Walker (1993) have presented a formalised auxiliary theory of decision costs—or the labour theory of cognition and decision-making—in order to incorporate costly action into the utility theoretical framework. Their idea has been that the details of a person's cognitive process can be omitted by the introduction of the notion of a balance between the benefits of a better decision and the costs of the decision (p. 260).

4. Broadening the view: the working equipment and institutions of inquiry

It took more than a decade for the new ideas to be adopted by a few economists—on the one hand, there were those interested in promoting experimental economics, and on the other, those who established a group calling themselves behavioural economists (see Yang and Lester, 1995; Loewenstein, 1999). It then took another decade or more before a formalisation of the decision cost theory was presented by Smith and Walker (1993) in a way that was adjustable (but is not generally adjusted) to the present mainstream framework of economic theorising. Parallel examples of the adoption of new ideas over the course of a long and complicated social process are easy to find in economics. The adoption of utility theory, for example, took some three-quarters of a century (Stigler, 1982, pp. 76–7), while a major consequence of the Allais paradox in the early 1950s eventually emerged in the discoveries of the new decision theories in the 1980s (Guala, 2000).

In the case of MSA the delays are understandable. Since the days of Adam Smith, the discipline itself had been regarded as non-experimental and, as Guala (2000, p. 67) explains, the Allais paradox in 1952 shifted the interpretation of expected utility theory from descriptive to normative—in so far as the theory is still descriptive, it describes only an ideal mode of rational behaviour. Not surprisingly, the results presented by Siegel and Simon, which suggested the necessity of reforms in both economic method and economic theorising, were ignored. They were, it may be argued, too costly to incorporate into the mainstream economics of the time. As Smith (1992, p. 277) explains, in the 1960s and 1970s there was little demand for experimental economics and economists' attitudes to experimental methods were critical.

The 1980s, however, saw an increase in both the demand and supply of experimental economics. On the demand side, general equilibrium theory, game theory and voting theory provided rival principles for economic phenomena and microeconomics provided alternative notions of equilibrium. Consequently, experimental economics was seen as an ideal tool for comparing alternative notions and predictions in economics (Friedman and Sunder, 1994, p. 123). In turn, on the supply side, experiments in the 1980s were no longer designed to mimic reality in as many details as possible. Instead, an experiment was seen as a competition between alternative models or theories (Plott, 1991, p. 906). In a sense, then, both economic theorising and experimental economics entered a phase where Simon's and Siegel's ideas gained greater relevance.

Where the consequences of the array of psychological choice anomalies produced by psychologists and responded to by experimental economists during the 1980s and 1990s are concerned, it would seem that these anomalies have given rise to significant consequences. As a review by Starmer (2000) on the development of theories concerned with decision-making under risk shows, psychological anomalies have given rise to a large body of theoretical modifications (for example, of expected utility theory) and also to alternative theories. A number of important lessons have been learned about theory-testing, and we now know more about the limitations of theorising and are, to some extent, more open to non-conventional strategies in theorising (theories formulated without maximising in the traditional sense). All in all, much of this satisfies the requirements of generally approvable scientific conduct: anomalies have helped economists to make discoveries and inventions and to study the scope and limits of economic theory. On the other hand, however, not only the development of the working equipment— a better ability of theories and theorists to incorporate new ideas—but also the institutions of inquiry have a bearing upon the length of the interval between the appearance of an anomaly and its consequences. In an extreme case, the institutions of inquiry, such as funding and publication, can even remove the long-run consequences of anomalies. Consider, for example, research into preference reversals. It has remained in a state of controversy which may make it difficult to exhaust the proper input of research into economic theory. This situation is the result, as Starmer (1999, p. 25) argues, partly of the fact that (1) research funding often goes to research whose solutions are regarded as immediately practical, and also from the fact that (2) professional journals often lose interest in long-drawn-out research which has lost its initial glamour.

5. Conclusion

It is a commonplace that economists are reluctant to respond to empirical anomalies in ways that would contribute to economic theory and theorising. If this supposition is correct, it should be regarded as an admonition at a time when a major part of the development of economics is based on the idea of expanding the domain of economic analysis beyond its traditional disciplinary boundaries—that is, into areas where one can expect economic theory to be repeatedly confronted with new empirical anomalies.

Closer scrutiny of various episodes related to the anomalies of economic theory can help in the rectification of any collective misunderstanding. The detailed study that has been made of the mixed strategy anomaly shows one way in which anomalies have influenced the development of economic theory and theorising. The evidence encourages the suggestion that there may also be other cases where anomalies have helped economists to make discoveries and to study the scope and limits of economic theory. Furthermore, the lessons learned from cases where economists have responded to anomalies in justifiable ways should then be used to criticise the kind of practices which tend to make economic theorising insensitive to empirical anomalies.

A question which deserves more attention is the division of cognitive labour between disciplines and sub-disciplines. Anomalies in economic theory are typically produced by non-economists whose own solutions, although addressed to economics, are difficult to incorporate into economics. Because the consequences of non-conventional solutions are often time consuming and less rewarding (at least in the short run), conventional solutions may precede and dominate in the official discussions (in journals) about anomalies. Furthermore, if research funding and the publication policy of journals favours the study of short-run practical and glamorous questions, the long-run consequences of anomalies can fade away unnoticed.

Notes

1 See, for example Backhouse (1994), Blaug (1980, ch. 15), Caldwell (1982, ch. 12), Hausman (1992, pp. 274–6).
2 Sidney Siegel (1916–61) received his PhD in psychology from Stanford University in 1953. Thereafter he became professor of psychology at Pennsylvania State University. With the economist Lawrence Fouraker, he co-authored two books on bargaining. Herbert Simon received his PhD in political science from the University of Chicago in 1943. Since 1965 he has been professor of computer sciences and psychology at Carnegie Mellon University. He has also been a consultant to the Cowles Commission and Rand Corporation. Amongst his many other awards, he has received the Nobel Prise for Economics in 1978, the American Psychological Foundation Gold Medal Award for Life Achievement in Psychological Science in 1988, and the John Von Neumann Theory Prize in 1988.
3 Indeed, Tversky and Edwards (1966) report on their own probability matching experiment without reference to Siegel. As noted by Smith (1991, p. 889), although Tversky and Edwards found that monetary incentives caused subjects' behaviour to shift closer to the predictions of the expected utility theory, they interpreted the shift to be insignificant. What is more, Tversky and Edwards refer to the possibility of producing a formal model of decision costs. However, an outline of such a model had already been provided by Siegel (1959, 1961), while its formalisation was made much later by Smith and Walker (1993).

Bibliography

Backhouse, R. 1994. The fixation of economic beliefs, *Journal of Economic Methodology*, vol. 1, 33–42

Backhouse, R. 1997. *Truth and Progress in Economic Knowledge*, Cheltenham, Edward Elgar

Blaug, M. 1980. *The Methodology of Economics*, Cambridge, Cambridge University Press

Caldwell, B. 1982. *Beyond Positivism: Economic Methodology in the Twentieth Century*, London, Allen & Unwin

Coats, A. W. 1976. Economics and psychology: the death and resurrection of a research programme, in Latsis, S. (ed.), *Method and Appraisal in Economics*, Cambridge, Cambridge University Press

Davis, R. L. 1954. Introduction, in Thrall, R. M., Coombs, C. H., and Davis, R. L. (eds), *Decision Processes*, New York, John Wiley

Davis, D. D. and Holt, C. A. 1993. *Experimental Economics*, Princeton, NJ, Prineton University Press

Estes, W. K. 1954. Individual behavior in uncertain situations: an interpretation in terms of statistical association theory, in Thrall, R. M., Coombs, C. H. and Davis, R. L. (eds), *Decision Processes*, New York, John Wiley

Flood, M. M. 1954. Environmental non-stationarity in a sequential decision-making experiment, in Thrall, R. M., Coombs, C. H. and Davis, R. L. (eds), *Decision Processes*, New York, John Wiley

Friedman, D. 1992. Theory and misbehavior of first-price auctions: comment, *American Economic Review*, vol. 82, 1374–8

Friedman, D. and Sunder, S. 1994. *Experimental Methods: A Primer for Economists*, Cambridge, Cambridge University Press

Friedman, M. and Savage, L. J. 1948. The utility analysis of choices involving risk, *Journal of Political Economy*, vol. 56, 279–304

Goldfarb, R. 1995. If empirical work in economics is not severe testing, what is it? in Rima, I. H. (ed.), *Measurement, Quantification and Economic Analysis: Numeracy in Economics*, London, Routledge

Goldfarb, R. 1997. Now you see it, now you don't: emerging contrary results in economics, *Journal of Economic Methodology*, vol. 4, 221–44

Guala, F. 2000. The logic of normative falsification: rationality and experiments in decision theory, *Journal of Economic Methodology*, vol. 7, 59–94

Harrison, G. 1989. Theory and misbehavior of first-price auctions, *American Economic Review*, vol. 79, 749–62

Harrison, G. 1992. Theory and misbehavior of first-price auctions: reply, *American Economic Review*, vol. 82, 1426–43

Hausman, D. 1991. On dogmatism in economics: the case of preference reversals, *Journal of Socio-Economics*, vol. 20, 205–55

Hausman, D. 1992. *The Inexact and Separate Science of Economics*, Cambridge, Cambridge University Press

Hausman, D. and Mongin, P. 1997. Economists' responses to anomalies: full cost pricing versus preference reversals, in Davis, J. B. (ed.), *New Economics and Its History* (Annual Supplement to Volume 29, *History of Political Economy*), Durham, NC, Duke University Press

Houthakker, H. S. 1950. Revealed preference and the utility function, *Economica*, vol. 17, 159–74

Kahneman, D. and Tversky, A. 1979. Prospect theory: an analysis of decision under risk, *Econometrica*, vol. 47, 263–91

Lewin, S. B. 1996. Economics and psychology: lessons for our own day from the early twentieth century. *Journal of Economic Literature*, vol. 34, 1293–323

Loewenstein, G. 1999. Experimental economics from the vantage-point of behavioural economics, *The Economic Journal*, vol. 109, F25–34

Merlo, A. and Schotter, A. 1992. Theory and misbehavior of first-price auctions: comment, *American Economic Review*, vol. 92, 1413–25

Mongin, P. 1992. The full-cost controversy of the 1949s and 1950s: a methodological assessment, *History of Political Economy*, vol. 24, 311–56

Mosteller, F. and Nogee, P. 1951. An experimental measurement of utility, *Journal of Political Economy*, vol. 59, 371–404

Musgrave, A. (1981) 'Unreal assumptions' in economic theory: the F-twist untwisted, *Kyklos*, vol. 34, 377–87

Plott, C. 1991. Will economics become an experimental science? *Southern Economic Journal*, vol. 57, 901–19

Rousseas, S. W. and Hart, A. G. 1951. Experimental verification of a composite indifference map, *Journal of Political Economy*, vol. 59, 288–318

Samuelson, P. 1948. Consumption theory in terms of revealed preference, *Economica*, vol. 15, 243–53

Siegel, S. 1959. Theoretical models of choice and strategy behavior: stable state behavior in the two-choice uncertain outcome situation, *Psychometrika*, vol. 24, 303–16

Siegel, S. 1961. Decision making and learning under varying conditions of reinforcement, *Annals of the New York Academy of Science*, vol. 89, 766–83

Siegel, S. and Andrews, J. M. 1962. Magnitude of reinforcement and choice behavior in children, *Journal of Experimental Psychology*, vol. 63, 337–41

Siegel, S. and Goldstein, D. A. 1959. Decision-making behavior in a two-choice uncertain outcome situation, *Journal of Experimental Psychology*, vol. 57, 37–42

Simon, H. 1955. A behavioural model of rational choice, *Quarterly Journal of Economics*, vol. 64, 99–118

Simon, H. 1956A. A comparison of game theory and learning theory, *Psychometrika*, vol. 21, 267–72

Simon, H. 1956B. Rational choice and the structure of the environment, *Psychological Review*, vol. 63, 129–38

Simon, H. 1959. Theories of decision-making in economics and behavioral science, *American Economic Review*, vol. 49, 253–83

Simon, H. 1991. *Models of My Life*, New York, Basic Books

Smith, V. 1976. Experimental economics: Induced value theory, *American Economic Review*, vol. 66, 274–9

Smith, V. 1978. Discussion (in psychology and economics), *American Economic Review*, vol. 68, 76–7

Smith, V. 1982. Microeconomics systems as an experimental science, *American Economic Review*, vol. 72, 923–55

Smith, V. 1991. Rational choice: the contrast between economics and psychology, *Journal of Political Economy*, vol. 99, 877–97

Smith, V. 1992. Game theory and experimental economics: beginnings and early influences, in Weintraub, R. (ed.), *Toward a History of Game Theory* (Annual Supplement to Vol. 24 *History of Political Economy*), Durham, NC, Duke University Press

Smith, V. and Walker, J. 1993. Monetary rewards and decision costs in experimental economics, *Economic Inquiry*, vol. 31, 245–61

Smithin, J. 1995. Econometrics and the 'facts of experience', in Rima, I. H. (ed.), *Measurement, Quantification and Economic Analysis: Numeracy in Economics*, London, Routledge

Starmer, C. 1999. Experiments in economics: should we trust the dismal scientists in white coats?, *Journal of Economic Methodology*, vol. 6, 1–30

Starmer, C. 2000. Developments in non-expected utility theory: the hunt for a descriptive theory of choice under risk, *Journal of Economic Literature*, vol. 38, 332–82

Stigler, G. 1982. The adoption of marginal utility theory, in *The Economist as a Preacher*, Oxford, Basil Blackwell

Tammi, T. 1999. Incentives and preference reversals: escape moves and community decisions in experimental economics, *Journal of Economic Methodology*, vol. 6, 351–80

Thrall, R. M., Coombs, C. H. and Davis, R. L. 1954. *Decision Processes*, New York, John Wiley

Thurstone, L. L. 1931. The indifference function, *Journal of Social Psychology*, vol. 2, 139–67

Tversky, A. and Edwards, W. 1966. Information versus reward in binary choices, *Journal of Experimental Psychology*, vol. 71, 680–3

Von Neumann, J. and Morgenstern, O. 1944/1947. *Theory of Games and Economic Behavior*, 1st/2nd edn, Princeton, Princeton University Press

Wallis, W. A. and Friedman, M. 1942. The empirical derivation of indifference functions, in Lange, O. (ed.), *Studies in Mathematical Economics and Econometrics*, Chicago, Chicago University Press

Yang, B. and Lester, D. 1995. New directions for economics, *Journal of Socio-Economics*, vol. 23, 433–47

56

A SELF-ADAPTATIVE STATISTICAL LANGUAGE MODEL FOR SPEECH RECOGNITION

Ye-Sho Chen*, P. Pete Chong and Jin-Soo Kim

Source: *Cybernetica*, 35:2 (1992), 103–127.

Abstract

Recent literature in speech recognition suggested that the statistical approach to language modeling to be a promising method. In this paper, we propose a self-adaptive statistical language model for speech recognition. The model is based on Herbert Simon's explanatory processes of imitation and association in text modeling. Three significant contributions can be identified. First, this model provides a constructive mechanism while incorporating three well-known empirical laws of text generation. Second, we show that the IBM's trigram language model in speech recognition is consistent with the imitation process. Third, the proposed self-adaptative model is based on the process of association.

1. Introduction

Natural language modeling is the analysis of syntax, semantics, pragmatism, dialogue, and knowledge of the speaker – in short, informations used in human communication (Waibel and Lee 1990); and it has been cited as an important approach in the study of speech recognition (Jelinek *et al.* 1983, Young *et al.* 1989, White 1990). Text modeling, on the other hand, is the study of how literary texts are generated, thus also a sub-field of the natural language modeling. Recent developments indicate that a statistical approach

* The first author's work was supported by a grant from the Council on Research at Louisiana State University.

to text modeling is a promising methodology to speech recognition; since by applying statistical models to text generations (Bahl *et al.* 1989), the probability of the occurrence of certain word strings (or speech patterns) can be determined, therefore increasing the capability of "recognizing" the subsequent words in a speech.

Section 2 describes one such model proposed recently by IBM. In IBM's statistical approach to text modeling a Markov chain model is used to generate texts that, in turn, are used to determine the words that are most probable to occur. Three other leading models – the multinomial urn model (Brainard 1982), the Simon-Yule model (Simon 1955), and the Mandelbrot-Shannon model (Mandelbrot 1953) – are discussed in Section 2 also. Each statistical model is based on different set of assumptions. For example, the Markov chain model assumes that the probability of choosing a certain word depends only on the previous n words chosen; while the multinomial urn model assumes that the number of an author's available vocabulary is fixed. Thus, it is rather difficult to conduct a comparative evaluation of these models effectively and objectively.

Herbert Simon (1968) proposed that appropriate assumptions must fulfill two requirements: (1) assumptions chosen must yield results resembling the empirical phenomena of text; and more importantly, (2) the underlying assumptions of the model shall provide a plausible explanatory mechanism for the phenomena. Simon has developed a model of text (Simon-Yule model) that would satisfy these two criteria. Section 3 is a discussion of how the Simon-Yule model aptly explains type-token identity, exponential recurrence distribution, and Zipf's laws – the three amazing empirical phenomena of text. Further in the section, we also show that the Simon-Yule model can be plausibly explained by Simon's assumption of the existence of the imitation and association process.

Section 4 shows that the IBM's statistical approach to natural language modeling is consistent with Simon's process of imitation involving natural language communication. Section 5 proposes a self-adaptive speech recognition framework that is based on Simon's process of association. To engineer the proposed framework, we introduce a self-adaptive mechanism in Section 6. Section 7 gives a simulation of how this mechanism enables the IBM's speech recognition system to adapt to the speaker by the constant updating of the word transition probabilities in the text generator. Finally, Section 8 is the concluding remarks.

2. Statistical language models for speech recognition

Figure 1 illustrates IBM's communication theory view of speech recognition (Jelinek *et al.* 1983). The speech recognition system consists of a text generator, a speaker, an acoustic processor, and a linguistic decoder, with the speaker and acoustic processor combined into an acoustic channel. The

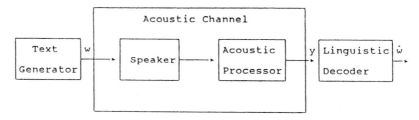

Figure 1 The IBM approach of speech recognition.

speaker transforms the text generated from the text generator into a speech wave form and the acoustic processor acts as a data transducer and compressor. The acoustic processor, serves as a phonetician, transcribes the speech wave form into a string of phonetic symbols, while the linguistic decoder translates the possibly garbled phonetic string into a string of words.

Let P(w | y) be the probability that the word string w was produced by the text generator given that the acoustic processor produced an output string y. The goal of the linguistic decoder is to find that word string ŵ which maximizes P(w | y). According to Bayes' rule:

$$P(w|y) = \frac{P(w)\ P(y|w)}{P(y)} \tag{1}$$

where P(w) is the probability that w is the generated word string, P(y | w) is the probability that the acoustic processor output the word string y after the speaker read w, and P(y) is the probability that y was produced from the acoustic processor. Let P(w,y) be the probability of the joint observation of the input-output pair w and y, then maximizing P(w | y) is equivalent to maximizing the likelihood P(w,y) = P(w)P(y | w), since P(y) does not depend on w.

Thus, the goal of the linguistic decoder is equivalent to finding a word string ŵ which maximizes P(w,y). To accomplish this goal, the linguistic decoder requires two models to supply the probabilities P(w) and P(y | w): (1) a statistical model of text which produces the information about the most probable words with respect to other words in the word string w, and (2) an acoustic channel model which produces information about the words that are most likely to occur given a word string w read by the speaker (Jelinek *et al.* 1983). Once the two models are in place the linguistic decoder can then determine directly the most likely ŵ (Jelinek 1985).

The statistical model of text for estimating P(w) in the IBM approach of speech recognition is the kth order (or k-gram) Markov chain, specifically k = 2. Jelinek pointed out in his invited 1985 IEEE conference paper (p. 1621) that there is "nothing to recommend the trigram language model

(k = 2) except its simplicity and ease of construction from training text."
Furthermore, "the selection of the exact classification scheme (for the conditional words), and its use in determining a large amount of text, is an
unsolved problem that will claim increasing attention of researchers" (p. 1618).
These comments underscore the need for an effective and objective evaluation procedure for statistical models of text.

Zipf discovered two amazing regularities of text (to be discussed in
Section 3.1.) in 1949. Since then there have been several attempts to explain
these regularities by means of statistical models, among which are the
multinomial urn model, the Simon-Yule model, and the Mandelbrot-shannon
model.

The multinomial urn model is a simplified version of the Markov chain
model and assumes that (1) the total number of the author's vocabularies is
fixed, and (2) the probability for the word selection is also fixed. Simon-
Yule model, a further generalization of the Markov chain model, was
proposed by Simon in 1955. Since this equation derived by Simon is equivalent to an earlier equation by Yule (1924) in a study of a biological
problem, it is usually cited as the Simon-Yule model of text. Finally, based
on Shannon's (1950) theory on the optimal coding of messages in communication systems, Mandelbrot (1953) assumes that in writing a text,
the author wants to obtain the maximum amount of information under
some cost constraints.

3. Evaluating the Simon-Yule model of text

This section is an evaluation of the Simon-Yule model of text with respect
to the two crucial criteria mentioned earlier in Section 1.

3.1. Three empirical phenomena of text

The type-token identity (Chen and Leimkuhler 1989) is the first empirical
phenomenon of text generation. First, let us define "the number of types"
to be the total number of distinct words used in the text and "the number
of tokens" as the total number of words used in the same text. Second, let
t = number of tokens used in a text and V_t = number of types found in the
same text, then the following identity is approximately true:

$$\frac{V_t}{t} + \frac{\ln V_t}{\ln t} = 1. \tag{2}$$

Chen and Leimkuhler (1989) showed that this type-token identity can be
derived from the Simon-Yule model.

The second empirical phenomena of text is the exponential recurrence
distribution of the gaps (Chen 1988). That is, For frequently used words in

English (such as "the," "a," "of," etc.), the distribution of gap lengths between successive occurrences of the same word is approximately exponential. Based on Simon-Yule model, Chen (1988) conducted simulation experiments on the most frequently used words and provided justification for the exponential recurrence distribution. The numerical results are consistent with the observed empirical phenomenon.

The third empirical phenomenon of text is the two Zipf's (1949) laws. The first law of Zipf states that if words are ranked by their frequencies of occurrence, then the product of any word's rank r and its frequency of occurrence, $g(r)$, will be approximately a constant. That is, if $g(r)$ is plotted against r on a log-log scale, then the resultant graph will be approximately a straight line with a slope of minus one.

Associated with the second law of Zipf are two interesting phenomena. Let $f(n)$ = the number of words having appeared n times in the text, then (1) the ratio of the number of words occurring once ($f(1)$) to the number of different words in the text is approximately a constant 0.5; and (2) the values of $f(n)/f(1)$, n = 1, 2, 3, 4, 5, show an approximate pattern of 1, 0.33, 0.17, 0.10, and 0.07. Chen (1989) showed that the Simon-Yule model provides a generating mechanism for the two laws of Zipf.

3.2. Explanatory processes of imitation and association

Embedded in all written materials are writers' writing styles which are characterized by writers' choices of words. How are these words put together to form sentences? One theory is that this combination occurs by associating a particular word with the context in mind. For instance, "robin" is associated with "bird" as well as Spring, therefore it is more likely to be chosen in a writing about Easter. Another theory is that writers learn to use a system of common rules (usually referred to as grammar) that is capable of producing sentences (Reed 1982). According to Anderson (1980) the language generation begins with the writer deciding what to say and how to say it. On the one hand, "what to say" represents the content of the information to be communicated, and upon which a class of words to be used are chosen. On the other hand, "how to say" represents the selection of words from that class and the method by which these words are arranged. In other words, the former determines the context and the latter the format of presentation.

Consistent with the literature, Simon explains that an author's word selection is a two-fold process: by imitation and by association, with imitation related to the format of the text and association related to the context. An author chooses words to write by sampling segments of word sequences from his other writings, from works of other authors, and from segments he has heard (imitation); he also samples his recent segments of the word sequence (association).

154

Simon demonstrated that, given two different sample texts A and B, same words would have similar ranks in either text. For example, the word "they" occurs 1010 times in text A and ranks 27th – a rank which is similar to that in text B (28th). More interestingly, 78 of the 100 most frequently used words in text A are among the top 100 in text B. Simon explained that the similarity in rankings of "common" words is due to the process of imitation – following the protocol, if you will, of the society.

The process of association is also evident. In text A, the proper noun "Bloom" occurs 926 times and ranks 30th. Simon argued that if the author had named the proper noun as "Smith" instead of "Bloom" it also would have ranked 30th, since this noun is associated with the context in which it appeared. In short, Simon (1955) believed that both imitation and association dictate which word is to be used, and the probability of occurrence for that word is somewhat proportional to (1) how often it is used in the language in general, and (2) how often it is used by this particular communicator.

4. Implication of imitation for speech recognition

The speech recognition system illustrated in Figure 1 indicates that the linguistic decoder requires a statistical language model to supply the probability, P(w), for the text generator to produce a word string w. As discussed in Section 2, Jelinek (1985) used a trigram Markov chain model to estimate P(w). In such a model,

$$P(w) = \prod_{i=1}^{n} P(w \mid w_{i-2}, w_{i-1}), \qquad (3)$$

where $w = w_1, w_2, \ldots, w_n$, denoting a string of n words. A matrix of word transition probabilities $P(w_i \mid w_{i-2}, w_{i-1})$ is constructed by analyzing a large set of training sentences (Young et al. 1989). In analyzing the sentences, the number of times the words w_{i-2}, w_{i-1} occur adjacent to each other is counted, disregard all other reasons that may result in the production of the same two words. Use the Raleigh language model (Jelinek et al. 1983) as an example (Figure 2), suppose that the previous two words are "each" and "large" (the left-most part in Figure 2), then the transition probabilities for next words may be given in Figure 3.

The estimated probability P(w) represents the frequency of occurrence of w in the language, with its value dependent of the training text used. Thus, if the training sentences are from an office text, then P(w) is the chance that the sentence w is written or spoken in the office environment. The estimate of equation (3) is based on the assumption that the choice of any sentence depends largely upon the "normal" or "traditional" choices of other writers or speakers. Since the office writing is usually restricted to what is deemed "correct" both grammatically and socially, writers are expected to follow

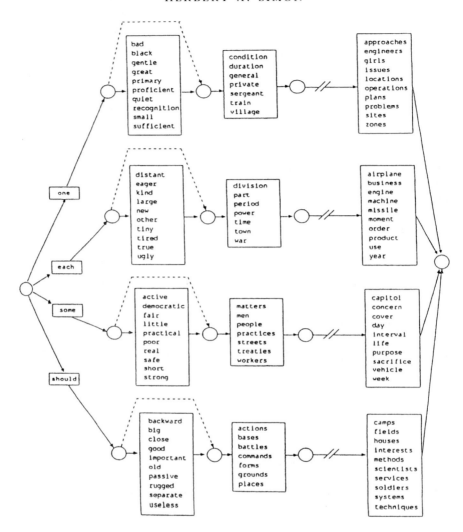

Figure 2 Portion of the Grammar of the Raleigh language in Jelinek *et al.* (1983).

(or imitate) certain formats or "styles." This assumption is consistent with Simon's process of imitation involving language communication.

5. Implication of association for speech recognition

The imitation part of the language production concentrates on the writer's cumulative and long-term experience with other materials, including his or her own past productions. However, according to Simon, the process also

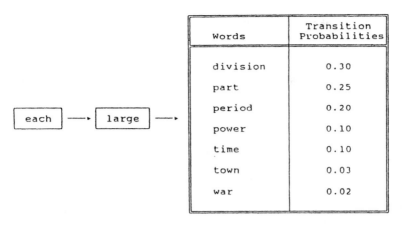

Words	Transition Probabilities
division	0.30
part	0.25
period	0.20
power	0.10
time	0.10
town	0.03
war	0.02

Figure 3 The transition probabilities corresponding to the word pair "each large."

involves the process of association, because the communicator tends to sample the more recent segments of his/her own writing or utterance. The process of association implies that the probability P(w) in equation (3) will be dynamic, adaptive, and increasing as the same sentence is repeated in the course of communication. An immediate example is that the probability of occurrence for the words "speech" and "recognition" will be much higher in this paper relative to a college student's term paper on finance. Also, for writers who prefer to write in third person, the chances for "I" or "we" to appear in the article are arbitrarily reduced.

A revised version of Figure 1 is suggested in Figure 4. This new framework of speech recognition system adapts to a speaker's usage pattern by

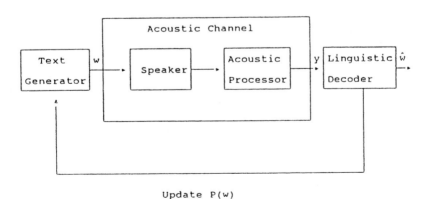

Figure 4 A revised version of Figure 1 based on Simon's process of association.

attempting to update constantly the probability P(w) in the text generator, thus generating texts in a more natural manner.

The following section discusses a self-adaptive linear search mechanism that is needed for engineering the above-mentioned framework into a working system.

6. Self-adaptive linear search mechanism

Linear search is a very simple method of data retrieval, and it has long been widely studied. In a linear search, the search progresses linearly from the first item to the last until the requested item is found. Thus, the search in Figure 3 after the word pair "each large" is a linear search. In practice, it is seldom that all items are searched the equal number of times; instead, some items would be accessed (therefore used) much more frequently than others. To take advantage of this usage-dependent phenomenon to enhance the performance of linear search, the order of the list must be dynamically arranged so that the frequently accessed items locate at the front of the list and the rarely accessed items are moved to the end. Assuming that the search is terminated once the searched item is found, a list that is arranged sequentially according to the access frequency of items would be much more efficient.

During the last few decades, various self-adaptive heuristics have been proposed to dynamically arrange the list according to the access frequency. The major difference among heuristics is the moving distance of the accessed item. The distance moved, on the other hand, depends on the schemes used by different heuristics and is either a constant or based on the location of the item or past events. Three of the most frequently cited heuristics are described below (Hester and Hirschberg 1985):

(1) Move-to-front: The accessed item is moved to the front of the list once it is found, if it is not already there. All the items that the accessed item passes are moved back one position.
(2) Transpose: If the accessed item is not at the front of the list, it swaps the position with the item just ahead of it.
(3) Count: When the item is accessed, the count of the accessed item is incremented by one; and that item is moved ahead items with lower counts. Thus, the list is always in decreasing order by the value of the access frequency of the items involved.

Several measurements – such as asymptotic cost, amortized cost, rate of convergence, and cost comparison with the optimal static ordering – have been suggested for the performance evaluation of the heuristics (Hester and

158

Hirschberg 1985). In general, based on those performance measurements count is shown to be superior to move-to-front and transpose. However, because the count method requires substantial amount of additional storage space, it has been considered as a separate class from move-to-front and transpose heuristics. Subsequently, the count method has received less attention (Bentley and McGeoch 1985) in the literature.

Fortunately, additional storage space for counter fields is not a major concern in IBM's statistical language model. As shown in Figure 3, counter fields are already in existence for tracking transition probabilities of each word in the system. Therefore, the count heuristic is recommended for the IBM's statistical language model; since in this case its superior performance is no longer realized at the cost of additional overheads.

7. A self-adaptive statistical language model

In this section, we develop a self-adaptive linear search mechanism for the proposed adaptive framework for speech recognition by incorporating count rule.

Consider the Raleigh language model shown in Figure 2. For each word there are fixed initial trigram transition probabilities that are stored in a secondary storage device (Jelinek 1985). When the speech recognition system is activated (such as during a training session), a counter field is added to each word in the primary memory to keep track of its usage frequencies. Throughout the system transactions the usage frequencies for each word are cumulated.

After the speech recognition system finishes processing its transactions, a self-adaptive mechanism incorporating count would be activated to update the trigram transition probabilities. For example, Column 3 of Table 1 lists

Table 1 Updating the transition probabilities shown in Figure 3.

(1) Words	(2) Transition Probabilities	(3) Usage Freqencies	(4) Updating (a)	(5) Updated Transition Probabilities	(a)/(b)
division	0.30	2	$0.30 \times (2/20) = 0.030$	0.190	
part	0.25	6	$0.25 \times (6/20) = 0.075$	0.475	
period	0.20	3	$0.20 \times (3/20) = 0.030$	0.190	
power	0.10	2	$0.10 \times (2/20) = 0.010$	0.062	
time	0.10	1	$0.10 \times (1/20) = 0.005$	0.032	
town	0.03	4	$0.03 \times (4/20) = 0.006$	0.038	
war	0.02	2	$0.02 \times (2/20) = 0.002$	0.013	
Sum	1.00	20	(b) 0.158	1.000	

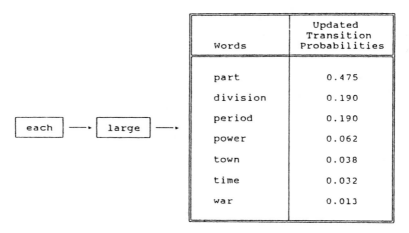

Words	Updated Transition Probabilities
part	0.475
division	0.190
period	0.190
power	0.062
town	0.038
time	0.032
war	0.013

Figure 5 The updated transition probabilities corresponding to the word pair "each large."

the cumulated usage frequencies of the words listed in Figure 3. As presented in Column 4, the updated transition probabilities can be obtained by multiplying the initial transition probabilities with the weighted frequencies. Since the summation of the updated frequencies is not equal to one, the results are normalized in Column 5 to provide the final updated transition probabilities.

Once the transition probabilities are updated, the count heuristic will sort the words according to the order of the updated probabilities. As a result, a new list of transition probabilities (Figure 5) corresponding to the word pair "each large" can be generated and stored in the secondary storage for the next batch of transactions. The counter fields would be deleted from the primary storage after each session to free up resources.

In summary, this proposed new framework of speech recognition system incorporates a self-adaptive statistical language model that adjusts to a speaker's speech pattern by constantly updating the probabilities P(w) in the text generator.

8. Conclusion

Conventional wisdom has it that the more one uses something, the more the same thing will be used again. The phenomenon has been found to be quite common in computer systems. For example, the well-known 80–20 rule states that 80% of computer usage involves only 20% of the resources (Heising 1953). As discussed in Section 3.1, similar phenomenon exists in the text generation also. It is logical then to maximize the usefulness and efficiency of speech recognition system according to this usage-dependent phenomenon. The most reasonable way is to reduce the time wasted in wadding through all seldom accessed data in order to find a frequently needed item in every search run. In other words, similar to arranging books in the study, put the most frequently needed references at the fingertip.

In this paper, a usage model (the Simon-Yule model) is introduced for the usage-dependent phenomenon in text generation. The model is able to explain the three amazing empirical phenomena of text; and based on the processes of imitation and association in human language communication, the model is also intuitively sound.

Based on the imitation-and-association process, a language model incorporating a self-adaptive mechanism is proposed for the IBM's statistical approach to speech recognition. Specifically, the count heuristic is chosen as the self-adaptive mechanism which allows the IBM's speech recognition system to update the trigram transition probabilities constantly without additional resource cost. As such, the text generator embedded in the speech recognition system will generate texts in a more natural manner.

References

Anderson, J. R. *Cognitive Psychology and Its Implications*. W. H. Freeman, pp. 437–453, 1980.

Bahl, L. R., *et al.*, "A tree based statistical language model for natural language speech recognition," *IEEE Trans. On Acoustic, Speech, and Signal Processing*, Vol. 37, No. 7, pp. 1001–1008, 1989.

Bentley, J. L. and McGeoch, C. C., "Amortized analyses of self-organizing sequential search heuristics," *Communications of the ACM*, Vol. 24, No. 4, pp. 404–411, 1985.

Brainard, B., "On the relation between the type-token and species area problems," *Journal of the Applied Probability*, Vol. 19, pp. 785–793, 1982.

Chen, Y. S., "An exponential recurrence distribution in the Simon-Yule model of text," *Cybernetics and Systems: An International Journal*, Vol. 19, pp. 521–545, 1988.

Chen, Y. S., "Zipf's laws in text modeling," *International Journal of General Systems*, Vol. 15, pp. 233–252, 1989.

Chen, Y. S. and Leimkuhler F. F., "A type-token identity in the Simon-Yule model of text," *Journal of the American Society for Information Science*, Vol. 40, No. 1, pp. 45–53, 1989.

Heising, W. P., "Note on random addressing techniques," *IBM Systems Journal*, Vol. 2, No. 2, pp. 112–116, June 1953.

Hester, J. H., and Hirschberg, D. S., "Self-organizing Linear Search," *Computing Surveys*, Vol. 17, No. 3, pp. 295–311, 1985.

Jelinek, F., Mercer, R. L., and Bahl, L. R., "A maximum likelihood approach to continuous speech recognition," *IEEE Transactions on Patterns Analysis and Machine Intelligence*, Vol. 5-PAMI, No. 2, pp. 179–190, 1983.

Jelinek, F., "The development of an experimental discrete dictation recognizer," *Proceedings of IEEE*, Vol. 73, No. 11, pp. 1616–1624, 1985.

Mandelbrot, B., "An information theory of statistical structure of language," *Proceedings of the Symposium on Applications of Communications Theory*, (London, September 1952), London: Butterworths, 1953, pp. 486–500.

Markov, A. A., "An example of a statistical investigation of the text of 'Eugen Onegin' illustrating the connection of trials in a chain," *Bulletinde L'Academie Imperiale des Science de St. Petersburg*, Vol. 7, 153, 1913.

Reed, S. K. *Cognition: Theory and Applications*. Brooks/Cole, pp. 232–237, 1982.

Shannon, C. E., "Prediction and entropy of printed English," *Bell Syst. Tech. J.*, Vol. 30, pp. 50–64, January 1951.

Simon, H. A., "On a class of skew distribution functions," *Biometrika*, Vol. 42, pp. 425–440, 1955.

Simon, H. A., "On judging the plausibility of theories, in B. van Rootselaar and J. F. Staal (eds.)," *Logic, Methodology and Philosophy of Sciences*, Vol. III, Amsterdam: North-Holland, 1968.

Waibel and Lee. *Readings in Speech Recognition*. San Mateo, California. Morgan Kaufmann Publishers, 1990.

White, G. M., "Natural language understanding and speech recognition," *Communications of the ACM*, Vol. 33, No. 8, pp. 72–82, 1990.

Young, S. R., *et al.*, "High level knowledge sources in usable speech recognition systems," *Communications of the ACM*, Vol. 32, No. 2, pp. 183–184, 1989.

Yule, G. U., *A Statistical Study of Vocabulary*, Cambridge, England: Cambridge University Press, 1944.

Zipf, G. K., *Human Behavior and the Principle of Least Effort*. Cambridge, MA: Addison-Wesley, 1949.

57

SATISFICING REVISITED

Michael A. Goodrich,
Wynn C. Stirling and Erwin R. Boer

Source: *Minds and Machines*, 10:1 (2000), 79–110.

Abstract

In the debate between simple inference heuristics and complex decision mechanisms, we take a position squarely in the middle. A decision making process that extends to both naturalistic and novel settings should extend beyond the confines of this debate; both simple heuristics and complex mechanisms are cognitive skills adapted to and appropriate for some circumstances but not for others. Rather than ask 'Which skill is better?' it is often more important to ask 'When is a skill justified?' The selection and application of an appropriate cognitive skill for a particular problem has both costs and benefits, and therefore requires the resolution of a tradeoff. In revisiting satisficing, we observe that the essence of satisficing is tradeoff. Unlike heuristics, which derive their justification from empirical phenomena, and unlike optimal solutions, which derive their justification by an evaluation of alternatives, satisficing decision-making derives its justification by an evaluation of consequences. We formulate and present a satisficing decision paradigm that has its motivation in Herbert Simon's work on bounded rationality. We characterize satisficing using a cost–benefit tradeoff, and generate a decision rule applicable to both designing intelligent machines as well as describing human behavior.

1. Introduction

While driving an automobile, many of us have experienced something similar to the following. We have been following a vehicle for an extended period of time even though there is very little traffic on the road. Suddenly, we realize that not only can we easily pass but also that we want to pass because the lead vehicle is going slower than our desired speed. We decide to pass, and act accordingly.

What are the factors that dictate our behavior in this situation? Can a characterization of the corresponding behavior-generation process be used to design better machines? This paper is written from two perspectives: first, from the perspective of a designer charged with the task of creating a machine capable of some degree of goal-directed autonomy and agency, and second from a perspective of describing goal-directed human behavior generation. Inherent in the resolution of these problems is the need to resolve tradeoffs. For machine intelligence, who resolves the tradeoffs, the designer or the machine? For humans, who resolves the tradeoffs, the human or societal/evolutionary forces?

There appear to be two disparate approaches to solving these problems. The first approach, a 'top-down' approach, contends that intelligence is tantamount to normative rationality and optimality. Representatives from this approach cite success in the philosophical foundations of cognitive science (a la psychology) and success in optimal decision theory (a la design) as evidence for a top-down description of intelligence. The second approach, a 'bottom-up' approach, contends that intelligence emerges from ecologically adapted behavioral and cognitive skills. Representatives from this approach cite evidence from the usefulness of cognitive heuristics (Gigerenzer and Goldstein, 1996) (a la psychology) and the success of, for example, ecological robotics (Brooks, 1986) (a la design). In both design and description, the top-down approach tends to rely on complex decision mechanisms whereas the bottom-up approach tends to rely on simple inference heuristics. A marriage between these extremes is necessary to ensure behavior that achieves a goal subject to environmental constraints.

1.1. Problem statement

From a machine intelligence perspective, goal-directed decision-makers capable of situated and continued existence must have the ability to self-police their behaviors. Included in self policing are the abilities to evaluate and anticipate performance internally, and the ability to resolve decision tradeoffs internally. These abilities can be accomplished to a limited extent by allowing a designer to specify complex decision mechanisms capable of handling all but the most subtle (and possibly most treacherous) situations. Alternatively, the designer can specify or identify simple inference heuristics and allow the machine to select among these heuristics as afforded by the environment. From a designer's perspective, the latter approach has the ability to scale to larger domains and is thus a useful approach but, unfortunately, this approach begs the question of how these heuristics are systematically created and managed.

Switching attention to descriptions of human-decision making, the distinction between simple inference heuristics and complex decision mechanisms appears to be somewhat artificial. Rational people can use either simple heuristics or complex mechanisms depending on which is more appropriate for the circumstances, and it is an open question as to how people select and obtain these skills. Both simple inference heuristics and complex decision mechanisms are *cognitive skills*, and a rational person naturally (either through instinctual responses, responses learned through external feedback, or responses learned through goal-directed internal feedback) employs tradeoffs and expected performance associated with each skill and chooses appropriately. The question of which skill is *more* correct is misguided because, from an agent's point of view, the environmentally afforded 'means' to reaching the decision are subjected to the goal-contextualized 'ends' produced by the decision, and any approach that efficiently uses means to generate productive ends is justifiable. Extending this thought, prescriptive approaches to decision-making should permit either simple heuristics or complex mechanisms provided that the expected result is good enough.

1.2. Solution approach

Cognitive skills can be treated as agents and organized into a society of Minskian agents (Minsky, 1986). Management of these skill-based agents is tantamount to a meta-decision problem that requires an appropriate notion of rationality. By framing the problem as one of skill management, the decision maker formulates a control problem wherein, given certain goals and a certain context, the decision maker controls which cognitive skill agent operates. This control problem is addressed by a meta-agent, whence the problem becomes one of coordinating agents in a multi-agent society. Multi-agent societies used to generate rational decisions that use cognitive skills require meta-choices which serve to resolve tradeoffs and assure rational agency.

An appeal to meta-rationality to settle a question of rationality is always risky. Too often, such appeals result in an endless chain of "how do I know that I know that I know . . ." Fortunately, if meta-choices are justifiable (from a prescriptive perspective) and produce a useful decision rule (from a descriptive perspective) then such an infinite regression can be avoided. Although in a prescriptive/design sense it may be desirable, such meta-rationality need not be explicitly possessed by the agent, but can instead be (and often is) imposed externally by a designer or through evolutionary forces. Our objective is to identify a decision rule that, from a descriptive perspective, is a useful heuristic in the spirit of Simon's notion of satisficing and that, from a prescriptive perspective, can be justified by an appeal to meta-rationality. In the end, we present a mathematical characterization of satisficing, discuss how Simon's original notion is compatible with this characterization, and describe how this characterization is manifest in observations of human decision making (including the car-following example).

1.3. Outline

This paper is organized as follows. In Section 2, we describe the elements of a decision problem and discuss the limits of both optimality and heuristics with an emphasis on justifiability and practicability. In Section 3, we discuss a decision mechanism for resolving tradeoffs and present a decision theoretic characterization of satisficing. In Section 4, we extend this characterization of satisficing decision making to include the interaction between two independent decision forces and the resulting coordination of Minskian agents. Then, in Section 5, we discuss the implications of this satisficing decision paradigm in the context of the debate between simple inference heuristics and complex decision mechanisms.

2. Elements of decision making

The elements of a decision problem are diagrammed in Figure 1. Given all observation $x \in X$ that is a function of the state of nature $\theta \in \Theta$, the decision task is to select an option $u \in U$ that produces acceptable (according to values and preferences) consequences. In decision making, there are two

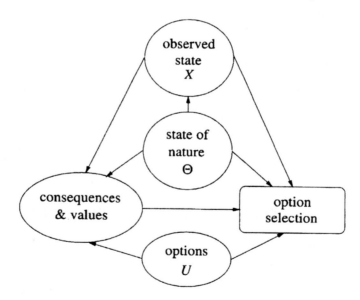

Figure 1 The decision problem. Arrows indicate either perceived (by the decision maker) or actual influence. For example, a consequence is the result of taking action $\mu \in U$ when $\theta \in \Theta$ obtains. Not all decision methodologies explicitly account for all influences. Typically, complex decision mechanisms seek to make all elements and influences explicit, whereas simple inference heuristics discard some of the influences or omit some of the elements.

conventional approaches: complex decision mechanisms based on seeking *superlative* decisions using normative rationality, and simple inference heuristics based on seeking *positive* decisions using empirically derived procedures. Superlative approaches seek to identify options U, estimate states Θ from sensory observations X, determine consequences using some causal model, and then extremize some performance metric that imposes a preference pattern on these consequences. By contrast, positive approaches short circuit some of these stages resulting in, for example, rules of the form 'if x then u.' The optimality-based literature, particularly that of optimal control theory and game theory, is overwhelmingly vast, reflecting many decades of serious research and development of ideas based on the superlative paradigm. The positive paradigm, manifest in the form of heuristics, procedurally rational decision making methods, and multitudinous *ad hoc* techniques, has also been well-represented in the computer science, social science, and engineering literatures.

There is an alternative to the superlative and positive paradigms. The most well known example of this *comparative* paradigm is Simon's notion of satisficing (Simon, 1955, 1996). A formally stated comparative paradigm, however, has not been well represented in the literature as a basis for a viable decision-making concept for general application. In this section, we first review the superlative and positive paradigms, and then discuss Simon's notion of satisficing to establish a foundation for our subsequent revisitation of satisficing. In the following subsections, we refer to the utility of accepting a decision and a utility of rejecting a decision. This discussion includes probabilistic inference as a special case where the utility of accepting a decision is unity if the decision is correct, and zero otherwise. Additionally, this allows us to treat optimality as the typical problem in normative rationality without loss of generality.

2.1. Superlative rationality: optimal decisions

When estimates of x and/or θ are distributed according to a known probability distribution, then a decision problem is said to be one of decision under *risk* (Luce and Raiffa, 1957). The conventional approach to decisions under risk is to define a utility function for each of the consequences and then select an option that produces the maximum expected utility (where the expectation is taken with respect to the distribution of states of nature). The option that maximizes expected utility is the optimal option u^* defined as

$$u^* = arg \max_{u \in U} \sum_{\theta} \upsilon(u, \theta) p(\theta | x) \tag{1}$$

where $v(u, \theta)$ is the utility of selecting option u given state θ, and $p(\theta | x)$ is the probability density function for θ given observation x. By contrast to decisions under risk, when the probabilities of x and Θ are completely unknown then the decision is said to be one of decision under *uncertainty* (Luce and Raiffa, 1957). The conventional approach to decisions under uncertainty is to use a maximin approach yielding

$$u^* = arg \max_{u \in U} \max_{\theta \in \Theta} \upsilon(u, \theta) \qquad (2)$$

where Θ is the set of feasible states given observation x. The function $\min_{\theta \in \Theta'} v(u, \theta)$ is called the security level for u and can be interpreted as an expectation with respect to a least favorable distribution of θ given x. Therefore, u^* is interpreted as the option that maximizes security.

These methods have been tremendously successful for certain applications. However, not all decision problems are optimization problems, nor should they be. Recalling a proverb from control theory, performing a study of nonlinear control problems is analogous to performing a study of 'non-elephant animals'; there are simply many more nonlinear control problems than linear control problems. Similarly, there are many problems addressable by 'non-optimal' approaches that are not amenable to optimal approaches. Although some may categorize the practice of 'non-optimal' choice as a species of irrationality, the quest for the successful development of intelligent machines rests, to some degree, upon the assumption that intelligence extends beyond naive optimization (Slote, 1989). Rationality is not tantamount to optimality.

2.2. Bounded rationality: the presence of tradeoffs in a superlative world

Many cognitive scientists recognize that insistence on optimality is a misplaced requirement in situations of limited resources and information, and that optimality inadequately describes observed behavior in naturalistic settings (Gigerenzer and Goldstein, 1996; Zsambok and Klein, 1997). For complex problems, there often exist information, memory, or computing limitations such that finding a strictly optimal solution is not feasible because (1) and (2) must be formulated and solved. Under these circumstances, a principle of *bounded rationality* is often recommended. Many such theories are based on Simon's well-known satisficing idea wherein a decision-maker uses "experience to construct an expectation of how good a solution we might reasonably achieve, and halting search as soon as a solution is reached that meets the expectation" (Simon, 1990, p. 9). Satisficing thus becomes a means of addressing when an option is 'good enough' in the sense that its utility exceeds an aspiration level. Determination of an aspiration level is based on experience-derived expectations of possible consequences, and a search algorithm is proposed that is compatible with limited computational resources and that terminates when an option is identified that exceeds the aspiration level.

Dissatisfied with this under-specified algorithm, some researchers have proposed other satisficing-like notions of bounded rationality such as augmenting the utility function with computational costs. Such methods are closely related to constrained optimization (see, for example, Kaufman, 1990; Zilberstein, 1996; Sandholm and Lesser, 1997), and yield optimal solutions according to a modified criterion. These algorithms appear to abandon Simon's original intention of comparing predicted consequences with expected potential consequences to justify good enough decisions. Instead, these procedures derive their justification by an appeal to optimality with respect to a modified performance criterion. Since no mention is made of how a situated decision maker might choose such a criterion, it appears that advocates of such approaches transform satisficing from a consequence-based justification to a procedure-based justification and thereby make a "virtue out of a necessity" (Levi, 1997, p. vii). However, insofar as justification can be derived through the process of optimization, these approaches are compatible with the goals of the proponents.

Regardless of the details of how a boundedly rational decision is obtained, it is clear that the ultimate rationale for adopting a decision obtained in such a way is that it is the resolution to a tradeoff between the goal-directed capabilities of a decision-maker and the environmental affordances relevant to that goal.

2.3. Positive rationality: heuristics

Once defined, approaches based on both optimality and non-Simon-like bounded rationality find the best possible solution (according to an implicit performance metric) given context-dependent constraints and imprecise information about the true state of nature. For real environments, a decision maker must also be able to determine not only the set of possible options U (the search space), but also something about the utility $v(u, \theta)$ of taking action[1] as well as the set of relevant states Θ. This can lead to intractable complexity, especially for the designers of machines. For example, control engineers sometimes use an explicit model to predict the consequences of a sequence of actions using a method termed 'model predictive control' (Mayne and Michalska, 1990; Richalet, 1993; Michalska and Mayne, 1995; Sistu and Bequette, 1996; Scokaert et al., 1997). The extent of the action sequence can be adjusted according to a receding planning horizon, and must often be very limited because of the combinatorial complexity of enumerating multiple action sequences. Often, when faced with such increasing complexity, the designer must resort to heuristics (consider the success of heuristic search techniques).

In effect, *heuristics are empirically derived cognitive shortcuts in a decision problem*. For example, under particular sensory influences x a decision maker might use the rule *if x then u*. A criticism of the use of heuristics is that they are unjustifiable and lead to capricious results because they are essentially *ad hoc* in nature (Kahneman and Tversky, 1996). *Ad hoc* procedures while producing good (maybe even very good) decisions, will not produce decisions that can be reliably established as being adequate in terms of performance, but are instead based on vague notions of desirability or convenience without any definitive measures of quality. Fortunately, some heuristics appear to be ecologically adapted to certain niches, and work is proceeding on identifying these niches and comparing the behaviors produced by these heuristics to more conventional approaches (see, for example, Chase *et al.*, 1998). The appropriate use of heuristics in machines and humans can increase capacity and can help generate solutions to non-optimal decision problems (Ho, 1999).

2.4. Interlude

The use of non-optimal decision mechanisms need not result in *ad hocism*. For example, Lotfi Zadeh, the father of fuzzy logic, can undoubtedly be included as someone who is interested in exploring non-optimal but justifiable choice. Near the beginning of his career he wrote an essay entitled 'What is optimal?' (Zadeh, 1958) and four decades later revisited the theme in his paper 'Maximizing Sets and Fuzzy Markoff Algorithms' (Zadeh, 1998). In these papers, Zadeh questions the feasibility (and wisdom) of seeking for optimality given limited resources. However, in resisting naive optimizing Zadeh does not abandon the quest for justifiability, but instead resorts to modifications of conventional logic that are compatible with linguistic and fuzzy understanding of nature and consequences. Other researchers, including many who have contributed to the area of optimal decision and control, have explored non-optimal but justifiable solution methodologies as exemplified in work in suboptimal decision making, ordinal optimization (Ho, 1994; Ho and Larson, 1995), probably approximately correct algorithms (Greiner and Orponen, 1996), multi-resolutional intelligence (Albus, 1991; Meystel, 1996), heuristic search, behavior-based/ecological robotics (Brooks, 1986, 1991; Duchon *et al.*, 1998), anytime algorithms (Zilberstein, 1996), and satisficing decision-making (Simon, 1996; Sen, 1998). It is interesting that each of these approaches seeks to resolve a tradeoff between the ultimate behavior of the agent or system and the practicable methods for generating this behavior.

2.5. Comparative rationality: being 'good enough'

The notion of being 'good enough' is an underlying issue in all decision problems and is an inseparable companion to the notion of a tradeoff. For example, under Simon's satisficing, rejecting an option that does not meet or exceed the aspiration level derives its justification from the observation that the option is rejected in favor of an unknown alternative that produces better consequences; we trade the would-be consequences of the rejected option for the expected consequences of an unidentified option. In machine intelligence, ensuring good enough performance has conventionally been the responsibility of the designer. By contrast, in human intelligence ensuring good enough performance is either the responsibility of the human or, in a much broader sense, the responsibility of the species subject to evolutionary forces. For an individual human, evaluating success in goal-directed behavior requires rational self policing.

Restricting attention to goal-directed behavior, self-policing becomes very important. Self-policing must include the ability to determine if a behavior produces good enough consequences and, if not, change or adapt behaviors. As part of this evaluative phase, a decision-maker may need to identify feasible alternatives, coherent beliefs, and consistent values. Another aspect of self-policing is the ability to, in the spirit of Simon's expectation-based aspiration level, anticipate the efficaciousness of an option. Regardless of whether heuristic or optimal, self-policing is essential for robust goal-directed behavior generation. Self-policing allows a decision-maker to evaluate and adapt (possibly context-dependent) 'means' subject to (possibly task-specific) 'ends' in an effort to produce good enough performance.

Recall the example of following a vehicle for an extended period of time even though passing it is a superior alternative. Unless a driver is a voracious optimizer capable of limitless attention, few would say that the behavior is irrational (although we reflect on the situation with mild amusement). The point is that being good enough is required, and being optimal is optional.

3. Satisficing and tradeoff

Too often, in a quest to impart intelligence to a machine we resort to one of two extremes. We either require the designer to have sufficient expertise to identify and encode a simple and effectual task-specific algorithm, or to determine and encode a complex context-free algorithm responsible for solving any and all task-specific problems. Similarly, in an effort to describe and prescribe human behavior we often resort to one of these extremes. Thus, we are forced into an artificial and unhealthy separation of task-specific/context-dependent (i.e., simple inference heuristics) and general-purpose/context-independent (i.e., complex decision mechanisms) methods. Both extremes tend to ignore the interdependence of 'means' and 'ends' (Connolly, 1999) as well as the requirement of simultaneously efficient and robust behavior.

Simon (1990) identifies the two factors that determine effectual behavior, "Human rational behavior . . . is shaped by a scissors whose two blades are the structure of task environments and the computational capabilities of the actor" (p. 7). Simon backs up this statement, albeit implicitly, in his development of satisficing. The computational capacities of the decision-maker are means, and the consequences produced by these means, evaluated in the context of overall goal-directed behavior, are evaluated against the standard for good enough ends. We wish to characterize the essence of satisficing as a cost-benefit tradeoff using a justifiable decision theoretic standard for performing rational self policing.

3.1. Some related characterizations of satisficing

Satisficing facilitates the development of a decision theoretic paradigm that differs from the de facto paradigm of optimality. One application of the concept of satisficing is in multi-attribute decision-making. "Aspiration levels provide a computational mechanism for satisficing. An alternative satisfices if it meets aspirations along all dimensions." (Simon, 1996, p. 30). Exploiting a parallelism between multiple attributes and multiple relevant states, this notion of satisficing has been mathematically formalized in (Mesarovic, 1970; Mesarovic and Takahara, 1972; Matsuda and Takatsu, 1979a,b; Takatsu, 1980, 1981). These developments compare a utility, $v(u, \theta)$, defined over the consequences of an option u given state θ, to a decision threshold (or aspiration level), $\rho(\theta)$. Note that this decision threshold depends only on observations and not on decision consequences. An option u is satisficing if and only if $v(u, \theta) \geq \rho(\theta)$ for all feasible θ. Our approach is similar to these other developments in that it is applicable to multiple states or attributes but, by contrast, compares two utilities defined over the consequences of a decision whence our approach mathematically generalizes these decision rules (i.e., the decision threshold $\rho(u, \theta)$ depends upon both control actions and the state of nature).

In this section, we characterize tradeoffs using two utility functions: one to represent the payoff for accepting an option and another for rejecting the same option. In our development and examples, we demonstrate why this generalization to an option-dependent threshold is useful. We then discuss two methods for combining these two utility functions to resolve tradeoffs. In Section 4, we discuss the applicability of each of these methods.

3.2. Epistemic utility theory: a related characterization

The philosopher Karl Popper made the following insightful comment regarding the goals of scientific inquiry, "... *truth is not the only aim of science.* We want more than mere truth: what we look for is *interesting truth.*" (Popper, 1965, p. 229). Although this statement is implicitly accepted by philosophers and scientists, most formal descriptions of scientific inquiry only implicitly accommodate this observation. By contrast, the epistemologist Isaac Levi made explicit this observation in his characterization of rational decision-making (Levi, 1980). A decision maker seeking to increase its knowledge is not only trying to learn truth but also trying to gain new and useful information. Such a decision maker is simultaneously playing two games: a game to obtain useful information and a game to preserve truth. Given a set of propositions, U, closed under negation (that is, if u is in the set then so is the negation, $\bar{u}$), information is gained whenever irrelevant or useless propositions $u \in U$ are rejected. This translates into a utility for rejecting proposition u or, equivalently, retaining proposition $\bar{u}$. On the other hand, identifying true propositions is one of the goals of epistemology which translates into a truth-based utility of accepting proposition u. Given these sometimes competing cognitive goals, the decision-maker engages in inquiry to identify true but informative propositions; stated simply, Levi asserts that error should be avoided (that is, truth should not be compromised) in the interest of adopting informative propositions. The lesson we learn from Levi is that truth and information are both essential elements of decision making and can be made explicit in the construction of a tradeoff-centered comparative rationality.

3.3. Comparing values: satisficing

Turning attention from the narrow world of epistemology to the broad world of practical decision making, we observe that truth is the epistemological manifestation of the practical decision-maker's goal of achieving success, and that information is the epistemological manifestation of the practical decision-maker's goal of efficiently using resources. In the practical decision-making arena, Popper's injunction can be rephrased to become *we want more than success — what we look for is efficient success.*

Building on Levi's work, tradeoffs can be thought of as a game between competing values. For most decision problems, there are not only reasons for accepting an option, but also reasons for rejecting an option. We need to translate these 'pros' and 'cons' into a decision rule that resolves these tradeoffs. Thus, we have two independent value functions: a payoff for selecting option u given θ, $J_1(u, \theta)$ (similar to Levi's truth support utility) and a payoff for rejecting option u given θ, $J_2(\bar{u}, \theta)$ (similar to Levi's informational value of rejection).

Returning again to Simon's notion of satisficing, we can think of an aspiration level as the utility of rejecting an option. In Simon's formulation, the aspiration level is derived from an expectation of possible consequences. By rejecting option u, the decision maker expects a payoff at least as great as the aspiration level. Thus, $J_2(\bar{u}, \theta)$ (which equals $\rho(\theta)$) encodes the aspiration level when the aspiration level is independent of the option. According to Simon, a decision is good enough only if $J_1(u, \theta) \geq J_2(\bar{u}, \theta) = \rho(\theta)$.

In the more general case when the payoff for rejecting an option depends on the option, we can think of the relationship of J_1 and J_2 as a tradeoff. The conventional approach to resolving tradeoffs is to combine the two utilities into a single utility and then to maximize the resulting hybrid utility; we discuss some aspects of this approach in the next subsection, but in this section we discuss an alternative formulation. Recall that a decision is optimal if, and only if, when compared to all other options, no other option is superior whence optimality is determined by comparing options against each other. By contrast, tradeoffs are resolved not by comparing options but rather by comparing values (defined over consequences) against each other, whence comparative rationality requires the evaluation of consequences. This is in the spirit of Simon's satisficing wherein the consequences of an option, encoded in the option's utility, are compared to the consequences of rejecting the option, encoded in the expected utility of an unidentified option.

An alternative to the optimization of an aggregated utility is to treat the resolution of a tradeoff as a meta-decision problem. Note that, in general, heuristics are used as fast and frugal ways to produce decisions and are therefore not decisions themselves but rather decision rules. Such decision rules are produced through a meta-decision process, sometimes the result of evolutionary forces, sometimes the result of external feedback, and sometimes the result of self-directed internal feedback. We construct a satisficing decision rule as the resolution of the tradeoff between J_1 and J_2 in the Appendix. Switching from the awkward notion of utility of rejecting u encoded in J_2 $(\bar{u}, \theta)$, we instead choose to think of the cost of choosing u and the benefit of choosing u encoded in, respectively, μ_L $(u; \theta) = J_2$ $(\bar{u}, \theta)$ and μ_A $(u; \theta) = J_1$ (u, θ). The satisficing decision rule, derived in the Appendix and presented as Equation (11) is repeated here for convenience

$$S_b = \{(u, \theta) : \mu_A(\mu; \theta) \geq b\mu_L(u; \theta)\}. \tag{3}$$

Under this rule, the consequences of decision u given observation θ are evaluated without reference to other decisions; an option is good enough if the consequences it produces are satisficing, and this characterization can be determined without reference to other options.

From (3) we see that the essence of satisficing, as determined from a tradeoff-centered resolution of indeterminate values, is a comparison. Intuitively speaking, this notion of satisficing requires that the payoff of selecting an option outweigh the payoff of rejecting that option. The definition of 'good enough' is based on comparing an option's benefit against the option's cost (and noting that the pay-off for rejecting an option is equivalent to a cost for accepting the option). This permits an agent-centered characterization of good-enough. An option is 'good enough' if benefit (as encoded in μ_A) outweighs cost (as encoded in μ_L). Satisficing therefore becomes a two-attribute decision problem with a benefit attribute (operationally termed *Accuracy*, meaning conformity to a given standard) and a cost attribute (operationally termed *Liability*, meaning susceptibility or exposure to to something undesirable). As mentioned earlier, Simon (1990) likened situated rationality to scissors with one blade the structure of the task environments and the other the computational capabilities of the actor. When these scissors operate, they produce two independent evaluations of consequences (the set of consequences are cut in two): a success-based evaluation called accuracy, and an efficiency-based evaluation called liability.

Given the satisficing decision rule, we can characterize the set of all states which are satisficing for a given u, and those skills which are satisficing given the state of nature θ, respectively defined as

$$S_b(u) = \{\theta : \mu_A(u, \theta) \geq b\mu_L(u, \theta)\} \tag{4}$$

$$S_b(\theta) = \{u : \mu_A(u, \theta) \geq b\mu_L(u, \theta)\}. \tag{5}$$

In practice, a decision-maker will not identify all elements of these sets, but will instead rely on the boundaries of these sets to detect when a behavior modification is mandatory. Suppose a cognitive skill $u \in U$ is being used to solve a decision problem. When $\theta \in S_b(u)$ then there is no need to resort to another approach. However, when $\theta \notin S_b(u)$, the current skill is inadequate and must be replaced with a different skill. Given the need to switch, any skill $u' \in S_b(\theta)$ can be employed. An evaluative algorithm can be outlined for tradeoff-based skill management as follows: If $\theta \in S_b(u)$ then $u' = u$; Else $u' \in S_b(\theta)$. This algorithm can be used to determine when a switch is mandatory. In other words, when θ is such that u is not satisficing then a new skill $u' \neq u$ must be selected.

3.4. Comparing alternatives: domination

Satisficing, as we have defined it, is a notion of rationality determined by comparing two aspects of the consequences of making a decision. Under this rationality, a decision can be admitted or rejected without reference to other decisions. However, learning, memory, and the ability to model the world sometimes permits an agent to compare the consequences of one decision against another. This allows a decision maker to compare the consequences of alternative decisions in an effort to improve performance. For every $u \in U$ let

$$B_A(u; \theta) = \{v \in U : \mu_L(v; \theta) < \mu_L(u; \theta) \ and \ \mu_A(v; \theta) \geq \mu_A(u; \theta)\}$$

$$B_L(u; \theta) = \{v \in U : \mu_L(v; \theta) < \mu_L(u; \theta) \ and \ \mu_A(v; \theta) \geq \mu_A(u; \theta)\} \tag{6}$$

and define the set of actions that are *strictly better* than u (i.e., set of actions that dominate u)

$$B(u; \theta) = B_A(u; \theta) \cup B_L(u; \theta); \tag{7}$$

that is, $B(u; \theta)$ consists of all possible actions that have lower liability but not lower accuracy than u, or have higher accuracy but not higher liability than u. If $B(u; \theta) = \emptyset$, then no actions can be preferred to u in both accuracy and liability, and u is a (weakly) non-dominated action with respect to θ. The *non-dominated* set

$$\varepsilon(\theta) = \{u \in U : B(u; \theta) = \emptyset\} \tag{8}$$

contains all non-dominated actions. It is interesting to note (see Goodrich *et al.*, 1998b) that the set $\varepsilon(\theta)$ is equivalent to the set of those options which maximize the aggregated utility $\alpha\mu_A(u; \theta) - (1 - \alpha) \mu_L(u; \theta)$ for some $\alpha \in [0, 1]$. In other words, $\varepsilon(\theta) = \{u : \exists \alpha \in [0, 1]$ for which u arg $\max_{u \in U} \alpha\mu_A(v; \theta) - (1 - \alpha) \mu_L(v; \theta)$. This means that the set of non-dominated options is equivalent to the set of maximizing options when the tradeoff parameter α is completely indeterminate.

It is important to note that the interpretation of $\varepsilon(\theta)$ as the set of optimal multi-attribute decisions is inadequate to justify selection of an option. Observe from (8) that $\varepsilon(\theta)$ is not a function of the consequences of making a decision, but rather a function of the state of nature. This distinction is important because decisions should be justified on the basis of their consequences and not simply because they are superior to some other decisions according to an arbitrary criterion. An element of $\varepsilon(\theta)$ might be optimal with respect to some criterion, but it may also produce unacceptable consequences. Thus, domination should act as a secondary criterion for determining the usefulness of an option and not as the primary criterion whence *domination is discretionary* (which is a companion to the notion that optimality is optional); it is a fact of life that sometimes the best option available to us is still unacceptable.

3.5. Postlude

To summarize the discussion of the preceding sections, two thoughts have emerged. First, decisions in the satisficing set are justified by the consequences, and decisions in the non-dominated set are justified by the alternatives. Second, satisficing is mandatory and domination is discretionary. One more point deserves mention before we end this section. One advantage of the aspiration-based satisficing approach is that multiple attributes (or, analogously, multiple states) decreases the size of the set of options that are satisficing. This implies that searching for a solution that is satisficing may take longer. However, once a satisficing option is identified it is likely to be robustly applicable under many circumstances.

Returning to our automobile driving example, following the vehicle is satisficing because the benefits of following, relative to our goal of reaching our destination, outweigh the costs of following, relative to time loss or risk. The passing behavior dominates the following behavior, but passing is optional so we feel no mandated need to pass. When cognitive resources permit, we may observe that passing dominates, but we need not pass since the current skill produces good enough consequences. Additionally, because car following is a skill that is satisficing under both heavy and light traffic densities, the skill is robust in that it affords safe but productive driving in many driving environments.

4. Intelligence through a multiple agent society

A large step toward resolving the debate between simple heuristics versus complex decision mechanisms is made by realizing that for goal-directed choice there exist meta-choice problems. For example, applying expected utility theory requires a meta-choice to determine the set of feasible options, beliefs, consequences, and utilities. From a machine intelligence perspective, the debate is often a discussion of whether these meta problems should be implicitly included in the choice problem (to produce complex decision mechanisms), or if simple skills and heuristics can be efficiently and explicitly (meta-)managed to produce the same intelligent results. From a human intelligence perspective, the debate is concerned with prescriptive versus descriptive models of rational choice; prescriptive models require the decision-maker to solve the meta-problems internally, and descriptive models suppose that these problems are solved through evolutionary or other externally imposed conditions (although there is nothing unnatural about learning to self-police our behaviors).

To justify the managed-skill hypothesis in describing human behavior or to encode this hypothesis in designing machine intelligence, we must address the theoretical issue of meta choices. Satisficing is a tradeoff-centered decision principle that applies to meta-decision problems and therefore decreases the gap between mind and machine, or in the quest to settle the debate between simple and complex decision mechanisms. Given that the essence of satisficing is tradeoff, the important issue is how, when, and by whom should tradeoffs be resolved. These questions are questions in meta-agency, that is, questions in self evaluation and self anticipation.

4.1. Situated decision makers

As we understand the philosopher Charles Peirce, meaning and therefore intelligence call only be present in a semiotic triad consisting of some kind of observation (firstness), some kind of consequent (secondness), and some kind of mapping from observation to consequent (thirdness) that turns

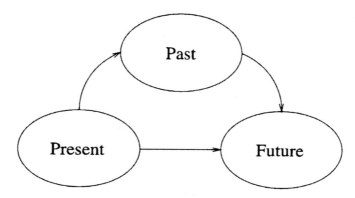

Figure 2 Interface between past, present, and future. Past experience, through explicit causal models or through utility elicitation, allows a decision-maker to map present observations and options into desirable future consequences.

firstness into secondness. Goal-directed agents capable of continued existence in real environments should have the capacity to respond to, interpret, and evaluate observations in terms of their capacities and skills. The key to doing this is to allow lessons learned from the past (in the form of values, models of causal behavior, etc.) to turn observations from the present into acceptable future consequences. As diagrammed in Figure 2, the past (thirdness) transforms the present (firstness) into the future (secondness).

The lesson we learn from this triad of situated agency is that much of reasoning is done in terms of either past experiences or expected future experiences. This can be extremely complex unless effective coping strategies are developed and used. A remarkably efficient coping strategy is to organize intelligence into modules appropriate for commonly encountered circumstances. We call these modules cognitive or behavioral skills and note that these skills determine the behavior of a situated decision maker. Such a decision maker can reason about the world in terms of the consequences afforded by these skills. With the emergence of multiple skills including the capacity for general-purpose problem solving, a decision maker can be capable of very sophisticated behaviors. In this context, an expert is one who has a skill that will produce satisficing consequences for any state θ in the domain of expertise Θ. This is diagrammed in Figure 3. Each closed curve represents a skill that produces satisficing consequences for the θ that it encloses. Note that multiple skills can be satisficing for a particular θ and that the skill set spans almost the entire domain of expertise Θ. In general, an expert in one domain Θ will not be an expert in all domains.

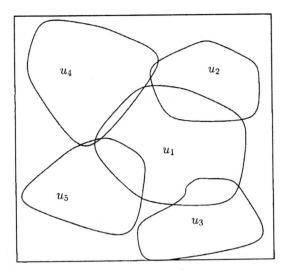

Figure 3 For a specific domain of expertise Θ, an expert has skills spanning the space that produce satisficing consequences. For any state, multiple skills can suffice.

4.2. Multiple agent society

Although many behavioral skills can be organized into a stimulus-response loop, cognitive skills require an appropriate organization. Borrowing on Minsky's *Society of Mind* (Minsky, 1986), we can treat each cognitive skill as an agent and organize these agents into a society. Recognizing that these agents must interact, we can include layers of agents managing agents (i.e., meta-agents), and agents managing agents managing agents, etc. These layers form a multi-resolutional hierarchical society of cognitive agents. Within this society, multiple forces can influence a decision. These forces include top-down forces from agents responsible for accomplishing certain goals, bottom-up forces from skilled agents responsible for acting in a particular context, and lateral forces from neighboring agents interacting to accomplish tasks that accommodate shared goals or require shared resources. Top-down forces evoke success-based evaluations of skills, and bottom-up forces evoke efficiency-based evaluations of skills.

4.3. Decision forces

Cognitive skills provide affordances for rational behavior. The term *affordance* is a term introduced by Gibson (1979) and extended by Norman to mean "those fundamental properties that determine just how the thing

179

[skill] could possibly be used" (Norman, 1988, p. 9). Skills whose affordances are compatible with top-down goals induce an attractive potential commensurate with their likely usefulness. In terms of the values involved in a tradeoff, J_1 (u; θ) represents this attractive potential. However, in addition to task specific goals there are also context-dependent constraints on the efficiency of these skills, and these constraints induce a repulsive potential commensurate with their likely inefficiency. The function J_2 ($\bar{u}$, θ) represents this repulsive potential.

Two independent descriptions of consequences can be thought of as the interplay between the two potential fields. Given the analogy of J_1 and J_2 as attractive and repulsive potentials, we can use this analogy to interpret the notion of satisficing. An option (skill) is satisficing if and only if the attractive potential is greater than the repulsive potential. Partitioning evaluations of consequences into these attributes recalls the generalized potential field (GPF) approach to path planning and obstacle avoidance (see, for example, Nam et al., 1996; Guldner and Utkin, 1993). In the GPF methodology, a goal is represented as an attractive potential, obstacles are represented as repulsive potentials, and the path along the negative gradient of the combined potentials is selected as a collision-free path. Although GPF approaches have traditionally been used to plan a feasible path (with a corresponding sequence of actions), the basic idea has been extended to dynamic environments wherein individual actions are identified as a function of current and projected future dynamic states (Nam et al., 1996). Unlike such GPF approaches which produce a unique best path (or unique best option), however, a tradeoff is resolved once a single skill is identified with attractive potential greater than repulsive potential. By contrast, non-dominated options are best in the GPF sense.

In this way, satisficing is a companion to a resolved tradeoff emerging from independent values. The interaction between meta-agents resolving meta problems and choice-agents resolving choice problems involves inherent indeterminacy. Simply put, a meta-agent does not know (nor especially care) what option a choice-agent will select, nor is it appropriate for the meta-agent to speculate about the expected choices of the choice-agent (doing so shifts all responsibility to the meta-agent and relegates the choice-agent to a vacuous role). The meta-agent is responsible for abductively framing the problem, and the choice-agent is responsible for inductively solving the problem. Since the consequences of framing a problem are different from the consequences of solving a problem, there is an indeterminate mapping between the consequences evaluated by the meta-agent and the consequences evaluated by the choice-agent. This indeterminacy requires that the meta-agent deal with sets of options and produces a decision rule used by the choice-agent to identify 'good enough' consequences.

180

4.4. Two stages of self-policing: evaluation and anticipation

As diagrammed in Figure 2, a minimum requirement for intelligence is a relationship between past, present, and future. To facilitate this relationship, there must be three phases for any choice problem: anticipating consequences, the 'moment of truth' when choice is made, and evaluating consequences. Anticipating future and evaluating past consequences are necessary stages in rational self-policing. By evaluating past consequences a decision-maker is evaluating its past choices, and is thus performing a third person (meta-)evaluation of a 'past self.' If performance is inadequate or if superior alternatives are manifest then the decision maker should adapt its future behavior. By anticipating future consequences, a decision maker is evaluating its future states, and is thus performing a third person (meta-)evaluation of a 'future self.' If expected performance is inadequate or if superior alternatives are recognized then the decision maker should act accordingly.

Unless anticipation and evaluation are simply re-enactments of the moment of truth, the decision maker should be seeking to identify feasible options. This is done in two ways: by identifying options that resolve tradeoffs and by identifying options that are non-dominated. In order of increasing complexity and necessity, satisficing-based rationality must be satisfied first (unless, for a particular world, non-domination guarantees satisficing) and then, if resources permit, domination-based rationality can be satisfied.

4.5. Problem solving

Let us now turn attention to a timeline for making rational decisions. Assume that the decision maker is situated, meaning that the decision maker has a known goal and exists in a particular context. A rational decision-maker should begin by identifying the set of possible states of nature Θ. By identifying relevant states, a process aided by familiarity with the situation or previous exposure to similar situations, the decision-maker is able to identify the goal-driven affordances from the suite of cognitive skills that it has available. Additionally, the decision-maker can recognize contextual factors that restrict the applicability of particular skills. Given an observation x and a subsequent understanding of the state of nature θ, the decision maker then enters the three phase process of decision making. This process consists of the two self-policing phases of anticipation and evaluation, and the moment of truth (i.e., choice) phase.

4.5.1. Anticipation

Given the state of nature, the meta-agent can determine the expected payoffs μ_A and μ_L of each skill through a deliberation process, through an

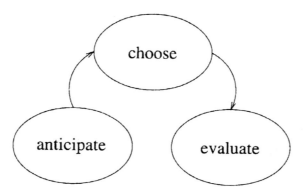

Figure 4 Three phases of the situated decision making. Choice is the *moment of truth* for a choice agent, and anticipation and evaluation are elements of (meta-)rational self-policing.

experience-based identification process, or through a stimulus–response mechanism. The meta-agent initiates a search for an appropriate skill, perhaps beginning at a default skill and then proceeding to other skills using some practiced procedure. Each possible skill is analyzed to see if its expected consequences resolve the tradeoff between goal-driven payoffs and context-dependent costs. If the decision maker has ample time and memory or a wealth of experience, multiple satisficing options might be identified yielding $G \subset S_h$ (θ). Furthermore, past experience may help the decision maker identify non-dominated options via lateral decision forces whence the search can be restricted to non-dominated option ε (θ).

4.5.2. Moment of truth

At the moment of truth, any $u \in G$ can be applied. Selecting among the alternatives can be done (a) via a constrained optimization policy such as selecting $u^* = \arg\max_{u \in G} \mu_A (v; \theta) - b\mu_L (u; \theta)$, (b) via an exploratory policy wherein an unexplored option $u \in G$ is randomly selected, or (c) through an arbitrary process wherein any $u \in G$ is randomly selected. The policy can be adapted to reflect the nuances present in the moment of truth. Regardless of the policy, the skill is expected to produce satisficing consequences and thus resolve the decision tradeoff because of the anticipation phase. In terms of modeling human behavior, it is important to note that not all behavioral variability is a result of noise and uncertainty. Instead, a portion of this variability results because, for a particular context and a particular task, many behaviors may be satisficing. This suggests that constrained optimization, though possibly appropriate for design, may not be readily applicable to describing the moment of truth in naturalistic settings.

4.5.3. Evaluation

Following the moment of truth, the consequences of the choice are evaluated. Any mismatch between anticipated and observed values can be used to tune these values for future use. Additionally, the meta-agent determines if the consequences are satisficing. If they are satisficing ($u \in S_b(\theta)$) and if cognitive resources are available, then the meta-agent might[2] compare u to other (remembered) options to refine the set of feasible options ε, or bias the search mechanism to use u again. If the consequences are not satisficing ($u \notin S_b(\theta)$) then the meta-agent might spawn a new search to find a skill $u' \in S_b(\theta)$ that is expected to produce satisficing consequences. If, after exploring and evaluating all known options, $S_b = \emptyset$ then the tradeoff is not resolvable given current options. The decision maker must then either adjust its expectations (decrease b) or acquire a new skill that will be appropriate for the circumstances.

5. Discussion and examples: simple inference heuristics versus complex decision mechanisms

Satisficing rationality provides a simple but justifiable method for determining when simple inference heuristics and/or complex decision mechanisms are justified. This allows the decision maker to perform cognitive and behavioral tasks with an appropriate mechanism by turning the meta-decision problem into one of controlling the selection of an appropriate skill. In this section, we give examples that support the hypothesis that intelligent behavior is organized into cognitive and behavior skills, and discuss how satisficing manifests itself in decision making.

5.1. Heuristics and biases: the existence of cognitive skills

In studies of human cognitive performance, Daniel Kahneman and Amos Tversky have led the way in identifying several heuristics and biases that systematically differ from standards of normative rationality (Kahneman and Tversky, 1979; Gardner, 1985). Among other observations, two seem most relevant to our discussion. The first observation is that people use and misapply cognitive shortcuts in inappropriate situations. The misapplication of cognitive shortcuts (i.e., heuristics) is evidence that people have and use these heuristics, and the fact that some cognitive biases disappear when the problem is reframed (e.g., the overconfidence bias can be overcome when data are presented as frequencies rather than probabilities (Gigerenzer, 1996; Kahneman and Tversky, 1996)) indicates that cognitive skills are ecologically adapted to certain domains. Additionally, the presence of robust but simple heuristics such as 'Take The Best' demonstrate that these heuristics can be very effective (Gigerenzer and Goldstein, 1996). The second observation is that untrained people are not very good at applying methods of normative rationality. One logical conclusion from the heuristics and biases literature is that if researchers want to fool subjects, they can probably succeed by inducing an incorrect cognitive skill.

5.2. Experts and naturalistic decision making: non-optimal choice

The naturalistic decision making community has emerged in response to dissatisfaction with using normative models of rationality in descriptions of expert behavior (Zsambok and Klein, 1997). A characteristic of naturalistic decision making descriptions of human intelligence is that experts organize intelligence into cognitive skills. The majority of time spent in expert decision making is spent searching and understanding the state of nature. Once the state space is accurately deciphered, an appropriate skill is invoked and the problem is efficiently solved. From Dreyfus and Dreyfus (1985), "[Experts] reflect upon the goal or perspective that seems evident to them and upon the action that seems appropriate to achieving that goal." They reason about the world in terms of afforded actions, and select action according to their stated goal. Experts do not reason using context independent and general purpose problem solvers, but rather with cognitive skills spanning the range of relevant states of nature (see Figure 3). Developing expertise is the process of spanning the states of nature and learning how to recognize and use the appropriate skill. Since acquiring a set of skills that span Θ is done during the process of becoming an expert, the majority of expert time is not spent in complex decision making but rather in identifying a skill appropriate for the circumstances.

5.3. Human interaction with automation: detailed example of explicit skill management

In this subsection, we give a detailed example of skill management in the context of human interaction with automation. Automation is ideal for illustrating skill management because when a human initiates automation they are consciously delegating a skill to the machine, and when they terminate automation they are consciously appropriating a skill from the machine. Both of these skill transitions provide a means to demonstrate how humans can manage skills. This section is largely taken from previously published work or from work currently in review (see Goodrich et al., 1998a, for a summary of the work under review).

5.3.1. Context

A mental model is an internal representation employed to encode, predict, and evaluate the consequences of perceived and intended changes to the system operator's current state within the dynamic environment. Humans interpret and respond to sensory input according to the context established by a mental model through task-specific filtering of the external world. Skilled action is organized into behavioral quanta that correspond to separate mental models each with their own perceptually delineated operational domain (Goodrich *et al.*, 1998). Many aspects of cognitive decision-making have been described in terms of mental models (Minsky, 1986; Johnson-Laird, 1988). Formally, a mental model $\mathcal{M}$ is a triple consisting of the perceived state of the environment Θ, a set of decisions or actions U, and a set of ordered consequences C that result from choosing $u \in U$ when $\theta \in \Theta$ obtains. According to this specification, a mental model not only encodes the relation between the input-action pair[3] (θ, u) and the predicted consequence c, but also induces an evaluation of preferences among consequences (see Figure 5, and compare to related figures in Meystel, 1996; Sheridan, 1992; Albus, 1991). In words, the mental model $\mathcal{M}$ provides the context for meaningfully interpreting sensory information and generating purposeful behavior and thus represents and encodes past experience within a decision problem.

Human behavior can be organized into a set of skilled activities that are applied when afforded by the environment (Gibson and Crooks, 1938; Norman, 1988). In this context, the term *activity*[4] means the human's actions on the system (e.g., a behavioral activity is pushing the brake pedal or turning the steering wheel, and a cognitive activity is adding two numbers or making a simple deduction). Formally, a *skill* can then be defined as *a learned sequence of human activities*. The human must map environmental

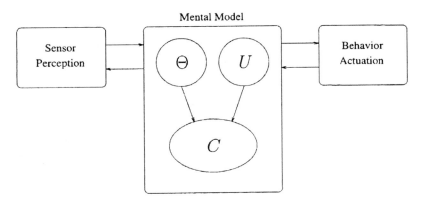

Figure 5 Working specification of a mental model. The arrows represent perceived or real influence. Consequences are a function of states and actions; behavior is generated through the operation of a mental model, but the mental model is constrained by the set of behavioral affordances; and sensory observations influence the mental model, but the mental model dictates active sensing of the environment.

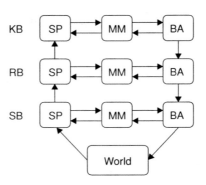

Figure 6 Interaction within a society of mental model agents. SP, sensor perception, MM, mental model, and BA, behavior actuation. The horizontal arrows are explained in the caption to Figure 5, and the vertical arrows indicate interaction of low level sensors/high level goals with high level representations/low level actions.

cues into selected activities; an efficient way to perform this mapping is to employ a pattern of activities specific for a particular task, and then implement this skill when appropriate. This approach uses a task-specific mental model to determine which skill is appropriate for the circumstances. Switches between skills are mandated when target perceptual states are not achievable by the currently enabled skill-based behavior or when enabled skills are not satisficing for the given state.

Human cognition can be described using multiple mental models (treated as agents) which can be organized into a society of interacting agents. This societal structure not only determines which agents contribute to human behavior, but also which agents can employ attentional resources. A three-level multi-resolutional society of interacting mental models organized into a hierarchical structure (see Figure 6) can be constructed corresponding to Rasmussen's knowledge-based (KB), rule-based (RB), and skill-based (SB) behaviors[5] (Rasmussen, 1976; Sheridan, 1992). At the KB level of this hierarchy, the agent role is supervisory; at the RB level, the agent role is task management; and at the SB level, the agent role is task execution. Intuitively speaking, the KB, RB, and SB agents think, monitor, and control, respectively. These mental model agents operate within the context of overall complex human behavior. SB agents are akin to cognitive skills, and RB agents are akin to meta-agents.

5.3.2. Experiment purpose and description

Automobile driving is a mix of cognitive and behavioral skills. When a driver delegates a task to automation, the vehicle assumes responsibility for a behavioral skill. However, the driver retains (meta-)responsibility for detecting the limits of the automation and responding appropriately. We conducted an experiment in which human subjects were placed in a driving simulator with a cruise control system engaged. At random intervals, a vehicle cut in front of the subject's vehicle and compelled the subject to determine if the automation can safely perform the skill or if the driver needed to intervene. Our objective in the experiment is to identify the perceptual boundary that delineates between when people use the skill performed by the cruise control and the skill of braking. To this end, we can obtain empirical estimates of accuracy and liability, as described below and as illustrated in Figure 7, after we have identified the top-down goal of driving and the bottom-up constraints on driving. Although people sometimes drive for pleasure and other related reasons, the predominant (top-down) reason for driving is to expediently reach a destination. Although fuel consumption and other factors can influence driving behavior, the predominant (bottom-up) constraint on driving is safety. In the next section, we associate expediency and safety with the perceptual variables time-to-contact and time headway, respectively defined as $T_c = R/v_R$ and $T_h = R/v$, where R is the distance (range) between two vehicles, v_R is the relative velocity between

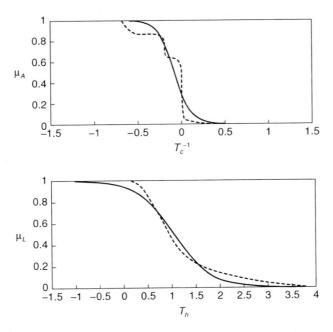

Figure 7 Actual (dashed line) and approximated (solid line) functions as a function of perceptually feasible observations: (a) accuracy as a function of time to collision T_c^{-1} and (b) liability as a function of time headway T_h.

the two vehicles, and v is the velocity of the subject vehicle. Intuitively speaking, time-to-contact is the amount of time before two vehicles collide, and time headway is the amount of time required for a vehicle to traverse the distance between itself and a lead vehicle (the commonly used role of maintaining a 2-s buffer between your vehicle and a lead vehicle is tantamount to requiring that $T_h \geq 2$). In practice, inverse time-to-contact is used because it retains perceptual plausibility[6] and is more amenable to computational modeling than time-to-contact (because T_c is infinite for any value of $v_R = 0$). These variables and the vehicle's speed v are ecologically valid state variables[7] that describe the state of the environment $\Theta = [T_h, T_c^{-1}, v]$ and span the domain of expertise Θ (Goodrich and Boer, 1998). The variables T_h and T_c^{-1} are used to delineate the region of satisficing cruise control usage, and v is the variable regulated by the cruise control system.

5.3.3. Empirical estimates

To identify μ_A and μ_L our objective is to find substates that trigger active braking. In the experiment, the subject was required to determine when the speed regulation (SR) skill of regulating v about a desired value via the cruise control must be replaced with a braking (BA) behavior. We therefore distinguish between nominal behavior[8] $u = SR$ and active braking behavior $u = BA$. Our goal is thus to find when $\theta \notin S_h (u)$ for $u = SR$. Nominal operating conditions occur when the brake pedal is not pressed (the term *nominal* implies that the driver persists in the currently chosen SR skill). The boundary of the perceptual region spanned by the SR skill, defined as $S_h (SR)$, is determined by identifying when the utility of terminating the SR skill (as determined in the context of safety) outweighs the utility of persisting in the SR skill (as determined in the context of expediency). T_h encodes safety-related information; low time headway indicates low safety because following too close implies high risk. T_c^{-1} encodes expediency-related information; low T_c^{-1}, which corresponds to low relative velocity, indicates high expediency because following at low relative velocity implies that the driver is likely to reach the destination expediently (without catastrophic incident).

For both nominal and braking conditions, we select representative sample points from each experimental trial and create two sets of $[T_c^{-1}, T_h]^T$ points: one set for nominal conditions, denoted NOM, and one set for braking conditions, denoted BRK. For trials when subjects actively brake, the subjects are demonstrating a switch to the BA skill whence the sub-state(s) $[T_c^{-1}, T_h]^T$ when braking is initiated is included in BRK, and the sub-state(s) $[T_c^{-1}, T_h]_T$ when braking is terminated (implying a switch back to the SR skill) is included in NOM; for trials when subjects do not brake, the subjects are demonstrating that the SR skill is satisficing whence the initial sub-state $[T_c^{-1}, T_h]^T$ in the trial is included in NOM; and for trials where subjects only brake (by anticipating the cut-in and then coming to a stop), the subjects are demonstrating that the SR skill is not satisficing whence the initial sub-state $[T_c^{-1}, T_h]^T$ in the trial is included in BRK.

For notational purposes in the subsequent sections, let $N\,(T = \tau\,|\,\text{CONDITION})$ denote the cardinality of the set of points $T = \tau$ given CONDITION. For example, $N\,(T_c^{-1} = \tau\,|\,\text{NOM})$ is the number of points in the set $\{\theta \in \text{NOM} : T_c^{-1} = \tau\}$. Under nominal conditions $\theta \in \text{NOM}$), relative velocity must be considered acceptable to the driver whence the distribution of T_c^{-1} under nominal conditions is an observable entity that provides information about when SR is an accurate skill. Clearly, if $T_c^{-1} = \tau_2$ is accurate then $\tau_1 < \tau_2$ must be at least as accurate (the expediency of the SR skill will not decrease as relative velocity decreases although another skill, such as a 'speed-up' skill, might dominate SR). This monotonicity property facilitates the computation of the accuracy function as the cumulative distribution function

$$\mu_A(T_c^{-1} = \tau) = 1 - F_{T_c^{-1}}(\tau\,|\,\text{NOM})$$

$$= 1 - \frac{N(T_c^{-1} \leq \tau\,|\,\text{NOM})}{N(T_c^{-1} \leq \infty\,|\,\text{NOM})}$$

For classification purposes, we fit (via least-squares) a sigma function of the form $1/e^{(a\tau+b)}$ to $\mu_A\,(\cdot)$ yielding the function shown in Figure 7(a).

When braking is initiated ($\theta \in \text{BRK}$), it must be because the driver considers the time headway values unacceptable, whence the distribution of time headways when the driver initiates braking is an observable entity that provides information about what is rejectable. Clearly, if $T_h = \tau_2$ is rejectable then $\tau_1 < \tau_2$ must be at least as rejectable (safety decreases as following distance decreases). This monotonicity property facilitates the computation of the liability function as the cumulative distribution function

$$\mu_L(T_h = \tau) = 1 - F_{T_h}(\tau\,|\,BRK)$$

$$= 1 - \frac{N(T_h \leq \tau\,|\,BRK)}{N(T_h \leq \infty\,|\,BRK)}.$$

For classification purposes, we fit (via least-squares) a sigma function of the form $1/e^{(-a\tau+b)}$ to $\mu_L(\cdot)$ yielding the function shown in Figure 7(b).

5.3.4. Classification results

For the driver to switch from one skill to another, it is necessary to identify when $u \notin S_b\,(\theta)$. Using $\mu_A\,(T_c^{-1})$ and $\mu_L\,(T_h$ from Figure 7, we can construct the set of states $S_b\,(\text{SR}) = \{\theta : \mu_A\,(T_c^{-1}) \geq b\mu_L\,(T_h)\}$ that support nominal behavior, and the set of states $S_b^c\,(\text{SR}) = \{\theta : \mu_A\,(T_c^{-1}) < b\mu_L\,(T_h)\}$ (superscript c denotes complement) that do not support nominal behavior. Thus,

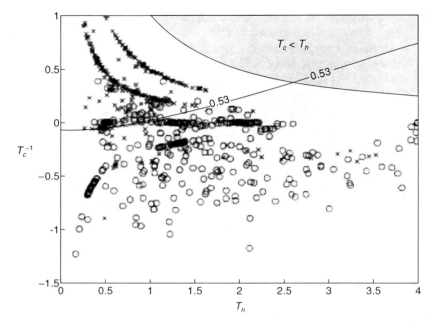

Figure 8 Scatter plot of nominal and braking perceptual states. The line represents the boundary of the nominal skill (states to the northwest of the line are unacceptable). The boundary of the braking skill is not identified in this plot. Compare this figure to Figure 3.

the line $\mu_A(T_c^{-1}) = b\mu_L(T_h)$ determines when behavior must be switched from nominal to braking. In other words, the line is the boundary of S_b (SR).

Given the empirically derived functions, we can determine the boundary between nominal and braking behaviors as a function of b by finding the perceptual states θ for which $\mu_A (T_c^{-1}) < b\mu_L (T_h)$. This is illustrated in Figure 8 for the data gathered in the simulator experiment, where $\bigcirc$ indicates $\theta \in$ NOM and $\times$ indicates $\theta \in$ BRK. To the northwest of the line, BA is satisficing but SR is not, and to the southeast of the line SR (and, perhaps, BA) is satisficing. Classification can be performed by finding the value of b that optimally separates braking from nominal behavior. Consider the following three performance indices: $J_1 (b)$ is the percentage of trials that are incorrectly classified (i.e., the total number of $\bigcirc$s above the line plus the total number of $\times$s below the line), $J_2 (b)$ is the percentage of nominal trials that are incorrectly classified as braking (i.e., number of $\bigcirc$s above the line), and $J_3 (b)$ is the percentage of braking trials that are incorrectly classified as nominal (i.e., number of $\times$s below the line). The value $b = 0.53$ is the minimax value $b = \arg \min_{b \geq 0} \max \{J_1 (b), J_2(b), J_3 (b)\}$ which attempts to balance the percentage of misclassifications ($J_1 (b)$), false alarms ($J_2 (b)$), and missed detections ($J_3 (b)$). The value $b = 0.20$ minimizes the number of samples

Table I Classification accuracies for different values of *b*.

b	% Misclassified	% False braking	% Missed braking
0.20	10.04	1.95	8.09
0.53	13.25	8.37	4.88

misclassified $b = \arg \min_{b \geq 0} J_1$ (b). The classification results for the different values of *b* are shown in Table I and indicate that, on the average, over 85% of samples are correctly classified.

These results were validated in a separate experiment using professional drivers in real vehicles responding to cut in events on a closed test track. To perform the classification, μ_A (T_c^{-1}) and μ_L (T_h) were estimated, and the *b* that minimizes the misclassification error was determined. The experiments generated one false alarm (○ above the line) and no missed detections (× below the line) in fifty trials at varying speeds. The results between the test track experiments and driving simulator experiments are very similar. The test track results produce a slightly smaller value of *b* ($b = 0.21$ for the test track versus an average value of $b = 0.53$ for the driving simulator) and a slight change in the liability function.[9]

5.4. Automobile driver behavior and navigation: implicit skill management

We can now return to the driving example given in the introduction. While driving an automobile, we have been following a vehicle for an extended period of time even though there is very little traffic on the road. Because following the vehicle is satisficing, we do not feel a need to consider changing our behavior but rather rest content with following the vehicle. Suddenly, we realize that we can easily pass and that we want to do so because the lead vehicle is going slower than our desired speed. Once we observe that an alternative behavior is still satisficing but dominates our current behavior, we select this behavior and act accordingly. This is possible because much of the behavior associated with speed management can be described by three simple skills: speed regulation, car following, and active braking. Speed regulation applies in the absence of other traffic, and is a simple perceptual regulation task where we manage the vehicle's speed to produce an optic flow consistent with our calibrated estimate of the vehicle's speed. Car following applies in the presence of other traffic, and is a simple perceptual regulation task where we manage the relative rate of optical expansion to stay within a threshold (Lee, 1976). Active braking is less sophisticated, and is tantamount to detecting an anomalous situation and defaulting to a safe behavior. Coordinating these behavioral skills is an exercise in meta-rationality with multiple satisficing skills overlapping for a given θ.

Navigation problems can be precisely solved by appealing to the topological layout of the city and a sense of direction. However, only a portion of the population actually navigates this way (Aginsky *et al.*, 1997). Many drivers use landmarks extensively; they maintain their course until a landmark triggers a behavioral response. Although the first method is more robust to errors for a well-informed driver, it requires complex representations of city and geography. By contrast, the landmark method is remarkably efficient in producing effective navigation, and requires minimal representation of the city. If the landmark is salient the driver can succeed with minimal knowledge of the street topology (Aginsky *et al.*, 1997). Both skills are justifiable for most of driving, and one is a simple heuristic method while the other is a complex decision method.

Both of these examples illustrate that simple heuristics can be used in dynamic operation of automobiles. Both are remarkably efficient in the required use of cognitive resources, and current evidence suggests that they are effective in producing desired behavior. Moreover, we are exploring how these different skills are managed, and preliminary evidence suggests that satisficing meta-rationality provides a useful mechanism for skill management (Boer and Goodrich, 1998; Boer *et al.*, 1998).

6. Conclusions

The essence of satisficing is tradeoff. Based on this theme, we constructed a decision-theoretic characterization of satisficing as a comparison of two independent evaluations of consequences: the consequence of accepting the option and the consequence of rejecting the option. Simon's original descriptions of satisficing fit nicely within this framework, but many variants of his ideas appear to abandon this comparative rationality in favor of variants of superlative rationality via constrained optimization. Since, as we have discussed, optimality is optional (and its companion domination is discretionary), satisficing, which is a mandatory evaluation of the consequences of a decision, deserves prominent attention in the decision-making community because being the best among the alternatives may not be acceptable, attainable, nor unambiguously definable. Additionally, satisficing provides a mechanism for spanning both simple inference heuristics and complex decision mechanisms; the satisficing decision rule manifests itself as a simple heuristic but has a meta-rationality justification.

We have presented several examples of satisficing and cognitive skill management. The most engaging example referred to automobile driver behavior in interacting with other traffic. The example illustrated why we consider it rational to do non-optimal things. In automobile driving, when drivers have limited attentional resources their superlative rationality is bounded and optimality is precluded — even for voracious optimizers. Nevertheless, drivers' comparative rationality permits the justification of rational driving behaviors. Extending from driving to other domains of goal-directed decision making, we observe that skills (be they heuristic or complex) are justified only if satisficing.

Appendix: A characterization of satisficing through meta-rationality

Resolving a tradeoff is not a decision itself, but rather a decision about how to decide, that is, a meta-decision or *decision rule*. In words, we want to identify conditions under which the tradeoff is resolved. We do this by deriving the satisficing decision rule by comparing all possible decision rules that combine a payoff for accepting and a payoff for rejecting an option. The result of this derivation is a decision rule which obtains its justification by an appeal to superlative meta-rationality, but which manifests itself as comparative rationality.

Let $\phi : \Theta \to \mathfrak{B}$, where $\mathfrak{B}$ is a sigma-algebra associated with U, denote a decision rule that maps the set of states of nature Θ to the subset $G \in \mathfrak{B}$ of possibilities. To resolve a tradeoff we must find the optimal decision rule ϕ subject to the constraint that u and $\bar{u}$ cannot simultaneously be accepted. The resulting decision rule represents the resolution of the tradeoffs in values J_1 and J_2. We can identify the utility of the decision rule ϕ as an aggregation of the two payoffs

$$H(\phi, x) = E_{\phi|x}[J(\phi(\theta), \theta)]$$

$$= E_{\theta|x}\left\{ \sum_{u \in U} [\alpha J_1(u, \theta)p(u \in \phi(\theta)) \right.$$

$$\left. + (1 - \alpha)J_2(\bar{u}, \theta)p(\bar{u} \in \phi(\theta))] \right\} \qquad (9)$$

where $p(u \in \phi(\theta))$ represents the probability that option $u \in U$ is an acceptable resolution to the tradeoff with $p(\bar{u} \in \phi(\theta))$ defined conversely, where α denotes a tradeoff parameter, and where $E_{\theta|x}(H)$ denotes the expectation of J with respect to the conditional probability $p(\theta \mid x)$, that is

$$E_{\phi|x}(H(\phi(\theta), \theta)) = \sum_{\theta \in \Theta} H(\phi(\theta), \theta)p(\theta) \mid x).$$

By choosing the decision rule ϕ we also choose the probabilities $p(\bar{u} \in \phi(\theta))$ and $p(u \in \phi(\theta))$. Our objective is to find a decision rule ϕ that maximizes (9) keeping in mind that the rule ϕ is a resolution between J_1 and J_2. Let

$$\mu_A(u; x) = \sum_{\theta \in \Theta} J_1(u, \theta)p(\theta \mid x)$$

$$\mu_L(u; x) = \sum_{\theta \in \Theta} J_2(\bar{u}, \theta)p(\theta \mid x)$$

Maximizing (9) over all possible tradeoffs yields the decision rule

193

$$\phi(x) = \begin{cases} u & \alpha\mu_A(u; x) \geq (1 - \alpha)\mu_L(y; x) \\ \bar{u} & \text{otherwise} \end{cases} \tag{10}$$

Without loss of generality, let observation x uniquely determine state θ whence we drop the dependence on x. The set of consequences that survive the resolution of the tradeoff is called the satisficing set and is given by

$$S_\alpha = \{ (u, \theta) : \alpha\mu_A(u; \theta) \geq (1 - \alpha)\mu_L(u; \theta) \}$$

or equivalently,

$$S_b - \{ (u, \theta) : \mu_A(u; \theta) \geq b\mu_L(u; \theta) \}, \tag{11}$$

where $b = 1 - \alpha/\alpha$. Thus, we see that resolving a tradeoff by maximizing over possible decision rules produces a weak rationality that eliminates obviously bad choices and admits good enough choices. Intuitively speaking, a tradeoff does not produce unique best decisions but rather a suspension of judgment between decisions that are 'good enough.' A *tradeoff is resolved if and only if at least one skill u can be identified whose expected benefits outweigh the expected costs, that is if and only if $S_b \neq \emptyset$.*

Notes

1 This can be determined directly by anticipating consequences via a model and then ranking the consequences, or indirectly by using a value function over state-action pairs (as in Q-learning), or some contribution of both.
2 Note that this approach of continuing to search if results are satisficing is not observed in studies of the design process (Ball *et al.*, 1996) because, simply put, if the results are good enough then there is very little motive to continue dedicating resources to determining another option.
3 A decision u is often treated as a mapping from Θ into the set of consequences (Fishburn, 1981).
4 There are many uses of the term activity in pattern recognition and design literature (see, for example, Bobick, 1997; Norman, 1998). For our purposes, we use activity to mean low-level movements which is yet another use of the term.
5 These layers correspond not only to Saridis's *organization, coordination,* and *execution* levels, respectively, for intelligent machine design (Saridis, 1989), but also the strategic, tactical, and operational levels of decision-making (Boer *et al.*, 1998).
6 Time-to-contact is perceivable via the relative rate of optical expansion defined as the ratio of the visual angle between any two points on the object and the rate of change in that visual angle. This ratio translates into an estimate of time-to-contact. Evidence suggests that the human visual system contains neurons sensitive to this ratio (Regan *et al.*, 1992). Such neurons will not distinguish between this ratio and its inverse whence inverse time-to-contact is perceptually feasible.
7 The justification of the statement that time headway is ecologically valid is based in the observation that time headway can be defined as the time-to-contact between the vehicle and stationary objects (textures, etc.) that exist in the same visual plane as the end of a lead vehicle.

8 This discussion ignores other perceptual skills relevant to regulating vehicle speed. Such perceptual skills include following another vehicle (which is tantamount to regulating T_h), overtaking, etc.

9 Let $T\max_h = \arg_{Th} \geq 0(\mu_L(T_h) = 1)$. For the test track, $T\max_h > 0$, whereas for the driving simulator $\max_h < 0$. These differences simply indicate that the costs of error are higher when real vehicles are used; in other words, a real collision on the test track is much more costly than a simulated collision in the driving simulator. Though the subjects were sincere and well-motivated, there is simply no substitute for the fear of death to motivate a driver. Additionally, the functional representation (obtained through least squares) of the empirical liability measure introduced a bias in the simulator study because the time headway space was not uniformly sampled.

References

Aginsky, B., Harris, C., Rensink, R. A. and Beusmans, J. (1997), 'Two strategies for learning a route in a driving simulator', *Journal of Environmental Psychology*, 17(4), pp. 317–331.

Albus, J. S. (1991), 'Outline for a theory of intelligence', *IEEE Transactions on Systems, Man, and Cybernetics*, 21 (3), pp. 473–509.

Ball, L. J., Maskill, L. and Ormerod, T. C. (1996), 'Satisficing in engineering design: causes, consequences and implications for design support', in *Proceedings of the First International Symposium on Descriptive Models of Design*, Istanbul, pp. 317–332.

Boer, E. R. and Goodrich, M. A. (1998), 'Mental models in micro worlds: Situated representations for the navigationally challenged', in *Proceedings of the 1998 IEEE International Conference on Systems, Man, and Cybernetics*, San Diego, CA, USA.

Boer, E. R., Hildreth, E. C. and Goodrich, M. A. (1998), 'The role of mental models in a driver's interaction with traffic', in *Proceedings of the 17th European Annual Conference on Human Decision Making and Control '98*, Valenciennes, France.

Brooks, R. A. (1986), 'A robust layered control system for a mobile robot', *IEEE Journal of Robotics and Automation*, 2, pp. 14–23.

Brooks, R. A. (1991), 'Intelligence without reason'. Technical Report A.I. Memo 1293, Massachusetts Institute of Technology Artificial Intelligence Laboratory.

Connolly, T. (1999), 'Action as a fast and frugal heuristic', *Minds and Machines*, 9(4), pp. 479–496.

Dreyfus, H. L. and Dreyfus, S. E. (1985), 'From socrates to expert systems: The limits and dangers of calculative rationality', in Mitcham, C. & Huning, A., eds., *Philosophy and Technology II: Information Technology and Computers in Theory and Practice*, Boston: Studies in the Philosphy of Science: Reidel.

Duchon, A. P., Warren, W. H. and Kaelbling, L. P. (1998), 'Ecological robotics' *Adaptive Behavior*, 6(3/4), pp. 471–505.

Fishburn, P. C. (1981), 'Subjective expected utility: A review of normative theories', *Theory and Decision*, 13, pp. 139–199.

Gardner, H. (1985), *The Mind's New Science: A History of the Cognitive Revolution*, ch. 13, New York: Basic Books, Inc.

Gibson, J. J. (1979), *The Ecological Approach to Visual Perception*, Boston: Houghton Mifflin.

Gibson, J. J. and Crooks, L. E. (1938), 'A theoretical field-analysis of automobile-driving', *The American Journal of Psychology*, 51(3).

Gigerenzer, G. (1996), 'On narrow norms and vague heuristics: A reply to Kahneman and Tversky (1996)', *Psychological Review* 103(3), pp. 592–596.

Gigerenzer, G. and Goldstein, D. G. (1996), 'Reasoning the fast and frugal way: Models of bounded rationality', *Psychological Review*, 103(4), pp. 650–669.

Goodrich, M. A. and Boer, E. R. (1998), 'Semiotics and mental models: Modeling automobile driver behavior', in *Joint Conference on Science and Technology of Intelligent Systems* ISIC/CIRA/ISAS'98 Proceedings, Gaithersburg, MD.

Goodrich, M. A., Boer, E. R. and Inoue, H. (1998), 'Brake initiation and braking dynamics: A human-centered study of desired ACC characteristics', Technical Report TR-98-5, Cambridge Basic Research, Nissan Research and Development, Inc., Cambridge, MA, USA.

Greiner, R. and Orponen, P. (1996), 'Probably approximately optimal satisficing stragies', *Artificial Intelligence*, 82, pp. 21–44.

Ho, Y.-C. (1994), 'Heuristics, rules of thumb, and the 80/20 proposition', *IEEE Transactions on Automatic Control*, 39(5), pp. 1025–1027.

Ho, Y.-C. (1999), 'The no free lunch theorem and the human-machine interface', *IEEE Control Systems*, pp. 8–10.

Ho, Y.-C. and Larson, M. E. (1995), 'Ordinal optimization approach to rare event probability problems', *Discrete Event Dynamic Systems: Theory and Applications*, 5, pp. 281–301.

Johnson-Laird, P. N. (1988), *The Computer and the Mind: An Introduction to Cognitive Science*. Cambridge, MA: Harvard University Press.

Kahneman, D. and Tversky, A. (1979), 'Prospect theory: an analysis of decision under risk'. *Econometrica*, 47(2), pp. 263–291.

Kahneman, D. and Tversky, A. (1996), 'On the reality of cognitive illusions', *Psychological Review*, 193(3), pp. 582–591.

Lee, D. N. (1976), 'A theory of visual control of braking based on information about time-to-collision'. *Perception*, pp. 437–459.

Levi, I. (1980), *The Enterprise of Knowledge*, Cambridge, MA: MIT Press.

Levi, I. (1997), *The Covenant of Reason: Rationality and the Commitments of Thought*, Cambridge University Press, Cambridge M.A.

Luce, R. D. and Raiffa, H. (1957), *Games and Decisions*, New York: John Wiley.

Matsuda, T. and Takatsu, S. (1979a), 'Algebraic properties of satisficing decision criterion'. *Information Sciences*, 17(3).

Matsuda, T. and Takatsu, S. (1979b), 'Characterization of satisficing decision criterion'. *Information Sciences*, 17(2), pp. 131–151.

Mayne, D. Q. and Michalska, H. (1990), 'Receding horizon control of nonlinear systems', *IEEE Transactions on Automatic Control*, 35, pp. 814–824.

Mesarovic, M. D. (1970), 'Systems theoretic approach to formal theory of problem solving', in Banerji, R. & Mesarovic, M. D., eds., *Theoretical Approaches to Non-Numerical Problem Solving*, Berlin: Springer, pp. 161–178.

Mesarovic, M. D. and Takahara, Y. (1972), 'On a qualitative theory of satisfactory control', *Information Sciences*, 4(4), pp. 291–313.

Meystel, A. (1996), 'Intelligent systems: A semiotic perspective', in *Proceedings of the IEEE International Symposium on Intelligent Control*, Dearborn, MI, USA.

Michalska, H. and Mayne, D. Q. (1995), 'Moving horizon observers and observer-based control', *IEEE Transactions on Automatic Control*, 40(6), pp. 995–1006.

Minsky, M. (1986), *The Society of Mind*. Simon and Schuster. New York.

Nam, Y. S., Lee, B. H. and Ko, N. Y. (1996), 'A view-time based potential field method for moving obstacle avoidance', *SICE*, pp. 1463–1468.

Norman, D. A. (1988), *The Design of Everyday Things*. Currency Doubleday. Previously published as *The Psychology of Everyday Things*.

Popper, K. R. (1965), *Conjectures and Refutations: The Growth of Scientific Knowledge*, New York: Harper and Row.

Rasmussen, J. (1976), 'Outlines of a hybrid model of the process plant operator', in Sheridan, T. B. and Johannsen, G., eds, *Monitoring Behavior and Supervisory Control*, New York: Plenum. pp. 371–383.

Regan, D., Hamstra, S. and Kaushal, S. (1992), 'Visual factors in the avoidance of front-to-rear-end highway collisions', in *Proceedings of the Human Factors Society 36th Annual Meeting*, pp. 1006–1010.

Richalet, J. (1993), 'Industrial applications of model based predictive control', *Automatica*, 29, pp. 1251–1274.

Saridis, G. N. (1989), 'Analytic formulation of the principle of increasing precision with decreasing intelligence for intelligent machines', *Automatica*, 25(3), pp. 461–467.

Scokaert, P. O. M., Rawlings, J. B. and Meadows, E. S. (1997), 'Discrete-time stability with perturbations: Application to model predictive control', *Automatica*, 33(3), pp. 463–470.

Sen, S., ed. (1998), *Satisficing Models*, Stanford, CA. AAAI Spring Symposium. Technical Report SS-98-05.

Sheridan, T. B. (1992), *Telerobotics, Automation, and Human Supervisory Control*. Cambridge, MA: MIT Press.

Simon, H. A. (1955), 'A behavioral model of rational choice', *Quart. J. Economics*, 59, pp. 99–118.

Simon, H. A. (1990), 'Invariants of human behavior', *Annuals. Reviews in Psychology*, 41, pp. 1–19.

Simon, H. A. (1996), *The Sciences of the Artificial*, 3rd edition, Cambridge, MA, MIT Press.

Sistu, P. B. and Bequette, B. W. (1996), 'Nonlinear model-predictive control: Closed-loop stability analysis', *AIChE Journal*, 42(12), pp. 3388–3402.

Slote, M. (1989), *Beyond Optimizing*, Cambridge, MA. Harvard University Press.

Takatsu, S. (1980), 'Decomposition of satisficing decision problems', *Information Sciences*, 22(2), pp. 139–148.

Takatsu, S. (1981), 'Latent satisficing decision criterion', *Information Sciences*, 25(2), pp. 145–152.

Zadeh, L. A. (1958), 'What is optimal?' *IRE Transactions on Information Theory*, 4(1), p. 3.

Zadeh, L. A. (1998), 'Maximizing sets and fuzzy markoff algorithms', *IEEE Transactions on Systems, Man, and Cybernetics – Part C: Applications and Reviews*, 28(1), pp. 9–15.

Zilberstein, S. (1996), 'Using anytime algorithms in intelligent systems', *AI Magazine*, pp. 73–83.

Zsambok, C. E. and Klein, G., eds. (1997), *Naturalistic Decision Making*, Hillsdale, NJ: Lawrence Erlbaum Associates.

58

HERBERT SIMON

Artificial intelligence as a framework for understanding intuition

Roger Frantz

Source: *Journal of Economic Psychology*, 24 (2003), 265–277.

Abstract

Herbert Simon made overlapping substantive contributions to the fields of economics, psychology, cognitive science, artificial intelligence, decision theory, and organization theory. Simon's work was motivated by the belief that neither the human mind, human thinking and decision making, nor human creativity need be mysterious. It was after he helped create "thinking" machines that Simon came to understand human intuition as subconscious pattern recognition. In doing so he showed that intuition need not be associated with magic and mysticism, and that it is complementary with analytical thinking. This paper will show how the overlaps in his work and especially his work on AI affected his view towards intuition.

1. Introduction

Herbert Simon made overlapping substantive contributions to the fields of economics, psychology, cognitive science, decision theory, and organization theory. Simon's work was motivated by the belief that neither the human mind, human thinking and decision making, nor human creativity need be mysterious. His life work was devoted to proving this point. His motto was "Wonderful, but not incomprehensible" (Simon, 1969, p. 4). Where he carried this out was at the intersection of economics, psychology, cognitive science, and organization theory. A major part of this intersection was creating computer programs which allow machines to "think" and make choices.

It was after he helped create "thinking" machines that Simon came to understand human intuition as subconscious pattern recognition. In doing so he showed that intuition need not be associated with magic and mysticism.[1]

He also showed that "intuition is not a process that operates independently of analysis; rather the two processes are essential complementary components of effective decision-making systems" (Simon & Gilmartin, 1973, p. 33).

Intuition is often described by what it is *not*: intuition is a residual concept. Intuition is not a conscious analytical – logical, sequential, step-by-step, and reasoned – process of thinking. The most common terms used for intuition reveal intuition's residual nature: gut feeling, educated hunch, sixth sense. Bunge (1962), in his book *Intuition and Science* states that intuition is what we call "all the intellectual mechanisms which we do not know how to analyze or even name with precision, or which we are not interested in analyzing or naming" (p. 68). The intellectual mechanisms Bunge cites include rapid reasoning, synthesizing disparate elements into a grand vision, and sound judgment. Simon's preference was to refer to intuition as subconscious pattern recognition.

Although the logical and analytical nature of economic thinking has kept intuition in the background of the profession, Simon is not the first economist to discuss intuition. Adam Smith (Frantz, 2000), John Stuart Mill (Frantz, 2001), Alfred Marshall (Frantz, 2002b), John Maynard Keynes (Moggridge, 1995), Schumpeter (1954), and Frank Knight (Frantz, 2002a) are other famous names who wrote about intuition. For the past 25 years it has become almost commonplace for an economist to state during a presentation that, "The intuition behind the model (and/or result) is . . ." In, *The Making of an Economist*, Klamer and Colander (1990) interviewed graduate students from various departments throughout the US. Students consider both mathematics and intuition to be important, and they express an appreciation for the intuitive elements in the work of their professors.

This paper will show some of the overlaps among Simon's work on economics, psychology, cognitive science, and organization theory, and how these overlaps affected his view towards intuition.

2. Intuition. The "problem" illustrated

Simon's philosophy of intuition may be said to begin with the publication of Chester Barnard's *The Functions of the Executive* (Barnard, 1942), specifically an appendix titled "Mind in Everyday Affairs" in which Barnard discusses intuition. Herbert Simon, in his lecture given in Stockholm upon receiving the Nobel Prize in Economics, referred to Barnard as an "intellectually curious business executive who distilled from his experience as president of New Jersey Bell Telephone Company . . . a profound book on decision making . . ." (Simon, 1965, p. 25). Yet, when it came to Barnard's philosophy of intuition, Simon says that Barnard, "presents an interesting, but perhaps too optimistic view of the 'intuitive' elements in administrative decisions . . ." (Simon, 1965, p. 60). What makes Barnard's presentation too optimistic for Simon?

Barnard's philosophy about intuition was stated matter-of-factly. First, intuition may seem abstract because it arises from the subconscious, but it is not abstract. Intuition is a non-logical process, defined by Barnard as a process which takes place in the subconscious or is so rapid as to seem subconscious, and hence also seems to be instantaneous and devoid of reasoning. Examples of intuition cited by Barnard include studying a complex balance sheet for only a few minutes or seconds before being able to derive a coherent picture of the company.

Second, intuition is as much an expression of intelligence as is logic. Third, intuition is useful and so people should use it. Fourth, many people use intuition at work but it is "frequently scorned" (Simon, 1996) because of psychological reasons. The reason is that many people feel the need to rationalize their beliefs and have them appear plausible, and hence do not want to admit using something that is unexplainable. The "most interesting and astounding contradiction in life" he says, is that regardless of intellect, people's insistence upon using logic is coupled with their inability to use it and to accept it when used by others. The bias against intuition among scientists is understandable, among non-scientists it is "unintelligent" (Simon, 1996).

Fifth, intuition is most appropriate when working with short time horizons and data which is either of poor quality and/or very limited. This covers according to Barnard the majority of situations used in every day affairs in both business and government. He says that it is "impossible effectively to apply the logical reasoning process to material that is so insecure that it cannot bear the weight of ponderous logic . . . The much ridiculed 'women's intuition' is the only mental process that can apply to it" (Simon, 1996, p. 310). Understanding organizations also calls for intuition. He says, "Our logical methods and our endless analysis of things has often blinded us to an appreciation of structure and organization . . . You cannot get organization by adding up the parts . . . To understand the society you live in, you must *feel* organization – which is exactly what you do with your non-logical minds . . ." (Barnard, 1942, p. 317).

Simon's approach was very different. As a scientist he needed to understand the phenomenon we call intuition. In the early part of his career there was not a scientific – rational, logical – theory of intuition, and so Simon considered intuition to be a mystery. In time and with advances in cognitive science and AI as a framework, Simon concluded that intuition is subconscious pattern recognition. Simon did not consider intuition to be irrational, he considered it to be a rational but not a conscious analytical method of decision making (Simon, 1987).

3. Rationality

For Simon, problem solving was a "search through a vast maze of possibilities, a maze that describes the environment" (Simon, 1982h, p. 66). Rationality is *bounded rationality* or limited by the vast maze of possibilities which is our environment. The maze makes the *procedures* we use in decision making, one of which is subconscious pattern recognition, more important than traditionally given in economics. And it means that the decisions we make are more *satisficing* than maximizing. Thus, Simon challenged the economic orthodoxy on the definition of rationality by proposing the concepts of bounded and procedural rationality, and satisficing.

The orthodox definition is represented by economic person (EP) who is a *substantively* rational maximizer of subjective expected utility. Substantive rationality occurs when behavior is appropriate to attain a given goal, under given conditions (constraints). In other words, substantive rationality is about *outcomes*. EP is substantively rational because she is assumed to have at least a sufficient amount of information about all relevant aspects of their environment, the ability to compute benefits and costs of available altern- ative courses of action, information about the probability of each outcome of each chosen behavior, and a willingness and ability to understand and consider simultaneously all current and future available alternatives. Assum- ing that individuals are substantially rational, and that they have a definite goal, economics can be "done" with calculus. And, it can be done without psychology. But, Simon says, ". . . there is a complete lack of evidence that, in actual human choice situations of any complexity, these computations can be, or are in fact, performed" (Simon, 1982a, p. 244).

Simon's ideas on bounded rationality (BR) were initially contained in the first (1947) and subsequent editions of *Administrative Behavior* (Simon, 1965), and in more formal models published in 1955 in the *Quarterly Journal of Economics* (Simon, 1982a), and in 1956 in the *Psychological Review* (Simon, 1982f). In 1956 Simon wrote a short story as an attempt at a "transmigra- tion of the soul" of his model of BR. The story, "The Apple: A Story of the Maze" (Simon, 1989a), is about a young man named Hugo who lived alone in a large castle. Hugo's problem was that he had to find food, which, mysteriously, was being left on the tables in some of the rooms. Some of the food left was of a variety he had never seen, so he had to discover his tastes and preferences for food. He also needed to save time at finding the right room so he began looking for *clues* to tell him which room had which variety of food. For example the rooms containing his favorite foods had various paintings on the wall. His preference for certain paintings had developed *unconsciously* as an *association* with certain preferred foods. With experience, finding his preferred foods became easier. Hugo's search for food did not continue until he found his favorite food. Hugo was often hungry and he did not know when he would find food again, so his searches ended when he found food which was satisfactory. His experience showed him that finding the right food depended upon the number of turns or choice points in the maze, the number of available paths at each choice point, the number of moves or steps between choice points, the number of

201

moves and choice points the individual can see ahead, and the ability of the individual to find clues (patterns) in order to avoid walking around in circles. The hungrier he was, the greater the number of food types and groups fell under the category of satisfactory. Hugo was a satisficer whose rationality was bounded by the shape of his world and the circumstances of his life. Associations or patterns were stored in memory and retrieved automatically from memory when it served to satisfy his goal. Hugo engaged in subconscious pattern recognition, that is, he engaged his intuition. Substantive rationality and global maximization in a maze is possible, but only when the maze is very small.

3.1. Substantive vs. bounded and procedural rationality

In contrast to EP, "bounded rational person" (BRP) lives in a world which offers a set of objectively available behavior alternatives, but a more limited set of "perceived" behavior alternatives. BRP lacks both the information and the computational capacities to be globally rational. RWP lives in a world with too much uncertainty – unintended consequences, and computational limits. Given our computational limits the environment that we are aware of is only a fraction of the "real" environment within which decisions are made. The number of possible alternatives is so immense that they cannot be examined. The best and only feasible solution is to find a satisfactory solution.

In psychology it is aspiration levels which perform this function. And "problem solving and decision making that sets an aspiration level, searches until an alternative is found that is satisfactory by the aspiration level criterion, and selects that alternative" (Simon, 1982j, p. 415) is called *satisficing*. The concept of satisficing is common within psychology (Simon, 1982c). It is part of a model of behavior in which the motivation to act comes from "drives," and the termination of action occurs when the drive is satisfied. The definition of drive-satisfaction varies upon aspirations and experience. Satisficing in economics is assumed to be less important because standard economics assumes that individuals are objectively or globally substantively rational expected utility maximizers. Of course these assumptions amount to nothing more than assuming away the importance of satisficing.

However, in the real world inhabited by BRP perception and cognition do not merely passively filter only a small part of the entire environment into our consciousness. Of the entire amount of new information generated by our entire environment, our senses filter out 99%+ before it reaches our consciousness. Given these facts, human behavior is in most cases restricted to satisficing behavior. Rationality is thus *bounded* by the complexity of the world we live in relative to our cognitive abilities. It seems intuitively obvious to the casual observer that BR is more descriptive of the way people with modest computational abilities make decisions, stay alive, and even thrive (Simon, 1983). Intuitive rationality (IR) is a subset of BR, but more about this later.

Because rationality is bounded the process we use in making the best decisions we can becomes more important. Simon thus considers behavior to be rational when it is the outcome of an appropriate deliberation *process*. Behavior is procedurally rational when it is the outcome of an appropriate deliberation process. Behavior is procedurally irrational when it is the outcome of impulsive behavior (Simon, 1982d, p. 426).

3.2. *Rationality and chess*

There are about 30 legal moves in a chess game. Each move and its response creates an average of about 1000 contingencies. In a 40 move chess game there are about 10^{120} contingencies. Chess masters are believed to look at no more than 100 contingencies, only 10% of the possibilities existing for *one* move and a response (Simon, 1982j). Beginning with an inordinately large number of possibilities, chess masters, and humans in general, humans search for outcomes whose utility values are at least satisfactory. Once found, the search stops. In other words, chess masters are satisficers, and their rationality is bounded by their limited cognitive capacity relative to their environment.

Chess grandmasters take so little time to decide on a move that Simon says that it is not possible for their moves to be the product of "careful analysis" (Simon, 1983, p. 133). A grandmaster takes 5 or 10 s before making a strong move, which 80–90% of the time proves to be correct and one that is "objectively best in the position" (Simon, 1983, p. 25). Their skill barely diminishes when they play 50 opponents at once rather than one opponent. How do they do it? When grandmasters are asked how they play they respond with the words intuition and professional judgment. Simon says that intuition is a "label for a *process*, not an explanation of it" (Simon, 1982h, p. 105; emphasis added). The process is subconscious pattern recognition based on experiences stored in memory and retrieved when needed. While short term memory can store only a relatively small amount of information, long term memory is, metaphorically speaking, a large encyclopedia with an elaborate index in which information is cross-referenced. Cross-referencing means that information is associative with one piece of information linked or associated with other associated thoughts. Cross-referencing and chunking makes subconscious pattern recognition or intuition easier.

Studies on recognition among chess masters have used eye movements to assess recognition abilities. Chess masters examining a previously unknown board position taken from an actual game immediately – within 2 s – shift their eyes to the most relevant part of the board. This means that they immediately grasp or "see" the most important relationships on the board.

Simon concludes that it is sufficient to state that a chess master's perform-ance is based on a knowledge of chess and an act of (subconscious) pattern recognition. In fact, Simon helped develop a computer program with the ability to mimic the eye movements of a chess master. His computer pro-gram and human chess masters make the same mistakes, and both recover in a similar way. For example, in one program a queen who was in trouble did exactly what a human would do to not only save their queen but to get their opponent in checkmate. Simon adds that the ultimate nature of human intellectual activity is best known through a chess playing machine. Human or machine experts at chess or in any field of activity experts are expert (in part) because of their ability for subconscious pattern recognition.

4. Artificial intelligence

Writing in 1966, Simon (1966a, 1966b) believed that the word mysterious was the adjective most often used to describe thinking, but that mysterious no longer applied. The reason was increases in knowledge about the process of thinking based on AI, that is, computer programs which mimic human problem solving (Simon, 1966b). Simon's view of thinking affected by AI is that thinking is a form of information-processing. Both human thinking, and information-processing programs perform three similar operations: they scan data for patterns, they store the patterns in memory, and they apply the patterns to make inferences or extrapolations. In fact, some programs reproduce and even outperform human experts at problem solving. Simon concluded that there is sufficient reason to believe that some kinds of human thinking closely parallel the operations of an information-processing computer program. AI also led him to conclude that intuition is a subset of thinking. The fact that the mind is a serial information processor, it per-forms one (or only a very few) operations at a time, places severe limits on human attention, binds our rationality, and limits our capabilities for problem solving to a set of satisficing rather than maximizing solutions.

Problem-solving thus involves two generalizations. First, a selective trial-and-error search is made which by necessity can only consider a relatively few possible solutions. The solution is thus a satisficing solution and the search is based on rules-of-thumb or heuristics. Second, one of the basic heuristics is means–end analysis. Means–end analysis involves three steps. First, the current situation is compared to a goal, and differences between them are noted. Second, a memory search is performed to identify an *oper-ator* which can bring the current situation more in line with the goal. Third, the operator is applied in the hope of getting closer to the goal.

Since computers solve problems as humans do using heuristics and means–end analysis, Simon concluded that computers display intelligence, defined as behavior which is appropriate to the goal and adaptive to the environ-ment. Intelligence allows the limited processing capacity of the organism, be it man or machine, to use efficient search procedures to generate possible solutions, with the most likely solutions being generated early in the search process (Newell & Simon, 1990). In order to test whether machines display intelligence, Simon (and his colleagues) identified tasks requiring intelligence and then built computer programs which carried out these tasks. These tasks include playing chess, solving math and physics problems, diagnosing disease, making discoveries in science, and even formulating hypotheses and testing them empirically. In doing these things, Simon showed that computers "think," and that they possess (artificial or man made) intelligence.

4.1. Machines who "think"

Simon's machine think in that they recognize patterns and apply "if–then" rules in making decisions. Boden (1990), in her book *The Creative Mind. Myths and Mechanisms*, uses the example of soybean diseases to show that a set of "if-then" rules incorporated into a computer program allows it to find patterns in a maze of data on soybean symptoms and then correctly diagnose soybean diseases. Programs such as the ID3 algorithm not only diagnose soybean diseases with an accuracy which would make any psychic jealous, but it does so with maximum efficiency. That is, it asks the right questions in the right order so as to make the right diagnoses in the minimum amount of time. ID3 has discovered patterns in data which humans have not, and it has discovered strategies in chess previously unknown by chess masters. Computer programs have been developed which input and output words, formula, images, and musical notations. These computer programs have been said to display creativity.

The first AI program, developed by Simon, is the logic theorist (LT). Written in 1956, LT discovers proofs for theorems contained in Alfred North Whitehead and Bertrand Russell's *Principia Mathematica* (Whitehead & Russell, 1962). In order to do this LT mimics expert human decision-makers by working "backward." Both LT and expert human decision-makers use information about the goal to eliminate many paths without having to try them. Human novices, on the other hand, solve problems in a more time consuming inefficient "forward" manner.

Work on LT demonstrated to Simon that trial-and-error (a procedure of science) and insight (an apparent discontinuity, or mystery) are complementary with each other. LT also lead Simon to conclude that the human brain is analogous to a digital computer. The value of the brain-as-computer metaphor is that it takes the mystery out of concepts such as intuition and insight (Simon, Newell, & Shaw, 1989b, p. 7).

The general problem solver (GPS), an early program developed in 1957 engaged in means–end analysis, a basic heuristic in problem-solving. The EPAM program (Feigenbaum & Simon, 1989) simulates human recognition or learning, while the MAPP program (Simon, 1989b) which simulates the ability to recognize patterns in a manner similar to chess (grand) masters. The "adaptive production system" (APS) program engages in learning-by-doing, and learning-by-example. The APS program learns-by-example to solve algebraic problems by inspecting each step in an algebraic problem placed in its memory. When faced with any algebraic problem it goes through the steps and arrives at a solution to a particular problem. APS programs learns-by-doing an algebraic problem, and then uses that example to learn how to solve other algebra problems.

Simon and his colleagues also developed several programs which make discoveries in science including BACON, BLACK, GLAUBER, and STAHL. BACON analyzes data sets and derives quantitative relationships among data sets. BACON "discovered" many well known scientific laws including Galileo's law of uniform acceleration, Kepler's third law, Boyle's law, and Ohm's law (Langley, Simon, Bradshaw, & Zytkow, 1987). And it does by considering the simplest explanation (pattern) first before moving on to more complex explanations. BLACK, named after Joseph Black, works on situations in which two substances are additive. If analyzing the data show that the two substances are not additive then BLACK finds one or more *unobservable* properties of the substances to explain non-additivity.

GLAUBER, named after the chemist Johann Glauber, divides substances into groups according to their observable properties. Similar to Glauber, GLAUBER uses a *sample* of acids and alkalis to infer correctly that *every* acid reacts with alkalis to form salt. STAHL, named after chemist Georg Stahl, is given a set of heuristics used by chemists and a list of experimental results on the nature of combustion in historical sequence. Similar to human chemists, STAHL's hypotheses about combustion are sometimes incorrect, but similar to human chemists STAHL reviews previous experimental results and corrects its mistakes. The result is that STAHL correctly reproduced the approximately 80 year development of the oxygen theory of combustion from the phlogiston theory.

5. Intuition. Simons early and later views

In the second edition of *Administrative Behavior* (Simon, 1965) Simon recognized the value of experience and habit in decision-making. Experience becomes human capital; habit becomes internalized as unconscious and automatic reflex actions. Decision-making using experience and habit relies on "clues." Whether clues are recognized consciously or known only to the subconscious, they enhance our understanding of particular situations, and improve decision-making. Experience and habit become part of effective procedures in decision making. Simon comments that "human rationality relies heavily upon the psychological and artificial associational and indexing devices that make the store of memory accessible when it is needed for the making of decisions" (Simon, 1965, p. 87). In the fourth edition of

Administrative Behavior, 1997, and having AI as his framework, Simon (1996) would refer to the associational and indexing devices of memory as intuition.

Another value of experience and habit in performing purposive or rational behavior is that it "permits conservation of mental effort by withdrawing from the area of conscious thought those aspects of the situation that are repetitive" (Simon, 1965, p. 88). And it permits similar stimuli or situations to be met with similar responses or reactions, without the need for a conscious rethinking of the decision to bring about the proper action (p. 88). In the fourth edition, Simon (1997) would also refer to this as intuition.

In the earlier additions of *Administration Behavior*, Simon did not discuss intuition because he was uncertain about the nature of subconscious thinking processes. In the fourth edition he introduced material about intuition because, he says, ". . . we have acquired a solid understanding of what the judgmental and intuitive processes are" (Simon, 1997, p. 31).

These processes are subconscious and/or rapid, and based on experience which by-passes a conscious "orderly sequential analysis" of a situation. Simon went so far as to say that intuition is actually analytical thinking "frozen into habit and into the capacity for rapid response through recognition of familiar kinds of situations" (Simon, 1997, p. 139). Intuition and analysis are complementary with each other and almost always present in all human decisions, including those of scientists. Thinking about the use of intuition among scientists in general and physicists in particular Simon spoke about "physical intuition,"[2] that is, intuition used by physicists or scientists in general.

The combination of intuition and analysis is present in chess grandmasters because chess "is usually believed to require a high level of intellect" (Simon, 1987, p. 28), and grandmasters use the word intuition when describing how they do what they do in chess. Chess grandmasters take only a very few seconds to decide on their next move and then a longer period of time verifying that their "educated hunch" is correct.

One test for the use of unobservable physical intuition was done with the use of protocol analysis in which a novice and an expert were given a physics problem to solve, and each person verbalized what they were thinking. The results showed that the more experienced person solved the problem in less time, required fewer steps to solve the problem, spent less time per step, did not write down as many relevant facts or equations to solve, and expressed more confidence in themselves. In essence, the skilled person took a series of appropriate short cuts and avoided conscious calculation of how to solve the problem. This is possible because an expert's knowledge is similar to an encyclopedia with a large index in which entries are cross-referenced. That is, not only does the expert have more knowledge than the novice, but the expert can more rapidly elicit relevant facts from memory.

The expert exhibits "the usual appearance of intuition," while the novice uses more "conscious and explicit analysis" (Simon, 1996, p. 136). The conclusion Simon reaches is that experience allows people to make decisions intuitively, or judgments "without careful analysis and calculation" (p. 136).

Simon says that intuition ". . . is no deeper than the explanation of your ability, in a matter of seconds, to recognize one of your friends whom you meet on the path tomorrow as you are going to class" (Simon, 1983, p. 26). Experience and knowledge is the key to intuition because paraphrasing Poincare, "inspiration comes only to the prepared mind" (p. 27). In other words, while the expert's approach is more "physical" or "primitive" (Simon & Simon, 1989, p. 224), the novice's approach is more algebraic. This capacity when observed among chess grandmasters and expert decision-makers in general is called intuition; when observed among physicists is called physical intuition.

5.1. Intuitive rationality

Intuition is useful, and it is a subset of BR. IR and BR are consistent with each other, and all "serious thinking" uses both. Both use search-like processes both lead to sudden recognition of underlying patterns, and the focus of one's attention plays a major role in the choices one makes. Intuition is said to be what is responsible for people finding solutions to problems "suddenly" and having the "aha" experience. Having AI as a framework, Simon understood these to be genuine experiences, and to lead to judgments which "frequently are correct" (Simon, 1983, p. 25). Simon helped create computer programs which mimic expert human decision-makers who use the word intuition as a label for how they make decisions. Creating machines that think led Simon to his "explanation" for that very human phenomenon called intuition.[3]

6. Summary and conclusions

Simon made significant overlapping contributions to various fields including economics, psychology, cognitive science, decision theory, and organization theory. Simon challenged economic theory by postulating that human rationality is bounded. He emphasized the limits in human computational abilities and memory relative to the information provided continuously by the environment. This concept of BR became relevant to his work on organizations, and; human decision making, problem solving, and scientific discovery. The concept of BR may be seen as the key interface between his work in economics and psychology.[4] BR also can be seen in his work on AI. After all, if human rationality and problem solving is limited by our computational capacities and memory, can computer programs with greater computational capacity and memory help extend our problem solving abilities?

Simon's challenge to economics and his work on AI led him to view human thinking as an example of information processing. It led him to view human and artificial intelligence as depending upon information processing leading to pattern recognition. And this lead him to his understanding that human intuition is subconscious information processing leading to subconscious pattern recognition. John Stuart Mill held similar views about intuition as subconscious pattern recognition. Unfortunately for him, he lived before Simon helped developed the field of AI.

Simon makes it clear that intuition or subconscious pattern recognition is a positive externality of an extensive period of study, and is part of the process of human information processing, albeit a subconscious part. With this in mind, intuition extends our ability to use our computational capacities and memory, extends the boundary of our ability for rational behavior, and hence enhances our ability for procedural rationality. The question is, can we enhance our intuition?

7. Uncited references

Hadamard (1945), McCorduck (1979), Simon (1977), Simon (1982b), Simon (1982e), Simon (1982g), Simon (1982i), Simon, Larkin, McDermott, and Simon (1989a), Tversky and Kahemann, 1981.

Acknowledgements

I wish to thank Mie Auguier, two anonymous referees, Andrea Salanti, Ray Boddy, Art Kartman, and Nancy O'Barr for helpful comments. All remaining errors of content and judgment are my own.

Notes

1 Simon had his own intuitive experiences. His preliminary exam in statistics for the University of Chicago in 1940 required that he produce a derivation of the chi-square statistic: he provided two derivations. He says, "While taking my shower on the morning of that exam, it came to me with blinding and unaccountable certainty that there would be a question on chi-square, and I boned up on it before setting out for the exam room. On no other occasion have I had such loving attention from my guardian angel" (Simon, 1996, p. 84). Simon had been contemplating programming computers to simulate chess playing since the early 1950's. In 1955 during a walk on the campus of Columbia University he says, "Suddenly, I had a clear conviction that we could program a machine to solve such problems" (p. 203). Speaking about government employees specializing in security he said, "Intuitively, they know that intellectuals seek to be loyal to abstractions like 'truth,' 'virtue,' or 'freedom,' rather than to a national state or its flag" (Simon, 1989a, p. 133).

2 In "New Age," and spiritual literature, physical intuition refers to physical sensations in your body. For example, when you meet someone for the first time, feeling an ache in your gut (gut feeling) is your intuition "telling" you that this

person is to be avoided. The difference in the use of the term physical intuition between Simon and New Age/spiritual literature is both startling and revealing of differences in approach to the topic of intuition.

3 Simon emphasized the role of the trained intellect in intuition. For an excellent discussion of the role of emotions, please see Hanoch (2002).

4 Augier (2001) has an excellent discussion of how Simon's concept of bounded rationality can be seen throughout his work in various fields.

References

Augier, M. (2001). Sublime Simon: The consistent vision of economic psychology's Nobel laureate. *Journal of Economics and Psychology*, *22*, 307–334.

Barnard, C. (1942). *The functions of the executive*. Cambridge, MA: Harvard University Press.

Boden, M. (1990). *The creative mind. Myths and mechanisms*. London: Weidenfeld & Nicolson.

Bunge, M. (1962). *Intuition and science*. New York: Prentice-Hall.

Feigenbaum, E. A., & Simon, H. (1989). EPAM-like models of recognition and learning. *Models of thought* (Vol. 2, pp. 145–166). New Haven, CT: Yale University Press.

Frantz, R. (2000). Intuitive elements in Adam Smith. *Journal of Socio-Economics*, *29*, 1–19.

Frantz, R. (2001). John Stuart Mill as an anti-intuitionist social reformer. *Journal of Socio-Economics*, *31*, 125–136.

Frantz, R. (2002a). *Frank Knight on the importance and difficulty of doing behavioral economics*. Paper Presented at History of Economics Society Annual Meetings, University of California Davis, July 2002.

Frantz, R. (2002b). *Marshall's economics as an economic application of the philosophy of Henry Mansel*. Working Paper.

Hadamard, J. (1945). *Essay on the psychology of invention in the mathematical field*. Princeton, NJ: Princeton University Press.

Hanoch, Y. (2002). Neither an angel nor an ant: Emotion as an aid to bounded rationality. *Journal of Economic Psychology*, *23*, 1–25.

Klamer, A., & Colander, D. (1990). *The making of an economist*. Boulder, CO: Westview Press.

Langley, P., Simon, H., Bradshaw, G., & Zytkow, J. (1987). *Scientific discovery. Computational explorations of the creative process*. Cambridge, MA: MIT Press.

McCorduck, P. (1979). *Machines who think*. San Francisco: W.H. Freeman Co.

Moggridge, D. E. (1995). *Maynard Keynes. An economist's biography*. London: Routledge.

Newell, A., & Simon, H. (1990). Computer science as empirical enquiry: Symbols and search. In M. Boden (Ed.), *The philosophy of artificial intelligence* (pp. 105–132). Oxford: Oxford University Press.

Schumpeter, J. (1954). *History of economic analysis*. New York: Oxford University Press.

Simon, H. (1965). *Administrative behavior* (2nd ed). New York: Free Press.

Simon, H. (1966a). Scientific discovery and the psychology of problem solving. In G. C. Robert (Ed.), *Mind and cosmos essays in contemporary science and philosophy* (pp. 22–40). Latham, MD: Center for the Philosophy of Science.

Simon, H. (1966b). Thinking by computers. In G. C. Robert (Ed.), *Mind and cosmos. Essays in contemporary science and philosophy* (pp. 3–21). Latham, MD: Center for the Philosophy of Science.

Simon, H. (1969). *The sciences of the artificial* (1st ed). Cambridge, MA: MIT Press.

Simon, H. (1977). *Models of discovery*. Boston: D. Reidel Pub. Co.

Simon, H. (1982a). A behavioral model of rational choice. In H. Simon (Ed.), *Models of bounded rationality. Behavioral economics and business organization* (Vol. 2, pp. 239–258). Cambridge, MA: MIT Press.

Simon, H. (1982b). Decision making as an economic resource. In H. Simon (Ed.), *Models of bounded rationality. Behavioral economics and business organization* (Vol. 2, pp. 84–108). Cambridge, MA: MIT Press.

Simon, H. (1982c). Economics and psychology. In H. Simon (Ed.), *Models of bounded rationality. Behavioral economics and business organization* (Vol. 2, pp. 318–355). Cambridge, MA: MIT Press.

Simon, H. (1982d). From substantive to procedural rationality. In H. Simon (Ed.), *Models of bounded rationality. Behavioral economics and business organization* (Vol. 2, pp. 424–443). Cambridge, MA: MIT Press.

Simon, H. (1982e). New developments in the theory of the firm. In H. Simon (Ed.), *Models of bounded rationality. Behavioral economics and business organization* (Vol. 2, pp. 56–70). Cambridge, MA: MIT Press.

Simon, H. (1982f). Rational choice and the structure of the environment. In H. Simon (Ed.), *Models of bounded rationality. Behavioral economics and business organization* (Vol. 2, pp. 259–268). Cambridge, MA: MIT Press.

Simon, H. (1982g). Rational decision making in business organizations. In H. Simon (Ed.), *Models of bounded rationality. Behavioral economics and business organization* (Vol. 2, pp. 474–494). Cambridge, MA: MIT Press.

Simon, H. (1982h). *The sciences of the artificial* (2nd ed). Cambridge, MA: MIT Press.

Simon, H. (1982i). The impact of new information-processing technology. In H. Simon (Ed.), *Models of bounded rationality. Behavioral economics and business organization* (Vol. 2, pp. 109–133). Cambridge, MA: MIT Press.

Simon, H. (1982j). Theories of bounded rationality. In H. Simon (Ed.), *Models of bounded rationality. Behavioral economics and business organization* (Vol. 2, pp. 408–423). Cambridge, MA: MIT Press.

Simon, H. (1983). *Reason in human affairs*. Stanford, CA: Stanford University Press.

Simon, H. (1987). Making management decisions: The role of intuition and emotion. In W. Agor (Ed.), *Intuition in organizations* (pp. 23–39). London: Sage.

Simon, H. (1989a). Otto Selz and information-processing psychology. In H. Simon (Ed.), *Models of thought* (Vol. 2, pp. 30–39). New Haven, CT: Yale University Press.

Simon, H. (1989b). The information-processing explanation of Gestalt phenomena. In H. Simon (Ed.), *Models of thought* (Vol. 2, pp. 481–493). New Haven, CT: Yale University Press.

Simon, H. (1996). *Models of my life*. Cambridge, MA: MIT Press.

Simon, H. (1997). *Administrative behavior* (4th ed). New York: Free Press.

Simon, H., & Gilmartin, K. (1973). A simulation of memory for chess positions. *Cognitive Psychology, 5*, 29–46.

Simon, H., Larkin, J. H., McDermott, J., & Simon, D. (1989a). Expert and novice performance in solving physics problems. In H. Simon (Ed.), *Models of thought* (Vol. 2, pp. 243–256). New Haven, CT: Yale University Press.

Simon, H., Newell, A., & Shaw, J. C. (1989b). Elements of a theory of human problem solving. In H. Simon (Ed.), *Models of thought* (Vol. 2, pp. 6–19). New Haven, CT: Yale University Press.

Simon, H., & Simon, D. (1989). Individual differences in solving physics problems. In H. Simon (Ed.), *Models of thought* (Vol. 2, pp. 215–231). New Haven, CT: Yale University Press.

Tversky, A., & Kahemann, D. (1981). The framing of decisions and the psychology of choice. *Science, 211*, 453–458.

Whitehead, A. N., & Russell, B. (1962). *Principia mathematica*. Cambridge: Cambridge University Press.

59

COGNITIVE COMPARATIVE ADVANTAGE AND THE ORGANIZATION OF WORK*

Lessons from Herbert Simon's vision of the future

Richard N. Langlois

Source: *Journal of Economic Psychology*, 24 (2003), 167–187.

Abstract

In a marvelous but somewhat neglected paper, "The Corporation: Will It Be Managed by Machines?" Herbert Simon articulated from the perspective of 1960 his vision of what we now call the New Economy – the machine-aided system of production and management of the late 20th century. Simon's analysis sprang from what I term the *principle of cognitive comparative advantage*: one has to understand the quite different cognitive structures of humans and machines (including computers) in order to explain and predict the tasks to which each will be most suited. Perhaps unlike Simon's better-known predictions about progress in artificial intelligence research, the predictions of this 1960 article hold up remarkably well and continue to offer important insights.

In what follows I attempt to tell a coherent story about the evolution of machines and the division of labor between humans and machines. Although inspired by Simon's 1960 paper, I weave many other strands into the tapestry, from classical discussions of the division of labor to present-day evolutionary psychology. The basic conclusion is that, with growth in the extent of the market, we should see humans "crowded into" tasks that call for the kinds of cognition for which humans have been equipped by biological evolution. These human

* Paper for a special issue of the *Journal of Economic Psychology* in memory of Herbert Simon to be edited by Mie Augier and James March.

213

cognitive abilities range from the exercise of judgment in situations of ambiguity and surprise to more mundane abilities in spatio-temporal perception and locomotion. Conversely, we should see machines "crowded into" tasks with a well-defined structure. This conclusion is not based (merely) on a claim that machines, including computers, are specialized idiots-savants today because of the limits (whether temporary or permanent) of artificial intelligence; rather, it rests on a claim that, for what are broadly "economic" reasons, it will continue to make economic sense to create machines that are idiots-savants.

1. Introduction

I had the chance to interact with Herbert Simon on only one occasion. But the circumstances were somewhat exotic. Simon and I were among a number of Western scholars invited to a conference in Warsaw in 1988, the year before everything changed. The objective of the conference was to interact with Polish scholars – philosophers, mostly – on the theme of "praxeology", the study of human action. I have vivid memories of sitting at a small table in our shabby hotel drinking terrible Romanian wine and listening to Simon and Donald McCloskey debating the merits of deconstructionism. (McCloskey thought deconstructionism had much to contribute; Simon thought it was the stupidest thing he had ever heard of.) I also remember Simon's general intellectual engagement and wide-ranging interests. He was the only one among us who made an attempt at the Polish language, and he tried to speak to people from his phrasebook whenever he could.

This encounter largely confirmed for me the impression of the man I had gained from reading his work over the years: a searching intellect, great originality, and a willingness to take strong and clear positions. I hope that all these attributes will also show through in this essay, which takes as its reading one of the more obscure works in the Simonian canon. In 1960, the editors of a volume challenged Simon to answer this question: "The Corporation: Will It Be Managed by Machines?"[1] In this marvelous but somewhat neglected paper, he articulated his vision of what the "knowledge economy" of the future – 1985! – would look like. Perhaps surprisingly for someone given to the most strident predictions of the speedy and inevitable success of artificial intelligence, Simon in this article is clear that computers and humans have fundamentally different cognitive comparative advantages.

[M]an's comparative advantage in energy production has been greatly reduced in most situations – to the point where he is no longer a significant source of power in our economy. He has been supplanted also in performing many relatively simple and repetitive eye–brain–

214

hand sequences. He has retained his greatest comparative advantage in: (1) the use of his brain as a flexible general-purpose problem-solving device, (2) the flexible use of his sensory organs and hands, and (3) the use of his legs, on rough terrain as well as smooth, to make this general-purpose sensing–thinking–manipulating system available wherever it is needed.

(Simon, 1960, p. 31)

In what follows I explore this notion of cognitive comparative advantage and use it to tell what (I hope) is a coherent story about the evolution of machines and of the division of labor between humans and machines. Although inspired by Simon's 1960 paper, my account weaves many additional strands into a tapestry of my own design, from classical discussions of the division of labor to present-day evolutionary psychology. I touch both on the history of what has been said about humans and machines and on the often fiery debates in artificial intelligence – debates in which Simon was so prominent. But I do not take on the difficult task of assessing and appraising those weighty topics comprehensively and fairly.

In the end, my basic conclusion is broadly consistent with that in Simon's 1960 paper. With growth in the extent of the market, we should see humans "crowded into" tasks that call for the kinds of cognition for which humans have been equipped by biological evolution. These human cognitive abilities range from the exercise of judgment in situations of ambiguity and surprise to more mundane abilities in spario-temporal perception and locomotion. This conclusion is not based (merely) on a claim that machines, including computers, are specialized *idiots-savants* today because of the limits (whether temporary or permanent) of artificial intelligence; rather, it rests on a claim that, for what are broadly "economic" reasons, it will continue to make sense to create machines that are idiots-savants.

2. The division of labor

At least since the first industrial revolution, people have pondered the relationship between humans and machines. How will machines change life and work? How will they change the role of humans? Although many have conceptualized the interaction between human and machine as a progressive displacement of the former by the latter, writers like Adam Smith and Charles Babbage envisaged a far more complex relationship.

In Smith's account, production is a matter of discrete tasks or stages, each with its own set of specialized tools. Under the sort of crafts production that precedes the division of labor, the artisan masters and coordinates multiple stages of production and wields a variety of specialized tools. As growth in the extent of the market makes it economical to subdivide labor, the artisans begins to specialize in a smaller subset of operations and tools.

To do this, the artisan must now cooperate with other artisans in a more carefully orchestrated way. Workers become complements to one another rather than substitutes (Leijonhufvud, 1986). And the coordination function that the artisans themselves once supplied must now be hardwired to a greater degree into the spatial and temporal "interfaces" among specialized operations and specialized operatives. Each operative must make his or her output relatively standardized so that the next operative down the line knows what to expect; and each operative must hand over that output at a predictable time, lest buffer inventories run dry and the entire production process come to a crashing halt.

Smith attributed the benefits of this organizational transformation to three sources: "first to the increase of dexterity in every particular workman; secondly, to the saving of the time which is commonly lost in passing from one species of work to another; and lastly, to the invention of a great number of machines which facilitate and abridge labor, and enable one man to do the work of many" (Smith, 1976, I.i.5).

The first source is clearly cognitive.[2] By narrowing their focus, the operatives are able to deepen their skills through learning by doing. Writing a few decades after Smith, Charles Babbage recognized the larger cognitive implications: that the division of labor applies to mental operations in general as much to as to mechanical ones. He recounts the story of the French mathematician Prony, who stumbled across a copy of the *Wealth of Nations* and suddenly realized that he could use the division of labor to calculate logarithm tables[3] (Babbage, 1835, Chapter 20). Babbage goes further, suggesting that a machine might take over from humans not only mechanical tasks but some of these intellectual tasks as well. What he had in mind, of course, was the never-finished "analytical engine" often hailed as the first computer. (Machines as information processors is major theme to which we will return.)

As an adherent to the British empiricist tradition – and as a good friend of David Hume – Smith believed that the mind starts out as essentially a tabula rasa and that differences in ability are the result of learning and not of any innate abilities.[4] But what if people are born with innately different abilities? Babbage pointed out that nature provides as much support for the division of labor as does nurture: unlike crafts production, the division of labor permits tasks to be allocated according to (innate) *comparative advantage*.[5] This famous principle of optimal resource allocation had lately been discovered by David Ricardo. It insists that allocation to tasks should be based not on who is *absolutely* better at the task but on who is *relatively* better. If person A is better than person B at both management and secretarial work, it may yet pay to assign B all the secretarial work if A is relatively better (is "more better", we might say) at management.[6] If one takes a middle-ground position in the nature–nurture debate, then clearly the division of labor offers benefits of both the Smith and Babbage kinds.[7]

Smith's third source of benefits from the division of labor brings us finally to the topic of machines. By concentrating their attention more narrowly on a smaller set of operations, he feels, operatives will naturally tend to invent devices that makes them more productive. The reason that specialized workers are able to perceive opportunities to successfully mechanize (parts of) their tasks is that, in narrowing the range of tasks and in standardizing the interfaces between tasks, the division of labor makes the work more routine.[8] It is a major theme of this essay that the human worker may need to retain discretion over some operations while delegating the most routine ones to machines. Nonetheless, in the pure Smithian model of the division of labor, the humans themselves become increasingly machine-like.

In the limit, this amounts to what Sabel (1982) has branded *fordism*. It was not really until the early 20th century that tools and machining techniques were precise enough to allow genuine standardization of parts (Hounshell, 1984). Such standardization enabled Henry Ford to take Smithian factory production to a new level by means of the moving assembly line and related techniques, which he and his engineering staff had begun implementing by 1913. The Ford assembly process was above all a system, one designed by specialized engineers rather than by the workers themselves. (This is of course another manifestation of the division of labor: the design of production becomes itself a specialized task.[9]) The system effected a complete redesign of production, breaking operations into simple sequences of routine activity that yielded standardized subassemblies.

By transferring control of systemic issues from the workers to engineers and industrial designers, fordism, in the phrase popularized by Marglin (1974), had rendered workers *deskilled*.[10] We need look no further than Smith himself for the dire implications of what fordist production would mean for the worker: "The man whose whole life is spent in performing a few simple operations, of which the effects are perhaps always the same, or very nearly the same, has no occasion to exert his understanding or to exercise his invention in finding out expedients for removing difficulties which never occur. He naturally loses, therefore, the habit of such exertion, and generally becomes as stupid and ignorant as it is possible for a human creature to become" (Smith, 1976, V.i.178).

3. Mechanization

For many, notably those intent on criticizing capitalist work organization, this is pretty nearly the end of the story. In fact, however, it is actually much nearer to the middle of the story. Recall Smith's assumptions. Tools start out specialized to the various activities involved in production, but labor is unspecialized. The division of labor consists in matching the specialization of labor to that of machines. But this does not exhaust the possibilities. Why cannot *machines* change their level of specialization? (Ames & Rosenberg, 1965)

When workers specialize, they reduce the range of activities in which they engage; but, if Smith is right, they also become more competent at the activities that remain. Specializing workers thus trade wide skills for deep skills. Let us for the moment take skill to mean the first concept, skill widening instead of skill deepening. Define skill as the number of activities an operative or machine engages in.[11] Clearly; a crafts artisan is more skilled in this sense than a fordist assembly-line worker. Define specialization as the reciprocal of skill: the number of doers (humans or machines) per activity. By this definition, specialization ranges between 0 (complete non-specialization) and 1 (complete specialization). Now consider a production process involving exactly three activities (a_1, a_2, a_3). The result is a set of possibilities summarized in Fig. 1. Technology A is what we called crafts production. One worker undertakes all three activities, but machines – which are clearly *tools* in this case – are specialized to activities. Technology B is what Smith had in mind: workers and tools are equally specialized to activities. Technology 3 is the forgotten alternative: workers are specialized, but machines – and now they are indeed *machines* not just tools – become less specialized.

What it means for the machines to become less specialized is that a single device has taken over – has automated – all three stages of production. Many have traditionally conceptualized such automation as a natural extension of the division of labor: each worker wields specialized tools, and automation is just a matter of hooking the relevant tools together (and typically connecting them to inanimate power) so that they run by themselves.[12] As we will see, however, creating skilled machines typically involves redesigning the work process, often in a radical way, so that it meets the needs of machine cognition. As a result, the process may no longer look a lot like a robotic version of the human division of labor. At the risk of

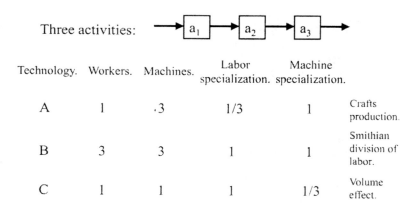

Figure 1 Labor and machine specialization.
Source: Ames and Rosenberg (1965).

drawing a distinction too sharply, we might say that a *tool* is a device that amplifies human skill applied directly to tasks, whereas a *machine* is a device that takes over (often integrated) tasks from the humans, who – as we will see – then direct their skills to tending, maintaining, and designing the machine rather than directly to the production process. A carpenter today still assembles a house with tools, even if those tools are now driven by small electric motors; but plywood is made by a machine. In effect, tools amplify human abilities – both mechanical and cognitive – without fundamentally changing the division of labor.

Machines are another matter. Smith tells us that growth in the extent of the market drives the progressive transition from Technology A to Technology B. But such growth also – and perhaps more importantly – drives a transition from Technology B to Technology C, which we can understand as a further manifestation of the larger division of labor with which Smith was concerned (Langlois, 1999a,b). One can see this point illustrated dramatically by visiting the Match Museum in the town of Jönköping, Sweden, which was the "match capital of the world" for much of the 19th and early 20th centuries. In the beginning, the industry took precisely the form Smith predicted. Cottagers in the town and surrounding countryside assumed a variety of subdivided tasks, from chopping and cutting the match wood to folding and gluing match boxes to the debilitating and ultimately gruesome task of coating the tips with chemicals.[13] But what thrust Jönköping to prominence in the industry was not a finer subdivision of putting-out tasks; rather, it was mechanization. In 1844, the brothers Johan and Carl Lundström opened a factory in Jönköping to capitalize on the recently invented safety match, improvements to which Johan had just patented. In 1870 they hired the inventor Alexander Lagerman to further mechanize the process of making matches. Lagerman's machines not only assumed the tasks of humans but – more significantly – combined within their operations what had been many previously separate tasks, and they did so in a way that often differed dramatically from the unmechanized sequence of tasks.[14]

If mechanization takes tasks entirely out of the hands of workers, are we left to infer, with Marx, that the progress of mechanization will inevitably relegate humans to an immiserated proletarian army of the unskilled and unemployed? The histories of the most-developed countries clearly demonstrate otherwise. But there are also theoretical reasons to see mechanization as producing quite a different and rather more benignant role for humans.[15]

Under Technology C, the human worker is still specialized, because he or she does only one thing. But that one thing is not any of the original activities; instead, it is the new activity of minding the machine. The invention of the power loom in 1787 increased productivity over the hand loom not only because it could weave faster (by the mid-1820s, at any rate) but because a single person, who was no longer providing the motive power, could operate more than one loom[16] (Landes, 1969, p. 86). Of course, we might well view "tending the machine" not as a single specialized activity but as a complex set of activities – perhaps more complex than the crafts activities the machine displaced. When automatic telephone switches replaced the activities of human switchboard operators, machine tending fell to highly trained technicians and (later) programmers. The backhoe, which replaced the activities of human ditch-diggers, required an operator with greater skill than any pick-and-shovel worker (Robertson & Alston, 1992, p. 336). In the telephony case, technological change increased the skill of workers because, as machines took over the more routine tasks, there remained (or were generated) certain complementary tasks to which machines are ill suited and that thus required the ministrations of skilled humans. In the backhoe case, technological change did not lead to a significant redesign of the work process. Instead, more-skilled machines not only aided humans in a skilled activity but actually called forth higher skill in the humans. Thus both skill-enhancing and skill-displacing technical change can be complementary to human skill.

4. Coordination and buffering

As we saw, production is largely a matter of the coordination among tasks.[17] And coordination means that each stage must somehow do the right things at the right time: each stage must make decisions that are appropriate in light of the decisions that came before and will come after. A crafts artisan is constantly interacting with and fiddling with the process of production at each step. But when labor is more finely divided, parts become standardized, and much of the coordination among stages is designed into the process.[18] What limits the use of such hard-wired coordination is the complexity and unpredictability of the environment. If a square hole awaits on the assembly line, the production process will work smoothly only if what arrives is always a square peg – and never a round peg, let alone a whale or a bowl of petunias. Indeed, the higher the throughput of a production system, the more vulnerable the system is to spurious variation. If a round peg appears when a square one is wanted, the entire system may come to a crashing halt.

As Simon tells us, there are fundamentally only two ways to deal with an unpredictable environment. "If we want an organism or mechanism to behave effectively in a complex and changing environment, we can design into it adaptive mechanisms that allow it to respond flexibly to the demands the environment places on it. Alternatively, we can try to simplify and stabilize the environment. We can adapt organism to environment or environment to organism" (Simon, 1960, p. 33). Consider the problem of crossing rough terrain – most of the American continent in the early 19th century, for example. Like the native Americans before them, the earliest western explorers used Simon's first technique: they took advantage of the adaptive mechanism of the human locomotion system. They walked and climbed, at least when there were not suitable rivers available. But once population began gravitating west, it became worthwhile to use the second approach. A steam locomotive is a high-throughput transportation system that works phenomenally well so long as one first prepares the environment in order to reduce variation almost to zero. So the railroad companies altered the terrain – they laid tracks – to accommodate this high-speed, high-volume, but inflexible technology.

A fordist assembly line is like a railroad. It increases throughput by eliminating variation, and thus makes itself vulnerable to whatever variation remains. It is for this reason that such systems need to *buffer* environmental influences (Thompson, 1967, p. 20) by placing human information processors between the uncertainty and the high-throughput production process. At the same time that fordism "deskills" assembly-line workers by making their tasks simpler and more routine, it also surrounds those workers (or the machines that inevitably take on the most simple and routine tasks) with a large number of more flexible (more widely skilled) workers at multiple levels – from maintenance workers to top management.[19] Uncertainty and variation can never be eliminated; at best they can be pushed "up the hierarchy" to be dealt with by adaptable and less-specialized humans.

As Stinchcombe (1990) sees it, these human "buffers" are information-processing systems that mediate between a complex and uncertain environment and the system in need of predictability.[20] Human cognition can often interpret complex data from the external world and translate that data into the kinds of routine information the productive system can use. For example, a professor translates the complex information on an essay exam into a letter grade that the Registrar's office can process; a physician translates the complex inputs from observation and medical instrumentation into a diagnosis, which results in a relatively unambiguous set of instructions for nurses, pharmacists, patients, etc.

5. Human versus machine

The first industrial revolution improved productivity by assigning the task of providing motive power to inanimate sources like water and steam. The hand weaver became a loom tender. At the same time, machines also began to take over some "relatively simple and repetitive eye–brain–hand sequences" (Simon, 1960, p. 31). To the extent that production had been (or could be) laid out as a sequence of simple coordinated steps, a machine could perform the steps (perhaps in a slightly different way or in a different sequence) with greater speed and precision. The specialized Smithian match maker gave way to the match-making machine. In the computer era, and especially in the last quarter century, machines have become faster not only at repetitive sequences of tasks in general but at repetitive calculations in particular. We often call such calculation "information processing". If, as I have argued, the human ability to buffer variation is a matter of information processing, will the computer eventually take over from the human buffers – including managers?

What makes this question especially intriguing is that Simon was a champion for the position that abstract symbol manipulation is the essence of thinking, and thus that computers, which manipulate symbols, can in principle be designed to think like humans (Newell & Simon, 1961). So we might expect to find Simon suggesting the opposite: that computers will surely begin to outdo humans in many if not all areas involving "information processing". In one sense, this was indeed Simon's view. He makes the characteristically bold claim that,

> because we can now write complex information-processing programs for computers, we are acquiring the technical capacity to replace humans with computers in a rapidly widening range of 'thinking' and 'deciding' tasks. Closely allied to the development of complex information-processing techniques for general-purpose computers is the rapid advance in the technique of automating all sorts of production and clerical tasks. Putting these two lines of development together, I am led to the following general predictions: Within the very near future – much less than 25 years – we shall have the *technical* capability of substituting machines for any and all human functions in organizations. Within the same period, we shall have acquired an extensive and empirically tested theory of human cognitive processes and their interaction with human emotions, attitudes, and values.
>
> (Simon, 1960, p. 22)

One way to resolve the apparent paradox is to remember that Simon's argument is based comparative advantage rather than absolute advantage. Under this logic, assignment to tasks is not a matter of who is better but, as we saw, of who is "more better". Just as it might be efficient to assign person B all the secretarial work even if A is better at both executive work and secretarial work, it might be efficient to assign to humans the tasks of flexible response and "buffering" even if computers are absolutely better at them, so long as computers are "more better" at routine and well-defined activities. As Simon puts it, to predict that humans will have the ability to make "thinking and deciding" machines "says nothing of how we shall use them". Instead, economics – not any inherent limits to AI – will determine the division of labor between humans and machines. "Thus, if computers are a 1000 times faster than bookkeepers in doing arithmetic, but only 100 times faster than stenographers in taking dictation, we shall expect the number of bookkeepers per thousand employees to decrease but the number of stenographers to increase. Similarly, if computers are a 100 times faster than executives in making investment decisions, but only 10 times faster in handling employee grievances (the quality of the decisions being held constant), then computers will be employed in making investment decisions, while executives will be employed in handling grievances" (Simon, 1960, p. 25).

There are many, of course, who would find this a singularly unsatisfying resolution, since it avoids the *sturm und drang* of the well-documented controversy over artificial intelligence. At one side of the debate, Simon always resolutely upheld the strongest version of the thesis that computers can in principle – and will soon in fact – be capable of essentially any cognitive task now undertaken by humans. At the other extreme have stood critics like Dreyfus (1979), who contend that human brains and computers work in very different ways, that the computer is not a good model of human cognition, and that computers will never be able to do what human brains can do. Simon's proclivity for the outrageous prediction has helped keep this pot boiling. My contention is that, far from sidestepping this debate, a bit of economic reasoning (of which the principle of comparative advantage is but one aspect) helps to clarify the issues – and indeed to demonstrate that the debate as it usually plays out is ill posed and misleading.

Clearly, the design of machines is importantly an economic matter. It pays to subdivide labor or mechanize production only when production runs are large enough. What may be less obvious is that the human machine is also in many respects a response to economic forces. The human brain (and the human being more generally) is an evolved product, and therefore one whose design reflects tradeoffs motivated by resource constraints. The field of evolutionary psychology (Cosmides & Tooby, 1987, 1994; Pinker, 1997) takes as a background premise that, like computers, human beings are information-processing machines, albeit ones designed by natural selection rather than by humans.[21] For scientists in this tradition, understanding the human mind involves "reverse engineering" the brain in light of the evolutionary problem or problems to which that brain proved to be a solution. The mind is thus a computer, designed for the manipulation of symbols; but is also a particular kind of machine, one designed for specific circumstances rather than for pure symbol manipulation in the manner of the digital computer.

Broadly speaking, the crucible of human cognition was the entire legacy of evolution, but critically the last 50,000 years, most of which our ancestors spent as hunter-gatherers. In this reading, evolution produced a mind well adapted to the needs of that lifestyle. Recall that, for Simon, human comparative advantage lies in two areas: (a) sensory, manipulative, and locomotive tasks and (b) problem-solving and decision-making tasks. Both of these sets of capabilities came in handy to the hunter-gatherers, and the two are probably interrelated both physiologically and in terms of evolutionary trajectory. An upright posture had its advantages, as did the sensitive ability to recognize objects and patterns and to grasp tools and other objects effectively. Having these skills required humans to develop amazingly complex robotics hardware and software.

But human problem-solving and decision-making abilities may have been even more crucial. Humans succeeded by seizing the *cognitive niche* (Tooby & DeVore, 1987). In evolutionary competition, species evolve distinctive traits to gain advantage. Their competitors – including their predators and their prey – must rely on evolution to counter that advantage. If lions become faster, zebra cannot immediately improve their agility or their camouflage. Not so humans. Like the Borg on *Star Trek*, they can quickly analyze and adapt to the offensive and defensive weapons of competitors. And they can do so on a time scale that is extraordinary short by evolutionary standards. This ability to learn, adapt, and solve problems in a creative way enabled humans to colonize and master virtually every kind of environment and every part of the planet. What made this success possible was the development of complex symbol-manipulation hardware and software, including language and the ability to amplify individual cognition through culture (Donald, 1991).

To Simon, sensory recognition, manipulation, and locomotion constitute the harder problem. "We are much further from replacing the eyes, the hands, and the legs" (Simon, 1960, p. 32). Despite some progress, we are still far from duplicating human perceptual-motor abilities more than 40 years after Simon wrote. But what about problem solving and decision making? Simon offered his characteristically bold prediction. "Duplicating the problem-solving and information-handling capabilities of the brain is not far off; it would be surprising if it were not accomplished within the next decade" (Simon, 1960, p. 32). We all remember the seventies for many things, but one of them is not the creation of computers that "duplicate" human cognitive skills. Indeed, that may or may not have happened yet, depending on what one wants to count as "duplicating".[22]

So, was Simon wrong? Again, I think the language of "prediction" and "duplication" obscures the real issues, which are that (a) human brains and computers are different machines with different designs and (b) what kinds of information-processing machines get designed will depend on economic considerations. (More on that below.) Moreover, that computers cannot (yet?) duplicate human abilities in creative decision making and open-ended problem solving is not so much a matter of the failure of computers as it is a reflection of the success of the human brain.

It is a staple of fiction that computers and robots are literal minded. When secret agent Maxwell Smart tells his android assistant Hymie to "kill the lights", Hymie pulls out a gun a shoots the light bulb. In fact, computers are literal minded at a much more fundamental level. The reason is that they are completely general symbol-manipulation engines. This can obviously be a great advantage. But it also poses the disadvantage that computers do not find ready at hand all the prepackaged pieces of information and all the purpose-built learning and processing systems we take for granted as "common sense". In cognitive science, this difficulty falls under the heading of the *frame problem*.

We all have an idea of what it means for tasks to be simple or easy. It turns out that what is simple or easy for a human may be damned hard for another kind of cognitive system. Reaching into the refrigerator and picking out an egg is easy – if you are a human not a mechanical robotic arm. Similarly, going to the same refrigerator to make a midnight snack (to use Dennett's example) is trivial for a human but a daunting piece of decision-making for a computer. The reason is that humans have a complex set of tacit understandings and expectations – some learned, some no doubt built in – that circumscribe the decision-making problem by excluding much of what is logically possible but irrelevant[23] (Dennett, 1998). People jump to conclusions and engage in other kinds of cognitive "cheating". This allows them to solve not only problems that would be impossibly complex for an axiomatic system but even problems that are overdetermined and thus have no unique analytic solution (Pinker, 1997).

Of course, Simon has also insisted that humans engage in a certain kind of cognitive "cheating". Because of the limitations of the human information-processing system, humans suffer from "bounded rationality". As a result, they must rely on *heuristics*, simplified rules that can find an approximate solution to a complex problem at a relatively lower cost of computation.[24] What has always seemed significant to me, however, is that Simon framed the notions of bounded rationality and heuristics in terms of the model of axiomatic general-purpose symbol processing (Langlois, 1986). "Rationality" is bounded because it cannot reach the correct analytical solution to a complex but well-defined problem (like winning in chess). And heuristics are therefore inferior or second-best solutions. To many writers on the cognitive foundations of behavior, this formulation has its eye to the wrong end of the telescope. Far from being inferior shortcuts to a general analytical solution, the rules humans follow may in fact represent a mode of approaching complex problems *superior* to that of general-purpose axiomatic symbol processing. In their seminal discussion of skills, routines, and capabilities Nelson and Winter (1982), invoke Simon's notion of heuristics as an example of a routine. But they move quickly to locate the ideas of skill and routine more firmly in the phenomenology of Simon's intellectual opponents. Skills, in the end, are inexplicit rules connected to specific human performances. They are *tacit knowledge*, in Polanyi's (1958) famous phrase.

Evolutionary psychology hints at why this is so. For many evolutionary psychologists, the physiological basis for human cognitive ability resides in the fact that the brain is the result of layers of historical evolution and thus consists not in a single central-processing unit (as in a von Neumann-style computer) but rather in a congeries of interacting organs or faculties each "designed" by evolution for a different role.[25] In computer terms, the brain is not a powerful CPU with a few simple support chips but rather a system of powerful but specialized co-processors governed by a relatively weak CPU. It is still unclear exactly how all of this works. And there is considerable controversy over what we may call the strong program of evolutionary psychology, namely, that much (most? all?) of human behavior can be explained in terms of specific hard-wired modules or faculties that evolved in specific evolutionary environments. But even researchers skeptical of the strong program are increasingly inclined to see the brain not as a pure engine of calculation but as a "layered, hybrid modern mind (that) is capable of experiencing, learning, knowing, and problem-solving, at all levels, sometimes employed at the same time, but in different ways" (Nelson & Nelson, 2002, pp. 723–724).

6. The future of work

The view from cognitive science informs our discussion in a number of ways. It is far from implausible, for example, to entertain the hypothesis that the evolutionary environment in which our ancestors found themselves may offer clues to the cognitive strengths and weaknesses of present-day humans as pieces of the productive system. Hunter-gatherers were clearly adaptors and creative problem solvers. They were highly skilled in the sense developed earlier: they needed to know many different routines and had the ability to switch among tasks. Surely most of the cognitive background assumptions of our ancestors's environment carry over to our own at all but the most superficial levels: objects still tend to fall down not up, etc. Thus, an information-processing system that is highly specialized and domain specific along a computational dimension becomes a general-purpose technology along an economic dimension. Human beings can do all sorts of things competently and flexibly, albeit at low rates of throughput. They are thus well suited to a wide range of tasks with similar cognitive profiles, from driving trucks to repairing trucks to running the Teamsters Union. Humans are natural "buffers".

At another level, the view from cognitive science suggests something about machines as well. In effect, nature solves the frame problem by enlisting the division of labor. Human "common sense" arises from specialization to the contours and demands of a specific environment. Moreover, the evolution of flexible cognition is the exception not the rule (Pinker, 1997, p. 154). Nature's tendency on the whole is to create idiots-savants not general-purpose problem solvers: lightning-fast cheetahs, bats that echolocate, birds that navigate by the stars.[26] The human brain itself may be a congeries of specialized idiots-savants who work together. So we as humans should not see it as odd that all we seem to be able to create are machines that do a narrow set of things well.

It makes good economic sense for machines to be idiots-savants, for the reasons Smith explained. Moreover, as robotics research has revealed, it is almost always cheaper to change the environment so that it demands less flexibility than it is to create an adaptation to a complex environment. If we want high throughput, we are well advised to stabilize the environment and simplify the computational demands of the task structure. If you want a personal computer built to your specifications, you can wander into your local mom-and-pop computer shop, where the proprietor can no doubt be induced to order the necessary parts and put them together for you. But if you want to produce personal computers to specification at extremely high volumes and significantly lower costs, you are far better off setting up an automated production and distribution system of the sort pioneered by Dell (Kraemer & Dedrick, 2001). The Dell system will not enquire about your grandchildren (unless some wag programs the website to do that), nor will it go home and fry up an egg for its son's supper. But the point is that we should not want it to.

Just as the human being is a general-purpose technology precisely because of its cognitive specialization, the computer is an idiot-savant because of its cognitive generality. Of course, the computer is a general-purpose technology in economic terms, since it can be reprogrammed easily to take on a wide variety of specialized computational tasks (Langlois, 2002). Giving a computer common sense is hard, but through software we can make computers into virtually any idiot-savant we choose. And that is exactly what we should want to do.

Even in the age of computers, high-throughput production is about altering the environment to reduce variation. In Ford's original version of the assembly line, everything was pre-programmed so that square pegs always appeared to match every square hole; eliminating variation meant eliminating round pegs not just whales and bowls of petunias. This is why it was an important part of Ford's manufacturing concept that the product be identical so as to permit as high a throughput at as low a cost as possible. At least since the jacquard loom, however, batch processing has actually been able to handle certain kinds of variety rather easily. So long as variety is predictable – that is, so long as variety means a selection from a restricted set of known possibilities – machines can be taught to recognize and deal with it. To resurrect some terminology I proposed a long time ago (Langlois, 1984), I will describe this as *parametric* variation – variation from within a known set mutually exclusive and collectively exhaustive possibilities. Any other kind of variation I will call *structural* variation.[27] Distinguishing among square, round, and triangular pegs is a parametric matter. Dealing with whales and bowls of petunias is a structural matter. Computers like those in the Dell production system have lowered the cost of managing parametric variation. You can choose from a wide menu of processors, memory, drives, etc.; but if it is not on the menu, you cannot have it.

It is for fundamentally economic reasons, then, that we should continue to see machines crowd humans out of tasks in which computers have comparative advantage, namely tasks involving predictable, repetitive sequences of activities, including potentially complex but well structured calculations. This also implies that humans will crowd into activities in which humans have comparative advantage, namely tasks involving flexibility and adaptability, especially in the areas of problem solving and perceptual-motor activities.

In her study of how information technology has altered the organization of work, Zuboff (1988) shows that this process has been going on for some time. Interestingly, this is especially clear in the realm of symbol-processing tasks like management and office work, where the need for judgment and buffering has long been moving up the hierarchy.

> Elements of managerial work most easily subjected to rationalization were "carved out" of the manager's activities. The foundational example of this process is the rationalization of executive work, which was accomplished by ejecting those elements that could be explicated and systematized, preserving intact the skills that comprise executive craft. It was the carving out of such elements that created the array of functions we now associate with middle management. A similar process accounts for the origins of clerical work. In each case, the most easily rationalized features of the activities at one level were carved out, pushed downward, and used to create wholly new lower-level jobs. In this process higher-level positions were not eliminated; on the contrary, they came to be seen more than ever as the depository of the organization's skills.
>
> (Zuboff, 1988, p. 98)

Although perhaps less obvious at first, change in mechanical tasks has followed a similar trajectory. The division of labor tends to make tasks more routine and therefore to "deskill" those who undertake those tasks. But, as we saw, that very routinization enables "skilled" integrative machines to displace those deskilled workers. It is such machinery (rather than to specialized humans) to which the most easily rationalized tasks are ultimately "ejected", leaving humans the more discretionary tasks of tending, maintenance, and design in which they have cognitive comparative advantage.

Both Simon (1997) and Zuboff cite a study of worker attitudes by Blauner (1964) that examined four kinds of industries: crafts (printing), fordist assembly (automobiles), machine tending (textiles), and continuous-process (chemicals). As one might expect, workers found fordist assembly and machine tending less pleasant than crafts production; but not so continuous-process production. In that type of industry, mechanization had proceeded farther, and machines had taken over most of the routine activities, leaving workers the more interesting – more crafts-like – tasks of maintenance and problem solving. Blauner is right to see continuous process technology as the future of mechanization. Because of their cognitive comparative advantage, machines are likely to continue to absorb routine and well-defined tasks, thereby becoming more integrated and thus making production more continuous.

The process of crowding humans into tasks suitable for human cognition is not confined to the shop floor or the interior of the firm. Within the larger market economy, we ought to expect the same general phenomenon. Simon envisioned humans filling a variety of roles.

- *Lower-level buffering workers*. These would include workers in small-scale tasks requiring human hand–eye–brain coordination. Such tasks would include routine or repetitive activities not worth automating or costly to automate. (The American system of road transport, designed for human drivers, comes to mind.)
- *Maintenance workers*, including those engaged in preventive maintenance. Someone has to clean up the mess when a whale or a bowl of petunias comes down the assembly line.
- *Bosses*. These are a kind of maintenance worker – people who deal with and plan for the non-routine. Simon notes, quite rightly, that redesign of production and mechanization is likely to lead to less need for management as "supervision".
- *Designers*, which includes not only designers of products and processes but also managers at the highest levels, who are designers of organizations.
- *Those involved in personal-service occupations*, who have to deal with the most unpredictable environment of all – other humans. Which occupations remain personal-service ones will depend, however, on which can be more cheaply redesigned to eliminate variation. In banking, automated tellers reduced the number of human tellers. But in the restaurant business, the automat of the 1950s failed miserably in displacing what we now refer to as the "waitperson".

Simon seems to suggest that, as automation proceeds, humans will progressively shift down this list, away from not-yet-automated assembly tasks and routine maintenance and into design, management, and personal service. Voilà the service economy, already clearly envisioned 40 years ago.

Will this be a better place? Clearly this sort of analysis cannot answer a question of such weight and complexity. But it does arguably cast light on one important aspect. Even the most routine sorts of jobs into which humans are likely to be shunted – like truck drivers or hairdressers – are clearly crafts occupations in the sense described earlier. They require the operative to switch among a wide set of routines and tasks, and they present that operative with a wide variety of stimuli. This speaks directly to one of the crucial considerations in the debate about technology: the issue of cognitive narrowing that so troubled Adam Smith and many others. Indeed, the present analysis would argue strongly against any criticism of mechanization aimed fundamentally at the issues of task narrowing or deskilling.

Of course, one could always conjure up unpleasant visions of a future knowledge economy (as the service economy is now called) on other grounds. In his cyber-punk short story "The Beautiful and the Sublime", Sterling (1989) gives us a future in which the advance of automation has moved the domain of human tasks so far down Simon's list that artists and aesthetes have become the rising dominant class. This is not necessarily all to the good, if the shallow and self-absorbed narrator and his friends are meant to be representative. Or maybe Simon is right in this as well: "perhaps more of us will be salesmen" (Simon, 1960, p. 38).

Acknowledgements

Thanks to Stefano Brusoni, Peter Earl, Giampaolo Garzarelli, Brian Loasby, Phil Mirowski, Keith Pavitt, Steve Postrel, Sid Winter, and an anonymous referee for helpful discussions and comments. None is implicated in the result.

Notes

1 The volume was intended to celebrate the tenth anniversary of the founding of the Graduate School of Industrial Administration at what was then Carnegie Tech.

2 Although not perhaps obvious at first, the benefits of less switching among tasks is also at base a cognitive matter, as Hendrik Houthakker explains. "The indivisibility of the individual consists in the fact that, although it may be capable of a great many different activities, it can perform only few activities simultaneously because most activities utilize the same resources and more particularly that coordinating resource which is known as the brain. The larger the number of simultaneous activities, the greater the difficulty of coordinating them and of carrying out each one properly, and the smaller therefore the output from each activity. This applies not only to simultaneous activities, but also to activities that are spread out over time. In the first place some shorter or longer interval is usually needed to switch from one activity to another; in the second place it is usually easier to perform activities that are known from previous experience than to perform them for the first time. All this, the economist will note at once, can be put in terms of increasing returns. We have increasing returns to the extent that, if several activities are replaced by a single one, there is less need for coordination and switching time and more scope for acquiring experience. The output

of the single activity may thus be raised above the combined outputs of the several activities" (Houthakker, 1956, p. 182).

3 Ironic indeed that the French needed Smith to teach them the division of labor, since Smith lifted his account of the making of pins from the French Encyclopédie.

4 "The difference of natural talents in different men is, in reality, much less than we are aware of; and the very different genius which appears to distinguish men of different professions, when grown up to maturity, is not upon many occasions so much the cause, as the effect of the division of labor. The difference between the most dissimilar characters, between a philosopher and a common street porter, for example, seems to arise not so much from nature, as from habit, custom, and education" (Smith, 1976, I.ii.4).

5 "We have seen, then, that the effect of the division of labor, both in mechanical and in mental operations, is, that it enables us to purchase and apply to each process precisely that quantity of skill and knowledge which is required for it: we avoid employing any part of the time of a man who can get eight or ten shillings a day by his skill in tempering needles, in turning a wheel, which can be done for sixpence a day; and we equally avoid the loss arising from the employment of an accomplished mathematician in performing the lowest processes of arithmetic" (Babbage, 1835, Section II, Chapter 20, Para 250).

6 Those who remember their Principles of Economics know that "more better" has a precise interpretation in terms of the slopes of production-possibilities curves.

7 Phrased this way, it is hard to disagree with the proposition that both nature and nurture matter. As I will suggest below, the issue once again becomes controversial as soon as one asks for specifics.

8 "It is generally agreed that Adam Smith, when he suggested that the division of labor leads to inventions because workmen engaged in specialised routine operations come to see better ways of accomplishing the same results, missed the main point. The important thing, of course, is that with the division of labor a group of complex processes is transformed into a succession of simpler processes, some of which, at least, lend themselves to the use of machinery" (Young, 1928, p. 530).

9 "All the improvements in machinery, however, have by no means been the inventions of those who had occasion to use the machines. Many improvements have been made by the ingenuity of the makers of the machines, when to make them became the business of a peculiar trade; and some by that of those who are called philosophers or men of speculation, whose trade it is not to do anything, but to observe every thing; and who, upon that account, are often capable of combining together the powers of the most distant and dissimilar objects. In the progress of society, philosophy or speculation becomes, like every other employment, the principal or sole trade and occupation of a particular class of citizens" (Smith, 1976, I.i.9, p. 21).

10 Of course, Marx noticed this long ago. "Intelligence in production expands in one direction, because it vanishes in many others. What is lost by the detail laborers, is concentrated in the capital that employs them" (Marx, 1961, Vol. 1, Part IV, Chapter XIV, p. 361). On this see also Braverman (1974).

11 The remainder of this paragraph follows Ames and Rosenberg (1965), who offer a more careful definition of terms than I attempt here.

12 Charles Babbage, for example: "When each process has been reduced to the use of some simple tool, the union of all these tools, actuated by one moving power, constitutes a machine" (Babbage, 1835, Chapter 19, Para 225). Similarly Karl Marx, who probably got the idea from Babbage: "The machine proper is therefore a mechanism that, after being set in motion, performs with its tools the same

operations that were formerly done by the workman with similar tools" (Marx, 1961, Vol. 1, Part IV, Chapter XIV, p. 374).

13 Which produced phosphorus necrosis in the workers. The transition to the safety match after 1844 had the happy effect of substituting less-toxic red phosphorus for the more dangerous yellow phosphorus (Karlsson, 1996).

14 A more familiar example illustrates the productivity gains to be had from this process. Smith (1976, I.1.3) describes the manufacture of pins in his day, in which 10 men, organized according to principles of the division of labor, could make about 48,000 pins a day, or almost 5000 per person per day. By Marx's era, making pins was already the business of machines, and a single machine could crank out 145,000 a day. One woman or girl could supervise four machines, which means almost 600,000 per person per day (Marx, 1961, Vol. 1, Part IV, Chapter XV, Section 8, p. 460). As of 1980, one person could supervise 24 machines, each making 500 pins a minute, or about 6 million pins per person per day (Pratten, 1980). That is a two orders of magnitude increase in productivity in the first century as machines replaced the division of hand labor but only (!) a single order of magnitude increase in productivity over the next century as machines improved.

15 In this respect, Alfred Marshall was closer to the mark than Marx. Machinery, he writes, "constantly supplants and renders unnecessary that purely manual skill, the attainment of which was, even up to Adam Smith's time, the chief advantage of division of labor. But this influence is more than countervailed by its tendency to increase the scale of manufactures and to make them more complex; and therefore to increase the opportunities for division of labor of all kinds, and especially in the matter of business management" (Marshall, 1961, IV.ix.3).

16 Landes (1969, p. 86) reports that "in 1833, a young man with a 12 year old assistant could run four looms and turn out as much as 20 times the output of a hand worker". Two looms may have been a more typical assignment, however, until the last quarter of the 19th century.

17 "Production", of course, means more than "making things" in the narrow sense and encompasses all the economic tasks necessary to get a product or service into the hands of the consumer. Indeed, the consumer may also need to engage in some "production" in order to be able to consume (Langlois & Coşgel, 1998).

18 Clearly, increases in the extent of the market make batch production more feasible. In a sufficiently large market, there is a demand for many instances of an identical object, which means, broadly speaking, that the production process for making the object will need to make many of the same decisions over and over again. In this respect, we can think of the move to high-volume production as a reduction in *variety* in the cybernetic sense (Ashby, 1956). This is implicit in most discussions of dominant designs and innovative regimes (e.g. Abernathy & Utterback, 1978), in which innovation stops being a matter of the trying out of many qualitatively different alternatives and becomes a matter of refining a single alternative. In the language of March (1991), high-volume production reflects a transition from *exploration* to *exploitation*. As I will suggest eventually, even the phenomenon of so-called mass customization is not an exception.

19 "There will generally be a separate set of skilled manual work departments (maintenance, tool and die making, and special departments that vary with the technology, such as the crew who lay firebricks inside steel furnaces) and skilled staff workers at the managerial levels (engineering, quality control and inspections scheduling and inventory)" (Stinchcombe, 1990, p. 64).

20 Frank Knight agrees. "In industrial life", he writes, "purely routine operations are inevitably taken over by machinery. The duties of the machine tender may

seem mechanical and uniform, but they are really not so throughout the operation. His function is to complete the carrying-out of the process to the point where it becomes entirely uniform so that the machine can take hold of it, or else to begin with the uniform output of the machine and start it on the way of diversification. Some part of the task will practically always be found to require conscious judgment, which is to say the meeting of uncertainty, the exercise of responsibility, in the ordinary sense of these terms" (Knight, 1921, III.X.7, pp. 294–295).

21 As many writers have pointed out, these design processes may not in the end be so very different (Nelson & Nelson, 2002).

22 In a 1994 interview in *Omni* magazine (and presumably elsewhere), Simon held that all of his predictions had come true except for the famous assertion that a computer would beat the human chess champion – and that one was off by only a factor of 4 (Stewart, 1994).

23 Phenomenological approaches to human action have long understood the importance of background understandings and experience, what Schüz and Luckmann (1973, p. 99) call the "stock of knowledge". It is this stock of knowledge that allows the agent to interpret reality. Some elements of the stock of knowledge are so fundamental that they are not merely non-conscious but are actually "a condition of every experience in the life-world and enter into the horizon of experience" (Schütz & Luckmann, 1973, p. 104). Dennett (1998, p. 188) has suggested extending phenomenology into "hetero-phenomenology", which would consider the demands of action not from the perspective of what is introspectively given to humans but from the perspective of the pure information demands of action.

24 A heuristic is "any principle or device that contributes to the reduction in the average search to solution" (Newell, Shaw, & Simon, 1962, p. 85).

25 And, if Damasio (1994) is right, organs and systems outside of the brain proper are also part of the cognitive process – of the mind.

26 In this and in earlier passages I have lapsed into the rhetorical trope of nature as designer. Of course I do not mean that literally, and the reader should take this locution as incorporating by reference a wholly Darwinian account of the sort so well expounded by Dawkins (1986).

27 Langlois and Coşgel (1993) argue that this distinction actually tracks Frank Knight's more famous (and widely misunderstood) distinction between risk and uncertainty.

References

Abernathy, W., & Utterback, J. M. (1978). Patterns of industrial innovation. *Technology Review* (June/July).

Ames, E., & Rosenberg, N. (1965). The progressive division and specialization of industries. *Journal of Development Studies, 1*(4), 363–383.

Ashby, W. R. (1956). *An introduction to cybernetics*. London: Chapman & Hall.

Babbage, C. (1835). *On the economy of machinery and manufactures* (4th ed). London: Charles Knight.

Blauner, R. (1964). *Alienation and freedom*. Chicago: University of Chicago Press.

Braverman, H. (1974). *Labor and monopoly capital*. New York: Monthly Review Press.

Cosmides, L., & Tooby, J. (1987). From evolution to behavior: Evolutionary psychology as the missing link. In J. Dupré (Ed.), *The latest on the best: Essays on evolution and optimality* (pp. 277–306). Cambridge, MA: MIT Press.

Cosmides, L., & Tooby, J. (1994). Better than rational: Evolutionary psychology and the invisible hand. *American Economic Review, 84*(2), 327–332.

Damasio, A. R. (1994). *Descartes' error: Emotion, reason, and the human brain.* New York: G.P. Putnam.

Dawkins, R. (1986). *The blind watchmaker.* New York: Norton.

Dennett, D. C. (1998). *Brainchildren.* Cambridge, MA: MIT Press.

Donald, M. (1991). *Origins of the modern mind.* Cambridge, MA: Harvard University Press.

Dreyfus, H. L. (1979). *What computers can't do: The limits of artificial intelligence.* New York: Harper Colophon, revised edition.

Hounshell, D. A. (1984). *From the American system to mass production, 1800–1932: The development of manufacturing technology in the United States.* Baltimore: Johns Hopkins University Press.

Houthakker, H. S. (1956). Economics and biology: Specialization and speciation. *Kyklos, 9,* 181–189.

Karlsson, F. (1996). *The history of Swedish match manufacture.* Available: http://enterprise.shv.hb.se/~match/history.html.

Knight, F. H. (1921). *Risk, uncertainty and profit.* Boston: Houghton-Mifflin.

Kraemer, K., & Dedrick, J. (2001). *Dell computer: Using E-commerce to support the virtual company.* Center for Research on Information Technology and Organizations, University of California, Irvine (June).

Landes, D. S. (1969). *The unbound Prometheus: Technological change and industrial development in western Europe from 1750 to the present.* Cambridge: Cambridge University Press.

Langlois, R. N. (1984). Internal organization in a dynamic context: Some theoretical considerations. In M. Jussawalla & H. Ebenfield (Eds.), *Communication and information economics: New perspectives* (pp. 23–49). Amsterdam: North-Holland.

Langlois, R. N. (1986). Rationality, institutions, and explanation. In R. N. Langlois (Ed.), *Economics as a process: Essays in the new institutional economics.* New York: Cambridge University Press.

Langlois, R. N. (1999a). The coevolution of technology and organization in the transition to the factory system. In P. L. Robertson (Ed.), *Authority and control in modern industry* (pp. 45–72). London: Routledge.

Langlois, R. N. (1999b). Scale, scope, and the reuse of knowledge. In S. C. Dow & P. E. Earl (Eds.), *Economic organization and economic knowledge: Essays in honour of Brian J. Loasby* (pp. 239–254). Aldershot: Edward Elgar.

Langlois, R. N. (2002). Digital technology and economic growth: The history of semiconductors and computers. In D. V. Benn Steil & R. R. Nelson (Eds.), *Technological innovation and economic performance* (pp. 265–284). Princeton, NJ: Princeton University Press for the Council on Foreign Relations.

Langlois, R. N., & Coşgel, M. M. (1993). Frank Knight on risk, uncertainty, and the firm: A new interpretation. *Economic Inquiry, 31*(July), 456–465.

Langlois, R. N., & Coşgel, M. M. (1998). The organization of consumption. In M. Bianchi (Ed.), *The active consumer* (pp. 107–121). London: Routledge.

Leijonhufvud, A. (1986). Capitalism and the factory system. In R. N. Langlois (Ed.), *Economics as a process: Essays in the new institutional economics.* New York: Cambridge University Press.

March, J. G. (1991). Exploration and exploitation in organisational learning. *Organization Science, 2,* 1–19.

Marglin, S. A. (1974). What do bosses do? *Review of Radical Political Economy,* 6(Summer), 33–60.

Marshall, A. (1961). *Principles of economics* (9th (variorum) ed., *Vol. I*). London: Macmillan.

Marx, K. (1961). *Capital (Vol. 1).* Moscow: Foreign Languages Publishing House.

Nelson, K., & Nelson, R. R. (2002). On the nature and evolution of human know-how. *Research Policy, 31,* 719–733.

Nelson, R. R., & Winter, S. G. (1982). *An evolutionary theory of economic change.* Cambridge, MA: The Belknap Press of Harvard University Press.

Newell, A., & Simon, H. A. (1961). Computer simulation of human thinking. *Science, 134,* 2011–2017.

Newell, A., Shaw, J. C., & Simon, H. A (1962). The problem of creative thinking. In H. E. Gruber, G. Terrell, & M. Wertheimer (Eds.), *Contemporary approaches to creative thinking.* New York: Atherton Press.

Pinker, S. (1997). *How the mind works.* New York: W.W. Norton.

Polanyi, M. (1958). *Personal knowledge.* Chicago: University of Chicago Press.

Pratten, C. F. (1980). The manufacture of pins. *Journal of Economic Literature,* 18(1), 93–96.

Robertson, P. L., & Alston, L. J. (1992). Technological choice and the organization of work in capitalist firms. *Economic History Review,* 45(2), 330–349.

Sabel, C. F. (1982). *Work and politics: The division of labor in industry.* New York: Cambridge University Press.

Schütz, A., & Luckmann, T. (1973). *The structures of the life-world* (R. M. Zaner, H. T. Engelhardt Jr., Trans.). Evanston, IL: Northwestern University Press.

Simon, H. A. (1960). The corporation: Will it be managed by machines? In M. L. Anshen & G. L. Bach (Eds.), *Management and the corporations, 1985* (pp. 17–55). New York: McGraw-Hill.

Simon, H. A. (1997). On the alienation of workers and management. *Models of Bounded Rationality (Vol. 3,* pp. 183–196). Cambridge, MA: MIT Press.

Smith, A. (1976). *An enquiry into the nature and causes of the wealth of nations* (Glasgow ed). Oxford: Clarendon Press (first published in 1776).

Sterling, B. (1989). The beautiful and the sublime. In *Crystal express.* Sauk City, WI: Arkham House.

Stewart, D. (1994). Herbert Simon: Thinking machines. *Omni* (June). Available: http://www.omnimag.com/archives/interviews/simon.html.

Stinchcombe, A. L. (1990). *Information and organizations.* Berkeley, CA: University of California Press.

Thompson, J. D. (1967). *Organizations in action.* New York: McGraw-Hill.

Tooby, J., & DeVore, I. (1987). The reconstruction of hominid behavioral evolution through strategic modeling. In W. G. Kinzey (Ed.), *The evolution of human behavior: Primate models.* Albany, NY: State University of New York Press.

Young, A. A. (1928). Increasing returns and economic progress. *The Economic Journal, 38,* 527–542.

Zuboff, S. (1988). *In the age of the smart machine.* New York: Basic Books.

60

NEO-DARWINISM AND SIMON'S BUREAUCRATIC ANTIHERO

Linda F. Dennard

Source: *Administration & Society*, 26:4 (1995), 464–487.

Decision making, as a form of Darwinism, has reduced our sense of what it means to be a human being to the practical art of adaptation to a hostile environment. In reality, however, the practicality of decision making to the survival of the species or the American culture is marginal. For Herbert Simon to be able to prescribe administrative behavior, which is essentially problem solving, he must also reduce the heroic nature of human beings to the dreary and uninspiring task of satisficing. Satisficing does not draw on the human capacity for proactive choice and purposeful change. Simon bases his theories on an incomplete view of evolution—especially human evolution. Simon's neo-Darwinism is illustrated and then compared with emerging views on the nature of evolution, the brain, and the human enterprise. The conclusion drawn here is that whether or not we have bounded rationality is really a matter of the choice we make about human purpose.

Modern administrative consciousness has been described by C. Wright Mills as the bureaucratic ethos—an exclusionary network of ideas and action that seems to operate in spite of citizens, instead of with them (1978, pp. 101–118). This ethos is, at least in part, the outcome of an intellectual crisis among those who prescribe administrative reform; a crisis energized by the attempts of economists like Herbert Simon to free the public arena of the conflict that comes from human influences. Indeed, neo-Darwinists, like Simon, enamored of skills, techniques, tasks, and programs, have made light of the very human need for idealism and aspiration—emotional

236

dispositions that could lead to a more humane world than that which rational economics can conceptually muster.

Human orientations, and the values that reflect them, have been allowed into administrative discourse only to the extent that they have fed the basic adversarial premises of economics. (Boggs, 1993, p. 77; Osborne & Gaebler, 1992) *Customer*, as the current economic vernacular for citizen, for example, assigns the public a manageable bit part in government as the demanding and critical patron of administrative services. Yet such an adversarial role for citizens is not likely to produce a more democratic government. It is just as likely to reinforce public administration's abiding attitude that it must adapt to and survive the hostile environment of politics—an attitude that is a long way from democratic.

The reduction of democratic public administration to customer relations is one manifestation of government's almost unconditional embrace of the social Darwinism of economic theory. Yet after all, it is with the unhappy principles of Darwin (1909; Schubert, 1989) that Herbert Simon helped create a profoundly sullen and negative identity for public administration —as the necessary but evil twin of democracy. Although many new theories exist that rival Simon's epistemology, the effect of his *rational man* on the administrative consciousness remains. This is so because the presumptions of natural selection, which are inherent in his methods, reinforce the continuing Madisonian disposition of public administration, which sees itself as a detached mediator of conflict among inequitable and warring factions that threaten the social order (Bruce, 1989; Ford, 1992; Mills, 1978; Nelson, 1982; Wolin, 1960).

A reality confirmed

Indeed, the disheartening legacy of interest-group liberalism seems to suggest that perhaps social Darwinism is an accurate description of American political life. Maybe politics is just the recreation of the natural struggle for supremacy translated into the pedestrian and economically sanctioned practice of the marketing of political ideas (Schubert, 1989; Spencer, 1967). Yet, if this is indeed political reality, it may be so because it is actively reinforced by the mediation of government agencies operating according to rules of administrative behavior like Simon's and not because it is an immutable reality per se.

For example, public agencies often structure encounters with citizens so that the attendant dialogue is organized by the demands of bureaucratic procedure—this, rather than public encounters being a free exchange of ideas. In so doing, agencies reinforce both predictable constituent behavior and their own power base by teaching people the common "rules of their game" (Harmon, 1981; Moe, 1989; Nelson, 1982). It appears that the administration is behaving equitably while also maintaining system stability because everyone is operating by the same rule book. Indeed, these chronic adaptations to environmental demands often pass for system accountability and responsiveness.

Yet, the bureaucracy is not truly changing by simply adapting to these demands from the premises of its own bureaucratic ethic. But then, change does not really appear to be the goal of bureaucratic adaptation. Instead, administrative response can as often be understood as the attempt to control the apparent chaos of democratic complexity. It does this by relating all political action to the common gameboard of decision-making procedure as it serves the bureaucracy's need to comply with the political agendas of the executive branch (Seidman & Gilmour, 1986). Bureaucracy seems to feel compelled to adapt to democratic life in this way because of the underlying presumption that it must reduce the conflict or risk system disequilibrium; this, at the same time it is reinforcing the outdated Hobbesian belief that interests have nothing in common to begin with, which might make their conflict productive (Rohr, 1978; Wolin, 1960).

Yet, this concern for order is not necessarily a consciously evil intent of individual bureaucrats, or even of economists like Simon. It seems rather to be the underlying ontological presumption that government, as Hobbes prescribed, is responsible for controlling the excesses of human behavior and that the decision-making model helps create the needed conditions of prediction and control by which equilibrium is created and maintained (Melossi, 1992, Wolin, 1960). One might fairly say that this attitude is as much a sense of responsibility as it is a fondness for the power such strategic adaptability seems to grant public institutions.

Unfortunately such presumptions, however well intended, deny the ever present potential that citizens have the ability and the capacity to understand each other, love each other, and move beyond the dismal horizons of social Darwinism. Indeed, if America cannot seem to overcome its differences, accept diversity, or allay its violence, it seems due, at least in part, to rational administrative practices that cast citizens as potential villains—environmental threats that must be rationally controlled for their own good.

Bureaucratic neo-Darwinism is marked by several distinctive and characteristically undemocratic traits associated in particular with Simon's models for administrative action: (a) a need to distance administrative action from human emotion and human relationship, (b) a distrust in ways of knowing other than rational decision making, (c) a disposition toward isolation from citizens and other "nonexperts," (d) a belief that knowledge is finite and can be applied instrumentally through strategic, homogenized plans in a programmed eradication of problems, and (e) a distrust of the political process. These overlapping characteristics may also be summarized by stating that Darwinistic public administration is primarily concerned with the maintenance of social equilibrium, and it does this by application of rational formulas for conflict management through social programs (Wolin, 1960). It is this desire to maintain stability in the face of human strife and competition that seems to be best served by the calculated methods of decision making (Simon, 1992, pp. 85–88). It is also this desire for control that appears to put bureaucracy at odds with democracy (Hummel, 1987). Bureaucratic neo-Darwinism then can be defined as the intertwining of the process of decision making with the tenets of natural selection and survival of the fittest. What emerges is the social justification for a methodology that isolates individual actions from the seemingly dangerous world of political life.

The isolated bureaucratic brain

Neo-Darwinism, as a modern state of bureaucratic consciousness, is rooted in a particular Western view of the evolution of the mind. The conventional understanding of evolution often equates the mind with the brain and, in particular, with the theorizing neo-cortex (Simon, 1992, pp. 272–273). The body is made to be a prior evolution to the more recent and therefore more superior neo-cortex in this understanding (Olstein & Sobel, 1987, pp. 55–70). For example, the Darwinian concept of natural selection made it appear to social theorists, like Simon, that the neo-cortex evolved away from, not with, the rest of the body and now exists as an isolated and defensive artifact of human history. The neo-cortex is then used to wage a battle with those human forces that would undermine the realities that it creates in its isolation (Simon, 1992, p. 273).

By analogy, then, the bureaucratic ethos might also be described, as anthropologist J. T. Fraser does, as the uncontrolled growth of the brain—the linear accumulation of self-affirming ideas caused by the reinforcement of the reductive and isolated tendencies of the neo-cortex (1990, pp. 235–282). Indeed, the now ingrained practice of public decision making depends, almost exclusively, on the rationalizing tendencies of the neo-cortex to create and then re-create narrow social realities based on lifeless linear models stored in memory as "expertise." (Simon, 1982, 1992). Neo-Darwinism not only reinforces the cortex's ability to theorize based on selective memory in this manner, it also creates the philosophic rationale whereby the neo-cortex can morally exclude all other brain functions in the name of survival of the species—particularly those associated with emotions, sensations, and our ability to imagine other potentialities. Indeed, the human species and its continued evolution is reduced by this reasoning to what the neo-cortex can do (Fraser, 1990, p. 235).

This linear model of the brain was not new with Simon, of course, but instead it is encompassed by the breadth of Western philosophical tradition. The adversarial relationship of human beings and the natural world, first defined by Plato for example, made it appear that the evolutions prior to rationality were to be left behind as vestiges of a chaotic nature or, at a minimum, controlled for their defects by the new evolutionary state. As a result those prerational processes associated with the body—sense and emotions—have most often been viewed as problematic and often expendable (Hatub, 1990; Taylor, 1989). Over time, through the influences of Descartes and his inheritors, the rejection of emotions and senses became a tradition of the emerging modern consciousness; thus human interactions—especially those related to politics and shared community—became suspect because of their dependence on emotive and often conflicted human relationships (Merchant, 1980).

Ironically, Darwin's evolutionary theory was initially an important step toward reintegration of the mind and body, which had been conceptually torn apart in the work of Plato, Aristotle, and St. Thomas Aquinas, among others. Darwin introduced the idea that the brain was a product of an evolutionary process of development; it was not simply a new brain function added to the human machinery at some arbitrary point in time. Rather, the higher functions of the mind were derivative of the so-called lower functions, including most specifically the senses (Darwin, 1909; Ho & Fox, 1986). However, because of the historical backdrop to Darwin's work, which included the competitive tenets of social contract theory, as well as the predictions of social strife in the population growth studies of Malthus, natural selection (as the determinant of inferior and superior behavior) was an idea that suited the times (Ho & Fox, 1986; Ho & Saunders, 1984). As a result, the new consciousness of the neo-cortex was seen as a movement to a superior state that marked a victory over the emotive limbic system (Ho & Fox, 1986; Olstein & Sobel, 1987, pp. 35–55). Human consciousness, then, became a symbol of the competitive isolation of individuals that seemed to mark the times—the tool by which we survived each other.

This narrow understanding of the mind as the neo-cortex—a tool for instrumentally reducing complexity and fending off a hostile environment —has had a limiting effect on public administration's ability to perceive that the democratic components of choice making and diversity are positive and practical elements of life in a naturally complex world. Instead, rational public administration, as the expert "brain" of the social system, has often perceived itself as the metaphorical guardian against such an influx of potentialities generated in the sensory and emotional relationships of an individual (Bruce, 1989, pp. 197–200). The effect has been that aspirational dialogue about the future of the human condition has been replaced by myopic, fragmented, and often isolated problem solving (Long, 1962; O'Toole, 1984, pp. 141–167).

For example, the liberal tradition, which emerged most clearly in the new public administration of the 1970s, approached social issues as opportunities to even the score among competitive and unequal interests through strategic problem solving (Radin & Cooper, 1989; Marini, 1971). Even Simon portrays himself as a liberal humanist concerned with righting social wrongs (1992). Yet, what produced the social fragmentation of interest-group liberalism was not the humane desire to help fellow citizens. It was perhaps more that the empowerment movements of that era promoted strategic competition as the regulator of economic and social relationships (Rawls, 1971; Rosenbloom, 1993; Sullivan, 1982). In this manner, the Darwinistic tendencies of economics that produced the inequalities were simply reinforced. Individuals still had to muster the political and economic strength to beat out the competition in the policy arena. Nothing seemed to exist that would free public administration of its felt need to manage conflict. In fact, through the methodologies of social theorists like Simon, government found ways to rationally manage social inequalities rather than engage in the creation of a culture that could exceed those inequalities (Piven, 1993).

Ironically perhaps, Simon's own portrait of neo-Darwinism serves as a frame of reference for the democratic analysis of bureaucratic systems—one that helps identify the nature of the American administrative state's struggle to define itself in democratic terms. It perhaps even suggests a way out of the mire of the bureaucratic ethos. This particular identity is described best in the personal accounts of Simon's autobiography, *Models of My Life* (1992). There is perhaps no other source from which a sense of the particular consciousness of this architect of modern thought can be so clearly extracted.

The travel theorem

A presumption exists in Simon's (1992)[1] work that the evolution of the neocortex may mark the end of human involvement in the natural process of evolution—at least evolution that has some connection to the body (p. 366). This finality of the human evolutionary process appears to be necessary to affect the conditions of control and management prescribed by Simon's methodology. His models create and continuously reaffirm a certain reality that appears to reduce conflict and improve efficiency. This artificial reality is not renewed with interaction in the environment but rather is reinforced at a given, presumably predictable and controllable historical point. That is to say, the risks to system equilibrium and control—inherent particularly in emotive human relationships—are minimized by having a preconceived principle like bureaucratic procedure to which all environmental conditions are related (Newell & Simon, 1972; Simon, 1982).

For example, Simon's travel theorem (1992, pp. 306, 308, 312, 313) offers a practical disposition for people wanting to conduct efficient business trips. It begins from the reductive premise that there is not much new in the world, at least not much that cannot be more efficiently learned through the reading of authoritative texts. By his own account, Simon's travels are structured by the understandings acquired through reading books, books that for him carry more legitimacy and more promise of certainty than lived experience (pp. 306, 307).

Simon went to China in 1989 as a management consultant, for example, and was thrown into the dramatic events of Tiananmen Square. Although Simon confesses to being moved by this democratic "incident," he chooses not to connect those feelings in any way to the purposes of his trip to China. The passions he encounters exist as extraneous accidents to the purposes of his information gathering journey. They are interesting, perhaps historically significant, and a source of sentimentality, but are not especially useful (p. 313). In this manner Simon allocates portions of the human experience to certain accidental categories—meaning that some things can be said to be unrelated to others.

The China trip is only one of the many trips that Simon describes in his autobiography. Each trip seems to confirm his theory that little of value is acquired when one travels on short business trips. The Taj Mahal by moonlight, for example, is a cliché, according to Simon, who relates what he sees and feels first to what he has read and thereby avoids the direct experience of the phenomena that may distort his original premise (p. 308). In this way, each encounter is only an affirmation of the original idea, not an engagement of the moment. Further, the experience—as a flat arrangement of facts, structure, color, and smell—can likely be replicated elsewhere given the same materials (p. 308). The experience has no intrinsic value, only a kind of functionality connected to the significance it has been given in literature or history—it is only information, not knowledge. As Simon explains:

> Anyone who espouses the travel theorem becomes the target of constant gibes if he traveled or plans to travel anywhere. One way to defend against such gibes is to plan your travel itineraries in such a way as to guarantee that you will not learn anything new. Our first trip to Europe in the summer of 1965, will provide an example. We resolved that we would not see anything on the trip that we did not know better already from books and pictures. . . . We took as our targets Paul Cezanne and Marice Utrillo among painters . . . Coming out of Switzerland we followed the route of Napoleon (known from history books) down to Aix-en-Provence . . . We spent our days visiting every spot we could find where Cezanne had stood when he painted Mont Ste. Victoire. Note only did we find the sites, but it was easy to determine within three feet exactly where Cezanne's easel had stood. And when we stood on those spots, the mountain looked exactly as it had on Cezanne's glowing canvasses: the literalness if his landscapes is almost beyond belief. We learned nothing new; we had already seen the paintings.
>
> (p. 309)

Simon does not say whether or not it was thrilling to stand at the spot where the painter he admired had stood. It was, perhaps, but the point to be made here is that the thrill was unrelated to the experience of the mountain. Instead, the mountain graciously reinforced Simon's preconception about it, a preconception that had been created by Cezanne's paintings and the interpretations of those paintings by historians and other artists. The mountain itself is only a reflection of what Simon imagines it to be. In fact, Simon quotes Oscar Wilde in this context, "Where were the fogs of London before Turner painted them? Nature as usual," Simon adds in a footnote, "imitating art" (p. 309).

The direct experience, however, is more than just extraneous and irrelevant to the information-gathering process; it also seems to be problematic. For example, Simon cautions against the distortions of peasants speaking the native language and conveying their versions of culture. Simon seems to imply that not only can human experience be segregated and prioritized, but that one can, and indeed must, also rank people—in a very undemocratic manner—by reason of their recognized expertise. Responding to an implied question that bilinguals in a foreign country might help the traveler with the more subtle nuances of culture, Simon remarks:

> But local bilinguals can tell you about them, can't they? Yes indeed, but so can books. And with books you can exercise some quality control over the information. You can make sure that their authors are qualified as experts and interpreters of the language ... If you are unsure how to make up such reading lists, librarians are always glad to help.
>
> (p. 308)

Simon's work certainly recognizes the existence of contingencies. Not everything can be planned for, but one is more prepared for such "accidents" if one already has an authoritative framework from which to interpret them. The accidents themselves exist only as they can be related to the already conceived framework. Traveling then becomes the process of bringing cultural contingencies in line with the already existing "objective" point of reference—one created and bounded by prior factual interpretations existing in books and the opinions of recognized experts.

For Simon to have learned anything new from his near adventure in Tiananmen Square, for example, he would have had to feel that change occurs in relationship with an event or a person that cannot always be anticipated or controlled. That is, he would have had to see the struggle for democracy in China as being part of his own human system of interrelationship and interdependence, rather than simply as another fact of history to be recorded. Although Simon confesses a felling of "great sadness" about the events in China, the feeling does not carry with it a clear connection between the purposes of his trip and the historic drama he witnessed. He could declare, despite the sadness, that on his trip to China, he still had learned nothing new (p. 355). It is a similar attitude of detachment that is perhaps at the basis of the complaints about public administration —that it has no real feel for the positive dynamics of democratic process. Rather, by categorizing and analyzing the behavior of individuals through programs and planning, it exhibits the more defensive feeling of fear or anxiety about the disequilibrium such dynamics seem to cause (Bruce, 1989; Simon, p. 271).

Neuro-Darwinism: reinforcing bounded rationality

Despite their obvious incongruence with democratic ideals, however, Simon's prescriptions for the rational man have the power of appearing sensible and observable. This is perhaps because decision making enhances the intrinsically reductive and theorizing processes of the neo-cortex and therefore feels like a natural methodology. These processes of the brain, which Simon prescribes and describes by extension, are also described as neuro-Darwinism by physicist Matthew Bergstrom (Briggs, 1988).

Neuro-Darwinism refers to the process by which the neo-cortex selects and interprets sensory data coming from the brain stem. It is the way the human brain creates and reinforces "realities" (Briggs, 1988). When the random fields of neuroelectric impulse from the brain stem meet the information-packed impulses from the cortex, a selection process takes place, according to Bergstrom (Briggs, 1988). The random bursts from the brain stem mix up some of the information coming from the cortex and from the memory retrieving limbic systems. The result is new information, new thoughts, and the possibility of new behavior. Bergstrom calls this a possibility cloud that contains mutations, variants, and error that struggle with the old firing patterns of the sympatic system. The strongest signals in relation tot he whole context of signals at that instance will survive. A signal's survival is "like the survival of a variant animal most suited to the environment at the moment" (Briggs, 1988, p. 45).

Thoughts themselves, neuro-physicists William Gray (1979) and Paul LaViolette (1979, 1980) say, are stereotyped or simplified emotional themes. When we form thoughts, we abstract from the complexity of sensory nuances brought to us through the evolutionarily older brain stem. As these emotional themes circulate through the Papez Circuit they call up long-term memories that have similar nuance characteristics. These memories become part of the evolving theme. There is always a sense of wondering and incompleteness, Gray says, but in the normal course of events this wondering and incompleteness is obscured by the transformation of the theme into an organization of thought—an emotional cognitive structure (Briggs, 1988; Gray, 1979). Once these structures are formed, they are changed with great difficulty and particularly so if reductive thinking like that employed in decision making is practiced religiously (Briggs, 1988, p. 48).

Simon's work, characterized by his travel theorem, appears to refine this action of the cortex as rational decision making. That is to say that only those signals that can easily be reinforced by limbic memory are allowed to survive. The result is that a frame of reference is continually reinforced and begins to appear to be reality—much like Simon's view of Mont Ste. Victoire. It becomes reality because any other signals that might distort it are suppressed by the increasingly strong signals that the cortex chooses from the limbic system. Indeed, new research indicates that there can be no new thought without emotional and sensory input. This is also supported by the chaos work of Nonaka (1988).

For example, Simon describes the inability of administrators to neatly separate rational fact and emotionally subjective values as the limits of rationality. Clearly, human emotions are not seen by Simon as the way to expand consciousness—as new brain research indicates—but as a deficiency in the order of rationality (p. 244). This deficiency clouds the decision-making process because it appears to disrupt the strategic thinking that results in a decision about right action according to a preexisting model (Harmon, 1989, 1992). What must happen to correct this supposed dysfunction of human nature is for values to be objectified—in much the manner that Simon attempts to strip language of the emotional power of its life in culture. In fact, Simon promotes cybernetics as an alternative language that avoids the ambiguities of human discourse by clearly connecting action with the arrangement of objective, single-meaning symbols (p. 193). This need for certainty, however, makes it appear that realities, like cultural diversity, are problems to be managed. Indeed, however, they may well be the enriching source of the information-laden nuance by which human consciousness is expanded.

The idea of satisficing, for example, which was central to Simon's early book, *Models of Man* (1957b), defines human purpose as a Darwinian struggle for survival and nothing more (pp. 274–275). On reflection, in his autobiography 35 years later, Simon equates satisficing with a kind of "it'll do" natural selection.

> Bracketing satisficing with Darwinism may appear contradictory, for evolutionists sometimes talk about survival of the fittest. But, in fact, natural selection only predicts that survivors will be fit enough—that is fitter than their losing competitors; it postulates satisficing not optimizing.
>
> (p. 166)

Simon's prescription for right decision making is to select among those sensory nuances that allow individuals to compete with the opposition. What becomes competitive is repeatedly reinforced in the interactions of human beings, all of whom share the minimalist purpose of satisficing. Satisficing is thereby made a reality by the process of decision making, a reality that re-creates itself by its repeated and exclusive accommodation of its own principles. It is therefore a process that can be replicated in the programming of computers (Simon, 1957a).

Indeed, Simon's interest in artificial intelligence seems really a radical attempt to move the rationalizing functions of the neo-cortex away from the threat to certainty posed by the sensory nuances that bombard the physical body (1992, p. 362). By placing the neo-cortex in a computer, the disengaged mind is free to create its models of reality and achieve perfection in relation to those models without sensory interference. As Simon says, "The area of rationality is the area of adaptability to these nonrational elements" (p. 88). By standardizing and objectifying values—that is, by limiting the play of environmental accidents by always relating them to immutable values detached from their emotional life, the manager can guarantee that organizational members will always arrive at the same "rational" decision (p. 88).

Yet the broader implication for democratic public administration is that decision making, as problem solving, inhibits sensory signals from developing into mature emotional themes, as chaos theorists understand the process. Indeed, decisions made without an awareness of the positive role of senses and emotions in the creation of new thought not only stereotype whatever sensory information comes in but also impoverish the individual's ability to create new thought in changing contexts. The result is a "flat" system of thought, as physicist Paul Rapp would term it, which inhibits the individual's ability to produce new solutions to old problems (Nonaka, 1988).

By contrast, LaViolette suggests that listening to sensory and emotional nuance is likely to have a positive effect on the quality of the decision made. "It is good to tune into feelings before they get abstracted into thought," he says. Further, "People who can do this are able to directly tune into data of far greater complexity." Such sensitivity fosters creativity and the ability to see things in new ways (1979, p. 20).

The feeling of nostalgia might serve as an example of LaViolette's reasoning regarding public policy. If nostalgia is thought to be an attachment to a particular set of historical circumstances—like middle-class family values—and that thought is consciously used to filter out any new feelings, a stereotype of the good-old-days of family values is likely to be reinforced. A disposition is thereby created that rejects change and provides no avenue for the values to be renewed. However, if nostalgia is felt in relation to a broad range of contextual nuance and is allowed to circulate freely in the brain, it is possible that a new thought will emerge that integrates the old with the new context to form a transcendent, more contextually relevant value.

The individual is thereby able to accommodate the changed environment without being forced to reject a treasured memory.

This indicates that Simon's methodology, far from reducing conflict, impedes the natural processes by which difference is accommodated and social stability is maintained. Instead, it seems to reinforce stereotypes based on preconceived, expert models and only resolves the dilemma of this by denying that people have the ability or the altruistic desire to create more real and more democratic perceptions of each other (p. 175). It is Simon's general method, for example, to dismiss any affront to his principles simply by denying the relevance and even the existence of any arguments other than those that appear to be only the opposite of his own. For example, he mocks those who cannot imagine that computers can think:

> There is a knock-down argument that is supposed to answer the question instantly. It goes like this: Computers are machines; machines cannot think; hence computers cannot think. Human beings are also (biological) machines; therefore, if machines cannot think, human beings cannot think.
>
> (pp. 272–273)

When the premises of this retort are not embraced, Simon laments that proving the reality of computer thought is like Darwin trying to prove the evolution of human beings from monkeys (p. 273). He thereby ignores the human capacity to participate in evolution by making choices and also dismisses the fact that human beings do not necessarily see their next highest evolution being the perfected machine. In fact, they may not see themselves as machines at all. Therefore, the automatic evolution to computer excellence is not necessarily a conscious (and therefore democratic) choice but more an adaptive acquiescence to technology (Appleyard, 1992). Indeed, modern physics, with its emphasis on organic systems, has long since made the notion of "mechanical humans" outdated (e.g., Olstein & Sobel, 1987). Yet, Simon limits his own options because of his reluctance to engage history, choosing instead to avoid conflict and true choice. There can be no transforming heroics in this case, no transcendence of the dreary history he critiques. Simon can only prove his point or become martyred for failing.

Making choices, not decisions

It is human aspiration, however, that makes it seem ironic that, although the cortex is responsible for reducing sensory data to what fits preexisting models of thought (i.e., satisficing), it also houses the human capability for intentionality and choice (Argyros, 1991; Briggs, 1988). That is to say that whether or not we limit our consciousness as human beings to a bounded rationality may really be a choice we make about the purposes of human action. For example, we might ask ourselves: Is the purpose of human action simply to discover certain truths and replicate them, or is the purpose of human action to create knowledge and continue in the evolutionary movement such knowledge generates? The strongest irony of Simon's work is that it is perhaps a brilliant recognition of a current incomplete state of human consciousness. However, rather than attempting to exceed that bounded state Simon's rational man seeks to reinforce and glorify it. He does this by disengaging from the complexity of the broader environment. In turn, Simon uses the principles of this disengaged reason to reaffirm the validity of his theories. Simon creates an alternative, narrow reality in this sense. By so doing, however, he condemns the human enterprise to the bounded limits of the memory of its own history.

This repetitive act of theory affirmation is evident in the public arena. For example, academics are pleaded with to be more practical—to address realities as they are—not as they should or might be (Brown, 1989). This affirmation of the existing patterns of relationships, however dysfunctional those relationships may be to democracy, has come to equate public management, as Simon does, with ordinariness. So administrators and citizens are taught ways to survive the adversarial policy environment rather than being encouraged to think about how to change that desperate reality. The result has been the reduction of public dialogue to a competitive and defensive exchange of information for the purposes of winning policy arguments mediated by a problem-solving public administration (Blake, 1990; Giddens, 1990).

Aspirations, a they come to reflect themselves in values, however, must be recognized for their compelling relationship to the capacity of human beings to make choices about the nature of their future—such choices being perhaps the primal democratic act. One might, for example, as Simon does, choose to structure and control nuance so that "nothing new is learned" and be quite successful at it because the neo-cortex has become so adept at that kind of filtering. Yet these designs must—by design—limit choice to decisions about acceptable alternatives. As such, rational decision making is a limitation on choice, even in the minimalist understanding of democracy, as simply the right to choose.

Yet an individual also may choose to reject this bounded rationality in search of a broader consciousness and new possibilities. It is not then that bounded rationality is simply an end point of human capability. Of course, to choose to engage the evolutionary forces of nature means that conflict between the rationalizing forces of the neo-cortex and the new thoughts pushing to be formed is simply inevitable and no doubt uncomfortable for the defensive mind. It is this state of discomfort that concerns Simon because his view of human purpose is the avoidance of such discomfort and uncertainty—but not necessarily by choice but also because of limited capability to choose. To Simon, bounded rationality is at once a mental limit-ation and a human disposition toward fear of the unknown (pp. 365–366).

For Simon's prescriptions to work, however, he must do more than simply advocate a methodology for rationalizing a complex world; he must create a human being to fit the sterile environment the methodology pro-duces. For example, after completing *Rational Choice and the Structure of the Environment* in 1956, Simon says, in his autobiography, that he was so pleased with the work that he felt compelled to write a short story about it (p. 175). This compulsion was revitalized with the outcome of an unlikely interview with Argentinean poet, Jorge Luis Borges, years later.

Hugo, the bureaucratic antihero

Simon asked for an interview with Borges during a trip to Argentina in 1970 where Simon was giving a management lecture. He was interested in Borges' use of labyrinths as a central theme of his prose (Borges, 1978). Simon wondered if his own attempts to understand human behavior by means of mathematical models might somehow be reinforced by Borges' understand-ing of the maze-like labyrinth (pp. 175–176). Simon projected that Borges' use of the maze as a metaphor in his stories supported to his belief that human beings spend their existence working their way through complex mental mazes. The maze indeed, in Simon's understanding, determines human goals so that an act of conscious responsibility is simply not possible. The maze allows only adaptation to its circumstances and not meaningful or moral action (p. 88).

However, despite Simon's attempts to engage Borges in a discussion about the nature of decision making, the poet resisted a categorization of his work as an explanation of anything—except as some aspect of his soul that demanded expression in his works (p. 179). Simon then seemed to conclude that Borges was suffering the same fate as everyone else—a kind of limited consciousness that did not allow him to recognize the rational models implicit in his own work (p. 179). Because Borges' response had been inad-equate (i.e., it did not meet the preconceptions Simon brought to the conversation), Simon's response was to rationalize the labyrinth myth by writing his own short story to explain his theory of bounded rationality.

"The Apple," a short story in *Models of my Life*, is a recount of the life of the functionalist Hugo. Hugo is forced by an initial need to eat and, by the maze-like structure of his castle (Simon's metaphor for the mind), to develop tastes for certain foods—his choices being determined at first by which door he chooses, the types of food on the table, and the degree of his hunger. To cut down on the time searching for the food he has come to prefer, Hugo keeps records. When the records do not increase the efficiency of finding the foods he enjoys, Hugo begins to notice more things in his environment that might be affecting his taste—a particular painting in a particular room, for example. The worst aspect of Hugo's existence is the burden of choice:

> Now he (Hugo) felt the burden of choice—choice for the present and the future. While the largest part of his mind was enjoying its leisure—playing with his thoughts or examining the murals— another small part of it was holding the half-suppressed memory of aspirations to be satisfied, of plans to be made, of the need for rationing his leisure to leave time for his work. It would not be fair to call him unhappy, not accurate to say that he was satisfied, for the rising and falling tides of his aspirations always kept close synchrony with the level of the attainable and the possible. Above all, he realized that he would never again be free from care.
>
> (p. 184)

The rational, ordinary man is mainly anxious—about things left undone, about survival, about meeting the imperatives of his goals. He avoids the dangers of life outside the castle by responding to the details of the system. The system, as Simon portrays it, is separate from people and mocks any moral purpose that might assign meaning to the complexity Hugo avoids. Simon writes:

> The story provides no heroics, no Theseus to seek out some fearsome Minotaur at its center and then escape by following the thread given by Ariadner. Its central figure is not Theseus but Hugo, an ordinary man. The story describes Hugo's life, much like every human life, as a search through a maze. In doing so it strips the mathematical wrapping from the technical paper that provided the metaphor.
>
> (p. 175)

Hugo is ordinary in the most reductive sense of the word. He has a limited desire to do more than accommodate his environment. in fact, Hugo, until he is forced by the demands of efficiency and hunger, resists any urge to expand his horizons or tackle the ambiguities implicit in the systemized order of his castle. His limited consciousness remains fixed on outcomes that are likely to be no more satisfying than a meal taken from a limited menu. Even leisure time is an expressionless and lonely task of playing with his thoughts:

> Fortunately for him (Hugo), he found these pictures and his own thoughts sufficiently pleasant and of sufficient interest to guard him from boredom, and he had become so accustomed to the solitary life that he was not bothered by loneliness . . .
>
> (p. 177)

In Simon's view, isolation in a lonely mental castle is not only a fact of human existence, the superior rational man also chooses to be there. But the choice is only the selection of what appears to be the lesser of two evils. Because Simon sees human action as being essentially power driven, rather than relational and interdependent (e.g., chap. 9), Hugo has no real choice except to be alone and anxious about survival. For example, one of Simon's metaphors about scientific life is the "island" as the "locus for innovation;" the "place where scientists might be protected from the need to defend the tender mutants" (p. 147).

The island metaphor, borrowed from Darwin, would appear to limit responsible action in the name of community to the protection of truths which, to remain intact, must exist in suspicion of the community they seek to serve. Yet for Simon to make sense of his own methodology, the pattern of human relationships has to be understood as something other than cooperative, dialogic, and potentially loving. Simon therefore champions the ordinary man, the one he says has no interest in anything broader than a comfortable survival in a competitive world.

Yet, Simon seems to empower the rational, expert administrator at the same time he denigrates the ordinary man by glorifying the low road of human endeavor with a terse, bone-dry methodology for coping with life one decision at a time. Indeed, Simon raises the manager to the level of a ruling elite by minimizing the aspirations of ordinary human beings— aspirations that threaten the premises of Simon's rationality. The manager becomes the Everyperson's (p. 363) hero—the one who has categorically figured out how to resolve the complexity of existence. Simon's manager makes the neo-Darwinistic presumption that those who have mastered the reductive processes of filtering achieved by the neo-cortex are by definition superior to those who live their lives in less calculated ways (Bologh, 1990, pp. 91–138). The ordinary man only retains the dubious honor of "ordinary" if he also succumbs to a reduction of his morality and will to what fits Simon's model of rationality. In this way, Simon perhaps shows less compassion for the ordinary man in his tale of Hugo than disdain for his continuing bondage to human emotion and human relationship.

The creative judgment

Reviving the potentiality of a grander human spirit than what Hugo can imagine, however, means government must assert its own ability to make choices by engaging political life rather than simply managing it. The generative basis of such an enriched social dialogue may well be what has historically been meant as a judgment. Judgment is perhaps not simply comparing the facts of the context to an existing value framework as Simon might describe it. Instead making a judgment may be the process of absorbing as many nuances as possible and allowing them free interplay with the forms of existing value stored in memory. It is here that diversity in an administrator's environment ceases simply to be a mass of complex problems to be simplified and solved and becomes the creative seedbed for new thought and action.

The difference between Simon's rational decision and an emotive judgment is illustrated by comparing the orthodoxy of Weber and that of Hegel, as Shaw does (1992). For Weber (1943), decisions rest on technical expertise. Such expertise is understood as knowledge of the system of rule that constitutes the policy arena and the systemic application of those rules to presenting cases. Rules achieve political outcomes and reduce arbitrary action with a standard of equity (Shaw, p. 384). According to Shaw, Weber's ideal of bureaucracy grants administrative legitimacy through adherence to the rules, rules being stable, universally applicable, and learnable (p. 384).

It is this rule-based expertise that Simon ennobles. Indeed, Simon equates the reduction of liberal education to the repetitive principles of technical professionalism as a democratization of academia. The implication is that the creations of democracy are ordinary and to assume they can be of any other complexity is elitist (pp. 263–268). Hegel, on the other hand, replaces rational decision making with subsumption—a process of judgment by which bureaucrats mediate between universal legal norms and individual cases to ascertain what is right. In this case, the bureaucrat legitimates action by the degree of reflection, the judgment itself being based on the validity of discretion. This discretion distinguishes the judgment defined here from a decision that is only a critical comparison between the context an the ideal. The act of discretion is one of accommodation of contextual different rather than judgmental evaluation. A judgment then begins from the democratic premise of acceptance.

Such discretion, Shaw says of Hegel, expands the possibilities in any situation from simply accepting or rejecting an idea based on how well it fits the mental framework of rules and/or a virtuous ideal (p. 385). The implication is that the relationship between the old knowledge, as it is expressed in law and value, and the new context is one of dialogue rather than competition; the goal of reflection is the creation of a new judgment applicable to the setting—not the suppression of elements that are extraneous, inferior, or superfluous to the old value system. A judgment then is not disengaged reason in search of a static ideal as prescribed by Descartes and Locke (Taylor, 1989, pp. 111–199). It is the "law of the situation" as Follett described it (1965). As a praxis between memory and context, judgment is the creation of the engaged "organic intellectual" of Antonio Gramsci—the practitioner/academic who is grounded in law and value, but who is also a listening participant in history (Gramsci, 1971, pp. 6, 12–15, 330).

The further democratic implication is that judgment emerges from the dialogue in which both bureaucrats and citizens are active participants.

Ordinariness might be seen in a less reductive light in this case—as the state of both accepting and engaging reality as it is but not for the purposes of analyzing it for its deficiencies but for the purpose of enhancing and renewing it through cooperative, creative thought.

A judgment would seem to require a well-defined awareness of the nature of old thought patterns like values and their history. But, a judgment also requires an equally intense sensory absorption in the historical context that Simon denies the Rational Man.

It may be that the role of values in the process of judgment making are not merely the imbedded principles for right action. Instead, they are simply known, as previously created structures in the way an artist might recognize a just-finished painting. The meaning of values, however, is never quite the same in each new view of them even as their intrinsic structure endures. Values are much like Mont Ste. Victoire for Simon—once they are removed from the dynamics of the political world, they cease to exist as social influences but become only reflections of a defensive ideological memory. The democratic value of equality, for example, must be discovered and rediscovered in the dynamics of democratic life. Equality therefore cannot be assigned, imposed, granted, or managed from a distance. It must be practiced. Such a practice begins with the belief that citizens have the evolutionary drive to take on such a mutually enlightening dialogue—that they have something to contribute and that democratic issues do matter to the ordinary person.

Of mazes and labyrinths

It is no small irony that Simon chooses to rationalize the myth of the Minotaur in his short story, "The Apple." It is the hero's journey in that myth and the angst of creativity implicit in Borges' tales of the labyrinth that most threaten the idea of the rational man. Borges tells the story of the Minotaur, Asterion, and his paradoxical life in the labyrinth of the great architect Daedalus. The labyrinth of Borges may well serve as a metaphor of the mind as Simon indicates, but of the mind as it is part of a connected universe, not as the utilitarian, isolated computer-brain of Hugo. It is a mind whose function is to create—a function that requires freedom and the absence of final truths. The universe to Asterion is not a limited box of safe alternatives but a "mythic universe pregnant with unformulated ideas" (Wheelock, 1989, p. 148).

Unlike, Simon's Hugo, Asterion is conscious of the responsibility implicit in having the capability to create his own identity. Certainly Asterion suffers more in this consciousness than Hugo, the satisficing antihero, who Simon describes as being only threatened by the potential of boredom and an inarticulated malaise (p. 177). Being responsible for one's own development is a painful burden . . . "an existential terror which befalls the ego-centered man as he awakes to the preceding," (p. 148). The terror arises from the uncertainty of an existence that is in constant renewal.

Simon's rational man, by contrast, is the quintessential modern liberal, who, in Rorty's view, would seek to avoid the pain and cruelty of the contingent human existence (Rorty, 1989). The moralism with which Simon addresses his work—his willingness to shift responsibility from the individual to the concept of a computer mind—perhaps reflects his liberal desire to stop the discomfort inherent in the human condition. Yet in doing so, he also denies the potential of meaningful, creative action, and personal development that may be the purpose of the uniquely human evolutionary process. Ironically, perhaps, this process, if freed from the reductive presumptions of behaviorism, is the very way in which Simon's bounded rationality is exceeded.

The paradox of Asterion's labyrinth is perhaps that of Gawthrop's (1993) "Barefoot Administrator" who must assume the awesome responsibility of acting in the public good but who must, at the same time, humbly submit to the democratic processes of community. A genuine love of service and of the public is what mitigates action rather than the expertise for such an administrator. He or she does not seek power but instead strives for enlightenment and compassionate action. This sharply contrasts with Simon's attitude about the nature of democratic leadership. The democratic manager, Simon says, is always free to listen to input:

> Management does not have to the weak to be "participative." All it requires is a manager who is strong enough in his inner convictions not to feel obliged to defend himself from ideas that come from without.

> (p. 149)

Such an attitude has serious implications for democratic accountability and the respect afforded citizens. Public administration has largely accepted the uncentered and unreflexive identity described by Simon whereby "The nature of the task to be accomplished and the pressure of the task requirement of the organization shapes the agency" (p. 118). The metaphor of Asterion's creative labyrinth, however, may suggest an identity for public administration that better serves the field than the beleaguered notions of objectivity, political adaptability, and decision making.

The self-conscious public administrator would maintain a vision of the purpose of democratic action—not by methodically picking among limited alternatives—but in the manner of freeing himself or herself from historical interests and the attendant details to seek an understanding of the broader good through creative dialogue. In other words, the self-conscious administrator would conduct his or her professional life within the more enduring processes of the community rather than in response to the temporal artifacts of decision making (Walzer, 1988; Wolfe, 1989). Key to this is the reengagement of public administrators with citizens through meaningful, relational dialogue, free of guile and strategy. It is in this loving relationship that the administrator may encounter new thought in a manner than nurtures the evolution of community and culture.

In his autobiography, Simon portrays public administration schools as the stagnant "backwater" of academia system (p. 114). Given Simon's representations of neo-Darwinistic thought, what might backwater mean? Perhaps it is a place teeming with chaos, diversity, conflict, "wicked" problems, emotive relationships, and moral dilemmas—all the conditions of a primordial fight for the survival of the "fit enough." Yet these are also the preconditions for evolutionary movement and the processes of a responsible democratic society. But like backwater behind a dam, public administration (and its students) are held back from developing a democratic consciousness because the dynamic elements of the political environment are viewed, by academics and practitioners alike, as problematic when indeed they are positive and inevitable aspects of democratic life.

Changing this sense of identity, however, would seem to require more than a reintroduction of democratic values into the dialogue of public administration. It would also seem to require less concern for certainty and more concern for making room for diversity through creative thought. Indeed, it would require a new identity for public administration that legitimates the use of discretion and judgment. Simon has shown us the loneliness and isolation of the practiced art of detached observation. For there to be meaning in our actions as administrators, we must embrace the chaos of our citizens' lives. But finding meaning in the very human processes of democratic life requires an evolutionary move to a more vital consciousness than that afforded by neo-Darwinism and Hugo, the tragic antihero, laboring in a lonely bureaucratic maze.

Note

1 Unless otherwise noted, citations to Simon refer to *Models of my Life*, 1992.

References

Appleyard, B. (1992). *Understanding the present: Science and the soul of man.* New York: Doubleday.

Argyros, A. (1991). *A blessed rage for order: Deconstruction, evolution, and chaos.* Ann Arbor: University of Michigan Press.

Blake, C. N. (1990). *Beloved community: The cultural criticism of Randolph Bourne, Van Wyck Brooks, Waldo Frank, and Lewis Mumford.* Chapel Hill: University of North Carolina Press.

Boggs, C. (1993). *Intellectuals and the crisis of modernity.* Albany: State University of New York Press.

Bolough, R. (1990). *Love or greatness: Max Weber and masculine thinking—A feminist inquiry.* London: Unwin Hyman.

Borges, L. J. (1978). *The Aleph and other stories, 1993–1969* (N. T. di Giovani, Ed. & Trans.). New York: E. P. Dutton.

Briggs, J. (1988). *Fire in the crucible: The alchemy of creative genius.* New York: St. Martin.

Brown, B. (1989). The search for public administration: Roads not followed. *Public Administration Review, 49* (2), 215–216.

Bruce, W. (1989). A response to C. J. McSwain's & O. F. White, Jr.: Transfiguring the golem: Actions speak louder than words. *Public Administration Review, 49,* 197–200.

Darwin, C. (1909). The origin of species. New York: P. C. Collier & Son.

Follette, M. P. (1965). *The new state: Group organization, the solution of popular government.* Gloucester, MA: Peter Smith.

Ford, M. E. (1992). *Motivating humans: Goals, emotions, and personal agency beliefs.* Newbury Park, CA: Sage.

Fraser, J. T. (1990). *Of time, passion, and knowledge: Reflections on the strategies of existence.* New Brunswick, NJ: Princeton University Press.

Gawthrop, L. C. (1993, February), *Ethics and democracy: A call for barefoot bureaucrats.* Inaugural lecture delivered on the occasion of the acceptance of the Tinbergn Chair professorship at Erasmus Universeit Rotterdam, the Netherlands.

Giddens, A. (1990). *The consequences of modernity.* Stanford, CA: Stanford University Press.

Gramsci, A. (1971). *Selections from the prison notebooks.* London: Lawrence & Wishart.

Gray, W. (1979). Understanding creative thought processes: An early formulation of the emotional-cognitive structure theory. *Man Environment Systems, 9,* 3–10.

Harmon, M. (1981). *Action theory for public administration.* New York: Longman.

Harmon, M. M. (1989, March–April). Decision and action as contrasting perspectives in organization theory. *Public Administration Review,* 144–149.

Harmon, M. M. (in press). Decision and action: Changing perspectives in organization theory. In R. C. Chandler & H. F. Frederickson (Eds.), *Public administration theory: The Minnowbrook perspective.*

Hatub, L. J. (1990). *Myth and philosophy: A contest of truths.* LaSalle, IL: Open Court Press.

Ho, M.-W. & Fox, S. W. (1986). *Evolutionary processes and metaphors.* Chichester, England: Wiley.

Ho, M.-W. & Saunders, P. T. (1984). *Beyond neo-Darwinism: An introduction to the new evolutionary paradigm.* London: Academic Press.

Hummel, R. (1987). *The bureaucratic experience.* New York: St. Martin.

LaViolette, P. A. (1979). Thoughts about thoughts, about thoughts. *Man Environment Systems, 9,* 20.

LaViolette, P. A. (1980). Thermodynamics of the "Aha" experience. Paper presented at 24th annual North American meeting of the Society for General Systems Research, Symposium on Psychotherapy, Mind, and Brain, San Francisco.

Long, N. (1962). *The polity.* Chicago: Rand McNally.

Marini, F. (Ed.). (1971). *Toward a new public administration: The Minnowbrook perspective.* London: Chandler.

Melossi, D. (1992). *The state of the social contract: A sociological study of concepts of state and social control in the making of democracy.* New York: St. Martin.

Merchant, C. (1980). *The death of nature: Women, ecology, and the scientific revolution.* New York: Harper & Row.

Mills, C. W. (1978). *The sociological imagination.* Oxford: Oxford University Press.

Moe, T. (1989). The Politics of bureaucratic structure. In J. E. Chubb & P. E. Peterson (Eds.), *Can government govern?* (pp. 267–329). Washington, DC: Brookings.

Nelson, M. (1982). A short, ironic history of American national bureaucracy. *Journal of Politics, 22,* 747–776.

Newell, A., & Simon, H. A. (1972). *Human problem solving.* Englewood Cliffs, NJ: Prentice Hall.

Nonaka, M. (1988, Spring). Creating organization order out of chaos: Self-renewal in Japanese forms. *California Management Review,* 57–53.

Olstein, R., & Sobel, D. (1987). *The healing brain: Breakthrough discoveries about how the brain keeps us healthy.* New York: Simon & Schuster.

Osborne, D. E., & Gaebler, T. (1992). *Reinventing government: How the entrepreneurial spirit is transforming the public sector.* Reading, MA: Addison-Wesley.

O'Toole, L. (1984). American public administration and the idea of reform. *Administration and Society, 16,* 141–166.

Piven, F. (1993). *Regulating the poor.* New York: Vintage.

Radin, B., & Cooper, T. (1989). From public action to public administration: Where does it lead? *Public Administration Review, 49,* (z), 167–170.

Rawls, J. (1971). *A theory of justice.* Cambridge: Cambridge University Press.

Rohr, J. (1978). *Ethics for bureaucrats: An essay on law and values.* New York: Marcel Bekker.

Rorty, R. (1989). *Contingency, irony, and solidarity.* Cambridge: Cambridge University Press.

Rosenbloom, D. (1993). Have an administrative RX. Don't forget the politics. *Public Administration Review, 53*(6), 503–507.

Schubert, G. (1989). *Evolutionary politics.* Carbondale: Southern Illinois University Press.

Seidman, H., & Gilmour, R. (1986). *Politics, position, and power: From the positive to the regulatory state.* New York: Oxford University Press.

Shaw, C. (1992, June). Hegel's theory of modern bureaucracy. *American Political Science Review,* 381–389.

Simon, H. A. (1957a). *Administrative behavior: A study of the decision-making process.* New York: Macmillan.

Simon, H. A. (1957b). Models of man: Mathematical essays on rational human behavior in social setting. New York: Wiley.

Simon, H. A. (1982). *Models of bounded rationality.* Cambridge: MIT Press.

Simon, H. A. (1983). *Reason and human affairs.* Stanford, CA: Stanford University Press.

Simon, H. A. (1992). *Models of my life.* New York: Basic Books.

Spencer, H. (1967). *The evolution of society: Selections from Herbert Spencer's principles of sociology.* Chicago: University of Chicago Press.

Sullivan, W. M. (1982). *Reconstructing public philosophy.* Berkeley: University of California Press.

257

Taylor, C. (1989). *Sources of the self: The making of the modern identity*. Cambridge, MA: Harvard University Press.

Waltzer, M. (1988, Spring). A better vision: The idea of a civil society: A path to social reconstruction. *Dissent*, 298.

Weber, M. (1947). *The theory of social and economic organizations*. London: Cambridge University Press.

Wheelock, C. (1989). *The mythmaker: A study of motif and symbol in the short stories of Jorge Luis Borges*. Austin: University of Texas Press.

Wolfe, A. (1989). *Whose keeper: Social science and moral obligation*. Berkeley: University of California Press.

Wolin, S. (1960). *Politics and vision: Continuity and innovation in western political thought*. Boston: Little, Brown.

61

COMPETING MODELS OF STABILITY IN COMPLEX, EVOLVING SYSTEMS

Kauffman vs. Simon

Tadeusz W. Zawidzki

Source: *Biology and Philosophy*, 13 (1998), 541–554.

Abstract

I criticize Herbert Simon's argument for the claim that complex natural systems must constitute decomposable, mereological or functional hierarchies. The argument depends on certain assumptions about the requirements for the successful evolution of complex systems, most importantly, the existence of stable, intermediate stages in evolution. Simon offers an abstract model of any process that succeeds in meeting these requirements. This model necessarily involves construction through a decomposable hierarchy, and thus suggests that any complex, natural, i.e., evolved, system is constituted by a decomposable hierarchy. I argue that Stuart Kauffman's recent models of genetic regulatory networks succeed in specifying processes that could meet Simon's requirements for evolvability without requiring construction through a decomposable hierarchy. Since Kauffman's models are at least as plausible as Simon's model, Simon's argument that complex natural systems *must* constitute decomposable, mereological or functional hierarchies does not succeed.

Introduction

In *The Sciences of the Artificial* (1969) Herbert Simon offers a theoretical argument for the claim that complex natural systems constitute decomposable, mereological hierarchies (pp. 92–98). The argument depends on the premise that the construction of complex systems out of simple elements is much easier, and takes much less time, if it proceeds piecemeal rather than all at once. If the elements are first organized into only slightly more complex subsystems, which are then organized into higher level subsystems, which are then organized into still higher level subsystems, until the complex whole is assembled, then, assuming a certain amount of noise in the construction process, construction proceeds much faster than if the complex whole is assembled directly from the simplest elements. Simon claims that evolution is just the type of noisy construction process that is optimized through the iterated assembly of elements into ever more complex subsystems until the whole is complete. Consequently, evolved, natural systems ought to constitute decomposable, mereological hierarchies.

Simon can be understood as arguing that the evolution of complex systems requires stages of stability between the simplest element stage and the complex whole stage (ibid., p. 97). For Simon, these intermediate stages of stability consist in the existence of systems of simple elements, which later become subsystems of complex wholes. However Simon's image of a mereological hierarchy is misleading in the context of the evolution of biological systems. Parts of organisms, in their current form, have never existed in isolation from those organisms. There are no fossil records of autonomous, individual human skin cells for example. Thus it is not literally the case that the subsystems which constitute the mereological hierarchy that an organism can be decomposed into existed as stable, autonomous units in the organism's evolutionary history. For Simon's argument to work, there must be some type of module or component used in the construction of our simple, evolutionary precursors, that has been conserved, and is still used, in conjunction with other components or modules, in the construction of the phenotypes of complex organisms like humans. Functional sub-systems of the genomes of complex organisms are plausible candidates. Genes or groups of genes encode solutions to specific problems that evolution must solve in order to produce complex, adaptive systems. These solutions are embodied in the phenotypic traits which these genes or groups of genes express. Now, once evolution hits on one such solution, via selection of a certain gene or group of genes, in some simple species, if the more complex species that evolve from this simple species need to solve the same problem, in addition to other problems, it seems plausible that the original solution is conserved across evolution, i.e., that the genes which code for the solution in the simpler species form a functional sub-system responsible for solving the same problem in the genome of the more complex species that evolves from it.

Thus, for the purposes of this paper, I propose the following, more biologically plausible re-interpretation of Simon's argument. The genomes of complex species can be decomposed into sub-systems of genes conserved, by evolution, from earlier, less complex species, because they encode phenotypic traits which constitute solutions to problems faced both by the earlier, less complex species and by the later, more complex species. It is because such progressive accumulation of genetic information is a necessary condition on the evolution of complex species that the genomes of complex species, and the phenotypic solutions they encode, are guaranteed to be hierarchically decomposable. The hierarchies that genomes can be decomposed into need not be mereological, i.e., functional sub-systems of genes need not literally be physical parts of higher-order systems of genes, for Simon's argument to work. A functional hierarchy is sufficient: a group of genes might form a sub-system of a larger group of genes in virtue of cooperating to perform some function that is a component of the overall function performed by the larger group of genes. We can think of Simon as proposing that genomes are organized much like computer programs: they can be decomposed into a hierarchy of modules such that the function performed by a higher level module is implemented by the functions performed by the lower level modules which constitute its functional sub-systems (see below). On this interpretation, Simon's claim is compatible with Dawkins' argument that the seemingly highly improbable organized complexity of evolved systems can only be explained if we assume that natural selection conserves, and progressively accumulates genetically encoded solutions (Dawkins 1996, Ch. 3, especially p. 81).

In the following I bring Stuart Kauffman's recent models of genetic systems to bear on Simon's argument. Kauffman's models are explicit attempts to explain the stability and evolvability of complex genetic systems (Kauffman 1993, pp. 441–443 & p. 523). Kauffman is impressed by the complexity of the regulatory interconnections between individual genes in a typical genome. Rather than coding for the construction of morphological structures, many genes function primarily to regulate the activity of other genes. For this reason, rather than assuming a Simonesque functional hierarchy of genes, Kauffman's models begin with the assumption that genomes consist of complex, regulatory networks of genes (ibid., pp. 441–443). The activity of any gene is located in a web of dependency on the activity of a potentially arbitrary number of other genes. Kauffman's project is to explain how order, stability, and evolvability emerge in such networks (ibid.). My discussion proceeds in four stages. First, I provide a detailed analysis of the problem that the evolution of complex systems from simple elements poses for Simon, and an explanation of how gradual assembly through a mereological or functional hierarchy is supposed to solve it. Second, I argue that Kauffman's models of genetic networks address a closely related problem, yet his proposed solution is, *prima facie*, radically different from Simon's. Third, I consider and argue against the claim that Kauffman's solution actually reduces to a detailed implementation of Simon's basic idea. I conclude by drawing out some implications for hierarchical decomposition as a research strategy in the study of complex, natural systems.

I. The problem of evolved complexity and Simon's solution

The problem that the evolution of complex systems from simple elements poses for Simon can be understood in several different ways. Simon offers the following abstract characterization of the problem. He asks us to imagine a small volume into which elementary parts are entering at a constant rate. The coexistence of a number of these parts in the small volume constitutes a partially completed subassembly of those parts. This construction process is 'noisy' because Simon assumes that there is a constant probability that a part currently in the volume is dispersed before another part is added unless the assembly reaches a stable state. Given these conditions, Simon argues that "the time required for the evolution of a complex form from simple elements depends critically on the numbers and distribution of potential intermediate stable forms" (Simon 1969, p. 93). If the completed, complex whole is the only stable configuration of elementary parts that can exist in the small volume, then it is exceedingly unlikely that the complex whole will form because it is exceedingly unlikely that all the parts will coexist in the small volume at the same time, given the probability that parts disperse before new ones are added. However, if we assume that there are subsystems of elements which are independently stable, then the assembly of the whole becomes much more likely. For the assembly of a stable subsystem requires fewer elementary parts to coexist in the small volume than the assembly of the whole. Thus, a stable subsystem is more likely to form before some of the parts it requires disperse. Once a subsystem is formed, all of the parts which compose it can no longer disperse. Thus, as stable subsystems gradually form, more and more of the elementary parts required to construct the complex whole become 'trapped' in the small volume, until all the necessary parts coexist, 'trapped' in different subsystems which are then assembled into the complex whole. Construction through a mereological hierarchy seems to solve the problem.

Simon also suggests that the problem of the evolution of complex systems can be understood as a search problem. The complex whole is a configuration of elementary parts that evolution is 'searching' for in the space of all possible configurations of those parts. The difficulty of the search problem increases exponentially with the complexity of the whole being constructed, i.e., with the number of elementary parts in the configuration that constitutes the whole, because the space of possible configurations increases exponentially with the number of elementary parts. The larger the space of possible configurations, the less probable the discovery of a particular configuration, and the less probable the discovery of a particular configuration, the longer the time required to discover that particular configuration (ibid., note 7, pp. 91–92). However this combinatorial explosion can be mitigated if we assume that search through the space is 'hierarchical'. Suppose that stable sub-configurations of elementary parts constitute sub-goals in the search for the complete configuration. A sub-configuration is easier to find since it contains fewer parts. If some combination of such sub-configurations is equivalent to the complete configuration, then piecemeal search for the appropriate sub-configurations drastically reduces search time. The sub-configurations constrain further search. In this sense, evolution is analogous to Simon's model of human problem solving: "in problem solving, a partial result that represents recognizable progress toward the goal plays the role of a stable subassembly" (ibid., p. 96).

This statement of Simon's argument provides exegetical support for my earlier claim that Simon can be interpreted as arguing that the genomes of complex organisms are decomposable into functional, modular hierarchies, similar to the standard architecture of computer programs, because their evolution requires the conservation and progressive accumulation of genetically encoded solutions, in Dawkins' sense. According to this view, the biological 'problem' solved by a complex species can be decomposed into 'sub-problems' solved at some point in the species' evolutionary pedigree. These earlier solutions are encoded in 'genetic modules' that constrain the further development of the genome in the following sense. The modules have to be used to solve the same problem when it is faced, as a 'sub-problem', in the construction and maintenance of the more complex species.

II. Kauffman's alternative approach

Simon's abstract characterization of the problem of the evolution of complex wholes from simple parts is not easily mapped onto the problems of genetic stability and evolvability addressed by Kauffman's models. Simon interprets the evolution of complex systems as the organization of increasing numbers of elementary parts. However, although evolution sometimes involves the addition of genetic material, many important evolutionary innovations involve the re-organization of the same genetic material (Kauffman 1993, pp. 487–488). Kauffman's models tend to address only the latter form of evolution. Kauffman asks the following questions. Given a fixed number of genes, what sorts of networks of dependency among those genes are stable, and how do such networks evolve through re-organization? Although Kauffman addresses the stability of the genetic networks themselves, his focus is on the stability of states of those networks. Assuming that each gene in a network can be in either an active or an inactive state, the state of an entire network can be specified in terms of the simultaneous activity or inactivity of the different genes. Kauffman is interested in which states or sequences of states of a network are stable and recurring. Stability is defined in terms of a genetic network's reaction to mutations, i.e., to transient changes in the states of some of its genes, and to permanent changes in the patterns of dependency among the genes. He understands evolution as the search for the best adapted stable, recurring sequences of states. If these sequences of states of a genetic network are understood as ordered sets of 'commands' which determine the construction of a phenotype, then the best adapted sequences are those which construct the best adapted phenotype. If we define evolvability as the capacity for orderly progression through ever more adapted, stable, recurring sequences of states of the network, then Kauffman's project can be interpreted as highly analogous to Simon's. However before the analogies are made clear, Kauffman's framework must be presented more rigorously and precisely.

Kauffman employs a class of models known as NK Random Boolean Networks to model genetic systems (ibid., pp. 188–191). The N units in a Boolean network can each take on one of two values: 0 or 1. Each unit represents a gene that is either active or inactive. The state of a Boolean network at any given time t can be represented as a point in the network's activation space. The axes which define the activation space correspond to the units in the network. The state of the network changes over time in the following way. To determine its activation at time $t + 1$, each unit takes as input the activations of K other units at time t. Thus, each unit receives as input a string of K 1s and 0s. Each unit's activation at $t + 1$ is a randomly assigned Boolean function of these inputs. The exact units from which each unit receives input are also randomly assigned.[1] Only the N and K parameters are controlled for in the simplest models, i.e., for each network, we only know the number of units it has, and the number of inputs that each unit receives. Thus, each combination of values for N and K defines an ensemble of Boolean networks whose units can implement arbitrarily different Boolean functions on inputs from arbitrarily different sets of K units in the network (ibid.). Beginning with some random state of a given network, represented by a point in its activation space, the network changes state with each iteration of the functions implemented by its units. This sequence of states can be represented as a trajectory through the network's activation space. In some network, a single state might constitute a stable 'attractor'. The trajectory representing the network's sequence of states would reach this attractor state, represented by a point in activation space, and stay there indefinitely, through the remaining iterations. In some other network, a 'cycle' of states might constitute a stable attractor. Since the dynamics of the network are fully deterministic, if the network ever 'visits' a state twice, it will cycle through the sequence of states that follows and returns to that state indefinitely. This type of trajectory shows up as a cycle in the network's activation space (ibid., p. 190).

Suppose that, with Kauffman, we interpret the state cycles of certain Boolean networks as sequences of genetic activity which code for specific cell types (ibid., pp. 467–469). A given network can have up to 2^N state cycles (ibid., p. 190). Thus, in Kauffman's framework, the problem of evolution becomes the problem of searching for the viable state cycles in this immense space of possible state cycles. Once one viable state cycle is found, it must remain stable, and it must have the capacity to evolve, i.e., different state cycles which code for better adapted cell types must be accessible from it. Thus, in terms of Kauffman's models, only networks which settle into highly constrained patterns of activity 'solve' the problems of stability and adaptability. For example, to be viable, a network's state cycle cannot contain too many states, yet given the constraints of Kauffman's models, a state cycle potentially consists of all the 2^N possible states of the network. Given Kauffman's interpretation, a cell type is expressed every time the appropriate state cycle is completed, but if the state cycle is so long that it would take biologically implausible amounts of time for the cell type to be expressed, then that state cycle cannot be viable (ibid., p. 483). Only a limited number of the possible state cycles are short enough to be viable.

Furthermore, only state cycles robust enough to recover homeostatically from mutations have the capacity to specify stable, evolvable cell types. In Kauffman's models, there are two types of mutations: "minimal perturbations" in the activations of particular units, and "structural mutations," such as changes in the functions implemented by particular units or changes in the sources of input to particular units (i.e., changes in the wiring diagram of the network) (ibid., pp. 469–470). A transient change in the activation of any unit, or a permanent change in the function implemented by any unit, or a permanent change in the wiring diagram, causes any network to change state unpredictably, thereby leaving the state cycle that it is currently on. If all such deviations have permanent effects on the dynamics of a network, if the network cannot recover from any mutation by returning to the state cycle it was on, then the network is not stable against mutations, and it can easily be thrown into unviable state cycles. Only networks that are able to recover from most mutations, returning to their normal, viable state cycles, are stable enough to constitute evolvable systems (ibid., pp. 531–533). In the best genetic networks, the dynamics are only changed permanently by favorable mutations, i.e., the state cycles of the best genetic networks are only altered permanently by mutations if the mutations shift them to better adapted state cycles.

It is now possible to see the isomorphism between Simon and Kauffman's frameworks for understanding the problems of stability and evolvability in complex systems. Instead of seeing the problem of 'noisy construction' in- terms of a small volume constantly gaining and losing elementary parts, as Simon does, we can follow Kauffman and see it in terms of a constant rate of mutation affecting a genetic network on a state cycle. If the genetic network tends to have unstable state cycles, then it is not stable enough to evolve: any mutation shifts it to a new state cycle which, given the immense space of possible state cycles, is unlikely to produce a viable phenotype. A stable, viable state cycle plays the same role in Kauffman's framework that stable, independent subsystems play in Simon's framework. In order for less adapted state cycles to evolve to more adapted state cycles, the less adapted state cycles must remain viable long enough for favorable mutations to occur, shifting them to more adapted state cycles. But if a less adapted state cycle is fragile, if any mutation alters it permanently, then the probability that it is transformed into an unviable state cycle, before it is transformed into a more adapted state cycle, is overwhelming. Much like Simon, Kauffman sees evolution as a search in an immense space of possibilities. But for Kauffman the search space is not only a space of possible configurations of parts, it is also a space of possible sequences of activity by particular configurations of parts. And the search does not proceed through a mereological or functional hierarchy of subsystems. Rather, it proceeds through a sequence of increasingly well adapted, viable and stable, state cycles.

Above, I have offered only the simplest possible interpretation of Kauffman's models. A given NK Random Boolean Network defines a space of possible state cycles. Thus, evolution, or development (ibid., pp. 489–495), can be defined as a search through this space. However, any combination of values for N and K defines a space of possible networks with N nodes implementing arbitrarily different Boolean functions on inputs from arbitrarily different sets of K nodes in the network. Thus, we might define evolution as a search through this space. Finally, the range of combinations of values that N and K can assume defines yet another, much larger space of possible networks. Evolution might also be defined as a search through this immense space. Kauffman's simulations show that networks where $K = 2$ are the only networks which meet the requirements for stability and evolvability. With $K = 2$ networks, the median number of states on a state cycle is only $N^{1/2}$, out of a possible 2^N. However with $K > 2$ networks, the median number of states on a state cycle expands exponentially (ibid., p. 479). Cell types coded for by such patterns of genetic activity would be unviable as the times required for the full patterns to be expressed are biologically unrealistic (ibid., pp. 483–482). All networks except $K = 2$ networks show very low homeostatic stability. Minimal mutations in the activations of individual units, or structural mutations such as changing the Boolean function implemented by some unit, or changing the wiring diagram of the network, are highly disruptive in all except $K = 2$ networks (ibid., p. 193). Remarkably, of all the 2^N state cycles which are *prima facie* accessible to $K = 2$ networks, these networks can only access $N^{1/2}$ state cycles, all of which exhibit homeostatic stability and biologically plausible lengths (ibid., p. 479).

The fact that $K = 2$ networks exhibit homeostatic recovery from most but not all minimal and structural mutations, suggests that $K = 2$ networks are capable of orderly evolution through both the space of all possible state cycles accessible to a given network, and through the space of all possible wiring diagrams and Boolean function sets consistent with $K = 2$. On the basis of these and other results, Kauffman concludes that only $K = 2$

networks meet the conditions for the stability and evolvability of genetic networks (ibid., pp. 531–533). And he speculates that genetic networks may even have evolved *toward* the $K = 2$ regime (ibid.). In any case, Simon's requirement that evolution constitute an orderly search through intermediate stable states toward a maximally adapted state can only be met by $K = 2$ networks. Yet these networks do not seem to be distinguished from other networks by their decomposability into a mereological or functional hierarchy. If $K = 2$ networks are relevantly accurate models of genetic networks, then intermediate, stable stages of evolution are not necessarily constituted by independently stable subsystems of the complex whole that is evolving. First and foremost, the intermediate stages are constituted by certain patterns of genetic activity, by certain state cycles of the genetic network.

Thus, it seems that Kauffman's results constitute a counterexample to Simon's claim that stability and evolvability are only possible in complex systems which are decomposable into mereological or functional hierarchies. However a number of caveats are necessary. Kauffman's models only address evolution through reorganization of the genome. However, there has been a significant increase in the size of the genome during evolution as well (ibid., p. 488). Perhaps the evolution of the size of the genome has proceeded through a Simonesque decomposable hierarchy. Also, it is important to remember that evolution is not the only example of the assembly of complex systems from simple parts in nature. The process of development in individual organisms, *controlled* by evolved genomes, is also an example of the assembly of a complex natural system from simple elements. Perhaps this process involves construction through a decomposable hierarchy, even if the structure that controls the process, the genetic network, evolves according to different principles. Finally, Kauffman's speculative explanation for why $K = 2$ networks are stable and evolvable has a Simonesque flavor. He suggests that in $K = 2$ networks, functionally isolated "frozen islands" of genes emerge, and are organized into a control hierarchy (ibid., pp. 495–505).

III. Are Kauffman's models mere implementations of Simon's idea?

A large proportion of the units in any $K = 2$ network implement what Kauffman calls "canalizing functions" (ibid., pp. 498–499). These are Boolean functions where only one of the inputs is sufficient to determine the activation of the unit. For example, the 'AND' and 'OR' functions are both canalizing. In the former case, if just one of the inputs to the function is a '0', then the function must return a '0', and in the latter case, if just one of the inputs to the function is a '1', the function must return a '1'. The 'XOR' function is an example of a non-canalizing function. For $K > 2$ networks, the proportion of units implementing canalizing functions drops (ibid.,

p. 498). The functionally isolated, frozen islands of genetic activity are a direct result of the preponderance of canalyzing functions in $K = 2$ networks (ibid.). Briefly, the frozen islands emerge in the following way. Suppose, for example, that a 'loop' of units, all implementing the 'AND' function, is set up in the randomly chosen wiring diagram of a $K = 2$ network. If the first unit in the loop is set to '0', then the next unit in the loop, which gets input from the first unit, will take on the '0' value. This continues around the loop of units until the loop is closed when the last unit passes a '0' value to the first unit. This guarantees that the first unit, and therefore every other unit in the loop, retain the '0' value indefinitely, through the remainder of the network's state cycle (ibid., pp. 496–497). Such "forcing" loops can form 'walls' around groups of units whose activity is more dynamic, changing with each iteration. These 'islands' of activity constitute functionally isolated groups of units. In a $K = 2$ network several such islands might emerge (ibid., pp. 499–500).

Kauffman's frozen islands of genetic activity explain many of the favorable features of $K = 2$ networks. For example, the stability of such networks against most mutations is explained by the fact that mutations within frozen islands of activity cannot propagate across the walls set up by the canalizing loops (ibid., p. 505). Furthermore, networks with frozen islands of activity meet some of Simon's conditions for decomposability. For example, interactions between units within the islands are much more frequent than interactions between units in different islands. This is analogous to Simon's claim that interactions between subsystems are much weaker than interactions within subsystems (Simon 1969, p. 99). And Kauffman suggests that the frozen islands might form a control hierarchy. The limited communication between islands, made possible by transient mutations in the units constituting the frozen walls for example, might be organized such that groups of islands fall under the control of single islands, which then form groups with other 'control' islands such that these higher level groupings fall under the control of still higher level islands (Kauffman 1993, pp. 500–501). Kauffman admits that such suggestions are highly speculative (ibid.). It has not been ascertained whether such control hierarchies actually form in NK Random Boolean Networks, let alone in actual genomes. However the suggestions do have a very Simonesque flavor.

Even if the strong hierarchical explanation of the stability and evolvability of $K = 2$ networks turns out to be true, there remain significant differences between Kauffman and Simon's models. The hierarchies which emerge in Kauffman's networks are very fluid. Control cannot be localized to particular units, for the role that a unit plays in an emergent control hierarchy depends on the activity of many other units in the network. For example, Kauffman suggests that, depending on an individual organism's stage of development, a given gene might be part of an isolated island of activity at one time, part of a frozen wall at another time, and part of a completely different isolated island of activity at still another time (ibid., pp. 504–505). Such variability of role is also possible if we interpret the networks as models of change at the evolutionary scale. The functionally isolated islands of activity that are Kauffman's analogs to Simon's subsystems *are not necessarily conserved* across development and evolution. New stages of development or evolution, i.e., new state cycles, can involve radical re-organization of the control hierarchy. If Kauffman's models are relevantly accurate, then evolution and development are not constrained by the sub-systems available, rather they are constrained by the state cycles accessible to a genetic network from the state cycle that it is currently on. Thus, even if subsystems do form in Kauffman's $K = 2$ networks, they are not the stable building blocks of evolution and development. The hierarchies that Kauffman speculates about are radically different from Simon's mereo-logical hierarchies.

Conclusion

If Kauffman's models of genetic evolution are relevantly accurate, then Simon's argument that complex, adaptive systems, like organisms, are neces-sarily decomposable into functional or mereological hierarchies, *because* they can only evolve via the progressive accumulation of genetic modules from earlier and simpler stages of evolution, is thrown into jeopardy. The key property of Kauffman's models responsible for this confutation of Simon's argument is the following: intermediate stages of stability are not necessarily constituted by modules that are conserved for use as sub-systems in later stages of stability. Kauffman is in agreement with Simon on two points: intermediate stages of stability are required for evolvability, and a good way of maintaining such stability is through some kind of modular, and perhaps hierarchical organization, as displayed, for example, in $K = 2$ networks. However, for Kauffman, these constraints are not derived from supposedly universal constraints on the *construction* of complex systems. For Simon's argument to work, evolution must *require* that genetic modules used in the construction of earlier, simpler forms be conserved and used in the construction of later, more complex forms. However, in Kauffman's models, the hierarchical, modular structure of a genetic network at a particular, stable stage of evolution is 'emergent': it is not necessarily composed of modules present at earlier stages, rather it is 'discovered' by the network as it settles into a new state cycle. The construction of new forms does not require the conservation of modules used in the construction of earlier forms. The only constraint on the construction of a new form is that it must be constituted by a state cycle of the network that is accessible from the state cycle that constitutes the construction of its immediate precursor. Given the preponderance of canalyzing functions in $K = 2$ net-works, the network is likely to display a hierarchical, modular organization, both in the earlier state cycle, and in the later state cycle. However, it is compatible with the accessibility of the later state cycle from the earlier, that the network's modular organization in the later state cycle is radically different from its modular organization in the earlier state cycle. Thus, although Kauffman agrees with Simon that intermediate stages of stability, guaranteed, in some sense, by modular hierarchical organization, are necessary for the evolution of complex, biological systems, his explanation for this is radically different from Simon's. The constraints on future stages of stability are not derived from the modular hierarchical organization that each stage displays. Rather, these constraints are derived from the dynamics of the genetic network, from the accessibility relations between different state cycles.

If Kauffman is right then there are at least three interesting theoretical consequences for the study of evolved systems. First, the modules that such systems can be decomposed into are not central to the explanation of biological change. Decomposition may be useful for descriptive purposes, but it does not isolate stable building blocks which constrain long-term, evolutionary dynamics. For example, if we assume the accuracy of Kauffman's models, then identifying some decomposable, modular hierarchy that the genome happens to temporarily settle into does not help explain or predict the re-organization of the genome in evolution. The modules in such temporary hierarchies do not constrain further change. Rather, the state cycles accessible from the state cycle that the genome is on at a particular time constrain fresher change.[2]

Second, the explanatory limitations of hierarchical, modular decomposition, with respect to the problem of biological change, may provide a more general methodological lesson for students of biological systems. As Bechtel and Richardson argue, the decomposition of complex systems into mereological or functional hierarchies of subsystems has been a popular strategy in the explanation of complex systems since the dawn of modern science (Bechtel & Richardson 1993, pp. 23–31). Simon's theoretical argument for the preponderance of such decomposable systems in nature supports the claim that such strategies are not merely of instrumental value: if there are good, evolutionary reasons why complex systems are *constituted* by decomposable hierarchies, then we should expect strategies of decomposition to produce *accurate* descriptions and explanations of complex systems. Kauffman's models can be used to argue against such a claim. At the very least, these models suggest that decomposing biological systems into functional or mereological hierarchies is not sufficient for, and perhaps not even central to, the satisfactory explanation of such systems.

Third, if Kauffman's models are accurate, then they constitute a sobering corrective to excessively progressive and adaptationist construals of evolution. Simon's argument assumes that evolution is constituted by the accumulation of solutions to problems: earlier organisms express 'partial' solutions to the problems solved more completely by later organisms. Thus, evolutionary change is driven exclusively by the natural selection of increasingly well-adapted forms, i.e., increasingly better 'solutions', and evolutionary change is progressive in Dawkins' sense: it involves the accumulation of the most adaptive 'solutions' (see Dawkins 1996, Ch. 3). In contrast, Kauffman's models locate many constraints on evolutionary change in the actual structures of evolving, genetic systems. Adaptation is de-emphasized because the problems that need solving are not the only source of constraints on evolution. The state-cycles accessible from a particular state-cycle of some genetic network are largely determined by the inherent dynamics of the network, independently of any adaptational constraints extrinsic to the network. Furthermore, because, in Kauffman's models, the functional sub-systems that genomes can be decomposed into at some stage of evolution are not necessarily conserved in later stages, these models seem incompatible with the alleged progressiveness of evolution, especially as defined by Dawkins. Certainly there is change, and change involves the 'discovery' of new solutions to new problems, however if this change is not constituted by the accumulation and use of old solutions to old problems, if new solutions to new problems are not straightforward functions of old solutions to old problems, then it is hard to see what the alleged progressivenes of evolution consists in.

Acknowledgements

I wish to thank two anonymous reviewers, Bill Bechtel, Andy Clark, Pete Mandik, participants in my PNP Works-in-Progress-Seminar (fall 1995), and members of the PNP Research Group for helpful comments. I also thank the Social Sciences and Humanities Research Council of Canada (Doctoral Fellowship #752-93-0222) and the James S. McDonnell Foundation (PNP Doctoral Fellowship, 1995–96) for financial support.

Notes

1 Functions and sources of input are assigned randomly only once, when the network is constructed, and, except for mutations, remain constant throughout the network's 'career'.

2 One might argue that even if this is the best way to explain the re-organization of the genome in evolution, the *growth* of the genome can only be explained in terms of more Simonesque principles. However this depends on how the genome in fact increases in size. For example, if such growth involves only the piecemeal addition of individual genes which are not parts of modules dedicated to specific functions, and further, if each such addition requires substantial re-organization of the existing genome, with its potential for the radical alteration of the genome's modular, hierarchical structure, then it is unclear in what sense the growth of the genome exhibits Simonesque principles.

References

Bechtel, William and Richardson, Robert C.: 1993, *Discovering Complexity*, Princeton University Press, Princeton.

Dawkins, Richard: 1996, *Climbing Mount Improbable*, Viking, London.

Kauffman, Stuart: 1993, *The Origins of Order*, Oxford University Press, New York.

Simon, Herbert A.: 1969, *The Sciences of the Artificial*, The MIT Press, Cambridge, MA.

62

SIMON'S SELECTION THEORY

Why docility evolves to
breed successful altruism

Thorbjørn Knudsen

Source: *Journal of Economic Psychology*, 24 (2003), 229–244.

Abstract

In light of the under-explored potential of Simon's theory of altruism, the purpose of the present article is to review his explanation of altruism and to point out some of its implications for behavioural economics and theories of economic organization. In the course of the argument, this article relates Simon's theory of altruism to Hamilton's theory of kinship selection and then proceeds to examine a critical assumption of Simon's model that social organizations know better than individuals. Within the parameters of Simon's own model, the paper suggests how this assumption can be justified. The paper concludes by noting that Simon offered a new and so far under-explored mechanism for the emergence of altruism in biological populations and suggests a controlled experiment to test Simon's explanation against Hamilton's. Finally, it is noteworthy that Simon's theory has immediate implications for the understanding of human nature that invites revision and development of behavioural economics and theories of economic organization.

1. Introduction

Although altruism seems a ubiquitous feature of nature and society, it is hard to explain how it can be sustained when defined as providing a benefit for others at a cost to the provider. From the viewpoint of evolutionary theory, altruism carries the cost of a reduction in the altruist's fitness.[1] That is, the altruist will on average have less offspring than the selfish organism. Therefore, the population share of altruistic organisms will eventually vanish, and the selfish ones will prevail. If altruism is a hardwired trait, the genetic configuration that codes for it will cease to exist, and if it is a learned trait, unlearning will set in. The logic appears flawless, and yet altruism is thriving in nature and society. Why? Assuming altruism to be a hard-wired trait, kinship selection was the convincing mechanism identified by Hamilton (1964). Close kin to a high degree share genes. It is therefore possible that the fitness reduction of altruism is less than the fitness increase weighted by the coefficient of relatedness. As relatedness increases, the probability of the sustained presence of altruism in a population also increases.

Hamilton's (1964) formulation was later extended to encompass clustering in geographical space as a general condition favouring the emergence of altruism (Bergstrom, 2002; Hamilton, 1975; Myerson, Pollock, & Swinkels, 1991). The effect of the tendency to cluster, termed assortment or viscosity, is that altruism may evolve if the population is genetically related or spatially clustered. Hamilton's rule, that the cost of altruism must be less than the benefit weighted by relatedness, is thought to be a general hurdle for altruism that can be surpassed only under rather specific circumstances (Axelrod, 1997; Bergstrom, 2002; Knudsen, 2002a; Myerson et al., 1991; Sella & Lachmann, 2000). Thus, an alternative explanation for the viability of altruism that differs from both kin-selection and geographical clustering is a repeated game in which agents may develop reciprocal altruism (Axelrod, 1997). If a repeated game ends with a probability less than one, altruism may survive, even if this would be impossible, were it known at which time step the game ended.

As indicated by the amount of effort allocated to develop convincing models that can explain the viability of altruism, it is an important issue in understanding observed biological, social and economic behaviour. It is therefore interesting that Simon in a stream of publications (Simon, 1983, 1990, 1991, 1993, 1997) offered a convincing explanation for the viability of altruism that differed from those mentioned above. It is here important to note that Simon's model is defined on the basis of an "even if" argument that makes it applicable to both economics and biology. Even if genes are the controlling sites of natural selection, Simon's model shows that the general capacity to learn at the socio-economic level may cause positive selection of altruism. As discussed below, the implication is that Simon's model deserves further attention both in economics and biology.

In light of the under-explored potential of Simon's theory of altruism, the purpose of the present article is to review his explanation of altruism and to point out some of its implications for behavioural economics and theories of economic organization. In the course of the argument I relate Simon's theory of altruism to Hamilton's (1964, 1975) theory of kinship selection and structured populations and then proceed to examine a critical assumption of Simon's model that organizations know better than individuals. Within the parameters of Simon's own model, it is suggested how this assumption can be justified.

2. How altruism may spring from the capacity to be instructed

Simon's model of altruism was based on the two assumptions of bounded rationality and docility, both introduced as empirical assumptions to characterise fundamentally the human condition (Simon, 1947, 1955, 1956, 1979, 1987).

Bounded rationality refers to limits of knowledge and computational power of individuals, and the implications of these limits in terms of the possible alternatives of an action that can be known, and the possibility of evaluating the consequences of each alternative. For instance, people consider treatments for physical symptoms of illness by including some but not all possible treatments. And in the course of evaluating a set of treatments, the screening of information is imperfect in the sense that a good treatment may be rejected, and a bad treatment accepted. Or the uncertainty regarding the consequences of alternative treatments may be so high that the choice is based on a procedure that is akin to the flipping of a coin.

Docility refers to the capacity for being instructed and the tendency to accept and believe instructions received through social channels. In an evolutionary perspective, "docility" must be seen as an evolved capacity expressed as "the tendency to depend on suggestions, recommendations, persuasion, and information obtained through social channels as a major basis for choice" (Simon, 1997, p. 244). It must be noted here that Simon was not entirely satisfied with the term docility because of its passive overtones and would have preferred the term "socializability", were it not so awkward (Simon, 1997, p. 3). Rather than being passive, Simon viewed a docile person as one that readily learned in a social setting and tended to acquire socially approved behaviours and beliefs.

Simon's definition of docility encompassed a cognitive and a motivational component. The cognitive component referred to the tendency to form beliefs on the basis of information received from legitimate or "qualified" sources rather than relying on a personal evaluation. For example, in evaluating a treatment for a physical symptom of illness a docile person would tend to rely on advice from a certified professional member of a medical institution rather than cooking up a treatment on the basis of personal studies. Today, the docile person would on average experience a great advantage over the non-docile by tapping in to the cumulated wisdom of the medical profession. By the same token, in a different time and social context, a docile person would tend to accept the treatment prescribed by a witchdoctor. Perhaps the advantage of docility in this case lies more in the comfort of tapping in to a well-known set of values than basing the cure on objective evidence. This possibility is an expression of the motivational component of docility, to accept information on the basis of social approval rather than individually held motives that are not socially acquired.

With bounded rationality and docility in place, the road is cleared for Simon's evolutionary explanation of altruism to unfold. Consider a population composed of p altruists and $1 - p$ selfish individuals, and let X be the fitness of a population considered within their current environment. Define F_S as the fitness of selfish individuals and F_A as the fitness of altruists. By definition, the typical altruist will sacrifice c units of offspring to contribute b units of offspring to the population (including self). The fitness functions are:

$$F_S = X + bP, \tag{1}$$

$$F_A = X + bp - c. \tag{2}$$

It is clear from these fitness functions that the altruists suffer a comparative disadvantage of c and will eventually vanish.

At this point it is interesting to briefly visit Hamilton's (1975) model of structured populations. Hamilton (1975) used the Price (1970, 1972) equations to introduce an assortment procedure so the correlation in two randomly selected members of a population is F. According to Hamilton, the positive correlation F, also referred to as the viscosity parameter, can be interpreted as the chance that the b units of fitness are definitely given to a fellow altruist; while with chance $(1 - F)$ they are given (as they always were) to a random member of the population. Then, if the altruist gives up c units of fitness to add b units to joint fitness, the above fitness functions become:

$$F_S = X + bp(1 - F), \tag{3}$$

$$F_A = X + bp(1 - F) + bF - c. \tag{4}$$

This implies that the criterion for positive selection of altruism, known as Hamilton's rule, is

$$bF > c \Leftrightarrow b/c > 1/F. \tag{5}$$

Hamilton's rule is general for asexual models with non-overlapping generations, and it also holds for diploid biological models. In other words, it is general to both social and biological populations. The main conclusion to be drawn from Hamilton's model is that altruism or costly cooperation can evolve only if the population is genetically related or spatially clustered so the viscosity parameter $F > 0$.

Since Hamilton's rule is commonly thought to be a general hurdle for altruism to evolve, it is interesting to note that Simon devised a simple alternative mechanism that works, even if Hamilton's rule is not obeyed. That is, if a population is completely homogeneous, so $F = 0$. For this reason Simon's model deserves much more attention than it has so far received.

Invoking the assumption of bounded rationality, Simon argued that human beings and other creatures do not behave optimally for their fitness because they do not possess the knowledge and computational power required to support optimisation. In the terminology introduced above, people are only capable of considering a limited subset of the possible actions that may bear on their fitness and are, at best, only capable of an imperfect screening of information regarding the consequences of each action.

Because of bounded rationality, people (and organisms) will on average benefit from receiving and relying on the information received through social channels. Unless society and its organizations generally cumulate bad information, docile people who enjoy a capacity to be instructed by society and to acquire skills on the basis of this socially transmitted information will experience a fitness advantage over those lacking the capacity. Thus, according to Simon, docile individuals experience a fitness advantage of d units over non-docile people because of their use of socially transmitted skills and their conformity to socially sanctioned behaviour. This fitness advantage may now be "taxed" by society through influencing the docile people to engage in behaviours that are useful to society in the sense that they contribute to net fitness. If society imposes a "tax" on docility by prescribing behaviours that reduce fitness by c units, the fitness functions for a homogeneous population are:

$$F_S = X + bp, \tag{6}$$

$$F_A = X + bp + (d - c). \tag{7}$$

Note first that the tax c contributes to the net fitness of society, and therefore it is a measurement of altruism. Note further that altruism will dominate selfish behaviour as long as the fitness advantage from docility is larger than the fitness reducing tax imposed by society, i.e. whenever $d > c$. But why do smart altruists accept instructions indiscriminately? Why do they not avoid the contribution c to society? According to Simon, there are two reasons for this. First, referring to the assumption of bounded rationality, even smart people have too limited knowledge and computational power to screen off the fitness decreasing instructions received through social channels. Second, the tendency to conform to social norms and accept information on the basis of social approval will reinforce the individual's limited ability to discriminate between fitness increasing and fitness decreasing instructions. This completes Simon's model of altruism.

In summary, altruism is in this model a by-product of docility. Because of bounded rationality, a docile person must indiscriminately accept the fitness advantage d and the fitness reducing cost c. And whenever d is larger than c, there is positive selection for docility. In Simon's model, altruism springs from docility, an evolved capacity to be instructed. A further force supporting the positive selection of docility is the emergence of social sanctions curbing deviant behaviour. Altruism therefore includes norms that encourage time spent on instructing others in proper social behaviours as well as enforcing proper behaviours by encouragement, detection and punishment of deviant behaviour.

One assumption of Simon's model, that society and its organizations know better than individuals, however, invites to further consideration. If we use Simon's model and by implication assume, it is valid also for social organizations, the question will be whether it is reasonable to infer that organizations know better than individuals? If this were not the case, the term d becomes negative since the docile individual would receive fitness reducing instructions through social channels. There would thus be selection against docility. Although this problem seems irrelevant in view of today's advances in the accumulation of societal knowledge, it must be remembered that Simon's argument relies on the possibility that the capacity for docility was positively selected also in ancient times when "society" was no more than a band of hunters and gatherers. In this case, as in the case of modern social organizations, the question whether an organization of N individuals better screens the distribution of prospects on offer than the sum of N independent individuals must be answered in the affirmative. To further justify Simon's model of altruism, it is therefore necessary to show that organizations, at least in some instances, better screen information than the members would do as independent agents. This is done in the following.

Before turning to this problem, Hamilton's model of altruism is revisited and integrated with Simon's. The point is to show that in the case of a clustered population there may be positive selection for altruism, even if society imposes a fitness reducing tax c that is higher than the fitness advantage d associated with docility. By considering the possibility that a population may be clustered, as measured by the viscosity parameter F, we get:

$$F_S = X + bp(1 - F), \tag{8}$$

$$F_A = X + bp(1 - F) + bF + (d - c). \tag{9}$$

In a clustered population, altruism dominates selfish behaviour whenever $d > c - bF$. Thus altruism may evolve in a clustered society imposing a tax that is almost bF units of fitness larger than the benefit d of docility. According to Simon's model, we should expect altruism to be a pervasive feature of every society, clustered or not. As the fitness advantage of docility increases by society's accumulation of useful empirically tested knowledge and processes that further utilize the members' capacity to be instructed, the term d will grow and the possibility of a correspondingly large term c arises. As

Simon (1997, p. 246) notes, there is indeed room for a lot of altruism in a modern high-tech society. But also in a low-tech society, some level of altruism is possible despite a negative contribution of docility. In early times, there was room for some level of docility, even if the members of a social group on average received bad advice. In particular, as long as the docile person would tend to team up with other docile people, and the less docile person tends to wander off, altruism would evolve, but only slowly. As societies grew increasingly homogeneous and accumulated increasingly more sound knowledge, a strong positive selection for docility would eventually occur. In this explanation, bounded rationality may be seen as a universal primordial feature characterising every being, whereas docility is a capacity that may evolve, given the right conditions. The primary condition favouring the evolution of docility is the appearance of (social) organisations that accumulate increasingly useful knowledge. To be convincing, Simon's explanation of altruism must therefore ideally be supported by an argument showing that the pure structural features of social organisations, independent of any form of technological advances, can lead to better screening of the prospects offered by the environment. In this case, there would be selection for docility, even in the ancient times when the media of storing knowledge were rudimentary or limited to primitive behavioural programmes.

3. Altruism in social organizations

In a summary of his work on altruism, Simon (1997) notes that people in recent theories of economic organization (the new institutional economics) are solely motivated by economic gains while the empirical facts apparently also include motives such as organizational loyalty and identification. Simon (1997, p. 199) further notes, "[w]orking my way through this conundrum has been the greatest challenge in my economic research in the past two decades." As we have seen above, one outcome of this work is a model of successful altruism to complement Hamilton's and its recent extensions. Another outcome, to be the focus of this section, is that docility obviously may be at work at the level of social organizations and therefore support the evolution of extensive altruism also in modern business organizations.

Why do employees often work hard? Arguing that purely economic rewards only provide some of the explanation, Simon (1991, 1993, 1997) identified a number of alternative mechanisms that may secure adherence to organizational goals. The most important is organizational identification. It is an empirical fact, Simon (1991, 1993, 1997) argued, that society is permeated by loyalties to various groups, including ethnic, religious and family groups and that such loyalties provide a crucial basis for altruism.

As noted above, the docility argument can be extended to any form of social group. When there is positive selection for docility, the member of any social group will tend to accept the instructions transmitted within the group. These quite possibly include instructions serving to inculcate organizational loyalties among its members and to further the members' identification with the goals of the organization. As Simon (1991, 1993, 1997) noted, such instructions that serve to build organizational identification will have a tendency to clearly discriminate between the members of the organization and the non-members.

From the viewpoint also of the modern business organization, the promotion of organizational identification by instilling organizational pride, loyalty and values therefore has an obvious advantage in motivating the employees to actively pursue the goals of the organization (Simon, 1991, 1993, 1997). For the individual employee, Simon's (1991, 1993, 1997) argument established that pride, loyalty, and values associated with membership of an organization are important motivating factors along with material rewards.

One very important implication of this argument is that it helps explain why an employee would not consistently act in economic self-interest but often attempt to aim at realising the goals of the organization, e.g. to maximize organizational profits. As Simon (1991, 1993) repeatedly emphasized, contrary to the assumptions adopted by the new institutional economics, a theory that includes aspects of motivation should begin with empirically valid postulates about real people in real organizations. In particular, he argued that assuming employees will inadvertently maximize their personal utility by shirking and cheating seems unfounded in the face of the available evidence supporting the competing argument that employees may indeed adopt organizational goals as their own. Yet this implies that employees may actually accept instructions at a personal disadvantage. Why would this be the case? Why does the individual employee not sharply discriminate between the instructions providing personal advantage (in terms of wealth or utility) and those providing a disadvantage?

First, because of the assumption of bounded rationality, the individual is incapable of perfectly screening the consequences associated with each instruction. Second, according to Simon's selection argument, people will generally tend to be docile and therefore accept the instructions received through social channels. The typical employee will therefore tend to be docile and to accept most instructions transmitted within the organization. Also, the possibility that the individual may limit the set of the possible goals to include only those of the organization (or organizational subunit) offers the employee a convenient means to simplify an otherwise more complex situation. Note here that Simon's (1991, 1993, 1997) argument implies that over time the employee will increasingly rely on the instructions received within the membership organization and increasingly ignore instructions and information transmitted from alternative sources.

This opens the question whether an organization of N individuals better screen the distribution of prospects on offer than the sum of N independent individuals. If this was not the case, it seems possible that the tendency to develop organizational identification would eventually weaken, because independent producers and traders would consistently outperform organizations. In the following, it is shown by example that organizations, at least in some instances, better screen information than the members would as independent agents. Since this possibility remains and since it would be very hard for the individual to infer what kind of organizational structures actually help make better decisions, we conclude that Simon's model of altruism rests on firm ground as an explanation of the emergence of altruism in any form of social organization.

4. Why social organizations sometimes know better than individuals

If a collection of independent individuals were always better off compared to a social organization including these individuals as members, the docility term in Simon's model would be negative and altruism could not evolve. It is therefore critical to show that, at least in some instances, the social organization helps structure the information flows among individuals to improve their ability to screen the distribution of prospects currently offered by the environment. Here, a prospect may refer to any opportunity that de- or increases the agent's benefit by whatever dimension(s) of benefit we wish to analyse. To keep things simple and consistent with Simon's model of altruism, we define the distribution of offers in terms of fitness (expected number of offspring). In the following, some necessary terminology is first introduced. Then comes the argument supporting Simon's model of altruism.

Within the parameters of Simon's model, bounded rationality implies that individuals are at best only capable of imperfectly screening a distribution of prospects. That is, individuals sometimes reject good offers (Type I error) and accept bad offers (Type II error). A useful way to model this problem is to impute to the individual a screening function that maps the distribution of offers onto the probability of accepting an offer. To do this, the distribution of offers is indexed with respect to its consequences (e.g. fitness, profit or utility) and the probabilities are constrained within the closed interval [0,1]. Given a distribution of offers, the condition of bounded rationality may be modelled as a screening function f mapping the offer x onto the probability p that an individual accepts the offer, so $p = f(x)$. The more severe the condition of bounded rationality, the larger the deviation from the perfect screening function, i.e. the higher the incidence of Types I and II error. In the most severe case, the agent simply has no clue about the distribution of prospects and picks an arbitrary constant $K \in [0, 1]$, and the screening function becomes $K = f(x)$.

In order to proceed, it is useful to conceptualise the structure of a social organization as a connected finite graph G including all possible paths of traversal of prospects among its members. The traversal of prospects can be denned in terms of a dynamic rule that determines where a member can or must send a prospect when it is accepted or rejected. A prospect can either be finally rejected or accepted. In the case of acceptance, the prospect adds to the accumulated knowledge of the organization. This can be symbolized by including the prospect in the organization's "final portfolio."

Given this terminology, the ability of the social organization to support its members' screening of prospects can be defined in terms of the graph screening function G and the probability P (not necessarily a "hard" probability) that the social organization will accept a prospect x, so $P = G(f(x))$. An analytical expression of G can always be derived by recursively traversing all the possible acceptance and rejection paths among the agents of a structure (Christensen & Knudsen, 2002a).

The simplest structures of some interest, a serial and a parallel connection of two agents were analysed by Sah and Stiglitz (1986, 1988). Intimately connected with the structure of two serially connected agents, referred to as a "hierarchy", Sah and Stiglitz (1986, 1988) defined a dynamic rule according to which the second agent only received the prospect if the first agent accepted it. Or the other way around, in a serial connection, any agent has the authority to reject a prospect. A parallel connection, referred to as a "polyarchy", was defined in the following way: with probability 0.5 one of two agents first receives a prospect. If this agent chooses to accept, it is accepted by the social organization and included in its final portfolio. If, on the other hand, this agent chooses to reject it, the second agent receives the prospect. If the second agent accepts the prospect, it is accepted by the social organization and included in its final portfolio. If the second agent, however, also chooses to reject it, this prospect is rejected for good and dumped by the organization.

Note here that the dynamic rule imputed to the polyarchy structure cannot be inferred by the structure itself, a difficulty preventing any straightforward generalisation of this structure defined by Sah and Stiglitz (1986). As Christensen and Knudsen (2002a) note, it is necessary to define a rule for polyarchy-rejection and -acceptance in order to generalise the polyarchy to structures including three or more agents.

For the current purpose, the important point is that Sah and Stiglitz (1986, 1988) showed that a hierarchy is the best performing structure in bad times, defined in terms of an expected value of the distribution of prospects less than zero. In good times, the polyarchy is the best performing structure. Since Sah and Stiglitz (1986, 1988) omit a comparison between the individual agent and the structure and since their analysis is limited to explicit structures including only two agents, it would be important in order to support Simon's docility argument if at least some large structures including three or more agents could be shown to perform better than the members would as independent agents. As Christensen and Knudsen (2002b) show, it is indeed possible that any graph (including deterministic and stochastic graphs as well as graphs with feedback) for some cost models may outperform a collection of independent agents equal in number to those employed in a social organization.

As indicated above, it is useful for the purpose of analysing screening functions to conceptualise a social organization as a graph. In order to generalise the prospect evaluation model, it is further useful to distinguish between stochastic and deterministic graphs. In a stochastic graph the receiving agent is picked at random by the sender. Given a dynamic rule, the receiver may be fixed, however, in which case the graph is called outward deterministic; or the sender may be fixed, in which case the graph is called inward deterministic. A stochastic graph thus represents a completely unstructured social organization, whereas a deterministic graph (both inward and outward) represents a social organization with the highest degree of internal structure. From the viewpoint of modelling real word social organizations, deterministic graphs seem the most relevant. Since employing meta-agents in nested structures easily reduces stochastic graphs, including three or more agents, to a manageable size, deterministic graphs also appear most interesting from a technical viewpoint (Christensen & Knudsen, 2002a).

The following example, Fig. 1 above, shows a deterministic graph in which information always enters the social organization at the coordinate (1,1). In the case of serial processing, a dynamic rule is used that generalizes Sah and Stiglitz's (1986) accept and reject-rule for hierarchies: if an agent accepts the prospect, it is sent to the member in the next layer (column in the sketch of the graph shown in Fig. 1). If the agent in the last layer also accepts the prospect, it is stored in the final portfolio of this social organization. To model parallel processing, we chose one of the possible ways to extend Sah and Stiglitz' (1986) accept- and reject-rule for polyarchies: if an agent accepts a prospect, it is sent to one in the next layer and possibly stored in the final portfolio. If an agent rejects a prospect, it is sent to the next immediate neighbour. Only if all agents within a layer have all rejected a prospect, it is dumped for good. Note here that the chosen dynamic rule for polyarchies ensures that members belonging to the same hierarchical layer are endowed with equal decision-making competence.

The purpose of the example shown in Fig. 1 above is to illustrate that some social organizations may indeed support the individual's ability to screen information. The perfect screening function is the step function shown in Fig. 1. If agents were equipped with this perfect screening function, there would be no need for any structure to support their decision. But accepting Simon's assumption of bounded rationality, individuals are at best capable of a limited screening of information. This is modelled by imputing a screening function to the agent that deviates from the step function of perfect screening. The more the deviation, the more severe the condition of bounded

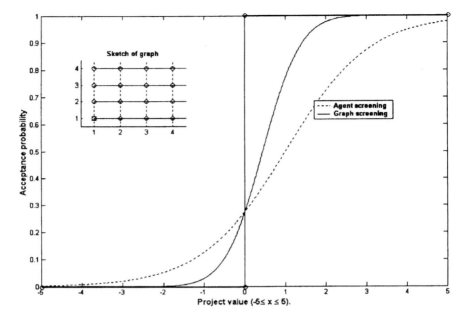

Figure 1 Agent versus graph screening. The example was constructed so the graph, for any project distribution, provides better screening than the individual agent, unless all mass of the project distribution cumulates at 0 (in this case the graph and the agent screen equally good).

rationality. Moreover, a non-monotonic screening function could be used to model "traps". For the purpose of the present example, however, agents are equipped with a monotone screening function as shown in Fig. 1.

The example is so constructed that the graph screening function, representing the social organization's ability to screen information, dominates the individual's agent screening function for any value of prospects different from zero. That is, no matter what the distribution of prospects, as long as all the mass of the prospect distribution does not cumulate at zero, the social organization represented in Fig. 1 would always do better than a comparable collection of independent agents, subject to the constraint that the costs of organization are not excessive.[2]

If we think of the above example in terms of the individual's ability to screen the distribution of fitness de- and increasing prospects offered by the environment within which the agent lives, we have by way of example shown that it is possible, in some instances, that the social organization helps structure the information flows among individuals to increase their individual fitness. In relation to Simon's theory of altruism, the significance of this example lies in the possibility that individuals who organize in a social group may accumulate knowledge, symbolized by the composition of the final portfolio in the above example, that would give each member of the group a fitness advantage compared to a situation where the members are independent individuals. This social organization would accumulate knowledge that left docile individuals with a fitness advantage over the individuals that had to instruct themselves or were less susceptible to instruction.

We have thus shown that a positive docility term upon which Simon's theory of altruism pivots would indeed be possible, even in the ancient and prehistoric times long before effective media of storage and transmission of social knowledge had been invented. Whether the social groups actually adopted such fitness enhancing structures is an open empirical question. Since it can be shown that structures of two members (Sah & Stiglitz, 1986, 1988), or any finite number of organization members (Christensen & Knudsen, 2002b), exist in which the screening of the social organization dominates the individual's screening ability in either good or bad times, Simon's theory of altruism appears to rest on very secure grounds.

5. Discussion

The above review of Simon's selection theory, according to which docility evolves to breed successful altruism, indicated that this theory rests on a very secure ground and therefore deserves serious consideration from biologists as well as social scientists. It was further indicated that Simon's selection theory is remarkable in pointing to a different mechanism to bring about altruism than the kinship selection and structured population models that have emerged from Hamilton's (1964, 1975) work.

As we have seen, Simon's theory is consistent with Hamilton's. According to Simon's model, we should expect altruism to be a pervasive feature of every society, clustered or not. In Simon's model docility gives the individual a possible fitness advantage to be realised in social organizations and societies that transmit useful instructions to individuals. As the fitness advantage of docility increases by society's accumulation of useful empirically tested knowledge, the possibility will increase that a society or a social organization may tax the individual by also conveying instructions that lead to fitness-reducing behaviour.

Integrating Hamilton's (1964) model into Simon's showed that in a clustered society there was room for some level of docility, even if the members of a social organization on average received bad advice. As long as the docile persons would tend to team up with other docile people, and the less docile persons tend to wander off, altruism would evolve, but only slowly. As societies grew increasingly homogeneous and accumulated increasingly more sound knowledge, a strong positive selection for docility would eventually occur. Hamilton's (1964) model thus supports Simon's theory of altruism.

When the positive selection of docility picks up speed, Simon's argument, however, relies on the critical assumption that organizations know better than individuals. It is assumed that the individual member of a social organization on average is better off because of the instructions received within the social organization. While this assumption seems self-supporting in the face of the modern scientific and technological advances, it must be remembered that Simon's argument is biological as well as social. Docility is an evolved property of human organisms and other creatures. Therefore, the challenge is to show that a positive docility term would be possible even in the ancient and prehistoric times long before effective media of storage and transmission of social knowledge had been invented. In order to do this, it was argued by example that it is possible, in some instances, that the social organization helps structure the information flows among individuals to improve their individual fitness. As mentioned above, the significance of this example lies in the possibility that individuals organized in a social group may accumulate knowledge that would give each member of the group a fitness advantage, compared to a situation where the members were independent individuals.

Simon's model is a biological model, to be sure, but it is defined on the basis of an even if argument that also makes it applicable to economics. Simon explicitly relates his model to "neo-Darwinian theory" (e.g. Simon, 1993, p. 156) according to which the criterion for success is biological fitness. Yet Simon (1990, p. 1665) himself regards his argument as an even if argument. Even if genes of individual persons are the controlling sites for natural selection, Simon's model identifies a mechanism that selects for altruistic behaviour well beyond altruism to close kin, beyond support from expected reciprocity or social enforcement, and beyond support from positive assortment and viscosity. This mechanism is the transmission of socially learned behaviours and beliefs that can be received by docile individuals. Even if altruistic behaviour is penalized because genes of individual persons are the controlling sites for natural selection, the general capacity to learn at the socio-economic level may contribute with an offsetting positive fitness effect. For this reason Simon's model is applicable to both economics and biology. Note here that Simon's model requires a general capacity to learn at the socio-economic level, but acknowledges additional specific factors that are not present in the model. Such factors include the actual forms of social transmission and learning as well as the actual forms of social organizations and societies that have emerged through history. The emergence of docile individuals may well have favoured the emergence of particular social organisations particularly well suited to benefit from their members ability to receive, accept and believe instructions, which in turn may have helped the further emergence of docility, and so on. This points to an explanatory circle that both involves upwards causation: from docile individuals to new forms of social organisation, and downwards causation: from particular organisational forms to a shift in the expression of docility.[3]

The possibility that selection may operate simultaneously on docility and the social organization within which the advantage of docility is expressed further indicates an unexplored potential of Simon's theory of altruism. Two promising pathways for further exploration of Simon's altruism theory have been indicated in the course of the above argument. First, Simon's theory deserves to be exposed to empirical test by biologists in a design that allows examination of the veracity of the competing explanations of clustering and docility. Second, Simon's theory deserves to be examined in a design that traces the nested effects of docility and the screening properties of social organizations. Regarding the first point, it is straightforward to base predictions on a classical controlled experiment including the four treatments: (a) docile + clustered, (b) docile + homogeneous, (c) less docile + clustered, (d) less docile + homogeneous. Here "docile" refers to the current characteristic of an organism, e.g. to be inferred by the period it takes a newborn organism to reach maturity. One could therefore select two types of organism and expose these organisms to a "clustered" or "homogeneous" environment. If the ranking of the outcome variable altruism were $a > b > c > d$ (or even better, $a,b > c,d$), we would conclude that Simon's docility effect is probably more important, whereas the ranking $a > c > b > d$ (or better still, $a,c > b,d$) indicates that Hamilton's viscosity effect is most important.

A number of further implications arise for behavioural economics and theories of economic organization. From the viewpoint of behavioural economics, a particularly important implication of Simon's argument relates to the motivation of employees. Simon repeatedly emphasized that the promotion of organizational identification by instilling organizational pride, loyalty and values has an obvious advantage in motivating the employees to actively pursue the goals of the organization. Because of docility and bounded rationality, Simon's argument established why an employee would not consistently act in economic self-interest but often attempt to aim at realising the goals of the organization.

The implications for current behavioural economics, and in particular the branch known as the new institutional economics, are profound. The new institutional economics relies extensively on opportunism to explain the existence, structure, and boundaries of the firm. Simon's argument, however, implies that altruism as a by-product of docility may significantly benefit firms seeking to exploit the possibility of inculcating the employees with organizational pride, loyalty and values. This argument suggests that the new institutional economics may benefit from integrating the docility assumption along with the assumption of bounded rationality that was always a keystone in its foundations. This indicates that a promising path of development for the new institutional economics would be to consider issues of organizational identification and learning along with issues of contracting.

Finally, and related, Simon's theory of altruism points to the need for further development of the evolutionary theory of the firm, extending some of the shared overlap of Cyert and March (1963), March and Simon (1958), Nelson and Winter (1982) and Simon (1947) by developing a detailed theory of the micro-evolutionary processes that give rise to the evolution of economic organizations. In particular, Simon's emphasis of the relation between docility and organizational identification points to further consideration of organizational routines as the medium in which instructions are stored, and organizational identities as the expression of these instructions. That is, organizational routines, a term introduced by Simon (1947) and further developed by Nelson and Winter (1982), may be viewed as a "replicator", the code containing the accumulated organizational instructions which are replicated when new members of the organization are instructed in organizational procedures, norms and values. And the organizational or social identity may be viewed as an "interactor", the expression of the routines that enables interaction among the members of an organization. This conceptualisation, here invited by Simon's emphasis of docility and his extension of the argument to encompass organizational identification, may be used as the foundation of a theory of linguistic selection (Knudsen, 2002b) and as an extension of the behavioural aspects of Nelson and Winter's (1982) evolutionary theory.

6. Conclusion

It is a noteworthy characteristic of Simon's theory of altruism that it is applicable to biology as a complement to the usual biological theory of kinship selection and its recent extensions. Because of the evolved property of docility, the typical human being is endowed with a great potential for being instructed, and because of bounded rationality, the individual cannot discriminate well between the instructions that further selfish goals and the instructions that, at a cost to the individual, contribute to furthering the goals of others. That Simon's theory is biological is noteworthy because it offers a new, convincing and so far under-explored mechanism for the emergence of altruism in biological populations. It is further noteworthy that Simon's model, because it is based on a mechanism of social learning, is also applicable to economics and has immediate implications for the understanding of human nature that invites revision and development of behavioural economics and some of its most important branches, including the new institutional economics and the evolutionary theory of the firm. For these reasons Simon's selection theory deserves further attention. Simon's selection theory is finally noteworthy because it is evidence of his wide scientific reach and taste in scientific problems.

Acknowledgements

The author appreciates helpful suggestions from Meta Andrés, Mie Augier and James G. March. All remaining errors were produced without any help.

Notes

1 Simon uses the term "altruism" in a technical sense that must be distinguished from its broader meaning in ordinary parlance as the unselfish concern for the welfare of others. Thus Simon defines altruism according to its use in evolutionary theory (genetics) as forgoing progeny to the benefit of others. For example, Simon (1990, p. 1665) defines altruism as "behavior that increases, on average, the reproductive fitness of others at the expense of the fitness of the altruist".
2 For this example, the agent screening function was defined as $f(x) = (\tanh((x - 1)/dx) + 1)/2$, $dx = 2.068564969066327$. The analytical expression of the graph screening function, a polynomial of degree seventeen, was derived by a recursive procedure provided by Christensen and Knudsen (2002a). In this case the graph screening function simplifies to $G(f(x)) = y^4(y - 2)^4(y^2 - 2y + 2)$, $y = f(x)$. As the reader can verify, according to this example: $x = 0 \Rightarrow G(f(x)) = f(x)$, $x < 0 \Rightarrow G(f(x)) < f(x)$, and $x > 0 \Rightarrow G(f(x)) > f(x)$.
3 Campbell (1974) and Sperry (1969, 1991) provide a description of the concept of downward causation and its use in scientific explanations. See Hodgson (1998) and Hodgson and Knudsen (2001) for its potential use in economics.

References

Axelrod, R. (1997). *The complexity of cooperation. Agent-based models of competition and collaboration.*
Princeton, NJ: Princeton University Press.
Bergstrom, T. C. The algebra of assortative encounters and the evolution of cooperation. In R. Amir, J.
Bergin, & T. Knudsen, (Eds.), *International game theory review, special issue*, in press.
Campbell, D. T. (1974). "Downward causation" in hierarchically organized biological systems. In F. J. Ayala & T. Dobzhansky (Eds.), *Studies in the philosophy of biology* (pp. 179–186). London, Berkeley and Los Angeles: Macmillan and University of California Press.
Christensen, M., & Knudsen, T. (2002a). *The architecture of economic systems: Towards a general framework.* Odense, Denmark: University of Southern Denmark, unpublished mimeo.
Christensen, M., & Knudsen, T. (2002b). *Extremal screening, cost and performance of economic architectures.* Odense, Denmark: University of Southern Denmark, unpublished mimeo.
Cyert, R. M., & March, J. G. (1963). *A behavioral theory of the firm.* Cambridge, MA: Blackwell Publishers.
Hamilton, W. D. (1964). The genetic evolution of social behaviour. *Journal of Theoretical Biology, 7,* 1–52.

Hamilton, W. D. (1975). Innate social aptitudes of man: An approach from evolutionary genetics. In R. Fox (Ed.), *Biosocial anthropology* (pp. 133–155). New York: John Wiley and Sons.

Hodgson, G. M. (1998). The approach of institutional economics. *Journal of Economic Literature*, *36*(1), 166–192.

Hodgson, G. M., & Knudsen, T. (2001). *The complex evolution of a simple traffic convention: The functions and implications of habit.* Hertfordshire, UK: University of Hertfordshire, unpublished mimeo.

Knudsen, T. (2002a). The evolution of cooperation in structured populations. *Constitutional Political Economy*, *13*(2), 129–148.

Knudsen, T. (2002b). The significance of tacit knowledge in the evolution of human language. *Selection*, *3*(1), 93–112.

March, J. G., & Simon, H. A. (1958). *Organizations*. New York: John Wiley.

Myerson, R. B., Pollock, G. B., & Swinkels, J. M. (1991). Viscous population equilibria. *Games and Economic Behavior*, *3*, 101–109.

Nelson, R. R., & Winter, S. G. (1982). *An evolutionary theory of economic change.* Cambridge, MA: Harvard University Press.

Price, G. R. (1970). Selection and covariance. *Nature*, *227*, 520–521.

Price, G. R. (1972). Extension of covariance selection mathematics. *Annals of Human Genetics*, *35*, 485–490.

Sah, R. K., & Stiglitz, J. E. (1986). The architecture of economic systems: Hierarchies and polyarchies. *American Economic Review*, *76*(4), 716–727.

Sah, R. K., & Stiglitz, J. E. (1988). Comittees, hierarchies and polyarchies. *Economic Journal*, *98*, 451–470.

Sella, G., & Lachmann, M. (2000). On the dynamic persistence of cooperation: How lower individual fitness induces higher survivability. *Journal of Theoretical Biology*, *206*, 465–485.

Simon (1947). *Administrative behavior* (4th ed). New York: The Free Press (1997).

Simon, H. A. (1955). A behavioral model of rational choice. *Quarterly Journal of Economics*, *69*, 99–118.

Simon, H. A. (1956). Rational choice and the structure of the environment. *Psychological Review*, *63*(3), 129–138.

Simon, H. A. (1979). Rational decision making in business organizations. *The American Economic Review* (September), 493–513.

Simon, H. A. (1983). *Reason in human affairs.* Stanford, CA: Stanford University Press.

Simon, H. A. (1987). Rationality in psychology and economics. In R. M. Hogarth & M. W. Reder (Eds.), *Rational choice: The contrast between economics and psychology* (pp. 25–40). Chicago: University of Chicago Press.

Simon, H. A. (1990). A mechanism for social selection and successful altruism. *Science*, *250*(December), 1665–1668.

Simon, H. A. (1991). Organizations and markets. *Journal of Economic Perspectives*, *5*(2), 25–44.

Simon, H. A. (1993). Altruism and economics. *The American Economic Review*, *83*(2), 156–161.

Simon, H. A. (1997). *Models of bounded rationality. Vol. 3. Empirically grounded economic reason.* Cambridge, MA: The MIT Press.

Sperry, R. W. (1969). A modified concept of consciousness. *Psychological Review*, 76(6), 532–536.
Sperry, R. W. (1991). In defense of mentalism and emergent interaction. *Journal of Mind and Behavior*, 12(2), 221–246.

63

THE AGENT–ENVIRONMENT INTERFACE

Simon's indirect or Gibson's direct coupling?

Robert Shaw

Source: Ecological Psychology, 15:1 (2003), 37–106.

A fundamental problem for ecological and cognitive psychology alike is to explain how agents are situated, that is, functionally coupled to their environments so as to facilitate adaptive actions. Herbert Simon (1969/1996) argued that such coupling is artifactual (rule governed), being mediated by symbol functions and necessarily involving information processing. An alternative to this computational approach is offered by James Gibson's (1979/1986) view that the interface is natural (law governed), being a direct informational coupling rather than a symbolically mediated one. This latter view necessarily involves the agent's awareness, whereas the former, being mechanistic, does not. I review the coupling problem from historical, logical, and semantic perspectives. I give arguments that the computational approach provides an inadequate account of situated adaptive actions and founders on the symbol grounding problem, whereas the ecological approach does a better job on both. Personal comments are interspersed throughout, providing an autobiographical perspective on issues germane to these topics.

Perhaps the composition and layout of surfaces constitute what they afford. If so, to perceive them is to perceive what they afford. This is a radical hypothesis, for it implies that the "values" and "meanings" of things in the environment can be directly perceived. Moreover, it would explain the sense in which values and meanings are external to the perceiver.

—James J. Gibson (1979/1986)

But, actually, an affordance is neither an objective property nor a subjective property; or it is both if you like. An affordance cuts across the dichotomy of subjective–objective and helps us to understand its inadequacy. It is equally a fact of the environment and a fact of behavior. It is both physical and psychical, yet neither. An affordance points both ways, to the environment and to the observer.

—James J. Gibson (1979/1986, p. 129)

An artifact can be thought of as a meeting point—an "interface" in today's terms—between an "inner" environment, the substance and organization of the artifact itself, and an "outer" environment, the surroundings in which it operates. If the inner environment is appropriate to the outer environment, or vice versa, the artifact will serve its purpose.

—Herbert Simon (1969/1996, p. 6)

Ironically, affordances, far from removing the need for internal representations, are carefully and simply encoded internal representations of complex configurations of external objects, the encodings capturing the functional significance of the objects.

—Alonso Vera and Herbert Simon (1993, p. 41)

Contrary to Gibson's (1977) view, the thing that corresponds to an affordance is a symbol stored in central memory.

—Alonso Vera and Herbert Simon (1993, p. 20)

Sir, I have found you an explanation, but I am not obliged to find you an understanding.

—Samuel Johnson (Boswell, 1791/1998)

In this article, I give, in part, an eyewitness account of some of the events and attitudes surrounding the original publication of Simon's (1969/1996) influential book *The Sciences of the Artificial* and furnish an appraisal of where things now stand after the publication of the third edition of this book in 1996. The tone of many of my remarks are personal and should be recognized as such. It is hoped that an occasional first-person voice will help the reader recognize that these issues of $3^1/_2$ decades ago are still unresolved and of paramount significance to our field today. The autobiographical thread, I hope, will also convey some of their historical vibrancy without being too discursive (of course being somewhat discursive is in the nature of chronicles).

The preceding epigraphs provide a convenient summary of the main issues and attitudes to be discussed. Please read them carefully, and return to them every so often as the commentary develops.

I offer a final word: One position is a foil for another if it makes the latter position seem better by comparison. In this commentary, Simon's (1969/1996) computational view is used somewhat mercilessly, I must admit, as a foil for Gibson's (1979/1986) ecological view, which he sharply attacks (Vera & Simon, 1993). A more sympathetic and, I hope, balanced account of these same issues can be found in Shaw and Shockley (2003), and a more comprehensive account of issues touched on here can be found in Shaw (2001) and Shaw and Turvey (1999).

Setting the stage

The late Herbert A. Simon, a Nobel Laureate for 1978 and one of the founders of computational psychology, was the quintessential representationalist of the extreme computationalism variety. In 1957, according to Dreyfus (1972), Simon had prophesied that within 10 years most theories in psychology would take the form of computer programs. Although much progress has been made in cognitive science with respect to computational techniques and the general use of computers in psychology has explosively expanded, nothing even close to Simon's prediction has yet materialized. For Simon was not predicting merely the widespread use of computers in psychology but that programs themselves would be devised that adequately modeled human thought, perception, and action.

Yet surprising to me was to discover that Simon was nevertheless somewhat ecological in his attitudes and sensitivities. This does not mean he was a Gibsonian or even sympathetic to the program, for he had strong misgivings and was the primary architect of an alternative approach that was quite antithetical to it. This article provides a commentary on some of the chief ideas of the third edition of Simon's (1969/1996) *The Sciences of the Artificial* published in 1996 but tailored to reveal certain fundamental similarities and contrasts with the thought of James J. Gibson (1966, 1979/1986). Hence, there is no attempt to review the book in its entirety.

Also, much of this commentary has been motivated by an important article by Vera and Simon (1993), which appeared as the target of discussion in a special issue of *Cognitive Science* dedicated to the topic of situated action. As far as I know, this article is the only place in which Simon contrasts his computational psychology with Gibson's ecological psychology, especially challenging Gibson's interpretation of "affordances" and repudiating his notion that perception is direct and unmediated. I found it more than a little curious that Simon would on one hand accept the legitimacy and usefulness of the affordance concept, and reject the main reasons

Gibson gave for introducing the term on the other. What hubris allowed him to do such a thing?

Consequently, exploring Simon's anti-Gibsonian but quasi-ecological attitudes are the main topics of this article. In the process, I use the occasion to defend Gibson and attempt to clarify his views along the lines that my colleagues (Michael Turvey and William Mace) and I have been developing for about 3 decades. Whether such efforts have made us neo-Gibsonians rather than strict Gibsonians is a fair question. Of course, I believe we are interpreting Gibson rather than revising him, but this is more a question of scholarship than intent. I sometimes think that had he lived until now, Gibson himself may have become a neo-Gibsonian, even a revisionist, as he had done at least twice before. Gibson would have continued to refashion old ideas and to introduce new and exciting ones. Hence, we would be in the best of company.

An inherent limitation of the Vera and Simon (1993) criticism of Gibson's theory is that apparently their only source was an early chapter on affordances published in Shaw and Bransford (1977). I seriously doubt that this early source is an adequate substitute for having read Gibson's (1950, 1966, 1979/ 1986) books in their entirety—many times! This was Vera and Simon's choice, and although this narrowness in scholarship makes little logical difference to the argument they make in defense of their own position, it does make their arguments seem more ex cathedra than enlightened and their criticism of the ecological approach more cavalier than reasoned. Often one receives an indelicate whiff of argumentum ad fiat.

Nevertheless, we should appreciate the criticism because serious attempts to answer critics' complaints can help raise the level of mutual understanding of the participants while helping neutral parties better grasp the significance of what each position stands for. An immediate dividend gained from these two sources alone, Simon's (1969/1996) book and the Vera and Simon (1993) article, is recognition that a prima facie case can be made that Simon's computational psychology is both unexpectedly *ecological* and unavoidably *situated*—in the current use of the terms. Indeed, Simon was forced to make this begrudging admission to fend off critics' charges that his theory of information processing was too narrow. The generous reader might see adumbrated in Vera and Simon the harbinger of a computational ecological psychology—a thesis more deliberatively proposed and adroitly defended by Wells (2002) and far better explored by Clancey (1997) and Clark (1997). Effken and Shaw (1992) also discussed the "new AI [artificial intelligence]" from an ecological psychology perspective.

In the late 1960s I was a neophyte in cognitive psychology when the movers and the shakers of the new field began contesting the most promising avenues for its future development. Reviewing these alternatives will help psychologists assess our progress as a science and perhaps suggest what still remains to be done. Considering the competing forms of computationalism will also put Simon's extreme computationalism in perspective by revealing that a less popular computational philosophy existed that was more congenial to ecological psychology than either the simulation or AI approaches. This third alternative was called the *synergy* approach (unrelated to Haken's synergetics approach). I fancy that had it been in the driver's seat for the last 30 years rather than AI, we Gibsonians might look today on efforts to develop a computational ecological psychology with greater approbation and less pessimism.

Diverse computational philosophies

In 1968 I was invited to lecture at the California Institute of Technology (Cal Tech) on the application of abstract machine theory to cognitive psychology—my unique forte at the time. Cal Tech, Massachusetts Institute of Technology (MIT), and Carnegie Mellon University were each home to one of three fledgling computational philosophies and therefore were struggling for hegemony in the new field. My host explained to me how Cal Tech's philosophy differed from its two competitors:

> Imagine you are given a contract to develop a computer application for playing chess as expertly as possible. Depending on your venue, there are three strategies you might consider: the simulation approach under development at Carnegie Mellon (by Simon and Newell), the artificial intelligence approach being promoted at MIT, or, finally, the synergistic approach favored here at Cal Tech.

He went on to explain that at Carnegie Mellon the computer model would likely take the form of a program designed to simulate the play of a Russian grandmaster on the assumption that human experts have insights and competencies that a machine did not but might be programmed to emulate. By contrast, if you were at MIT, you might instead apply AI techniques to try to build a program that played the best game of chess possible, whether or not it did so as humans do—all that matters is that it play brilliantly.

At Cal Tech the computational philosophy differed from those of the other two universities. The aim was not to simulate human experts, or even to create artificial experts, but to treat the computer as a tool designed to serve the purposes of human agents rather than to be a stand-alone device capable of autonomous goal-directed activities. Hence the program, if successful, should couple the computer with a human expert so as to create a maximally effective synergistic partnership. As a synergy, the successful human–computer system should play a better game of chess than either a human expert or computer expert alone. A successful synergistic program is designed to facilitate the interactive accommodation of the best features of both components while allowing them to compensate reciprocally for each other's intrinsic limitations.

Whereas the aim of the first two strategies is to contrive context-free computational mechanisms that can be plugged into any chosen task domain—chess playing, medical diagnostics, or whatever—the synergistic approach cannot aim for context-free mechanisms because its program cannot, in principle, stand alone. It depends on the expertise of a cooperative human agent. Essentially, it seeks to form a human–computer partnership. Compared to simulation and AI programs, this lack of perfect autonomy may be seen as detracting from the usefulness of synergistic programs because they depend on a human interface to interact with real-world task situations.

This complaint that the synergistic models lack autonomy would be legitimate if it were avoidable and if the other two approaches were unqualified successes—an opinion that even the staunchest proponents would have to admit is arguable. Their autonomy is limited no less than the synergistic strategy by a need to be interpreted, debugged, attuned, and reattuned to real-world situations by a human agent. Hence, the demonstrable lack of autonomy of each kind of model could be taken as evidence that favors the validity of the synergy method because of the three views, only it recognizes the recalcitrant fact of failed autonomy—indeed, it is designed to exploit this fact.

On the other hand, if all the synergy style of modeling amounts to is business as usual with computers, such business as is required for all programming—non-modeling as well as modeling tasks—then it hardly counts as a distinct modeling strategy. However, one may argue that because a synergy is sought that essentially seeks to form a human–computer partnership—a kind of cooperative, "social" dyad, as it were—then this is a bit more than business as usual with computers. It requires a specific theory and clever solutions to some outstanding human–computer interaction problems—problems that today are referred to as situated action and situated cognition problems. Did the synergy approach foreshadow a computational approach to ecological psychology? At least one might argue that although their philosophies and methodologies may differ, the scientific feasibility of one is logically linked to the other because they both depend on modeling a "smart" coupling between agents and their environments

Next, I take a look at Simon's (1969/1996) information processing approach as represented in his book and in Vera and Simon (1993) and simultaneously, as promised, use it as a foil to help clarify Gibson's view.

Simon's book in the context of the times

There is much to admire about Simon's (1969/1996) modest little book, *The Sciences of the Artificial*, originally published in 1969 and now in its third edition. This book stimulated the interest of many psychologists and social scientists in the budding field of cognitive science. The author blessed us with elegant, uncluttered prose so one might better concentrate on the substance of his hypotheses and arguments without being distracted by too much niggling detail. He spoke simply and directly with the authority of one who truly believes in the promise of a fledgling field and yet is quite aware of its difficulties and modest accomplishments. Most remarkably, he managed to communicate the book's technical thesis without pages of dense equations, programs, or extensive flow diagrams. The language is nearly jargon free, therefore, even today one might well recommend it to those who wish a relatively painless introduction by a major founder of the field to the origins and aspirations of the field of AI during the period of its inception.

Simon's (1969/1996) book was revised in 1981 (second edition) with the addition of an important chapter, "The Architecture of Complexity," and again in 1996 (third edition) with another new chapter, "Alternative Views of Complexity," being inserted to introduce the former chapter. This newest chapter considers concepts and tools for the analysis of complexity but in no way qualifies Simon's previous thesis or blunts the message of "The Architecture of Complexity" chapter. Simon's innovative thesis is that life forms are basically simple, inheriting their apparent complexity from their environments. Simon said: "The thesis is that certain phenomena are 'artificial' in a very specific sense: They are as they are [e.g., complex] only because of a system's being molded, by goals or purposes, to the environment in which it lives" (p. xi).

This thesis stands in refreshing contrast to the typical cognitivist thesis that the mind and brain system is inherently complex, with layers on layers of computations making it perhaps more complex than anything else in nature. For Simon, however, such complexity is more apparent than real —being true of the expressed behavior, whereas the computations that produce that behavior remain simple. To this end, Simon constructed a syllogism to support his belief in the following man–machine analogy.

First premise

As we succeed in broadening and deepening our knowledge— theoretical and empirical—about computers, we discover that in large part their behavior is governed by simple general laws, that what appeared as complexity in the computer program was to a considerable extent complexity of the environment to which the program was seeking to adapt its behavior.

(Simon, 1969/1996, p. 21)

Simon parlays this observation into what is, for him, an important methodological insight: namely, that the relation of program to environment invites us to see computers as being organized like human programmers—at least intellectively. If so, then the next major premise follows.

Second premise

For if it is the organization of components, and not their physical properties, that largely determines behavior . . . then the computer becomes an obvious device for exploring the consequences of alternative organizational assumptions for human behavior.

(Simon, 1969/1996, p. 21)

Thus, psychology need not wait for solutions to problems of neurological organization but can move forward by studying how computers do what they do whenever they do anything that humans do. This brings us to the final premise.

Third premise

But I have argued that people—or at least their intellective component—may be relatively simple, that most of the complexity of their behavior [like that of computers] may be drawn from their environment, from their search for good designs.

(Simon, 1969/1996, p. 138)

From these premises Simon asserts the following conclusion.

Conclusion

Instead of just studying experimentally and observing naturalistically how humans adapt to a complex environment, one might instead and more conveniently study computer simulations of such adaptive behaviors, with realistic expectations of discovering the design principles underwriting their organizations (Simon, 1969/1996).

I now take a closer look at some of the problems raised by this simulation thesis.

Grounding and situating of symbols

A potential criticism of Simon's simulation thesis is that it fails to address two very important issues.

First, how do symbols conjure up in our understanding the objects, events, or circumstances to which they refer? If we label something, then the label is the symbol and the something is the referent that grounds the symbol's meaning in some original denotative context. Without such grounding, the symbol's meaning is left "free floating."

Second, and of equal importance as the grounding question, is to ask, "How is a symbol situated?" Situating a symbol requires establishing its conventions (rules) for use in different contexts. Whereas the grounding involves a symbol's denotative contexts, situating involves its connotative contexts. Consider an example.

If I tell a friend who is a healthy, robust athlete that he looks well, it means something quite different than my telling the same friend after a grueling battle against cancer that he looks well. In both cases, although denotatively speaking we refer to the same thing—our friend's state of health—common usage allows for connotative differences; these connotative differences are revealed by making explicit the tacitly agreed on implicit phrase "under the prevailing circumstances and standards" (e.g., referring to $fitness_1$ standards, as applied to athletes, as opposed to $fitness_2$ standards, as applied to terminal cancer patients). If we interchange the situations and use the wrong standards—$fitness_1$ in the place of $fitness_2$ and vice versa—our statements would be inappropriate and misleading, although they continue to refer to the same grounding, namely, my friend's state of health.

Thus, there are two kinds of conventional rules involved here: Grounding requires rules of reference that specify what the symbol denotes (refers to), whereas situating requires rules of usage that specify what the symbol connotes (means in context). Usually such rules are not explicit but come as part of the presuppositional framework shared by native speakers of the same language culture.

Furthermore, as a shorthand for the previous discussion, I shall speak of such denotative and connotative conventions being "reducible" for a symbol if both its grounding referent and situating contexts can, in principle, be made explicit by perceptual means (e.g., by demonstration or example). I shall have occasion to return to the grounding and situating of symbols, in cases in which their conventions are either reducible or irreducible, as the case may be.

In anticipation, a case is made that unless direct specification (in Gibson's sense) is involved in both the grounding and situating of symbols, Simon's simulation approach is unable to guarantee that the involved conventions are reducible. Consider a case that illustrates how ungrounded symbols might nevertheless take on a life of their own when situating efforts are rather extreme. The main point of the example is to suggest a way that symbolic representations (internal models) may assume a kind of fictive or virtual reality even when their conventions are irreducible.

Cost of making ungrounded symbols come alive

Imagine a slightly delusional bride who, as an orphaned child with no known relatives and to avoid loneliness, invents a fictitious sister as a playmate. She convinces her new husband that although she has no sister, he must act as if she did if he wants her to be happy. Because he wishes only for her happiness, he agrees to cooperate in every way. Thus, they set out to orchestrate carefully all the various and sundry ways that others might be persuaded of her existence. They invent a place for her in their lives thereafter, even setting an extra place for her at the dinner table. They are so convincing in their scam that friends, neighbors, and the husband's relatives come to believe in the fictitious sister's existence. Over the years this ruse begins to steamroll, precipitating a full-blown clinical case of folie à deux (shared delusion).

For instance, they begin to place presents for the mythical sister under the Christmas tree, put her in their wills, get her a post-office box, subscriptions to magazines, memberships in social organizations, a place on donor lists of charity and political organizations, a social security number, an e-mail address, a Web page, a driver's license, declare her beneficiary to their insurance policies, co-owner of their home, a telemarketing job that she does from her home, payment of her taxes, a disabled dependent on their income tax, collect her social security retirement checks, and finally—because all good things must come to an end—a funeral, complete with the burial of her coffin marked by an elaborate headstone, followed by the lighting of votive candles in the cathedral and annual pilgrimages to weep by the grave side on the anniversary of the sister's "death." In this way, we can see how symbols, although merely virtual entities, may become situated in the real world by taking up actual space in virtual environments (i.e., being listed, counted, and corresponded with), having an institutional, social, and familial identity, and using actual resources.

As pointed out, grounding and situating symbols necessarily involve reducing conventions through perceptual means. One criticism of Simon's simulation strategy is that it does not involve such perceptual means where they are most needed. Here is one reason for this criticism.

It is often said that the proper study of mankind is man himself; Simon suggested the corollary that a proper study of mankind might also be computers that may serve as a convenient source of solutions that also apply to humans. The study of the artificial is a surrogate for life forms. This simulation strategy has been attacked for being too reductionistic in flavor (Clancey, 1997; Clark, 1997; Rosen, 1991). For if we study only the intellective analogies between artificial and human systems, are we not ignoring the embodiment problems in which actions are guided by perception in real-world situations? Simon did not suggest that this should be our only study, but his emphasis is clearly on the side of intellective modeling rather than situated modeling, and his technique of choice is clearly simulation. This approach favors the goals of systems that stand alone, outside of contexts, and belies any claim of strategic interest in situated cognition.

As is seen a little later, ecological psychology takes an entirely different tack, being more in line with the notion of synergy modeling with its natural concerns for how systems are situated. Under attack from theorists who thought he had shortchanged the problem of situated cognition and situated action (Clancey, 1997; Costall & Leudar, 1996; Greeno, 1989; Lave, 1988; Suchman, 1987), Simon made a belated attempt to show that his approach had always been in line with situated action and even to some extent with ecological psychology (Vera & Simon, 1993). Simon's critics were not appeased.

Was Simon justified in his claim of being a proponent of ecological or situated theory? I consider his case.

Simon's brush with ecological psychology

Another way of framing Simon's thesis is to say that the agent is made to look complex by using relatively simple decision making and control capabilities in response to the complicated demands and local vicissitudes of the task environment. Viewed this way, the complexity arises in situ and de novo at each engagement of a new task but is not present in the agent per se otherwise. If so, Simon's syllogism implies that very simple rule systems might be used to simulate goal-directed behaviors even though the behaviors themselves appear inordinately complex. This however puts me in mind of something I once said.

Once as a budding young cognitive psychologist, I was challenged by a radical behaviorist of some repute to explain how the new psychology would explain the abundant evidence supporting stimulus–response association theory. My brief answer was quite irksome to him. I said, "I think association theory only applies when the 'mind' is turned off." One might likewise conjecture that, according to Simon, the principles of computational psychology appear in their most elegant and unvarnished form when the system fails to engage a situated task, that is, when the requirement for being situated is also "turned off."

If so, in Simon's view, then a theory of complexity is needed for the environment and for understanding the agent's interactions with task situations but not for understanding the agent taken in isolation. The agent, whether computer or life form, will be a simple system of rules. This is Simon's ploy for avoiding complexity that has so bedeviled simulation theory. However, do agents and their agency as psychological creatures functioning in real-world tasks have any meaning when they are de-situated and not ecologically involved? Is a simple rule system even capable of being an agent in the full psychological sense of the word? I consider the daunting requirements.

Local exigencies are the inevitable demands placed on an agent in controlling its behavior by the details of the current context that may thwart or misdirect its efforts. *Local expedients* are the tailored solutions that the agent brings to bear to nullify the local exigencies and thereby accommodate its behavior to the current task demands. *Situational dynamics* is a term I use to denote the processes by which such context conditioned variability is imposed on the agent's behavior by the perturbing details of real-world contexts (e.g., a bicycle rider zig-zagging to avoid potholes while trying to stay on course). Such perturbing details are surely typical and ubiquitous.

I can now summarize what I mean by situated action, that is, the actions of a situated agent: To be a situated agent, a system must apply local expedients that are capable of overcoming local exigencies that arise inevitably from any real-world situation. Notice that by situating agents one situates all the agent's capabilities at once; hence, situated action, situated perception, situated cognition, situated problem solving, and so forth are as unnecessary and as misleading as early attempts of psychologists to isolate mental faculties. Such attempts are a throwback to the reductionistic strategy of mechanists who believed that to divide was to conquer. It now seems that such divisions simply eliminate the truly interesting and challenging properties of complex systems. By situating the agent, it is unnecessary that each of these faculties be treated separately. Ecological psychology should have as its goal a theory of situated agency at the ecological scale, and let the rest follow as it may.

Here is the major thwart to a simulation strategy. No rule for predicting the contextual exigencies can be written; no way is known for simulating specific contexts because their denotative richness and their connotative implications are unbounded. A theory of contexts, as characterized by different kinds of challenging details, would be just as hard to come by as a description of the commonsense knowledge used in different real-world (connotative) contexts. Both are too broad and unpredictable to be simulated.

Nature, however, has solved this problem by endowing agents with perceptual means to become situationally aware of those affordances that serve the agent's interests (intentions) and sufficiently effective in their actions to realize the relevant goals afforded. Furthermore, being situationally aware is a simpler requirement for agents evolved for such duty than being computationally able to simulate such a capability. The inability to achieve the latter has nothing to do with having the ability to achieve the former.

Whereas a programmer must be able to describe all relevant situations before they can be entered into a simulation program, agents need only be aware of what the details afford. Indeed, awareness is needed to apply any rule, even a simple one. This clearly cannot be accomplished by writing a prior rule, for such leads to an infinite regress without awareness ever becoming grounded. *Hence, it is a gross and flagrant error to think that there can be a rule-based simulation of awareness when awareness is needed for the detail to which the rule must apply.* This point cannot be emphasized too strongly!

Being situationally aware of all relevant detail may be like having a look-up table with endless entries prescribing what is to be done when certain thwarting detail is encountered in every case imaginable; but how would the look-up table ever get constructed for each agent, and even if it did, how would the retrieval issues get resolved? An agent who had to consult such a table would be stultified at every move seeking the proper prescriptions for behavior. An agent who had to have such a table to act would be forever exploring every context with every possible intent in mind to see what detail might be appropriate to that given intent. There must be a better way. Consider the attempt to simulate a master chess player.

It is cheating to begin with the playing of a game, for the first requirement is for the agent to recognize in what situations it is appropriate to play the game. Just seeing a chessboard and pieces is not sufficient. Is it your board or someone else's (e.g., on the counter at a store, or one someone else is getting ready to use, or one belonging to a person who wants to play but is known to become homicidal when he loses)? How well should you play against a young child, against a person who is terminally ill that you would like to cheer up, against another master? In tournament play, which classical strategies should you choose at which point in a game against whom? A simulation must have a look-up table for all strategies, indexed against all social situations on all different occasions, played under all possible varieties of provisional conditions. Describing all the relevant detail and factors needed to situate a symbolic agent in a virtual game is only feasible because the virtual situation is virtual and not real.

In real-world situations it would be wise to include a real agent in the loop as the synergy approach admonishes so that at least one system component might comtribute the requisite situational awareness—especially because there is no substitute. Computational resources might then be used to help focus the agent where needed or broaden its perspective.

In short, even assuming that rules for simulating the awareness of real-world contexts were possible, the list of ad hoc provisos that would be needed to allow a programmer to take into consideration all situations and their provisions is a demand impossible to fulfill operationally. The fallacy committed by thinking that such unrealistic demands might be satisfied is known as Tristram Shandy's paradox—the fallacy of trying to describe in words (or formulae or programs) that which is experienced in real time in real-world situations. Because any radical simulation project inescapably encounters this paradox, we would do well to examine it.

The Tristram Shandy paradox

From 1760 to 1767, Laurence Sterne (1760–1767/1983) published nine volumes of a comic novel titled *The Life and Opinions of Tristram Shandy, Gentleman*, as an "autobiography" of Tristram Shandy who is committed to the impossible task of omitting nothing from his life's story. Sterne's volumes are actually a meditation on performatory storytelling putatively describing, in nonlinear episodes, Shandy's view of his own life. Sterne has Shandy write so slowly that it takes him a year to complete only 1 day in his life; given the unfinished result, this is still way too fast. Thus, the most recent event recorded is the day that occurred 1 year ago, the 2nd day 2 years ago, and so forth. Each additional day takes him another year to complete. The threads of events splay out in all directions, as one tangent after another is engaged in a futile effort to omit nothing of consequence —resulting in a hopeless jumble of discursive narratives, with cause and effect chains never quite reaching closure.

The question is why does 1 day take a year to describe—even incompletely and incomprehensibly? The answer is obvious in this one regard: Whereas narrative logic of events must be organized sequentially by the writer using explanatory "time tags," the natural logic by which the events unfold requires no such imposed order; and so, it is with futile attempts at simulations of real-time situated events. Time tags are not required for real events that have an intrinsic time course but are indispensable for those same events when symbolic conventions are employed in their description— making them appear as endless digressions.

This is the difference between knowledge by description as opposed to knowledge by acquaintance, between third-person attempts to describe from the outside first-person events experienced from the inside. Simulations are always necessarily of this sort in their vain effort to replace direct perceptions with indirect ones involving representations.

Perhaps the closest a third-person description may approach first-person experiences would be in hypertext formulations of the narrative. However, even then real nonlinear choices that happen spontaneously in life must be organized by a judicious and laborious adherence to conventions that steer the reader down multilinear avenues and byways, often ending in cul-de-sacs or simply petering out. Such conventions must be changeable in a nearly arbitrary fashion, as later events reveal facts that require recasting the interpretation of earlier events. Hence, some rules for updating what has already been written would make continual revision unavoidable and, I fear, unspecifiable by any rule. No wonder Sterne's Shandy is a frustrated autobiographer who alternates between the comical and the pathetic.

Guthrie (n.d.) makes the so-called Tristram Shandy paradox explicit:

> For a precise view of the problem, I will show the paradox numerically. The paradox posits an autobiographer who writes on every day passed. Since it takes Shandy one year (=365 days) to complete one day, then in terms of a one-to-one correspondence it would appear to be futile on a finite level:

Observed History: 1 day, 2 days, 3 days, 4 days, 5 days, . . .
Recorded History: 365 days, 730 days, 1095 days, 1460 days,
1825 days, . . .

It would seem mathematically impossible for Shandy to complete
writing on all the days passed. Since each day yields an additional
365 days to write then it would seem that the longer Shandy wrote,
the further behind he would get.

An even more intriguing insight into the Tristram Shandy paradox as
a logic of digression was suggested by Parker (1997). She suggested that
Sterne (1760–1767/1983) conceived of Tristram Shandy's autobiography as
a way to subvert linear narratives of its time, which move predictably to a
steady state in which their action ceases. Moreover, if Sterne had had access
to the graphical representations of contemporary nonlinear dynamical
systems theory (i.e., chaos theory), then his narrative might have been
appropriately represented as a chaotic, or strange, attractor such as the
butterfly attractor (see Figure 1).

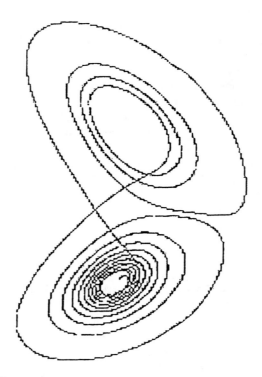

Figure 1 Butterfly attractor.

Although here we see only a two-dimensional representation of this strange attractor, it actually evolves in a multidimensional state space. Its trajectories diverge at one time and almost converge at another but never actually intersect. Instead, they are attracted to unstable points that are never reached. Tristram Shandy's complex narrative with its digressive logic behaves like a chaotic dynamical system that explores a bounded arena of infinite possibility. This is worse than an NP-complete problem, although both show that linear excursions can never express the totality of nonlinear ones involved. (NP problems are those that can be-solved by a nondeterministic Turing machine in polynomial time, e.g., the traveling salesman problem. Unfortunately, at this time the only algorithms we have are exponential in rime as a function of the problem size. In a landmark paper, Karp, 1972, showed that 21 intractable combinatorial computational problems are all NP complete.)

I think Parker (1997) hit the nail on the head, just as did von Neumann (1949/1966), who expressed pessimism at the prospect of giving explicit formulations of complex phenomena in either words or formulae. Some levels of complexity cannot ever be simulated; they must be directly experienced to be fully appreciated. The Tristram Shandy paradox is the metaphor for the theme explored in this article—the decline of mechanism.

The general semantic fallacy: where symbols take on a life of their own

Simon (1969/1996) explained that the kinds of symbols he had in mind are physical rather than abstract:

> Symbol systems are called "physical" to remind the reader that they exist as real-world devices, fabricated of glass and metal (computers) or flesh and blood (brains). In the past we have been more accustomed to thinking of the symbol systems of mathematics and logic as abstract and disembodied, leaving out of account the paper and pencil and human minds that were required actually to bring them to life.
>
> (p. 22)

If, like Simon, one treats symbols as physical objects, then their existence and manipulation should require work be done to sustain them in their role as representations (Shaw & McIntyre, 1974). In addition to the physical role of a symbol, it has a primary semantic role as a representation. We recognize that different physical symbols may play identical semantic roles, as in the case of written words and the words spoken by different voices or notes on a musical score and the same notes played by different instruments. However, to confuse the physical symbol with the semantic referent is to pervert the role of the symbol as a semantic function.

307

It is for this reason that it is wise to distinguish the *symbol vehicle* (physical object that functions as a symbol) from the *symbol function*, which may be carried out by different symbol vehicles. Not to make this distinction is to confuse the meaning of the symbol with the symbol vehicle, as when we confuse flesh and blood individuals with the social stereotypes we have set up, or react to the shouted warning "Fire!" as if there is a fire. The general semantic fallacy is the unwarranted identification of the two. This is why prejudice, being based on a fallacy, is deservedly abhorred. Of course there is no fallacy if the identification of the two is warranted; rather, the symbol function serves its legitimate purpose, for example, as in escaping from a fire because of an early warning.

I dramatize this fallacy to make clear how serious the abuse of symbol functions can be and how extreme forms of radical representationalism may create a kind of virtual but false reality by exploiting them—a pseudo-reality that simulates nothing real but is utterly fictitious and yet can incur real costs.

The situating process, such as the symbolic sister cum sister-in-law, can be insinuated as symbols of great import and significance into people's lives to whatever extent people allow themselves to become obsessively delusional. In a nonpejorative sense, people should recognize that ideals expressed institutionally become situated into their lives and the culture in just this way—ideals ranging from legends like Robin Hood, Santa Claus, and the tooth fairy to national heroes (e.g., Tomb of the Unknown Soldier) and religious icons (e.g., recall Albert Schweitzer's famous book *In Search of the Historical Jesus*).

I should not forget to mention scientific ideals that are later repudiated (e.g., phlogiston, the ether) or innocent people wrongly convicted by kangaroo courts on trumped up charges, the Spanish inquisition, the Salem witch trials, the infamous Nazi conspiratorial campaign against European Jews, gypsies, and political dissenters, and the unfounded propaganda, in general, that for centuries has moved nations to go to war against other nations for distorted and ill-conceived motives such as religious differences (e.g., the Crusades and other so-called holy wars). Situating ungrounded symbols is no less serious business because it is fictive.

To return to my earlier example, we saw how a social contrivance such as a mythical sister can be made to enjoy symbolic familial relationships as well as communal, social, and even legal ones. As this network of relationships becomes more extensive and its details more complete, the symbol becomes a "living" symbol with its own biographical history. The main point of the sham-sister example is to illustrate what is meant by the idea of *generative closure*, the idea that a complex of real objects can exhibit more mutual entailments than there are objects actually in the complex. The complex is a kind of functional scheme that organizes parents, siblings, sons and daughters, aunts and uncles, and brothers and sisters by shared blood lines.

However, it also can be legally extended by marriage contracts to "relatives-in-law." Here the abstract schema for the complex (e.g., family tree) comprises all relations a wife might have and not just the ones that the wife in question does have, hence the potential for unaccounted for sisters who may be unseen or previously unknown. Circumstantial evidence, as opposed to eye-witness grounding of the mythical sister, may be sufficient as long as no recalcitrant skeptic decides to check all credentials back to their source.

More generally, having generative closure over the functional relations of a complex means that if a real object in the complex were removed, it would leave a "hole" that might be filled by a symbolic surrogate. It also means the manufacture of whatever credentials and relationships that a real object in the complex might have had can be inherited by a surrogate that replaces it. An only child still belongs to the complex with a potential for siblings. This is what "only" here connotes. By contrast to this generative *completion*, as the filling of empty places in an incomplete complex schema, one can also see generative *impletion* at work whenever the truth is embroidered in people's attempts to pay homage to departed friends, relatives, and public figures—especially as shown in ancestor worship and the forging of heroic legendary figures from more modest factual lives.

In this way, in the case of the sham sister, one can see how even an ungrounded symbol can have a place manufactured for it by situating it in the relational complex. When formalized, this is called *possible worlds logic*, in which interpretations of objects and events are taken as pragmatically true if they remain consistent over the greatest number of interlocking scenarios (i.e., possible worlds) that attempt to incorporate the putative facts. Here history books are different from historical fiction in just this way. Also, the judgment of good science fiction as opposed to bad science fiction is based on how well the former fits with accepted scientific facts and principles and how poorly the latter does.

The fact that symbols may be situated even when they are not grounded in existence shows clearly that the situating of a symbol and its grounding are logically distinct; one may situate an ungrounded symbol (unfounded beliefs that control behavior) but one cannot ground a symbol without situating it to some extent (to see its grounding is to see its situation). Situating can be achieved through secondhand knowledge dissemination, but grounding requires firsthand experience.

These cases show that a symbol functions best when it fits most tightly into our possible world scenarios. This is the way that a symbol becomes situated. Grounding a symbol requires, in addition, that one can be made ostensively aware of the direct specification of the symbol's referent. Without that, people have no firsthand knowledge and must rely on the situating of that knowledge secondhand in their belief systems. It is the playing off of situating as a kind of coherence theory of truth and meaning against grounding, a kind of correspondence theory, which perhaps characterizes best the ecological theory of meaning. In it there is room for both direct specification vis-à-vis grounding and indirect specification vis-à-vis situating. These are dual processes pertaining, respectively, to increasing the scope of a symbol's insinuation into people's experiences as opposed to the precision with which it is incorporated.

If I see something bizarre that is utterly alien to me and label this experience, then that label is grounded, if not very well situated, beyond the context in which I experienced it. Conversely, if I see something so familiar that I scarcely take note of it but can readily label it if called on to do so, then that label is well situated in my experience but not very well grounded. In conclusion, one can see that a symbol serves as a virtual (fictive) substitute for real entities with real relationships to other real entities that it itself cannot fully enjoy. As a fiction, the symbol can only inherit those meanings bestowed on it by virtue of its membership in the relational complex. Take away its grounding situation in the real complex and the symbol becomes only a naked object stripped of its power to represent.

The success of actors, magicians, propagandists, advertising agencies, and con artists rests on how well they can promote the general semantic fallacy convincingly to a segment of the public for a certain length of time. Their incomes and uses of facilities and resources are real costs that may or may not serve legitimate purposes. They do serve a legitimate purpose if both of the following conditions are satisfied: first, the referent of the symbol function exists so the representations are grounded; and second, if they are properly situated in that what they afford is clearly specified.

In science, the general semantic fallacy gives rise to theories whose models may, at best, be consistent but untrue. Hence, there is no substitute for models being held to empirical accountability.

Simon and the Gibsonian alternative

There is a real danger that simulation models may unwittingly promote the general semantic fallacy and waste substantial resources because they blindly pursue goals blocked by the Tristram Shandy paradox. Is it wise to shift the lion's share of the burden of explanation to simulation environments, as Simon admonished us to do, where complexities may be too easily fabricated through symbol function abuse? Is this not going to make the simulation approach to interface design theory too chancy and costly to pursue? I am not suggesting that simulation is useless—in restricted contexts it can be a useful tool (e.g., doing dry runs to train people when the actual trial runs would prove too dangerous or costly)—only that it would be too dangerous to depend on it as a sole or primary means to theory construction and evaluation.

A viable alternative is to be sought in synergy approaches that appreciate and demand embodiment, situating, and grounding. I am not alone in recommending this cautionary advice. One articulate defender of the need for embodied and embedded cognition, such as what robots might require, made this appraisal of the simulation approach:

> Simulation offers at best an impoverished version of the real-world arena, and a version impoverished in some dangerous ways: ways that threaten to distort our image of the operation of agents by obscuring the contributions of environmental features and of real physical bodies.
>
> (Clark, 1997, p. 96)

The Gibsonian thesis is of course different from Simon's, which argues for a simple agent but a complex environment: Ecological psychology, being synergistic, aims to strike a balance between the two components of eco-systems so as not to obscure the contribution of either to the interaction. This strategy involves moving to higher levels of environmental description, that of objects and events and their invariant information that specify their affordance properties—those functional descriptions that allow the environment to be seen in terms of the actions and choices organisms might actually need to make. Simon made statements that seem on the surface to repudiate Clark's (1997) criticism of the simulation approach while also being consistent with the ecological thesis just offered:

> This position should not be interpreted as suggesting that internal representations should be the central focus of investigation in understanding the relation between behavior and cognition. On the contrary, information processing theories fundamentally and neces-sarily involve the architecture's relation to the environment. The symbolic approach does not focus narrowly on what is in the head without concern for the relation between the intelligent system and its surround. . . . A fundamental problem for cognitive modelers is to interleave internal and external states in order to achieve natur-alistic behavior.
>
> (Vera & Simon, 1993, p. 12)

Also, just as others have attempted to align ecological psychology with situated action or cognition theory (Clancey, 1997; Costall & Leudar, 1996; Greeno, 1989; Lave, 1988; Suchman, 1987), so Simon tried to co-opt his critics by aligning his computationalism with situated action or cognition theory. For instance, in opening their article, Vera and Simon (1993) declared the following:

> In this article, we wish to examine whether SA [i.e., situated action] is actually antithetical to symbolic manipulation. To anticipate our

conclusions, we find that there is no such antithesis: SA systems are symbolic systems, and some past and present symbolic systems are SA systems. The symbolic systems appropriate to tasks calling for situated action do, however, have special characteristics that are interesting in their own right.

(p. 8)

One must wonder what it tells us about situated action or cognition theory that attempts have been made to align it with both computational and ecological psychology? Can it really stand on such neutral ground, or can ecological and computational psychology actually be so similar in spirit? Simon thought situated action theory can be neutral but that situated action theorists do not see this because they have unfortunately and mistakenly thrown in with ecological psychology in denouncing representational theory. These issues are a little slippery at first because Simon clearly implied that his view is ecological, but it soon becomes clear that it is not ecological in the Gibsonian sense. Like Gibson, Simon's theory is philosophically layered; hence, it is possible to find different degrees of agreement and disagreement at different layers.

Although an unrepentant cognitivist and unrelenting mediation theorist, Simon, like Gibson, was also a functionalist. Furthermore, he not only used the term *affordance* but gave a kind of begrudging recognition of its centrality to his cognitive computationalism. This brief isolated flirtation with ecological psychology and situated action or cognition theory seems to have been only a temporary expedient designed to confound his critics. If so, then one is not surprised that Simon (so far as I have been able to determine) never returned to these issues after the special issue of *Cognitive Science* in 1993 ("Situated Action," 1993). Neither is one terribly surprised that he used the concept of affordance so perversely, violating Gibson's original intent when he coined it, as clearly indicated by the quote in the epigraphs asserting that an "affordance is a symbol stored in central memory" (Vera & Simon, 1993, p. 79).

Despite Simon's tentative embrace of ecological psychology, it is still instructive to ask why he did so at all. Simon was too serious a scientist and scholar to merely act perversely. I suggest another reason. He saw the ecological approach as anathema to his own view, recognizing that if it stood, then his must fail. Both could not be simultaneously true. A coupling between an organism and its environment could not be accomplished by direct specification (information in Gibson's sense) but only by symbolic mediation (information in Simon's sense). His attitude toward this competitive theory was dismissive if not contemptuous. I see no evidence that he ever seriously tried to understand it. I could be wrong, but this was the impression I gained from my few personal conversations with him. His apparent disinterest in our approach might justify our disinterest in his approach, but it does not diminish the value of using him as a foil for understanding Gibson.

Another point of intersection and conflict concerns Simon's and Gibson's inconsistent hypotheses regarding how organisms as perceiving, acting, and thinking agents interface with their environments so as to perceive it, act on it, and think about it (e.g., make plans and decisions about goals). Simon and Gibson had two diametrically opposed hypotheses regarding how agents and environments interfaced: For Simon it was indirect, being mediated through symbolic representations; for Gibson it was direct, being unmediated and achieved by specification.

Perhaps, the key comparison to be made is whether the coupling envisioned is assumed to be law or rule governed. A rule, as intuitively conceived in cognitive science, is akin to the notion of a recursive rule as used in abstract machine theory, the mathematical foundation of computational science. Not always recognized, or left unemphasized if recognized, is that Gibson also used the term *rule* but in a quite different sense than recursive. Because these might be confused, I need to make their differences clear. In fact, one of the main aims of this commentary is to explore this issue. One chief difference to be discovered is that whereas Gibson's use of rules holds because it is underwritten by law, Simon's are only underwritten by convention.

The key issue in both cases is how these two conceptions of rule relate to or rely on the deeper notion of natural laws. A full understanding of this topic suggests that I delve still deeper into Simon's (1969/1996) motivations for *The Sciences of the Artificial*. Consequently, I do so next in a way tailored to my purposes.

The sciences of the artificial

As clear as Simon's (1969/1996) book is overall, there are certain difficulties faced by any reviewer of any persuasion. One difficulty is that Simon sometimes makes equivocal pronouncements where one might have hoped for something more definite. This is not to say his views are wishy-washy, only that in his candor and conservatism Simon refused to feign a clarity that seems to him unjustified by the state of current knowledge. For example, he used such phrases as "to hedge my bets" rather than just "making a bet," or "having the air of necessity" rather than simply "being necessary."

In fairness, however, such circumlocutions do not detract from Simon's theses but actually strengthens their credibility although by no means makes them entirely convincing. Moreover, by judiciously avoiding the temptation to make overclaims, Simon's judgment in other matters seems more prudent and trustworthy. Furthermore, Simon's prose, in addition to being eloquent, has a most remarkable rational appeal, even to one whose orientation may be quite different. I often found myself liking the way Simon said something even when I disagreed with what he said.

Mostly, however, the book (Simon, 1969/1996) is for those who buy into the general computational philosophy. Whether a champion of AI or simulation, the appeal for the computationalist is that Simon's arguments project clear directions for theory and research. Alternatively, even those who are neither computer scientists nor psychologists might expect to find in this book issues of fundamental importance to their fields. I review his chief claims.

Simon (1969/1996) recognized four properties as indicative of the artificial:

1. Artificial things are synthesized by human agents—either intentionally or unintentionally.
2. Artificial things may simulate natural things in some ways but not all.
3. Artificial things can be characterized intentionally in terms of functions, goals, and adaptation.
4. Artificial things connote the imperative as well as the descriptive.

Under the broad heading of the *sciences of the artificial* and in contrast to the sciences of the natural, Simon addressed a number of issues of significance to cognitive psychology, an important one being how we should conceptualize life forms as opposed to inanimate objects. He offered many important, difficult, and often surprising theses, and defended them most eloquently if not always cogently—a fact, however, which seems not to have lessened their general appeal among cognitivists and computationalists.

By contrast, because they focus on the natural, the theses of ecological psychology, it seems to me, arise in contradistinction to the theses Simon proposed for the artificial. Hence, careful consideration of his theses may help us understand our own a little better.

An ecological exegesis of Simon's main theses

Simon listed the following characteristics among his most significant claims about artificial phenomena. Following each, I note the exceptions ecological psychologists might take, which in all but one case implies a counter thesis.

Psychology deals primarily with the artificial rather than the natural

Here, assuming I take the natural as being law governed and the artificial as rule governed, ecological and computational psychology are at loggerheads regarding whether laws or rules are the most appropriate explanatory construct. Gibson (1979/1986) himself introduced the notion of a rule for the perceptual control of action (e.g., locomotion or manipulation). Does this imply agreement with Simon's thesis? No, as Gibson's attempt to elucidate his sense of rule makes clear:

> I asserted that behavior was controlled by *rules*. Surely, however, they are not rules enforced by an authority. The rules are not commands from a brain; they emerge from the animal–environment system. But the only way to describe rules is in words, and a rule expressed in words is a command. I am faced with a paradox. The rules for the control of locomotion will sound like commands, although they are not intended to. I can only suggest that the reader should interpret them as rules *not formulated in words*.
>
> (pp. 232–233)

One could just as easily substitute the term *symbol* for the term *word* without changing Gibson's intent, and thus rule out programs represented in the head as a means for reifying the imperative thrust of rules for the perceptual control of actions. This is, perhaps, Gibson's most explicit statement about the meaning of rule as he used it. It implies a clear rejection of Simon's computational thesis. Perhaps what he had in mind was more akin to the medieval logicians' notion of deontic law than to a recursive rule.

The *deontic law* is the basis for an imperative logic, one that governs the obligatory actions that must be taken because they are needed to attain some sought after end (i.e., if z is the end sought and w must be done to achieve z, then one is obliged to do w to have z). As Simon (1969/1996) pointed out, there seems to be a need for "a distinct logic of imperatives, or a normative, deontic logic" (p. 115); therefore, it is not surprising that "there have been a number of constructions of modal logic for handling 'should,' 'shalts,' and 'oughts' of various kinds" (p. 115). Although Simon's means–ends analysis seems a natural expression of a deontic law and might have made this medieval notion central to his approach, he demurred from its pursuit because in his opinion "none of these systems has been sufficiently developed or sufficiently widely applied to demonstrate that it is adequate to handle the logical requirements of the process of design" (p. 115). (Later we shall see that Gibson posed rules for action that have need of a logic of imperatives. Moreover, a law at the ecological scale is deontic in just this sense.)

Consequently, although Simon (1969/1996) was quite aware of the relevance of deontic laws to his notion of means–ends analysis, he rightly demurred from such treatment because he found the current understanding of the logic of such laws both flawed and incomplete. In spite of this, and with a renewed interpretation of deontic law, it seems to me that both Simon's and Gibson's rules for intentional actions may be appropriately treated as different renditions of the notion of a deontic law. This claim deserves treatment at another time. (This promissory note is offered because I have, for some years, worked toward an acceptable interpretation of the deontic law for ecological psychology.)

One should also note carefully that both ecological and artificial sciences do not differ because the former is *physical* and the latter *mental*—in keeping with the old Cartesian chestnut—but rather both sciences putatively have physical foundations. Indeed, it would quite miss the point if Simon were simply dismissed as being a mentalist. Although he did rely on symbolic representations as mediating internal states, symbols are for Simon physical objects that have psychological consequences.

Consequently, it is nearer the truth to say that Simon's science of the artificial has more to do with Gibson's indirect perception by means of artifacts than it does with Gibson's direct perception that does not depend on artifacts at all. For this reason, it behooved Simon to try to relegate direct perception to being a derivative epiphenomenon of efficient computational architecture, as he indeed did.

Finally, Simon divided the world into natural and artificial phenomena, whereas Gibson, not denying the existence of artifacts, strongly disagreed that this should be a fundamental distinction:

> Why has man changed the shapes and substances of his environment? To change what it affords him . . . this is not a new environment—an artificial environment distinct from the natural environment—but the same old environment modified by man. It is a mistake to separate the natural from the artificial as if there were two environments, artifacts have to be manufactured from natural substances. It is also a mistake to separate the cultural environment from the natural environment, as if there were a world of mental products distinct from the world of material products. There is only one world, however diverse, and all animals live in it, although we human animals have altered it to suit ourselves. We have done so wastefully, thoughtlessly and, if we do not mend our ways, fatally.
>
> (Gibson, 1979/1986, p. 130)

For Gibson affordances are most natural, and all things have them, artifacts not excluded; hence, artifacts are as natural in their affordances as anything else in the environment. Some things have bad affordance and some good regardless of their origin; our job is to act so as to maximize the good ones and minimize the bad ones. Thus, any design theory to be of ecological significance, must shoulder this responsibility.

The inner environment is simple, whereas the outer environment is complex

Here Simon meant by the *outer environment* a physical environment that gives rise to functional meanings, and by *inner environment* he meant the constitution and organization of the agent biologically. How the functional description is to be handled vis-à-vis the notion of affordances is the issue and a source of disagreement. Still there is broad agreement on where a smart coupling is required. Ecological psychologists should, then, applaud Simon's choice of problems as well as his general functionalism—if not the exact form it takes.

The interface sought should relate rather than cleave the seam separating agents from their environments and, unlike Simon, I think it theoretically more useful to seek a balance in complexity across the two components —that there must be a fit between what the environment furnishes and what the agent can attain—if adaptability is to be achieved and sustained.

On the other hand, we should not agree with Simon's second claim that the organism and environment are disproportionally complex. The complexity of the environmental situation and the organism should be functionally matched at the moment the agent commits itself to an action that proves successful. Failure may result, however, from the inability of the actor to solve Bernstein's degrees of freedom problem, for example, in achieving macrocoordination over its microneuromuscular-skeletal variables. How and why this functional balance should be achieved has been spelled out in mathematical detail (but I fear generally ignored because it is too abstract). The case for favoring theoretical interpretations of the agent–environment coupling that keeps complexity functionally balanced across the ecological interface can be found in Shaw, Flascher, and Kadar (1995) and Shaw, Kadar, Sim, and Repperger (1992).

Finally, tacitly, if not explicitly, such a balance principle provides the theoretical and methodological foundations for what has been called *ecological interface design* (Effken, Kim, & Shaw, 1997; Vicente, 1999). Moreover, for this reason my colleagues and I (Shaw & Kinsella-Shaw, 1988; Shaw, Kugler, & Kinsella-Shaw, 1990; Shaw & Todd, 1980) were motivated to introduce the idea of intentional dynamics as a way to explain how effectivities can match affordances under conditions that allow actions to succeed in goal attainment.

Complex systems can be reduced to simpler form by proper description

On its face, this claim seems unquestionably valid but surprisingly an opposing case can be made that, for systems beyond a certain level of finite complexity, no verbal description or mathematical formulation can reduce its complexity. In fact, an even more pessimistic conjecture may be warranted. John von Neumann (1949/1966), the great Hungarian American mathematician and to many the father of the computer revolution in the United States, as Turing was in Great Britain, made a startlingly pessimistic claim about the difficulties faced by those who would design so-called pattern recognition programs:

> It is not absolutely clear a priori that there is any simpler description of what constitutes a visual analogy than a description of the visual brain. . . . Normally a literary description of what an automaton is supposed to do is simpler than the complete diagram of the automaton. It is not true a priori that this will also be so. There is a good deal in formal logics to indicate that the description of the functions of an automaton is simpler than the automaton itself, as long as the automaton is not very complicated, but that when you get to high complications, the actual object is simpler than the literary description.
>
> (p. 47)

A little later in this book, von Neumann (1949/1966) gave a hint as to what he might have had in mind:

> It is characteristic of objects of low complexity that it is easier to talk about the object than produce it and easier to predict its properties than to build it. But in the complicated parts of formal logic it is always one order of magnitude harder to tell what an object can do than to produce the object. *The domain of validity of the question is of a higher type than the question itself* [italics added].
>
> (p. 51)

It is interesting to note that von Neumann (1949/1966) posed this conjecture decades before the class of NP-complete problems were identified by Cook (1971) and the search for them came into vogue (Karp, 1972). This and more recent developments in the study of complex systems lends credence to von Neumann's conjecture being prescient rather than merely speculative. As von Neumann said, "there is a good deal in formal logics" (p. 47) to support this conjecture. What sort of evidence might be germane?

It is clear that in the green years of the field there was little sympathy for taking von Neumann's (1949/1966) conjecture seriously, in spite of his prominence. Cognitive psychology in the 1960s was on the upswing and many of us as psychologists were holding onto the coattails of McCulloch and Pitts (1943), Craik (1943), Chomsky (1957, 1965), and Miller, Galanter, and Pribram (1960).

318

Simon's (1969/1996) attitude in the first edition of his book was as typical of its day as his attitude in the third edition is for today. For instance, Miller *et al.* (1960) voiced the sentiments of most cognitive psychologists in their classic book when they claimed the following:

> It seems to the present authors, that attempts to simulate psychological processes with machines are motivated in large measure by the desire to test—or to demonstrate—the designer's understanding of the theory he espouses. History suggests that man can create almost anything he can visualize clearly. The creation of a model is proof of the clarity of the vision. If you understand how a thing works well enough to build your own, then your understanding must be nearly perfect.
>
> (p. 46)

It is not clear at all that the history to which Miller *et al.* (1960) referred recounts any successes with complex systems. In 1976 I gave the following response to Miller *et al.*, which I still endorse today with even more confidence:

> Moreover, contrary to what Miller *et al.* claim, history shows that the mere knowledge of how to construct something, whether it be fire, a table-top planetarium, a picture, a cake, or an internal combustion engine, is far from being sufficient for a scientific understanding of the object created. *To be able to do something implies only that you know how to do it, not that you understand what it is you did* [italics added]. This is analogous to the fact that the learning of a skill may be quite different from the execution of the skill or that the programming of a computer may not involve the principles necessary to understand the most significant functioning of that program. The *skill, like the program, may serve as nothing more than a link in an immensely large nomological net of facts and principles which provide the full context required to understand the real significance of either skill or program* [italics added].
>
> (Shaw, 1976, p. 163)

As one who had struggled vainly with the problem of contexts for two decades—first as a Chomskian psycholinguist, then as a Piagetian, and finally as a Gibsonian—I fancy I had caught a glimmer of what was later to be celebrated as the problem of situated cognition and learning (Clancey, 1997). The problem proved both as recalcitrant as it was slippery.

In 1969, after some scathing reviews, I was finally able to publish an article reviewing the conjecture. The article was written while I was participating in a seminar on computational complexity taught by Juris Hartmanis at Cornell (Shaw, 1969, 1976). The article had already received high marks from Hartmanis—a pioneer and leader in the new field of computational complexity theory. At his insistence, my article only attempted to review a few fundamental theorems from formal logics and mathematics that von Neumann (1949/1966) might have used to make his case had they existed at the time. I was careful to avoid philosophical declarations but restricted myself to arguments based on the current state of the art of complexity that seemed to give foundation to von Neumann's conjecture: such issues as "speed-up" theorems (Blum, 1967; Hartmanis & Stearns, 1965), decomposability methods (Hartmanis & Stearns, 1966), and order–type complexity indexes (Minsky & Papert, 1969).

Despite this, I was pilloried and attacked in the field for daring to suggest that there may have been a rational basis for taking the conjecture seriously—especially because Gödel had himself thought there may have been something to it. Gödel gave this account of what he thought von Neumann (1949/1966) must have meant:

I think the theorem of mine which von Neumann refers to is not that on the existence of undecidable propositions or that on the lengths of proofs but rather the fact that a complete epistemological description of a language A cannot be given in the same language A, because the concept of truth of sentences A cannot be defined in A. It is this theorem which is the true reason for the existence of undecidable propositions in the formal systems containing arithmetic. . . . Now this theorem certainly shows that the description of what a mechanism is doing in certain cases is more involved than the description of the mechanism, in the sense that it requires new and more abstract primitive terms, namely higher types.
(as cited in von Neumann, 1949/1966, pp. 55–56)

Gödel went on to say that his same theorem was proved by Tarski a little earlier. With two notable logicians backing up von Neumann's conjecture, one might have thought it would have been taken more seriously than it was.

Ironically, despite the criticism I received for publicizing this conjecture, or perhaps because of it, I was still granted a lucrative and prestigious 5-year National Institutes of Health career development award to study such issues as they pertained to psychological modeling. I was surprised but felt partly vindicated. Still nothing much came of these efforts until Penrose (1989, 1994) and later Rosen (1991, 1999) revived this criticism in their arguments that living systems are complex exactly because they exhibit behaviors not algorithmically computable—a topic that has generated much controversy. The field has a habit of either ignoring what it cannot abide or trying to kill the messenger's credibility.

Many people who favored rule-governed learning and championed the budding field of computational psychology were extremely put off by my publicizing and defending this pessimistic conjecture and told me so in no uncertain terms. One of these was Simon, who told me at a later conference in Vail, Colorado (see Klahr, 1976), more or less, that I should not be surprised at being attacked because if the conjecture were true it cast aspersions on the new field of simulation at just the time support was needed if progress was to be made.

Not surprising, given the field's tendency for killing the messenger, Penrose (1989, 1994), who has severely criticized the strong computational thesis in two much publicized books, has himself in return been roundly criticized by ardent computationalists (e.g., see Penrose, 1996, in the electronic journal *Psyche*). From a history and sociology of science perspective, it is interesting to note that the temper of such debates has not changed.

Penrose (1996) expressed chagrin at the response of those true believers who take strong exception to his use of Gödel's theorem to justify rejecting the extreme computationalism thesis:

> For those who are wedded to computationalism, explanations of this nature may indeed seem plausible. But why should we be wedded to computationalism? I do not know why so many people seem to be. Yet, some apparently hold to such a view with almost religious fervour. (Indeed, they may often resort to unreasonable rudeness when they feel this position to be threatened!) Perhaps, computationalism can indeed explain the facts of human mentality —but perhaps it cannot. It is a matter for dispassionate discussion, and certainly not for abuse!

Miller *et al.* (1960) might have applauded the reprise of their optimistic theses a quarter of a century later, as echoed by the two notable cognitive scientists, Churchland and Churchland: "Church's Thesis says that whatever is computable is Turing computable. Assuming, with some safety, that what the mind-brain does is computable, then it can in principle be simulated by a computer" (Churchland & Churchland, 1983, p. 6).

However, Churchland and Churchland misunderstood the import of the Church–Turing thesis. It does not imply results that entail "that a standard digital computer, given only the right program, a large enough memory and sufficient time, can . . . display any systematic pattern of responses to the environment whatsoever" (Churchland & Churchland, 1990, p. 26). As Copeland (1997) observed:

> This no doubt explains why they think they can assume "with some safety" that what the mind-brain does is computable, for on their understanding of matters this is to assume only that the mind-brain

exhibits a systematic pattern of responses, or is characterized by a "rule-governed" input–output function.

Copeland (1997) was quite right to point out that the Church–Turing thesis does not entail that the brain (or the mind or consciousness) can be modeled by a Turing machine program, even when buttressed by the belief that the functional brain (or mind) is amenable to precise scientific description, or even if it exhibits invariant patterns of responses to the environment that seem to conform to certain rules. (For details, see Copeland, 1997, author of the Church–Turing Thesis entry to the online *Stanford Encyclopedia of Philosophy*.)

Miller *et al.*'s (1960) optimism about how simulation would solve our problems seems, in more recent times, like a child whistling in the dark, for numerous unforeseen problems and mysterious structures have been shown to emerge from increased complication (e.g., fractal sets, nonlinear dynamics, criticality; Casti, 1994). These surprises lurking in the depths of even simple dimensions of complication should make us more mathematically circumspect and scientifically prudent, discouraging sweeping generalizations about truly complex systems. Perhaps the jury is still out on von Neumann's (1949/1966) conjecture, but I suspect its pessimism now seems more realistic than fanciful.

Life forms seek satisficing rather than optimal solutions to their problems

Most ecological psychologists strongly agree; we recognize that although optimality may be a useful idea for analytical mathematical modeling, it is pragmatically false. Consequently, I find this last thesis the least objectionable, as long as we do not confuse a satisfactory outcome with an unlawful one. To protect the law concept, we must admit to a kind of graded control, or determinism with an admixture of nondeterminism, if one prefers.

In quantum physics there is a model for how to represent such tolerant but suboptimal solutions that are, more realistically, encountered in psychology. Hamilton's principle, by which particles somehow select the least action path, is an idea that carries over to optimal control theory—with one important difference: There the initial conditions for the control law may be modified to conform to particular constraint conditions. Felicitous modifications of initial conditions, something not possible in physics, in contrast to inert particles, allows a system with a proper control law to find an acceptable path; it can do so by minimizing a cost functional such as least time, least distance, or least fuel. Mathematically, this is accomplished by application of a technique known as the *calculus of variations*.

Unfortunately, even these control theoretic solutions are analytically too exact to mirror how real agents perform on situated tasks. Such solutions are too idealized to be appropriate in either quantum mechanics or psychology because of the limitations imposed by uncertainty in the former and indecision in the latter.

A more realistic path for a particle (or an agent) to follow is one that expresses the so-called effective action, the least action path overlaid with uncertainty. This, in effect, hides the ideal path solution inside a kind of blurred strip—yielding at best a path corridor comprising the superposition of all possible alternative path solutions satisfying the cost functional (Mensky, 1993). In situated tasks for agents rather than particles, one should expect something similar. The paths that present themselves on repeated trials will be found to meander and involve detours that avoid situational thwarts or that reflect less than perfect control. These blurry path corridors are what is meant by tolerant suboptimal solutions—solutions that depart from analytic perfection because of local exigencies but that are still satisfactory (or "satisficing," to use Simon's apt expression).

For Gibson, a path solution is tolerant if, in spite of the small errors, it nevertheless realizes the affordance goal that the agent intends. *Intentional dynamics* is the name I have given for the collection of methods (e.g., various Monte Carlo methods) that discover the controls on initial conditions that are sufficiently adequate to get the job done intended by the agent. Unlike the initial conditions on dynamical laws controlling particles, these initial conditions are altered to agree with the intended final condition. I say more about this later when I discuss rules for the perceptual control of actions or, as Simon (1969/1996) denoted them, *means—ends analyses*.

In what follows, I discuss how closely Simon's approach agrees with Gibson's, paying special attention to Simon's brand of ecological functionalism. If, as Gibson supposed, a goal (e.g., an affordance) is directly perceived, then how the relevant initial conditions can be tailored to achieve intended final conditions, that is, finding the proper control law, is explained. *The agent simply sees what is to be done to eradicate the differences between current information and the information specific to the goal.* As unlikely as this may sound, reasons are given later for its plausibility.

On the one hand, if, as Simon supposed, perception cannot be direct but must be mediated by symbolic representations that specify the goal, then the problem, it seems to me, is made enormously more difficult. I argue that it is not only made more difficult but may even become intractable when situated rather than idealized tasks are considered.

Clearly, the Gibsonian strategy depends on direct perception being a feasible alternative to mediating symbolic expressions. Hence, I consider this problem next.

Simon on the direct perception of affordances

Direct perception is so central a concept for ecological psychologists that it naturally penetrates deeply into the ontological assumptions of the whole field of psychology, meaning that to understand how perception can be direct is to understand the world in quite a different way than traditional psychology, indeed, even than traditional physics and materialistic philosophy allow. The objects of direct perception, depending on whom you read, are some or all of the following: (a) things, (b) events, or (c) the affordances of things and events (see the special issue of *Ecological Psychology*, "How Are Affordances Related to Events?" 2000). Even more iconoclastic is the claim that (d) affordances per se are all that we truly perceive—an ontological claim that I have called *affordance imperialism* (Sanders, 1997; Stofffegen, 2000).

On the contrary, Gibson (1979/1986) gave a list of things that might be perceived along with their affordances:

> My description of the environment . . . and of the changes that can occur in it . . . implies that places, attached objects, objects, and substances *are what are mainly perceived* [italics added], together with events, which are changes of these things. To see these things is to perceive what they afford.
>
> (p. 240)

Here it is clear that it is not only affordances that one perceives, although one also perceive them in the same act of perceiving these other things. What would it mean, and how useful could it be, to perceive affordances but not to perceive those things that do the affording? For example, how plausible is it to say that one sees the pourability of water but not the water that is pourable? This has been an "in-house" argument that probably concerns few if any outsiders.

As the captions clearly show, although Simon deigned to use the term *affordance*, he and Vera interpreted it quite contrary to Gibson's intended usage (Vera & Simon, 1993). Regardless of which of the four interpretations one endorses as defining the objects of direct perception, none are consistent with Simon's indirect interpretation. How could Simon go so far astray from the intended use? How could he defend treating affordances in such a disparate fashion from its conventional usage?

For Simon, affordances were not empirical primitives but derived from computational primitives. To my mind (Shaw & Shockley, 2003), Simon made a grave mistake in his criticism of Gibson's notion of *direct* when Vera and Simon (1993) wrote the following:

> A functional description of the world (i.e., a description in terms of something like affordances) is one that allows simple mappings

between our functional models of what is out there (e.g., road curves to the left) and our functional actions (e.g., turn to left). However, the resulting simplicity of the relation between these two functional representations does not imply that the relation is somehow "direct" or unmediated. It is, in fact, complexity of mediation (in the form of many representational layers) that affords this simplicity. Simplicity, in turn, gives the relation the phenomenological character of being direct.

(p. 21)

I call this a grave mistake because it is wrong in two ways: It implies a solution is in hand for a problem that still has the status of a mystery while at the same time committing an egregious category error; it mistakes a symbol for the referent it denotes—a case of the general semantic fallacy discussed earlier. Why would Simon make such an undefended and perhaps indefensible assertion? Simon did so because he had no choice given his commitment to the precept that all psychological functions are reducible to computation, that is, symbol manipulations. Hence, Simon seeks in one grand gesture to bring Gibson's ecological psychology under his own theory. For Simon, psychology is one of the sciences of the artificial in which rules governing the design of artifacts are paramount. Should the reader think it preposterous to attribute such extreme computational reductionism to the 1978 Nobel Laureate, consider Simon's (1969/1996) own words:

The thesis is that certain phenomena are "artificial" in a very specific sense: They are as they are only because of a system's being molded, by goals or purposes, to the environment in which it lives. If natural phenomena have an air of "necessity" about them in their subservience to natural law, artificial phenomena have an air of "contingency" in their malleability by the environment.

(p. xi)

Hence, any system or phenomenon is deemed artificial if they have about their character the "air of 'contingency,'" such that they might have been otherwise, and natural if they have about them the "air of 'necessity,'" meaning presumably that they could not have been otherwise. Moreover, and most surprising, is that because living systems are adapted for purposeful behaviors, the same conditions that make a system such as a computer, a hammer, or a farm artificial apply to them as well. Simon (1969/1996) declared:

Notice that this way of viewing artifacts . . . applies equally well to many things that are not man-made—to all things that can be regarded in fact as adapted to some situation; and in particular *it applies to the living systems* [italics added] that have evolved through forces of organic evolution.

(p. 6)

Hence, humans and animals belong to the category of the artificial as well and, thus, like any man-made artifacts, fall under Simons' proposed new science.

By an act of redefining category boundaries, Simon settled by fiat the age-old mind–body problem, for if one class of artificial mechanism can have "minds," then why cannot other less wonderful mechanisms, such as robots, computers, and toasters have at least graded mental capacity? They all have symbol functions in their make up. This shows Simon's hubris and allowed him to deny without virtue of argument the aspirations of ecological psychologists who strive to attain the status of a natural science for psychology. It also excludes biology as well from deserving such status. A successful theory of AI would, presumably, explain them all.

Surely, there is no reason to follow Simon in the a priori exclusion of psychology and biology from the natural sciences. The issue is not whether they are the results of an evolutionary process that might have been otherwise but whether there are laws that allow for graded determinism. Since the decline of the rigid notion of 19th-century mechanism with its assumption of absolute determinism, laws for nondeterministic simple phenomena have been found in quantum and statistical physics, and there is a growing scientific industry that seeks natural laws for complex phenomena (Wolfram's, 2002, efforts notwithstanding).

Ecological psychologists have worked on both fronts to make a strong case for psychology being one of the natural sciences of complex (graded) nondeterministic phenomena. We need not let Simon's own aspirations displace ours and reduce our science to the bedrock form of extreme computationalism that he espouses.

If we disallow his postulate that life forms are artificial because they are adapted to affordance goals requisite to their survival, then neither do we need to accept his belabored and facile characterization of affordances as symbols to be computationally manipulated as representations stored in central memory, and neither would we wish to reify information for affordances in this way.

Recall the earlier quoted passage in which Simon allowed that affordances might be used to name "a functional description of the world" that permits "simple mappings between our functional models of what is out there . . . and our functional actions" (Vera & Simon, 1993, p. 21). Simon would have us believe that directness in our awareness of them is not really primary; rather, it is no more than an epiphenomenon that somehow rides piggyback on computationally layered architectures—but this somehow is never even addressed. In fact Simon (1969/1996) himself acknowledged elsewhere that we do not yet have a clue to understanding this problem. This is recognized as Chalmer's (1996) "hard" problem, namely, discovering how our experiences have the character they do because our neurophysiology processes function the way they do—a problem in need of philosophical clarification before sensible scientific hypotheses can be framed.

Gibson offered a solution but it would not make the mechanist happy: Direct perception follows from the ecological realist's thesis that things appear as they do because that is the way they are, as taken in reference to the perceiver as actor at the ecological scale. However, notice this is not naive realism as sometimes claimed. Naïve realism is absolute: Things appear exactly as they are, unconditionally.

Perhaps, then, one can concur:

> So long as Simon maintains that the inner environment of the symbol functions is not the central issue, and admits that we presently know nothing about how our phenomenological experiences originate in neural functions, then his attempt to reduce direct experiences to indirect symbolic representations is little more than hand waving.
>
> (Shaw & Shockley, 2003, pp. 430–431)

Simon spoke apodictically but really had not made his case as fully as needed to be convincing.

Peroration of similarities and differences

Let us pause to review Gibson's and Simon's most important points of agreement and disagreement. First and foremost, they were both functionalists of roughly the same generation rather than behaviorists or mechanists (with Gibson, born 1904, being 12 years senior to Simon, born 1916). Simon, however, was a reductionist; Gibson was not. They sharply differed also as to the nature of the functionalism espoused. Although both exhibited ecological sensibilities, they were not ecological in exactly the same way. Likewise, they were both friends to situated analyses—with Simon leaning more toward situated cognition than situated action (see the special issue of *Cognitive Science*, "Situated Action," 1993) and Gibson the other way around (see the special issue of *Ecological Psychology*, "Situating Action," Costall & Leudar, 1996).

For both theorists, situated analyses remained implicit. Gibson's whole approach emphasized the active agent behaving in its environment, doing the work of adaptive living, whereas Simon's approach emphasized the agent's deciding which next step might be most adaptive and yet practical. In general, Gibson's actor navigates with intuitive awareness through a complex world by detecting invariant information for socially shared affordances according to ecological laws, that is, deontic rules for the perceptual control of goal-directed actions. By contrast, Simon's thinker must consult an internal model for each situation—a model that must be continuously updated "online"—and then apply a deontic rule (means–ends analysis) to decide at each moment what next step to take to reach its goal.

For Gibson, the intuitive agent can be any organism, from microbes to insects and from insects to fish, birds, mammals, and humans as long as they have evolved adaptive intentions and sufficient situational awareness to conform to the relevant deontic laws at the ecological scale. For Simon, the agent must also have situational awareness or its functional equivalent, awareness of the situation's internal model, and in addition, sufficient cognitive abilities to make proper deontic decisions based on means–ends analysis. Thus, Simon's approach seems more elitist than Gibson's in having restricted application to agents with highly evolved cognitive capacities.

However, of course, one of the tasks of Simon's design theory is to avoid this restriction by endowing all creatures with cleverly designed interfaces. Unfortunately, there is no hint of how nature might have evolved such designs except where the intuitions of human programmers are allowed. For by Simon's own admission, computers are designed in humans' images for human purposes. There are none designed by insects or other life forms; there are only the life forms themselves. Although the simulation strategy can still be applied, one must ask if it is appropriate.

For Gibson, the functional coupling of organisms with their environments is direct, having no need to reify an informational interface (beyond its causal support), its design arising naturally as a product of evolutionary preattunement as well as ongoing attunement through learning and the education of attention; for Simon, by contrast, a whole new science of artifacts (symbolic representations) is required to deal with the problems of how the interface was or should be designed and reified. Also, for Gibson, the design arises lawfully at the ecological scale, whereas for Simon it is contrived by rules of symbol production and manipulation that emerge somehow from some kind of computational roots in a way never entirely clear.

Simon and Gibson were both information theorists—but not of the Shannon variety. Whereas Simon believed information had to be symbolically represented and processed to be meaningful, Gibson thought information only had to be detected to yield its secrets. It is not "out there" (purely objective), as so many critics and interpreters have enoneously claimed; nor is it "in there" (purely subjective), as so many psychologists feel compelled to believe. Rather, information is relationally duplex, pointing people both toward their environment and toward themselves; it bridges between what traditionally was called the *subject* and the *object*, the first-person (direct) experiences (knowledge by acquaintance) and the (indirect) experiences shared secondhand (knowledge by description)—although the latter depend on the former (Grote, 1865; James, 1911; Russell, 1912). For Simon, information comes in only one form—symbols; there is no direct specification only indirect representation.

Simon, like Gibson, recognized the coevolution of animals and their environments but saw information as inhering in the agent's changing attitudes toward the environment—attitudes that were learned. The environment is physical and law governed, being coupled to rule-governed symbols housed in the agent's memory. By processing these symbols, the agent is able to make reference to external artifacts (e.g., books, maps, movies, recipes, etc.); hence, not all information is stored in the agent but may be stored in the external environment as well—a notion with which Gibson agreed.

Gibson's view contrasts sharply with Simon's on the priority indirect perception deserves and the role secondhand information plays. For Gibson, firsthand information was not carried by representations, although representations may convey secondhand information. *Simons notion of artificial sciences, as interpreted through his information processing theory, fits rather nicely under Gibsons notion of indirect perception.* This insight is worth strong emphasis; please take note of it. Thus, Simon's theory is extremely limited because it leaves no room for direct perception and thus leaves unexplained the act of ostensive specification by which symbols, as physical objects, come to refer beyond themselves (Shaw, 2001). In short, if direct perception is not primary, symbol functions of objects have no point of origin.

Simon believed an agent must engage in information processing before acting; Gibson did not. Rather, Gibson believed that information just needs to be picked up and used by an agent. Simon's information processing necessarily introduces mediation by symbol structure manipulation. If we are to use Simon's view as a foil for clarifying Gibson's direct perception, one needs to be clear about what Simon meant by indirectness—mediation by symbolic representations. Symbol systems manipulate symbols. Here is what Simon (1969/1996) said symbols are (for more details, see Newell & Simon, 1976):

1. Symbols are physical patterns (e.g., chalk marks, electrical impulses) that can be constituents of symbolic expressions (i.e., symbol structures).
2. A symbol's actual meaning comprises the pattern of activations between associated symbol structures that some outside stimulus induces.
3. A symbol's potential meaning comprises the entire framework of associations and connections that might be activated by imposed stimulus.
4. A symbol's linguistic, historical, and environmental context adds meaning to it.
5. Symbols may designate objects and processes that the symbol system to which it belongs can interpret and execute.

In addition, Simon (1969/1996) stated the defining properties of a physical symbol system:

6. A symbol system (e.g., a computer, a person) has processes capable of manipulating symbolic expressions—"processes that create, modify, copy, and destroy symbols" (p. 22).
7. A physical symbol system evolves over time, producing and developing a collection of symbol structures that can and often do serve as internal representations (e.g., images) of environmental properties and structures to which the symbol system seeks to adapt.
8. A symbol system has "windows on the world and hands, too" (p. 22) by which it acquires information to be encoded into internal symbols as well as produces symbols that initiate actions back onto the world.
9. All cognitive, perceptual, memorial, and reasoning processes involve symbol manipulation, as does the preparation for and initiation of actions.

There are many criticisms that maybe levied against the physical symbol hypothesis as a theory of meaning, most of which have already been raised against Locke's associative theory of meaning and its more contemporary renditions (Dreyfus, 1995; Korb, 1995). Most critical are the criticisms that it fails to explain reference, how symbols are grounded, and to delimit the expansion of irrelevant meanings built up by associations in the arbitrary situating of symbols. The idea of the generative closure of coalitions developed throughout this article is my suggestion for how an ecological theory of meaning (invariant specification of affordances) avoids both of these criticisms by offering a new look on grounding and situating.

In summary, to fully appreciate Simon, one must see that his theoretical psychology is founded on a commitment to symbols as the vehicles of thought, and thought as dominant over perception and action. To fully appreciate Gibson, one must come to see that direct perception is a conclusion rather than an assumption, that perception is the primary source of all adaptive thinking, that perception and action are equal partners, that they mutually interact and reciprocally dominate one another (i.e., a perceiving–acting cycle), and that cognitive abilities are elaborations of these more evolutionary primitive processes. Few battle lines have ever been so clearly drawn.

Earlier, I discussed how generative closure can lead to the creation of living symbols that have imputed physical existence and live as parasitic epiphenomena. The very property that allows this abuse in the symbol function also allows the generative closure needed to underwrite direct perception.

330

Coalitions: a historical note

For ease of reference, I call any system with the kind of functional closure that arises from situating and grounding experiences and that conforms to the four kinds of information control (discussed later) a *coalition*—a term I originally introduced in a book to describe how aphasic errors, although propagating insidiously, only make sense with respect to the function they have in the pragmatics of normal language use (Jenkins, Jimenez-Pabon, Shaw, & Sefer, 1975). The term was used more abstractly later to try to express the *generative closure* properties in which meanings and intentions are involved (Shaw & Turvey, 1981; Turvey, Shaw, & Mace, 1979). The complex of functionally defined relationships endows the invariant properties of agents and their environments with meaning and intentionality so that the properties make reference to other components in the complex through the generative closure property, fashioned after a similar property in mathematical group theory. Let us see how this works.

The group property of generative closure says that any member of the complex generatively specifies the total membership of the complex, that to be a member of the complex is to be directly cospecified by the other members. *Directly* means that nothing is cospecified indirectly through something else brought in from the outside, for the something else would be an interloper falling outside the closure property and might be eliminated without injury to the integrity of the complex. Say, for example, we did artificially interpolate a chain of mediators between two natural members of the complex. Finding a direct route through a complex of such indirectly connected sites amounts to finding the shortest shortcut, that is, one that puts each natural member just a step away from another natural member.

Relational complexes with this power to eliminate the interpolated artifacts are said to exhibit *commutativity*—the fundamental property that also allows natural parts to add up to structured wholes that surpass the natural parts in aggregation—an intuition the gestaltists appreciated. Relational complexes that can be reduced to one step cospecifications are said to be involutional and may be modeled by the involutional group. The involutional group is usually modeled by a scheme involving four complex numbers:

$$(i^0, i^1, i^2, i^3) = i^n \text{ for } n = (1, 2, \ldots, 4) \text{ and } i = (-1)^{1/2}.$$

For example, $i \times i = -1$, $i \times i \times i = -i$, and so forth. I do not go further into this here because the argument has been presented in detail elsewhere (Shaw *et al.*, 1990). Also, the notion of generative closure as based on the (cyclic) group closure property has been experimentally illustrated by Shaw and Wilson (1976). Here is the background on this idea and Simon's and Gibson's reaction to it around the time that I had come up with it. (It was the key idea funded by my 1970–1975 career development award.)

I had the opportunity to present the argument for generative closure (an idea I generalized from Chomsky's, 1957, 1965, more restricted idea of generative grammars) at the first cognition and instruction conference held in Vail, Colorado, in June 1974. Simon, who was a discussant of the paper, made favorable comments—but I suspect this was because the elimination of extraneous artifacts idea (discussed later) was not a part of the original paper (Shaw & Wilson, 1976). This is what the editor of the conference report had to say about this work in the preface of the published volume (Klahr, 1976):

> Shaw and Wilson . . . address issues of process and structure from a more abstract—almost philosophical—position, but they also provide concrete examples from Shaw's work on perception. The central issues concern the ability to understand an entire concept from experience with just a subset of its instances. Such an ability, Shaw and Wilson argue, lies at the heart of understanding invariance.
>
> (p. xi)

I think this is still true.

Ironically, the idea originated from Gibson's (1950) discussions of transformational groups and the properties they leave invariant, which he had borrowed from Ernst Cassirer's 1944 paper titled "The Concept of Group and the Theory of Perception." Around this same time, I discussed this idea of generative closure with Gibson and thanked him for putting me on to it. To my great surprise, Gibson staunchly denied ever having read Cassirer— not relinquishing his denial until I pointed out his use of Cassirer's ideas in his first book (Gibson, 1950, pp. 153, 193). Gibson laughed, shaking his head.

For the record, among other things Gibson said in 1950 was the following:

> The geometry of transformations is therefore of considerable importance for vision, and it is conceivable that the clue to the whole problem of pattern-perception might be found here. . . . A transformation is a regular and lawful event which leaves certain properties of the pattern invariant.
>
> (p. 153)

Gibson also said later: "If we are ever to understand exactly what yields a perception of shape we must study the dimensions of variation of various shapes" (p. 193).

For years to come, I was to parlay these insights of Cassirer, Gibson, and Chomsky into a theory of event perception (Kim, Effken, & Shaw, 1995; Shaw & Cutting, 1980; Shaw, Flascher, & Mace, 1996; Shaw, McIntyre, & Mace, 1974; Shaw & Pittenger, 1979; Warren & Shaw, 1985), which to my delight finally appeared as a topic in its own right in Gibson's (1979/1986) last book. Interest in the topic also, with help of many, led us to hold the first event perception conference at the University of Connecticut in 1981, from which the idea for an International . Society of Ecological Psychology got its initial boost (Warren & Shaw, 1985).

I now take a closer look at the idea of generative closure, which in one of several incarnations has appealed to such dissimilar minds as Chomsky, Simon, and Gibson.

Generative closure: a closer look

The generative closure property makes integrable compositions possible whose differentiations cannot exhaust their essential properties. Closure bestows the gestalt property on an integrable but possibly undifferentiable complex. I suspect Gibson coined the term *affordance* because he needed some way to label this fourfold emergent ecological complex—fourfold because it is simultaneously an expression of the *exterospecific, propriospecific, expropriospecific*, and *proexterospecific* forms of information. (The same terms can usefully be applied to control as well.) The closure property not only explains what makes information ecological (relationally defined between agents and their environments) but also what makes it direct. Mainly, for our purposes, it shows how directness is a conclusion not an assumption.

Figure 2 tries to make this important point clear and places the main logical difference between Simon and Gibson in sharp relief. The nodes designated E and O can be taken as representing Simon's outer and inner environments, respectively. As Simon (1969/1996) said: "The artificial world is centered precisely on this interface between the inner and the outer environments; it is concerned with attaining goals by adapting the former to the latter" (p. 118). Because nodes E–O and O–E mediate the ordered relations between the outer environment E and the inner environment O, Simon would have one represent these indirect relationships by symbols denoting cognitive representations. Such symbols constitute what Simon (1969/1996) meant by "the artifact as interface" (p. 6).

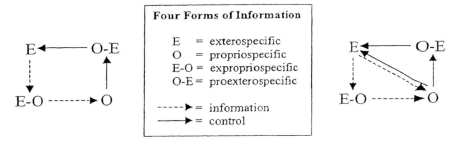

Figure 2 Cyclic closure (left) and direct commutators (right).

My take on Gibson's idea is more parsimonious; it would have one recognize that indirect (artifactual) closure is a lower order description than is needed and replace it by its direct commutator description—indicated in the figure by a pair of dual diagonal arrows. (Of course Gibson would never characterize direct specification in these terms; they are mine, but I fancy he would not disapprove!) The right diagram introduces the notion of a commutative relation (or commutator). Whereas ordinary commutators select alternative paths to a given path, a direct commutator always makes an indirect path into a direct path by connecting its initial and terminal nodes while ignoring what goes on in between. Thus, the mediating chains of multiple nodes may be ignored because they play no necessary role.

Logically speaking, then, one must conclude that the diagrams for Simon and Gibson are fundamentally different, with Simon's being contained in Gibson's as a subdiagram. This allows the use of indirect means of specification whenever legitimate—that is, when secondhand information is substituted for firsthand information. Ultimately, at the level of direct perception of affordances or other environmental properties, the symbolic representations are not needed and become semantically superfluous whenever the closure property of higher order information holds. This is what I called "elimination of extraneous artifacts" earlier. Here is a little more on this idea.

Reducibility of conventions and laws

Simon (1969/1996) recognized the essential role intention must play if symbols are to do their job:

> An artifact can be thought of as a meeting point—an "interface" in today's terms—between an "inner" environment, the substance and organization of the artifact itself, and an "outer" environment, the surroundings in which it operates. If the inner environment is appropriate to the outer environment, or vice versa, *the artifact will serve its purpose* [italics added].
>
> (p. 6)

Again, we are told by Simon (1969/1996) that "the outer environment determines the goals of the inner environment" (p. 11). In essence, design strategies orchestrate properties of the inner environment so that they serve the goals of the outer environment. Central to the nature of artifacts "are the goals that link the inner to the outer environment" (pp. 10–11).

The coupling of the inner and outer environments can be hypothesized as indirect, as in Simon's thesis, which invokes information processing by symbol manipulations, or direct, as in Gibson's thesis (in my words, not Gibson's), bringing direct commutators to the forefront as the purveyors of direct specification. This thesis was made even clearer by Gibson (1966):

We tend to think of direct stimuli from the terrestrial environment as being like words and pictures instead of realizing that words and pictures are at best man-made substitutes for these direct stimuli. Language and art yield perceptions at second-hand. This second-hand perception no doubt works backwards on direct perception [on the direct commutators], but knowledge *about* the world rests on *acquaintance* with the world, in the last analysis, and this is our first problem.

(p. 28)

This is such an important point, I look at a variety of ways to illustrate it.

Gibson (1979/1986) stated: "What the philosopher called foresight is what I call the *perception of the affordance*. To see at a distance what the object affords on contact is 'necessary for the preservation of the animal'" (p. 232). Here adaptive success depends on prospective control, which in turn depends on anticipatory information. Such information may come to us firsthand by direct apprehension or secondhand by indirect means. Here are some cases that elucidate this fact in several different ways, each providing an entree to a different set of issues and concerns.

Case 1: Firsthand versus secondhand knowledge

If I ask you for a favor directly, I can have your response directly, but if I ask a mutual friend to ask you for me, then I can have your response only indirectly, requiring the mutual friend to act as a mediator. This means not only can I then not know your response until the friend responds, but if the friend is unable to respond or chooses not to, the closure is broken and the symbol function thwarted. The mediating friend performs a kind of symbol function for my request, which is roundabout and secondhand. Here it is clear that without my original request of the friend to mediate for me, the friend would serve no function and become superfluous.

Therefore, here is the main pnint once again. The original request carries the root intention of the social transaction; this root intention requires that a direct commutator exist in principle. To Gibson, symbolic representations are just such superfluous entities having no power to get the epistemic process going, although they may play the role of connecting meanings after the process is initiated.

Case 2: Epistemic grounding of symbols

Simon placed great stock in the notion that his symbols are physical rather than abstract. Simon's theory stands to Gibson's as remembering the combination code for opening a safe stands to cracking the safe by feeling the tumblers fall into place and thereby learning the combination. The sequence of left–right turns by a specific number of degrees is a physical code that defines a successful path to the goal of opening the safe for whatever reason—to alter or check on the contents of the safe.

An analysis of the relation between using a code to open the safe versus opening a safe to discover the code is instructive. It illustrates, by analogy and example, the major similarities and differences between Simon's theory of interface design and the Gibson-inspired ecological interface design (Vicente, 1999). The code is information specific to a goal—opening the safe—which is used to guide the action. One perceives to act (specifically, uses code to guide opening the safe) and conversely one acts to perceive (specifically, e.g., to check contents in the safe).

The conventions for the use of symbols must be reducible. If they are, then they are underwritten by natural law. Conventions are reducible in the current sense in those cases and only those cases in which an effective action achieves realization of an intended goal, that is, by following a rule whose convention rests on realizable affordances. In this example, the relevant convention specifies how if the dial on a safe is manipulated according to a sequence of symbols (e.g., 0, right twice stopping at 16, left to 23, right back to 0), the action affords opening the safe. The idea of reducibility may be made clearer by considering a case in which the convention is not reducible, and in which there is no effective action—such as when the combination on a safe is changed so the previous action is now ineffectual.

However, even here a new effective action may be discovered by safe cracking techniques (say, by listening to or feeling the tumblers fall into place). Here a new code can be associated with the effective action by reading off the dial the code sequence corresponding to the points where the tumblers fall.

Notice that a symbol or symbol sequence is useless if its intention fails to reduce to an affordance–effectivity fit through an effective action. One can adjust the intention, for example, by having a pseudo-code to confound any unauthorized person trying to open the safe. A pseudo-code is a double convention code, one rule for translating the false code into the true code and the other to apply the code to guide the interfacing of actions (twiddling the knob) to the safe. Note that the rule translating one code into another is useless if it is not followed by a rule for realizing the code's intention by effective action. When this is the case, then one can say the rule conventions satisfy the reducibility condition. This condition satisfies a symmetry condition between the agents effectivities and the affordances supporting the actions. To reiterate: This is what we mean by an affordance–effectivity fit—a shorthand for the reducibility of convention argument.

Hence, by this analysis, Simon's view of affordances is wrong in two fundamental ways: First, an affordance cannot be a symbol, as he claimed, because as a goal it is essential to a symbol's convention being reduced. Second, an affordance can be realized as a goal by an effective action whether or not there is a symbol at all. Finally, I strongly emphasize that *symbols are useful if and only if their conventions are reducible.* Such is the case when the symmetry condition holds between affordance and the effectivity (effective action) that realizes it.

Later, we shall see that the symmetry condition expresses how symbols depend on ecological laws for their validity. This is tantamount to saying that rules that satisfy the reducibility condition are underwritten by laws.

Case 3: Informational transparency

Consider one of my favorite examples of direct perception. I perceive the shape of the cavity in my back molar by probing its boundaries with a three inch metal pick. Clearly I am in contact with this dental tool, which is in contact with my molar's cavity, but I am also in contact with my tooth. How can this be? It can be because probing with a tool not only coimplicates both the probed and the probing agent but is a successful action only if the probe (tool) is infomationally transparent to both the object probed and the control of the action required to guide the probe.

This transparency condition for information here in the case of tool use is a formal analogy to the reducibility condition for symbols. This is a crucial insight for beginning the approach to an ecological study of language—or better, of communication. It starts with the realization that communication through language (reducibility of conventions) and communication through tool use (transparency of media to information) have much in common. Ecological psychologists will, in my opinion, not make progress on the language problem until this analogy is explicitly understood.

To be direct is an either–or proposition in the sense of an exclusive disjunct (i.e., either–or but not both). It matters not how remote or how near the ends of the linkage are. All that matters is whether in the final analysis the linkage, in its entirety, is a medium over which the influence is transparent from one end to the other. Specification fills the gap regardless of its breadth or the complication of the medium. It could include the central nervous systems, tools, or other linkages. A ship whose signal gets weaker and weaker as it increases its distance from the shore is still in contact with its shore base until the medium of support for the signal collapses under a severely lopsided signal-to-noise ratio. This remote sensing brings me to the next case.

Case 4: Insight as direct apprehension

Like the ship, an actor navigating in the world may perceive the direct effects of its intended remote target over arbitrary distances—as long as the medium for the information field does not collapse, then it can maintain contact with the target. In a more abstract vein, imagine the insight that

337

allows a creative person to see the most elegant route to the end of a task or to the solution of a problem. The gestaltists called this ability to apprehend directly the solution to a problem *insight*.

Insight that allows a mathematician to prove a theorem is no different in kind than insight that allows a person to select a navigable path to a final destination. More generally, *insight* might be denned as an intuitive act of maintaining awareness of the final consequence of a train of choices of arbitrary length. Here, as with any other medium, the train of choices must be a medium transparent to goal-specific information. Such direct apprehension of remote intended effects are as common among artists as they are among mathematicians who intuit the theorem to be proved ahead of time (how else?) or soccer players who position themselves for a header because they see the cross developing from other players.

To reiterate my main point, direct epistemic acts are no more perceptual than they are cognitive, nor more cognitive than they are action based. Gibson's magnificent insight was to see how epistemic directness could be teased apart from causal mediation if one only recognizes that the function of information is different from the physical media that support it. Although information is no less physical than other aspects of energy distributions, it acts directly, as a veritable action-at-a distance, to keep the agent in contact with affordances of consequence.

Without affordances the information would signify nothing, and without the information agents would roam aimless (if they perchance to exist). Directness means that affordances are knowable at a distance ahead of time; hence anticipation forecasting, and planning are possible. My colleagues and I have not seriously studied the affordances of solution spaces to problem sets, but we have made a beginning (Barab, Cherkes-Julkowski, Swenson, Garrett, & Shaw, 1999; Shaw, Efflcen, Fagen, Garrett, & Morris, 1997).

Case 5: Invariant optical information

I ask that you carefully ponder this: The way an optical instrument (e.g., telescope or microscope) produces an image from a real-world scene is evidence *not that we see the world (indirectly) as images* but that *we directly detect the invariant optical information specific to the scene*—which also produces the image.

Whereas the image is appropriate to the simple, flat, homogeneous screen on which it may be focused, the invariant optical information is appropriate to the complex, multidimensional, multilayered, multifaceted resonating detector systems of the central nervous system. Whereas it takes the latter to view the former, the former cannot under any circumstances view the latter. Whereas it takes the whole organism to react meaningfully and purposively to the invariant information specific to an environmental situation (and thereby to produced properly situated actions), no computational, symbol manipulating system can do likewise; it is to meanings (affordances) and not symbols that actions must be directed if a system is to be situated.

In sum, to be *in*directed to symbols is to be misdirected from meaning unless the symbols are made transparent by direct specification of their referents regardless of the length or indirectness of symbol chains. Symbols as object have no intrinsic power to specify; as objects per se they are referentially opaque and only become transparent by virtue of such direct specification. I return to elaborate this point later. First, let us try a more cognitive example to see if the notions of *direct* and *indirect* generalize from perceptually driven to cognitively driven actions.

Case 6: Situating rules

One may follow a recipe and produce an ethnic dish from unfamiliar ingredients by comparing their labels to the names in the recipe and apportion by cook's measures the recipe's stated quantities. Similarly, one may mechanically follow the steps in preparation and cooking as stated in the cookbook. Of course, this is not the same as a master chef who constructed the recipe as a record of his or her situated actions—defined here as taste experiments involving years of trials combining and apportioning a broad range of varied ingredients as well as successes and failures with a plethora of preparation and cooking strategies. Hence, the novice's use of the recipe is the indirect result of the master chef's attunement of the selection, preparation, and performance stages of cooking through extended direct experience.

In short, although it is true that a novice without being properly situated in his or her cooking actions can produce a crude approximation to the expert's properly situated actions, he or she will lack facility to improvise when faced by less than felicitous means. As in Locke's nightmare (discussed later), the novice who cannot properly situate his or her actions may produce something by rote that he or she scarcely, if at all, understands. The hedge "scarcely" is needed here because in the mere attempt he or she will begin accruing direct experience that may, depending on talent, initiate the situating process; the direct perception of what the cooking situation affords may produce resonances across subsequent situations whose information is invariant with prior situations.

In this way, the novice's actions begin insinuating themselves into all situations to the degree that they share the same affordances. Recipes do not resonate, cooks do—meaning that resonance to invariant information in cases of properly situated action require that the agent be insinuated into that situation by an *adaptive resonance process*. It does not work if the agent is only in a symbolic representation of the real situation, although the agent might become adept at using the symbols (e.g., like mechanically following a recipe by rote rather than by direct participation through resonances to taste and cooking experiences).

It is just that where perception is concerned, the evidence is the experience of the functionally defined, temporally extended, ecologically scaled environment. Given how much confusion has surrounded this point, it is worth taking a moment to review what *indirect* means in hope of sharpening our appreciation of what *direct* must mean. My chief aim is to shed light on how the direct perceiving of affordances is synonymous with keeping in contact with the environment.

Indirect means of encountering the world through description and depiction cannot and should not be made fundamental. To duplicate facsimiles, shove the copies into the head, and call them the memorial basis for perception was to Gibson ludicrous and superfluous, not to mention unparsimonious, for it makes perception an internal process with no access to the world except through a dictionary look-up table that is impossible to validate independently. It also leaves as a mystery how such a look-up table could come to be in the first place if no direct perception were involved.

It ultimately confounds the semantic problem of intentionality with Locke's claustrophobic nightmare. In Locke's nightmare, each of us is trapped in his or her own mind like being in a locked trunk with no key. Perception then becomes cognition in the sense of reflection. All one can do is rummage around through one's own ideas as if they were curios whose provenance is long lost. Action fares no better because we are no longer able to act on or even toward the world but are restricted to acting on symbols and then toward their mental dictionary representations. Thus, Locke's nightmare precludes there being knowledge of the world if all knowledge is secondhand.

Earlier I considered some formal intuitions (generative specification, group closure, and direct commutators) that might suggest ways to mathematize the theory of direct specification. I say *direct specification* to cover all bases: direct perception, direct memory access, direct control of action, direct inference, direct learning, direct problem solving, direct concept acquisition, and so forth. The theory of directness as the absence of mediation is not limited to perception. It is not a casual idea, sometimes holding and sometimes not holding, as some commentators on Gibson seem to think. It is a bold assault on the claim that indirectness can be a primary source of knowledge.

It is not, however, a denial of the reality of symbol functions; that is, it still allows that certain objects, when treated consistently by learned conventional rules, can promote indirect specification of the direct circumstances under which the rules were learned. Why is such an easily dispelled misunderstanding so often repeated?

When something challenges the status quo in science but is not understood, then myths grow up around the offending view aimed, either wittingly or unwittingly, at making it seem preposterous and undeserving of serious consideration. This has happened time and time again in the case of ecological psychology and especially in regard to direct perception—around which an aura of mystery has grown up. It might be wise to dispel some of these most obvious myths before proceeding.

Myths about direct perception

Myth 1: Ecological psychologists do not believe in indirect perception

This is patently false. Gibson also allowed perception to be indirect where paintings, photographs, TV, movies, virtual realities, and other facsimiles of reality are concerned, although he strongly opposed the traditional attempts to reduce all perception and cognition to being indirect, that is, mediated by memorial states or inferential processes.

Gibson was no fool; he would never deny anything so obvious and, in fact, wrote extensively on this topic (see, for instance, Part 4 of his 1979/1986 book, in which he discussed depiction and the structuring of light by artifice; see also Turvey & Shaw, 1979, on the primacy of perceiving). Such indirect processes have their place, but Gibson was quite sure it was foolish to try to replace direct processes with them.

Myth 2: Ecological psychologists do not believe in memory

This is also false. Acceptance of direct specification does not entail the rejection of memory as persisting knowing nor memory as portable knowledge, but it does lead one to treat memory differently from orthodoxy. We reject the computer metaphor that treats memory as storage; memory is not for us a receptacle in which things are placed—whether those things be ideas, images, facts, or charges that cloak internal states with symbolic representations (Carello, Turvey, Kugler, & Shaw, 1984; Shaw & McIntyre, 1974). I prefer to think of it as an attunement of a resonance process rather than as an "item-in-the-box" theory (Turvey & Shaw, 1979). I say more about resonance theory later.

Myth 3: Ecological psychologists do not believe in inference

This is also quite false. We do not and should not deny a legitimate role to inference as a cognitive process; however, we prefer to construe it as a way of linking current indirect evidence, perhaps through mediating propositions, to future or past direct experiences. To evaluate the indirect evidence one must ultimately link it up to directly specified evidence. This is why we call it *direct inference*. Even some of the staunchest critics of the direct perception hypothesis have had to relinquish this point. For instance, Fodor and Pylyshyn (1981) made this candid realist's admission:

Even theories that hold that perception of many properties is inferentially mediated must assume that the detection of *some* properties
is direct (in the sense of *not* inferentially mediated). Fundamentally,
this is because inferences are processes in which one belief causes
another. Unless some beliefs are fixed in some way other than by
inference, it is hard to see how the inferential processes could get
started. Inferences need premises.

(p. 155)

Also, I add, the premises need to be reducible (grounded).

I find little to disagree with here—except I would amend their statement
to read "it is impossible to see how the inferential processes could get started."
As was seen earlier, Simon (1969/1996) also recognized that "symbols must
have windows on the world and hands too" (p. 22). One wonders if a
rapprochement is possible if other prejudices could be overcome. Clancey
(1997) made a strong case that Fodor and Pylyshyn (1981) simply missed
the point of Gibson's ecological level of description. Fodor and Pylyshyn
missed the point because they did not relinquish internal state descriptions
in favor of relational ones.

Satisfying the inheritability of truth conditions either makes or breaks an
entailment theory. Grounding a proposition so it can be evaluated in terms
of its pragmatic truth value requires evaluation in a real-world context.
Although quite relevant, situated logic is a technical study in its own right,
and therefore I will not explore it here (but see Barwise & Perry, 1984).

Ecological psychologists also recognize that indirect perception is the meat
and potatoes of being an artist, photographer, or composer, just as indirect
inference is the staple technique for historians, archeologists, and sleuths, as
well as being involved in forecasting by medical doctors, weathermen, economists, pollsters, and political pundits.

The depth of misunderstanding of Gibson's radical hypothesis is illustrated by a quote from a leading author (Clark, 1997) of an otherwise
interesting and insightful book:

A related view of internal representation was pioneered by the
psychologist James Gibson (1950, 1966, 1979/1986). This work made
the mistake, however, of seeming to attack the notion of complex
mediating inner states *tout court*. Despite this rhetorical slip,
Gibsonian approaches are most engagingly seen only as opposing
the encoding or mirroring view of internal representation.

(p. 50)

Clark (1997) missed the mark in his understanding of what is theoretically
at stake. Neither Gibson nor his followers reject mediation *tout court* but
repudiate the mentalist use of internal states as well as the behaviorist's use

of external states in trying to model what is primary in epistemic activities. A pox on both their houses! Such models never succeed, although failure does not seem to discourage a futile succession of repeated attempts. In their stead, as I have been at pains to show, we favor the use of relational (dual) states as being primary.

It seems to me, speaking abstractly, that the rock bottom level of description that best serves psychology is to be found at the ecological scale where the direct commutators live—unfortunately, the sense of this claim is that direct perception is a natural outcome of describing systems at the ecological scale. To me this is such a crucial postulate of the ecological approach that to ignore it is to misunderstand completely the strength and plausibility of the approach. If internal states are not needed, then much of the force is removed from criticisms of the direct specification thesis. Are they needed?

Can we improve on internal state space analysis?

Having converted to ecological psychology in the 1970s from being a committed computational cognitivist in the 1960s, I became increasingly suspicious of internal states—except when treated as ancillary physical or neurological constructs. Here is a quick sketch of why my attitude changed from being cognitive to ecological.

Like so many young Turks, under James Jenkins tutelage during my Minnesota postdoctoral studies (1965–1967), I had rebelled against the establishment that was thoroughly and rigidly behavioristic. The behaviorists were coming under increasingly harsh criticism by such cognitivist gurus as Noam Chomsky, James Jenkins, Jean Piaget, George Miller, Karl Pribram, and Ulric Neisser. Like so many others, I became profoundly convinced that psychology needed a nonbehavioristic alternative to explain language acquisition and cognitive development. The answer seemed at the time to require something akin to Craik's (1943) internal model theory.

Craik (1943) proposed the hypothesis that thought models or parallels reality, that the essential problem for psychology was not the mind, self, or sense data but symbolism. Such symbolism is instantiated in mechanical devices designed to aid human thought in calculation. Furthermore, Craik argued, that thought performs a simulative function by providing a convenient small-scale model of natural processes. Simon appealed to us at the time because he seemed to have been squarely in Craik's corner. The first crack in my allegiance to internal state theory (e.g., simulation models) came when I visited Cal Tech, as reported earlier.

The synergy strategy takes issue with this simulative proposition by avoiding what we later called a FOIF—a *first-order isomorphism fallacy* (Shaw & Turvey, 1981). Simulation theories assume that features of (mental, neural) representations can be mapped one to one onto the environmental state of affairs they represent, for this is how they accrue their meaning. Gestalt theories emphatically disagree and consider this a fallacy; instead, they are concerned about how things become organized in similar ways, their organization as wholes, and thus not their individual features. Such laws of organization are considered transposable over different concrete instantiations of a pattern (e.g., circles drawn on a blackboard with chalk or made by giant stones at Stonehenge; a melody played on different instruments or hummed by different voices).

Gestaltists (e.g., Koffka, 1935) rejected the FOIF in favor of a second-order isomorphism between the laws that explain the organization of the environmental state of affairs and those that account for the organization of the (neural) representation. As a budding theoretical psychologist, this move away from the crass correspondence theory of meaning promoted by Craik (1943) and Miller *et al.* (1960) and endorsed by Simon (1969/1996) sounded better to me, especially when I later learned that Gibson (1979/1986) said that one of his prime motivations was to ecologize Gestalt psychology. Soon I came to believe the gestaltist had a better idea. From the gestaltists I discovered Gibson, who seemed to me to have an even better idea as an answer to the question, "Why reproduce that which can be dealt with more directly and elegantly by invariant specification?" This was, after all, in keeping with my belief in the rightness of von Neumann's (1949/1966) conjecture.

Let us look at FOIFs more closely with an eye on what they imply. Whereas feature correspondence is first-order isomorphism, correspondence of the transposable holistic properties of representations is second-order isomorphism because it is of a higher type. To try to reduce the latter to the former is to try to reduce a thing of a higher type to something of a lower type, and this buys into the fallacy of reductionism—the vain attempt to legitimize FOIFs. Von Neumann (1949/1966) suspected that there were reasons why reductionism is a dangerous intellectual game, and the logician Gödel and the formal semanticist Tarski proved it independently (see the editor's introduction to von Neumann, 1949/1966).

The gestaitists were as unhappy with Craik's (1943) type of solution as Gibson, arguing instead that a more useful strategy involves second-order isomorphisms. These models instead express invariant principles of organization that are transposable over the configurational properties of situations, thus treating particular instances as tokens of a more abstract class of situations. Because Gibson (1979/1986) had admitted that one of his goals was to ecologize Gestalt psychology, he replaced their phenomenalism and its dependency on subjective experience with the social invariants we all share, and their configurational properties with those invariants that inhere in relational properties that couple organisms to their environment. Affordances are an example of such interactional invariants. Moving from the gestaitists' phenomenalism to ecological realism was to me Gibson's better idea.

Simon, however, is not guilty of this fallacy in all aspects of his theory but seemed to argue for both forms of isomorphism—first-order for the representations achieved by simulation and second-order for the sharing of organizational principles in his search for common laws of design. However, the latter is corrupted by the former, and therefore the whole theory is tainted by his endorsement of the radical simulation hypothesis—an indefensible endorsement of the FOIF.

If Simon's laws of design were not based on this FOIF, then he would perhaps have been more open to Gibson's move to still higher order forms of isomorphism. We (Shaw & Turvey, 1981) argued, in the explanation of Gibson's ecologically scaled functionalism, that his notion of affordances as *invariants of invariants* (i.e., compound invariants) demands a still higher order isomorphism. We (Shaw & Turvey, 1981) called this *third-order isomorphism* and claimed it implicates even a fourth-order one—the latter we called *coalitional* to distinguish its concern from that of lower order gestalt holism that deals with only invariants over structures. The fourth-order isomorphism of a coalition adds the property of generative closure, as already discussed. Whereas the third-order isomorphism deals with invariants of invariants over structure (i.e., invariant properties of second-order isomorphs), coalitions express the closure of third-order isomorphism under ecological boundary conditions.

An agent's actions are guaranteed to be successful if and only if they are embedded in its ecosystem treated as a coalition (Shaw & Turvey, 1981). To be coalitional is to exhibit generative closure, as discussed earlier. Actions, no less than symbol functions, must be grounded and situated at the ecological scale. This means they must be defined over dual states of an ecosystem—states that coimplicate, deontically speaking, both the relevant environmental affordances and the agent's effectivities needed for realizing the action in question. The organism's effectivity for utilizing the environmental support involved in realizing an affordance goal must follow directly from a rule for the perceptual control of action, and most important, this rule must be underwritten by an ecological law.

I appreciate the difficulty of comprehending these ideas without elaborate discussions and illustrations. For this reason, the rest of the article is aimed at developing these ideas further. Key to this topic is seeing how the generative closure property of coalitions allow direct specification as the basis for actions as well as perceptions. This requires gaining an understanding of two notions: first, ecological states as dual states that coimplicate the agent and its environment simultaneously; and second, models of systems that manage to carry out goal-directed behaviors without entailing internal states.

In the next section I offer a first pass on these two topics.

345

Dual state machines: relational systems without
internal representations

In the early 1970s, after the scales fell from my eyes and I became a cognitivist reprobate, I began seeking both the best way to formally interpret ecological states and a way that internal states might be reconceptualized so as to retain their methodological usefulness, even if shorn of their putative explanatory value. The proposal for a dual-state machine that Todd and I (Shaw & Todd, 1980) offered three decades ago still seems to me to be on the right track and worthy of serious consideration by those with a computational bent but who do not uncritically assume internal state representations are necessary to psychological explanations:

> In fact the ecological approach to perception . . . proceeds upon the assumption that they [organism and environment] must be treated jointly and that they entail a mutually defined, integral unit of analysis whose "states" are neither internal nor external. Although it may be useful for methodological reasons to focus temporarily on a single interpretation in isolation, one cannot lose sight of their reciprocal nature without losing something essential.
>
> (Shaw & Todd, 1980, p. 400)

We go on to elaborate what general purpose internal state descriptions serve in modeling psychological systems, as seen from our ecological perspective:

> The existence of so-called "internal states," Q(t), is nothing more than a convenient fiction of contemporary computer science methodology, which allows the programmer, in lieu of evolution and learning opportunities, to provide machines which have no natural histories, H(t), with artificial ones. . . . Algorithmic models of perceptual phenomena . . . may provide a useful summary of the complex histories of animal–environment transactions by which the perceptual systems under study might have become attuned.
>
> (Shaw & Todd, 1980, p. 400)

On the other hand, such theorists seeking models should not fall under the spell of mechanistic reductionism. Reductionistic idealism is just as bad as reductionistic materialism, for they both depend on being fixated at the level of the FOIF. But why reductionism at all when there is good reason to incorporate higher order isomorphisms into one's theory—either as a gestaltist (second-order) because of transposability, or as a traditional ecological psychologist (third-order) because of affordances as invariants of invariants, or as one who adopts coalitions (fourth-order) as models of ecosystems because of the generative closure property, as I do?

In any case, theorists are admonished to be circumspect and not take the internal state description fostered by this methodological tool of programming as license to reify the ghostly states of mind. An excellent review of Shaw and Todd (1980) and perspicuous discussion of the consequences of this old way of thinking for cognitive neuroscience has been given by Clancey (1997, chap. 12), for which I am appreciative.

If one rejects Simon's physical symbol hypothesis with its reliance on simulation as being an instance of a FOIF because it requires correspondence between the world and internal states, then there are new options to consider in state space analysis. State space analysis is popular because of the history and usefulness of differential equations in physics and engineering. As pointed out, Todd and I (Shaw & Todd, 1980) introduced the rudiments for a new kind of state space analysis in 1980 in a short BBS commentary on Ullman's (1980) target article attacking Gibson's direct perception. Todd and I (Shaw & Todd, 1980) believed then, as I do now, that a state space comprising relational states might serve us better than ordinary state space with its singular states. This followed from seeing the need of states that have one foot in the environment and the other foot in the organism to model affordances.

Thus, what we had in mind might better be called *dual-state* space analysis. I have had a hand in developing this idea further with every generation of students who have worked with me since then. Only in the place of states, even dual states, we have come to appreciate the additional power and appropriateness of dual path descriptions (for an introduction into path spaces for psychology, see Kadar & Shaw, 2000; Shaw, Kadar, & Kinsella-Shaw, 1995; Shaw, Kadar, Sim, & Repperger, 1992; Shaw & Kinsella-Shaw, 1988).

The use of internal states as the primary construct in psychological modeling carries an insidious flaw, a danger of leaving perceptual knowledge unfounded as well as short-circuiting the ability for staying in contact with the world through the grounding of the actions of situated agents. Simon (1969/1996) agreed in part with this dual-state space sentiment. I find it perplexing that he could hold to internal (cognitive) state descriptions while at the same time harboring the following dual (ecological) state sentiments:

> The artificial world is centered precisely on this interface between the inner and the outer environments; it is concerned with attaining goals by adapting the former to the latter. The proper study of those who are concerned with the artificial is the way in which the adaptation of means to environments is brought about—and central to that is the process of design itself.
>
> (p. 113)

Simon (1969/1996) further argued: "Symbol systems are almost the quintessential artifacts, for adaptivity to an environment is their whole *raison d'etre*. They are goal-seeking, information-processing systems, usually enlisted in the service of the larger systems in which they are incorporated" (p. 22). Yet, Simon also argued that "symbol structures can, and commonly do, serve as internal representations (e.g., 'mental images') of the environments to which the system is seeking to adapt" (p. 22).

Simon (1969/1996) recognized also that for a symbol system to be useful, it

> must have windows on the world and hands, too. It must have means for acquiring information from the external environment that can be encoded into internal symbols, as well as means for producing symbols that initiate action upon the environment.
>
> (p. 22)

How can symbols have "windows" unless we admit, as even Fodor and Pylyshyn (1981) did, that at some time or other they were either directly perceived as grounded or as being situated with other symbols that were?

From the preceding quote, one sees that Simon (1969/1996) clearly recognized that symbols must be relational in at least one sense; they are assigned two simultaneous locations (i.e., dual states). Although they reside in the agent as mental constructs, they must designate properties and events in the world. They must have, as it were, one foot in each camp. A convention must be learned to make this relationship hold. Sans convention, this is reminiscent of Gibson. For Gibson (1979/1986), this symbol function is supplanted in perception by what I earlier called *direct commutators*, the purveyors of the ecological relations born, in general, by information and more specifically by affordances:

> But, actually, an affordance is neither an objective property nor a subjective property; or it is both if you like. An affordance cuts across the dichotomy of subjective–objective and helps us to understand its inadequacy. It is equally a fact of the environment and a fact of behavior. It is both physical and psychical, yet neither. An affordance points both ways, to the environment and to the observer.
>
> (p. 129)

Hence, it would seem that what separates Simon and Gibson is not what they believe must take place if adaptive knowledge is to be possible, but how it could. Little wonder that when Simon was confronted with the affordance concept, he identified it with a symbol—for he had no place else to hang its function except on an internal state. One sees this in the following quotation:

Contrary to Gibson's (1977) view, the thing that corresponds to an affordance is a symbol stored in central memory denoting the encoding in functional terms of a complex visual display, the latter produced, in turn, by the actual physical scene that is being viewed.

(Vera & Simon, 1993, p. 20)

The nub of Simon's and Gibson's disagreement seems to devolve on the willingness to use internal states in their explanations of how agents can know their environments. Can Gibsonians really get by with a theory of this knowing relation that avoids the FOIF implied by using internal states? In spite of arguments to the contrary (e.g., Wells, 2002), I think they can. I consider this question next.

A science in the first-person voice

Although using internal states is bad, it is not so bad as reifying them. The tricky issue for most computationalists to grasp is that one does not necessarily have to assume that states of being aware of something are internal. They may instead be dual states, which is tantamount to requiring that the description of states of awareness be cast at the ecological scale. Why the temptation to treat them as internal? Here is one reason.

From a third-person perspective, for example, that of the scientist or programmer, states of being aware of something are seen as being private because they are not shared at the moment by others. However, private experiences are still observed and therefore observable. If one person or species can participate in such experiences (notice the locution here!), logic does not allow excluding the possibility that others do as well. For on what grounds could they be excluded other than philosophical prejudice? Gibson (1979/1986) like Simon had his own syllogism that underwrites his theory:

At the ecological scale, the basic premise is compounded and fourfold:

A thing means what it is. (ontological premise)
To perceive is to be aware. (epistemological premise)
To be aware is to be aware of some thing. (psychological premise)
To be aware of some thing is to know its meaning. (intentionality premise)

Therefore:

To perceive something is to know its meaning. (direct perception conclusion)

There are no terms omitted from this argument; hence, there is no room for the addition of mediating constructs or anything else to this syllogism.

The conclusion follows directly from the premises. Collectively, the four premises as a compound define the relational complex that is identified as the basic ecological premise. The total meaning of perception being direct is conveyed fully by the whole argument (the compound ecological premise); also, as promised earlier, it is revealed to be not an assumption but a conclusion. Because this is so, if one buys into the compound ecological premise, one cannot avoid accepting direct perception as an unavoidable implication—indeed, as a direct inference.

Therefore, it is difficult to see Simon as an ecological psychologist despite his obvious ecological sentiments because he refuses to buy into the premises of the Gibsonian syllogism—which makes direct perception a theorem of ecological psychology.

Furthermore, this argument also implies that ecological psychology is science to be done in the first-person voice of the actor-perceiver, unlike other natural sciences that are carried out in the third-person voice of the scientist as observer-experimenter. The former is expropriospecific and proexterospecific (ecological psychology), whereas the latter is either exterospecific (objective physics) or propriospecific (subjective psychology).

Ecological psychology puts the first-person voice into a science of agents—agents who are trying to sustain adaptive behaviors by maintaining dynamical contact, in some felicitous way, with a potentially changing reality where threats and opportunities abound. On the spot, opportunistic awareness of what is changing and what is persisting is demanded. Direct perception is evolution's answer to this demand for situational awareness as well as for the grounding of actions so they can be realistic rather than fanciful. Grounded situational awareness is the agent's direct perception of what surrounds it, what is changing, and what is emerging. Moreover, in keeping with the Tristram Shandy paradox, there is no time for the agent's cognitive machinery to grind out representations, nor any need for it.

Direct perception answers the question of how agents can stay grounded in reality rather than merely having knowledge of it in the form of true beliefs. One need not assume animals have belief systems to believe that they have realistic expectations; their having attunement to the relevant affordances is truth enough. No belief is involved. Actions that succeed need not be believed to exist to have the consequences they do. The field of cognitive psychology has been too preoccupied with illusions, false beliefs, misperceptions, and other anomalies and not sufficiently occupied with discovering the ecological laws animals follow in functioning as adaptive as they are observed to do. Seeing that this is so is one consequence of adopting the first-person voice in science.

Conversely, by treating agents as artifacts, Simon's science retains the traditional third-person voice used by mechanists. Structuralists such as Titchener tried to have a science in the first-person voice, just as behaviorism tried to have a science in the third-person voice. Both failed because they isolated their respective premises, destroying the integrity of the compound ecological premise. Both quantum physics and relativity physics have placeholders for agents who observe and hence leave open the possibility of introducing the first-person voice into science. However, quantum physics fails because of the measurement problem (collapse of the wave function) and relativity theory because of frame discrepancies (breakdown of general covariance over reference frames).

Unfortunately, in both physical cases they can only approximate the ecological stance through extralogical concessions to the imperfections in the respective theory: Quantum physics allows it only where the mathematics of the wave equation fails to explain collapse and relativity physics only where the principle of general covariance fails to hold (i.e., where no tensor invariant solutions hold over frames). What is needed is a science not based on the weaknesses of other sciences but on its own inherent strengths. Since Simon's ploy of reducing all systems that have been adapted or that are self-adapting to artifacts, they become fodder for the sciences of the artificial, and the first-person voice is lost.

Not so with Gibson. In accepting no less than the compound ecological premise, agents retain their voices and their proper share of responsibility for success or failure in adaptation. Mechanism, on the other hand, fails. Because of its inherent dependency on less than the full complement of premises, it cannot be relational; not being relational, it cannot be intentional (in the broad sense of making reference beyond itself).

Thus, mechanisms serve awareness but cannot specify its content. To truly serve well they must have malleable rather than fixed state sets. Becoming aware *of this* when before you were aware of *that* is to change from a state set that includes *this* to one that includes *that*. Systems governed by rules cannot react to spontaneity; rules are hindered by too much inertia. Rules may work for persistent phenomena, but try to imagine a rule for recognizing spontaneity in happenings.

Consequently, I have always found it more than a little ironic that the most common complaint raised against ecological psychology is that it cares too little about mechanism, as if it should. We as ecological psychologists are warned that our approach will not command attention from the scientific community until it couches its explanations in mechanistic terms—as if the mechanistic philosophy would rule forever! On the contrary, it is well recognized that the reliance on mechanism in science is in general decline (d'Abro, 1952). Here is a typical example of such shortsighted criticism:

> One might claim that certain information about the world is picked up without processing intermediate types of information, but in support, one must produce the smart device itself and show the secret of its operation. . . . This type of analysis is still missing from the Gibsonian approach. . . . We believe that their call for a radical

reconceptualization of perceptual psychology will not meet with much favorable reaction until the mechanism underlying some *perceptual* process is revealed.

(Kubovy & Pomerantz, 1981, p. 450)

Of course, Kubovy and Pomerantz (1981) were quite right in their expectations of what the field would accept as an explanation but quite wrong in implying that a mechanistic explanation is all that should be scientifically acceptable. For ecological psychologists and contemporary physics, laws rather than mechanisms are the preferred basis for explanations (d'Abro, 1952; Feynman, 1967). In the long run, one might well ask: Will scientific contempt be more likely deserved by ecological psychology or mechanistic psychology? Which is more in keeping with contemporary scientific trends and which more old fashioned?

The role of awareness is of paramount importance to science in the first-person voice because it is synonymous with direct perception. Next I show why.

Awareness as directness

I am not aware of something being directly perceived, I am only aware of the something. Put differently, directness and awareness are the same; one is not an accompaniment or a garnish for the other, and they are both self-presenting the way pains and colors are—being incapable of being mediated. The semantics here are the same as for noticing. I cannot notice that x is the case without being aware of x, and I cannot notice x and not do so directly. The problem that traditionalists have who accept Cartesian mind–matter dualism is that they want to place awareness on the psychical side of the "epistemic cut" and the object of awareness on the material side. Gibson would not allow this: For him my direct perception of an environmental property, object, or event is also the awareness of a mutual property of self to which that property, object, or event is referred. Under this mutuality of cospecification, the agent and environment components retain their distinction but their separateness is no longer real.

There is no object of my awareness other than the object itself taken in reference to me. No addition to me is necessary; no internal state is required, for it is the whole system that resonates, not some local part (as Grossberg, 1980, argued). There is no awareness of a second object, which acts as a symbol or representation of the first object, that makes me notice the first object, for if there were, then by such direct noticing the mediator is made superfluous. If a mediator can be made superfluous, why is it needed in the first place? How did its mediation function originate?

How could a symbol become associated with its referent object without my noticing the referent object being associated with the symbol? It would be like Alice noticing the smile of the Cheshire cat without noticing the cat, or noticing the affordance without noticing the object that exhibits the affordance, or one object as being in an adjacency relationship without noticing at the same time that a second object is as well. There can no more be just one object noticed in associations, adjacencies, symbol functions, or representations than there can be the sound of one hand clapping. Because such subtle logic rarely wins any converts to the theory of direct perception, I try a different line of attack.

This logic denies that the epistemic cut should follow the fault line of the Cartesian mind–matter dichotomy. Instead, Gibson suggested that no cut at all be placed at the organism–environment synergy. However, with respect to epistemic cut of knower versus known, where most psychologists and philosophers are happy naming the divide the subjective–objective, Gibson would rather we repair the cut entirely by a kind of relational integration, for this is the main purpose for introducing ecological scaling in the first place.

If Gibson would have us replace the word *objective* with *socially invariant*, with what should we replace the word *subjective*? In its place Gibson used the term *awareness* in a way that is not meant to connote the person being in a particular internal state, namely, a state of consciousness. About this Gibson (1979/1986) wrote the following:

> Perceiving is an achievement of the individual, not an appearance in the theater of the mind. It is a keeping-in touch with the world, an experiencing of things rather than a having of experiences. It involves awareness-of instead of just awareness. It may be an awareness of something in the environment or something in the observer or both at once, bur there is no content of awareness independent of that which one is aware.
>
> (p. 239)

One might quibble and ask: Is not being aware synonymous to being in an internal state of awareness? For Gibson, as for James (1911), the answer has to be an emphatic "no!" For although an experience with concurrent awareness of the world and the self must surely have both physical external (environmental) support and internal neurological support—on this point Simon and Gibson agree—the ecological function and the psychological meaning of this necessary condition is first and foremost its socially invariant function. Here Simon and all other critics that I have read misunderstand Gibson's take on the issue—with Clancey (1997) being perhaps a notable exception. I tried to make the ecological position clear in a recent *Ecological Psychology* article (Shaw, 2001), but I try again in this context.

This idea of being aware of *x* is akin to James's (1911) radical empiricistic notion that we are in the experience rather than the experience being in us.

Dewey (1896) also understood this and made it a cornerstone of his brand of functionalism. He claimed that we interpolate into the core meaning of a stimulus what our actions with respect to it should be, as opposed to tacking responses onto it as associated linkages. This idea is also reflected by Mace's (1977) apt title that admonishes one to "ask not what's inside your head, but what your head's inside of." Such an experience involves an awareness of the other and the self concurrently. Therefore, it is neither internal nor external, nor both, if you prefer. It exhibits simultaneously a mutuality of environmental information and a reciprocity of perspectival information. It expresses awareness of the world in a chorus of first, second, and third voices.

To refer to such experiences as being internal states is simply grossly inappropriate because they are *observables* (in my extended use of the physicist's term); they are socially shareable rather than private. Hence, ecologically invariant experiences are really not objective but social, not external (belonging only to the environment) nor internal (belonging only to the agent).

Finally, let us return to where we came in and reconsider the case in favor of laws at the ecological scale.

Rules and laws in lieu of mechanism

Ecological rules are expressed in the imperative mood (i.e., are deontic), as Simon proposed for his rules, but apply to the agent as actor and not to the programmer or designer attempting to simulate agents (although such rules may help inform programmers of what rules need to be simulated or help interface designers set up their problems so that solutions are possible).

Experiences may be shared by others on the same or different occasions because they are not always private but common public social experiences. Humans have all shared the same types of experience such as pain, love, fear, anger, joy, and so forth, even if the token experiences were different, that is, the objects of those experiences differed. Gibson's notion of invariant environmental information allows one to go beyond the claim that we as humans can share only the same types of experiences to validate the claim that because we are aware of the same affordances, we can share the very same experiences.

If this claim seems strained or strange to you, then it is likely that you treat experiences as mental rather than as social constructs and concentrate unduly on their differences rather than their invariant core of similarities. It is not just information about the environment; it is socially invariant information about the environment. It is socially invariant because it remains invariant over different points of observations that might be occupied by different observers of similar design and attunement at different times. This is a consequence of generative closure and the most crucial feature of experiences as ecologically construed (i.e., as coalitional). To drive this point home, I Typically cite the insightful title of the paper by Mace (1977) given earlier. It bears repeating as the ecological mantra:

Ask not what's inside your head, but what your head's inside of!

Mace, of course, asked that one situate the agent as a whole and not just his head.

Because all creatures, from insects to humans, share the same general environment, although different habitats (where they live in that general environment) and niches (how they live there), they will share all affordances that hold in general and some others that are invariant over their habitats and relevant to their niches. This is what Gibson meant by affordances and information being objective is some sense. Such objective (socially invariant) information is lawful to the extent that it can be counted on when acted upon.

In his 1979 book, Gibson (1979/1986) gave 10 examples of ecological laws, each of which can be used to underwrite a rule for the perceptual control of action. Such rules are deontic in the sense discussed earlier because they follow the law of obligation on which imperative logics should be based. I also mentioned earlier that I had something to say on this issue; here is a sketch of what needs to be explained more elaborately at some other time:

> *For each ecological law identified, it is possible to write over it a rule that uses the law so as to allow perceptual information to control an action. I ask you to note carefully the deontic structure of the rule and how it is underwritten by a law at the ecological scale while all the time preserving the first-person perspective of the agent of choice. The rule is, of course, to he followed by the agent—whether available through the agent having discovered it and then learned it or having it evolved into the agent's design. This is the essence of the ecological interface design problem.*

Here are some examples of ecological laws from Gibson's (1979/1986) list that have universal application across all properly situated and attuned members of any species of agents:

> Flow of the ambient array specifies locomotion, and non flow specifies stasis.
>
> (p. 227)

Here Gibson (1979/1986) meant the *optic* array and that if the flow is *global*, it specifies *self*-locomotion, whereas if *local*, then it specifies that something else moves. A rule for the perceptual control of action can easily be devised from an information law by simply finding its first-person voice, changing the mood of the statement from the indicative to the imperative, and incorporating a controlling final condition (purpose) set in the optative mood (the mood in which needs, wants, and intents are defined). To wit:

If I want to move, then I must cause the optic array to undergo a global transformation!

As a hypothetical conditional, it is not yet well posed. It needs to be unconditional, namely, it must provide a definite answer to the question (interrogative mood), Do I want to move (optative mood) ? Yes? Then I must follow this rule (imperative mood) that abides by the relevant law (indicative mood). An important implication is that agents are not compelled to act by a law but must learn the rules that apply the law appropriate to their intents. Particles have no option but to move as the law dictates—once initialized for them. Agents have the option to alter their intents; however, once the intent is in place and the law adopted that can finalize that intent (help reach the goal unless thwarted by unforeseen circumstances), then the agent must abide by the law. This conveys the imperative import of ecological law and reveals clearly its deontic nature.

Hence, an ecological law applies just as inexorably for agents as dynamical laws do for particles. Whereas the dynamical law must be initialized to apply, the ecological law must be finalized. (Both must satisfy a set of boundary conditions impressed by the law being situated in a particular case.) Finalizing an ecological law may require that the agent select, from the set of rules that it knows, the proper one for satisfying the intention it holds. Elsewhere this has been called the *fundamental problem of intentional dynamics*; for Simon, it is the. fundamental problem of design theory. The two approaches are very similar, both being related to but not reducible to traditional optimizing techniques and utility theory.

Here is another ecological law that is less general—applying only to certain kinds of actors but is nested under the previous law:

Flow of the textural ambient array just behind certain occluding protrusions into the field of view specifies locomotion by an animal with feet.

(Gibson, 1979/1986, p. 229)

This law is specific to pedal animals and thus, unlike the first law, does not apply to all animals. It is nevertheless general to all pedally locomotive creatures and underwrites a rule for action as well:

If you want to walk, then cause the optic array to undergo a global transformation such that the leading edge of the feet delete the textual array and the trailing edge accretes it!

In this, one sees that ecological laws and the action rules they underwrite may be graded from the universal to the specific.

The key point to recognize is that these are rules that hold in the first-person and not just for one person but for all persons that fall within its range of application. To reiterate, whereas some laws are sufficiently general to be considered universal laws at the ecological scale in that they hold without exception (e.g., the first law mentioned previously), other laws may be less general (e.g., laws that underwrite rules for aquatic, arboreal, or flying creatures). Laws therefore need to be graded for the rules they enforce, from less to more general, up to their maximum degree of social invariance.

One of the virtues of being able to treat psychological phenomena as law governed is the economy it gives to explanations. If one has laws, then one does not have to worry about discovering underlying, deeply rooted mechanisms to have an explanation. Law-based explanations, unlike mechanisms, tend to be logically shallow and highly ramified. The more general the law, the more shallow and more ramified its application. Mechanisms that are "smart" in Runeson's (1977) sense become unwieldy and fragile if allowed to grow too large. This is, I truly believe, a consequence of the truth of von Neumann's (1949/1966) conjecture. Have you ever had to redo a program or a proof because it got so unwieldy that it was safer and less time consuming just to do it over?

Reducing the wonderful in nature to the commonplace in science

One must be careful not to romanticize nature. Hardheaded scientists who think that to be objective one must dispel wonder in favor of the familiar, even if banal, will never accept Gibson's use of a phenomenological basis to his science (Kadar & Effken, 1994). It is recognized that awareness is not a third-person observable but a first-person experience. Observables can be formalized, experiences cannot; but they might be shared. Note that because of this sharing (social invariants), Gibson's phenomenological basis to ecological science avoids the subjective flaw (introspective method) that precludes mentalism from making serious advances. Having awareness of x as a social invariant is like having cake and eating it too—one gets subjectivity and objectivity wrapped up in a single package.

Simon (1969/1996) also wanted his cake and to eat it too. Here is what he said is the goal of science: "The central task is a natural science is to make the wonderful commonplace: to show that complexity, correctly viewed, is only a mask for simplicity; to find a pattern in apparent chaos" (p. 1). In short, to make the wonderful comprehensible by decomposing it into simple parts and simple movements, the dream of every mechanist is a love affair with reductionism. Simon, though, wanted it all: wonder as comprehendible, complexity as simplicity. Forgive me, but this sounds a little like Orwellian doublespeak. Simon must have realized that he damaged his credibility by speaking too plainly of his goals; therefore, he amended his statement:

> This is the task of natural science: to show that the wonderful is not incomprehendible, to show how it can be comprehended—but not to destroy wonder. For when we have explained the wonderful, unmasked the hidden pattern, *a new wonder arises at how complexity was woven out of simplicity* [italics added].
>
> (p. 3)

I am indeed nearly seduced by the eloquence of these last lines, but it hides an insidious assumption, and one I believe, as von Neumann (1949/1966) did, likely to be quite false. The phrase "how complexity was woven out of simplicity" assumes that complexity is predicative and hence recursive —that if one only uses a divide and conquer, all will be well. Yet, what if complexity is neither predicative (e.g., decidable in the logician's sense) nor recursive? Ironically, being recursive and predicative is what the systems theorist par excellence Rosen (1991, 1999) called the defining characteristics of simple systems. What if complexity is by nature rather than artifice (formal description) a limitless source of generatively specified impredicativities, that is, undecidable predicates, as von Neumann, Penrose, and Rosen all suspected? What then?

Complex systems that can be reduced to simple systems are not complex at all but mistakenly described. Wonders that reduce to the banal are not wonderful at all but sadly denuded spectacles. Magicians' tricks may be so reduced, but nature is no magician to have its secrets so easily revealed. Still one knows of the wonder because one can directly perceive it; it is a self-presenting fact about the universe, not a symbol stored in central memory. Of course, this is an attitude to be shared, not an argument to be won.

A more manageable query that needs attention that grows from this aesthetic sense of wonder and our stubborn concupiscence as rationalists is this: How can some systems be so shallow in terms of logical layers and yet so ramified in their generality? Gibson (1979/1986) approached an answer to this question with his notion of invariants of invariants (what was earlier encountered as third-order isomorphism). He recognized that the difficulty psychologists typically have had in understanding his concept of invariants (second-order isomorphism) would be exacerbated in the case of affordances as higher order invariants. With respect to the typical psychologist, Gibson made this pessimistic prediction:

He may concede the invariants of structured stimulation that specify surfaces and how they are laid out and what they are made of.
But he may boggle at the invariant combinations of invariants
that specify the affordances of the environment for an observer.
The skeptic familiar with the experimental control of stimulus variables has enough trouble understanding the invariant variables I
have been proposing without being asked to accept invariants of
invariants.

(p. 140)

Gibson opened the door for going even further toward generality to be
obtained by composing invariants of invariants to get higher and higher
order affordances: "Nevertheless, a unique combination of invariants, a
compound invariant, is just another invariant. It is a unit, and the components do not have to be combined or associated" (Gibson, 1979/1986,
pp. 140–141). In this way explanations might be achieved that become
more logically shallow as they become more highly ramified. Coalitions
then, as fourth-order isomorphisms, should give us models that are most
shallow and most highly ramified in their applications to nature.

In fairness, it should be pointed out that Simon (1969/1996) surely agreed
that systems should be broader but less deep and has discussed extensively
how symbol processing systems might capitalize on these desirable properties. For instance, he told the story of two watchmakers, Tempus and
Hora, one who benefits from modular construction if the watch is dropped,
and the other who does not. If one has hierarchic depth in a system to
contend with, then modularity can help insulate against mistakes made at one
level from propagating across all levels. This has been a popular context-
free strategy where situating and grounding the components is ignored.

Hence, there is a clear difference between Gibson's and Simon's two
proposals, for modularity is mechanistic and invokes layers and layers of
mediation, whereas compounding invariants keeps each higher order level
just as direct as the one below it and hence as situated. For Gibson, situational
awareness is defined over these higher order invariants under which the
contextual meanings are nested and recoverable by differentiation of the
available information. For Simon, the recoverability seems both less assured
and more mysterious.

Prospective control by anticipatory information is a necessary ingredient
for any adequate theory of situated action. On this Simon and Gibson
agreed, as is seen next.

Prospective control

In 1709 Bishop Berkeley reminded us that the chief end of perception is to
enable agents "to foresee the benefit or injury which is like to ensue upon

application of their own bodies to this or that body which is at a distance."
Two hundred seventy years later, as mentioned earlier, Gibson (1979/1986)
endorsed this adaptive function for vision:

> What the philosopher called foresight is what I call the *perception
> of the affordance*. To see at a distance what the object affords on
> contact is "necessary for the preservation of the animal." . . . But it
> must be able to see affordances from afar. A rule for the visual
> control of locomotion might be this: so move as to obtain bene-
> ficial encounters with objects and places and to prevent injurious
> encounters.
>
> (p. 232)

Simon (1969/1996) provided a very similar formulation of rules for action
as produced by means–end analysis:

> The distinction between the world as sensed and the world as acted
> upon defines the basic condition for the survival of adaptive
> organisms. The organism must develop correlations between goals
> in the sensed world and actions in the world of process. When they
> are made conscious and verbalized, these correlations correspond
> to what we usually call means—ends analysis.
>
> (p. 210)

It is obvious that Gibson's rule for the perceptual control of action, like
Simon's, must also have the agent develop such correlations between the
information it intends to receive and the information that it comes to
receive after proper movements. Simon (1969/1996) goes on to summarize
the rule this way: "Given a desired state of affairs and an existing state of
affairs, the task of an adaptive organism is to find the difference between
these two states and then to find the correlating process that will erase the
difference" (p. 210). If one did not know it was Simon speaking, one might
have well imagined it to be Gibson.

There are two conditions that such rules for adaptive action should satisfy. First, it does not matter how one erases the difference between the
information specifying a current state of affairs and information specifying
the future state of intended affairs as long as it gets erased. This means that,
as in quantum theory, the only measurements that need be compared are
remote before and after termini; what goes on in between is only important
insofar as it is the means that contribute to the ends intended.

Second, what is to be established is a correlation between goals and
actions such that the latter eventually comes into phase with the former.
Hence, the adaptive process is one of establishing phase correlations, not
one of constructing mediating causal chains. This may sound like the same

thing, but it is not. As all students are taught in a first statistics class, *correlation does not mean causation*—meaning that just because two remote events are correlated does not imply that they are causally related. Hence, explanations based on correlations are not mechanistic because they need not be mediated by causal chains.

Likewise, they need not be mediated by anything else either, not by mental representations, ethereal ether, or ghostly ectoplasm. The correlation may just as well be thought of as a direct specification that it performs lawfully as an action-at-a- distance.

Conclusions

Here I have aired my prejudices so that there can be no misunderstanding as to what I believe is at stake, namely, that some radical, ecological version of science must replace the mechanistic science most psychologists adopt uncritically. Also, the new ecological science should, to remain a science, retain the fundamental appearance of the old science in its appeal to laws of nature. Simon and others of his ilk challenge the idea of the new ecological science that puts knowing agents back into the equation. They make a rebellious countermove away from traditional law-based science—a move that makes the Lockean solipsistic nightmare unavoidable.

Recall that Locke argued that all thought is about ideas and that these ideas either come from perception or reflection—no other source. Hence, he is only recognizing this fact when he says: "Whatsoever the mind perceives in itself, or is the immediate object of perception, thought, or understanding, that I call an idea" (Locke, 1706/1974, pp. 111–112). Locke placed ideas, by definition, as the sole objects of thought, just as Simon placed symbols. Both condoned the cognitive paradox by which one can then only know the virtual objects of thought—ideas and symbols—and not their real-world referents. Locke himself recognized this paradox and merely avoided discussing it, producing instead a new theory later in his treatise (*An Essay Concerning Human Understanding*) that was inconsistent with the earlier one (Russell, 1945).

I do not see how Simon, or any other representationalist for that matter, either avoids Locke's paradox or resolves it. For Gibson the task is different but not easier. Although Gibson took the objects of thought, like Locke, to be the objects of perception, those objects are not virtual objects (ideas or symbols) but the real objects themselves (reread captions). The difficulty with this direct realist's view, not confronted by the indirect realist's account, is that perception takes time; therefore, the object perceived cannot be the present object but must be a retrospective one. If retrospective, how then can it avoid being like a persisting image, or memory trace, a virtual object? In such a case, perception is indeed indirect in that it is mediated somehow by these virtual objects.

To my mind, Gibson offered a brilliant solution to this apparent direct realist's paradox: This difficulty is overcome by getting rid of "objects" of perception treated as being at a fixed punctiform moment in time (James's, 1911, so-called specious moment); these are replaced with events whose temporal courses dynamically express invariant properties. (This is the reason that in my work I have adopted paths rather than states, as indicated earlier.) It is these temporally sustained invariant properties of process (persistence over change) that one experiences directly—not some retrospective object of a frozen past moment. These processes (objects of perception construed as paths) resonate over time and space and remain the same objects of memory or thought at later moments if their invariants are preserved. For they are their invariants and not something else! Thus, no virtual objects are needed if one carefully reformulates what is the real object, as perceived or otherwise referred to.

A final word

Where have we come? In opposition to Simons clearly stated "axioms" for a design theory for how artificial systems couple to their environments, I can now state the axioms for an ecological interface design theory:

- Direct perception is a consequence of the self-referentiality of ecological law.
- Rules underwritten by such laws require no mechanism—indeed, can have none.
- Direct specification is a consequence of a system's generative closure property.

These axioms have three corollaries:

- Law-based symbol systems have reducible conventions and require no rule-based mechanism.
- Symbol systems not based on law have irreducible conventions and so require a rule-based mechanism.
- Information underwritten by ecological law is direct specification (acts at a distance); all other forms of information require a symbol manipulation mechanism.

Whereas the set of axioms and corollaries express the sense of both direct and indirect perception, or more generally specification nee information, the last two corollaries locate the place where computational theories enter legitimately—under indirect specification. There is no room whatsoever for extreme computationalism. Recall Gibson's (1979/1986) radical thesis: "If so, to perceive them is to perceive what they afford. This is a radical

362

hypothesis, for it implies that the 'values' and 'meanings' of things in the environment can be directly perceived" (p. 127).

If one accepts these conclusions and their implications, then it is time to make a beginning toward the new ecological science that Gibson's radical hypothesis called for. To his critics who reject direct perception out of hand, Gibson might have echoed Dr. Samuel Johnson, who is reputed to have said (by Boswell, 1791/1998) in response to a dim carping critic: "Sir, I am obliged to give you an explanation but I am not obliged to give you an understanding."

Gibson's congenial nature, however, would never have allowed him to inflict so unkind a cut. At least Gibson did succeed in giving us an opportunity for understanding a vision of psychology that is quite superior, in my opinion, to the competing view of extreme computationalism and its attendant philosophy of mechanism. Also, quite rightly, it does not rule out an important role for a computational ecological psychology—the latter will just not be center stage.

Acknowledgements

I thank Peter Kugler for helpful comments on earlier portions of this article, as well as the students in my graduate seminar: Bruno Galantucci, Steve Harrison, Mike Richardson, and Theo Rhodes. Special thanks to Bill Mace who offered much needed help on all aspects of the article. My apologies to them all for any problems that remain, for which I am of course solely responsible.

References

Barab, S., Cherkes-Julkowski, M., Swenson, R., Garrett, S., & Shaw, R. (1999). Principles of self-organization: Ecologizing the learner-facilitator system. *The Journal of the Learning Sciences, 8*, 349–390.

Barwise, J., & Perry, J. (1984). *Situations and attitudes*. Cambridge, MA: MIT Press.

Berkeley, G. (1709). *An essay towards a new theory of vision* (4th ed., Classics in the History of Psychology). Toronto, Ontario, Canada: York University. Retrieved from http://psychclassics.yorku.ca/Berkeley/vision.htm

Blum, M. (1967). A machine-independent theory of the complexity of recursive functions. *Journal of the ACM, 14*, 322–336.

Boswell, J. (1791). *Life of Johnson*. Project Gutenberg Release No. 1564 (December 1998). Retrieved from http://digital.library.upenn.edu/webbin/gutbook/lookup?num.1564

Carello, C., Turvey, M., Kugler, P., & Shaw, R. (1984). Inadequacies of the computer metaphor. In M. S. Gazzaniga (Ed.), *Handbook of cognitive neuroscience* (pp. 229–248). New York: Plenum.

Cassirer, E. (1944). The concept of group and the theory of perception. *Philosophical and Phenomenological Research, 5*, 1–35.

Casti, J. (1994). *Complexification: Explaining a paradoxical world through the science of surprise.* New York: HarperCollins.

Chalmers, D. J. (1996). *The conscious mind.* New York: Oxford Universiry Press.

Chomsky, N. (1957). *Syntactic structures.* The Hague, The Netherlands: Mouton.

Chomsky, N. (1965). *Aspects of the theory of syntax.* Cambridge, MA: MIT Press.

Churchland, P. M., & Churchland, P. S. (1983). Stalking the wild epistemic engine. *Nous, 17,* 5–18.

Churchland, P. M., & Churchland, P. S. (1990, January). Could a machine think? *Scientific American, 262,* 26–31.

Clancey, W. (1997). *Situated cognition: On human knowledge and computer representations.* Cambridge, England: Cambridge University Press.

Clark, A. (1997). *Being there: Puttingbrain, body, and world together again.* Cambridge, MA: MIT Press.

Cook, S. (1971). The complexity of theorem-proving procedures. In *ACM Symposium on Theory of Computing* (pp. 151–158).

Copeland, B. J. (1997). The Church–Turing thesis. In E. N. Zaka (Ed.), *The Stanford encyclopedia of philosophy* (Fall 2002). Retrieved February 20, 2003, from http://plato.stanford.edu/archives/fall2002/entries/church-turing/

Costall, A., & Leudar, I. (Eds.). (1996). Situating action [Special issue]. *Ecological Psychology, 8*(2).

Craik, K. (1943). *The nature of explanation.* Cambridge, England: Cambridge University Press.

d'Abro, A. (1952). *The rise of the new physics; its mathematical and physical theories* (2nd ed.). New York: Dover.

Dewey, J. (1896). The reflex arc concept in psychology. *Psychological Review, 3,* 357–370.

Dreyfus, H. (1972). *What computers can't do: A critique of artificial reason.* New York: Harper & Row.

Dreyfus, H. (1995). Simon's simple solutions. *The Stanford Electronic Humanities Review, 4*(1). Retrieved February 18, 2003, from http://www.stanford.edu/group/SHR/4-1/text/dreyfus.commentary.html

Effken, J. A., Kim, N.-G., & Shaw, R. E. (1997). Making the constraints visible: Testing the ecological approach to interface design. *Ergonomics, 40,* 1–27.

Effken, J., & Shaw, R. (1992). Ecological perspectives on the new artificial intelligence. *Ecological Psychology, 4,* 247–270.

Feynman, R. (1967). *The character of physical law.* Cambridge, MA: MIT Press.

Fodor, J., & Pylyshyn, Z. (1981). How direct is visual perception?: Some reflections on Gibson's "ecological approach." *Cognition, 9,* 139–196.

Gibson, J. (1950). *The perception of the visual world.* Boston: Houghton Mifflin.

Gibson, J. (1966). *The senses considered as perceptual systems.* Boston: Houghton Mifflin.

Gibson, J. (1977). The theory of affordances. In R. Shaw & J. Bransford (Eds.), *Perceiving, acting and knowing: Toward an ecological psychology* (pp. 67–82). Hillsdale, NJ: Lawrence Erlbaum Associates, Inc.

Gibson, J. (1986). *The ecological approach to visual perception.* Hillsdale, NJ: Lawrence Erlbaum Associates, Inc. (Original work published 1979)

Greeno, J. (1989). Situation, mental models and generative knowledge. In D. Klahr & K. Kotovsky (Eds.), *Complex information processing: The impact of Herbert A. Simon*. Hillsdale, NJ: Lawrence Erlbaum Associates, Inc.

Grossberg, S. (1980). Direct perception or adaptive resonance? *Behavioral and Brain Science. 3*, 385–386.

Grote, J. (1865). *Exploratio phihsophica*. Cambridge, England: Deighton, Bell.

Guthrie, S. (n.d.). *Russell, infinity, and the Tristram Shandy paradox*. Retrieved February 17, 2003, from http://sguthrie.net/infinity.htm

Hartmanis, J., & Steams, R. (1965). On the computational complexity of algorithms. *Transactions of the American Mathematical Society, 117*, 285–307.

Hartmanis, J., & Stearns, R. (1966). *Algebraic theory of sequential machines*. Englewood Cliffs, NJ: Prentice Hall.

How are affordances related to events? An exchange of views [Special issue]. (2000). *Ecological Psychology, 12*(1).

James, W. (1911). *The meaning of truth*. New York: Longman Green.

Jenkins, J., Jimenez-Pabon, E., Shaw, R., & Sefer, J. (1975). *Schuell's aphasia in adults*. New York: Harper & Row.

Kadar, E., & Effken, J. (1994). Heideggerian meditations on an alternative ontology for ecological psychology: A response to Turvey's (1992) proposal. *Ecological Psychology, 6*, 297–341.

Kadar, E. E., & Shaw, R. E. (2000). Toward an ecological field theory of perceptual control of information. *Ecological Psychology, 12*, 141–180.

Karp, R. (1972). Reducibility among combinatorial problems. In R. E. Miller & J. W. Thatcher (Eds.), *Complexity of computer computations* (pp. 85–103). New York: Plenum.

Kim, N.-G., Effken, J., & Shaw, R. (1995). Perceiving persistence under change and over structure. *Ecological Psychology, 7*, 217–256.

Klahr, D. (Ed.). (1976). *Cognition and instruction: Tenth annual Carnegie-Mellon symposium on information processing*. Hillsdale, NJ: Lawrence Erlbaum Associates, Inc.

Koffka, K. (1935). *Principles of Gestalt psychology*. New York: Harcourt Brace.

Korb, K. (1995). The meanings of "meaning." *The Stanford Electronic Humanities Review, 4*(1) . Retrieved February 18, 2003, from http://www.stanford.edu/group/SHR/4-l/text/korb.commentary.html

Kubovy, M., & Pomerantz, J. (Eds.). (1981). *Perceptual organization*. Hillsdale, NJ: Lawrence Erlbaum Associates, Inc.

Lave, J. (1988). *Cognition in practice*. Cambridge, England: Cambridge University Press.

Locke, J. (1974). *An essay concerning human understanding* (5th ed., A. D. Woozley, Ed.). New York: New American Library. (Original work published 1706)

Mace, W. (1977). James J. Gibson's strategy for perceiving: Ask not what's inside your head, but what your head's inside of. In R. Shaw & J. Bransford (Eds.), *Perceiving, acting and knowing: Toward an ecological psychology* (43–66). Hillsdale, NJ: Lawrence Erlbaum Associates, Inc.

McCulloch, W., & Pitts, W. (1943). *Embodiments of mind*. Cambridge, MA: MIT Press.

Mensky, M. (1993). *Continuous quantum measurements and path integrals*. Bristol, England: Institute of Physics.

Miller, G., Galanter, E., & Pribram, K. (1960). *Plans and structures of behavior.* New York: Holt.

Minsky, M., & Papert, S. (1969). *Perceptrons: An introduction to computational geometry.* Cambridge, MA: MIT Press.

Newell, A., & Simon, H. (1976, March). Computer science as empirical enquiry. *Communications of the ACM, 19,* 113–126.

Parker, J. (1997). Spiraling down "the gutter of time": Tristram Shandy and the strange attractor of death. *Electronic Book Review (ebr): Science, Technology & the Arts: Weber Studies,* 14(1, Suppl.). Retrieved February 21, 2003, from http://www.altx.com/ebr/w(ebr)/essays/parker.html

Penrose, R. (1989). *The emperor's new mind: Concerning computers, minds, and the laws of physics.* New York: Oxford University Press.

Penrose, R. (1994). *Shadows of the mind: A search for the missing science of consciousness.* New York: Oxford University Press.

Penrose, R. (1996, January). Beyond the doubting of a shadow: A reply to commentaries on *Shadows of the Mind. Psyche,* 2(23). Retrieved February 22, 2003, from http://psyche.cs.monash.edu.au/v2/psyche-2-23-penrose.html

Rosen, R. (1991). *Life itself: A comprehensive inquiry into the nature, origin, and fabrication of life.* New York: Columbia University Press.

Rosen, R. (1999). *Essays on life itself.* New York: Columbia University Press.

Runeson, S. (1977). On the possibility of "smart" perceptual mechanisms. *Scandinavian Jortmal of Psychology, 18,* 172–179.

Russell, B. (1912). *The problems of philosophy.* New York: Home University Library.

Russell, B. (1945). *A history of western philosophy.* New York: Simon & Schuster.

Sanders, J. (1997). An ontology of affordances. *Ecological Psychology, 9,* 97–112.

Shaw, R. (1969). Cognition, simulation and the problem of complexity. *Journal of Structural Learning, 2,* 31–44.

Shaw, R. (1976). Simulation and the problem of complexity. In J. Scandura (Ed.), *Structural learning* (pp. 197–221). New York: Gordon & Breach.

Shaw, R. (2001). Processes, acts, and experiences: Three stances on the problem of intentionaliry. *Ecological Psychology, 13,* 275–314.

Shaw, R., & Bransford, J. (Eds.). (1977). *Perceiving, acting and knowing: Toward an ecological psychology.* Hillsdale, NJ: Lawrence Erlbaum Associates, Inc.

Shaw, R., & Cutting, J. (1980). Biological constraints on linguistic forms: Clues from the ecological theory of event perception. In U. Bellugi & M. Studdert-Kennedy (Eds.), *Biological constraints on linguistic form* (pp. 57–84). Berlin, Germany: Dahlem Konferenzen.

Shaw, R., Effken, J., Fagen, B., Garrett, S., & Morris, A. (1997). An ecological approach to the on-line assessment of problem-solving paths: Principles and applications. *Instructional Science, 25,* 151–166.

Shaw, R., Flascher, O., & Kadar, E. (1995). Dimensionless invariants for intentional systems: Measuring the fit of vehicular activities to environmental layout. In J. Flach, P. Hancock, J. Caird, &. K. Vicente (Eds.), *Global perspectives on the ecology of human–machine systems* (Vol. 1, pp. 293–357). Hillsdale, NJ: Lawrence Erlbaum Associates, Inc.

Shaw, R., Flascher, O., & Mace, W. (1996). Dimensions of event perception. In W. Prinz & B. Bridgeman (Eds.), *Handbook of perception and action* (Vol. 1, pp. 345–395). London: Academic.

Shaw, R., Kadar, E., & Kinsella-Shaw, J. (1995). Modeling systems with intentional dynamics: A lesson from quantum mechanics. In K. Pribram (Ed.), *Appalacia II: Origins of self-organization* (pp. 53–101). Hillsdale, NJ: Lawrence Erlbaum Associates, Inc.

Shaw, R., Kadar, E., Sim, M., & Repperger, D. (1992). The intentional spring: A strategy for modeling systems that learn to perform intentional acts. *Journal of Motor Behavior, 1* (24), 3–28.

Shaw, R., & Kinsella-Shaw, J. (1988). Ecological mechanics: A physical geometry for intentional constraints. *Human Movement Science, 7*, 155.

Shaw, R., Kugler, P, & Kinsella-Shaw, J. (1990). Reciprocities of intentional systems. In R. Warren & A. Wertheim (Eds.), *Control of self-motion* (pp. 579–619). Hillsdale, NJ: Lawrence Erlbaum Associates, Inc.

Shaw, R., & McIntyre, M. (1974). Algoristic foundations for cognitive psychology. In W. Weimer & D. Palermo (Eds.), *Cognition and symbolic processes* (pp. 305–362). Hillsdale, NJ: Lawrence Erlbaum Associates, Inc.

Shaw, R., McIntyre, M., & Mace, W. (1974). The role of symmetry in event perception. In H. Pick & R. MacLeod (Eds.), *Studies in perception: Essays in honor of J. J. Gibson* (pp. 276–310). Ithaca, NY: Cornell University Press.

Shaw, R., & Pittenger, J. (1979). Perceiving change. In H. Pick & E. Saltzman (Eds.), *Modes of perceiving and processing information* (pp. 187–204). Hillsdale, NJ: Lawrence Erlbaum Associates, Inc.

Shaw, R., & Shockley, K. (2003). An ecological science of the artificial? *The Journal of the Learning Sciences, 12*, 427–435.

Shaw, R., & Todd, J. (1980). Abstract machine theory and direct perception. *Behavioral and Brain Sciences, 3*, 400–401.

Shaw, R., & Turvey, M. (1981). Coalitions as models for ecosystems: A realist perspective on perceptual organization. In M. Kubovy & J. Pomerantz (Eds.), *Perceptual organization* (pp. 343–415). Hillsdale, NJ: Lawrence Erlbaum Associates, Inc.

Shaw, R., & Turvey, M. (1999). Ecological foundations of cognition: II. Degrees of freedom and conserved quantities in animal–environment. *Journal of Consciousness Studies, 6*(11–12), 111–123.

Shaw, R., & Wilson, B. (1976). Abstract conceptual knowledge: How we know what we know. In D. Klahr (Ed.), *Cognition and instruction: Tenth annual Carnegie-Mellon symposium on information processing* (pp. 197–222). Hillsdale, NJ: Lawrence Erlbaum Associates, Inc.

Simon, H. (1996). *The sciences of the artificial* (3rd ed.). Cambridge, MA: MIT Press. (Original work published 1969)

Situated action [Special issue]. (1993). *Cognitive Science, 17*.

Sterne, L. (1983). *The life and opinions of Tristram Shandy, gentleman.* Oxford, England: Oxford University Press. (Reprinted from *The Complete Works and Life of Laurence Sterne*, by W. L. Cross, Ed., 1904, New York: J. F. Taylor. Original work published 1760–1767)

Stofxregen, T. (2000). Affordances and events. *Ecological Psychology, 12*, 1–28.

Suchman, L. (1987). *Plans and situated actions: The problem of human machine communication.* Cambridge, England: Cambridge University Press.

Turvey, M., & Shaw, R. (1979). The primacy of perceiving: An ecological reformulation for understanding memory. In L. G. Nilsson (Ed.), *Perspective on memory research: Essays in honor of Uppsala University's 500th Anniversary* (pp. 167–222). Hillsdale, NJ: Lawrence Erlbaum Associates, Inc.

Turvey, M., Shaw, R., &. Mace, W. (1979). Issues in the theory of action. In J. Requin (Ed.), *Attention and performance VII* (pp. 557–595). Hillsdale, NJ: Lawrence Erlbaum Associates, Inc.

Ullman, S. (1980). Against direct perception. *Behavior and Brain Sciences, 3,* 373–415.

Vera, A., & Simon, H. (1993). Situated action: A symbolic interpretation. *Cognitive Science, 17,* 1–48.

Vicente, K. J. (1999). *Cognitive work analysis: Towards safe, productive, and healthy computer-based work.*

Mahwah, NJ: Lawrence Erlbaum Associates, Inc.

von Neumann, J. (1966). *Theory of self-reproducing automata.* Urbana: University of Illinois Press. (Original work published 1949)

Warren, W., & Shaw, R. (Eds.). (1985). *Change and persistence: The first international conference on event perception.* Hillsdale, NJ: Lawrence Erlbaum Associates, Inc.

Wells, A. J. (2002). Gibson's affordances and Turing's theory of computation. *Ecological Psychology, 14,* 140–180.

Wolfram, S. (2002). *A new kind of science.* Champaign, IL: Wolfram Media.

64

HERBERT SIMON'S COMPUTATIONAL MODELS OF SCIENTIFIC DISCOVERY

Stephen Downes

Source: *PSA: Proceedings of the Biennial Meeting of the Philosophy of Science Association*, (Vol. 1: Contributed Papers). Chicago: University of Chicago Press, 1990, pp.97–108.

1. Introduction

Herbert Simon's work on scientific discovery deserves serious attention by philosophers of science for several reasons. First, Simon was an early advocate of rational scientific discovery, contra Popper and logical empiricist philosophers of science (Simon 1966). This proposal spurred on investigation of scientific discovery in philosophy of science, as philosophers used and developed Simon's notions of "problem solving" and "heuristics" in attempts to provide rational accounts of scientific discovery (See Nickles 1980a, Wimsatt 1980). Second, Simon promoted and developed many of the crucial techniques and methods used in cognitive science. One is the use of computers to model internal psychological processes, a technique central to his account of scientific discovery. Another is protocol analysis, the use of the verbal reports of experimental subjects in psychology to construct accounts of their psychological processes. Protocol analysis is given a detailed formulation by Simon (Simon and Ericsson 1984), and is modified for use in the study of scientific cognition in the paper on Krebs (Kulkarni and Simon 1988). Third, Simon introduces normative proposals for science based on his computational investigations of scientific discovery (See also Zytkow and Simon 1988). Simon's work can be viewed as a contribution to naturalized philosophy of science, which centrally features the derivation of normative proposals from descriptive accounts of science. His work can also be viewed as a contribution to the growing field of "cognitive science of science," which uses techniques from the cognitive sciences to tackle issues in the philosophy of science.

In this paper I critically evaluate Simon's recent work on scientific discovery.[1] I focus primarily on Scientific Discovery (Langley *et al.* 1987), which documents many computer programs that purportedly make scientific discoveries, and "The Process of Scientific Discovery" (Kulkarni and Simon 1988), which is a detailed investigation of Krebs discovery of the ornithine cycle. I present several distinct criticisms of Simon's work. First I argue that Simon's descriptive account cannot distinguish discoveries as the product of an individual scientist's psychological processes or as the product of a social process involving several scientists. Yet Simon argues that scientific discovery can be adequately accounted for by appealing to psychological processes. I offer two lines of argument to establish that this latter step is unjustified. The first is that Simon's method of protocol analysis does not provide sufficient evidence for the existence of the distinct psychological processes he claims underlie scientific discoveries. The second is that scientific discovery has a crucial social component that Simon cannot account for. I conclude that as a result of these failures Simon's descriptive characterization of scientific discovery is inadequate, and further that this inadequacy is due to what I call "cognitive individualism." I conclude the paper by considering the normative dimension of Simon's account, and argue that his computer models of scientific discovery can be best understood as contributions to what Clark Glymour has called "android epistemology."

2. An outline of Simon's project

In *Scientific Discovery* (Langley *et al.* 1987) Simon describes a set of computer systems that purportedly make scientific discoveries. Primarily he is concerned with systems that can make data driven discoveries, or discoveries of a particular relationship in a certain (usually numerical) data set. The systems use a set of production rules (conditional statements) that represent heuristics (rules of thumb), which constrain operations on the data, Such a rule (or heuristic) for detecting regularities in numerical data is: "If the values of two numerical terms increase together, then consider their ratio" (Langley *et al.* 1987, p.66). The "discovery" of Kepler's Third Law by such a system is characterized as a problem solving task, involving a search through the data, the "problem space," to produce the desired goal, the law. The data are values for the periods of the planets (P) and their distances from the sun (D), and the desired relationship (goal state) is $D^3/P^2 = c$.

Simon claims that the systems' potential application extends beyond the particular scientific discoveries investigated, to providing an account of scientific discovery in general. The computer programs, the BACON programs, and other related programs, are progressively developed to deal with gradually more complex data, for example data requiring qualitative laws and attribute ascription. *Scientific Discovery* documents a large array of programs that Simon claims have discovered Kepler's Third Law, Boyle's Law, Snell's Law and many more.

Simon claims that the work

> ... seeks to investigate the psychology of the discovery process, and to provide an empirically tested theory of the information-processing mechanisms that are implicated in that process.
>
> (Langley *et al.* 1987, p.4)

The work is firmly embedded in his overall information processing approach in cognitive science (See e.g. Simon 1969, Newell and Simon 1972). According to Simon, "the research is mainly limited to finding a set of mechanisms that is sufficient to account for discovery" (Langley *et al.* 1987, p.4). So Simon's claims are that scientific discovery is a psychological process, and that a sufficient account of this process will be provided by the computer models.

In "The Processes of Scientific Discovery: The Strategy of Experimentation" (Kulkami and Simon 1988) Simon discusses Krebs experiments that led to the discovery of the ornithine cycle. Simon explains that the BACON programs did not broach the issue of where data came from in data driven discovery. He claims that the processes of designing experiments and observation were not investigated and that these latter are investigated in the work on Krebs. Simon's computational analysis of scientific discovery is governed by a guiding principle that scientific discovery is a collection of psychological processes and that these can be elicited by studying the work of scientists throughout history who have made important discoveries. Therefore the production system resulting from the work on Krebs is intended to complement the BACON discovery systems.

Simon argues that he can provide a reliable account of the psychological processes involved in Krebs' discovery of the ornithine cycle by relying on Holmes' (Holmes 1980) historical work on Krebs'. Holmes' account is constructed from a combination of Krebs' published work, his and his assistant's laboratory notebooks and interviews with Krebs made years after the discovery. Holmes' account provides the necessary protocols from which Simon derives heuristics, the proposed psychological mechanisms that produced Krebs' discovery. These heuristics have been embodied in the production system KEKADA, which simulates Krebs' discovery. Overall Simon claims that Krebs' discovery of the ornithine cycle was due to a set of psychological processes that Krebs possessed, and that these are derived from his scientific writings used as protocols, and captured in the computer program KEKADA.

3. The descriptive adequacy of Simon's account

Philosophers of science have turned to studies of scientific discovery as a reaction to the claims of Popper and the logical empiricist philosophers that discovery was not amenable to rational explanation (See e.g. Nickles 1980b). Scientific discovery is also the subject of investigation of historians and sociologists of science (See e.g. Brannigan 1981, Pickering 1984, Galison 1987). The picture of discovery that arises from these investigations is by no means monolithic, rather one of a complex and varied activity. Discovery is part psychological activity, part sociology of group acceptance, and pan historical accident and timeliness. In contrast we see that Simon's account centers around the development of computer programs that arrive at the same results as great scientists in history. Simon argues that this approach provides a sufficient set of mechanisms to account for scientific discovery (Langley *et al.*, p.4). Further he argues that the success of these computer programs will "show how simple information processes . . . can give an adequate account of the discovery process" (Langley *et al.*, p.33). Simon's descriptive account of scientific discovery shares none of the richness of the picture that arises from research in philosophy, sociology and history of science, and I argue that this makes it an insufficient account of scientific discovery.

Let us begin with the use of protocols. Simon's own observations about the weaknesses of the method of protocol analysis can be extended into arguments against his use of this method to elicit the psychological processes involved in scientific discovery. I conclude that protocol analysis provides insufficient evidence to support the existence of the proposed psychological processes underlying in scientific discovery.

Two methods of direct verbalizations are used to generate verbal reports from psychology subjects: Thinking aloud and retrospective accounts (My account follows Simon and Ericsson 1984 and Ericsson and Oliver 1988). The former are recorded as the subject carries out the task under study, and the latter are recorded immediately after the activity under study has taken place to make sure that the subject still has the relevant information in short term memory. In the paper on Krebs Simon claims that scientist's laboratory notebooks are closer in nature to retrospective reports than thinking aloud reports (Kulkarni and Simon 1988). We have no thinking aloud reports in the Krebs case as the protocols are from a historical study not a psychology experiment. When retrospective reports are used in psychology experiments they are made according to specific guidelines for remembering what was thought about during task performance (Ericsson and Oliver 1988). So Simon's comparison between laboratory notebooks and retrospective reports is a weak one. Although laboratory notes are taken at the end of particular tasks (and even at the end of the day or the week), they are not taken at the end of a particular psychological process. The notion of coming to the end of a psychological process is not a relevant factor for a scientist determining when to make notes in their laboratory notebook.

Scientists do not primarily aim at recording their thought processes during experiments when making laboratory notebooks. For example Millikan's notebooks (see Holton 1978) contained columns of figures and comments such as "beautiful, publish this." This is good evidence that he was not always concerned with recording his psychological processes, rather with recording his results and commenting on their usefulness. Scientists in the laboratory record important results, or outline replicable procedures for themselves to use on a future occasion, or for graduate students or technicians to use in their absence.[2] Laboratory notebooks do provide useful data about scientific practice, but it is not necessarily evidence for the existence of particular psychological processes of a particular scientist.[3] Such writings could also be used to generate an account of the social processes involved in a discovery (see Latour and Woolgar 1979). On the evidence of laboratory notebooks it is not only difficult to distinguish between different psychological processes, but it is also difficult to distinguish between the psychological processes of individual scientists and the more interactive processes of all the participants in the laboratory. The type of evidence provided by scientists' writings does not force one to the conclusion that particular psychological processes underlie scientific discovery.

In conclusion the analogy between verbal reports in psychology experiments, and laboratory notebooks as a resource for work on scientific discovery is strained for two reasons. First laboratory notebooks contain recollections, which may not have been made immediately after the putative psychological process they relate to occurred. Second, the laboratory notebooks do not contain information specifically about psychological processes. The laboratory notebooks can only be used as data from which an attempt to derive an account of psychological processes is made, and they could equally be used to derive an account of social processes.

The use of scientists more public writings to gain information about their psychological processes is even more problematic. One of the problems with retrospective reports in psychology is that subjects often "fill in" their reports with information not directly reproduced from memory (Simon and Ericsson 1984). They will perhaps give some plausible reasons for a particular activity instead of trying to remember the actual processes they went through (Cf. Nisbett and Wilson 1977). In a scientist's published work she is almost exclusively concerned with giving a plausible account of her results (in the form of reasons for these results), she is rarely if ever required to remember her psychological processes at the time of producing such results. Further she does not attempt to distinguish between reasons for results, and the psychological processes that led to such results. No principled method is available to distinguish between the two types of *post facto* reports: Ones that present psychological processes, and ones that present plausible reasons for a particular act (Cf. Nisbett and Wilson).

Leaving the issues surrounding protocols as insufficient evidence for the existence of psychological processes, a second line of argument challenges Simon's claim that such processes provide a "sufficient" account of scientific discovery. Drawing evidence from work in the sociology of science, I conclude that his cognitive individualist account of scientific discovery is not sufficient as it cannot account for the social nature of scientific discovery.

Simon's approach to explaining scientific discovery is directed by his information processing psychology. Simon investigates scientific discovery as a process of "thinking man" (or thinking machine) (Simon 1969). His position is that the scientists under investigation use one or more of a common stock of psychological processes. These processes are heuristic driven search mechanisms. An important question is why one person's use of some shared psychological processes would produce a scientific discovery, whilst another person's use of it would not. Simon claims in earlier work that the environment is the essential governing factor in producing different results with the same processes (Simon 1969, 1957), and yet he devotes no time in *Scientific Discovery* to describing *how* the environment is instrumental in producing the particular scientific discoveries he investigates, It is consistent with Simon's information processing psychology to argue that, given our shared psychological processes any human could come up with scientific discoveries, if he or she were put in the right environment. Putting it another way, it is consistent with Simon's account that factors other than the simple psychological processes he claims we possess are instrumental in producing scientific discoveries, and yet he leaves no room for such factors. Despite this deficiency he claims that he provides a sufficient account of scientific discovery. I now consider some factors that a sufficient account of scientific discovery must to account for.

Simon pays no attention to the issue of how one establishes that a scientific discovery has been made. A discovery's acceptance by the relevant scientific community is essential to its status as a discovery. And it is hard to separate this acceptance procedure from the process of discovery itself, a point argued by Brannigan in his *Social Basis of Scientific Discovery* (1981). Brannigan uses several examples from the history of science and exploring to illustrate his claim that the acceptance of a discovery by the relevant social group (the social context of the discovery), and the actual psychological process of discovery are indistinguishable (Cf. Woolgar 1988, pp.58–65). For example he assesses Columbus' "discovery" of America (Brannigan 1981, pp.120–142) and Mendel's "neglected" discovery of the genetic basis of inheritance (Brannigan 1981, pp.89–119). In both cases Brannigan argues that the special social contexts determined these discoveries. He argues that it was the preparations for Columbus' voyage and the recognition of his achievement by royal sponsors that distinguish his discovery of America. And for Mendel it was the emergence of a context within modern biology for his work that rendered it a significant discovery, and it was not until such a context arose that it became a significant discovery.

The distinction between acceptance and discovery could perhaps be cashed out in terms of a clear distinction between cognitive and social factors of the scientific discovery process. On this distinction the cognitive component of the discovery would be that part explained by Simon's psychological models, say chronologically the part of a discovery up to the submission of a paper reporting the findings. The social component of the discovery could be the particular peer review process that led to the acceptance of the paper by a distinguished journal. But this hypothetical picture is too limited and obscures the complexity of scientific discovery. Simon's own account of Krebs' discovery of the ornithine cycle gives us enough information to question any account based on such a straightforward distinction between cognitive and social factors.

Krebs' work on the ornithine cycle was carried out with an assistant. For much of the time Krebs' assistant Henseleit did all the experimental work and took all the laboratory notes, whilst Krebs was pursuing more theoretical work on this and other projects (Holmes 1980). Simon paraphrases Holmes' account of the discovery, which includes an account of Henseleit's contributions, yet KEKADA models the putative psychological processes of an individual scientist. Whether Krebs *could* have carried out the work leading to his discovery by himself is irrelevant here, as Simon aims to explain the *actual* discovery of the ornithine cycle (Kulkarni and Simon 1988, pp.140–143). But this discovery was produced by two cognitive agents whose interactions were instrumental in the discovery. KEKADA however is an idealized version of the possible psychological processes of an individual discoverer of the ornithine cycle. Thus KEKADA is not a model of the actual discovery of the ornithine cycle. Here we have a clear example of a scientific discovery, the relevant cognitive product, which was produced by more than one working scientist, or by social interaction.

If the interactive nature of scientific discovery were accepted, there would still be nothing in principle that prevents computer modelling of such activity.[4] For example Simon could claim that he was modelling the discovery of the ornithine cycle by producing a production system that characterized two heuristic based problem solvers, and embodied them in a system that combined and synthesized their results. But Simon is a cognitive individualist with regard to scientific discovery.[5] He holds that the cognitive process of scientific discovery can be accounted for by a model of an individual's psychological processes. The cognitive individualist approach prevents him from being able to provide a sufficient account of scientific discovery as it leaves important facets of scientific discovery unaccounted for, such as the interactions of a group of researchers essential to the eventual production of the scientific discovery, the relevant cognitive product.

For Simon scientific discoveries are produced by the psychological processes of an individual system, be it an individual scientist or computer program. Yet Simon's method of protocol analysis does not provide sufficient evidence to establish the existence of these psychological processes. Even if an account of the relevant psychological processes could be provided it would not provide a sufficient account of scientific discovery, as it cannot account for scientific discoveries arising from social interaction. Simon's cognitive individualist account cannot encompass the richness of scientific discovery revealed by sociologists and historians of science.

4. Normative accounts of scientific discovery and android epistemology

Simon's computational models of discovery may not provide a sufficient account of scientific discovery, but perhaps they fulfill the role of refuting the claim, once held by the majority of philosophers of science, that scientific discovery is not amenable to rational analysis. Certainly Simon claims that his programs do this, but can this claim be sustained? Simon quotes what I call "Popper's challenge" from *The Logic of Scientific Discovery*:

> The work of the scientist consists in putting forward and testing theories. The initial stage, the act of conceiving or inventing a theory, seems to me neither to call for logical analysis nor be susceptible to it.
>
> (Langley *et al.* 1987, p.38)

In contrast Simon claims that there can be a normative theory of discovery. But if Simon has not provided a sufficient descriptive account of scientific discovery, what becomes of his normative account? I will suggest that Simon's normative account is best understood as a contribution to what Glymour has called "android epistemology" (Glymour 1987).

Logical empiricist philosophers and Popper concentrated on the development of theories of confirmation or justification of scientific theories. They assumed a split between discovery and justification; the former was not amenable to logical analysis, whilst the latter was. Since Hanson's work in the late fifties and sixties (see e.g. Hanson 1958), the most sustained philosophical discussion of scientific discovery in the literature is collected in Nickles' two volumes on scientific discovery (Nickles 1980b). The philosophers represented in this volume are still, like Popper and the logical empiricists, concerned with the normative dimension of science, but the "friends of scientific discovery" (Nickles 1980a) hold that normative accounts of scientific discovery are possible. For example some ways of going about scientific discovery are better than others. Most "friends of scientific discovery" have been concerned with elevating the status of scientific discovery from a mysterious process to a process amenable to rational analysis. The latter task involves providing a normative account of discovery. These philosophers also aim to provide accurate descriptive accounts of various scientific discoveries (See Nickles 1980b, Vol. II). They borrow historical or sociological methods to achieve this aim. An assumption driving this work is that if an accurate descriptive picture can be given of a great scientific discovery, it will inform the derivation of a normative account of scientific discovery in general (Nickles 1980a).

Simon has a similar project to the historically oriented philosophers of science (friends of scientific discovery), as he also aims to move from a descriptive to a normative account; the descriptive account constrains the norms derived. Simon focuses on both regulative and evaluative norms. Philosophers of science have traditionally been concerned with evaluative norms, for example norms for assessing a good theory. Regulative norms are those which, if followed, should produce effective procedures, including scientific discoveries. This distinction between regulative and evaluative norms is parallel to the one proposed by Nickles, who calls them "generative" and "consequentialist" norms (Nickles 1987).

Simon introduces his normative theory of discovery with the following claim: "The efficacy ("rationality," "logicality") [sic.] of the discovery process is as susceptible to evaluation and criticism as is the process of verification" (Langley *et al.* 1987, p.39). Simon is explicitly addressing Popper and the logical empiricists and their separation of the context of confirmation, or verification, from that of discovery. He claims that "a normative theory of discovery would be a set of criteria for judging the efficacy and the efficiency of processes used to discover scientific theories" (Langley *et al.*, p.45). Simon claims that this theory "rests on contingent propositions such as 'If process X is to be efficacious for attaining goal Y, then it should have properties A,B, and C'" (ibid.) (the evaluative normative concern), and that "given such norms, we would be justified in saying that a person who adhered to them would be a better scientist" (ibid.) (the regulative normative concern).

Simon's work in *Scientific Discovery* is based on the assumption that there is no one scientific method, rather that there are several methods applicable over many domains of science. He calls these "weak methods" to contrast them with more powerful specific methods within a particular domain of research. According to Simon weak methods are to be judged against the limiting case of random search. He claims that scientists are very seldom involved in random search, and rational activity is distinguished from random search by the fact that the *best* use of weak methods is employed. So in the formula for the normative theory of discovery quoted above, variables A,B, and C correspond to weak methods. Simon goes on to substitute "heuristics" for the notion of "weak methods." Hence the normative theory of discovery is restated as: "Rationality for a scientist consists in using the best means he has available – the best heuristics – for narrowing the search down to manageable proportions" (Langley *et al.* 1987, p.47).

Simon's normative theory looks less like a normative theory of scientific discovery in general, than a theory of rationality construed as efficient search through a problem space. Of course Simon's descriptive theory treats discovery as a form of problem solving, and on his account problem solving is just an heuristics based search through a problem space. So, from the point of view of his information processing perspective, rationality and rational scientific discovery may amount to nothing more than efficient search. But this is not a general normative theory of scientific discovery. It is still an open question whether Simon's descriptive account captures scientists' psychological processes, and hence whether a scientist who adopted Simon's regulative norms, or more specifically used the best heuristics, would make better discoveries. It may well be true that if scientists were information processors whose work was best characterized by search through a problem space, they would become better discoverers if they used the best heuristics available. But as we have already seen Simon's descriptive account of discovery is far too limited, so a normative theory derived from this account can have only a limited application.

Simon's work is minimally consistent with that of naturalistic philosophers of science (for example historically oriented philosophers of science) who claim that a normative account of scientific discovery can only be developed on the basis of, and at the same time as a descriptive account (Cf. Laudan 1977). The problem for Simon is that his descriptive account does not do justice to the complexity of the scientific discovery process, for example the social relations involved in the process. Consequently the normative account he derives can provide no directives for groups of scientists. Further it provides no directives for different instances of complexity in scientific practice, such as when it would be best to move to a different level of explanation to solve a scientific problem. In biology, for example, the solution to a particular problem might require shifting from the cellular to the biochemical level. What Simon's account does provide is a set of norms for guiding the simulation of further scientific discoveries, provided simulation can be achieved by representing the activity in terms of an heuristics based search through a problem space. Simon even claims his approach cannot "replicate the historical details of various scientific discoveries" (Langley *et al.*, p.62). Instead it can provide models of how such discoveries *"might* occur." If this is the overall claim of *Scientific Discovery*, then it is an entirely normative one, but we have seen that Simon also aimed to provide a descriptive account. I will conclude by suggesting that Simon's normative claims may be best understood as guidelines to assist in building good scientific discovery machines, and so his work is best understood as a contribution to what Glymour has called "android epistemology" (Glymour 1987).

Glymour has proposed the name "android epistemology" for the production of the norms that regulate machines such as Buchanan and Mitchell's meta-DENDRAL (Buchanan and Mitchell 1978), which have attained some level of success in scientific discovery (Glymour 1987). This project involves the development of machines to solve problems that humans have been accustomed to solving, especially problems that have traditionally interested philosophers. Scientific discovery is of central interest to many philosophers, so for Glymour the development of norms for machines that make scientific discoveries is work in "android epistemology."

Glymour has proposed a logic of scientific discovery implemented as a computer program (Glymour *et al.* 1988, and Glymour and Kelly 1989). The explicit difference between Glymour's approach and Simon's is that Glymour is not concerned with modelling actual human psychological processes (Glymour 1987, 1988). Glymour claims that "conventional artificial intelligence programs are little theories. The more theories look like theories of reasoning, the more the description of the program looks like a piece of philosophy" (Glymour 1988, p.200). Glymour's view of philosophy is close to logical empiricism. He claims that the philosopher's concern is to give a "reconstruction of a domain of knowledge or form of reasoning" (Glymour 1988, p.201. Cf. Glymour 1981). Glymour shares with the logical empiricists the assumption that reasoning processes can be abstracted from their context. In the case of scientific practice it is argued that the scientists' reasoning can be appraised independently of other scientific practices. Glymour diverges from the logical empiricists in arguing that one *can* provide a logic of scientific discovery, which for him is a theory of the reasoning that produces scientific discoveries. He claims that AI programs provide him with the formal capability of presenting such a theory. Finally, Glymour's account is an entirely normative one. His normative theory of discovery is proposed as a theory of how to make the best scientific discoveries (regulative norms). Or even stronger: How to go about discovering the truth. Recently he has claimed that he can give an account of the reasoning involved in discovering "the truth and nothing but the truth" (Glymour and Kelly 1989). Setting the external standards by which his norms are judged very high.

Simon's and Glymour's normative accounts share the same goals. Simon aims to provide an account of how the best scientific discoveries will be made. The way the account is implemented is in the construction of computer programs. Such programs bear little relation to the actual practice of scientific discovery, and so they fulfill one of Glymour's requirements for contributions to android epistemology, as they do not replicate human endeavor (Glymour 1987). The requirement is that the android epistemologist avoid what Glymour calls the "anthropocentric constraint": "[T]hat the algorithms executed by an android in performing a cask must, at some appropriate level of description, be the *very same* algorithms that people execute in performing that task" (Glymour 1987, p.74). While Glymour explicitly avoids the "anthropocentric constraint," Simon avoids it by default, due to the insufficiency of his descriptive account of scientific discovery.

Simon's and Glymour's accounts of scientific discovery are in direct competition if they are both understood as android epistemology. The decision between the two accounts may be determined by generality of application, say by the scope of the regulative norms in each account. If we consider the applicability of regulative norms in terms of the maxim "ought implies can," then neither account is generally applicable to human scientists. If one is concerned with the production of good science *per se*, then it is an empirical question which account is more generally applicable. The answer will depend on the quality of the new scientific work that the relevant normguided computers produce in the future.

Android epistemology is only one facet of the enterprise of cognitive science of science, others concern the description and explanation of human cognitive practices.[6] Glymour explicitly rejects this latter project. Simon, on the other hand, arrives at android epistemology by default, due to the inadequacy of his descriptive account. He provides guidelines for the design of efficient computer programs. Simon's account of scientific discovery does little to increase our understanding of scientific discoveries made by humans throughout history, and provides no useful regulative norms for groups of scientists practicing research currently. These are two of the goals that a cognitive science of science might achieve, and Simon's work fails to reach them.

Some more general proposals about naturalistic yet normative philosophy of science arise from this analysis. The first is that if a naturalized philosophy of science is to make any claims of descriptive adequacy, it must make use of empirical work in sociology and history of science as well as in cognitive science. The second is that if we are concerned with providing either regulative or evaluative norms for science, we should be concerned with their potential for application. The naturalistic turn in philosophy adds a new challenge to those who produce norms, which is that the norms must be applicable by human agents within certain constrained situations. The difference between android epistemology and a more general normative naturalistic epistemology is that the latter should aim to apply to human scientists who have limited psychological capacities and must always act in social contexts.

Notes

1 throughout the paper I will refer to Simon's collaborative work by Simon's name alone. The citations credit his co-workers.

2 It is worth noting that graduate students and technicians often make entries in the laboratory notebooks, Certainly they cannot be recording the internal psychological processes of their supervisor. We see below that Henseleit, Kreb's assistant, took many of the notes the Holmes study was based on, yet Simon treats these as protocols.

3 Cf. Tweney (1989) who derives an interesting account of what he calls "external memory" from a study of Faraday's notebooks. (See also Gooding and James 1985.)

4 Rob Cummins' SOFT program is an example of a program that models the cognitive activity of groups of people (Cummins 1983).

5 It is important to note the qualification "with regard to scientific discovery." In Simon's work on administrative behavior and his use of the notion of satisficing, the claim that the individual was the prime unit of analysis was not central. See for example his *Models of Man* (1957), which is interestingly subtitled "Mathematical Essays on Rational Human behavior in a Social Setting." Simon's work in information processing psychology has many affinities with his work in organizational behavior, which was neutral with regards its units of analysis. The work was applicable to individuals or groups, such as business organizations. I detect a tension between Simon's work on organizations and his work on scientific discovery, the former is neutral over its units of analysis and the latter is cognitive individualist. A possible resolution would be to view scientific discoveries as produced by organizations, and so the relevant heuristics would govern group behavior. Simon nowhere indicates that this is the way his work on scientific discovery should be understood.

6 Of course one cannot hold this sharp division between the goals of android epistemology and other more descriptive goals of cognitive science of science if one presupposes that humans and computers cognitive capacities are both computationally bounded. Much empirical work in cognitive science shows that although there are many deficiencies of human cognitive practices, the important bounds to human cognition are not purely computational (See e.g., Faust 1984, cf. Cherniak 1986).

References

Baars, B. J. (1986), *The Cognitive Revolution in Psychology*. New York: Guildford Press.

Brannigan, A. (1981), *The Social Basis of Scientific Discoveries*. Cambridge, UK: Cambridge University Press.

Buchanan, B. G. and Mitchell, T. M. (1978), "Model Directed Learning of Production Rules," in Waterman and Hayes-Roth (eds.) (1978).

Cherniak, C. (1986), *Minimal Rationality*. Cambridge, Mass: MIT Press.

R. G. Colodny, (ed.) (1966), *Mind and Cosmos*. Pittsburgh: University of Pittsburg Press.

Cummins, R. C. (1983), "SOFT," in *The Proceedings of the Conference on Artificial Intelligence*, Oakland University.

Ericsson, K. A. and Oliver, W. L. (1988). "Methodology for Laboratory Research on Thinking: Task Selection, Collection of Observations, and Data Analysis," in Sternberg and Smith (eds.), pp.392–428.

Faust, D. (1984), *The Limits of Scientific Reasoning*. Minneapolis: University of Minnesota Press.

Fetzer, J. H. (ed.) (1988), *Aspects of Artificial Intelligence*. Dordrecht: Kluwer.

Galison, P. (1987), *How Experiments End*. Chicago: University of Chicago Press.

Ghotson, B., Shadish, W. R., Neimeyer, R. A., and Houts, A. C. (eds.) (1989), *Psychology of Science: Contributions to Metascience*, Cambridge University Press: Cambridge, U.K.

Glymour, C. (1988), "Philosophy is Artificial Intelligence," in Fetzer (ed.), pp.195–207,

——. (1987), "Android Epistemology and the Frame Problem," in Pylyshyn (ed.) (1987), pp.65–75.

——. (1981), *Theory and Evidence*. Princeton, NJ: Princeton University Press.

——. and Kelly, K. (1989), "Convergence to the Truth and Nothing but the Truth," in *Philosophy of Science* 56.

Glymour, G., Kelly, K. and Spirtes, P. (1988), "Philosophy of Science and the Logic of Discovery," unpublished manuscript.

Gooding, D. and James, F. A. (eds.) (1985), *Faraday Reconsidered*. New York: Stockton Press.

Hanson, N. R. (1958), *Patterns of Discovery*. Cambridge Cambridge, U.K.: University Press.

Holton, G. (1978), *The Scientific Imagination*. Cambridge, U.K.: Cambridge University Press.

Kulkarni, D. and Simon, H. A. (1988), "The Process of Scientific Discovery: The Strategy of Experimentation," *Cognitive Science* 12: 139–176.

Langley, P., Bradshaw, G. L, Simon, H. A. and Zytgow, J. M. (1987), *Scientific Discovery*. Cambridge, Mass: MIT Press.

Latour, B. and Woolgar, S. (1979), *Laboratory Life*. London: Sage.

Laudan, L. (1977), *Progress and its Problems*. Berkeley: University of California Press.

Nersessian, N. (ed.) (1987), *The Process of Science*. Dordrecht: Nihjoff.

Nickles, T. (1987), "Twixt Method and Madness," in Nersessian (ed.) 1987.

——. (1980), "Scientific Discovery and the Future of Philosophy of Science," in Nickles (ed.), pp.1–63.

——. (ed.) (1980), *Scientific Discovery*. 2 Volumes, Dordrecht: Reidel.

Nisbett, R. and Wilson, T. D. (1977) "Telling More than we can Know: Verbal Reports on Mental Processes," *Psychological Review* 84: 231–259.

Pickering, A. (1984), *Constructing Quarks: A Sociological History of Particle Physics*. University of Chicago Press: Chicago.

Pylyshyn, Z. W. (ed.) (1987), *The Robot's Dilemma*. Ablex: New Jersey.

Simon, H. A. and Ericsson, A. (1984) *Protocol Analysis: Verbal Reports as Data*. MIT Press: Cambridge, Mass.

——. (1977), *Models of Discovery*. Reidel: Dordrecht.

——. and Newell, A. (1972) *Human Problem Solving*. Prentice-Hall: New Jersey.

——. (1969), *The Sciences of the Artificial*. MIT Press: Cambridge, Mass.

——. (1966), "The Psychology of Scientific Problem Solving," in R. G. Colodny, (ed.) 1966.

——. (1957), *Models of Man*. John Wiley and Sons, Inc.: New York.

Sternberg, R. J. and Smith, E. E. Eds. (1988), *The Psychology of Human Thought*. Cambridge University Press: Cambridge, U.K.

Twcney, R. D. (1989), "A Framework for the Cognitive Psychology of Science," in Gholson *et al.* (eds.), pp.342–366.

Waterman, D. A. and Hayes-Roth, F. (eds) (1978), *Pattern Directed Inference Systems*. Academic Press: New York.

Wimsatt, W. C. (1980), "Reductionist Research Strategies and their Biases in the Units of Selection Controversy," in Nickles (ed.), 231–259.

Woolgar, S. (1988), *Science: The Very Idea*. Tavistock: London.

Zytgow, J. M. and Simon, H. A. (1988), "Normative Systems of Discovery and Logic of Search," *Synthese* 74: 65–90.

382

65

CONTEXTUAL LIMITS ON VALIDITY ATTAINMENT

An artificial science perspective on program evaluation

Jonathan Z. Shapiro

Source: *Evaluation and Program Planning*, 12 (1989), 367–374.

Abstract

This article presents a conceptual framework, based on the work of Herbert Simon and Christopher Alexander, which promotes a contextual perspective on understanding and conducting program evaluation. The basic argument is that evaluation should be context responsive, and therefore the pursuit of evaluation goals, such as validity attainment, must be tempered by the demands of the context within which the evaluation will take place. This notion of evaluation as artifact is exemplified using the Chen and Rossi model of theory-based evaluation research.

One of the enduring arguments in the field of program evaluation concerns the significance of attaining different types of research validity in the process of assessing social programs. One position, suggested in the field research literature, principally by Campbell and Stanley (1966) and Cook and Campbell (1979), asserts that the need to insure correct causal inference requires primary attention to the maximization of internal validity. In expanding the original Campbell and Stanley argument, Cook and Campbell (1979) go on to enumerate two additional validity issues, separating out statistical conclusion and construct validity as sufficiently distinct from internal and external validity to warrant their own consideration. They argue for the relative importance of statistical conclusion, construct and external validity as being dependent upon the purpose of the research, applied or basic, and they construct different priority orderings of validities for the two research settings. However, in both instances, internal validity is taken to be most important to pursue and attain.

An alternative view is advanced by others in the field (Cronbach, 1980, 1982; Shapiro, 1982) who assert that because the primary purpose of evaluation is to serve the needs of decision makers rather than evaluation researchers themselves, external validity should be of primary importance because decision makers will find causally flawed but generalizable program information to be of greater value than correct but historically limited information (Shapiro, 1984a).

A third view of validity priority in program evaluation has been advanced by Chen and Rossi (1983, 1987) who take the position that instead of making maximizing validity choices, evaluators can employ a variety of statistical techniques which can achieve satisfactory levels of validity attainment for all four validity types. In their article describing the theory-driven approach to validity, Chen and Rossi (1987) argue that instead of making choices among validity concerns, researchers can adopt an approach, based upon a theoretical view of programs, which will permit the attainment of satisfactory levels of all four types of validity described by Cook and Campbell (1979). Chen and Rossi's (1987) solutions to the problems confronting evaluators in the pursuit of validity are based upon the use of appropriate methodological techniques — sufficient samples for statistical conclusion validity; random assignment for internal validity; explicit theoretical specification for external validity; and measurement models for construct validity. They further suggest that certain aspects of modeling programs theoretically will assist in these pursuits of validity.

The intention of this paper is to advance another view on the significance of alternative validities in the assessment of social programs. The main argument is that the choices of validity pursuit are often limited by the nature of the setting or context within which program evaluation takes place. It is argued in this paper that the context of program evaluation often limits the degree to which validity can be attained. Employing the analytical framework developed by Simon (1981) in his book *The Sciences of the Artificial*, this paper considers several aspects of the press of context on the pursuit of validity in the evaluation of social programs.

The first section of this paper presents the basic notions developed by Simon, and related ideas in the work of Alexander (1967). The framework is then considered as it relates to evaluation as an artificial phenomenon or artifact. This is followed by a suggested approach for analyzing the interface between the pursuit of validity and the context of program evaluation. The concluding section advances some possible implications for tradeoff decisions likely to confront evaluators intent on producing useful research information for social program decision making.

Simon's approach to the analysis of artifacts

In his work, Simon begins by distinguishing naturally occurring phenomena from person-made creations which he calls artifacts. Simon (1981) has observed that

> ... certain phenomena are "artificial" in a very specific sense: they are as they are only because of a system's being molded, by goals or purposes, to the environment in which it lives. If natural phenomena have an air of necessity about them in their subservience to natural law, artificial phenomena have an air of "contingency" in their malleability by environment.
>
> (p. IX)

The central question in Simon's work is whether "... empirical propositions can be made at all about systems that, given different circumstances, might be quite other than they are" (1981, p. X). Simon's response to that question forms the basis for the sciences of the artificial.

The purpose of this section is to present the major aspects of Simon's work on the analysis of artificial phenomena, although the notions will be modified to some degree. The analysis of artifacts is based upon the interrelation of three factors: the goal or purpose of the artifact, the structure and organization of the artifact labeled the "inner environment," and the context within which the artifact operates labeled the "outer environment." The function of the artifact is to mediate the influence of the outer environment on the inner environment in order to attain the goal. The artifact is therefore a meeting place or interface between the inner and outer environment. If the inner environment is structured appropriately to meet the demands of the outer environment, the artifact will serve its intended purpose.

This formulation portrays the sciences of the artificial as the analysis of design, the assessment of the degree to which artifacts can adapt to impinging outer environments such that goals are achieved. Simon acknowledges this by stating

> ... I thought I began to see in the problem of artificiality an explanation of the difficulty that has been experienced in filling engineering and other professions with empirical and theoretical substance distinct from the substance of their supporting sciences. Engineering, medicine, business, architecture and painting are concerned not with the necessary but with the contingent — not with how things are but with how they might be — in short with design. The possibility of creating a science or sciences of design is exactly as great as the possibility of creating any science of the artificial. The two possibilities stand or fall together.
>
> (1981, p. X)

The notion of purposive activity as design is at the heart of the sciences of the artificial. In pursuit of goals, one designs inner environments which respond to the demands imposed by the elements of the outer environment. From this perspective, program evaluation as artifact is portrayed as the attempt to design evaluation approaches which achieve evaluation goals within the setting imposed by the social program context.

Related arguments concerning the relationships among design, context, and goals are offered by Alexander (1967). In discussing the analysis of design problems, mainly in architecture, Alexander (1967) points out that the focus of analysis is the suitability or "fitness" between an artifact and its context.[1] The inner environment is the solution to the problem, the outer environment defines the problem. Alexander labels the inner and outer environments the "ensemble," to emphasize that the real object of design problems is not the artifact itself, but the artifact within a given context. Thus, in the sciences of the artificial, inner and outer environments must be analyzed simultaneously.

The contingent relationship among inner environment, outer environment, and goal yields several directions for research on the artificial. One can analyze the fitness of a specific goal, inner environment, and outer environment. For a given goal and fixed inner environment, one can determine which of a series of outer environments would constitute fitted ensembles. For a given goal and a fixed outer environment, one can identify the set of inner environments which would constitute fitted ensembles. Finally, for a fixed inner and outer environment, one can explore the set of feasible artificial goals.

Simon suggests that, given a goal, decomposing an artifact into inner environment, outer environment, and interface leads to a highly useful form of functional analysis. This approach permits analysts to achieve functional explanations of artificial phenomena by considering only the goal and the outer environment. He exemplifies this, noting that many animals in the Arctic have white fur. This is because white is the best color for escaping detection in the Arctic. Simon (1981) emphasizes that this kind of explanation demands an understanding mainly of the outer environment, with little reference to the biological structure (the inner environment) of the animals. He concludes that ". . . the first advantage of dividing inner from outer environment in studying an adaptive or artificial system is that we can often predict behavior from knowledge of the system's goals and outer environment with only minimal assumptions about its inner environment" (p. 11). For example, one could explain the failure of evaluation data to influence a decision by referring to the degree of politicization of the decision setting; in that instance the characteristics of the evaluation itself mostly are irrelevant.

Simon argues further that, under very different circumstances, whether or not an artifact achieves its goal may depend mainly on the structure of the inner environment and only minimally on the characteristics of the outer environment. In accounting for the behavior of a thermostat, the focus is on the invariant relationship between inner system and goal maintained over a wide range of outer environments. In program evaluation, the establishment of a trust relationship between evaluator and client may facilitate utilization in decision settings of various degrees of politicization.

Finally, Simon proposes that it may be possible to synthesize these two analytic foci and minimize the elaborate structural descriptions of both the inner and outer environments. This could be accomplished by creating a science of the artificial that would depend on the relative simplicity of the interface as its primary source of abstraction and generality. Such an approach would require identification only of the relatively few elements of the inner and outer environments which interact with one another.

In focusing on the interface, the design problem concerns the way in which the properties of the inner environment are molded to achieve the goal in a demanding outer environment. The outer environment is generally assumed to be less malleable than the inner environment. Alexander (1967) takes a stronger position on this issue, contending that the most rational approach to design is to presume a fixed outer environment and concentrate on molding the inner environment to respond to the most significant problematic elements in the outer environment. He further asserts that within the amalgam of outer environmental elements, it is best to focus on the negatively competitive elements, those which are most likely to interfere with goal attainment. Alexander argues that when the ensemble contains misfits between the inner and outer environment, goal attainment suffers. He concludes that designs must be adaptable, in order to minimize the misfit with the outer environment.

Both Simon's decomposition and Alexander's minimization of misfit involve the identification of those elements of the outer environment which impinge upon the ability of the artifact to achieve its goal, as well as those properties of the inner environment which respond to the outer environmental press. Simon asserts that because the inner environment is constrained by conformity to natural law, it is usually the case that artifacts can adapt to the outer environment only approximately.

It is in the limits of adaptability, that is, the inability to design perfectly adaptive artifacts, that empirical inference becomes possible. It is in this inability that the limiting characteristics of the inner environment can be detected. For example, one can identify the limits of a teacher's ability to manage a classroom by adding students until control is lost. Similarly, one can identify limiting characteristics of the social policy-making process by examining problems that the political system is unable to resolve. For program evaluation, one can identify the limits of evaluation designs by identifying the conditions under which particular evaluation goals, such as utilization, are not achieved.

Simon observes that in a benign environment one can learn from an artifact only what it has been called upon to do. In a taxing environment one can learn something about the internal structure of the artifact, specifically about those aspects of the internal structure that were chiefly instrumental in limiting performance. He argues therefore that the analysis of an artifact can suggest more than the normative rules of behavior. It can also identify the limiting characteristics of the inner environment, that is, the empirical content of the phenomenon. Simon describes this aspect of an artifact as the necessary that rises above the contingent, revealed in the inability of the artifact to adapt perfectly to its environment.

Program evaluation as artifact: implications of the Simon/Alexander model

It has been argued (Shapiro, 1984b) that program evaluation can be viewed as an artifact. This entails an extremely macro-level view of program evaluation, where the metaphor is evaluation as purposive human endeavor. The contrast with more typical metaphors, for example evaluation as research or evaluation as information production, suggests the relatively high level of abstraction at which the artificial analysis of evaluation is conceptualized.

The artificial science perspective requires the identification of the inner environment, the outer environment, and goals of program evaluation. The interface would consist of those elements of the inner and outer environment which interact or interfere with each other in the pursuit of evaluation goals.

As conceived of here, the inner environment of evaluation consists of activities often labeled as evaluation practice. The inner environment would consist of activities or designs that evaluators can control or manipulate. Thus, the choice of research designs; the decision to gather quantitative or qualitative data, or a combination of the two; the choice of data analysis procedures and methods for recruiting subjects; and decisions on how to present and disseminate evaluation findings can all be treated as elements of the inner environment.

The outer environment then consists of aspects of the setting within which evaluation takes place which at least impinge (to use Simon's notion) if not directly interfere with (Alexander's notion) the ability of the inner environment to achieve its goal. Shapiro (1985) has identified three outer environments or subcontexts which often impinge upon the conduct of program evaluation as the ethical, organizational, and political contexts. Other literature includes these as well as an interpersonal context (Caplan, 1979; Cronbach et al., 1980), which reflects the significance of the personal interactions between the evaluator and program personnel.

In a recent review of the literature on evaluation utilization, Cousins and Leithwood (1986) identify 12 factors related to the utilization of evaluation findings. Six factors are labeled implementation factors. They are evaluation quality, credibility, relevance, communication quality, findings, and timeliness (p. 350). From the artificial science perspective, these factors would be considered elements of the inner environment of evaluation because they fall more directly under the control and manipulability of the evaluator.

Cousins and Leithwood refer to the six remaining factors influencing utilization as decision or policy setting factors. They are information needs, decision characteristics, political climate, competing information, personal characteristics and commitment, or receptiveness to the evaluation (p. 351). These factors, from the artificial science perspective, would constitute the outer environment of evaluation since these elements may influence the utilization of findings but they are relatively beyond the control of the evaluator with respect to direct manipulation.

It is interesting that in the Cousins and Leithwood article, two sets of influences on utilization, labeled here as inner and outer environment, are identified. However, the nature of the relationship between the two sets of factors is not considered in their analysis. Rather, Cousins and Leithwood assess the relationship of each of the 12 factors and utilization as independent variables. In effect, the inner and outer environment are portrayed as orthogonal influences on use. This is equivalent to presuming that the interface does not exist.

The crucial issue suggested by the sciences of the artificial concerns the need to consider the interface as a significant determinant of the success of an evaluation effort. The primary analytic focus is the interaction between the inner and outer environments and the effect of that interaction on utilization. In extending the Cousins and Leithwood research, an artificial science analysis would raise the question of which of the six inner environmental factors interface with which of the six outer environmental factors to influence the degree of use. Employing Simon's perspective, the interface may promote or may diminish the likelihood of utilization. From Alexander's perspective, the outer environment should be viewed as a set of problems which will diminish the likelihood of use unless the misfits are minimized.

In the following section, the principles of the sciences of the artificial are applied to the study and conduct of validity attainment in the context of program evaluation. The following section proposes a conceptual model for employing the notions of the sciences of the artificial in the analysis of this question.

A framework for analyzing the contextual press on validity

This section of the paper considers how the ideas developed by Simon and Alexander can be employed to study the effects of context on validity attainment. The attainment of the four validity types — statistical conclusion, internal, external, and construct — constitute the goal of the artifact. The design employed to achieve this goal is deferred to the last section of the paper, where the Chen and Rossi (1987) design is treated as an inner environment. The third component of the analysis, the outer environment must be constructed. For this paper, it is argued that relevant impinging elements of the program evaluation context can be grouped as members of an ethical, organizational, or political subcontext (Shapiro, 1985).

Among possible contextual presses identified in the literature are ethical elements such as informed consent and right to privacy (Riecken & Boruch, 1974), assignment of treatment to individuals or individuals to treatment by social welfare distribution criteria (Shapiro, 1984c), and the withholding of treatment to deserving individuals (Cook & Campbell, 1979). Organizational elements may include the loose coupling of bureaucracy (Weick, 1976), the significance of cultural and informal norms in the operation of organizations (Meyer & Rowan, 1977; Meyer & Scott, 1983), and the resistance to environmental pressure most organizations develop (March & Simon, 1958; March & Olsen, 1976). Aspects of the political context involve the nature of decision making (DeYoung & Conner, 1982; Shapiro, 1984), the information sources typically employed in politics (Fiorina, 1974; Heclo, 1979), the symbolic role of information (Feldman & March, 1981) and the influence of competing interest groups (Dahl, 1956; Lindblom, 1980).

Using the notions developed by Simon and Alexander, the question of the contextual press on validity can be phrased as what elements of the social program context interface with what elements of the artifact designed to attain validity such that validity attainment is difficult. Further, using Alexander's notion of the misfit of negative contextual elements, it is appropriate to focus on those negative aspects of the context most likely to generate the greatest obstacles to validity.

It is possible to conceptualize the interface between context and validity attainment as a cross tabulation table. Consider the following figure:

| | Context | | |
Validity	Ethical	Organizational	Political
Statistical Conclusion	A	B	C
Internal	D	E	F
External	F	G	H
Construct	I	J	K

Several interesting implications of the contextual press on validity attainment can be derived from the contingency table notion. One is that thinking down the columns implies that the contextual elements may impinge on different evaluation goals. Secondly, thinking across rows implies that any evaluation goal can be influenced by various contextual elements. Most interesting, however, and consistent with the ideas developed by Simon and Alexander, is the idea of interface implied by the individual cells. In this representation the cell contents consist of elements of the inner environment designed to achieve the goal implied in the row and impinging elements of the outer environment implied in the column. Thus, the cell represents the location of the interface between inner and outer environment.

Cell A, for example would contain the elements of the inner environment designed to achieve statistical conclusion validity. Cell A would also contain elements of the ethical context which would impinge on the evaluation researcher's ability to achieve statistical conclusion validity. The analysis of the misfit between the two sets of elements would identify the interface between a design for attaining statistical conclusion validity and those elements of the context which would be most likely to obstruct that attainment. Similarly, Cell B would represent the interface between a design for statistical conclusion validity and impinging elements of the organizational context while Cell D would represent the interface between a design for internal validity and ethical obstacles to attaining that validity.

The contingency table notion focuses the attention of the context analyst on the interface between design and context in the interactions symbolized by the table cells. The last section of this paper illustrates how this framework may be employed to analyze program evaluation by examining aspects of the Chen and Rossi (1987) model of validity attainment as an inner environmental design and considering how significant structural design elements may constitute misfits with aspects of the program evaluation context.

The contextual press on validity attainment: implications for program assessment

The intention in this section is to illustrate the use of the artificial science approach by examining the possible misfits between aspects of the Chen and Rossi design and the contextual elements suggested above. To accomplish this, consideration of the first row and first column of the contingency table are offered. The ultimate purpose is to suggest that the choice of validity priorities may be shaped, at least in part, by the nature of the setting within which the evaluation of programs takes place. To support this contention, the contingency framework is employed to identify significant limiting characteristics of the context on the pursuit of research goals in social action settings.

Using the contingent structure outlined in the previous section, the first row of the table would represent the design for achieving statistical conclusion validity specified by Chen and Rossi. Their design calls for sufficient statistical power and minimal residual variance. The significant elements of their design include large samples and standardized treatment levels, ranges and delivery (1987, p. 99).

The cells in the first row represent elements of the program context which would interfere with the successful implementation of sufficient samples and standardization. Cell A, for example, suggests the interface of elements of the ethical context of program evaluation that impinge on the attainment of statistical conclusion validity. Ethical aspects of social programs which would constitute misfits with large samples and standardized treatments might include a liberal social welfare distribution criterion (House, 1978) for example, where the treatment of individuals based on an equity criterion would require variance in treatment as a function of variance in need. Such a criterion can be found in the notions of special education or mental health treatments where individual differences or needs are supposed to be ameliorated on an individual basis.

Similarly, medical ethics may call for the treatment of clients with rare diseases, compelling program samples to consist of small numbers of subjects. When evaluation of these programs is undertaken, statistical conclusion validity will suffer.

Cell B represents the interface between aspects of the organizational context and statistical conclusion validity. The key question here concerns the degree to which aspects of organizational process and structure will impinge upon the ability of researchers to generate large samples and standardized treatment. For example, to the degree that bureaucracies are loosely coupled (Weick, 1976), multiple site programs or programs requiring coordination across subunits of an organization are likely to be relatively unstandardized in their delivery of treatment. Smith and Bissell (1970), for example, suggest that the method by which Project Head Start was implemented led to significant variation across sites in the nature, purpose, and structure of local operations.

Cell C would represent the limiting aspects of politics on the ability of a researcher to achieve valid statistical conclusions. It is perhaps less clear how aspects of politics and decision making, who gets what, when, and how, would impinge upon the size of treatment groups or standardization in any sort of systematic fashion. This suggests that contextual threats do not apply equally across evaluation goals, and therefore contextual analysis can indicate under what conditions which threats to the attainment of a particular goal require the evaluator's attention. The first column of the contingency table represents the interface of the ethical context with the four validity types. It has already been suggested that the ethical press on validity would pose problems for creating large samples and standardized treatments.

Cell D represents the press of the ethical context on the attainment of internal validity. For Chen and Rossi (1987, pp. 98–99), internal validity is maximized when random assignment to groups is coupled with model specification. Two ethical elements can press on this design. One involves the random allocation of treatment or policy when other ethical distribution criteria, such as Rawlsian justice or Pareto optimality, are operative or more appropriate in social settings (House, 1984; Shapiro, 1984). The other concerns the ethical problem of denying treatment to deserving individuals when such treatment is available. (Cook & Campbell, 1979; Shapiro, 1985).

Cell F represents the interface between external validity and the ethical context. According to the Chen and Rossi design (1987, pp. 100–102), the essential elements of the inner environment involve random selection when the future program population is well defined and explicit modeling of the program process when the causal relationships are to be generalized. It is argued here that, in the absence of ethical obstacles to random selection, the design of external validity is relatively independent of the ethical context. Similar to the argument above that for particular goals, the degree of contextual press will vary, so it is asserted that for a particular context, the degree of press on different goals will vary.

Taken together, the two arguments imply that certain goals and certain contextual presses are likely to be more prominent than others, that is, certain cells will produce greater misfits. On a general level, it has been suggested (Shapiro, 1985) that the ethical context will press most on the design of evaluation, the organizational context will press most on the implementation of evaluation, and the political context will press most on the use of evaluation findings. The implication for practice is that it will be useful for evaluators to analyze the various interfaces and determine which cells should be accorded the greatest amount of attention.

Finally, Cell I represents the interface between the ethical context and construct validity. According to Chen and Rossi (1987, pp. 99–100), the essential elements of the design for construct validity attainment is the use of a multivariate methodology which employs both measurement and structural modeling. This generally requires multiple indicators of theoretical measures and the testing of alternative theoretical explanations for observed outcomes. Perhaps the most significant ethical issue in this instance concerns the choice of the empirical indicators, such as culturally sensitive instruments for data collection with minority subjects.

Several implications of this analysis can be derived. The first is that the artificial science approach can serve as both an analytic framework for meta-evaluation and a useful heuristic for evaluation practitioners. For meta-evaluation purposes, the framework can be used to derive hypothesis, models, and theories about the compatibility of various evaluation goals, designs, and contexts. To the degree that the evaluation context can be viewed as generally fixed, for example by invoking various political science, organizational, and social welfare theories, it becomes possible to analyze the fit among sets of evaluation methodologies and intentions. This is exemplified in this paper by analyzing the fit of the Chen and Rossi design, the goal of attaining satisfactory levels of research validity, and the contextual elements identified above.

As a heuristic for practitioners, the framework suggests the utility of analyzing the particular context in which a specific evaluation is to take place, and then negotiating purposes and practice against this analysis. Thus, prior to the conduct of an evaluation, significant contextual elements need to be identified such that the purposes and design of the evaluation can be adapted to fit the context in order to produce a useful evaluation. Thus, the likely success of program evaluation depends on the evaluator's ability to articulate goals, identify the relevant contextual press, and then design an evaluation approach or strategy based on the most significant obstacles or detriments to the design. For those interested in pursuing valid research, the assessment of context will lead to designs most likely to achieve some measure of validity within the unique context of the evaluation of social programs.

Finally, the framework presented here can be interpreted as presenting an alternative basis for choosing among validity types to pursue in the evaluation of social programs. In effect, Cook and Campbell can be seen as arguing for the need to view internal validity as preeminent at all times, Cronbach as seeing external validity as most significant, and Chen and Rossi suggesting that rather than making forced choices, a case can be made for pursuing satisfactory levels of all validity types through a theoretically driven research design. To these can be added a fourth argument on making validity choices in evaluation — the choice depends upon what the context will permit in particular situations.

Note

1 Although Alexander and Simon appear to be dealing with similar concepts, they employ different labels for the same ideas. In order to clarify the presentation here, Simon's terms are used in expressing Alexander's arguments. In his book, Alexander employs the terms form, context, and ensemble for what Simon calls inner environment, outer environment, and interface.

References

ALEXANDER, C. (1967). *Notes on the synthesis of form.* Cambridge, MA: Harvard University Press.

CAMPBELL, D. T., & Stanley, J. C. (1966). *Experimental and quasi-experimental designs for research.* Chicago: Rand McNally.

CAPLAN, N. S. (1979). The two-community theory and knowledge utilization. *American Behavioral Scientist, 22,* 459–470.

CHEN, H. T., & Rossi, P. H. (1983). Evaluating with sense: The theory-driven approach, *Evaluation Review, 7,* 283–302.

CHEN, H. T., & ROSSI, P. H. (1987). The theory-driven approach to validity. *Evaluation and Program Planning, 10,* 95–103.

COOK, T. D., & CAMPBELL, D. T. (1979). *Quasi-experimentation.* Boston, MA: Houghton Mifflin.

COUSINS, J. B., & LEITHWOOD, K. A. (1986). Current empirical research on evaluation utilization. *Review of Educational Research, 56,* 331–364.

CRONBACH, L. J. *et al.* (1980). *Toward reform of program evaluation: Aims, methods and institutional arrangements.* San Francisco: Jossey-Bass.

CRONBACH, L. J. (1982). *Designing evaluations of educational and social programs.* San Francisco: Jossey-Bass.

DAHL, R. A. (1956). *A preface to democratic theory.* Chicago: University of Chicago Press.

DeYOUNG, D. J., & CONNER, R. F. (1982). Evaluator preconceptions about organizational decision making. *Evaluation Review, 3,* 431–440.

FELDMAN, M. S., & MARCH, J. G. (1981). Information in organizations as symbol and signal. *Administrative Science Quarterly, 26,* 171–186.

FIORINA, M. P. (1974). *Representative, roll calls and constituencies.* Lexington, MA: D.C. Heath.

HECLO, H. (1979). Issue networks and the executive establishment. In A. King (Ed.), *The new American political system.* Washington, DC: American Enterprise Institute for Public Policy Research.

HOUSE, E. R. (1978). Assumptions underlying evaluation models. *Educational Researcher, 7,* 4–12.

HOUSE, E. R. (1984). How we think about evaluation. In R. F. Conner & Associates (Eds.), *Evaluation Studies Review Annual, Vol. 9.* Beverly Hills: Sage.

LINDBLOM, C. E. (1980). *The policy making process.* Englewood Cliffs, NJ: Prentice-Hall.

MARCH, J. G., & SIMON, H. A. (1958). *Organizations.* New York: Wiley.

MARCH, J. G., & OLSEN, J. P. (1976). *Ambiguity and choice in organizations.* Bergen, Norway: Universitetsforlaget.

MEYER, J. W., & ROWAN, B. (1977). Institutionalized organizations. *American Journal of Sociology, 83,* 340–363.

MEYER, J. W., & SCOTT, W. R. (1983). *Organizational environments: Ritual and Rationality.* Beverly Hills: Sage.

REICKEN, H. W., & BORUCH, R. F. (1974). *Social experimentation.* New York: Academic Press.

SHAPIRO, J. (1982). Evaluation as theory testing: An example from Head Start. *Educational Evaluation and Policy Analysis, 4,* 341–353.

SHAPIRO, J. Z. (1984a). On the application of econometric methodology to educational research: A meta-theoretical analysis. *Educational Researcher, 13,* 12–19.

SHAPIRO, J. Z. (1984b). *Toward the discipline of evaluation research: Lessons from the sciences of the artificial.* Paper presented at the joint meeting of Evaluation Network and Evaluation Research Society, San Francisco.

SHAPIRO, J. Z. (1984c). Social justice and educational evaluation: Normative implications of alternative criteria for program assessment. *Educational Theory, 34,* 137–149.

SHAPIRO, J. Z. (1985). Where we are and where we need to go. Educational evaluation and policy analysis. *Educational Evaluation and Policy Analysis, 7,* 245–248.

SIMON, H. A. (1981). *The sciences of the artificial* (2nd ed.). Cambridge, MA: The MIT Press.

SMITH, M., & BISSEL, J. (1970). Report analysis: The impact of Head Start. *Harvard Educational Review, 40,* 51–104.

66

SIMON'S TRAVEL THEOREM AND THE DEMAND FOR LIVE MUSIC

Peter E. Earl[1]

Source: *Journal of Economic Psychology*, 22 (2001), 335–358.

Abstract

This paper extends Herbert Simon's Travel Theorem to the market for live music. It is also designed to provoke interest in using the method of subjective personal introspection in economic analysis. Music is a structured flow of information and is readily stored for flexible and convenient use. Live music performances involve many costs that can be avoided by listening to recorded music, yet a significant market for live music still exists. Subjective personal introspection is used here to identify characteristics of live music performances that cannot be offered by recordings. Particular attention is given to psychological, social and ritualistic aspects, and to different opportunities for risk taking and risk management that the two modes of consumption present. © 2001 Elsevier Science B.V. All rights reserved.

1. Introduction

In his autobiography *Models of My Life* Herbert Simon discussed his travel experiences at some length and explored the extent to which they were consistent with his Travel Theorem. This theorem holds that 'Anything that can be learned by a normal American adult on a trip to a foreign country (of less than one year's duration) can be learned more quickly, cheaply and easily by visiting San Diego Public Library' (Simon, 1991, p. 306). Simon went on to point out that the theorem does not assert that travel is not enjoyable but rather that the theorem's function is 'to produce a well-justified guilt in those who seek to reconcile their passion for travel with the Protestant ethic. Epicureans and bon vivants should have no trouble with it'

(Simon, 1991, p. 307). Simon argued that if we are to understand the enthusiasm that people have for venturing overseas, we should not do so in terms of information-gathering economies even if travelers claim that their reason for experiencing particular destinations in the flesh was to 'find out what they are like'.

This paper generalizes the Travel Theorem to the music business: much of the demand for live performances of musical works is similarly mysterious if the enjoyment of live music is framed only in terms of gathering and processing information. Many of the arguments here are applicable also to live theater, sporting events and other public spectacles at which crowds gather. Marina Bianchi (personal communication, 22 March 2000) suggests that similar issues may arise with many other 'apparently inefficient' goods technologies. These include not merely books versus lectures or 'videos versus movies, movies versus theater, but also cooking versus heating prepared food [and possibly, if one is a skilled cook, eating at home versus eating in a restaurant], letter-writing versus e-mail, ... buying in shops versus buying via internet, newspaper reading versus television news ... and perhaps also copies versus originals (of every type).'

In addition to its objective of raising awareness of the Travel Theorem and its broader applications, this paper has a methodological objective: to generate interest in the possibility of using overt subjective personal introspection and a variety of informal ethnographic methods as means towards understanding why consumers make particular choices. When I say 'overt', I mean that my analysis is based *explicitly* on my own experiences as a consumer of both recorded and live music, with a penchant for classical music, opera, heavy rock and the progressive rock bands of the early 1970s. This mix of tastes no doubt marks me out as an atypical consumer, but I believe it at least raises some important issues that would be left out of mainstream analysis. Moreover, as Gould (1995, p. 710, emphasis in original), notes, 'the power of mindful *self*-observation is a strength not a weakness: one can never know as much about another's inner states as about one's own'.

The rest of the paper is structured as follows. Section 2 is a brief overview of music-related technological changes without which it would not be appropriate to generalize Simon's thinking to live music performances. The mixture of introspective and informal ethnographic methods that was employed is discussed in Section 3 and cast in the context of the relevant literature. In Section 4, I raise problems inherent in information-based analysis of the demand for live music performances. Section 5 is focused on characteristics of the live music performance, and its nature as a process, that cannot be captured simply by purchasing audio and video recordings. Section 6 is an examination of the modeling implications of the preceding sections and is followed by a brief conclusion.

2. Music technology and the travel theorem

Music is particularly suited to discussion in terms of Simon's Travel Theorem. Modern technology enables studio performances or concerts within the confines of a concert hall to be recorded with remarkable accuracy for both audio and visual senses. Until virtual reality technologies get better at capturing the ambiance and 360° panoramas of travel destinations, music will remain far more amenable than travel to storage and retrieval in digital information systems. Moreover, although people sometimes talk of the appeal of theatrical performances with reference to 'the smell of the greasepaint', by and large the musical context is not affected by problems that the written word has in terms of conveying smells. Exceptions include the smells of giant music festivals such as those held at Woodstock or the Isle of Wight: videos of these events can only hint at the aromas associated with dope-smoking, portaloos, and so on. (In respect of such smells, it might be unwise to follow Simon's (1991, p. 308), tongue-in-cheek challenge to the view that one needs to travel to sample the smells of a location: he suggested that it is quite easy to recreate the smell of, say, India in one's backyard.)

Over the past century and a quarter the need to attend live performances to appreciate music or to study the tricks of the trade of accomplished musicians has diminished relentlessly, yet records continue to be set in terms of seats sold in concert tours. Prior to the invention of the phonograph and the player-piano, the enjoyment of music required that consumers either invested much time in becoming able to play it personally, or that they attended live performances by others. Music involving more than one performer was of necessity a social pursuit, in which one was either active, as a member of a chamber group or orchestra, or passive, as part of a concert audience. The only exception to this was the case of the musician with the capacity to imagine vividly what music on a score would sound like.

The phonograph made possible the private consumption of ensemble music. Initially the technology was expensive, the quality of reproduction poor, and anything longer than a few minutes could not be enjoyed seamlessly owing to the need to keep changing short-playing cylinders and, subsequently, 78 rpm disks. However, for those living away from major cities, the development of recording technologies provided in its early days at least a low-fidelity opportunity to hear national or international orchestras and other recording artists rather than being restricted to performances by less gifted/less accomplished local musicians. By 1983, with the launch of compact discs, and with the emergence of cheaper and cheaper audio systems with high fidelity sound, there was no need to attend a live performance to achieve access to seamless music performed by artists of the highest caliber. The invention of the VCR – recently augmented by DVD and home theater technologies – likewise enabled operas, live concert films and instructional videotapes to be viewed time and again at home. Now, in-car entertainment systems or a Sony Walkman enable us to listen, en route to a concert, to the artist we are about to see – which raises the question of why we are going to the concert in the first place.

3. Toward introspective and ethnographic economics

The prejudice against introspection, which prevailed fifty years ago, always seemed to me absurd and the very opposite of the economist's proper attitude. How can we interpret the aims and efforts of others except by trying to understand our own?
(George Shackle, letter to Ludwig M. Lachmann, 9 August 1987, from the Shackle Archive in Cambridge University Library, quoted in Littlechild, 2000, p. 343).

The use of subjective personal introspection in the analysis of demand is unconventional in terms of modern mainstream economics and certainly does not figure in Vogel's (1998) standard text on the economics of the entertainment industry. Potential for introspective economics was recognized over a century ago by early writers in the a priorist tradition, who called it the 'psychological method'. As Hutchison notes,

[This] tradition of economists . . . coming down from Senior and Cairnes to Wieser and Mises maintained that far from greater difficulties *the economist started* with *great advantages compared with the natural scientist*: 'The economist starts with a knowledge of ultimate causes. He is already, at the outset of his enterprise, in the position which the physicist only attains after ages of laborious research.' (Cairnes.) Moreover: 'We can observe natural phenomena only from the outside, but ourselves from within . . . What a huge advantage for the natural scientist if the organic and inorganic world would clearly informed him of its laws, and why should we neglect such assistance?' (Wieser.)
(Hutchison, 1977, p. 159, emphasis in the original)

When seeking to make sense of the place of introspection in modern economics, it is important to go back to Hutchison's much earlier (1938) inquiry into economic method. It is to the influence of this work that Shackle alludes, in the passage taken as the epigraph to this section, when he writes of a 'prejudice' against introspection. The fact that Hutchison was writing in the era of Nazi Germany should be kept in mind when one attempts to understand why he was so keen to make a case for systematic empirical testability and falsification. Events in Germany in the mid-1930s showed horrified outsiders – and visitors such as the young Hutchison –

what could happen if policies were based purely on misguided subjective beliefs.

In his critique of the early followers of the 'psychological method',
Hutchison (1938, pp. 131–137), was careful to keep 'introspection' separate
from 'a priorism'. Despite his critical remarks (1938, pp. 137–141) about the
dangers of economists generalizing their own perspectives as if they applied
to all economic agents, Hutchison argued that introspection does have a
place in economics. That place is at the early stages of theory formation;
unlike the a priorists, he did not see it as a rival for a subsequent stage in
which theories are tested. Unfortunately, to judge from what has happened
subsequently, most economists failed to read Hutchison's writings closely
(despite his very clear (1938, p. 163) summary remarks) and have conflated
the two notions. As a consequence, they have not merely distanced themselves from a priorism but have also limited the extent to which they
let reflections on their own lives provide foundations for their theoretical
propositions.

Since the axioms of neoclassical consumer theory were neither selected
randomly nor in the light of the kind of psychological research that Simon
has used as a foundation for behavioral economics, it appears they *must*
reflect introspection. But either this is a very unimaginative kind of introspection, or the economists who do it lead very simple lives involving little
more than substitution between apples and oranges or complementarity
between tea and sugar. To judge from the theory they have produced, they
have no cultural passions of the kind that led Scitovsky (1976) to turn away
from such analysis to consider the psychology of *The Joyless Economy*. Nor
do their lives seem to entail the kinds of crucial, irreversible decisions that
preoccupied George Shackle, whose theory of choice under uncertainty was
based on deep reflection even though in its exposition it revealed very little
about his formative personal experiences.

The results of extensive introspection are presented in this paper not as an
attempt to construct a generally applicable a priori analysis but in order to
suggest empirical opportunities that might otherwise go unnoticed. In this
sense, the approach of the paper is entirely consistent with Hutchison's
perspective and should not provoke controversy. Rather, my hope is that I
can provoke readers to do some introspection of their own in this context
and thereby add to the agenda of issues that it may be useful to research
systematically if patterns of demand for live and recorded music are to be
better understood.

The fact that the paper refers to particular events within my personal
experience is, however, likely to seem unusual to most economists. It
includes a quite extensive reflection on a particular concert I attended in
Brisbane in November 1999, given by Yngwie Malmsteen, a Paganini-
influenced Swedish virtuoso rock guitarist whose latest live CD and video
performances I had added to my collection only a few weeks before. This

rhetorical technique gives readers an event to visualize and material to reflect upon from their own perspectives and may provide a trigger for their imaginations to notice things that I have missed, or to form alternative conjectures as to the likely significance of thing to which I draw attention. This style of writing about consumer behavior is borrowed from researchers such as Gould (1991, 1993) and Holbrook (1995) in marketing. Their use of introspective methods for analyzing consumer behavior is inspired by literature from philosophy and psychology extending back as far as confessional essayist Michel de Montaigne (1533–1592).

Even within marketing, introspection is a relatively recent method, part of a postmodern movement aimed at shifting the focus of research away from a policy-driven concentration on brand choice and towards a study of consumption experiences 'for their own sake' (see Hirschman & Holbrook, 1992; Holbrook, 1995). The seminal paper here, which introduced the fantasies, feelings and fun aspect of consumption is Holbrook and Hirschman (1982). This contrasts sharply with the seminal work of Bettman (1979), in which Simon's work on decision heuristics is rigorously applied to brand choice. However, the consumption experience should be of interest even to 'banausic' researchers – to use Holbrook's preferred term for an obsession with policy relevance – since experience may lead to changes in decision rules used subsequently. The papers that provided the basis for Holbrook's (1995) book make frequent use of its author's musical experiences (see Holbrook's, 1986, 1987), but do not address at any length the question of why one would bother to go to a jazz concert. This omission is understandable, given that Holbrook's account of his musical experiences mainly concerns listening to jazz and playing it as an amateur musician. Jazz is a genre that is relatively immune from the Travel Theorem since it is based so strongly around improvization: each performance is intended to be unique.

The introspective technique initially proved very controversial in marketing and there was debate about the kinds of introspective research that should be seen as legitimate. The budding research program was threatened by a critique of Gould (1991) launched by Wallendorf and Brucks (1993), who largely ignored earlier contributions by Holbrook about which they knew and to which their charges did not apply. It was vigorously rebuffed by Gould (1995), Holbrook (1995, especially pp. 251–254), and (Brown, 1998). The present paper carries the implication that Wallendorf and Brucks were wrong to claim, among other things, that the value of introspection is doubtful because people forget things, even though what people actually *do* remember may be the crucial thing in terms of the significance of an event to them. Many of the live performances referred to here were still vivid in my mind a couple of decades later. Nor do I think it legitimate to label as narcissists those who bare their musical souls in writing about the demand for musical products. A much fairer comment would be that such writing is partly evangelical in its intent: an aim is to encourage readers to try out the artists in question. However, Wallendorf and Brucks should be pleased to see that here I mingle introspection with some ethnographic input as a reality check and further source of insight.

The ethnographic inputs here are informal compared with those employed in experiential research regarding leisure activities such as white-water rafting and skydiving (see, respectively, Arnould & Price, 1993; Celsi, Rose, & Leigh, 1993) or the study of the experience of Harley Davidson ownership by Schouten and McAlexander (1995). A novel feature is the use of web-sites of major rock acts as a source of text from fans that have attended concerts. Seminar presentations of earlier versions of this paper worked rather like focus groups, while subsequent conversations with participants often involved them in recounting oral histories of their musical experiences. I also tested how friends reacted to the suggestion that I should not attend the Malmsteen concert since I would learn nothing that I could not get from my collection of his videos and recorded music. Despite the high volume levels at rock concerts I have been able also to engage in eavesdropping of conversations between audience members as well as observing their behavior, styles of dress and tendencies to wear earplugs.

4. The disadvantages of live performances

As a means of purchasing access to the information that comprises a particular artist's music, it is clear that in most cases the live concert is a hopelessly outmoded technology. A concert ticket typically costs at least as much as a compact disc or video cassette and, unlike the latter, can be neither shared nor used over and over again. In the case of top-ranking artists and ensembles, a ticket for a concert will cost significantly more than a recording. Of course, to use the latter entails the fixed costs of the playback technology, but these can be amortized across many years of use, including use in other contexts (non-music videos, for example). The live performance carries additional penalties, which can be illustrated by the following vignette concerning some of my experiences in attending Yngwie Malmsteen's 1999 Brisbane performance. (For another example of an introspective consumption vignette, see 'Morris Fears Flying', pp. 96–100 of Hirschman & Holbrook, 1992.)

> The concert took place at the Arena nightclub, which meant that children were not allowed to attend, and on a Sunday evening, which happened to be the time selected for major out-of-hours road resurfacing works near the venue and resulted in unexpected parking complications. A babysitter was arranged via a neighbor's recommendation but she failed to show up. Attempts to contact the babysitter (whose address we did not know) by phone were fruitless as the phone-line was persistently engaged because the teenager had

forgotten the arrangement and was surfing the internet. Fortunately, other neighbors agreed to baby-sit at a minute's notice once we promised to get back shortly after midnight.

After marveling en route at Malmsteen's extraordinary Concerto Suite for Electric Guitar and Orchestra via the car's audio system, we arrived about twenty minutes after the supposed starting time. The Arena was not yet open and we joined the end of a long line of expectant fans that stretched along the block. At least the mood of the crowd seemed very Malmsteen-friendly, in contrast to his show in Auckland a week before when, according to his fan club's website, few people showed up and one member of the audience even threw beer at him. When the doors were eventually opened there was no chance of getting anywhere near the front of this unseated venue. In any case, almost a quarter century before I had learned the hazards of being at the front, having been almost crushed into the stage of the Cambridge Corn Exchange on several occasions, and been hit by flying beer cans intended for support acts. I was normally nervous about being in the circle in a seated venue, having been terrified at the way the Glasgow Apollo's upstairs shook when fans stomped their feet during a Thin Lizzy concert. Sitting beneath could be even more hazardous as I had learnt in the mid-1970s, whilst watching Irish blues guitarist Rory Gallagher deliver a brilliant performance at the Rainbow Theatre in London. This was just before it closed for major refurbishing and I was hit by falling chunks of plaster from the balcony as the crowd above stomped their feet to the beat of 'Going to my home town'. The Arena was hardly the most salubrious venue (as I had discovered from a reconnaissance trip a few weeks before) but its gallery was closed to the public, so I would have no fears regarding its structural integrity. The unseated nature of the venue at least meant that I would not have to worry about having to stand precariously on a seat after everyone else had done so in fruitless attempts to improve their view – an experience I recalled from watching The Who at London's Empire Pool.

Eventually we decided to stand behind the mixer enclosure, right back and close to the bar, but with a far better view than further forward in the middle of the crowd. No drinks were allowed into the venue, so patrons faced a monopoly supplier in the form of the high-priced bar and with the PA system running it was necessary to shout orders and be lip-read by the bar staff. It was not until 9.00 p.m. that a local heavy metal band appeared on stage as the support act. By this stage I was already looking nervously at my watch and considering the implications of the babysitter situation.

Memories flooded back of having to leave Led Zeppelin's 1975 Earl's Court gig at the start of 'Stairway to Heaven', in order to avoid missing the last train home. Reports on earlier gigs in Malmsteen's tour had mentioned a three-hour set. Without the support band, we would have been OK, but though Malmsteen is the master of neoclassical electric guitar, this was not the neoclassical economics world of free disposal. The only crumb of comfort in watching the support act was the charitable feeling that, without such gigs, aspiring heavy rockers have few chances to play live (cf. Straw, 1993): Malmsteen needed no supporting act whatever, but the support band needed his audience.

In the end, we saw about 90 min of Malmsteen's performance, as he eventually arrived on stage at about 10.15 p.m. Because of the small stage, the light show was vastly inferior to that used in the massive concerts captured in his live videos. Given my limited time there, I would have preferred not to have the (admittedly impressive) drum solo. My partner offered to go home alone, suggesting that I should stay till the end and take a taxi. A major consideration in my not doing this was that I had had enough of the sheer volume of sound. Like a number of other fans I was wearing earplugs, but even with these, and fingers pressing on top of them, it was dangerously loud. Fellow economist–guitarist Jochen Runde, who had seen Malmsteen some years before, had warned me to expect this, saying that it felt like being machine-gunned in the chest each time the drummer used his tom-toms. Most of the time my chest felt as if it was being used as punch-bag for the bass guitarist. It was a relief to escape and hear a far better quality sound from the outside as we walked away in search of the car. At least on this occasion, unlike my earplug-free Gallagher concert, my ears did not ring painfully for three days afterwards. I was very sad that things had to be like that in heavy metal: Malmsteen's perfect pitch will be of little use if he goes deaf in the process of displaying his craft. The only good thing to be said for music played at 120 db was that it drowned out some of the audience noise. I was sad, too, that both the performer and so many of the audience should smoke, and annoyed that my clothes reeked of tobacco.

The vignette reveals a substantial set of negative attributes associated with attendance at, particularly, rock concerts. These are summarized in Table 1. Seen purely in these terms, the live music performance appears to be a doomed product, destined to give way to recorded music which has none of these price and non-price costs attached. Just as travel is an inefficient way of gathering information, so a concert is an inefficient way of

Table 1 The down-side of live music performances.

(i)	Transport-related costs
(ii)	Child-related costs
(iii)	Poor sound quality and excessive volume
(iv)	Difficulties in seeing the performers
(vi)	Disadvantages of social consumption
(vi)	Undesired supporting artists
(vii)	Limited editing opportunities
(viii)	Monopolistic suppliers of food and drink

obtaining access to music and know-how concerning musicianship. In my own case, many of these factors were important in reducing my willingness to attend live performances and my growing expenditure on CDs and music videos.

Classical concerts and live opera often offer more civilized consumption experiences than rock performances in vast arenas or sordid nightclubs. Yet, well before I discovered Simon's Travel Theorem I had all but abandoned attending classical performances. The decisive factor was that I found my attention wandering due to a preoccupation with work or domestic matters and I realized that if I spent the ticket price on a CD I would be able to listen to it many times over when in an attentive mood. Thus whereas early in my career subscriptions to Scottish Opera at both Glasgow and Edinburgh were a major indulgence, later in my career I could easily afford expensive tickets but I was too stressed out to find it worthwhile to purchase them. So, for psychological reasons, a night at the opera became in my case an inferior good. Berger (1989, pp. 216–223), thus seems wise to try to get economists to pay attention to the way that attention affects resource allocation. The sheer volume and fast-moving spectacle of a major-league rock concert has far greater capacity than an orchestral performance to arrest one's attention, though even that can be overwhelmed by anxieties upwelling from unconsciousness to conscious thought.

5. Positive experiences associated with attending live music performances

Despite the inherent inefficiencies of concerts in the terms just outlined, music-lovers continue to buy tickets for them. More peculiar still, they often do so as complements to, not substitutes for, purchasing sound and video recordings of the same artists. My introspection suggests that, in seeking to make sense of this phenomenon, we may do well to pursue a rather more psychological, sociological and anthropological research agenda than mainstream economics would normally follow. I suggest that the following lines of inquiry could be fruitful.

5.1. Curiosity and concert-specific music

Many performers are careful to limit the release of live CDs and videos of their live performances. For consumers who are impatient and/or who can never be sure precisely which concert tours will eventually appear in recorded form, this policy makes actual attendance the only means, bootlegs aside, of experiencing particular aspects of the artists' performance as a flow of information. For example, the movie and soundtrack 'The Song Remains the Same' by Led Zeppelin reveals things that I had previously discovered by attending live performances and which were only partially captured by reviews in the music press. These included: (a) the delights of a 20-min-plus version of the 6-min studio track 'Dazed and Confused', and (b) how Jimmy Page arranged his live performances to cover for his multi-tracked guitars on studio albums. Likewise, I might have attended many concerts by, say, Pink Floyd to experience in full their visual dimensions (flying pigs, etc.), even if the music itself faithfully reproduced the studio recording.

Much the same point can be made in terms of classical music and opera. Concert programs often comprise a cunning mix of familiar works with something rarely played on the radio and difficult if not impossible to obtain in recorded form. Opera seasons frequently entail both novel productions of familiar works (for example, Tosca relocated in time to fascist Italy) and rare opportunities to see works by lesser-known composers. With jazz, as noted in Section 3, and with much rock music, improvization makes each performance of a given work unique.

5.2. Living dangerously: The joy of live performances

Like trapeze artists or lion tamers at a circus, a live concert provides excitement that cannot be provided by a recording, in terms of the risk that one may observe a disaster. These arise due to things such as musical errors, onstage personnel disputes, equipment trouble, or the failure by artist or road-crew to catch a thrown guitar. For example, the Akkernet web-site of Dutch guitar virtuoso Jan Akkerman mentions a number of performances where he managed to recover seamlessly from broken guitar strings or even – at Montreux – from dropping his guitar after the strap came unhitched. With notable exceptions such the Portsmouth Symphonia, who knowingly made a hilarious art-form out of their inability to play competently, or affluent soprano Florence Foster Jenkins, who seemed blissfully unaware of her musical shortcomings, musicians are careful not to release recordings that contain mistakes. Most are thankful that modern digital recording and editing technologies make it very easy to assemble a seemingly flawless performance in the studio.

Whereas a failed serve in tennis may lose a point to the opposition without necessarily losing the match, an on-stage fiasco produces humiliation for the artist concerned and widespread feelings of embarrassment for members of the audience. With music that requires technical virtuosity and prodigious feats of memory, there is massive scope for disaster. This risk is present for most performers even if their music is not 'difficult' by the standards of those who are able to perform acts of virtuosity. It is perfectly possible to read a succession of concert reviews, that make it clear that the artist was completely in command, and yet be spellbound and awestruck whilst attending a subsequent concert which leaves one marveling that the performer could actually do what had been done.

There is something profoundly emotional about living through a concert with a performer who takes his or her art to the limit and emerges triumphant at the end with a perfect or frontier-moving performance (see also Holbrook, 1995, p. 262). Compared with listening to a recorded performance at home, the peak musical experience of witnessing a brilliant live performance has a far greater capacity to move onlookers emotionally and make the body tingle. Such experiences are well captured in Scitovsky's pioneering (1976, 1981) use of physiological psychology to make sense of well-being. Whereas comfort involves limiting the flow of novel/challenging information inputs to an optimal level, pleasure arises from departing from that optimum temporarily by living dangerously (a least vicariously). A definite cycle of heightened arousal followed by a process of winding down is evident, with skilled stagecraft entailing multiple musical orgasms for the audience. Scitovsky used this line of thinking to understand why affluence did not bring joy mainstream Americas, whom he stereotyped as opting for safe comfort rather than the Bohemian pleasures that come from living dangerously. If emotional highs are not a key part of safe, middle of the road performances by artists who challenge neither themselves nor their audiences, the popularity of such live acts must be found under other headings.

5.3. Sampling without commitment

Where potential customers do not know a musician's or group's work, they face a different kind of risk as they consider alternative ways of sampling it. If they do so by purchasing a recording, after being able to hear little or nothing in a record store, they not only risk wasting their money on something they dislike. Worse still, each time they subsequently choose which recording to play, they also have the product as a nagging physical reminder them of their error unless they trouble to sell it to a store that retails secondhand recordings. The 'trouble' here may not entail merely time to visit such a store and do a deal, something which is subject to scale economies. There may also be the issue of 'face' in front of the storekeeper. To trade in a single recording, may seem, paradoxically, to entail a far clearer admission of failure than if one were trading in a great stack of CDs.

(To raise cash for some particular goal? Because one is moving overseas?) By contrast, a concert lets me choose how durable the experience will be. If the music is awful, it simply vanishes into the ether unless I choose to store the memory of the event for future use in conversation at socially opportune moments. There is nothing concrete to signify that my competence in pre-judging music is not all I would like it to be. (Much the same considerations arise with the choice between getting a book from a library rather than buying it for oneself. This may not always hinge upon matters of price but rather it may sometimes lie in the very limited extent to which we sink part of our selves into obtaining a library book that can very easily be returned, barely read, no questions asked.) Concert tours provided a commitment-free way of sampling unfamiliar artists, familiar performers in unfamiliar contexts, or the latest albums of familiar acts. However, their future role in this respect will be limited as music lovers come to expect to be able to visit web-sites to download excerpts from recently released albums.

Scitovsky's (1976, 1981) focus on the relationship between novelty and arousal is relevant here, too. While a classical concert program may include something new or obscure in the midst of established repertoire items, concert promoters have learnt that it is commercially unwise to offer programs that consist entirely of unfamiliar material that challenges and hence discomforts the audience. Likewise, rock bands have learnt that even though they may ostensibly be touring to promote an album that they have very recently released, they should only intersperse selections from it among familiar favorites from earlier albums. A mixed program enables people to buy tickets confident that, at worse, only part of the concert could make them feel like they are out of their depths or wasting their time.

5.4. Hero worship

The tendency of many consumption objects and experiences to be shifted by consumers from the profane to the sacred has been explored at length by Belk, Wallendorf, and Sherry (1989). Many of their observations apply to the consumption of music in the home. These include the separation of particularly cherished artists' recordings from those of more mundane performers, and obsessive collecting of the former. The sacred dimension can be seen in different ways with regard to live performances. As well as providing opportunities in risk management, concerts enable mere mortals to get physically close to famous people of their time. The feedback sections of artists' web-sites attest to the fact that many fans regard sheer physical proximity as an intensely involving part of the live concert experience. For example, in writing about Yngwie Malmsteen's November 1999 concert at the Galaxy Theater, Santa Ana, CA, Carlos Umana (http://pd.net/yngwie/feedback/alchemyUSA.html) wrote that 'Last night I went to the Yngwie concert; he was so amazing. I was so close to him that I was touching him.

Mark Boals gave me a pick. When Yngwie came close to me, I reached over and he handed me his cigarette. I was able to get eight picks and two broken guitar strings.' Trophies such as signature guitar picks no doubt have a social as well as functional use for those who extract them from their gods. Physical contact achieved by front-row fans or those who lurk at the stage door is the ultimate in getting close. However, even for those in the audience at large there is a psychological payoff to being in the midst of a famous person that is far less readily achieved with other celebrities. Not only do artists become real as we experience their physical presence for ourselves and verify that we have not fallen prey to publicity hype and studio trickery, but the reality of oneself is to some extent changed in becoming part of the performance.

This line of thinking can be seen as an extension of McCracken's (1989) analysis of celebrity endorsements, in which he proposes a major role for celebrities in helping people assign meaning to their lives. Even if the performers are not famous people amongst the public at large, they often are significant to us personally and seeing them perform is a high-involvement experience. Their significance may arise in a variety of ways, for example:

(i)   They are doing precisely what we believe one should be capable of doing, possibly displaying valor in the face of critical disapproval or other forms of adversity;

(ii)   They have 'struck a chord' with us by previously showing us a way that seems the way to go;

(iii) They symbolize the possibility that we ourselves could have done precisely what they are doing had we not chosen other courses in life.

They are, in short, people we have reason to worship – hence the emergence of such phrases as 'guitar heroes' and the famous graffito 'Clapton is God'. Our journeying to, and attendance at, their concerts is a form of pilgrimage and paying of homage. That it entails all the negatives raised in the Section 4 is actually a plus from this standpoint: we make sacrifices or martyr ourselves because of our commitment to the artist. Attendance at a concert by an artist to whom we accord sacred status is an act of affirmation. It provides a far more direct and less anonymous way (even in a huge crowd, so we kid ourselves!) of saying 'we're with you, keep up the good work' than that entailed in buying a recording and letting a percentage of the price filter through to the artist's royalty statement.

In my case, it was practically *unthinkable* (both to myself and to those who know of my recent Malmsteen obsession) that I should not take the opportunity to see him playing live. This was despite the fact that, from CDs, videos and transcriptions, I knew all his material and the remarkable technical feats that its playing required. In the mid-1970s, when I began to listen to violin concertos, I began to dream that it might be possible to play an electric guitar as Paganini played the violin. I spent countless hours working out Paganini's Moto Perpetuo on the guitar and trying to play it fluently, little realizing the difference a really thick pick would have made to speed and articulation. Malmsteen, much younger than I, had had the same dream at around the same time and, after assiduously studying Paganini's 24 Caprices, had turned it into reality – something of which I had been oblivious for fifteen years. Discovering his work and his use of thick picks had transformed my playing. How could I not trouble to see him play, having previously troubled to see lesser guitarists play live? I was also worried that he might face the indignity of playing to a less than packed house, given that the relatively small venue chosen signified limited confidence that he would draw a large crowd. (I still recalled the guilt I had felt over twenty years before on reading that pianist Christina Ortiz, whom I had considered going to see in concert in my hometown, had played to an almost empty house.) My demand for live music thus had a moral dimension similar to that employed to explain why people bother voluntarily to vote in non-marginal constituencies: showing up is an *expressive* act, based on a sense of duty (cf. Etzioni, 1988).

5.5. *Opportunities for uninhibited forms of behavior*

A live concert allows opportunities for social behavior that may be precluded in a domestic setting. Sound levels somewhere between the potentially deafening and the sort of volumes that would annoy family or neighbors permit the physical power of music to be experienced in a manner not possible with a recording played through the weedy speakers of a home audio system. Better still, the volume, the darkness of the audience space, and the knowledge that one is in the midst of like minds, encourage even the most inhibited dance-phobics to move to the music as, for example, sound-intoxicated head-bangers and air-guitarists. Likewise, the bedroom-guitarists, who are never in a position to crank up their amplifiers and experience at first hand the delights of having an electric guitar come alive at their fingertips at high volume, can at least achieve the experience vicariously in such a setting.

5.6. *The social dimension*

The social side of a concert is something that mainstream economists would habitually ignore, but it appears to be a major component of such occasions. One obvious area for future research that relates to the previous two subsections is the way that some artists manage the responses of their audiences in much the same manner as a charismatic religious leader. These artists seem to operate as if they have knowledge of mob psychology and group activation effects. We often attend such events fully expecting to be whipped up into some kind of communal ecstatic frenzy. (Whether or not this happens in the event may depend in part on how full the venue is, rather than its capacity, per se: to be tightly packed with other spectators in an unseated venue may indeed feel physically dangerous but it can also be exhilarating.) This theme relates to the discussion of the ritual dimension in the next subsection but, prior to that, a variety of other social aspects can be noted.

First, consider matters of dress. A concert or a night at the opera is an occasion for using dress to affect one's feelings of well-being. In my twenties, as a lecturer at Stirling University, I would sometimes attend Scottish Opera performances in formal clothing, conforming to the norm and identifying with the typical wealthy patrons. (Since I normally traveled to the performance straight from the office, I would have to endure a day of bewildered looks from students and jibes from colleagues, such as 'When's the job interview?') At other times I would delight in registering my thoughts about the pretentious stuffiness of the mainly elderly audiences by showing up in jeans and bright red 'Scottish Opera' sweatshirt, later noting in *Scottish Opera News* letters about slipping standards of dress amongst the audience.

Less elite events provide opportunities for solidarity amongst those with rebellious intent (cf. Dolfsma, 1999). Rock and other 'popular' concerts have their own different styles of uniform in which many of the audience would be unlikely to be seen elsewhere and which, as with uninhibited gyrating and yelling, spectacularly break normal codes of conduct. (A good example is the T-shirt that inquires 'Yngwie who?' on the front and shouts 'Yngwie fuckin' Malmsteen!' on the back.) Often, clothing choices seem intended to emulate the performer, as with the case of the late Rory Gallagher, who in the age of 'glam-rock' maintained a no-image image and played to audiences in large part dressed like himself in checked lumberjack shirts and jeans.

Secondly, from eavesdropping on conversations at concerts and afterwards, it is possible to see their role as social meeting places and status conferring events. They are places at which to see, and be seen by, others, as well as to make new friends via chance encounters or introduction via mutual friends. They also provide opportunities to discover whether one is alone in one's social group in liking a particular type of music. They offer a sense of belonging and clues to how other people spend their lives. In my twenties, I felt like a fish out of water at the opera and wondered how the art-form kept going as its elderly patrons died off. In my forties, I am delighted to find other people of my generation at heavy rock concerts, as well as a new generation of fans not even born in the 1970s. Perhaps, in thirty years' time, staff in rest homes will have moved beyond exhorting their customers to 'do the hokey cokey' and will be playing to them music that might not even require a hearing aid!

Thirdly, compared with solitary listening to recordings, social interaction at live performances provides a fertile opportunity for sharing judgments about the performer's capabilities and works and setting them in a broader context. But technology is changing things here, too. In the past, the lone music lover otherwise could only share judgements via reviews in the music press, with limited chances for interaction via letters to the editor. Nowadays, however, the interactive opportunities of performers' web-sites are increasingly making it unnecessary actually to get together with others who are interested in the same artists in order to do this. Such web-sites can also help produce feelings of belonging when one might otherwise have felt like a lost soul.

Fourthly, there is the role of the live show as a safe courtship venue for couples whose relationships are at an early stage, such that an invitation to listen to music on a bedroom stereo would have the wrong connotations. For those who are well past this stage, there is the issue of nostalgia that has been raised by Holbrook and Schindler (1989) in the context of the demand for recorded music. Reunion-tours by long-defunct bands are hard to make sense of as efficient means of answering questions concerning the physical condition of the musicians, their ability to get on with each other, and so on. Such issues can be resolved by watching their television appearances and via their studio reunions. Rather, the demand for reunion concerts may be understood in terms of a broader reunion of people (audience as well as band) with something in common from the past, rather like a college alumni dinner. The all-too-familiar music merely provides a context for recapturing the past and reflecting on how far one has come since then.

Finally, we should note a point already hinted at, via the notion that hero-worshipping fans collect trophies at concerts: even those who come away armed only with memories may 'dine out' on them for years to come. 'Being there' provides status opportunities that a recording does not, even if the concert is a free event attended by several hundred thousand others. Travel provides exactly the same opportunities, as Simon (1991, p. 310), admits: 'After a quarter-century of this, we have become formidable competitors in one-upmanship when the conversation at dinners of cocktail parties turns to travel'.

5.7. The ritual dimension

Well before I discovered the scholarly writing on ritualistic consumer behavior by writers such as Rook (1985), it had become apparent to me that whenever I attended the opera or a concert of whatever kind I was participating in a ritual. (For a recent guide to the rituals literature, see Rook, 1998.) Every bit as much as Thanksgiving, graduation ceremonies and weddings, such events entail a set of stereotypical roles, a definite script in terms of a prescribed sequence of events, the use of a range of ritual artifacts, and an

412

audience. For example, many performances by guitar-heroes such as Yngwie Malmsteen or the late Stevie Ray Vaughan have included, close to the end, at least one item composed by their formative influence Jimi Hendrix. This tends to be followed by the Hendrix-style torture and setting fire to, or painful disemboweling of, a Fender Stratocaster (admittedly the strings ripped from the guitar would be steel rather than gut). Likewise, no heavy rock band would dare to project its sound by putting PA microphones in front of small combo amps rather than having a wall of Marshall 'stacks'. The movie 'Spinal Tap' is a wonderful parody of many other ritualistic aspects of this genre.

In the world of classical music, the Last Night of the Proms is the extreme manifestation of ritual, where almost the entire performance is utterly predictable. Yet Promenaders will queue for hours for entry rather than merely watch in lounge-room comfort (though no doubt they later do watch, vainly, for themselves on video-recordings of the event). Ritual elements include grooming prior to the concert, as well as the support act, the seemingly interminable delays before the headline band appears, the flowers presented to classical soloists and last, but not necessarily least, the journey home. (For members of Stirling University Music Society in the early 1980s, a key ingredient of a Friday night concert at the Usher Hall in Edinburgh was stopping the minibus for haggis and chips on the way back.)

To a limited extent, elements of concert rituals provide the same sort of coordinating role as institutions such as traffic signals, the legal framework and well-known personality characteristics or corporate strategies: if we know the ritual, we know where we are and can feel comfortable. With key elements missing, we feel cheated and uncomfortable about what life is coming to. (Examples include a performance featuring John Cage's challenging silent 'composition', or a concert by The Who in which Pete Townshend did not smash any guitars, or any rock event that fails to feature an encore or a performance of the artist's most famous piece of music.) In participating, we stand up to be counted as ready to play a particular social role in a way that simply cannot be matched by private consumption of a recording item of music. By reflecting on whether or not we feel comfortable in that role, we learn something about who we really are.

6. Implications for modeling the demand for live performances

Formally speaking, music is nothing more than an organized flow of information, capable of being relayed to consumers via a variety of delivery modes. Mainstream economists might find the analysis in Section 4 useful when formulating models of changing demands for different delivery modes. For example, a rise in the price of babysitting services would be predicted to lead to a substitution effect against live performances. So, too, would a fall in the price of music DVDs. One might even use hedonic price equations to try to disentangle the impact of particular characteristics, such as non-smoking venues or the projection of video images on a screen behind the performers, on the demand for live performances. Data from large sample sets of music consumer might make it possible to discover not merely the relative weights attached to the various characteristics of alternative music delivery modes but also how commonly associated any of them are with the use of decision procedures that have an intolerant component. For example, to the extent that the positive experiences of attending live performances exist, are they nonetheless swamped, for a significant number of people, by a concern that such events are, for example, '*too* loud', '*too* smoky', '*too* much hassle'? (For a critical analysis of hedonic pricing models and a comprehensive discussion of the economics of non-compensatory decision processes, see Earl, 1986.)

The analysis in Section 5 implies that much of the demand for live music should be understood as something other than a demand for the music itself. Moreover, to the extent that consumers bother to attend live perform-ances, their reasons for doing so may be very deeply rooted in their personal histories and/or reflect the social contexts in which they live. Unless they were engaging in 'sampling without commitment' in respect of unfamiliar artists, consumers with wide-ranging collections of recorded music might only bother to see particular artists to whom they ascribe some kind of heroic status or whose work has particular significance in some social/ nostalgic sense. Such considerations lead to questions about how fine-grained models of the demand for live music might need to be. Any large-sample research based on questionnaires obviously could not require subjects to engage in oral histories of their musical associations to tease out why some artists were ascribed hero status and others were not.

Aside from the practicalities of gathering data there is the problem that, if the demand for live performances by a particular artist could be traced back to a particular event in a consumer's life, aggregation across the sampled individuals may be ruled out. Complex individual life histories do not make for models that capture the essence of many people's choices. However, different causal starting points may result in consumption experiences that eventually converge on something that is a powerful predictor of their will-ingness to attend a live performance. For example, my obsession with Yngwie Malmsteen dates back to a vision I had in 1976, but someone else's might have nothing to do with Malmsteen's pursuit of *Paganinian* virtuosity in particular. Yet we both might rate him in our all-time top-five ranking of rock guitarists. If ascription of hero status determines concert attendance, the probability of the consumer doing this might be predicted merely from questionnaire information about the ranking given to the artist, with no need to inquire about the basis of the ranking. Were it not for the possibility that artists might be treated with great reverence very early in their careers, it might even be possible to base the probability of concert attendance on an objective measure such as the number of recordings of the artist already owned by the consumer. This number could serve as an indicator of ascription of hero status. The trouble with these kinds of simplifications is that they would reveal little about why the particular artist is viewed with a particular degree of reverence. It might therefore be preferable instead to question subjects about how they saw the characteristics of the performers and the playing of different artists and on this basis predict the probability of heroic status being ascribed. This could then be combined with other variables, such as those relating to nostalgia and the ritual dimension, to predict the relative likelihood of attendance at live performances of different artists.

Finally, it seems worth noting that the material in Section 5 has interesting implications in relation to the notion of diminishing marginal utility. Consider the following comment made by Morris Holbrook near the end of the review process for this paper:

> It occurred to me, in passing, that one reason we/I go to see musicians live is that I've never seen them before. Today, I can say that I actually saw Lester Young. At the time, he was in very poor shape and played rather badly. But, hey, I SAW the guy! Some of the same logic applies even to musicians I really like who are playing great. If I've already seen them a couple of times, I somehow feel I don't really need to see them again.
>
> (e-mail from Holbrook, 12 March 2001)

Performers will tend to have trouble generating repeat live performance ticket sales if people attend for the reasons outlined in this paper. Even a single live experience of a particular artist may be quite enough for resolving uncertainties about the artist's capabilities (in the absence of live recordings) and about whether one fits within a tribe, to gather socially valued memories, and to pay homage. Unless they can maintain the curiosity of their existing audiences, it appears that performers need continually to generate new audience cohorts if they are to maintain attendance levels through time. This may require them to change the products that they offer, which may be problematic for themselves as well as for anyone trying to model patterns of demand in this market. Reinventing oneself as an artist (as David Bowie has done several times) runs the risk of alienating existing audiences by unduly falsifying their expectations. Playing longer and longer concerts can only be pushed so far before both artist and audience are exhausted. Pushing musical virtuosity and staging beyond previous high levels may lead to music that becomes too esoteric and stage architecture that is impossibly expensive, promoting the kind of backlash that progressive rock suffered in the face of the 'New Wave' in the mid-1970s.

415

7. Concluding comment

The foregoing analysis is not intended to be the last word that could be offered to assist the modeling of demand in this market. It is likely that readers will have had different experiences with music and will wish to add their own suggestions to those already offered. Even prior to any formal modeling, it is evident that introspection has raised issues that would not have arisen if we restricted ourselves to mainstream economic theories of consumer choice, even those cast in characteristics/attributes space. Mainstream economics provides no clues of itself as to which characteristics of either music delivery mode might be worth investigating if the dynamics of demand are to be understood. Nor does it provide any hints about areas in which cross-disciplinary research might be fruitful. On the contrary, axiomatic economics actively discourages any social-psychological perspective. The mainstream approach might go as far as saying that recorded music and live performances are experience goods, but it would not normally set out to analyze what the respective experiences entail.

Note

1 Earlier versions of this paper were presented to seminars at Lincoln University, New Zealand and University College London; I am grateful for suggestions offered on those occasions. It has benefited from comments made by Aaron Ahuvia (as Action Editor for this Journal), Marina Bianchi, Morris Holbrook (a self-identifying referee) and Stephen J. Gould (originally an anonymous referee). The usual disclaimer applies.

References

Arnould, E. J., & Price, L. L. (1993). River magic: Extraordinary experiences and the extended service encounter. *Journal of Consumer Research, 20*, 24–45.

Belk, R. W., Wallendorf, M., & Sherry, J. F., Jr. (1989). The sacred and profane in consumer behavior: Theodicy on the Odyssey. *Journal of Consumer Research 16*, 1–38.

Berger, L. A. (1989). Economics and hermeneutics. *Economics and Philosophy, 5*, 209–233.

Bettman, J. R. (1979). *An information processing theory of consumer choice*. Reading, MA: Addison-Wesley.

Brown, S. (1998). The wind in the wallows: Literary theory, autobiographical criticism and subjective personal introspection. *Advances in Consumer Research, 25*, 25–30.

Celsi, R. L,, Rose, R. L., & Leigh, T. W. (1993). An exploration of high-risk leisure consumption through skydiving. *Journal of Consumer Research, 20*, 123.

Earl, P. E. (1986). *Lifestyle economics: Consumer behavior in a turbulent world*. New York: St Martin's Press.

Etzioni, A. (1988). *The moral dimension: Toward a new economics.* New York: Free Press.

Gould, S. J. (1991). The self-manipulation or my pervasive, perceived vital energy through product use: An Introspective-praxis perspective. *Journal of Consumer Research, 18,* 194–207.

Gould, S. J. (1993). The circle of projection and introjection: An introspective investigation of a proposed paradigm involving the mind as a "consuming organ". In J. A. Costa, & R. W. Belk (Eds.), *Research in consumer behavior* (pp. 185–230), Greenwich, CT.

Gould, S. J. (1995). Researcher introspection as a method in consumer research: Applications, issues and implications. *Journal of Consumer Research, 21,* 719–722.

Hirschman, E. C., & Holbrook, M. B. (1992). *Postmodern consumer research: The study of consumption as text.* Newbury Park, CA: Sage.

Holbrook, M. B. (1986). I'm hip: An autobiographical account of some musical consumption experiences. In R. J. Lutz (Ed.), *Advances in consumer research* (Vol. 13, pp. 614–618), Provo, UT.

Holbrook, M. B. (1987). An audiovisual inventory of some fanatic consumer behavior: The 25 cent tour of a jazz collector's home. In M. Wallendorf, & P. F. Anderson (Eds.), *Advances in consumer research,* (Vol. 14, pp. 144–149), Provo, UT.

Holbrook, M. B. (1995). *Consumer research: Introspective essays on the study of consumption.* Thousand Oaks, CA: Sage.

Holbrook, M. B., & Hirschman, E. C. (1982). The experiential aspects of consumption: Consumer fantasies feelings and fun. *Journal of Consumer Research, 9,* 132–140.

Holbrook, M. B., & Schindler, R. M. (1989). Some exploratory findings on the development of musical tastes. *Journal of Consumer Research, 16,* 119–124.

Hutchison, T. W. (1938). *The significance and basic postulates of economic theory.* New York: Augustus M. Kelley (reprinted in 1965). Hutchison, T. W. (1977). *Knowledge and ignorance in economics.* Oxford: Blackwell.

Littlechild, S. C. (2000). Disreputable adventures: The Shackle papers at Cambridge. In P. E. Earl, & S. F. Frowen (Eds.), *Economics as an art of though: Essays in memory of G.L.S. Shackle* (pp. 323–367). London: Routledge.

McCracken, G. (1989). Who is the celebrity endorser? Cultural foundations of the endorsement process. *Journal of Consumer Research, 16,* 310–321.

Rook, D. W. (1985). The ritual dimension of consumer behavior. *Journal of Consumer Research, 12,* 252–264.

Rook, D. W. (1998). Ritual. In P. E. Earl, & S. Kemp (Eds.), *The Elgar companion to consumer research and economic psychology* (pp. 506–511). Cheltenham, UK: Edward Elgar. Schouten, J. W., & McAlexander, J. H. (1995). Subcultures of consumption: An ethnography of the new bikers. *Journal of Consumer Research, 22*(1), 43–61.

Scitovsky, T. (1976). *The joyless economy.* New York: Oxford University Press.

Scitovsky, T. (1981). The desire for excitement in modern society. *Kyklos, 34* (1), 3–13.

Simon, H. A. (1991). *Models of my life.* New York: Basic Books.

Straw, W. (1993). Characterizing rock music culture: The case of heavy metal. In S. During (Ed.), *The cultural studies reader*. London: Routledge. Vogel, H. L. (1998). *Entertainment industry economics: A guide for financial analysis.* Cambridge and New York: Cambridge University Press.

Wallendorf, M., & Brucks, M. (1993). Introspection in consumer research: Implementation and implications. *Journal of Consumer Research, 20,* 339–359.

67

THE STATE IN POLITICAL SCIENCE

How we become what we study

Theodore J. Lowi

Source: *American Political Science Review*, 86:1 (1992), 1–7.

American political science is a product of the American state. There are political reasons why particular subdisciplines became hegemonic with the emergence of the "Second Republic" after World War II. The three hegemonic subdisciplines of our time are public opinion, public policy, and public choice. Each is a case study of consonance with the thought-ways and methods of a modern bureaucratized government committed to scientific decision making. Following Leviathan too closely results in three principal consequences: (1) failure to catch and evaluate the replacement of law by economics as the language of the state, (2) the loss of passion in political science discourse, and (3) the failure of political science to appreciate the significance of ideological sea changes accompanying regime changes.

This presidential pilgrimage is over, and I can report that the American Political Science Association is alive and well. But a pilgrimage is not a journey into happiness. A pilgrimage is a search, and no pilgrimage is fulfilled until the the pilgrim returns and shares the pains of discovery.

From out of their early pilgrimage, the Quakers cried, "Speak truth to power."From out of my pilgrimage I responded, "Who's listening?" and "What truths do we have to impart?" On my pilgrimage I listened in on the conversation between political science and power, and it is my duty to report that the terms of discourse have been set by power. We are not the teachers we thought ourselves to be.

419

The insights of my pilgrimage began with my awakening to three facts: (1) U.S. political science is itself a political phenomenon and, as such, is a product of the state; (2) there is not one science of politics but several, each the outcome of a particular adaptation to what it studies; and (3) even assuming that we are all sincerely searching for the truth (and it is more interesting to assume that), there are reasons other than the search for truth why we do the kinds of political science we do and why particular subdisciplines become hegemonic. In sum, every regime tends to produce a politics consonant with itself; therefore every regime tends to produce a political science consonant with itself. Consonance between the state and political science is a problem worthy of the attention of every political scientist.

To explore the relation between the state and political science, I have chosen case studies of the three hegemonic subdisciplines of our time— public opinion, public policy, and public choice—preceded by an overview of the transformation from the old to the new state and the old to the new political science. I will conclude with a brief evaluation of the consequences for political science of being a "dependent variable."

There is no need to document for political scientists the contention that the American state until the 1930s was virtually an oxymoron. The level of national government activity was almost as low in 1932 as it had been in 1832. However, although a number of large social movements had failed to expand the national government after the Civil War, they had succeeded in nationalizing the focus of U.S. politics. The Civil War and industrialization made us one nation in fact. *Wabash, St. Louis, and Pacific Railway* v. *Illinois* of 1886 (118 U.S. 557) contributed with the doctrine that the state governments were constitutionally incompetent to confront the nationalizing economy. The media transferred their dependence from the highly localized political parties to the corporations seeking mass sales through advertising.

Political science as a profession was a product of this nationalization of political focus. Intellectual historians such as Somit and Tannenhaus (1967) and Seidelman (1985) report that the APSA was part of the progressive reform movement. Somit/Tannenhaus report that only 20% of the first decade's membership were "professors and teachers" (p. 55). From out of the beginnings in the 1890s, where the writing was "legalistic, formalistic, conceptually barren and largely devoid of what would today be called empirical data" (p. 69), the founders of the association were committed to political realism, which meant facts, the here and now, and the exposure of the gap between the formal institutions and the realities. James Bryce in his address as the fourth association president in 1909, urged political scientists to "Keep close to the facts. Never lose yourself in abstractions. . . . The Fact is the first thing. Make sure of it. Get it perfectly clear. Polish it till it shines and sparkles like a gem" (quoted in Somit and Tannenhaus 1967, 70). The title of Woodrow Wilson's presidential address to the seventh annual meeting of the APSA was "The Law and the Facts." Early in his speech he said, "I take the science of politics to be the accurate and detailed observation of [the] processes by which the lessons of experience are brought into the field of consciousness, transmuted into active purposes, put under the scrutiny of discussion, sifted, and at last given determinate form in law" (1911, 2). But these were not facts for themselves alone. Some early political scientists were active reformers, others were radical muckrakers, and a few may have been completely aloof. But facts were to be put in the service of assessment: Did a given political institution meet its purpose? According to Wilson, political scientists should serve as a kind of "self-constituted commission . . . to discover, amidst our present economic chaos, a common interest, so that we might legislate for the whole country instead of this, that, or the other interest, one by one" (pp. 6–7).

There is no evidence to suggest that the founding generation were trying to form an *intelligentsia*, defined as an organization of intellectuals in opposition to the state. There was, in fact, no state to organize against. If anything, there was a memory trace of the two states that conducted the most devastating total war in history up to 1865. But both states were dismantled quickly after the Civil War and were folded back into the "stateless polity" of the restored Union (Bensel 1990). One could say, however, that the early APSA was a kind of *counter*intelligentsia formed in defense of a state that did not yet exist. The political science of the entire first generation of the APSA was formed around politics—the observable, the immediate, and the short-run purpose to be served. But politics was not only a phenomenon, it was a problem. For example, to Goodnow, the purpose of the political science was to show "particularly from a consideration of political conditions as they now exist in the U.S., that the formal governmental system as set forth in the law is not always the same as the actual system" (quoted in Ross 1991, 274). And for most of them, there was a handy solution to the problem of politics—government, properly characterized as the "building of a new American state" (Skowronek 1982). This goal of a new American state can, in turn, be characterized as a stateless government, or an enlightened administration. Woodrow Wilson, while still an obscure professor of political science at Johns Hopkins, sounded the call for the study of administration in 1887. This should be understood, however, within the context of his still larger declaration that the era of constitution making was closed "so far as the establishment of essential principles is concerned" (quoted in Ross 1991, 275). Administration could be a solution to politics because, in Wilson's words, we could have the Prussian state breathe free American air (Wilson 1887). As Seidelman puts it, "the study of politics for Wilson thus had to evolve into a study of America's cultural uniqueness and European administration" (1985, 44). Wilson was confirming the unarticulated major premise of political science, namely, that the American system was permanent and that the science of politics involved the study and assessment of political things within a permanent and unique context. We were one republic, then and forever. Political scientists could remain a counterintelligentsia not because all members shared the Lockean liberal consensus but because they were scientists in the state-building business even while, as with Bentley, they were attacking the very concept of the state as "soul stuff" (ibid., 70–71). For the same reason, political science was atheoretical. Works produced by the founding generation stand up well even by today's standards of science and are superior to most of ours in the quality of the knowledge they brought to bear and in their use of the English language. But the work remained essentially empirical and became almost technocratic in its participation in the reform movement, primarily because it had no concept of an alternative regime in the United States.

It should have been unmistakably clear to any political scientist of 1887 or later that the American system after the Civil War was a new regime, deserving a new name. Why not the Second Republic? The answer is that that would have suggested an impermanence to the American regime. If a Second Republic, why not a Third and Fourth? My wife sometimes introduces me to her friends as her first husband. That is a sobering sobriquet. Political science was atheoretical because it had no concept of a Second Republic or of any other alternative regime. Eventually, political scientists would virtually rewrite democratic theory to accommodate political parties and would rewrite republican theory to accommodate the devolution of constitutional powers from Congress to the presidency. But this was not a self-conscious act of political theory; it was part of "the study of political conditions as they exist." In the stateless polity of the founding epoch, the science of politics was the study of politics and of political institutions within a timeless, as well as a uniquely American, framework.

In my opinion, the golden age of U.S. political science came toward the end of this founding epoch, which corresponds, of course, with the end of the stateless polity. Works of political science of the 1930s and 1940s were magnificent in their ability to describe a complex political whole; thorough, honest, and imaginative in their use of statistics to describe a dynamic reality; and powerful and cogent in pointing out flaws and departures from U.S. ideals. But this was the sentimental part of my journey. To yearn for those particular studies of elections, case studies of interest groups and policymaking, histories of party systems, and representation in Congress is to yearn also for the luxury of the First Republic, now that we are irreversibly in the Second and possess at least the bare beginnings of an awareness of the possibility of regime change in the United States.

Surely by now there has been, in fact, a change of regime, which I call the Second Republic, for lack of an established enumeration. It is not the French state or the Prussian state; but at least, we can say that the American state is no longer an oxymoron. Here, all too briefly, are its relevant high spots: (1) it is a positive, not a reactive, state, from the start centered on the executive branch; (2) constitutional limits on the powers of the national government over the economy and on the distribution of power among the branches within the national government were very quickly laid to rest; (3) many aspects of politics that had traditionally been private (e.g., registration, ballots, election administration, nomination, job patronage, polling, and campaign finance) have been governmentalized—that is, modern government has assumed responsibility for its own politics; (4) political parties, like nuclear families, have declined for lack of enough to do; (5) bureaucracy, independent of patty and Congress, has expanded in size and scale approaching autonomy as a social force; and, (6) intimately connected with (5), government has become intensely committed to science. This was no accident, and it is no mere policy. Science is an inherent part of the new, bureaucratized state, in at least two dimensions: First, it involves a commitment to building science as an institution, that is, a commitment to government *for* science; and second, it involves a commitment to government *by* science—that is to say, it involves scientific decision making. This has been properly characterized as *technocratization*, which I take to mean "to predict in order to control" (compare Mills 1959, 113). But another to-me-more-interesting but less appreciated part of this aspect of the expansion of science is that *economics has replaced law as the language of the state.*

What Tocqueville said of the First Republic we may say of the Second: "A new science of politics is needed for a new world" (quoted in Wood 1969, v). But life is not quite so simple. If modern states are differentiated, there are almost certain to be several sciences of politics, rather than just one. We tend to call these subdisciplines; but despite continuities and overlaps, they are quite distinct. Each can be understood as a product of the phenomena it studies; but I am concerned here not to explain or place them all but only to understand the "hegemonics" of disciplines—why public opinion, public policy, and public choice became hot topics and when.

Some call public opinion behavioral science. I think I am more accurate calling it public opinion. Observers from an alien intellectual planet would find it most peculiar that the study of individual opinions and attitudes could be called behavioral—until they deconstructed the discourse between the new bureaucratized state and the new political science. Here is my deconstruction:

1. If science is to be public, it must be neutral.
2. It must also be rational and therefore concern itself with rational phenomena, that is, orderly, repeatable, predictable phenomena. This is precisely what makes science and bureaucracy so compatible. Karl Mannheim, in 1929, over 20 years before the behavioral revolution, wrote, "Bureaucratic thought is permeated by measurement, formalization, and systematization on the basis of fixed axioms. . . . [such that]

only those forms of knowledge were legitimate which touched and appealed to what is common to all human beings" (1936, 167).

3. Science also has to be microscopic, down to the irreducibly smallest unit. It is no paradox that as our state grew larger, the units of analysis in our social science became smaller. This is a profoundly important aspect of rationality: out of small units, large numbers grow; and large numbers behave according to the regularities of mathematical probability. (In this context it is easy to understand why Arthur Bentley's appeal "to fashion a tool" with the group as the smallest unit of analysis was first uttered in 1907 and not really heard, or responded to, until over 40 years later [see Seidelman 1985, 72–74].)

4. Science, like administration, has to follow a prescribed method. As Robert Wiebe put it, "Bureaucratic thought . . . made 'science' practically synonymous with 'scientific method'. Science had become a procedure . . . rather than a body of results" (1967, 147).

5. The language itself has to be microscopic; that is, science has to be translated into the language of variables.

The phenomena and methodology of public opinion obviously meet all the requirements of a science that would be consonant with bureaucratic thinking. And now consider the units of analysis within the sample surveys that give public opinion its link to political behavior: voting and participation. These display an even stronger consonance with the state, in that these are approved political behavior (i.e., political behavior sponsored by the state and needed by regimes and elites to maintain their legitimacy).

Some see behavioral science as a large step toward hard science and, through that, an advancement toward greater enlightenment about society and politics. I do not disagree. But my political analysis tells me also that the hegemony of the subdiscipline of behavioral science or public opinion was to a large extent a product of its compatibility with bureaucratic thought-ways, rather than the result of successful discourse within political science.

It is important to emphasize, however, that the hegemony of the sub-discipline of public opinion is a case of natural selection, not one of political maneuvering or intellectual opportunism. Anyone personally acquainted with the people who made the behavioral revolution in political science would agree that if political skill were required to succeed, there would be no survey research centers—probably no behavioral science at all. It is their very lack of attention to playing the political game that makes the success of their field so interesting. The explanation is to be found not in politics in the vulgar sense but politics in the higher sense—the politics of state building.

The Second Republic, having put a new emphasis on science, also determined what that science would be. The capacity to engage in public opinion research in political science had been in existence since at least the late nineteenth century. Statistics, which takes its name from *state* and *statist*,

reached maturity still earlier in the nineteenth century and grew in importance as states democratized and individuals began to "count" for something.
Sampling was also well advanced and widely practiced, especially in the
agricultural sciences (Porter 1986, 23–25). Even opinion polling in political
campaigns was actually tried at least as early as 1892, albeit over the
objections of many defenders of the sanctity of elections (Jensen 1969, 228–
229)—and was picked up by advertising companies and newspapers soon
after. Yet public opinion did not become the hegemonic subdiscipline of
political science until the Second Republic.

Public policy as a subdiscipline of political science has an even longer
genealogy than public opinion, although it was more than a decade later in
emerging as a hegemonic subdiscipline. The study of public policy begins, of
course, with the study of legislation, whose history is usually traced out
from divine law through common law to something called positive law, to
indicate the demystification of law and the deliberateness of modern laws.
There is, then, one later stage called public policy, indicating the inter-
vention of administration between legislature and citizen. Public policy
is a term of art reflecting the interpenetration of liberal government and
society, suggesting greater flexibility and reciprocity than such unilateralist
synonyms as *law, statute, ordinance, edict*, and so on. Public policy began
to gain some currency in public administration in the 1930s; and public
administration had been one of the hegemonic subdisciplines in the political
science of the stateless polity I refer to as the First Republic. The decline
and transfiguration of public administration gives us the key to public policy.
Traditional public administration was almost driven out of the APSA
by the work of a single, diabolical mind, that of Herbert Simon. Simon transformed the field by lowering the discourse. He reduced the bureaucratic
phenomenon to the smallest possible unit, the decision, and introduced
rationality to tie decisions to a system—not to any system but to an economic system. His doctorate was in political science; his Nobel award
was in economics.

Now, Simon did not accomplish this all by himself. His intellectual
tour de force was made possible by actual changes in the administrative
institutions of the Second Republic. Administrative authority in the First
Republic partook of a fairly well established tradition of separating public
from private life by a variety of legal rules and procedures that comprise
what Joseph Vining calls the "masterful myth of the 'rule of law'"; in the
Second Republic, these rules and myths broke down—not spontaneously,
but in face of the rise of economic thinking in the corporate world, as well
as in government (1978, 27).

It is in this context that modern public policy became a hegemonic
subdiscipline in political science, overshadowing behavioralism itself. The
study of public policy in the political science of the First Republic drew
upon public law and institutional economics. Some of that old-fashioned

public policy study exists today. But the modern approach is more appropriately called public policy analysis, which draws upon macroeconomic methods and economic systems thinking. The best way to demonstrate the size and character of this new subdiscipline of political science is to point to the presence of the policy analysis courses within political science departments and the explosive growth of the separate policy analysis programs and the economics requirements in the schools of public affairs and public policy and in the law schools. All the students in those places are learning the new language of the state.

It does no disservice to the subdiscipline of public choice to tie it to another of Karl Mannheim's observations dating from 1929, namely, that in the political science of a bureaucratic state "an economic man, a political man, etc., irrespective of time and race, could be constructed on the basis of a few axiomatic characteristics" (1936, 167–68). Mannheim continues: "Only what could be known by the application of these axioms was considered as knowable. Everything else was due to the perverse 'manifoldness of the real', concerning which 'pure' theory need not worry itself" (p. 168). Compare this to Kenneth Arrow's assertion made in a boastful spirit nearly 40 years later that any assumption other than the rational actor leads to mysticism and irrationality (Gold-field and Gilbert 1990, 14–15). This gives us a start toward a political explanation for why public choice has become probably the hottest thing going in political science today.

Quite aside from whatever merits it may have as a method and however true its truths may be, public choice is hegemonic today for political reasons or (to be more dignified about it) for reasons of state. Let me dramatize this in quite tangible rational actor terms: most of the luminaries in this subfield of political science came from, serve in, or are substantially associated with the same freshwater universities that kept burning the flame of laissez-faire ideology: Chicago, Rochester, Washington University of Saint Louis (nor should we overlook the Saint Louis Federal Reserve staff) (Johnson 1991). Here, again, we are confronting not political opportunism but institutional consonance—a symbiotic relationship between state and political science.

The affinity between modern bureaucratic government and economics—already strong—was further strengthened by the revival of the political popularity of laissez-faire ideology within the Republican party. For most of this century, laissez-faire liberalism (erroneously called conservative) had been the Republican party's center of gravity; but after the Depression, it had had little effect on voters and even less on intellectuals in the social sciences. Few intellectuals figured in national Republican party circles. *Conservative intellectual* was just another oxymoron. Today, of course, Republican administrations are overflowing with intellectuals, as are affiliated think tanks and the op-ed pages of the major newspapers. I see no signs yet of a Republican takeover of the APSA; but I do see one beneficiary of the Republican party era in political science, namely, public choice. People of merit inhabit this subfield, but its hegemony has little to do with their merit. Their success as a group was entirely fortuitous.

We political scientists enjoy the primitive wisdom of Mr. Dooley; and probably Mr. Dooley's best-known scientific proposition was, "No matter whether th' constitution follows th' flag or not, th' supreme court follows th' iliction returns." A more dignified Dooley would say, "The APSA follows Leviathan." I conclude with what are to me the three principal consequences of following Leviathan too closely. First, we have as a consequence failed to catch and evaluate the significance of the coming of economics as the language of the state. Second, we have failed to appreciate how this language made *us* a dismal science like economics. Third, having been so close to Leviathan, we failed to catch, characterize, and evaluate the great ideological sea changes accompanying the changes of regime.

First, then, why economics? Of what use is economic analysis to politics? Since economics was always a deeply flawed predictive science, why was it so attractive to policymakers and bureaucrats in the new state? Why was it so attractive to political science? My evaluation was inspired in part by an observation made 30 years ago by the distinguished economic philosopher Joan Robinson: "Economics . . . has always been partly a vehicle for the ruling ideology of each period as well as partly a method of scientific investigation" (1962, 1). My answer is that economic analysis is politically useful because it closes off debate, especially in a highly public representative assembly like Congress. The rise of economics as the language of the state parallels the decline of Congress as a creative legislature. (I argue this point more extensively in Lowi 1991.) Policymaking powers are delegated less to the agency and more to the decisionmaking formulas residing in the agency. The use of economic analysis to close off debate was strengthened as Republicans discovered that economic analysis could be used as effectively for them as for the Democrats—by manipulating the cost, rather than the benefit, side of cost–benefit analysis. I recommend John Schwarz's evaluation of Murray Weidenbaum's outrageous manipulation of the "costs of regulation" that supported the Reagan administration's commitment to deregulation (1988, 90–99). But I must confess that both the Democratic and the Republican politicians were smarter than the political scientists, because they took the stuff as weaponry, while we took it as science. We swallowed economics before subjecting it to a political analysis.

We should have seen that economics rarely even pretends to speak truth to power. If substantive truths were claimed, there would be room for argument. But economics, particularly as a policy science, stresses method above all. And the key to the method is the vocabulary of economics, which is the *index*. An index is not a truth but an agreement or convention among its users about what will be the next best thing to truth. M_1, the Dow, the CPI, unemployment, GNP: This is the new representative government—an index representing a truth. Indices have analytic power because they fit into defined systems; and of course, systems are also not truths but only useful fictions. (This, by the way, is not an attack on indices *or* systems. It is just a political evaluation of indices and systems.)

Now to the second of my consequences, that is, that the modern bureaucratic state has made political science just another dismal science. By *dismal* I do not mean merely the making of gloomy forecasts, in the Malthusian tradition: I mean the absence of *passion*.

During my pilgrimage, the most frequent complaints I heard were against the *American Political Science Review*. I join in at least one of these, which I do not limit to the *APSR*. Too few of the articles seek to transcend their analysis to join a more inclusive level of discourse. There is consequently little substantive controversy. The response is that a scientific journal must be dedicated to replication and disproof. But actually, very few pieces independently replicate anything; and even if they did, replication alone is dismal stuff. Political science is a harder science than the so-called hard sciences because we confront an *un*natural universe that requires judgment and evaluation. Without this, there can be no love of subject, only vocational commitment to method and process. The modern state has made us a dismal science, and we have made it worse by the scientific practice of removing ourselves two or three levels away from sensory experience. Political scientists have always quantified whatever and whenever they could, and most tried to be rigorous; but they stayed close to sensory experience. Even with our original mechanical helper, the counter–sorter device, it was possible to maintain a sensory relation to the data. What a pleasure it was to watch the cards seek their slots! And what a pity today that the empiricists have only their printout!

Finally, I turn to our failure to catch or evaluate adequately the ideological sea changes accompanying the changes of regime. Time permits only the barest inventory of missed opportunities, but I think they will speak for themselves.

The perspective of nearly 50 years makes it easy to see what we did not catch about the New Deal as a regime change. Although political scientists caught the new liberalism in the air, they failed to evaluate whether all the elements of this ideology were consistent with liberalism or with constitutionalism. They failed, for example, to capture and evaluate the significance of "administrative law." They noticed, but merely celebrated, the delegation of power from Congress to the executive branch. At the time it meant only the fulfillment of the New Deal program. Even as time passed, our tendency was to render each change consistent with our existing model of the political system. There was virtually no serious political science inquiry into whether the changes in constitutional doctrine, governmental structure, and policy commitments constituted a regime change. Some Republicans suggested that the United States had become a socialist regime, but political science did not respond to this challenging formulation. It should be a matter of ultimate interest, as well as enjoyment, to fight intensely over the identification of criteria for determining when a political change is sufficient to constitute a regime change. The New Deal helped give us a new political science but did not provide sufficient inclination to evaluate what was new.

We are at this moment in the presence of another failure, namely, a failure to catch the nature and significance of the ideological shift accompanying the current Republican era. The inability of the Reagan administration to terminate any important Mew Deal programs should at least have led to a reflection on the nature of the New Deal as a regime change. Even a post hoc evaluation would be useful. Meanwhile, the Republican era has brought with it some profound ideological changes that political science is failing to capture even though our own public opinion polls are sensing them. Political science has failed to catch and evaluate the two separate components of the Republican coalition: the old, laissez-faire liberalism and the genuine, native conservatism. Political science has stood by and permitted Republican candidates and staff intellectuals to treat the traditional laissez-faire core of the Republican party as conservative and then to compound the felony by stigmatizing liberalism as an alien belief system akin to socialism. This profound misuse of rich terminology is literally poisoning political discourse in the United States, and political science has to take a lot of the blame for this. We also did not catch the rise of the genuine conservatism; although our polls were picking up significant reactionary movements, we continued to treat the Falwell phenomenon and such predecessors as the Christian Anti-communist Crusade as aberrant. And we have passively witnessed the joining of laissez-faire liberalism with genuine right-wing conservatism as though they are consistent in their opposition to big government. Laissez-faire liberal Republicans, supported by their economists, embrace an ideal of radical individualism and view all government as a threat to freedom. In contrast, genuine conservatives are not individualists but statists. The state they want consists of tight and restrictive police control by state and local governments, but they are statists nevertheless. Genuine conservatives were never really at home with purely market relations; and they have never espoused the ideal (much less the methodology) of rational individualism. (Many conservative Catholic lay intellectuals have tried in vain to establish a comfortable concordance with free market liberalism.) Conservative intellectuals ate now writing the poetry of executive power and are the authors of most of the writing that bashes Congress and the politics of representative government. Just as political scientists did not catch the ideological significance of the propresidential power writings of the New Deal supporters in the 1950s and early 1960s, we ate now not catching the significance of the fact that most of the current propresidential power writing is by the Far Right. The far right-wing intellectuals are also writing a significant proportion of the new work on the founding intended not only to contribute to historical scholarship but to reconstitute the constitution in such a way as to place the presidency above the law and affirmative action beneath it.

No effort has been made to camouflage my antagonism to Republican era ideology. But my own personal position is irrelevant. Political scientists of the Left, Right, and center are a unity in their failure to maintain a cleat and critical consciousness of political consciousness. Causal and formal analyses of the relations among clusters of variables just will not suffice. Nor will meticulous analysis of original intent. It is time we became intellectuals.

At the end of my pilgrimage, I have come to the conclusion that among the sins of omission of modern political science, the greatest of all has been the omission of passion. There are no qualifications for membership in the APSA; but if I had the power to establish such standards, they would be that a member should love politics, love a good constitution, take joy in exploring the relation between the two, and be prepared to lose some domestic and even some foreign policy battles to keep alive a positive relation between the two. I do not speak for the passion of ideology, though I do not count it out. I speak for the pleasure of finding a pattern, the inspiration of a well-rounded argument, the satisfaction in having made a good guess about what makes democracy work and a good stab at improving the prospect of rationality in human behavior.

Regime changes throughout the world since 1989 ought to give us a clearer perspective on some new sciences of politics. Although only a few of the world's regime changes will be liberal democracies, they are stimulating tremendous demand for transferrable insights about the workings of liberal democratic institutions, especially U.S. institutions. May this demand draw U.S. political scientists out of the shadow of Leviathan upward and outward toward a level of discourse worthy of the problem. This is not an opportunity to play philosopher–king. It is an opportunity to meet our own intellectual needs while serving the public interest. And we need not worry how to speak truth to power. It is enough to speak truth to ourselves.

Note

My thanks to Professors Mauro Calise, Raymond Seidelman, David Collier, Walter Mebane, Richard Bensel, and Michael Goldfield for their help along the way.

References

Bensel, Richard F. 1990. *Yankee Leviathan—the Origins of Central State Authority in America, 1859–1877*. New York: Cambridge University Press.

Goldfield, Michael, and Alan Gilbert. 1990. "The Limits of Rational Choice Theory." Presented at the annual meeting of the American Political Science Association, San Francisco.

Jensen, Richard. 1969. "American Election Analysis." In *Politics and the Social Sciences*, ed. Seymour Martin Lipset. New York: Oxford University Press.

Lowi, Theodore J. 1991. "Knowledge, Power, and the Congress." In *Knowledge, Power, and the Congress*, ed. William H. Robinson and H. Wellborn Clay. Washington: Congressional Quarterly.

Mannheim, Karl. 1936. *Ideology and Utopia*. New York Harcourt Brace Jovanovich.

Mills, C. Wright. 1959. *The Sociological Imagination*. New York: Oxford University Press.

Porter, Theodore M. 1986. *The Rise of Statistical Thinking, 1820–1900*. Princeton: Princeton University Press.

Robinson, Joan. 1962. *Economic Philosophy*. New York: Doubleday Anchor.

Ross, Dorothy. 1991. *The Origins of American Social Science*. New York: Cambridge University Press.

Schwarz, John E. 1988. *America's Hidden Success*. New York: W. W. Norton.

Seidelman, Raymond. 1985. *Disenchanted Realists: Political Science and the American Crisis, 1884–1984*. Albany: State University of New York Press.

Skowronek, Stephen. 1982. *Building a New American State: The Expansion of National Administrative Capacities, 1877–1920*. New York: Cambridge University Press.

Somit, Albert, and Joseph Tannenhaus. 1967. *The Development of Political Science: From Burgess to Behavioralism*. Boston: Allyn & Bacon.

Vining, Joseph. 1978. *Legal Identity: The Coming of Age of Public Law*. New Haven: Yale University Press.

Wiebe, Robert. 1967. *The Search for Order, 1877–1920*. New York: Hill & Wang.

Wilson, Woodrow. 1887. "The Study of Administration." *The Political Science Quarterly* 2:202–17.

Wilson, Woodrow. 1911. "The Law and the Facts." *American Political Science Review* 5:1–11.

Wood, Gordon S. 1969. *The Creation of the American Republic, 1776–1787*. New York: Norton.

68

THE STATE OF AMERICAN POLITICAL SCIENCE

Professor Lowi's view of our discipline

Herbert A. Simon

Source: *PS: Political Science and Politics*, 26:1 (1993), 49–51.

This note questions both some of the premises and some of the conclusions of Theodore J. Lowi's diagnosis, in the March 1992 *American Political Science Review*, of the state of the political science discipline. Since I am given a prominent, if undeserved role, in his analysis of historical trends, perhaps I may be pardoned if it begins by refuting that part of his argument.[1]

Surely one should feel great (and devilish) delight at learning that one has exercised diabolical influence over the shaping of political science. Alas, I am wholly lacking in the power that Professor Lowi attributes to me in his paper. Alas also, if I were armed, my gun was not aimed in the direction he supposes it was. I am not at all in sympathy with the Third American Government whose (confused) economics-based ideology he presumes I created, as anyone will recognize who has read the foreword to the recent re-issue of the Simon-Smithburg-Thompson textbook, *Public Administration*,[2] or the earlier work, *Administrative Behavior (AB)*,[3] or the more recent *Reason in Human Affairs*.[4] Are these books written so obscurely that Professor Lowi could not see that the rationality celebrated in them (if any rationality is celebrated at all) is a weak, muddled, bounded rationality that is rejected out of hand by the economists who espouse public choice and neoclassical laissez-faire theory?

From whence derive Professor Lowi's errors? First, he does not understand the so-called "behavioralist" revolution that reshaped political science in the 1930s and 1940s, and its relation to the much later, and unrelated, attempt of economists to colonize political science. Second, he does not have the slightest clue to my own relation, or that of the other behavioralists in political science and economics, to the dominant neoclassical orthodoxy in the discipline of economics or to public choice. In short, his essay is bad social history.

The behavioralist revolution in political science was a celebration, not of reason but of real human behavior, as earlier described in *The Federalist* and by such commentators as de Tocqueville and Bryce. It was closely allied (as Professor Lowi correctly perceives) with American Progressivism. It aimed at replacing the legalism and traditional theorizing that still flourished in the discipline with empirical evidence (including observation) and theory based on evidence. It was quantitative when quantities were relevant and could be measured, but was not obsessed with equations or numbers. (Has Professor Lowi counted the number of equations in my books, listed above, or in the works of the major behavioralists?) Although most of the behavioralists of that (and perhaps this) time were New Dealers, they generally believed that understanding must precede advocacy, and to a limited extent were able to separate their roles as scientists from their roles as citizens, a separation that is still eminently desirable if clear thought is to prevail in the discipline.

Behavioralism flowered in the Chicago School during Charles Mercian's chairmanship there (see Chapter 4 of my autobiography, *Models of My Life[5]*). The School for several decades provided half of Professor Lowi's distinguished predecessors as presidents of the American Political Science Association. This "Chicago School" had not the slightest resemblance to the present Chicago School of neoclassical economics, whose forefathers (e.g., Frank Knight, Henry Simons, von Hayek) were barely on speaking terms with Merriam and his colleagues. Perusal of recent issues of the *American Political Science Review*, including the one in which Professor Lowi's essay appears, will show that behavioralism still represents the mainstream of the profession, and has not been replaced by (though it competes vigorously with) the alien imports from economics of game theory and public choice.[6]

Anyone who does not know the difference between behavioralists and the advocates of economic rationality should reread Harold Lasswell, the leading behavioralist of them all, or Charles Merriam or Harold Gosnell. Freud plays a far more central role in Lasswell's thought than Dewey, and Adam Smith no role at all. And the products of Chicago, such distinguished political scientists as Gabriel Almond, David Easton, V. O. Key, Avery Leiserson, David Truman—one could go on and on—are no more rationalists than were Lasswell or his colleagues.

And where was the Devil during this period? He was a very junior partner in the enterprise, contributing *AB* (1947), and later (1950) the public administration textbook mentioned above. Was he, unlike the rest of the Chicago School, a rationalist? Professor Lowi reads *AB* in a most peculiar way. This book and my other writings proclaim a very limited form of human rationality (later christened "bounded rationality") that acknowledges the whole person: values, emotions, stupidities, cupidities, loyalties, ignorance, and all. Madison, Hamilton, and Jay would have had no difficulty seeing in the administrator of *AB* the same Homo politicus that they described in the pages of *The Federalist*.

Far from supporting neoclassical economic orthodoxy, the research and writings by me and others on bounded rationality have been consistently anathematized by mainstream economists, who are only now just beginning to sense that human beings are not global utility maximizers. Those who are viewed by economists as behavioralists have used the concept of bounded rationality to castigate the orthodox and to show them the error of their excessive adoration of an unachievable rationality and their failure to provide empirical support for their assumptions about human choice. Small thanks they get from Professor Lowi for braving the arrows of the neo-classicists, the game theorists, and the public choice theorists. In his war against the economists, he would be wise to accept all the help he can find, especially from those who have already been engaged in the battle for over 40 years.

My paper in *The American Political Science Review*,[7] the talk I gave on receiving the James Madison Award, warned political scientists against the missionaries of economic rationality and public choice theory. Professor Lowi will find in that paper a strong plea for studying the focus of public attention as a central variable in understanding political phenomena. In the behavioralist literature, the individual decision maker is never taken as an uncaused–cause, independent of society. In fact, *AB* is at pains to point out that human rationality, even bounded rationality, is possible only in a social setting.

Professor Lowi is also in error in associating a decision-making approach with a preoccupation with rationality. Again, if he will consult *AB* (e.g., Chapters 3, 9, 12, 16, 10, 15), he will find that decisions begin with goals and values, and are strongly conditioned by organizational loyalties and perceptions. Rationality enters because people generally have reasons for what they do; Freud found no conflict between that idea and the idea that they also have powerful emotions.

But what of the reductionism of the decision-making approach? I hear an echo of a cry that has been raised in other sciences, e.g., "molecular biologists don't understand the whole living organism." Indeed they don't; but they have taught us an enormous amount about the processes that make the organism live and function. And they do not deny an essential complementary scientific role to cell biologists, physiologists, ethologists, ecologists, or population geneticists, who adopt more holistic views.

Theorists of decision making don't understand the whole polity either; but they have taught us an enormous amount about the minds (and emotions) of the human characters who play roles in the political drama: voters, office-holders, civil servants, lobbyists. They have told us much about how these actors think, what they know, and what they value. Without that knowledge, accounts of events at the global, holistic level become pointless (if hair-raising) dramas without plot or motives.

No one argues that all political studies should take decision making as their organizing thread. But for all that, it has been an extremely effective organizer, shaping much of the most useful work in the discipline. And for larger systems (e.g., in studying public administration), the underlying structure of decision-making processes illuminates the coherence of the whole, the contributions of the parts to that whole, the organization's functions and its malfunctions.

One of Professor Lowi's central themes is that political science has blown with the winds of political power. Has political science in fact prostituted itself to serving as the PR voice, first of the New Deal, then of the New Conservatism (a.k.a. Classical Liberalism)? The trends that Professor Lowi discerns in American government since the Great Depression are surely there, as many others have noticed long ago. But the response of political science to these trends has surely not been uncritical. Professor Lowi must be aware of the many critics that the New Deal had in the profession, as well as its many friends. Has he missed the extensive literature on pressure groups, on centralization and decentralization, on the presidency in its relation to Congress, on the Court Bill controversy? (These works do not appear prominently among his references.) If political science prostituted herself to power, the mistress seems to have been frequently ungrateful to her protector.

And did Professor Lowi notice only analyses at the individual level, and not such socio-centered works as the Chicago School's "making of citizens" series, or the continuation of that theme by Gabriel Almond and others? Or for that matter, Merriarn's own *Political Power*? The behavioralists suggest neither that individual values are brought by the Tooth Fairy, nor that people are the Leibnitzian monads described by public choice and Libertarian theory.

One has equal difficulty in sharing Professor Lowi's despair about the present state of the discipline. It is quite true that game theorists and public choice theorists have entered into political analysis with enthusiasm, often rediscovering truths that had long been established in the political science literature, sometimes proposing hypotheses that assume an outrageously unlikely level of rationality. But my simple count of articles in the *APSR* shows that they do not enjoy the hegemony that Professor Lowi deplores. What evidence supports his claim (page 5) that "the modern state has made us a dismal science, and we have made it worse by the scientific practice of removing ourselves two or three levels away from sensory experience." If the public choice framework is fundamentally flawed, as he and I believe it to be, it is not going to be overthrown by emotional rhetoric. It is going to be overthrown, if empirically incorrect, by carefully amassing and analyzing empirical evidence—that is, by behavioralism.

435

But behavioralists should not reject Professor Lowi's whole message just because he misunderstands theirs so egregiously; nor should we reject him as a johnny-come-lately in the struggle against the excesses of rational analysis. It is better that we welcome him as an ally (if he is willing to join with the Devil). But before he enlists in the behavioralist movement's struggle against excessive rationalism, he must get his facts straight, and the names of the players right.

Notes

1 It is a little boorish of me to complain about Professor Lowi's treatment of me in an issue of the *Review* where on pages 196–98, in a review of my autobiography, my views are treated accurately, and even quoted at length. But some readers may not persist from page 4 to page 198, Professor Wahlke, in his generous review, does make one mistake. He erroneously states that I have retired. No way.
2 New Brunswick, NJ: Transaction Publishers, (1950) 1991.
3 New York: The Free Press, 3rd edition, 1976.
4 Stanford, CA: Stanford University Press, 1983.
5 New York: Basic Books, 1991.
6 A review of the articles in the March 1992 issue (other than two essays on the history of theory) shows those by Warren, Swank, Huckfeldt and Sprague, Mouw and Mackuen, and Weatherford to be behavioral, while those by Lake, Abramson, *et al.*, and Green belong to the public choice stream. To quantify, the score is 5 to 3.
7 "Human Nature in Politics: The Dialogue of Psychology with Political Science," *APSR*, 79: 293–305 (1985).

69

A REVIEW OF HERBERT SIMON'S REVIEW OF MY VIEW OF THE DISCIPLINE

Theodore J. Lowi

Source: *PS: Political Science and Politics*, 26:1 (1993), 51–52.

Dear Professor Simon:

It is an honor to be read, and read carefully, by someone of your distinction. But since you missed the major premise of my March 1992 essay, it is virtually impossible to engage in a point-by-point rebuttal. In fact, few of your propositions I'd care to rebut, not only because they are irrelevant to my argument but also because I tend to agree with you. After all, I am a product of your work of the 1940s and early 1950s, as I am of the writings of the various Chicago political scientists you singled out for praise—having read their every word, including yours, and having studied with some of them as a student and served with some as a colleague. I contributed to the revival of Gosnell's *Machine Politics—Chicago Model* with a foreword (1968), in which I said, among other things, "It is a masterpiece in the imaginative use of aggregate data in the study of political phenomena. A direct predecessor to the work of V. O. Key, this study is unexcelled to this day as an effort to understand political behavior in its institutional setting" (vii).

The essay to which you object can be said to have arisen out of the loss of hegemony of these very people. What you call behavioralism associated with Chicago lost out to the behavioralism most people would associate with the University of Michigan, which some would call the genuine behavioralism precisely because it is constructed unit-by-unit and professes to operate hypothesis-to-hypothesis. Also declining in hegemony at the same time was empirical public administration, or as they called it, the "politics of administration" That kind of public administration for which Chicago was well known lost out to the unit-by-unit approach to administrative behavior

that I associate with you. And note well that you are one of the few of that
Chicago epoch that stayed in administrative studies. Others who, like you,
began in Chicago with public administration, got out of it altogether—Key,
Truman, Almond, Leiserson, and, yes, Pritchett. Many of them got out of it
and into the study of electorates and other aspects of political behavior,
it seems to me, precisely because by the 1950s, the unit-by-unit approach
associated with the University of Michigan seemed to be the best way to
go. And I don't think they were particularly good at it. Key's best work was
his institution-level, aggregate data empirical approach to political parties
and elections *qua* institutions. Truman's best work was not in his study of
congressional behavior but in his equally empirical but distinctly not unit-
by-unit analysis of the group process. In my piece I referred to their work
(and yours) as

> The golden age of U.S. political science. . . . Works of political sci-
> ence in the 1930's and 1940's were magnificent in their ability to
> describe a complex political whole; thorough, honest, and imagin-
> ative in their use of statistics to describe a dynamic reality; and
> powerful and cogent in pointing out flaws and departures from
> U.S. ideals.
>
> (p. 2)

But that's not what my argument was all about. The previous passage continued as follows: "But this was the sentimental part of my
journey. To yearn for those particular studies of elections, case studies
of interest groups and policymaking, histories of party systems, and
representation in Congress is to yearn also for the luxury of the First
Republic. . . ."

This leads me back to my major premise, which is about power—not your
power or that of any other political scientist but about *government power*
and how it shapes us. You seemed to feel I was accusing you of being in
sympathy with a particular administration or ideology or of supporting a
particular "economic ideology" (p. 3) in order to have personal influence
or recognition. Not at all. At one point I actually tried to head off that possible misinterpretation:

> It is important to emphasize . . . that the hegemony of [a]
> subdiscipline . . . is a case of natural selection, not one of political
> maneuvering or intellectual opportunism. . . . [If] political skill were
> required to succeed, there would have been no survey research
> centers—probably no behavioral science at all. It is their very lack
> of attention to playing the political game that makes the success of
> their field so interesting.
>
> (p. 3)

You also seemed to think that my argument had something to do with establishing a direct association between behavioralism and economics, in particular with neoclassicism or with rational choice (pp. 1–2). Again, that may be an interesting point to pursue somewhere else, but not here. For me, those are two different subdisciplines in two different epochs, sharing, for my purposes, only those aspects of method and structure that were relevant to the interests of the "state" in the Second Republic.

That's where power came into my analysis: My argument is based on a Darwinian, not a political process or a political ambition, analysis. The ideas, methods, and subdisciplines that became hegemonic were those most consonant with the political environment in which they were operating; and that relation of consonance between a subdiscipline and the state became more important and easier to perceive after the National Science Foundation and other government R&D programs decided to include the social sciences—with the foundations pretty much following the mode or fashion. And the fashion was set largely by those scholars engaged in peer review whose leadership in the most consonant subdisciplines made them attractive to the authorities who appointed the peer review committees. This is not and never was a matter of a conspiracy or a political faction imposing its will. The consonance of which I speak is a web of reinforcing relationships grounded in and fostered by consonance with the needs and interests of state power as this is lodged in the minds and perspectives of career bureaucrats in the Executive Branch and on the staffs of major congressional committees. Their requirement for a scientific social science was an absolutely necessary political strategy, one made necessary by the tremendous amount of discretion given them in the Second Republic. They had to have some basis for avoiding political power based upon factions and voting and the other matters that were more important in the First Republic. The politics of the hegemony of the disciplines will have to be studied in terms of the discourses of science that were relevant to the games being played by these career bureaucrats.

Mr. Simon, I hate to have to tell you this but you are a product of the state. It's a bit of a lottery, I suppose in the same sense that natural selection is. You, and not Lasswell, became our most important product. Your concept of administration—which, in my opinion, became a concept of organizations without politics, based on the decision rather than the policy as the key unit—became the hegemonic view, one that continues to be influential in political science but is far more influential in the business schools and schools of public affairs where the test of their eminence is the power held by their MBAs and MPAs. Your view replaced the "politics of administration" advanced by those wonderful scholars who contributed to Fritz Morstein-Marx's volume (*Elements of Public Administration*), and those who contributed to the Wallace Sayre volume for the American Assembly (*The Federal Government Service*). These scholars are certainly a vital part of the American political science literature, but they axe nevertheless largely in the past. You are very much still in the present, but I do not think it is irrelevant—nor do I think it is sour grapes on my part—to observe that you became a professor of psychology and computer science, you refused an offer to be president of the American Political Science Association, and you received the highest honor given a political scientist, but it was in economics—the Nobel. I make no prejudicial comment whatsoever about your marvelous accomplishment by saying that power, state power, state interest, political need, had something to do with this. At least it's an interesting hypothesis.

As for rational choice, it became a hegemonic subdiscipline not because Bill Riker and others had political ambitions or because they were ideologically committed to Ronald Reagan's program. But neither did it become a hegemonic subdiscipline because it was truer or better in dealing with factions or life in committees or policy making or presidential power. (I'd personally welcome a wider circulation of your misgivings about rational choice, but that's beside the point here.) I argue simply that the Ronald Reagan epoch provided the most favorable environment for rational choice.

Other subdisciplines go on their way. Neither administrative behavior nor behavioralism at large nor rational choice is actually the mainstream in political science. Each of the subdisciplines I identified, and without question still others, became hot disciplines, with influence beyond the dreams of the adherents, for Darwinian reasons, not for reasons of virtue or truth. So I argue. I repeat in conclusion that at least this is an interesting hypothesis. And it has one particular value, whether I am right or whether I am wrong. It has the value of shocking political scientists into an awareness of their place in history and of their own place in the political process. Since we are not and cannot be neutral, no matter how hard we try, we should make ourselves part of our political analysis.